PROVERB LITERATURE

PROVERB LITERATURE

A Bibliography of Works
relating to Proverbs

EDITED BY

WILFRID BONSER, B.A., Ph.D.

LIBRARIAN TO THE UNIVERSITY OF BIRMINGHAM AND
LATE HON. LIBRARIAN TO THE FOLK-LORE SOCIETY

COMPILED FROM MATERIALS LEFT BY THE LATE

T. A. STEPHENS

MEMBER OF THE FOLK-LORE SOCIETY

PUBLISHED FOR THE FOLK-LORE SOCIETY

WILLIAM GLAISHER, LTD.

265 HIGH HOLBORN, LONDON, W.C. 1

1930

[LXXXIX]

PRINTED IN GREAT BRITAIN BY ROBERT MACLEHOSE AND CO. LTD.
THE UNIVERSITY PRESS, GLASGOW.

CONTENTS

v

CONTENTS

CONTENTS

vii

CONTENTS

To face Page ix.

MEMOIR

THOMAS ARTHUR STEPHENS was born on May 25th, 1852, and died on November 15th, 1925. He was the son of Charles Viret Stephens, who was for many years in the Bank of England. It is of interest that " Kitty " Stephens, the operatic prima donna, who late in her career was married to the fifth Earl of Essex, was his great aunt.

Arthur Stephens followed his father into the Bank of England, where he remained for nearly forty years. He retired owing to ill-health at the age of 59.

He was the author of a small volume of poems, which was published by Fisher Unwin under the title *Hope's Gospel*. He also compiled *A Bibliography of the Bank of England*, which was published by Effingham Wilson in 1897. The actual printing was carried out at the presses of the Bank : 250 copies only were printed.

During the last years of his life he found great enjoyment in the collection of material for the present volume, but his own ill-health and that of his wife retarded his labours. He left an incomplete introduction, together with several books of notes and a list of some 1500 titles. The generosity of Mrs. Stephens has enabled the work to be completed and published, and to stand as a memorial of him and the ambitious scheme he was not permitted to carry through. His collection of some 60 volumes relating to proverbs he bequeathed to the Library of the Folk-lore Society.

MEMOIR

Arthur Stephens was a man of wide reading, and it was seldom that a subject was discussed in his presence without his being able to throw fresh light upon it. He was an admirable raconteur with a great fund of entertaining stories. He was one of the original members of the Bath Club. " What struck one most about Arthur Stephens," says an intimate friend, " was his intense ' curiosity ' and mental alertness. He seemed to have an inexhaustible store of out-of-the-way information : nothing seemed to escape his notice, and he was not satisfied until he had placed any new fact in its proper niche. Even his last illness was not allowed to remain unprobed by his inquisitive mind, for he read most of the literature dealing with the disease which eventually killed him. His hobbies included microscopy, photography, cactus-growing, and chess."

INTRODUCTION

By the late T. A. STEPHENS

[The following introduction was written somewhat in haste by Mr. Stephens just before his death, in 1925. It has been printed as he left it but for the necessary textual corrections. He had intended to develop the subject further and continue.—W. B.]

THE compilation of a complete Bibliography of Proverbs, even if not impossible, would be a work to occupy the lifetime of the longest liver, had he the desire, even in his youth, to commence such a gigantic task.

It is, however, a desire not likely to exist in a young man, for, although to the middle-aged student (half of whose life has been already lived) proverbs and their literature possess a fascination not easily understood by the uninitiated, youth is the time of action, scarcely that of meditation on or acceptance of old saws, however witty or wise.

Haller, in the preface to his "Altspanische Sprüchwörter," says he had been hard at work for three years (he was then 73!), and the book only goes as far as the letter A! Before further remark let us see what has been done in paremiology by comparison of the material existing early in the nineteenth century with that now at our disposal.

Omissions.—I have, for lack of room in this present volume, been compelled to omit some of the titles given by Gratet-Duplessis, *e.g.*, those of books which treat only of one proverb. Those anxious to explore such fields will find in the pages of Nopitsch and Gratet-Duplessis ample references to enable them to pursue such special investigations.*

About 100 years ago, John Wade (writing under the pseudonym of Thomas Fielding), in the introduction to his little book (*q.v.*, **195**) on proverbs, says, "The Germans are not remarkable for their proverbs, probably from an aversion to the aphoristic style; they have doubtless their proverbial phrases like all other countries, but I have not seen any regular collection of them."

Fielding was a true lover of proverbs, and in his unpretentious volume has left us a richer legacy than is contained in many a

---

* The index-volumes of "Notes and Queries" should also be consulted.—W. B.

fat octavo, but he lacked the wealth of opportunity we have in 1926 to examine the proverbial literature of almost every race, living on the earth now or in the past, that has accumulated during the last century or that has been recovered from ancient sources by our Flinders Petrie and Wallis Budge and their co-workers of all nationalities. Fielding was evidently unaware that only two years before, in 1822, Nopitsch had published his " Literatur der Sprüchwörter," which consisted of 284 pages.

Nopitsch, as the pioneer bibliographer of the subject, had in his day not only the handicap of being the first in the field, but suffered further from the disadvantage of limitation of facilities of reference to many libraries, and the published catalogues of them now in international circulation, e.g., the Bibliothèque Nationale and the British Museum.

In 1847 Gratet-Duplessis published his " Bibliographie parémiologique "—an admirable book both in matter and arrangement, but in which only 44 English books are given, and they, from our national point of view, scarcely treated satisfactorily. This bibliography includes 893 books in 35 languages.

In this present volume I have given upwards of 1500 * titles, at the same time omitting deliberately many of those included by Gratet-Duplessis.

K. F. W. Wander, in 1863, in his " Deutsches Sprichwörter Lexicon " made a distinct advance in his treatment of the individual proverbs and those related to them in other tongues than his own.

In 1872 those devoted workers, the Reinsberg-Düringsfelds, still further improved things, notably in their bibliographical sections.

The year 1883 saw the birth of both Strafforello's " Sapienza del Mondo " and Haller's " Altspanische Sprichwörter."

In 1905 came out a new edition of Trench, " Proverbs and their lessons," with a bibliographical list of 277 books in many languages. Beyond this and Stirling-Maxwell's " Books at Keir " there seem to have been no serious attempts at a bibliography in English of existing proverbial literature.

During the nineteenth century, especially the latter half, missionaries and explorers all over the world had been gathering the proverbs current amongst the natives of the regions in which they worked, and now the time has come when some attempt can be made to fill this gap in English literature to which Hazlitt refers in a note to his " English Proverbs " (1907). In the present volume I have endeavoured to supply the deficiency as far as personal limitations have permitted me.

I must here mention the names of some of the men who have collected by word of mouth the proverbs of races amongst whom no systematic collections of their proverbs had been made :—

* Enlarged since Mr. Stephens' death to over 4000 titles.—W. B.

T. Roebuck in 1824 in Persian and Hindustani; Percival in Tamil, 1842; Carr, Mainwaring, Temple in Hindustani, 1886. In this twentieth century, Burton in West Africa, N. W. Thomas (Ibo), Rattray in Ashanti, Hausa and Chinyanja, and Ris in Oji and Akwapim, 1853-54. In Japan, Lafcadio Hearn, Sir E. J. Reed.

Again, individual nations had commenced scientific treatment of their own proverbs:—Capponi, Giuseppe Giusti, Pitrè, Pasqualijo, in Italy. Caballero, Sbarbi in Spain—the monograph of the latter certainly ranks with Pitrè and Wander. In Dutch and Flemish, Harrebomée and recently Stoen. In France, Mesangère, Gratet-Duplessis, Le Roux de Lincy, De Méry. In Scotland, Henderson, Hislop, Macintosh, Maclean, Nicholson and Cheviot. The Classical Erasmus always first, *facile princeps*, also Otto and Binder.

In ecclesiastical processions the highest dignitary comes last, and so in our own tongue. Heywood in the sixteenth century, Howell, Ray and Camden. In the eighteenth, Fuller. In the nineteenth, Fielding (1853), Trench in his delightful " Proverbs and their lessons," and again 1905 by Smythe Palmer, editor; E. P. Hood, Cheates, Bohn's two books—(*a*) " Reprint of Ray "; (*b*) " Polyglot of Foreign Proverbs " (both indexed); Inwards and Swainson in " Weather Proverbs " and W. C. Hazlitt in the latest edition of " English Proverbs " in the twentieth century (1907). Malan Tay and W. O. E. Oesterley in Old Testament and Apocryphal Wisdom books.

In monographs and books alone the field is so vast that practically articles in journals, newspapers, reviews and other periodicals cannot herein be dealt with.* Here I have indicated in the briefest possible manner some of the more prominent features of the work that has been done in proverb literature—or may we not say paremiology?—for the growth of the subject, now well past the stage of infancy, surely entitles it to a distinctive baptismal name.

Although the aim of this book is bibliographical, a few words may be said here as to the different modes of treatment of which the subject is susceptible.

I know that some of my fellow-members of the Folk-lore Society regard it as a special department of folklore, and so it is, and the thing may be done merely from that point of view. Valuable results may so be obtained, especially of the correlative conditions of culture and customs growing from climatic and local causes prevalent amongst the races using the sayings.

Secondly, the philologist finds that by looking at the matter from his *locus standi* much light is reflected on the history and

---

* These have been included when found, but indexes to periodicals have not been systematically examined, except in a few obvious cases, owing to their enormous scope.—W. B.

derivation of words; and intimately associated with this side of the subject is what may be termed, *faute de mieux*, differentiation of expression from other causes than those given above.

There still remains what many consider the most valuable function and precious property resident in proverbs, and again first comes last: their virtue as affecting the conduct of life, rightly and, alas, sometimes wrongly (traces of vice, of adverse influence). These latter are few in number and so may be at once dealt with and " dismissed with a caution."

Samples from several languages are given below.

" De mortuis nil nisi bene " (or bonum).   (595.)*

" Man darf nur sterben um gelobt zu werden."   (716.)

" Mit Schweigen verräth man sich nicht."   (668.)

" Den letzten beissen die Hunde."   (696.)

Schöner's Sprüchwort, " Womit sich laue Christen behelfen."   (719.)

" Einmal ist keinmal "; " Une fois ne compte pas "; " Once is never.' (737.)

C. Gerber, " Unerkannte Sünden der Welt."   (Nopitsch, 52; 1703, 19 and 25.   Gratet-Duplessis, 584.)

" Charity begins at home."

" Each for himself and God for us all."

" Mieux un raisin pour moi que deux figues pour toi."   (French.)

" Zelf is de man."   (Dutch.)

" As well be hanged for a sheep as a lamb."

" Hard for an empty sack to stand straight."

" Peccato celato mezzo perdonato."

" Blessed is the son whose father went to the devil."

" Draw the snake from its hole by another's hand."

" One must howl with the wolves."

" Consonus esto lupis, cum quibus esse cupis."

" Ich bin mir selbst der nächste "; " Proximus sum egomet mihi."   (598.)

" Comptez après votre père."

" Over shoes over boots."

As Trench says, a little seeking would reveal many such black sheep in our large flock.

There is a vast difference between a healthy maxim coarsely worded in the language of the period when originally popular, and one intentionally nasty and dirty, however elegantly expressed : with this latter category we have no concern. It is astonishing that more than one nineteenth century paremiologist should have thought fit to publish a special list of such weeds, instead of leaving them to decay in the mire of oblivion. In the first case, trifling trouble would yield plenty of later similar maxims, cleanlier in matter and quite as forcible in expression, which have succeeded them in popular use. It is easy to remove

---

* These numbers refer to the entries in Duplessis.

the dust of antiquity by substituting modern clean expressions for nauseous ancient ones.

The proverb " De mortuis nil nisi bonum " may have arisen probably more from superstition and fear of spiteful spooks than from any feeling of commiseration with departed souls. But its vice is obvious as being prohibitive of the execration of dead villains and their vileness. If to praise the memory of the good be right—and it is—surely it is permissible to hold up for condemnation the bad examples of the wicked.

All things psychical had their physical parallels, and here the readiest to hand are the finger-posts pointing the way to reach our destination, and the cautions and danger-boards showing what we should avoid. The German " We need only die in order to be praised " is a gloss on " De mortuis nil nisi bonum." C. Gerber in his " Unerkannte Sünden der Welt " comments on hurtful proverbs, as does Trench in his " Proverbs and their lessons," in which the evil influence of some of the other proverbs in the above list is well pointed out.

Many proverbs in all languages exist of the " ca' canny " order, from the old Egyptian (3440: Precepts of Ptah Hotep): " A wife will be doubly attached if her chain is pleasant," down to the recent Yankee: " Early to bed and early to rise ain't never no good if you don't advertise," and those advocating wisdom of a mere worldly-wise type.

Proverbs as to marriage, love and women abound from Solomon's time downwards. Amongst these, some only half-true, appear: " A good wife is the workmanship of a good husband "; " All of us know that frequently excellent women have vile mates." " Every man can tame a shrew but he that hath her " points to experience.

In the Russian, " The devil is poor; he has no God," a deeper and richer vein is struck, and its gloss " An atheist has got one point beyond the devil "; " Cheer up; God is where he was " (this was before Browning's " God's in His heaven; all's right with the world "); " Do not evil to get good thereby, which never yet happened to any "; the Chinese, " Sweep the snow from thine own door before carping at the frost on thy neighbour's tiles "; " Frost and fraud both end in foul "; " Guilt is always jealous "; " He who resolves to amend has God on his side "; " Take away fuel, take away flame "; " Wise men care not for what they cannot have "; " Who ever suffered for not speaking ill of others."

The Old and New Testaments, the Apocrypha, and the Talmud have a literature of their own; to deal adequately with it would need a special bibliography.*

* Therefore these are not given in detail.—W. B.

EDITOR'S INTRODUCTION

VARIOUS attempts have been made to define a proverb from the time of Erasmus (" Celebre dictum scita quadam novitate insigne ") onwards. Risley * gives a very entertaining discussion on the essentials of a proverb, and points out that most definitions fail to emphasise the important fact that the saying must be current in the mouths of the common folk. It is this which makes the proverb of interest to the folklorist. The more primitive the race, the more meagre its written literature, and the more important the proverb as an expression of the thought and life of the folk, since it represents tribal wisdom which could be handed down in an easily remembered form. Mr. Raymond Firth has shown in a recent number of our journal † how " the proverbs of a native people are interwoven with the details of their daily life, and must be studied in that context." He defines the proverb as " a concise and expressive, often figurative, saying in common use, which acts as a conveniently formulated means of expression, charged with emotional significance, to indicate and transmit the facts of experience, or to point out by injunction or prohibition an ideal of social conduct and behaviour."‡

This bibliography, however, deals with the proverbs of civilised European countries, as well as those of primitive peoples, and the bulk of the European material far surpasses that of all the other continents. Local and dialect proverbs are here specially of interest to the folklorist, since they illustrate local conditions, and since the life of the peasant approximates more closely to that of the primitive races than does that of the better-educated townsman or the courtier.

Works on literary proverbs, *i.e.*, those collected from the writings of famous men, have usually been omitted, since these are the furthest from the primitive and the true proverb, and therefore do not come within the scope of this work.

It would be possible, and profitable, to arrange the material contained in this bibliography in at least three different ways: topographically, ethnographically, or linguistically. It has seemed best to arrange as far as possible topographically, since this

---

* Sir H. Risley, " The People of India," pp. 128 *et seq.* 1915.

† " Folk-Lore," Vol. 37, pp. 134-53, 245-70. 1926.

‡ *Op. cit.*, pp. 265-66.

method appears to be the simplest. In such cases as Latin, Jewish, etc., this method has had to give way to a linguistic and ethnographical arrangement: difficulties also arise in connection with such categories as *niederdeutsch, plattdeutsch*,* where the historical element as well as the linguistic enters in.

The topographical method has occasionally to be modified, also, where modern political divisions and the dictates of the Treaty of Versailles have rendered the strict classification under countries inconvenient. For instance, " borderland proverbs " partake of the characteristics of both countries to which they are adjacent: therefore proverbs from Alsace-Lorraine, which are partly in French and partly in German, have been placed in a division of their own: so have Basque proverbs, which are possibly of an older stratum than either French or Spanish: while those of the Ladin Valleys, which politically should be divided between Trentino and Venetia among the local Italian, have also been treated as a special unit.

In France, the older provinces—Normandy, Brittany, Provence, etc.—have been taken as the units of classification rather than the smaller and more machine-made departments. Similarly, in Asia and Africa, large areas have been taken as units rather than individual states or tribes.

Any classification, however carefully considered, will by some be considered arbitrary: a glance at the contents will help the student, and it is hoped that the index will settle most queries.

The following particulars, wherever possible, are given: name of author, title of work, place of publication, publisher and date; the pages relevant, the price at which it was published, the library in London in which the work may most conveniently be found, and references to other bibliographies in which it occurs. Notes, where possible those left by Mr. Stephens, have been added to indicate the scope and value of each work. No works in a non-European script have been included. The earliest and latest editions of which information is available have been given: details of other editions only in special circumstances.

It cannot be pretended that this present bibliography is anything like complete. No systematic attempt has been made to collect articles from periodicals, though these have been included whenever found: the same applies to odd chapters in books of travel and ethnology, which often contain paremiological material. Such collecting, as Mr. Stephens justly remarks, is the work of a lifetime.

Short notices on proverbs in general and on individual proverbs abound in " Notes and Queries." These have not been included here, and the reader is referred to the general index-volumes of this periodical.

* In this classification *niederdeutsch* (general) means all Low German speech, while *plattdeutsch* refers only to Low German speech within the boundaries of modern Germany.

Mr. Stephens, in his introduction, mentions various persons who have attempted bibliographies of works relating to proverbs in the past. Perhaps more detailed information as to some of these would be useful and helpful, since their works are quoted in the notes to the various entries throughout this book.

P. A. Gratet-Duplessis in 1847 published a " Bibliographie parémiologique." Reference has been made to all his entries which have been included here, and the entries have, as far as possible, been checked before incorporation. Duplessis' entry-number has been given. His notes are often long and verbose : here they have been abbreviated as much as possible. He includes hardly any material outside Europe and Asia.

Ignacy Bernstein, a Pole, published in 1900 a " Catalogue des livres parémiologiques," which is one of his own library of works on proverbs, emblems,* maxims,* etc., and contains some 4000 entries. His notes are in Polish, and in a great many cases it has not been possible to verify his references, since the books do not exist in the library of the British Museum. A reference to " Bernstein " indicates him as the sole authority.

Conrad Christian Nopitsch published in 1822, and again in 1833, his " Literatur der Sprichwörter," which deals especially with those of Germany. He does not, however, as Duplessis complains, confine himself to proverbs proper.

In 1905 Carl Friesland issued a bibliography of 498 entries of works on French proverbs which had appeared since the bibliography of Duplessis. He unfortunately does not give the size (4°, 8°, etc.) of the works he includes, which means that entries for which he is the sole source of information are here also deficient in that particular.

In 1887 Giuseppe Fumagalli issued a " Bibliografia paremiologica italiana," with 408 entries. This was continued for two more years in " Archivio delle tradizioni popolari."

Giuseppe Pitrè published in 1894 a work entitled " Bibliografia delle tradizioni popolari d'Italia," of which a large section, containing over a thousand entries, deals with proverbs. This has been incorporated, but not in its entirety, since many of his entries deal with single proverbs and other minutiae which are not required here.

V. S. Lean, of " Collectanea " fame, left his library of proverb literature to the Bristol Public Library, which issued a catalogue of the collection in 1903. This has been incorporated.

C. Mayreder put a notice in " Polybiblon " in 1877, stating his intentions of composing a bibliography of proverb literature, and inviting co-operation. The subsequent numbers of this periodical contain the response to this appeal. No trace, however, has been found of the published work, and Bernstein states that Mayreder died soon after.

---

* Omitted here as not being relevant.

Mr. Stephens left a list of some 1500 entries, and several books containing notes. Most of the remaining material was added by Miss Norah K. Lewis of the University of London School of Librarianship. Miss Lewis has checked all Mr. Stephens' entries, and also made her own additions from the books themselves whenever they exist in the libraries of the Folk-Lore Society, University College, London, the Royal Anthropological Institute, and the British Museum.

I have to acknowledge my very great indebtedness to Mr. L. C. Wharton of the British Museum for his help with the Slavonic entries, and for reading through the proofs. Dr. M. F. Liddell, of the University of Birmingham, has also kindly read through the German entries in proof. I have also to thank Mr. A. R. Wright for general, and Mr. F. W. H. Migeod for African, material provided; Mr. F. J. Richards for assistance in the classification of the Asiatic, and Rev. Edwin W. Smith of the African entries, and Mr. B. Maxwell Stephens for his kindly interest and encouragement throughout. The Society is also under a very deep debt of gratitude to Mrs. T. A. Stephens for her financial aid, without which it would have been impossible for the book to have been produced.

WILFRID BONSER

ABBREVIATIONS

(Indicating Libraries in which copies may be found.)

B.M. = British Museum.
U.C.L. = University College, London.
F.-L.S. = Folk-Lore Society.
L.L. = London Library.
R.A.I. = Royal Anthropological Institute.

To ensure correct alphabetical order, " ä," " ö," " ü " have been written " ae," " oe," " ue " in the first word of each entry.

Anonymous works are entered under the first noun or important word in the title.

GENERAL

(including collections in three or more languages).

1. Abercrombie (Ralph). Echoes of texts, proverbs, and street voices, *etc.* pp. viii, 188. 1870.

Pp. 159-174, the proverb element in literature. An essay on the origin, moral significance, and suggestiveness of proverbs.

2. Ács (Károly). Magyar, nemet, olász, román(olah), cseh-tót és szerb beszelgetések, *etc.* pp. [ix], 287.
2.20 kr. 8°. Pest, *Lauffer és Stolp*, 1859.

A conversation book in Hungarian, German, Italian, Roumanian, Bohemian, Slovak and Serbian. Pp. 78-84, 76 proverbs in the above languages. These proverbs in three languages only are also to be found in a Hungarian-German-Bohemian (or Czecho-Slowakian) conversation book, published by the same author, same place and date. [B.M.

3. Adagia. Adagia, *i.e.* proverbiorum . . . quae apud Graecos, Latinos, Hebraeos, Arabes, *etc.*, in usu fuerunt, collectio.
fol. Francof. ad M., 1629.
Another edition. fol. Francof. ad M., 1670.

4. Adler-Mesnard (E.). Anleitung zur deutschen, englischen, französischen und italienischen Umgangssprache. . . . Enthaltend: ein Verzeichnis der . . . Sprichwörter, *etc.* pp. xii, 736. 32°. Leipzig, *Weber*, 1841.

5. Albrecht (August). Redensarten und Sprichwörter in vier Sprachen: deutsch, französisch, englisch und italienisch. pp. 200. 8°. Leipzig, *Fries*, 1864.

Arranged alphabetically by the keywords of the German. Contains rather more phrases than proverbs. [B.M.

6. Almanach. Almanach proverbial pour l'année 1886. pp. 128.
12°.

Bernstein, 66. The only year mentioned by him. Librairie des villes et des campagnes.

7. Azbuka. Русская азбука съ раскрашенными картинами, *etc.* pp. [8], 47. 12°. Варшава, *Кельтеръ*, 1860.

Pp. 44-46, Пословицы: Русскія. Латинскія. Французскія. Нѣмецкія.

A

8. Bacon (Francis), *Viscount St. Albans.* The promus of formularies and elegancies . . . by F. B., illustrated and elucidated by passages from Shakespeare. By Mrs. Henry Pott, etc. pp. xix, 628.

8°. London, Longmans, 1883 [1882].

Another edition. Francis Bacon's Promus of formularies and elegancies. Being a literal reprint, *etc.* pp. 63.

8°. London, 1898.

A collection of 1655 sentences in Latin, French, English, Greek, Spanish and Italian, without arrangement. Some are original, but most are either quotations from the Bible, Ovid, *etc.*, or proverbs. In the 1883 edition the proverbs are compared and contrasted with others, or with passages from the Bible or from Shakespeare.   [B.M.

9. Barros (José). Verdaderos principios de la lengua castellana, *etc.* 2 pts.   4/-. 12°. Belfast, *Longman*, 1827.

Pp. 106-116, equivalent proverbs in Spanish, French and English.   [B.M.

10. Bartels (J. H.). Dissertatio de proverbiorum fontibus.

4°. Witembergae, 1725.

Gratet-Duplessis, 3.

11. Bechtel (John H.). Proverbs. Maxims and phrases drawn from all lands and times, *etc.* pp. 201.

8°. London, Gay & Bird, 1906.

Proverbs in English classified by subjects. No notes.   [B.M.

12. Becker, *Dr.* Das Sprichwort in nationaler Bedeutung.

4°. Wittenberg, 1851.

In Programm des Gymnasiums zu Wittenberg, 1851, pp. 1-24.

13. Bemerkungen. Einige Bemerkungen über das Wesen der Sprichwörter.   4°. Stuttgart, München, *Cotta*, 1883.

In Das Ausland, 1883, No. 9, pp. 177-178. A commentary.   [B.M.

14. Benas (Baron Louis). On the proverbs of European nations.
8°. London, Longmans, Liverpool, Marples, 1878.

In Proceedings of the Literary and Philosophical Society of Liverpool . . . 1877-78, No. 32, pp. 291-332. A general study with many examples from the French, Italian, Spanish, German, Dutch and Scandinavian.   [B.M.

15. Bernstein (Ignacy). Catalogue des livres parémiologiques composant la bibliothèque de Ignace Bernstein. 2 tom.

8°. Varsovie, Drugutin, 1900.

Two large volumes comprising 4761 entries. Full bibliographical details are given, and in many cases whole title-pages are reproduced. Each entry is given in the language and characters of the original. Each volume has a second title-page and introduction in Polish; the notes are given in Polish only. This catalogue was reviewed by P. Teza in the Rivista Bibliografica Italiana, 1903, and some copies of the review were printed separately.   [B.M.

16. Beronius (M. O.). Dissertatio de proverbiis, praeside Joh. Upmark, respondente M. O. Beronio. Upsaliae, 1816.

Gratet-Duplessis, 5, gives Gottland's De proverbiis Feniciis as his authority for this entry, but no indications of scope, *etc.*, are given.

17. Bibliographie. Bibliographie des proverbes.
8°. Paris, 1877-1878.

In Polybiblion, Deuxième Série, Tome 5, pp. 192, 280-285, 287-288, 384, 474-476, 477-478, 560-561; Tome 6, pp. 96, 287-288, 384, 464, 557-559; Tome 7, pp. 287-288. Correspondence started by Ch. Mayreder, who announced his intention of compiling a bibliography of proverbs, and asked that details of relevant works should be published in Polybiblion. No such bibliography appears to have been published by Mayreder; *see* Bernstein, 2119. [B.M.

18. Blanchet (François). Apologues et contes orientaux, *etc.* pp. lvi, 285. 8°. Paris, *Debure*, 1784.

Pp. 197-210, Maximes et proverbes orientaux, italiens, espagnols et anglois. A few proverbs from each of the above languages translated into French.
[B.M.

19. Bland (Robert). Proverbs, chiefly taken from the Adagia of Erasmus, with explanations; and further illustrated by corresponding examples from the Spanish, Italian, French and English languages. 2 vols. 8°. London, *Egerton*, 1814.

Gratet-Duplessis, 854. Vol. 1 and Vol. 2, pp. 5-223, proverbs; Vol. 2, pp. 225-248, index. Reviewed in the Quarterly Review, Vol. 125, pp. 217-254. Contains nothing unusual, but is quite readable. The comparisons with proverbs of other nations are neither many nor interesting. [U.C.L.

20. Boecklen (A.). 3553 Sprichwörter. Proverbes. Proverbj. Proverbios. 8°. Stuttgart, 1922.

21. Bohn (Henry George). A polyglot of foreign proverbs, comprising French, Italian, German, Dutch, Spanish, Portuguese, and Danish, with English translations, and a general index. pp. iv, 579. *First edition.* 8°. London, 1857.
Another edition. pp. 579.
5/-. sm. 8°. London, *Bell*, 1867.

Bohn's Antiquarian Library. A good general collection, arranged alphabetically under countries. No notes, no illustrations. Reviewed in an article in the Quarterly Review, Vol. 125, pp. 217-254. [F.L.S. (Stephens collection).

22. Boinvilliers ( ). Code moral, ou choix de sentences et de proverbes grecs, latins, français, anglais, espagnols, italiens et orientaux, *etc.* pp. viii, 330.
12°. Paris, *Eymery*, 1825.

Gratet-Duplessis, 30. Proverbs and moral maxims with French translations. lacking the notes and explanations which would have made it interesting and useful.

23. Borràs (José). Diccionario citador de maximas, proverbios, frases, *etc.* pp. 399.
8°. Barcelona, *Imprenta de Indar*, 1836.

Maxims, proverbs, phrases, *etc.*, from English, Latin, French and Italian authors.

24. Bouhours, *Père.* Explication de divers termes françois que beaucoup de gens confondent faute d'en avoir une notion exacte.   1701.

Gratet-Duplessis, 7. Published posthumously in the Journal de Trevoux, septembre et octobre, 1701. Reprinted by Duplessis in the appendix to his Bibliographie parémiologique, pp. 427-438. The author gives the exact definition of such words as : aphorisme, sentence, maxime, proverbe, apophthegme, *etc.*

25. Brassicanus (Johannes Alexander). Adagiorum symmicta, *etc.* pp. 89.   12°. 1532.

Also in various editions of Erasmus and Grynaeus.

Proverbiorum symmicta, *etc.* pp. [vii], 89.

sm. 8°. Viennae-Austriae, *Vietor,* 1529.

Gratet-Duplessis, 13. Comparatively rare book containing 127 Greek or Latin proverbs with some notes. It is a work of little importance, and was reprinted at the end of various editions of the Adagia of Erasmus, notably those of Paris 1579, and Frankfort 1612.   [B.M.

26. Brunet (G.). Bibliographie des proverbes.

8°. Bruxelles, *etc.,* 1852.

In Bulletin du Bibliophile belge, Tome 9, pp. 233-240. Indicates some 30 odd works not included in Duplessis, and gives fuller details about others.

[B.M.

27. Buchler (Johann). Syntaxis proverbialium sententiarum.

8°. Coloniae, 1600.

Another edition.   12°. Moguntiae, 1614.

Gratet-Duplessis, 145.

28. ——— : Thesaurus proverbialium sententiarum uberrimus, ex Germanicis, Latinis, Gallicis, Graecisque parœmijs, *etc.*

12°. Coloniae, *Gualtherus,* 1623.

Gratet-Duplessis, 145. Very mediocre.

29. Bukvar. Букварь для обученія юношества чтенію по Россійски и по Польски, *etc.* pp. 80.

8°. w Wilnie, *w drukarni uniwersyteckiey,* 1819.

Pp. 77-79, Пословицы: Русскія. Латинскія. Французскія. Нѣмецкія.

30. Bulbena y Tusell (Antoni). Aforistica universal. Nou recull de proverbis, *etc.* pp. 240.

32°. Barcelona, *Stampa Elzeviriana,* 1905.

A collection of proverbs of different countries with Catalan translations.

31. Cahier (Charles). Quelques six mille proverbes et aphorismes usuels empruntés à notre âge et aux siècles derniers. pp. xiii, 579.   12°. Paris, *Lanier,* 1856.

Reviewed in the Quarterly Magazine, 125, pp. 217-254. French, German, English, Scottish, Flemish, Italian, Spanish, Arabic, Chinese, Indian, Hebrew, Russian and Turkish proverbs, the last six being given in French only, but the others in their native languages as well. The book concludes with some legal and philosophic axioms.   [B.M.

32. Callières (François de). Du bon et du mauvais usage dans
les manières de s'exprimer, *etc.* pp. 241.

12°. Paris, *Barbin*, 1693.

Another edition. 12°. Paris, *Brunet*, 1698.

Gratet-Duplessis, 6. This book is a continuation of " Des mots à la mode
et des nouvelles façons de parler," *etc.* The second conversation contains a
very just appreciation of the proper use of proverbs. [B.M.

33. Cats (Jacob). Spiegel van den ouden ende nieuwen tijdt,
bestaende wyt spreek-woorden ende sin-spreucken, ontleent
van de voorige ende jegen-woordige eeuwe, *etc.* [Illustrated.]

4°. 's Graven-Hage, *Burchoorn*, 1632.

Another edition.

la. 8°. Amsterdam, Utrecht, *Diederichs*, 1828.

Gratet-Duplessis, 17. Pitrè, 2552-63, quotes 11 other editions, of which
Duplessis particularises several. Proverbs of all centuries and from all countries
commented on by appropriate verses or illustrations. There is little method in
the arrangement, though a certain number of proverbial maxims bearing on
the same subject have been collected together in each of the three appendices.
See also **142.** [B.M. (various editions).

34. ——— and Farlie (Robert). Moral emblems with aphorismes,
adages and proverbs of all ages and nations . . . edited . . .
by Richard Pigot. . . . 3rd edition. pp. xvi, 242.

4°. London, *Longmans*, 1865.

Each page is surrounded by four proverbs; there are also others in the body
of the text. [B.M.

35. Chalumeau de Verneuil (F. T. A.). Grammaire espagnole
. . . augmentée . . . de proverbes et d'idiotismes espagnols,
français et anglais, *etc.* pp. 955.

8°. Paris, *Samson*, 1821.

Pp. 878-902, Spanish, French and English proverbs. [B.M.

36. Chamberlain (Alexander F.). Proverbs in the making: some
scientific commonplaces. 8°. Boston, 1904.

In Journal of American Folk-Lore, Vol. 17, pp. 161-170, 268-278. 450 succinct
quotations from various authors which might in time become proverbs. [B.M.

37. ———: Race character and local color in proverbs.

8°. Boston, 1904.

In Journal of American Folk-Lore, Vol. 17, pp. 28-31. 45 Negro-English or
Yoruba proverbs, in English. [B.M.

38. Champion (Selwyn Gurney) and **Mavrogordato** (Ethel).
Wayside sayings. pp. 122.

sm. 8°. London, *Duckworth* [1922].

Second Series. pp. xvi, 284.

8°. London, *Duckworth*, [1924].

Proverbs in English from many countries, classified by languages. The
second series contains a larger and better selection than the first. Series 2,
pp. xiii-xvi, Authorities consulted. No notes.

[Series 1, F.-L.S. (Stephens collection); Series 2, B.M.

39. Cheales (Alan Benjamin). Proverbial folk-lore. pp. 165.
 8°. Dorking [printed], London, *Simpkin Marshall*, [1874].
Second edition. pp. 173.
 8°. Dorking [printed], London, *Simpkin Marshall*, [1875].
Reviewed in the Folk-Lore Record, Vol. 3, Pt. 2. First edition anonymous.
A study of proverbial wisdom with numerous examples, arranged under subject
headings.   [B.M.

40. Chesnel de la Charbouclais (Louis Pierre François Adolphe
 de), *Marquis*. Dictionnaire de la sagesse populaire, *etc.*
 7 fr. 8°. Paris, *Migne*, 1855.
Migne's 3e Encyclopédie théologique, Vol. ii. A dictionary of proverbs,
phrases, maxims, precepts, sayings, apophthegms, *etc.*, of all times and all
countries. The proverbs are given in French, and are accompanied by notes.
Under the word proverb, some English, Latin, German, Spanish and Italian
ones are given in the original.   [B.M.

41. Choix. Choix de maximes, pensées morales et proverbes tirés
 de divers philosophes anciens et de différens peuples. pp.
 304.   18°. Londres, Paris, 1785.
Gratet-Duplessis, 23. Pp. 51-130, proverbs.

42. Christy (Robert). Proverbs, maxims, and phrases of all ages,
 etc. 2 vols.   8°. London, *Fisher Unwin*, 1888.
Another edition. 2 vols. 8°. London, *Fisher Unwin*, 1898.
Proverbs in English arranged alphabetically under subject headings. No
notes.   [B.M.

43. Coleman (A. N.). Proverbial wisdom. 3rd edition.
 New York, *Eckler*, 1903.

44. Collins (John Churton). The posthumous essays. Edited by
 L. C. Collins, pp. vi, 287 and frontispiece.
 8°. London, *Dent*, New York, *Dutton*, 1912.
Pp. 256-279, Curiosities of popular proverbs. An essay on proverbs in general,
giving many examples and sources.   [U.C.L.

45. Conklin (George W.). The world's best proverbs.
 Philadelphia, *Mackay*.

46. Connor (James). Manuel de conversation, en Français, en
 Allemand et en Anglais. . . . Elfte verbesserte Auflage. pp.
 viii, 277.   12°. Heidelberg, *Winter*, n.d.
Pp. 264-275, proverbs and idioms in the three languages.

47. Coulon (H.). Proverbes d'autrefois. pp. 174, and fac-simile.
 8°. Cambrai, 1902.

48. Coursier (Édouard). Русско - французско - нѣмецкіе обще-
 ственные разговоры, *etc.* [Fifth edition].
 2 tom., 8°. St. Petersburg, 1861.
Another edition.   2 tom., 8°. С.-Петербургъ, (1896).
Contains a section of proverbs in Russian, French, and German. The
French and German are probably the same as those in Coursier's German-
French Manual.   [B.M.

49. Decsi (János), *Baronyai.* Adagiorum Graeco Latino Ungaricorum chiliades quinque, *etc.* pp. [xiv], 424.

12°. Bartphae, *Klöss*, 1598.

A rare book.

50. Denis (Jean Ferdinand). Le Brahme voyageur, ou la sagesse populaire de toutes les nations. pp. 108. 18°. Paris, 1832.

Gratet-Duplessis, 34. A little book forming part of the " Bibliothèque populaire " of Ajasson de Grandsagne, and containing a number of moral proverbs from all nations, especially the Oriental ones. This work was published earlier, with the same title, accompanied by an " Essai sur la philosophie de Sancho." This last does not appear in the popular edition given above, but it has been reprinted by Leroux de Lincy in his " Livre des proverbes français." The Essai is also found translated into Spanish by Sbarbi, in the latter's " Refranero general español," Vol. 5. [B.M.

51. Dennys (E. M.). Proverbs and quotations of many nations. pp. 56. 8°. London, *Simpkin Marshall*, [1890].

Proverbs in English, two for each day of the year. No notes. [B.M.

52. Desaivre (Léo). Croyances, présages . . . et proverbes, *etc.* pp. 39. 8°. Niort, *Clouzot*, 1881.

53. Dictionnaire. Dictionnaire d'anecdotes, de traits singuliers . . . Nouvelle édition, augmentée. 2 tom. 8°. Paris, 1767.

Another edition. 2 tom. 8°. Paris, *La Combe*, 1787.

A brief list of French, Russian, Italian, Spanish, Dutch and Asiatic proverbs. [B.M.

54. ———: Dictionnaire portatif des proverbes et des idiotismes français, allemands et anglais, comparés entre eux, avec un quadruple vocabulaire, *etc.*

la. 16°. Nuremberg, *Schrag*, 1827.

Gratet-Duplessis, 31, remarks that it is a book which might be useful for occasional reference only; it has neither notes nor philological commentary.

55. D'Israeli (Isaac). A second series of Curiosities of literature, *etc.* 3 vols. 8°. London, *Murray*, 1823.

Another edition. pp. xii, 578.

la. 8°. London, *Moxon*, 1854.

Another edition. pp. xv, 582.

8°. London, *etc.*, *Routledge*, 1889.

Gratet-Duplessis, 10. Contains an excellent essay on the philosophy of proverbs, which is only to be found in editions containing the second or both series. A commentary on the origin, use, and importance of proverbs, with many and varied examples.

[(1854 edition) U.C.L., B.M. (various editions).

56. Dizionario. Il dizionario di un originale. Volume unico. pp. 144. 12°. Bologna, *Foschini*, 1866.

Pp. 87-113, many proverbs of different countries.

57. Draxe (Thomas). Bibliotheca scholastica instructissima, or a treasury of ancient adagies and sententious proverbs, selected out of the English, Greeke, Latine, French, Italian, and Spanish ranked in alphabetical order and suited to one and the same sense, *etc.* pp. [vi], 248.

8°. Londini, *Billius*, 1616.

Another edition. pp. [vi], 247. 8°. London, *Kirton*, 1654.

Gratet-Duplessis, 150. The proverbs are arranged alphabetically by subject; Latin ones predominate. [B.M. (various editions).

58. Dumont (Antoine). Traité de la prudence, contenant un grand nombre d'instructions, de sentences, et de proverbes choisis. 12°. 1733.

Gratet-Duplessis, 309. Nodier thinks it was printed at Besançon; Duplessis that it comes from Holland. Very rare, but of little importance. The name Antoine Dumont, supposed to be the pseudonym of a certain Abbé Arnoux, is given at the end of the table des matières.

59. Ehlers (Johannes). Deutsche, französische und englische Sprichwörter. pp. 20. 12°. Prenzlau, *Mieck*, 1874.

100 proverbs in each of the three languages.

60. Epigrammatum. Epigrammatum delectus . . . cum brevioribus sententiis seu proverbiis latinis, graecis, hispanis, italis, *etc.* pp. [lviii], 590. 8°. Parisiis, *Savreux*, 1659.

Thirteenth edition. pp. [xlviii], 311, 24.

12°. Londini, *Rivington*, 1762.

Gratet-Duplessis, 500. Attributed to Nicole of Port-Royal. Contains : Sententiae breves ex illustrioribus autoribus Grecis, Latinis, et Hispanis excerptae; Sentences courtes et proverbes pleins de sens . . . traduits en françois. There are also numerous quotations, phrases and excerpts from the Classics. The 13th edition does not contain the Spanish and Italian proverbs with their French translations. [B.M.

61. Erasmus (Desiderius). Desiderii Erasmi Roterodami veterum maximeque insignium parœmiarum, id est, adagiorum collectanea, *etc.* 4°. Parisii, 1500.

Another edition. [Vol. 2 of complete works.]

fol. Lugduni Batavorum, 1703.

Another edition. sm. 8°. Lipsiæ, 1759.

Gratet-Duplessis, 12. An enormous collection of Greek and Latin proverbial sayings which has proved a treasure mine for all later writers on, and collectors of, proverbs. Erasmus made this book the vehicle, not only for proverbs and notes thereon, but also for his political and theological opinions, which led to the censoring of the work in later editions. There are a great many editions, both complete and abridged. The first, of 1500, contained the explanation of 800 proverbial sayings; one which appeared at Basle, 1536, contained over 4000. With the edition of 1575 begins the system of ecclesiastical censure prescribed by the Council of Trent; in these all controversial passages have been suppressed. The editions of 1650 and 1759 are abridgements of the completed work; the second of these contains a good preface on Erasmus and his work. Duplessis gives full details of Erasmus and his work. Reviewed in the Quarterly Review, 125, pp. 217-254. *See also* **19, 182, 189.**

[U.C.L. (various editions).

62. Everybody. Everybody's book of proverbs and quotations, *etc.* pp. 160. 16°. London, *Saxon*, 1910.

Proverbs, quotations, *etc.*, in English, arranged under arbitrary headings. Unimportant. [B.M.

63. Farrer (James A.). Primitive manners and customs. pp. xxx, 315. 8°. London, *Chatto & Windus*, 1879.

Chapter 3, pp. 78-100, some savage proverbs. A commentary, with many examples in English, on savage proverbs compared and contrasted with those of civilised communities. [F.-L.S.

64. ———: Some savage proverbs. 8°. London, 1877.

In Gentleman's Magazine, April, 1877, pp. 477-88. Proverbs on vindictiveness.

Fielding (Thomas), *pseud. See* **195.**

65. Floriati (Muzio). Proverbiorum trilinguium collectanea latina, itala et hispana, *etc.* pp. [x], 323.
4°. Neapoli, *Scoringius*, 1636.

Gratet-Duplessis, 159. Arranged alphabetically by the Italian. Latin proverbs are taken from Manuzio and the Classics, Italian ones from Buoni, and Spanish ones from Nuñez. Duplessis says the book is of little importance. [B.M.

66. Freixa y Rasabo (Eusebio). El crisol de centenares de libros, *etc.* pp. 256. sm. 8°. Madrid, *Freixa y Rasabo*, 1879.

Pp. 149-156, Provervios de varias naciones. Some ninety proverbs of different countries, in Spanish. [B.M.

67. Freund (Leonhard). Aus der Spruchweisheit des Auslandes. Parömiologische Skizzen. pp. 48.
8°. Hannover, *Meyer*, 1893.

Proverbs, sayings, *etc.*, in French, Italian, Russian, *etc.*, with German translations.

68. Fries (M. M.) and **Lavezzari** (   ). Französische und italienische Sprachübungen. Nebst einer Sammlung der . . . Sprichwörter und sprichwörtliche Redensarten. pp. 198.
8°. Erlangen, *Enke*, 1845.

Pp. 185-198, proverbs and idioms in French, German, and Italian.

69. Fuller (Thomas). Gnomologia; adages and proverbs, . . . ancient and modern, foreign and British. pp. x, 297.
12°. London, *printed for B. Barker*, 1732.

Another edition . . . to which is added Ramsay's collection of Scottish proverbs. pp. viii, 280. 12°. London, 1819.

Gratet-Duplessis, 28. A simple list of 6496 proverbs, *etc.*, in English, in alphabetical order. No notes. [B.M.

70. Fyvie *afterwards* **Mayo** (Isabella). Stories and sayings from many lands. 6 pts. 6d. each. 8°. London, *Daniel*, [1912].

Fables and tales interspersed with lists of proverbs and sayings in English. [B.M.

71. Gaal (Georg von). Sprüchwörterbuch in sechs Sprachen; deutsch, englisch, latein, italienisch, französisch und ungarisch. pp. x, 324.   12°. Wien, *Volke*, 1830.

Gratet-Duplessis, 33. 1808 German proverbs arranged alphabetically, followed by their equivalents in the five other languages given above.   [B.M.

72. Gaichiés, *Père.* Maximes sur le ministère de la chaire. Third edition.   12°. Paris, 1739.

Another edition. pp. xv, 367. 8°. Paris, *Estienne*, 1743.

Gratet-Duplessis, 8. Contains a "Dialogue dans lequel on examine l'usage que l'on doit faire des proverbes," an interesting and well written study. Duplessis mentions, without details, the earlier editions of these Maximes which appeared anonymously in 1710, but he declares that of 1739 to be the best.
                                                                              [B.M.

73. Gambini (   ). Carnet de l'ignorant, *etc.* pp. 404, xx.
                                                  8°. Paris, *Fayard*, n.d.

Pp. 313-404, les citations mythologiques; les principaux adages et proverbes espagnols, italiens, arabes, persans, turcs et chinois, *etc.*

74. Golshukh (Ivan). Пословицы, поговорки и изреченія или народная мудрость на трехъ языкахъ: русскомъ, французскомъ и нѣмецкомъ, *etc.* pp. 103.
                              8°. Казань, *Императорскій Университетъ*, 1887.
1004 entries.

75. Gomme (*Sir* George Laurence). The handbook of folklore. Edited by G. L. Gomme. pp. vii, 193.   8°. London, 1890.

New edition, revised and enlarged by C. S. Burne. pp. x, 364.   8°. London, 1914.

Publications of the Folk-Lore Society, 20 and 73. Contains chapters on proverbs, indicating their importance in the study of folk-lore and giving examples. A very valuable and useful work.   [F.-L.S.

76. Gould (Sabine Baring-). National characteristics.
                                                  8°. London, 1888.

In Cassell's Family Magazine, Vol. 14, pp. 30-32. Proverbs concerning various countries.   [B.M.

77. Grassow (A.). 5500 Sprichwörter, sprichwörtliche Redensarten und dergleichen in deutscher, englischer, and französischer Sprache, *etc.* pp. 104.   8°. Kassel, *Kegel*, 1879.

Proverbs arranged alphabetically by the German, followed by equivalents in French and English, and occasionally in other languages.   [B.M.

78. Gratet-Duplessis (Pierre Alexandre). Bibliographie parémiologique. Études bibliographiques . . . Suivies d'un appendice, contenant un choix de curiosités parémiographiques. pp. viii, 520.   8°. Paris, *Potier*, 1847.

Classified by languages; the standard bibliography up to 1847.
                                                  [F.-L.S. (Stephens collection).

79. ————: Catalogue des livres . . . composant la bibliothèque de feu M. Gratet-Duplessis, *etc.* pp. xx.
                                                  8°. Paris, *Potier*, 1856.

Pp. 150-179, catalogue of books on proverbs, about 200 items.   [B.M.

80. Gruter (Jan). Florilegium ethico-politicum, *etc.* 3 vols.
8°. Francofurti, *Rhodius*, 1610-1612.

Gratet-Duplessis, 16, gives the full titles of all three volumes, and full notes. This is the most voluminous single collection of maxims, sentences, and proverbs that exists. Each volume is divided into two parts. The first is composed of an alphabetical list of sentences and maxims, *etc.*, in Latin, of a selection of maxims from Greek authors, and, finally, of fairly comprehensive notes. The second part, with its own pagination, consists of a list of proverbs divided by languages, but without any translation, explanation or comment whatsoever, except in the case of the Spanish proverbs (Vol. 1), which are accompanied by the French translation of Cesar Oudin. In each volume there is a list of authorities. The book, though interesting, would have been more useful if the proverbs had been distinguished from the maxims, *etc.*, and if the author had given notes to the modern as well as the ancient ones. The Italian proverbs are taken from Pescetti.
[B.M.

81. Grynæus (Johann Jacob). Adagia, id est, proverbiorum, parœmiarum et parabolarum omnium quae apud Graecos, Latinos, Hebraeos, Arabes, *etc.*, in usu fuerunt, collectio, *etc. First edition.*
fol. Francofurti ad Maenum, *sumptibus C. Schleichii & P. de Zetter*, 1629.
Another edition.
fol. Francofurti ad Maenum, *typis Wechelianis*, 1646.

Gratet-Duplessis, 18. The compiler has adopted an entirely different form and order from that of Erasmus. There were various editions. Of little importance.

82. Gsel (Johann). Nucleus sententiarum . . . Durch Johannem Gsel alias Gallum, Medicum. pp. [16].
4°. Greiffswalt, 1627.

A brief collection of Latin, German, Spanish, Italian and French proverbs.

83. Guericke (Otto von). Sammlung lateinischer, französischer, italienischer, holländischer und deutscher Sinnsprüche, *etc.* pp. 51. M.1. 4°. Magdeburg, *Baensch*, 1885.

This book is notable as one of the best early attempts to bring together correlative proverbs from several languages.
[B.M.

84. H. (D. G. C.). Flores trilingues . . . Sententiae Latino-Germanico-Polonicae, nec non proverbia . . . editi a D. G. C. H. pp. [x], 192. 8°. Gedani, *Stollius*, 1702.

Contains over a thousand proverbs, phrases, maxims, *etc.*, in the three languages.

85. Hécart (Gabriel-Antoine-Joseph). Bibliographie parémiologique, ou revue alphabétique des recueils de proverbes. pp. 36. 8°. Valenciennes, 1841.

Gratet-Duplessis, 2. Published after the author's death in the Mémoires de la Société d'Agriculture, des Sciences et des Arts de l'arrond. de Valenciennes, tome 3, pp. 36-81. Very incomplete and limited, with a few exceptions, to the best known French collections. Contains, however, some useful information.

86. Heckenauer (Johann). Parœmiae et dialogi trilingues: oder, kurze Vorstellung 1340 ausserlesener Sprüchwörter . . . in teutsch, französisch und italiänischer Sprache verfasset. 2 pts.   8°. Ulm, *Kühnen*, 1700.

Gratet-Duplessis, 583.   [B.M.

87. Helps (*Sir* Arthur). Friends in council . . . A new series. 2 vols.   8°. London, *Parker*, 1859.

Vol. 1, pp. 211-226, two dialogues on proverbs.   [B.M.

88. Hensel (J.). Collection polyglotte de proverbes, *etc.* pp. 48. 8°. Berlin, *Kortkampf*, [1879].

750 entries in German, English, French, Italian and Latin.

89. Hesekiel (Johann Georg Ludwig). Land und Stadt in Volks- munde, *etc.* pp. 60.   8°. Berlin, *Janke*, 1867.

A collection of sayings and rhymes, mostly in German, characterising different countries, towns and peoples.   [B.M.

90. Hood (Edwin Paxton). The world of proverb and parable, *etc.* pp. 563.   8°. London, *Hodder & Stoughton*, 1885.

An excellent and varied book, containing chapters on proverbs in general, proverbs concerning sun-dials, kicking dead lions, about birds, *etc.* In each case many examples are given, and these are always well-selected. The essays are above the average.   [B.M.

91. Howell (James). Parœmiographia . . . collected by J[ames] H[owell].   fol. London, *Bee*, 1659.

Gratet-Duplessis, 841. This collection, though with its own title page and pagination, forms an integral part of Howell's " Lexicon tetraglotton," *etc.* fol. London, *Tonson*, 1660. It is a polyglot collection, containing a large selection of English, French, Italian and Spanish proverbs in English, current at the beginning of the 17th century. The English ones are sometimes accom- panied by brief explanations; some are translated into French, Italian and Spanish. Various letters in proverbs such as those of Arsiccio Intronato and Blasco de Garay are given. There is a list of Cambrian proverbs with English translations, and 500 " New sayings, which may serve for proverbs to posterity," some 80 of which are quoted by Duplessis. Reviewed in the Quarterly Review, 125, pp. 217-257.   [B.M.

92. Hoyt (J. K.) and **Ward** (Anna L.). The cyclopædia of prac- tical quotations . . . with proverbs from the Latin and modern foreign languages. Third edition. pp. iv, 899. 8°. New York, *Funk & Wagnall*, 1882.

Another edition. pp. xxxi, 1343. 8°. New York, London, *Funk & Wagnall*, 1922.

The 1882 edition contains some thirty pages of proverbs and mottoes in Latin, French, Spanish, German and Italian, with English translations, but without notes. The later editions contain a brief selection of English proverbs, but only mottoes in other languages.   [B.M.

93. **Hulme** (Frederick Edward). Proverb lore. Many sayings, wise or otherwise, on many subjects, gleaned from many sources. pp. vii, 269.   7/6. 8°. London, *Stock*, 1902.
Another edition.   5/-. 8°. London, *Stock*, 1906.

A book about proverbs, not a collection of them.
[F.-L.S. (Stephens collection).

94. **Humière** (J. P. d'), *Abbé.* Recueil de proverbes français, latins, espagnols, italiens, allemands, hollandais, juifs, américains, russes, turcs. Par le citoyen d'H[umière]. pp. 72. 8°. Paris, *Bureau de la Correspondance des villes et des campagnes*, [1790].

Gratet-Duplessis, 24. A collection of proverbs, in French, arranged under various headings, in alphabetical order. It was to have formed the basis of a larger work, but this was never published. Comparatively unimportant. With very slight modifications and omissions this book was published anonymously under the title : Recueil de proverbes de différens peuples, *etc.* 12°. Valence, 1829. (Gratet-Duplessis, 32.)   [B.M.

95. **Jones** (Hugh Percy). Dictionary of foreign phrases and classical quotations, *etc.* pp. xx, 532.
8°. London, *Deacon*, 1900.
Another edition.   8°. Edinburgh, 1925.

Successor to Deacon's Dictionary of foreign phrases. Alphabetical arrangement. Contains many proverbs.   [B.M.

96. **Keitges** (John). Proverbs and quotations for school and home.   Chicago, *Flanagan*, 1905.

97. **Kelly** (Walter Keating). Proverbs of all nations, compared, explained, and illustrated. pp. viii, 238.
3/6 (out of print). sm. 8°. London, *Kent*, 1859.
Another edition. pp. viii, 226.   8°. London, [1877].

Lists of proverbs, classified by subject, the originals of foreign ones given in footnotes, with an index. Reviewed in an article in the Quarterly Review, Vol. 125, pp. 217-254. The 1877 edition forms part of Diprose's Railway Library.
[F.-L.S. (Stephens collection).

98. **Ketcham** (Henry). Handbook of proverbs. New York, *Burt.*

99. **King** (William Francis Henry). Classical and foreign quotations, *etc.* pp. viii, 608.   8°. London, *Whittaker*, 1887.
Another edition. pp. xii, 624.   8°. London, 1889.
Another edition. pp. xi, 412.   8°. London, 1904.

Contains a good number of proverbs amongst the quotations. A useful book.   [B.M.

100. **Kirchner,** *Dr.* Parömiologische Studien. 2 pt.
4°. Ostern, 1879-80.

Reviewed by A. M. Ottow in : Archiv für Litteraturgeschichte, Bd. 9, pp. 399-409.

101. Knox (Vicesimus). Elegant extracts . . . in prose . . . New
edition. [Edited by Vicesimus Knox]. pp. xvi, 1019.

8°. London, *Dilly*, [1770?].

Another edition. 2 vols.   8°. London, *Mawman*, 1816.

Another edition.   la. 8°. London, *Rivington*, 1824.

Gratet-Duplessis, 456, 516, 858. Contains three lists of English proverbs, old
Italian proverbs, and old Spanish proverbs, in English. These proverbs are
not to be found in the 1842 (6 vols.) edition.   [B.M.

102. Langius (Josephus). Adagia, sive sententiae proverbiales
Graecae, Latinae, Germanicae, *etc.* pp. 546.

8°. [Francofurti], *Rihelius*, 1596.

Another edition.   fol. Francofurti, 1681.

Gratet-Duplessis, 96, 143. Also published under the title of : Polyanthea, *etc.*
[B.M.

103. Lawson (J. G.). The world's best proverbs and maxims.

8°. New York, *Doran*, 1926.

104. Lean (Vincent Stuckey). Bristol public libraries. Reference
library. The Stuckey Lean collection. Edited by Norris
Mathews. pp. viii, 268.   4°. Bristol, 1903.

Pp. 73-123, Section 2. Works relating to proverbs.   [B.M.

105. ———: Lean's collectanea. Collections . . . of proverbs,
English and foreign, folk-lore, and superstitions, also com-
pilations towards dictionaries of proverbial phrases and words,
old and disused. [Edited by T. W. Williams, with a memoir
of the author by Miss J. L. Woodward]. 4 vols [in 5].

la. 8°. Bristol, *Arrowsmith*, London, *Simpkin Marshall*,
1902-04 (out of print).

Each of the volumes contains about 500 pp. Vol. 1, pp. 1-277, proverbs
relating to the United Kingdom and to localities therein, arranged under the
county divisions; pp. 278-285, proverbs relating to colonies, dependencies, and
the United States of America; pp. 287-343, Gl' Italiani da suoi stessi dipinti :
proverbs in their own tongue concerning people and places in Italy; pp. 345-509,
proverbs and popular sayings relating to the calendar and natural phenomena.
Vol. 2, part 2, pp. 657-752, proverbs by reference to authors using them, proverbial witticisms. Vol. 3, pp. 279-371, phrases with examples of their use
[containing some proverbs]; pp. 373-512, and Vol. 4, pp. 1-206, English
aphorisms, proverbs and proverbial phrases, with references to authors by whom
the same are used. Vol. 4, pp. 207-263, contributions to Notes and Queries
containing various proverbs.   [F.-L.S. (Stephens collection).

106. Leibius (Joannes). Studentica, hoc est, apophthegmata,
symbola, et proverbia . . . Germanico-Latino-Italica, *etc.*

16°. Coburgi, *Grunerus*, 1627.
[B.M.

107. Lewis (*Rt. Hon. Sir* George Cornewall), *Bart.* An essay on
the influence of authority in matters of opinion. pp. xii, 424.

8°. London, *Parker*, 1849.

Second edition. pp. **x**, 296.   8°. London, *Longmans*, 1875.

Chap. 6 contains a brief commentary on the value of proverbs as the expression
of popular opinion.   [U.C.L.

108. Lipperheide (Franz Joseph von), *Baron.* Sprüchwörterbuch, *etc.* pp. vii, 1069. 8°. Berlin, *Lipperheide*, 1906-07.

An enormous collection of proverbs, phrases, quotations, *etc.*, in all languages, though principally in German. Arranged alphabetically by the German. Originally issued in monthly parts. [B.M.

109. Long (James). Bible teaching and preaching for the million, by emblems and proverbs. pp. 8. 8°. [London?], 1875.

A paper read at a conference of Church of England clergy and Sunday-school teachers. [B.M.

110. ———: Proverbs: English and Keltic, with their Eastern relations. 8°. London, 1880.

In Folk-Lore Record, Vol. 3, pt. 1, pp. 56-79. With many examples. [F.-L.S.

111. Lorin (Theodore). Essai sur quelques proverbes contestés et contestables. pp. 30.

8°. Soissons, *Fossé Darcosse*, 1850.

An essay on the truth or injustice of certain proverbs, chiefly French. [B.M.

112. Ludwig (Christian). Gründliche Anleitung zur englischen Sprache, *etc.* pp. [xiv], 997, [ii].

8°. Leipzig, *Fritsch*, 1717.

Pp. 942-976, Die nützlichsten und gebräuchlichsten Sprüchwörter nach der alphabetischen Ordnung der gleichgültigen Lateinischen. Equivalent proverbs in Latin, German and English. [B.M.

113. Makarov (N.). Латинскія, итальянскія и англійскія поговорки, пословицы и тексты, *etc.* pp. 56.

8°. С.-Петербургъ, *Тренке и Фюсно*, 1878.
Bernstein, 2043.

114. Manuzio (Paolo). Adagia quaecumque ad hanc diem exierunt, [the Adagia of Erasmus] Paulli Mannuccii studio, *etc.* fol. Florentiae, 1575.
Another edition. 4°. Venetiis, *Muschius*, 1609.

[B.M.

115. Mapletoft (John). Select proverbs, Italian, Spanish, French, English, Scottish, British, *etc.*, chiefly moral. pp. [xii], 126. sm. 8°. London, *Monckton*, 1707.

Gratet-Duplessis, 22. Not a very interesting collection. Contains English translations of all the foreign proverbs. D'Israeli in his " Philosophy of proverbs " speaks of it as an excellent collection, and as anonymous; but really edited and translated by Mapletoft. [B.M.

116. Marin (Carl). Ordspråk och Talesätt, på svenska, latin, franska, tyska, italienska och engelska, *etc.*

Stockholm, 1863.
Another edition. 8°. Stockholm, *Haeggström*, 1867.

117. Marvin (Dwight Edwards). The antiquity of proverbs, *etc.*
pp. xiii, 329.   8°. New York, London, *Putnam*, 1922.

Pp. ix-xiii, authorities consulted. Notes and comments on fifty different proverbs are given, followed by lists of variant and allied proverbs from different countries, in English. Some of the sections are too overloaded with comments.
[B.M.

118. ———: Curiosities in proverbs, *etc.* pp. xi, 428.
7/6. sm. 8°. New York, London, *Putnam*, 1916.

The author-index contains some printer's errors. There are some evidences of haste throughout the book. Pp. vii-xi, authorities consulted.
[F.-L.S. (Stephens collection).

119. Masson (Moritz). Die Weisheit des Volkes. Einiges aus dem Sprichwörterschatz der Deutschen, Russen, Franzosen und anderer, ihnen stammverwandter Nationen, *etc.* pp. viii, 390.   1 r. 75 kop. 8°. St. Petersburg, *Glasunoff*, 1868.

There is another title page in Russian. Equivalent proverbs in German, Russian and French, frequently compared with English, Italian, Serbian, *etc.*, examples.   [B.M.

120. Master. The eloquent master of languages, *etc.*
8°. Hamburg, *T. von Wiering*, 1693.

This curious little grammar book contains various lists of proverbs in English, French, German and Italian.   [B.M.

121. Matras (Daniel). Proverbes, sentences, et mots dorés, recueillis des meilleurs autheurs qui ont escrit de cette matière en François, Danois, Italien et Allemand.
8°. Copenhague, *Marzan*, 1633.

Another edition.   12°. Copenhague, 1643.
Gratet-Duplessis, 826.   [B.M.

122. Maunder (Samuel). Maunder's treasury of knowledge and library of reference. Parts 1 and 2.
12°. London, *for S. Maunder*, 1830.

Another edition. pp. 899. 12°. London, *Longman*, 1859.

Gratet-Duplessis, 865. Contains a section of proverbs, terms and phrases in Latin, French, Spanish and Italian, with English translations. Each page is also surrounded by four English proverbs or maxims in the margin. [B.M.

123. Mawer (E. B.). Analogous proverbs in ten languages.
pp. 113.   8°. London, *Elliot Stock*, 1885.

Proverbs in English, Roumanian, French, German, Italian, Spanish, Dutch, Danish, Portuguese, Latin. The proverbs are arranged alphabetically under the English version, which is followed by the foreign equivalents. No notes or explanations. Of more interest philologically than parœmiologically, as the proverbs are all well known.   [B.M.

124. ———: Proverbele Rômanîlor. English proverbs, *etc.*
pp. 64. 12°. London, *Kerby & Endean*, Bucuresci, [1882].

Proverbs in Roumanian, English, French and German, without notes or explanations.   [B.M.

125. Mayreder (C.). Die polyglotte Sprichwörterliteratur. Eine bibliographische Skizze, als Ergänzung zu M. G. Duplessis' " Bibliographie parémiologique," etc.

8°. Torino, etc., 1877.

In Rivista di letteratura popolare, Vol. 1, pp. 241-265. *See also* **17.**

126. Megiser (Hieronymus). Παροιμιολογίας, pars prima, etc.

8°. Graecii Stiriae, *Widmanstadius*, 1592.
Parœmiologia polyglottos, etc. pp. 240.

8°. Lipsiae, *Grosius*, 1605.

Another edition. fol. Lipsiae, 1606.

Gratet-Duplessis, 15, gives details of the life and works of the author. Proverbs and sentences chiefly in Latin, Greek, French and German, arranged under subjects. [B.M.

127. Méry (C. de). Histoire générale des proverbes, etc. 3 tom.

8°. Paris, *Delongchamps*, 1828-29.

Gratet-Duplessis, 11. This book does not fulfil the promise of its title; however, there are a good number of proverbs collected from little-known books which would be difficult to procure. Vol. 1 consists of proverbs arranged under different nations, with explanations taken from various authors, and followed by another collection arranged under such headings as, historical, general, etc. Vols. 2 and 3 consist of maxims, sentences, etc., taken from famous writers, and proverbs and proverbial sayings arranged under various headings, followed by some biographical notices of authors of collections of proverbs. Not a very important book. [B.M.

128. Meurier (Gabriel). Recueil de sentences notables . . . proverbes, . . . traduits la plus part de Latin, Italien et Espagnol, et réduits selon l'ordre alphabétic.

sm. 8°. Anvers, *Waesberghe*, 1568.

Another edition. Trésor de sentences dorées et argentées, etc.
pp. 332. sm. 8°. Cologny, *Le Febure*, 1617.

Gratet-Duplessis, 14. This collection of proverbs is not a learned work, but it is very interesting, since it preserves a record of a number of sayings now obsolete.

129. Middlemore (James). Proverbs, sayings and comparisons in various languages. Collected and arranged by James Middlemore. pp. vi. 458. 7/6. sm. 8°. London, *Isbister*, 1889.

Pp. 1-375, proverbs and sayings; pp. 376-443, proverbs in five languages; pp. 443-458, comparisons. Arranged alphabetically under the English version with foreign translations and equivalents beneath.

[F.-L.S. (Stephens collection).

130. Mikhelson (M. I.). Мѣткія и ходячія слова, etc. pp. vi, 690.

8°. St. Petersburg, Яблонскій, 1894.

A book of quotations, proverbs, familiar phrases, etc., in Russian, German, English, French, and Latin. [B.M.

131. Mombert (J. I.). A chapter on proverbs.

8°. Andover, London, 1881.

In The Bibliotheca Sacra, Vol. 38, pp. 593-621. A general survey containing numerous examples. [B.M.

B

132. Montlong (   ). Quintessenz der Conversation, oder 3000
Sprichwörter in 14 Sprachen, als: deutsch, französisch,
englisch, italienisch, spanisch, ungarisch, polnisch, serbisch,
lateinisch, griechisch, türkisch, arabisch, persisch, und
hebraeisch, im Originaltexte und mit deutsch-französischer
Uebersetzung, *etc.*   8°. Wien, *Beck*, 1862.

Only the first two parts are in the British Museum, though twelve were
announced.   [B.M.

132a. Moorhead (J. K.). A dictionary of quotations and proverbs. With an introduction by J. K. Moorhead. 2 vols.
                                        8°. London, *Dent*, 1928.

Everyman Library, Nos. 809-810.   [B.M.

133. Mosing (Irma von). Sprichwörter in vier Weltsprachen.
Deutsch, Englisch, Französisch, Italienisch. pp. 47.
                                        8°. Dresden, [1911].

134. Muroulides (Bas. A.). Φιλοσοφικὰ ψιχία ἤτοι συλλογὴ παροιμιῶν
Ἑλλήνων, Λατίνων, Γάλλων, Ἰταλῶν, Ἑβραίων, Ἀράβων, etc. pp.
320.   8°. Ἐν Ἀθήναις, 1897.

135. Nannus Mirabellius (Dominicus). Polyanthea, *etc.*
                                    fol. Venetiis, 1507.

Florilegii magni, seu polyantheae floribus novissimis sparsae
libri xx, *etc.* fol. Lugduni, *A. de Harsy & P. Ravaud*, 1620.

Abstract subjects, with a collection of precepts, maxims, extracts from famous
authors, *etc.*, relating to them. Lists of adagia, Latin and Greek, are given
under most of the headings in the later editions.   [B.M.

136. Nomenclatura. Nomenclatura brevis reformata . . . una cum
duplici centenario proverbiorum Anglo-Latino-Graecorum ac
aliis nonnullis. Editio auctior, *etc.*   8°. London, 1684.

137. Nopitsch (Christian Conrad). Literatur der Sprichwörter.
Ein Handbuch für Literarhistoriker, Bibliographen und
Bibliothecaren. Zweite Ausgabe. pp. viii, 284.
                                    8°. Nürnberg, *Lechner*, 1822.
Second edition. pp. viii, 284. 8°. Nürnberg, *Ebner*, 1833.

Gratet-Duplessis, 1. The second edition is the same as the first of 1822, with
a new frontispiece. Very good for German parœmiology, but rather incomplete
for other nations. Contains too many entries concerning maxims and thoughts
rather than proverbs. His work has been more or less superseded by that of
Wander, Reinsberg-Düringsfeld and others, but it is still of interest and use.
He is rather superfluously particular over the various editions of any one book.
Difficult to refer to, as there is no index.   [B.M.

138. O'Leary (C. F.). The world's best proverbs and proverbial
phrases.   St. Louis, *Herder*, 1907.

139. Opdyke (George H.). The world's best proverbs and short
quotations.   Chicago, *Laird*.

140. Orton (James). Proverbs illustrated by parallel, or relative passages of the poets, to which are added Latin, French, Spanish and Italian proverbs, with translations, *etc.* [Illustrated.] 8°. Philadelphia, 1852.

141. Ottow (A. M.). Beiträge zur Sprichwörterlitteratur.
8°. Leipzig, *Weigel*, 1867.

In Serapeum, Zeitschrift für Bibliothekwissenschaft, *etc.*, Jahrgang 28, pp. 326-331. [B.M.

142. Ozenfant (Émile). Les proverbes de Jacob Cats.
8°. Paris, 1892-1896.

In La Tradition, tome 6, pp. 33-38, 86-88, 186-190, 335-339; tome 7, pp. 24-26, 101-104, 147-149, 211-215; tome 8, pp. 37-41, 71-77, 214-222. A brief notice of J. Cats, followed by selections from his proverbs. [B.M.

143. Palmer (Charles). A collection of select aphorisms and maxims, with several historical observations extracted from the most eminent authors. pp. [viii], 322.
4°. London, *printed by E. Cave*, 1748.

Not arranged in any order. Origin only given occasionally. [U.C.L.

144. Pianzola (Bernardino). Dizionario, gramatiche, e dialoghi per apprendere le lingue italiana, greca volgara, e turca. *First edition.* 2 tom. 8°. Padova, 1781.
Third edition. 3 tom. 8°. Venezia, *Zatta*, 1801.

The Dialoghi contain a chapter of proverbs in all three languages. [B.M.

145. Pissot (Noel Laurent). Histoire des proverbes, rédigée par le traducteur de la Galerie Anglaise, [*i.e.* N. L. Pissot]. pp. 249. 12°. Paris, *Durosier*, 1803.

Stirling Maxwell, p. 46.

146. Pokornuy (A.). Параллельно — синонимическій лексиконъ пословицъ, поговорокъ, цитатъ, *etc.* 8°. Одесса, 1895.

In Одесскій Альманахъ ... на ... 1895, pp. 109-112. Bernstein, 2627.

147. Prantl (Carl von). Die Philosophie in den Sprichwörtern. pp. 24. 4°. München, *Kaiser*, 1858.
[B.M.

148. Proverbes. Plus de deux mille proverbes rassemblés en divers pays. pp. 231. sm. 8°. Bruxelles, *Kiessling*, 1871.

807 French proverbs; 35 Russian; 15 Indian; 232 Arabic; 62 Jewish; 173 Chinese; 52 English; 66 German; 402 Spanish; 95 Italian; and 89 Dutch proverbs. Those of the last five countries mentioned are in the original languages.

149. ———: Proverbes rassemblés en divers pays, par un voyageur parœmiophile. pp. 231.
sm. 8°. Bruxelles, 1854.

Stirling Maxwell, p. 73.

150. Proverbs. Dropped proverbs. 8°. London, 1867.
In All the Year Round, Vol. 17, pp. 423-7. [U.C.L.

151. ———: On the use of proverbs in grave composition.
8°. London, 1857.
In Fraser's Magazine, Vol. 56, pp. 710-718. [B.M.

152. ———: Popular proverbs. pp. 24.
8°. Cleveland, Ohio, *Cleveland Educational Bureau*, 1882.
Books for the people, edited by C. E. Bolton, No. 2. English, Welsh, Scottish and foreign proverbs in English, arranged alphabetically. Quite unimportant.
[B.M.

153. ———: Proverbs. 8°. London, 1857.
In The Leisure Hour, Vol. 6, pp. 574-576, 597-599, 618-620. [B.M.

154. ———: Proverbs. 8°. Edinburgh, London, 1860.
In Blackwood's Edinburgh Magazine, Vol. 88, pp. 472-484. A general survey.
[B.M.

155. ———: Proverbs, ancient and modern. 8°. [London, 1868].
In Quarterly Review, Vol. 125, pp. 218-254. An article reviewing 19 books of proverbs, an excellent introduction to the study of the subject: pp. 237-239, a selection of proverbs from Talmudical sources.
[F.-L.S. (Stephens collection).

156. ———: Proverbs of different nations. 8°. London, 1835.
In The Westminster Review, Vol. 22, pp. 343-361. A review of D'Israeli's " Curiosities of Literature," but worthy to be considered on its own account.
[U.C.L.

157. ———: Proverbs ; or the manual of wisdom ; being an alpha-betical arrangement of the best English, French, Spanish, Italian, and other proverbs, *etc.* 12°. Oxford, 1803.
Second edition. pp. vi, 146. 8°. London, *Tabart*, 1804.
Gratet-Duplessis, 26. A list of proverbs from various countries, in English.
[B.M.

158. R. (N.). Proverbs, English, French, Dutch, Italian and Spanish. All Englished and alphabetically digested by N. R., gent. pp. [viii], 151. 12°. London, *Midar*, 1659.
Gratet-Duplessis, 19. An alphabetical list of English, French, Italian, Spanish and Dutch proverbs in English. No notes. [B.M.

159. Ragusa-Moleti (Girolamo). I proverbi dei popoli barbari. pp. 62. 8°. Palermo, *Vena*, 1893.
An interesting study in parœmiology, with a good sprinkling of proverbs of the Basutos, Maoris, Abyssinians, *etc.*, translated into Italian. [B.M.

160. Ray (John). Nomenclator classicus, sive dictionariolum trilingue. . . . Fifth edition. 8°. London, *Taylor*, 1706.
Eighth edition. 12°. Dublin, *Dillon*, 1735.
The earlier of the above editions contains : A century of proverbs and pro-verbial speeches, in English, Latin and Greek ; in the later edition only the English and Latin are given. These proverbs are not in an edition of the Dictionariolum trilingue, dated 1685. *See also* **630,** later editions, for General proverbs.
[B.M.

161. Reinsberg-Düringsfeld (Ida von), *Baroness*, and **Reinsberg-Düringsfeld** (Otto von), *Baron*. Sprichwörter der germanischen und romanischen Sprachen, *etc.* 2 Bde.
8°. Leipzig, *Fries*, 1872-1875.

An important work demonstrating the similarity, and in some cases, identicality, of proverbs of the Germanic and Latin peoples. The proverbs are arranged alphabetically by the German, with equivalents from most European languages following. Bd. 2, pp. 629-638, bibliography. An excellent and painstaking work, which might have been called a comparative dictionary of proverbs.
[B.M.

162. Rijnenberg (J.). Spreekt gij Maleisch? *etc.* pp. 147.
8°. Leiden, *Sijthoff*, [1873].
Third edition. obl. 8°. Leiden, [1890].

Contains a brief list of proverbs and phrases in Dutch, Malay, French, German and English.
[B.M.

163. Rohde (Ulric Andreas). De veterum poetarum sapientia gnomica, Hebraeorum in primis et Graecorum commentatus est. pp. viii, 29, 346. 8°. Havniæ, *Schubote*, 1799.

Gratet-Duplessis, 4. Not concerned particularly with proverbs, but Duplessis thinks it should be included, since the author proves that many moral maxims of the poets have in the course of time become proverbial. Duplessis quotes a passage dealing with this. Re-issued in 1800, with a new title-page. [B.M.

164. S. (E.). Words of human wisdom. Collected and arranged by E. S. With a preface by H. P. Liddon. pp. xv, 148.
3/6. 16°. London, *Murray*, 1873.

Alphabetical list of proverbs, epigrams, axioms, *etc.*
F. L.S. (Stephens collection).

165. Sadashew Wishwanáth. Select proverbs of all nations. Four thousand and upwards . . . translated into Marathi couplets. pp. [xi], 465, [18]. 8°. Bombay, *Crishnajee*, 1858.

166. Samenhof (M. F.). Phraséologie parallèle des langues russe, française et allemande . . . Vergleichende russisch-französisch-deutsche Phraseologie oder Sammlung von Sprichwörtern, Denksprüchen, *etc.* 3 Thle. 8°. Warschau, 1873.

167. Sayings. The proverbial and wise sayings of the English, Scotch, Italians and Spaniards, *etc.* 12°. London, n.d.
The proverbs are translated into English.

167a. ———: Proverbial sayings; or a collection of the best English proverbs by John Ray; Scots proverbs by Allan Ramsay; Italian proverbs by Orlando Pescetti; Spanish proverbs by Ferdinand Nuñez. With the wise sayings and maxims of the ancients. 12°. 1800.

168. Schiepek (Josef). Bemerkungen zur psychologischen Grundlage des Sprichwortes. 8°. Saaz, 1890.

In Programm des Kais. Kön. Staats-Ober-Gymnasiums zu Saaz, 1890, pp. 1-16.

169. Schiepek (Josef). Ueber die mnemotechnische Seite des
sprichwörtlichen Ausdruckes.   8°. Saaz, 1891.

In Programm des Kais. Kön. Staats-Ober-Gymnasiums zu Saaz, 1891, pp.
1-24.

170. Scholz (G.). Short proverbs for grammar analysis.
Chicago, *Flanagan*, 1903.

171. Schwabhaeuser (M.). Sprichwörter-Schatz in vier Sprachen.
8°. Heidelberg, 1915.

172. Schweitzeren (Joannes à). Thesaurus quinque Germanicae,
Latinae, Hispanicae, Gallicae et Italicae linguarum funda-
mentalis, *etc.* [Dedication signed Joannes à Schweitzeren].
pp. [xiv], 962.   4°. Viennae Austriae, *Rickesin*, 1665.

Pp. 744-774, lists of proverbs in each of the above languages.   [B.M.

173. Seelbach (Carl). Proverbial treasury. English and foreign
proverbs, *etc.* pp. iv, 190.
8°. New York, *Seelbach*, Leipzig, *Hartmann*, 1880.

A collection of proverbs in English, in alphabetical order, with references and
explanations where necessary. Presumably this was meant to be continued, as
only letter A is dealt with.   [B.M.

174. Septuagenarian. Anecdotes, aphorisms and proverbs. Collected by a septuagenarian. pp. 183.
8°. London, *Griffith, Farran*, [1906].

Pp. 167-183, English, Spanish and Turkish proverbs in English.   [B.M.

175. Sessa (Giuseppe). Dottrina popolare in quattro lingue. . . .
Seconda edizione, *etc.* pp. 211. 12°. Milano, *Hoepli*, 1891.

Pp. 182-211, proverbs in Italian, French, English and German.

176. Shearer (William John). Wisdom of the world, in proverbs
of all nations.   New York, *Macmillan*, 1904.

177. Smith (J.). Grammatica quadrilinguis; or, brief instructions for the French, Italian, Spanish and English tongues,
with the proverbs of each language, *etc.* pp. 264.
8°. London, *Newman*, 1674.

Stirling Maxwell, 89. Pp. 61-68, French proverbs; pp. 123-132, Italian proverbs; pp. 197-205, Spanish proverbs; pp. 257-264, Anglicana proverbia.

178. Sprichwoerter. Russische Sprichwörter — Italienische
Sprichwörter—Deutsche Sprichwörter—Französische Sprichwörter—Spanische Sprichwörter.
4°. Frankfurt-am-Main, 1835.

Several articles in : Didaskalia, 1835, Nos. 248, 269, 273. The proverbs are
translated into German.

179. Standing (B.). Anecdotes, aphorisms, and proverbs, *etc.*
pp. 183.   8°. London, *Griffith, Farran*, 1891.

Pp. 167-183, a few English, Spanish, and Turkish proverbs, the two latter
being also in English. A brief list, no notes.   [B.M.

180. Stirling, *afterwards* **Stirling-Maxwell** (*Sir* William), *Bart.*
An essay towards a collection of books relating to proverbs
. . . being a catalogue of those at Keir. pp. vi, 244.

8°. London, *privately printed*, 75 *copies only*, 1860.

The book consists of three sections, the first, pp. 1-107, dealing with books
of proverbs; the second, with emblems; and the third, with apophthegms, epitaphs, *etc.* The books or editions unnoticed by Duplessis are distinguished from
those which were published since the appearance of his " Bibliographie parémiologique." The arrangement is alphabetical, and the books are described with
meticulous care. A useful list, but it is to be regretted that the author did not
attempt to indicate the scope of the various works. [B.M.

181. ———: Lemmata proverbiala. pp. 24.

4°. Londini, 1851.
Only ten copies printed.

182. ———: On the first edition of the Adagia of Erasmus.
pp. 5. sm. 4°. London, 1854.

Also as Bibliographical and Historical Miscellanies of the Philobiblon Society,
Vol. 1, item 7. Also reprinted in the author's works, Vol. 6, pp. 51-53, 1891.
The author gives an exact transcript of the title-page of the first edition of the
Adagia, and says the book is in 8°, whereas it is usually given as 4°.
[*Works*, F.-L.S. (Stephens collection).

183. Storckau (Joannes Christophorus). Parœmiae grecae,
latinae, germanicae, *etc.* ff. [48].

12°. Osterodae, *Trabethus*, 1668.

Gratet-Duplessis, 21. A small collection of Greek, Latin and German proverbs. Not very important. [B.M.

184. Strafforello (Gustavo). La sapienza del mondo, ovvero
dizionario universale dei proverbi di tutti i popoli, *etc.* 3 tom.

8°. Torino, *Negro*, 1883.

Was published in numbers of 24 pages each, from 1870-1883. Vol. 1, pp.
xiii-xxv, bibliography. The proverbs are arranged alphabetically by the
Italian, followed by the equivalents in different Italian dialects and from other
languages. All the foreign proverbs are given in Italian, except the French,
which are in the original. A thoroughly workmanlike book. [B.M.

185. ———: La sapienza del popolo spiegata al popolo, *etc.* pp.
viii, 264.

L.2. 16°. Milano, *Editoria della Biblioteca Utile*, 1868.

Pitrè, 3307, says this book is purely a translation of Trench's " Proverbs and
their lessons," *q.v.* **191,** which Strafforello has had the audacity to pass off as
his own work. He compares both books in detail. Mr. Stephens has verified
this accusation and finds it absolutely true. Pp. 254-64, bibliography. [B.M.

186. Strings. Strings of proverbs. 8°. London, 1852.

In Household Words, Vol. 4, pp. 469-472, 524-526, 538-540. Comments on
numerous proverbs of different languages. [B.M.

187. Sumaran (Joannes Angelus von). Sprachbuch und gründlicher Wegweiser, *etc.* pp. [xxvi], 645.

sm. 8°. (Monachii), *Verlegung dess Authoris*, 1621.

Bernstein, 3633. Pp. 622-645, proverbs in French, Italian, Spanish and
German; 100 of each.

188. Sumaran (Angelus A.). Thesaurus linguarum. 3 vols.
4°. Ingolstadt, 1626.

Pitrè, 3310. Vol. 3, Nomenclatura et proverbia. Proverbs in Spanish, French, Italian and German. Author's name spelt thus by Pitrè; ? same book as last entry.

189. Taverner (Richard). Proverbes or adagies with newe addicions gathered out of the Chiliades of Erasmus, *etc.*
8°. London, *at the sygne of the Whyte Harte*, 1539.
Another edition. ff. lxxv. 8°. London, *Kele*, 1552.

Gratet-Duplessis, 834. A careful selection with delightful notes and comments.
[B.M.

190. Tobias (Anton). Beiträge zur Sprichwörter-Litteratur.
8°. Leipzig, *Weigel*, 1868, 1869.

In Serapeum, Zeitschrift für Bibliothekwissenschaft, *etc.*, Jahrgang 29, pp. 149-155; Jahrgang 30, p. 336. Gives bibliographical details of two or three books of proverbs. [B.M.

191. Trench (Richard Chevenix), *Archbishop of Canterbury.* On the lessons in proverbs, *etc.* pp. iv, 128.
8°. London, *Parker*, 1853.
Another edition. Proverbs and their lessons, pp. viii, 179.
8°. London, *Routledge*, New York, *Dutton*, 1905.

The edition of 1905 is an enlarged one, containing an extra chapter and a bibliography. The book consists of lectures on various aspects of proverbs; in every case the author quotes many examples. There is an appendix of metrical proverbs in the Middle Ages. Reviewed in the Quarterly Review, Vol. 125, pp. 217-25. [F.-L.S. (Stephens collection).

192. Valette (T. G. G.). Verzameling van spreekwoorden en spreekwoordelijke uitdrukkingen in vier talen. (Nederlandsch, fransch, hoogduitsch, engelsch), *etc.* pp. 76.
8°. Haarlem, *Bohn*, 1887.
Contains about 500 entries.

193. Varrini (Giulio). Scuola del volgo, cioè scielta de' più leggiadari e spiritosi detti, aforismi, e proverbi, *etc.* pp. [xxii], 287. sm. 12°. Verona, *Rossi*, 1642.
Third edition. Scielta dē proverbi e sentenze italiani, *etc.* pp. [xxiv], 287. 12°. Venetia, 1656.

Gratet-Duplessis, 20, quotes other editions. A large collection of proverbs from various languages translated into Italian, without either notes or commentary. Interesting, but without any great importance. [B.M.

194. Vaslet (Louis). Nomenclator trilinguis . . . cum proverbiis miscellaneis ducentis & duodecim. . . . Editio tertia, *etc.* pp. 151. 8°. Londini, *impensis auctoris*, 1713.

Pp. 126-147, Adagia miscellanea, *etc.* Latin, English, French. [B.M.

195. Wade (John).   Select proverbs of all nations, illustrated
with notes and comments, *etc.*   By Thomas Fielding.   [*pseud.*
of John Wade].   pp. xviii, 216.

12°.   London, *Berger*, [1824].

Gratet-Duplessis, 29.   Pp. vii-xviii, Introduction, indicating the unworked
field of paremiology : pp. 1-54, select proverbs of all nations, arranged alphabetically; pp. 55-127, proverbs arranged under subjects; pp. 128-140, English
local proverbs; pp. 141-156, proverbial rhymes, old saws, *etc.*; pp. 201-213,
sayings and maxims of the ancients and Fathers of the Church; pp. 213-216,
miscellaneous maxims.   The proverbs are mostly in English, but occasionally
foreign originals are given.   Reviewed in the Quarterly Review, Vol. 125, pp.
217-254.   [F.-L.S. (Stephens collection).

196. Walker (J.).   Handy book of proverbs.

New York, *Crowell*, 1910.

196a. Ward (C. A.).   Proverbs.   8°.   London, 1883.

In Time, Vol. 8, pp. 112-19.   Definitions and general discussion, with
examples from many races.   [B.M.

197. Ward (Caroline).   National proverbs in the principal languages of Europe.   pp. iv, 176.   16°.   London, *Parker*, 1842.

Gratet-Duplessis, 35.   630 proverbs in English, compared with as many
French, Italian, Spanish and German ones.   Lacking in notes and explanations.
                                                                   [B.M.

198. Wiltse (S. E.).   Folklore stories and proverbs.

Boston, *Ginn*, 1924.

199. Zeuschner (O.).   Internationaler Citatenschatz.   Lesefrüchte
aus heimischen und fremden Schriftstellern (Sprichwörter und
Sentenzen), *etc.*   pp. iv, 474.

M.4.   8°.   Leipzig, *Schloemp*, 1884.

Third edition, pp. iv, 503.   8°.   Leipzig, *Freund*, 1887.

Proverbs and quotations in German, English, Latin, French, *etc.*, in alphabetical order; the foreign ones with German translations.   [B.M.

200. Zubrodt (   ).   Adagia, *etc.*   Francfort, 1670.

LATIN

(Ancient, Mediæval, and Modern).

201. Adagia. Adagia selecta faciliora. 4°. Dilingae, 1647.
Gratet-Duplessis, 163.

202. Alberta (Joseph). Epitome adagiorum ex Grecis Latinsq.
scriptoribus excerptorum ordineq. alphabetico digestorum.
12°. Romae, 1574.
[Bristol Pub. Lib.

203. Andrelinus (Publius Faustus). Epistolae proverbiales et
morales. 4°. [Paris, 1508?].
Another edition. 8°. Moguntiae, *Schoeffer*, 1527.
Gratet-Duplessis, 122, says these letters had a great success when they were
first published, although they are without literary importance. There were
various other editions. [B.M.

204. Anger (Johann B.). Wörtliche und ursprüngliche Erklärung
. . . lateinischer Sprichwörter, *etc.* pp. 72.
8°. Wien, *Edlen*, 1798.
Bernstein, 103. Deals with 228 proverbs.

205. Apotheca. Apotheca scholastica, *etc.* pp. 112, [7].
8°. London, *Brooke*, 1666.
Pp. 30-58, adagia sententiae proverbiales.

206. Apparatus. Apparatus proverbiorum et adagiorum, *etc.*
pp. 127. 8°. Augustae Vindelicorum, *Gæbelius*, 1683.
Another edition. 8°. Augustae Vindelicorum, 1758.
Gratet-Duplessis, 175 and 202.

207. Arnoldus (Danielus). Sententiae proverbiales selectae opera
Arnoldi. 8°. Hamburgi, 1666.
Another edition. pp. 222. 8°. Helmestadii, *Müller*, 1674.
Gratet-Duplessis, 168. Latin proverbs with German translations or equi-
valents. [B.M.

208. Bartsch (Carl). Sprichwörter des xi. Jahrhunderts.
8°. Wien, 1873.
In Germania, Neue Reihe 6, pp. 310-353. [B.M.

209. Berluccius (Joannes Antonius). Adagia selecta, *etc.* pp. [30], 765.

8°. Coloniae Allobrogum, *Joann. de Tournes*, 1632.

Another edition. 8°. Genevae, 1672.

Gratet-Duplessis, 158. *See also* **278.**

210. Beroaldus (Philippus). Oratio proverbiorum, *etc.* pp. [54]. 4°. (Bononiae, *Hectoris*, 1499).

Another edition. 4°. Basle, 1517.

Gratet-Duplessis, 120. An uninteresting discourse, of which there were many other editions. Duplessis mentions some of them, and gives a brief sketch of Beroaldus. [B.M.

211. Binder (Wilhelm). Medulla proverbiorum latinorum, *etc.* pp. iv, 160. 16°. Stuttgart, *Metzler*, 1856.

1875 proverbs, arranged alphabetically by the first word of the Latin, with German translations and occasional German equivalents. A useful book. [B.M.

212. ———: Novus thesaurus adagiorum latinorum, *etc.* pp. xiv, 403. 8°. Stuttgart, *Fischhaber*, 1861.

3609 Latin proverbs arranged alphabetically, with German translations or equivalents. The place of origin is indicated in each case. Pp. ix-xiv, bibliography. Reviewed and discussed by W. H. D. Suringar in Tijdschrift voor de nederlandsche Gymnasiën voor 1861, pp. 135-185. [B.M.

213. Bolza (Giambattista). Motti, precetti e proverbi latini, colla versione italiana. 2 pts.

8°. Venezia, *Antonelli*, 1855-1856.

Another edition. pp. 96. 8°. Como, *Franchi*, 1865.

214. Borghi (Luigi Costantino). Proverbi e detti sapienziali latino-italici. pp. 37.

L.0.50. 8°. (Venezia, *Tipografia " La Venezia,"* 1882).

In some cases 1883 is found as the date of publication. Since 393 proverbs are given, this is presumably the book indicated by Pitrè, 2501. The proverbs are arranged alphabetically under the Latin, with Italian translations and equivalents underneath. No notes. [B.M.

215. ———: Altri proverbi e detti sapienziali latino-italiani. pp. 91. 8°. Venezia, *Istituto Coletti*, 1896.

Pitrè, 2502.

216. ———: Proverbi e detti sapienziali latini . . . confrontati con altri italiani. pp. 198. 8°. Venezia, *Visentini*, 1898.

Bernstein, 4271.

217. Bozon (Nicole). Les proverbes de bon enseignement de Nicole Bozon, publiés pour la première fois par A. Chr. Thorn. pp. xxxi, 65 and 3 tables.

5 kr. la. 8°. Lund, *Gleerup*, Leipzig, *Harrassowitz*, 1921.

In Lunds Universitets Årsskrift, N.F., Avd. 1, Bd. 17, Nr. 4. Latin proverbs translated into French verse. [U.C.L.

218. Capellanus (Georg). Sprechen Sie Lateinisch?, *etc.* pp.
107.   8°. Leipzig, *Koch*, 1880.
Second edition. pp. 115.   8°. Leipzig, 1892.
Contains a section : Sprichwörtliches. Latin proverbs with German translations.   [B.M.

219. Caviceo (Jacopo). *Begin :* Urbium dicta ad Maximilianu[m]
Federici Tertii coesaris [*sic*] filiu[m] romanor[um] Regem
triumphantissimu[m].   4°. (1491).
Gratet-Duplessis, 121. Contains a nomenclature of proverbial sayings characterising certain towns.   [B.M.

220. Corbellinus (Petrus). Adagiales flosculi. ff. 72.
                            4°. Parrhisijs, *Officina Chevallica*, 1520.
Another edition.   4°. Parisiis, *Chevallon*, 1580.
Gratet-Duplessis, 137.

221. Cordier (Mathurin). Sententiae proverbiales Gallicolatinae,
etc. pp. 78.   8°. Parisiis, *Paruus*, 1549.
Another edition.   8°. Lutetiae, *David*, 1561.
Gratet-Duplessis, 128. Separate editions of a small but good collection of
Latin and French proverbs, to be found in the same author's " Commentarius
puerorum . . . qui prius Liber de corrupti sermonis emendatione dicebatur,"
etc. Duplessis gives further details of Cordier's life and work.   [B.M.

222. Czapiński (Leopold). Księga przysłów, sentencji i wyrazów
łacińskich, *etc.* pp. ii, 524.
                            8°. Warszawa, *Orgelbrand*, 1892.
Arranged alphabetically, with full notes in Polish.   [B.M.

223. Dalpiaz (B.) and **Jülg** (Carlo). Gius. Steiner e Dr. Aug.
Scheindler. Libro di lettura e di esercizii latini . . . pubblicato
ad uso delle scuole italiane, da B. Dalpiaz e Carlo Dr. Jülg,
etc. pp. iv, 72.   8°. Trento, *Monauni*, 1890.
Pitrè, 2669. From the title it is impossible to discover which are the authors.
Pp. 68-71, an appendix containing 65 proverbs and sentences in Latin, with
Italian counterparts.

224. Egbert, *von Lüttich.* Fecunda ratis. Zum ersten Mal
herausgegeben . . . von Ernst Voigt. pp. lxv, 273.
                            8°. Halle a S., *Niemeyer*, 1889.
A long explanatory introduction, followed by the Latin proverbs or maxims
from the manuscript of Egbert von Lüttich.   [B.M.

225. Faselius (August). Latium, oder das alte Rom in seinen
Sprüchwörtern, *etc.* pp. xvi, 276. 8°. Weimar, *Voigt*, 1859.
Second edition. pp. xvi, 276.   8°. Weimar, *Voigt*, 1865.
A collection of Latin proverbs with German translations or equivalents, and
explanatory notes.   [B.M.

226. Feind (Bartholdus). Florilegium Germanico-Latinum sententiarum proverbialium. . . . Editio quinta, *etc.* pp. [206].
8°. Hamburgi, *Schillerus et Kisnerus*, 1720.
Sixth edition. 8°. Hamburgi, *Kisnerus*, 1734.

Contains 1000 Latin proverbs, with German equivalents. These are rather sentences from famous authors than popular proverbs. [B.M.

227. Ferrerio (Giovanni). Collectanea proverbiorum.
Colon[iae], 1612.

Also included in various editions of the Adagia of Erasmus.

228. Fitzgerald (Kathleen). Proverbs in Latin and English.
pp. 169. 32°. London, *Hill*, [1920].

Hill's Bilingual Series. [B.M.

229. Fleischner (J. M.). Handbüchlein sorgfältig ausgewählter lateinischer Sprichwörter und Denkverse, mit entsprechender teutscher Uebersetzung, *etc.* pp. xv, 120.
8°. Erlangen, *Palm & Enke*, 1829.
520 entries.

230. Fumagalli (Giuseppe). L'Ape latina. Dizionarietto di 2588 frasi, sentenze, proverbi, *etc.* pp. 353.
8°. Milano, *Hoepli*, 1911.
With Italian translations. [B.M.

231. Gartner (Andreas). Proverbialia dicteria, *etc.* ff. 115.
8°. [Erfurt], 1570.
Another edition. 8°. Francofurti, *Egenolphius*, 1591.
Another edition. 8°. Francofurti, 1598.

Gratet-Duplessis, 141. Divided into two parts, the first containing proverbial sayings in verse with German translations, the second consisting of various items, among which are a number of moral maxims taken from the Fathers of the Church. Duplessis gives details of the other items. [B.M.

232. Geffensis (Joannes). Carmina et proverbia magis obvia.
Antverpiae, 1617.

Gratet-Duplessis, 152, gives no details of author or book.

233. Gerbertus (Joannes). Chilias adagiorum communiorum Latino-Germanicorum. 1641.

234. Germbergius (Hermannus). Carminum proverbialium . . . loci communes, *etc.* pp. [xvi], 357.
8°. Basileae, *Officina Oporiniana*, 1582.
Latin, with occasional German translations or equivalents. [B.M.

235. Giselinus (Vict.). Adagiorum omnium . . . epitome.
8°. Antv., 1671.

These proverbs are also given in some of the numerous editions of the collections of Erasmus and Grynaeus.

236. Godofredus (Petrus). Proverbiorum liber. pp. 176.
sm. 8°. Parisiis, Stephanus, 1555.

Gratet-Duplessis, 132. 200 proverbs in Latin, mostly taken from the classics, accompanied by explanatory notes on their origin or sense. A rare book, a large part of which, however, was reprinted at the end of various editions of the Adagia of Erasmus, notably those of Paris, <i>Michel Sonnius</i>, 1579, and fol. Frankfort, 1612.   [B.M.

237. Gossmann (Johann Barth.). 777 lateinische Sprichwörter
. . . in alphabetischer Ordnung und mit freier Uebersetzung,
etc. pp. 50.   sm. 8°. Landau, Kaussler, 1844.

Gratet-Duplessis, 226. A collection of maxims, proverbs, etc., translated into German, but without notes.

238. Hanzely (K. J.). Erklärung lateinischer Sprichwörter für
die studierende Jugend.   Brünn, 1794.

239. Hartleben (Franc. Jos.). Dictionarium parœmiarium . . .
cum notis historico-mythologicis et proverbiis linguae germanicae, <i>etc.</i> pp. iv, 262.
la. 8°. Pesthini, Hartleben, 1818.
Gratet-Duplessis, 221.

240. Hartung (Carl). Ueber die Sprichwörter, besonders die
lateinischen.   4°. Sprottau, 1871.

In Realschule i. Ordnung zu Sprottau, 1871, pp. 1-22.

241. Hauer (Georg). <i>Begin.</i> Haverius (De partibus orationis,
etc.).
4°. Augustae Vindelicorum, in officina Millerana, 1516.
Another edition. ff. 49. 4°. Augustae Vindelicorum, 1520.

Gratet-Duplessis, 124. A Latin grammar, containing a selection of proverbs taken from Erasmus, in Latin and German. The proverbs are common ones which may be found anywhere; there are no notes.   [B.M.

242. Haupt (Moriz) and **Hoffmann** (Heinrich). Altdeutsche
Blätter. 2 Bde.   8°. Leipzig, <i>Brockhaus</i>, 1836-40.

Bd. 1, pp. 10-14, Latin proverbs; pp. 74-78, Altholländische Sprüche (in rhyme); Bd. 2, pp. 133-137, Sprüche und Sprichwörter, deutsch und lateinisch. Scarcely popular proverbs.   [B.M.

243. Hawenreuter (J. L.). Adagia classica, <i>etc.</i> pp. 302.
12°. Argentorati, Rihelius, 1573.
Gratet-Duplessis, 135.

244. Hegendorphius (Christ.). Adagiorum selectorum centuriae V.   8°. Cracov[iae], 1535.

245. Hempel (Hermann). Lateinischer Sentenzen- und Sprichwörter-Schatz. pp. viii, 237.
8°. Bremen, Heinsius, 1884.
4290 sentences and proverbs in Latin, with German equivalents.

246. Henderson (Alfred).   Latin proverbs and quotations.   With translations and parallel passages, *etc.*   pp. vii, 505.

4°.   London, *Sampson Low*, 1869.

[B.M.

247. Henningius (Johannes).   Parœmiologia Virgiliana.

12°.   Quedlinb., 1694.

248. Hilner (Joannes).   Certa, facili et delectabili methodo constans nomenclator rhythmicus brevior . . . et gnomologicum Latinogermanicum sextuplex, *etc.*

8°.   Lipsiae, *Voigt*, 1599.

Latin and German.   [B.M.

249. I. (S. A.).   Carminum proverbialium . . . loci communes, *etc.* pp. xv, 364.

sm. 8°.   Basileae, *ex officina Oporiniana*, 1576.

Another edition.

sm. 8°.   Londini, *impensis Richardi Thrale*, 1670.

Gratet-Duplessis, 136. The first edition contains also German translations of most of the items in the book; that of 1670 is in Latin only. A curious collection of proverbs, verses, maxims, epigrams, *etc.* Duplessis quotes a few extracts. Attributed by Nopitsch to Hermann Germberg.   [B.M.

250. ———: Sententiae proverbiales de moribus. . . . Cum interpretatione Germanica, *etc.* pp. 134.

8°.   Basileae, *ex officina Oporiniana*, 1568.

[B.M.

251. Junius (Hadrianus).   Adagiorum centuriae octo, *etc.* pp. 927.   8°.   Basileae, *Frobenius*, 1558.

Gratet-Duplessis, 133. These adages were reprinted in various editions of the Adagia of Erasmus, which they were meant to complete. The real name of Junius was Du Jon.   [B.M.

252. Kocher (Christianus Fridericus).   Manualis scholastici pars posterior, *etc.* pp. 118, 70, [17].

8°.   Stutgardia, *Müllerus*, 1722.

The second pagination of 70 pp. contains : Proverbia Latino-Germanica, *etc.*

253. Koeberus (J. F.).   Sylloge proverbiorum et gnomarum notabilium atque usitatiorum, *etc.* pp. [xxii], 199, [4].

12°.   Jenae, *Bielckius*, 1686.

253a. Kruse (C.).   Dactyliotheca.   Corpus sententiarum dactylicarum.   8°.   Sundiae, 1863.

Includes 1246 proverbs from Horace, Ovid, Vergil, *etc.*, with indications of their origin.

254. L. (P. D.).   Radices, sive, primitiva probatae Latinitatis vocabula, cum appendice adagiorum, *etc.* pp. 112.

8°.   Giessae, *Müllerus*, 1731.

Gratet-Duplessis, 201.

255. Lentz (A.). Lateinisches Vocabularium nach Gegenständen geordnet. . . . Zweite . . . Auflage. pp. vi, 86.

8°. Graudenz, *Röthe*, 1866.

Pp. 68-80, Anhang 1, Sprüchwörter. 202 Latin proverbs, with German equivalents.

256. Levasseur (Francis). Proverbes et expressions proverbiales des meilleurs auteurs latins, avec une traduction et les proverbes français correspondans en regard du texte. pp. 133.

12°. Paris, *L'Huillier*, 1811.

Gratet-Duplessis, 220. Of no great literary merit, but interesting because of the care with which the French equivalents have been chosen. At the end is a small selection of Italian and Spanish proverbs with French translations.

257. Lull (Ramón). Liber de mille proverbiis Latina simul et Lemovicensi lingua nunc primum editus. pp. [42], 183.

8°. Palmae Majoricarum, *Cerda, etc.*, 1746.

Moral maxims rather than popular proverbs. A collection of rhymed proverbs by Lull was also published in Romania, Tome 11, pp. 188-202. [B.M.

258. Manutius (Aldus). Thesaurus proverbiorum et sententiarum.

12°. Colon[iae], 1642.

259. Margalits (E.). Florilegium proverbiorum universae latinitatis, *etc.* (Supplementum, *etc.*). pp. 548, 283. 2 vols.

8°. Budapestini in Hungaria, *Kókai*, 1895-1910.

These two volumes form a large collection of Latin proverbs arranged alphabetically by their principal words. No notes. [B.M.

260. Marinoni (Petrus). Sylva proverbiorum et sententiarum, *etc.* pp. 48. 12°. Bassani, *Remondinus*, 1694.

Bernstein, 2082. 200 Latin proverbs, *etc.*, with Italian equivalents.

261. Mayer-Ahrdorff (Eduard). Alte Sprüche in neuem Gewande. . . . 200 Adagien, Proverbien und Sentenzen aus lateinischen Classikern frei und metrisch paraphrasiert. pp. xv, 224.

8°. Wien, *Braumüller*, 1878.

Each poem is headed by a proverb. [B.M.

262. Memmert (Johann Friedrich). Grammatik, *etc.*

8°. Erlangen, 1803.

Gratet-Duplessis, 721. Theil 1, pp. 154-248, Lateinische Sprichwörter und Sentenzen. Im Versuch einer . . . teutsch-lateinischen Sprachlehre, *etc.*

263. Montijn (J. F. L.). Spreekwoorden en spreekwoordelijke uitdrukkingen der Romeinen. pp. viii, 158.

8°. Utrecht, *Beijers*, 1893.

264. Muffany (M. H.). Proverbia Latina. Paris, *Hachette.*

265. Neipeius (Melchior). Adagia, *etc.*

Included in numerous editions of the Adagia of Erasmus and Grynaeus.

[B.M.

266. Nelin (Heinrich Gottfried). Bellaria deliciaeque juveniles, *etc.* pp. 80.   8°. Kopenhagen, *Hoecke*, 1788.

Bernstein, 229.   Over 1000 Latin proverbs, maxims, sentences, *etc.*, without notes.

267. Nicolaus (Chr.). Veterum sapientum exempla et adagia.
                    8°. Hafniae, 1618.

268. Oertel (   ). Auswahl der schönsten Denk- und Sittensprüche, Sprüchwörter, Räthsel . . . aus lateinischen Dichtern und Prosaikern gezogen, *etc.* pp. iv, 160.
                    8°. Nürnberg, *Campe*, 1842.

Gratet-Duplessis, 225.   No notes.

269. Orelli (Johann Conrad). Poetarum veterum Latinorum et recentiorum quorumdam carmina sententiosa, tomus prior, *etc.* pp. xxvi, 310. (Supplementum editionis, pp. iv, 56.)
                8°. Lipsiae, *Fleischer*, 1822-24.

Gratet-Duplessis, 115.   No more published. This does for the Latin moralists what Orelli's other work does for the Greek. Useful for the origin of a certain number of proverbs.

270. Otto (A.). Die Sprichwörter und sprichwörtlichen Redensarten der Römer, *etc.* pp. xlv, 436.
                8°. Leipzig, *Teubner*, 1890.

A large alphabetical collection, with German translations and notes. The prefatory notes are important. For additions to this work, *see* **295, 297, 298, 307.**   [B.M.

271. Palmireno (Juan Lorenzo). De vera & facili imitatione Ciceronis, *etc.* ff. [132].   8°. Çaragoça, *Bernuz*, 1560.

Ff. 121-128, Adagiorum centuriae quinq[ue].

272. Perbonus (Hieronymus). Oviliarum, lib. xxvi, *etc.*
                fol. (Mediolani, 1533).

Each of the 26 books finishes with a list of adagia. A rare book.   [B.M.

273. Philippi (Ferdinand). Lateinisch-deutsche Sprechübungen, *etc.* pp. 172.   8°. Leipzig, *Focke*, 1827.

Bernstein, 4626.   Pp. 108-172, Zweite Abtheilung. Die wichtigsten und gebräuchlichsten lateinischen Sprichwörter. Latin proverbs with German equivalents.

274. Pontanus (Joannes). Aristologia proverbialis, *etc.*
      8°. Francofordiae ad Oderam, *Eichorn*, [1600?].
Collectio proverbiorum . . . post Joannis Pontani et Jo. Friderici Koeberi . . . operam repetita, amplificata, emendata. Studio Jo. Gottfr. Hauptmanni. pp. 172, [20].
              8°. Francofurti, *Lipsiae*, 1743.
Another edition.   8°. Gerae, *Rothius*, 1778.

Gratet-Duplessis, 215, 216. A carefully formed collection of maxims, axioms, *etc.*, taken from the classics and given in German either by a literal translation or by a similar maxim. Amongst these are a certain number of true proverbs translated by their German equivalents.   [B.M.

c

275. Porta. Porta ad Germanam linguam Polonae iuventuti aperta, *etc.* pp. [xxiv], 144.

8°. *Typographia Brunsbergensis Societatis Jesu,* 1700.

Bernstein, 2644. Pp. 129-144, Sententiae et proverbia. Latin, with German translations.

276. Proverbi. Proverbi latini ed italiani, *etc.* pp. 45.

16°. Venezia, *Contarini,* 1825.

277. Proverbia. Proverbia Latino-Germanica e variis autoribus collecta et in alphabeti seriem digesta. pp. 327.

16°. (Halae Suevorum, *Gräter,* 1654).

Bernstein, 2795. He says that his copy lacks the title page, and that he has taken the above title from another page.

278. Rambot (Gustave). Bibliographie provençale. Les adages de Berluc. pp. 10. 8°. Marseille, *Boy,* 1855.

Bernstein, 2938. *See also* **209**.

279. Regius (Barth.). Adagia. 8°. Ticini, 1606.

Gratet-Duplessis, 146.

280. Richerius (Ludovicus Coelius), *Rhodiginus.* Adagia quaedam.

In various editions of the Adagia of Erasmus and Grynaeus.   [B.M.

281. Riley (Henry Thomas). Dictionary of Latin quotations, proverbs, maxims, and mottos, *etc.* pp. vi, 556.

8°. London, *Bohn,* 1856.

Arranged alphabetically. Reprinted 1860.

282. Ritzius (Andreas). Florilegium adagiorum et sententiarum Latino-Germanicum, *etc.* pp. 16, 1001.

8°. Basileae, *Brandmüller,* 1728.

Gratet-Duplessis, 196. Proverbs, sentences, maxims, *etc.*, taken from great authors.   [B.M.

283. Robert (Ulysse). Un vocabulaire latin-français . . . suivi d'un recueil d'anciens proverbes. 8°. Paris, *Picard,* 1873.

In Bibliothèque de l'École des Chartes, tome 34, pp. 33-46. This contains a list of French and Latin proverbs taken from a 14th century MS. in the Bibliothèque Nationale.   [B.M.

284. Rosenheyn (J. S.). Lateinisches Lesebuch. Dritter Cursus. la. 8°. Königsberg, 1810.

Gratet-Duplessis, 219. Pp. 67-74, 120 Latin proverbs.

285. Ruiz Bustamente (Juan). Adagiales ac metaphoricae formulae, *etc.* 16°. 1551.

Gratet-Duplessis, 131. A collection of Latin proverbs and proverbial sayings taken from different authors, translated into Spanish, with occasional notes. Of no great literary interest.

286. Schamelius (Johann Martin). Lateinische Sprichwörter und Maximen, *etc.* pp. 234, [14].
8°. Leipzig, *Erben*, [1716?].
Bernstein, 3218.

287. Schmidius (Johannes). Proverbiorum falsiverbiorum decades duae. 4°. 1692.
Gratet-Duplessis, 179.

288. Schmitt (Johann Joseph Hermann). Lateinische Sprichwörter, Redensarten, Musterstellen, *etc.* pp. 106.
8°. Edenkoben, *Kreiselmeyer*, 1886.
Bernstein, 3257.

289. Schonheim (Otto Wilhelm). Proverbia illustrata et applicata in usum juventutis illustris, *etc.*
8°. Leipsig, *Deer*, 1728.
Another edition, enlarged. 2 pts. 8°. Leipsig, *Deer*, 1734.
Gratet-Duplessis, 197. Explanations, *etc.*, in German. [B.M.

290. Schreger (Odilio). Studiosus jovialis. . . . Editio tertia, *etc.* pp. [vi], 840. 8°. Pedeponti, *Gastl*, 1752.
Seventh edition. pp. [viii], 704.
8°. Augustae Vindelicorum, *Rieger*, 1773.
Lustiger und nützlicher Zeit-Vertreiber . . . Sechste . . . Auflage. pp. [vi], 576. 8°. München, *Gastl*, 1765.
Gratet-Duplessis, 227. Contains a large selection of axioms, many of which are true proverbs. *See also* **299**. [B.M.

291. Secretarius. Der in Verfertigung allerhand Schreiben stets bereite und vielvermehrte Secretarius, *etc.* pp. 334.
16°. Nürnberg, *Buggel*, 1699.
Pp. 308-334, Anhang unterschiedlich-nützlicher Sententien und Sprüchwörter. Latin proverbs and maxims with German equivalents.

292. Sententiae. Sententiae et proverbia ex poetis Latinis, *etc.* pp. 226. 8°. Venetiis, 1547.
Bernstein, 3362.

293. Sententiae. Sententiae morales et proverbiales. pp. 63.
8°. Berolini, *apud A. Havde & Spenerum*, 1701.
Latin and German. [B.M.

294. Seybold (Johan Georg). Fasciculus adagiorum latinorum et germanicorum. 12°. Ulmiae, 1654.
Another edition. Viridarium . . . paroemiarum . . . Latino-Germanicarum . . . Lust-Garten von . . . Sprüchwörtern, *etc.*
8°. Nürnberg, *Endter & Erben*, 1677.
Another edition. Selectiora adagia Latino-Germanica, *etc.* Editio tertia. pp. 392 + index.
12°. Norimbergae, *Endterus*, 1669.
Gratet-Duplessis, 166, 572, gives details of various other editions. [B.M.

295. Sonny (A.).   Neue Sprichwörter und sprichwörtliche Redensarten.   8°.   Leipzig, 1893.

In Archiv für lateinische Lexikographie, Jahrgang 8, pp. 483-494; Jahrgang 9, pp. 53-80.   Supplementary to **307**.   [U.C.L.

296. Suringar (W. H. D.).   Lijst van geschriften over de
Latijnsche spreekwoorden.   Eine bijdrage voor de bibliographie.   8°.   Leiden, 1861.

In Tijdschrift voor de Nederlandsche Gymnasien voor 1861, pp. 111-134.
[B.M.

297. Sutphen (Morris Crater).   A collection of Latin proverbs
supplementing Otto's Sprichwörter, *etc.* [**270**].   pp. 391 and
frontispiece.   8°.   Baltimore, 1902.

Embodies and enlarges the additions to Otto by Szelinski **298**, Weyman **307**,
and Sonny **295**.   An arduous and scholarly work.   [B.M.

298. Szelinski (Victor).   Nachträge und Ergänzungen zu Otto.
[**270**].   Jena, 1892.

299. Tauber (Isidore).   Studiosus jovialis.   Ad modum libri . . .
quem olim . . . Odilo Schreger . . . collegit, denuo compilavit
Isidorus Tauber, *etc.*   pp. vi, 304.
                                          8°.   Viennae, *Doll*, 1846.

Gratet-Duplessis, 227.   Founded on, but by no means the same as, Schreger's
book, *q.v.* **290**.   Pp. 1-21, Proverbia et sententiae memorabiles latino-
germanicae; pp. 22-46, Ephemerides adagiorum, *etc.*

300. Torre (Antonius van).   Dialogi familiares. . . . Editio novissima, *etc.*   8°.   Leod, *Bourgign*, n.d.

Contains ten sections of Latin and French proverbs headed : Adagiorum decas
prima (-decima).

301. Ulpius (Joannes).   Epitome adagiorum.

In the Adagia of Erasmus and Grynaeus.   [B.M.

302. Vade-Mecum.   Vade-mecum classicum, seu conservatorium
mille et ducentorum axiomatum, proverbiorum, sententiarum,
etc.   pp. 168.
          8°.   Augustae Vindelicorum, *Officina Wolffiana*, 1857.
[B.M.

303. Vannucci (Atto).   Proverbi latini.   3 vols.
          Vol. 1, L.10; Vol. 2 and 3, L.6 each.
                              8°.   Milano, *Menozzi*, 1880-1883.

Arranged in chapters, according to subject.   Anticipatory chapters under the
same headings were published separately between 1865 and 1872; for details
see Pitrè, 3348-3353.   Many Italian dialect proverbs, particularly Istrian ones,
are to be found in the notes on these Latin proverbs.   The illustrative notes are
thoroughly well done.

304. Vergilius (Polydorus). Proverbiorum libellus. ff. [69].
4°. Venetiis, *per Christophorum de Pēsis*, 1498.
Another edition, enlarged. Adagiorum aeque humanorum et
sacrorum opus, *etc.* 8°. Basileae, 1550.

Gratet-Duplessis, 119. Polydore Vergil accused Erasmus of plagiarism in his
Adagia, since his work had appeared two years earlier. The work of
Erasmus is, however, immeasurably superior and more important. [B.M.

305. Walterus (Antonius). Gnomologia historico-proverbialis,
etc. pp. 908. 8°. Stetini, *Rhetius*, 1639.

Gratet-Duplessis, 160. A book of maxims, quotations, aphorisms and anecdotes, rather than a collection of proverbs, though a large number of these
are included.

306. Werner (Jakob). Lateinische Sprichwörter und Sinnsprüche
des Mittelalters aus Handschriften gesammelt. pp. viii, 112.
M.2.20. 8°. Heidelberg, *Winter*, 1912.

Hilka's Sammlung mittellateinischer Texte, No. 3. In alphabetical order.
[B.M.

307. Weyman (Carl). Zu den Sprichwörtern und sprichwörtlichen Redensarten der Römer. 8°. Leipzig, 1893.

In Archiv für lateinische Lexikographie, Jahrgang 8, pp. 23-38, 397-411.
Supplementary to Otto, **270.** [U.C.L.

308. Wideburg (Joan Joachim Gerard). Voces ac formulae
sollemnes, atque adagia scholiis illustrata, denique sententiae
morales, *etc.* pp. [xvi], 164.
8°. Halae Magdeb., *sumptibus Orphanotrophei*, 1768.

Pp. 39-94, Adagia. Latin and German. [B.M.

309. Wiegand (Carl). Das Proverbium in grammatischer Ver-
wendung bei dem Elementar-Unterricht in der lateinischen
Sprache, *etc.* pp. xvi, 105.
8°. Leipzig, *Klinkhardt*, 1861.

Over 1100 Latin proverbs and proverbial phrases, with German translations
and explanations. [B.M.
A közmondás nyelvtani alkalmazásban a latin nyelv elemi
oktatásában, *etc.* pp. xvii, 219. 16°. Pest, *Lampel*, 1864.

Bernstein, 4049.

310. Withals (John). A shorte dictionarie in Latine and English.
. . . Nowe lastlie augmented with more than six hundred
rythmicall verses, whereof many be proverbial, *etc.*
4°. London, *by Thomas Purfoot*, 1586.
A dictionary in English and Latine, *etc.* pp. [xiv], 623.
8°. London, *by Thomas Purfoot*, 1634.

The proverbs, *etc.*, are given as illustrations; a quaint and informative little
book. The edition of 1634 also contains a separate list of proverbs, Latin and
English. There is little in the way of proverbs in the first edition of 1568.
[B.M.

311. Woelfflin (   ).   Krieg und Frieden im Sprichworte der
Römer.   8°.   München, 1888.

In Sitzungsberichte der philos.-philol. Classe der k. b. Akademie der
Wissenschaften zu München, Bd. 1, pp. 197-215.   [B.M.

312. Woerter-Buechlein.   Teutsch-Lateinisches Wörter-Büchlein
zum Nutz und Ergötzung der Schul-Jugend zusammen
getragen, *etc.* pp. 256, 44, 47.
                          8°.   Noribergae, *Zieger*, 1713.

The 44 pages of the second pagination contain : Farrago sententiarum, a
collection of over 600 Latin and German proverbs, maxims, *etc.*

313. Wyss (Wilhelm von).   Die Sprüchwörter bei den römischen
Komikern. pp. 114.   2 Mk.   8°.   Zürich, *Schulthess*, 1889.

Reviewed in the Classical Review, Vol. 4, pp. 378-9.   Proverbs are not
sufficiently distinguished from idiomatic metaphors, otherwise a good collection.

See also index at end for references to Latin in other sections.

GREEK

(including Modern).

314. Apostolius (Michael). Παροιμίαι, *etc.*
8°. Basileae, *ex officina Hervagiana,* 1538.
Another edition. pp. [xvi], 387.
4°. Lugduni Batavorum, *Elsevier,* 1653.
Gratet-Duplessis, 99. The 1538 edition is in Greek only and very incomplete.
That of 1653 is, with the exception of a new title page, exactly the same
as one of 1619. There are Latin translations of the proverbs. These proverbs,
without the explanations, are included in various editions of the Clavis Homerica.
[B.M.

315. Arabantinos (Panogiotes). Παροιμιαστήριον, *etc.* pp. 183.
8°. ἐν Ἰωαννίνοις, 1863.
926 modern Greek proverbs, in alphabetical order. [B.M.

316. Archelaos (I. Sarantides). Ἡ Σινασός ἤτοι θέσις, *etc.* pp.
287. 8°. ἐν Ἀθήναις, Νικολαΐδου, 1899.
Bernstein, 4235. Pp. 171-188, Δημώδεις ἐν Σινασῷ παροιμίαι. [B.M.

317. Baar (A.). Sprichwörter und Sentenzen aus den griechischen
Idyllendichtern. Görz, 1887.

318. Bartholdy (Jacob L. Solomon). Bruchstücke zur nähern
Kentniss des heutigen Griechenlands . . . Erster Theil, *etc.*
pp. xii, 518 + plates, *etc.*
Pp. 443-453, 67 modern Greek proverbs transcribed and with German translations. [B.M.

319. Bauck (Ludovicus). De proverbiis aliisque locutionibus . . .
apud Aristophanem, *etc.* pp. 88.
8°. Regimonti Pr., *Leopold,* 1880.
Bernstein, 205.

320. Benizelos (I.). Παροιμίαι δημώδεις συλλεγεῖσαι, *etc.* pp. 134.
8°. ἐν Ἀθήναις, 1846.
Another edition. pp. viii, 360.
8°. ἐν Ἑρμουπόλει, Πατίρδος, 1867.
Bernstein, 244. [B.M.

321. Berettas (Ioannes Ph.). Συλλογὴ παροιμιῶν τῶν νεωτέρων
Ἑλλήνων μετὰ παραλληλισμοῦ πρὸς τὰς τῶν ἀρχαίων.
8°. ἐν Λαμίᾳ, 1860.
Proverbs, both ancient and modern, arranged in alphabetical order. [B.M.

39

322. Boissonade (J. F.). Poetae graeci gnomici, *etc.*
32°. Paris, *Lefèvre*, 1823.
Gratet-Duplessis, 89.

323. Bojadschi (Michael G.). Kurzgefasste neugriechische Sprachlehre, *etc.* pp. xxiv, 380.
8°. ἐν Βιέννῃ τῆς ᾿Αυστρίας, *Δαβιδοβίκη*, 1821.
Bernstein, 4268. Pp. 343-348, proverbs with German translations.

324. Brachmann (Friedrich). Quaestiones pseudo-Diogenianeae.
8°. Leipzig, *Teubner*, 1885.
In Jahrbücher für classische Philologie, Supplementband 14, Heft 2, pp. 339-416. Proverbs attributed to Diogenianus compared with others.   [B.M.

325. Brunck (R. F. P.). ᾿Ηθικὴ ποίησις, sive gnomici poetae graeci, *etc.*   8°. Argentorati, 1784.
Another edition.   8°. Lipsiae, 1817.
Gratet-Duplessis, 89.   [B.M.

326. Cohn (Leopold). Zu den Parœmiographen. Mitteilungen aus Handschriften. pp. 84.   8°. Breslau, *Koebner*, 1887.
Breslauer Philologische Abhandlungen, Bd. 2, Heft 2. With numerous examples.   [B.M.

327. Cousin (Gilbert). Gilberti Cognati Nozereni opera multifarii argumenti, *etc.*   fol. Basileæ.
Tom. 1, pp. 24-85, Zenodoti qui Didymum ac Tarraeum in compendium redegit, proverbia : Greek and Latin. Tom. 2, 86-171, παροιμιῶν συλλογὴ . . . quas Erasmus in suas chiliadas non retulit, *etc.*   [B.M.

328. Creuzer (Friedrich). Zur Geschichte der griechischen und römischen Literatur, *etc.* pp. 655.
8°. Leipzig, Darmstadt, *Leske*, 1847.
Forms Abtheilung 3, Bd. 2, of the author's " Deutsche Schriften." Pp. 303-326, Ueber die Parœmiographi Graeci.   [B.M.

329. Crusius (Otto). Paroemiographica. Textgeschichtliches zur alten Dichtung und Religion, *etc.* pp. 120.
8°. München, 1910.
Sitzungsberichte der kgl. bayerischen Akademie der Wissenschaften, philosophisch-philologische und historische Klasse, Jahrgang 1910, Abhandlung 4.   [B.M.

330. Darbaris (Demetrius N.). Χρηστομάθεια ἁπλοελληνικὴ, *etc.*
ἐν Βιέννῃ τῆς ᾿Αυστρίας, *Δαβιδοβίκη*, 1820.
Pp. 296-301, proverbs.   [B.M.

331. Diogenianus. Παροιμίαι δημώδεις. Vulgaria proverbia.
Contained in **324, 334, 351, 384.** Diogenianus of Heraclea was a Greek grammarian who flourished during the reign of Hadrian. This collection of proverbs is probably an abridgment from that made by himself from his lexicon.

332. Firmenich-Richartz (Johann Mathias). Τραγοίδια ρωμαϊκά. Neugriechische Volksgesänge, *etc.* 2 Theile.

8°. Berlin, *Heymann, Hertz*, 1840, 1867.

Theil 2, pp. 185-194, Neugriechische Sprichwörter. 100 proverbs with German translations. [B.M.

333. Fungerus (Joannes). Nova proverbiorum farrago, tam ex Graecis quam Latinis auctoribus collecta. pp. 213.

8°. Lugduni Batavorum, *Plantinus*, 1585.

Another edition. 8°. Lugduni Batavorum, *Plantinus*, 1595.

Gratet-Duplessis, 140. Proverbs and sayings, with notes more erudite than interesting. [B.M.

334. Gaisford (Thomas). Parœmiographi Graeci. Quorum pars nunc primum ex codicibus manuscriptis vulgatur. pp. xxiv, 432. 8°. Oxonii, *e Typographeo Academico*, 1836.

Another edition. 8°. Oxonii, 1863.

Gratet-Duplessis, 107, reproduces in part the work of Schottus, but with notable differences. In Greek with Latin notes. Contains : Proverbia e codice Bodleiano; proverbia ex codice Coisliniano, n. 177; proverbia Diogeniani; proverbia Zenobii. [U.C.L.

335. Geisler (Eugen). Beiträge zur Geschichte des griechischen Sprichwortes. 8°. Breslau, 1908.

[L.L.

336. Germbergius (Hermannus). Proverbiorum centuriae xiv, *etc.* pp. [viii], 388. 8°. Basileæ, *Henricpetri*, 1583.

Latin and Greek. [B.M.

336a. Goebel (M.). De graecarum civitatum proprietatibus proverbio notatis. pp. 172. la. 8°. Breslau, 1915.

337. Gousios (A. D.). Ἡ κατὰ τὸ Πάγγαιον χώρα.

ἐν Λειψίᾳ, 1894.

Pp. 87-103, proverbs and proverbial phrases.

338. Grasberger (Lorenz). Abhandlung über die griechischen Stichnamen. pp. 42. 4°. Würzburg, *Stahel*, 1877.

Second edition. pp. iv, 78. 8°. Würzburg, *Stahel*, 1883.

Contains a section : Die Sprichwörter der alten Griechen überhaupt. [B.M.

339. Graux (Charles). Les textes grecs . . . (Œuvres . . . Tome 2). pp. xiv, 551. 8°. Paris, *Vieweg*, 1886.

Pp. 117-138, Supplément au Corpus parœmiographorum Graecorum [of Leutsch & Schneidewin]. *q.v.* **351.**

340. Gruenwald (Eugen). Sprichwörter und sprichwörtliche Redensarten bei Plato. pp. 15. 4°. Berlin, 1893.

Bernstein, 1357.

341. Hotop (Augustus). De Eustathii proverbiis.
8°. Leipzig, 1888.

In Jahrbücher für classische Philologie, Supplementband 16, pp. 249-313.
Also published separately. Compares Greek proverbs taken from various authors.
[B.M.

342. Houghton (H. P.). The moral significance of animals as indicated in Greek proverbs.   Baltimore, *Hopkins*, 1915.

343. Jungblut (Henricus). Quaestionum de paroemiographis pars prior. De Zenobio. pp. 42.
8°. Halis Saxonum, *Karras*, 1882.

Also published in the Dissertationes philologicae Halenses, Vol. 5, pp. 201-244.
[B.M.

344. Kabadias (Georgios). Ὁ πρακτικὸς λόγος ἢ συλλογὴ 10,000 παροιμιῶν, γνωμικῶν, *etc.* pp. 104.
8°. ἐν Κερκύρᾳ, *Κάδμος,* 1876.

Bernstein, 1671. This is the first part, containing 1191 entries. No more appeared.

345. Kigallas (I.). Σύντομον δοκίμιον περὶ παροιμιῶν καὶ παροι-μιωδῶν ἐκφράσεων τῆς νεοελληνικῆς γλώσσης.
4°. 'Αθήνησι, 1853.

In Πανδώρα, Tom. 3, pp. 320-324. 126 entries.   [B.M.

346. Koch (Jo.). Quaestionum de proverbiis apud Æschylum, Sophoclem, Euripidem, *etc.* pp. 92.
8°. Regimonti, *Liedtkianis*, 1887.

Second Part.   8°. Bartenstein, 1892.
Bernstein, 1722.

347. Konstantinides (Michael). Neohellenica, *etc.* pp. xvi, 470.
8°. London, New York, *Macmillan*, 1892.

Pp. 245-248, Greek proverbs with literal translations and English equivalents.
[B.M.

348. Kretikake (P. N.). Πλανῆται ἤτοι συλλογὴ δημωδῶν παροιμιῶν. p. 32.   8°. ἐν Τριπόλει, 1883.

349. Kuriakides (A.). Ἑλληνικαὶ παροιμίαι ἀπανθισθεῖσαι ὑπὸ **A.** Κυριακίδου. pp. iii, 82.   16°. ἐν Λευκωσίᾳ, 1916.
In Greek only.   [B.M.

350. Leake (William Martin). Researches in Greece. pp. xix, 472.   4°. London, *Booth*, 1814.

Gratet-Duplessis, 109. Pp. 443-454, 90 modern Greek proverbs with English translations. Also published in the Classical Journal, Vol. 17, pp. 39-46, 1818.   [B.M.

351. Leutsch (Ernst Ludwig von) and **Schneidewin** (Friedrich & Wilhelm). Corpus parœmiographorum Græcorum, *etc.* 2 tom. la. 8°. Gottingae, *Vandenhoeck & Ruprecht* (Vol. 1), Libraria Dieterichiana (Vol. 2), 1839-1851.

Gratet-Duplessis, 108. This book is better than those of Schottus and Gaisford, though the former's work is not quite superseded, since he gives Latin translations and full notes, which the present authors do not. There is an interesting preface, in which one of the editors reviews the ancient grammarians, lexicographers, *etc.*, who dealt with proverbs. Duplessis quotes an extract dealing with the scope and plan of the book. Reviewed in the Quarterly Magazine, 125, pp. 218-254. For Supplement *see* **339**. [B.M.

352. Linde (C.). De proverbiorum apud tragicos Graecos usu.
Gotha, 1896.

353. Lingenberg (Johann Wilhelm). Platonische Bilder und Sprichwörter. pp. 21. 4°. Köln, *Greven*, [1874?].

Bernstein, 1943. Pp. 10-21, Sprichwörter bei Platon. [B.M.

354. Maniares (Ioannes Z.). Ἡ σφίγξ, ἤ συλλογὴ Ἑλληνικὴ παροιμιῶν, *etc.* ἐν Τεργεστῇ, 1832.

355. Manolakakes (Em.). Καρπαθιακὰ, *etc.* pp. 304.
8°. ἐν Ἀθήναις, *Καλαράκη*, 1896.

Pp. 270-290, δημώδεις παροιμίαι. 341 entries. [B.M.

356. Manolakakes (Joannes). Παροιμίαι, φρασεολογίαι, *etc.*
4°. ἐν Κωνσταντινουπόλει, 1891.

In Ζωγράφειος ἀγὼν ἤτοι μνημεῖα τῆς Ἑλλάδος ἀρχαιοτητὸς ζῶντα ἐν τῷ νῦν ἑλληνικῷ λαῷ, Τομ. Α, pp. 343-380. Pp. 343-369, 544 proverbs. [B.M.

357. Martin (Paul). Studien auf dem Gebiete des griechischen Sprichwortes, *etc.* pp. 34. 4°. Plauen i. V., *Neupert*, 1889. [B.M.

358. Martin du Tyrac (Marie Louis Jean André Charles de), *Count de Marcellus.* Chants populaires de la Grèce moderne, *etc.* pp. xvi, 335. 8°. Paris, *Michel Lévy*, 1860.

Pp. 302-324, proverbes, adages. 140 proverbs translated into French. [B.M.

359. Miller (E.). Mélanges de littérature grecque, *etc.* pp. xvi, 473. 8°. Paris, *Imprimerie Impériale*, 1868.

Bernstein, 2205. Pp. 341-384, recueil de proverbes.

360. Mommsen (August). Griechische Jahreszeiten, *etc.* 5 Hefte. 8°. Schleswig, *Bergas*, 1873-77.

Heft 1, Neugriechische Bauernregeln, *etc.* [B.M.

361. Nachtigall (Ottmar). Senarii Graecanici quingenti et eo amplius versi, singuli moralê quandâ sententiâ, aut typum proverbialem prae se ferētes, Othmaro Nachtgall . . . metaphraste. pp. 49. 4°. Argentoraci, *Knoblouch*, 1523.

Greek and Latin. [B.M.

362. Negris (Alexander).   A dictionary of modern Greek proverbs, with an English translation, explanatory remarks and philological illustrations.   pp. xi, 144.

12°.   Edinburgh, *Clark*, 1831.

Gratet-Duplessis, 111.   A book of unusual interest, worth reading from other points of view than the parœmiological.   Gives 950 proverbs, a fair proportion of which are peculiar to the country, and are expressed in a way nationally characteristic.   [B.M.

363. Nestorides (K.).   Παροιμίαι καὶ παροιμιώδεις φράσεις ἀνέκδοτοι.

8°.   ἐν ᾿Αθήναις, 1893.

In Παρνασσός, 1893, pp. 159-160, 469-477, 635-639, 878-880, 946-955.   [B.M.

364. Orelli (Johann Conrad von).   Opuscula Graecorum veterum sententiosa et moralia, graece et latine, *etc.*   2 vols.

8°.   Lipsiae, *in Libraria Weidmannia*, 1819-1821.

Gratet-Duplessis, 89, says that although this is hardly a book of proverbs, it is extremely useful as a study of gnomic literature.   He discusses the relationship between gnomic poetry and proverbs, and decides that some knowledge of the first is essential to a complete study of the second.   [U.C.L.

365. Pachalery (A.).   Le manuel de l'étudiant grec, ou choix d'homonymes, . . . proverbes, locutions proverbiales.   pp. 199.   *First edition.*

fr.3.50.   8°.   Constantinople, *Zellich*, 1877.

Eighth edition.   8°.   Constantinople, 1891.

366. Papadopoulos (A. I.).   ᾿Ανέκδοτοι δημώδεις παροιμίαι.   1873.

In ᾿Ανατολικὴ ἐπιθεώρησις, 1873, Τομ. Α, pp. 442-6, 451-3, 474-5, 510-11, 530-4, 558-62.

367. Papadopoulos Bretos (Marinus).   Mélanges néohelléniques, *etc.*   16°.   Athènes, *Imprimerie Royale*, 1856.

Pp. 43-46, 33 proverbs in French.   [B.M.

368. ——— : Proverbes de la Grèce moderne.   4°.   Paris, 1854.

In Athenæum français, Année 3, pp. 733-734.   31 modern Greek proverbs in French.   [B.M.

369. Planudes (Maximus).   Die Sprichwörtersammlung des Maximus Planudes, erläutert von Eduard Kurtz.   pp. 47.

8°.   Leipzig, *Neumann*, 1886.

Compares the proverbs of Planudes with Russian and modern Greek ones.   [B.M.

370. Platt (Hugh Edward Pigott).   Alia.   pp. 50.

8°.   Oxford, *Blackwood*, London, *Simpkin, Marshall*, 1904.

By-ways in the Classics, including Alia.   pp. vi, 146.

8°.   Oxford, *Blackwood*, London, *Simpkin, Marshall*, 1905.

A last ramble in the Classics.   pp. 208.

8°.   Oxford, *Blackwood*, London, *Simpkin, Marshall*, 1906.

Contains a chapter of proverbial phrases with classical equivalents.   The " Last ramble " is an entirely different book from the " Byways."   [B.M.

371. Plutarch. Plutarchi de proverbiis Alexandrinorum libellus ineditus, recensuit et praefatus est Otto Crusius. 2 pts.

4°. Lipsiae, *Teubnerus*, 1887-95.

[B.M.

372. Polites (Nikolaos G.). Μελέται περὶ τοῦ βίου καὶ τῆς γλώσσης τοῦ ἑλληνικοῦ λαοῦ . . . Παροιμίαι, *etc.* 4 tom.

ἐν 'Αθήναις, *Σακελλάριος*, 1899-1902.

Part of C. G. Marasles' Βιβλιοθήκη Μαράσλη. The first four volumes deal with proverbs. Teza's study, Dei proverbi popolari in Grecia, *q.v.* **390**, is concerned with the first volume of this work. The long introduction contains a bibliography. The work is a vast collection of Greek proverbs with erudite and extremely helpful notes. [B.M.

373. ———: Περὶ τῶν δημωδῶν παροιμιῶν. 1872.

In Παρθενῶν, Vol. 2, pp. 921-930.

374. Polulas (I.). Ἡ φιλολογική μας γλῶσσα. ἐν 'Αθήναις, 1892. Pp. 68-72, 32 proverbs.

375. Prittwitz-Gaffron (Erich von). Das Sprichwort im griechischen Epigramm. pp. 68. 8°. Giessen, *Töpelmann*, 1912.

[B.M.

376. Proverbi. Proverbi e motti bellissimi di diversi autori excellentissimi heroici greci et latini in rima.

Macerata, *Martellini*, 1585.

Pitrè, 3180.

377. Proverbs. Δημώδεις παροιμίαι. 8°. ἐν 'Αθήναις, 1871.

Νεοελληνικὰ ἀνάλεκτα, pp. 129-192. A collection of 530 proverbs contributed by various people. [B.M.

378. ———: Παροιμίαι. 8°. 'Αθήνησι, [1853].

In Πανδώρα, Τομ. 3, pp. 321-324. [B.M.

379. Rein (Theodor W.). Sprichwörter und sprichwörtliche Redensarten bei Lucian. Inaugural Dissertation. pp. 104.

8°. Tübingen, 1894.

Bernstein, 2994.

380. Ross (Ludwig). Reisen auf den griechischen Inseln. 3 Bde.

8°. Stuttgart, 1840-5.

Bd. 2, pp. 174-178, proverbs with German translations. [B.M.

381. Sanders (Daniel Hendel). Das Volksleben der Neugriechen, dargestellt und erklärt aus Liedern, Sprichwörtern, Kunstgedichten, *etc.* pp. xii, 358.

8°. Mannheim, *Bassermann*, 1844.

Gratet-Duplessis, 112. Pp. 219-233, Sprichwörter. 146 Greek proverbs with German translations. No notes. [U.C.L.

382. Schmidt (Wilhelm Constantin Moritz). Verisimilium capita duo, *etc.* pp. 32. 8°. Jenae, *Maukius*, 1861.

Pp. 1-22, De parœmiographis Graecis. A dissertation with various examples. [B.M.

383. Schoell (Fritz). Zu den sogenannten proverbia Alexandrina des Pseudo-Plutarch. 8°. Freiburg i. B., Tübingen, 1882.

In Festschrift zur Begrüssung der in Karlsruhe . . . tagenden 36. Philologen-Versammlung verfasst von den Philologischen Collegen an der Heidelberger Universität, 1882, pp. 37-57.

384. Schottus (Andreas). Παροιμίαι ἑλληνικαὶ. Adagia, sive proverbia Graecorum ex Zenobio, Diogeniano et Suidae collectaneis. (Proverbiorum Graecorum e Vaticana Bibliotheca appendix. Stromateus proverbialium versuum.) pp. [xx], 702. 4°. Antverpiae, *ex officina Plantiniana*, 1612.

Gratet-Duplessis, 98. A useful collection. There are 353 proverbs from the Vatican MS. The Latin translations are faithful and the notes useful. [B.M.

385. Seberus (Wolfgang). Florilegium Graecolatinum. . . . Adjecti sunt tres indices; quorum . . . tertius proverbia, sparsim ad illas citata enumerat, *etc.* pp. [xiv], 325, 224.
8°. Lipsiae, *Schürerus*, 1605.
Bernstein, 3314.

386. Serz (Georg Thomas). Handbuch der griechischen und lateinischen Sprichwörter. . . . Erster Theil. pp. 635.
8°. Nürnberg, *Strebner*, 1792.

Gratet-Duplessis, 103. Greek and Latin proverbs with brief explanations in German taken chiefly from the Adagia of Erasmus. The second part was never published. Not without a certain interest, but of no great importance. [B.M.

387. Solari (G.). La vita economica nei proverbi greci.
4°. Torino, *etc.*, 1898.

In Rivista italiana di Sociologia, Anno 2, pp. 187-206, 303-320.

388. Sprichwoerter. Sprichwörter der Neugriechen.
4°. München, 1820.

Gratet-Duplessis, 110. *In* Flora, No. 86.

389. Stromateus. Στρωματεὺς ἐμμετρῶν παροιμιῶν.
4°. Lutetiae Parisiorum, 1618.
See also **384.** [B.M.

390. Teza (E.). Dei proverbi popolari in Grecia raccolti da N. Politês. pp. 18. 8°. Venezia, *Ferrari*, 1899.

A commentary on the first volume of Politess' Μελέται, *etc.*, including numerous examples of proverbs. [B.M.

391. Treu (M.) and **Crusius** (Otto). Griechische Sprichwörter.
8°. Göttingen, 1889.
In Philologus, Neue Folge, Bd. 1, pp. 193-208. [U.C.L.

392. Tribukait (P.). De proverbiis vulgaribus que aliis locutionibus apud bucolicos Graecos obviis. Königsberg, 1899.

393. Vuisheslavtsev (M.). Анекдоты, изреченія и пословицы, *etc.* pp. 126. 12°. Новгородъ, *Тип. Губ. Правленія*, 1891.

Bernstein, 4156. Pp. 63-66, Греческія пословицы : pp. 115-124, Латинскія пословицы. 51 Greek and 139 Latin proverbs translated into Russian.

394. Wachsmuth (Curt). De gnomologio Palatino inedito.
8°. Berolini, *apud Weidmannos*, 1879.

In Satura Philologa, *etc.*, by Hermann Sauppe, pp. 7-42. A commentary with notes and examples of 161 proverbs. [B.M.

395. Warnkross (Maximilianus). De paroemiographis capita duo, etc. pp. 65. 8°. Gryphiswaldiae, 1881.

Pp. 1-26, de Zenobio : pp. 26-62, de Lucillo Tarrhaeo.

396. Wiesenthal (M.). Quaestiones de nominibus propriis quae Graecis hominibus in proverbio fuerunt, *etc.* pp. 62.
8°. Barmen, 1895.

Bernstein, 4054. Wissenschaftliche Beilage zum Jahresbericht des Gymnasiums zu Barmen.

397. Wunderer (Carl). Polybios-Forschungen, *etc.* 3 Thle.
8°. Leipzig, *Dietrich*, 1898-1909.

Theil 1, Sprichwörter und sprichwörtliche Redensarten bei Polybios, *etc.*
[B.M.

398. Zell (Carl). Ferienschriften. 3 pts.
8°. Freiburg im Breisgau, *Wagner*, 1826-33.

Gratet-Duplessis, 114. Pt. 1, pp. 91-124, Ueber die Sprichwörter der alten Griechen. Pt. 2 (which alone has the title, "Darstellung aus dem Leben und Literatur der Römer," given by Duplessis), pp. 1-96, Ueber die Sprichwörter der alten Römer. Two excellent critical essays. [B.M.

399. Zenobius. Ζηνοβίου ἐπιτομὴ τῶν Ταρραίου καὶ Διδύμου παροιμιῶν, *etc.* pp. 132. 4°. Florentie, *P. de Zunta*, 1497.
Another edition. [Edited by V. Obsopoeus]. pp. 149.
8°. Haganœ, 1535.

Gratet-Duplessis, 91. The proverbs of Zenobius are also to be found in the works of Cousin, **327**, Gaisford, Leutsch and Schneidewin, and Schottus. Zenobius was a Greek sophist who flourished at Rome in the reign of Hadrian. His collection of proverbs in three books is extant in an abridged form. It was compiled, according to Suidas, from Didymus of Alexandria and Lucillus of Tarrha (in Crete). [B.M.

See also index at end for references to Greek in other sections.

BYZANTINE.

399a. Gleye (C. E.). Die moskauer Sammlung mittelgriechischer Sprichwörter. pp. 36. 8°. Leipzig, 1913.

400. Krumbacher (Carl). Mittelgriechische Sprichwörter. pp. 272. 8°. München, *Akademie der Wissenschaften*, 1893.

Separate publication of an article in the Sitzungsberichte der philosophisch-philologischen und historischen Classe der k. b. Akademie der Wissenschaften zu München, Jahrgang 1893, Bd. 2. Pp. 28-32, bibliography. [B.M.

401. Krumbacher (Carl). Die moskauer Sammlung mittelgriechischer Sprichwörter. München, 1900.

402. ———: Eine Sammlung byzantinischer Sprichwörter.
8°. München, K. Akademie, 1888.

In Sitzungsberichte der philosophisch-philologischen und historischen Classe
der k. b. Akademie der Wissenschaften zu München, Jahrgang 1887, Bd. 2, pp.
43-96. [B.M.

403. Meyer (Gustav). Zu den mittelgriechischen Sprichwörtern.
8°. Leipzig, 1894.

In Byzantinische Zeitschrift, Bd. 3, pp. 396-408. An article concerned with
Krumbacher's work. [U.C.L.

404. Papageorgiu (Petros N.). Zu den mittelgriechischen Sprichwörtern. 8°. Leipzig, 1894.

In Byzantinische Zeitschrift, Bd. 3, pp. 553-580. Remarks on Krumbacher's
Mittelgriechische Sprichwörter. [U.C.L.

405. Polites (Nikolaos G.). Ἑρμηνευτικὰ εἰς τὰς Βυζαντινάς παροι-
μίας. 8°. ἐν Ἀθήναις, Μαῖσονερ καὶ Καργαδούρης, 1898.

In Ἐπετηρὶς τοῦ Παρνασσοῦ, 1898. [B.M.

406. ———: Δημώδεις παροιμίαι ἐν μεσαιωνικοῖς ἑλληνικοῖς ποιήμασι,
etc. pp. 17. 8°. ἐν Ἀθήναις, 1896.

In Ἐπετηρὶς τοῦ Παρνάσσου Α'.

407. Salzmann (E.). Sprichwörter und sprichwörtliche Redensarten bei Libanios. Tübingen, 1910.

408. Sathas (Constantine N.). Μεσαιωνικὴ βιβλιοθήκη, etc. 7 tom.
8°. ἐν Βενετίᾳ, 1872-94.

Vol. 5, pp. 525-569, proverbs and phrases from different mss., with
explanations. [B.M.

409. Timoshenko (Ivan). Византійскія пословицы и славянскія
параллели къ нимъ, etc. pp. 51. 8°. Варшава, 1895.

Originally published in Русскій Филологическій Вѣстникъ, Том. 32-34.
A dissertation on the similiarity of Byzantine and Slavonic proverbs,
suggested by two books, Krumbacher's " Mittelgriechische Sprichwörter " and
Kurtz " Sprichwörter-Sammlung des Maximus Planudes."

LOCAL AND DIALECTS.

410. Balabanes (I.). Μνημεῖα τῆς ἐν Πόντῳ δημοτικῆς Β'. παροιμίαι.
1870.

In Κωνσταντινουπόλις ἑπτάλοφος,1870, Τομ. Β. Pp. 349-381, proverbs.

411. Carnoy (Émile Henri) and **Nicolaïdès** (Jean). Traditions
populaires de l'Asie Mineure.
8°. Paris, Maisonneuve, 1889.

Les littératures populaires de toutes les nations, Tom. 28. Pp. 283-290,
proverbes. In French. [B.M.

412. Dekigallas (I.). Γενική στατιστική τῆς νήσου Θήρας. pp. 126.
8°. ἐν 'Ερμουπόλει, 1850.
Another edition. pp. 320. 1852.
Contains a list of proverbs.

413. Phrantzeskakes (Em. D.). 'Η ἀριάδνη ἤτοι συλλογή Κρητικῶν ἀσμάτων καὶ παροιμιῶν διατεταγμένων κατ' ἀλφάβητον συλλεγέντων καὶ ἐκδοθέντων. pp. 128. 8°. ἐν 'Αθήναις, Τρίμη, 1883.
Bernstein, 4420. Pp. 105-117, Διάφοροι, παροιμίαι. Modern Cretan proverbs.

414. Georgeakis (G.) and **Pineau** (Léon). Le folk-lore de Lesbos.
pp. xx, 372. 8°. Paris, *Maisonneuve,* 1894.
Les littératures populaires de toutes les nations, Tom. 31. Pp. 281-287, proverbes. In French. [B.M.

415. Giannares (Antonios N.). 'Αισματα Κρητικὰ μετὰ διστιχῶν καὶ παροιμιῶν, *etc.* pp. vii, 386.
8°. Leipzig, *Brockhaus,* 1876.
Pp. 291-314, proverbs. 201 proverbs, some with German equivalents. [B.M.

416. Ionnides (Sab.). 'Ιστορία καὶ στατιστική Τρπεζοῦντος [*sic*], *etc.* ἐν Κωνσταντινουπόλει, 1870.
Pp. 268-270, 85 proverbs.

417. Kalaïsakes (G. I.). Κρητικαὶ παροιμίαι.
8°. ἐν 'Αθήναις, 1894.
In Παρνασσός, 1894, pp. 479-480, 559-560, 635-638, 878-880. [B.M.

418. Kanellakes (Konstantinos N.). Χιακὰ ἀνάλεκτα ἤτοι συλλογή ἠθιμῶν, *etc.* pp. viii, 592. 8°. ἐν 'Αθήναις, Πέρρη, 1890.
Pp. 213-318, Παροιμίαι. 793 entries with notes. [B.M.

419. Louis Salvator, *Archduke of Austria.* Paxos und Antipaxos.
pp. xv, 480 + plates. 4°. Würzburg, Wien, *Woerl,* 1887.
Pp. 44-49, proverbs from Paxos with German translations. [B.M.

420. Loukas (G.). Φιλολογικαὶ ἐπισκέψεις, *etc.* pp. 200.
8°. ἐν 'Αθήναις, 1874.
Pp. 142-148, Παροιμίαι καὶ γνωμικὰ τῶν Κυπρίων. [B.M.

421. Papadopoulos (Georgios). Γλωσσική ὕλη τῆς νήσου Νισύρου, *etc.* 4°. ἐν Κωνσταντινουπόλει, 1891.
In Ζωγράφειος ἀγὼν ἤτοι μνημεῖα τῆς 'Ελλάδος ἀρχαιότητος ζῶντα ἐν τῷ νῦν ἑλληνικῷ λαῷ, Τομ. Α, pp. 381-417. Pp. 410-413, 78 proverbs. [B.M.

422. Sakellarios (Athanasios A.). Τὰ Κυπριακὰ ἤτοι γεογραφία, ἱστορία καὶ γλῶσσα τῆς νήσου Κύπρου, *etc.* 2 vols.
8°. ἐν 'Αθήναις, Σακελλαρίος, [1890-91].
Vol. 2, pp. 277-289, 400 proverbs from Cyprus. [B.M.

423. Trimes (Konstantinos A.). Κυμαϊκὰ ἤτοι ἱστορία και τοπογραφία τῆς Κύμης. pp. 80. 8°. ἐν 'Αθήναις, Φέξης, 1894.
Bernstein, 3752. Pp. 62-70, Παροιμίαι. [B.M.

D

JEWISH

(Including Yiddish).

424. Adalberg (Samuel). Przysłowia Żydowskie, *etc.* pp. 22.
8°. Warszawa, *Jeżyński*, 1890.
Separate publication of an article in : Wisła, Tom 4.

425. Aquin (Ludovicus Henricus d'). Sententiae et proverbia
Rabbinorum, *etc.* pp. [iv], 159.
16°. Lutetiae Parisiorum, *Cramoisy*, 1620.
Stirling-Maxwell, p. 18. Maxims in Hebrew and Latin. [B.M.

426. Benczer (Benjamin). Sprichwörter galizischer Juden.
8°. Leiden, *Brill*, 1897.
In Der Urquell, N.F., Bd. 1, pp. 14-15. 28 proverbs. [B.M.

427. Bernstein (Ignacy). Jüdische Sprichwörter. Aus einem
Manuscript des Herrn I. B. 2 pts.
4°. Warschau, 1888-1889.
Separat-Abdruck aus dem " Hausfreund," herausgegeben von M. Spektor.

428. ———: Jüdische Sprichwörter und Redensarten . . . Zweite
. . . Auflage, *etc.* pp. xv, ff. 328, pp. 84.
8°. Warschau, *Kauffmann,* 1908.
Nearly 4000 proverbs and phrases in Yiddish, transliterated on the opposite
pages, and with notes in German. [B.M.

429. Bible.
The Bible, especially the Book of Proverbs and such apocryphal books as
Ecclesiasticus, is an almost inexhaustible storehouse of proverbs, sayings and
maxims. It does not, however, lie within the scope of this bibliography to
enumerate its editions or the commentaries to which it has given rise, and a
general mention is all that can be given here. Bernstein gives a lengthy list
of books of Proverbs of Solomon, Sentences of Jesus Serach, Ben-Sirae, *etc.*

429a. Bjoerck (Gustav Ludwig). Agurs och Lemuels ordspråk,
etc. pp. 33.
8°. Upsala, *Kongl. Akad. Boktryckeriet*, 1865.
Bernstein, 314.

430. Blass (Moritz). Jüdische Sprichwörter, *etc.* pp. 30.
8°. Leipzig, *Gerhard*, 1857.
Stirling-Maxwell, p. 8. Jewish proverbs in German, arranged alphabetically.
[B.M.

431. Blass (Moritz). Sammlung sinnreicher jüdisch-deutscher Spruchwörter. pp. 30.
8°. Budapest, *Selbstverlag des Herausgebers*, 1897.

Although with a different title page and a preface signed Nathan der Weise, this is nothing but a plagiarism of the last entry.

432. Bock (Moyse Hirsch). L'ami des enfans Israélites, *etc.*
8°. Berlin, 1811.

Gratet-Duplessis, 50. In Hebrew, French and German. Contains (1) Moralisches A.B.C. in Sprüchen aus dem Talmud und andern (heiligen) Büchern. (2) Moralisches A.B.C. in Sprichwörtern aus dem gemeinen Leben.

433. Bonyhády (Benjamin). Sprichwörter kroatischer und slavonischer Juden. 8°. Lunden, 1896.

In Am Ur-Quell, Bd. 6, pp. 33-34. 20 entries. [B.M.

434. Bruell (N.). Sprüchwörter in der nachtalmudischen Literatur des Judenthums.
8°. Frankfurt am Main, *Erras*, 1885.

In Jahrbücher für jüdische Geschichte und Literatur, Jahrgang 7, pp. 18-30. 47 entries, with German translations and notes. [B.M.

435. Buchner (A.). Kwiaty wschodnie. Zbiór zasad moralnych, teleogicznych przysłów . . . wyjętych z Talmudi i pism ówczesnych. pp. xxvii, 260, [8].
8°. Warszawa, *Chmielewski*, 1842.

436. Burder (Samuel). Oriental customs: or an illustration of the Sacred Scriptures, *etc.* pp. xvi, 400.
8°. London, *Longman*, 1802.
Another edition. 2 vols. 8°. London, 1822.
Another edition. 4 vols. 8°. London, 1827.
Oriental literature . . . designed as a sequel to Oriental Customs. 2 vols. 8°. London, 1822.
Oriental customs applied to the illustration of the Sacred Scriptures. [Articles selected from the two previous books with extracts from other authors.] 8°. London, 1831.
Another edition. pp. xiv, 475. 8°. London, 1837.

Gratet-Duplessis, 52. These contain a number of proverbs scattered throughout. [B.M.

437. Burger (S.). Sprichwörter deutscher Juden.
8°. Lunden, 1891.

In Am Ur-Quell, Bd. 2, pp. 26-27. [B.M.

438. Buxtorfius (Johannes). Florilegium Hebraicum, *etc.* pp. [xvi], 390, [8]. 8°. Basileæ, *Koenig*, 1648.

Gratet-Duplessis, 43. Sixty Hebrew proverbs from the Florilegium were inserted in Hartmann's " Chrestomathie hébraïque," Marburg, 1797. The book is a collection of proverbs, phrases, apophthegms, *etc.* [B.M.

439. Charap (J. A.). Sprichwörter galizischer Juden.
8°. Lunden, 1893.

In Am Ur-Quell, Bd. 4, pp. 194, 212-213. [B.M.

439a. Clouston (William Alexander).　Flowers from a Persian
garden, and other papers.　pp. xii, 368.
8°.　London, Nutt, 1890.
Pp. 259-267, Wise Sayings of the Rabbis.　　　　　　　　[F.-L.S.

440. Cohen (Abraham).　Ancient Jewish proverbs.　pp. 127.
8°.　London, Murray, 1911.
Wisdom of the East Series.　A good introduction to the study of the subject.
The illustrations to the 350 proverbs are copious and to the point.　Proverbs are
only given in English.　　　　　　　　　　　　　　　　[B.M.

441. Cohen (Henry).　Talmudic sayings, selected and arranged
. . . by Henry Cohen.　pp. xii, 94.
8°.　Cincinnati, Chicago, Bloch, [1894].
In English.　　　　　　　　　　　　　　　　　　　　[B.M.

442. Dessauer (Julius).　Spruch-Lexikon des Talmud und Midrasch, <i>etc.</i>　pp. xiii, 259.　　　　　　8°.　Budapest, 1876.

443. Drusius (Joannes).　Proverbiorum classes duae, <i>etc.</i>　pp.
[xii], 329, [16].　　　　　4°.　Franckerae, <i>Raderus</i>, 1590.
Another edition.　　　　　　　　　fol.　Londini, 1660.
Another edition.　　　　　　　　　fol.　Tiguri, 1753.
Apophthegmata Ebraeorum ac Arabum, <i>etc.</i>　pp. [viii], 87.
4°.　Franckerae, Raderus, 1591.
Another edition.　　　　　　　　4°.　Franckerae, 1612.
Proverbia Ben-Sirae, <i>etc.</i>　pp. [viii], 122.
4°.　Franckerae, Raderus, 1597.
Another edition.　　　　　　　　　fol.　Londini, 1660.
Les sentences de Ben-Syra . . . traduits de Caldee en
françois et commentées par Barthelemy du Poix.
16°.　Angers, R. Piquenot, 1569.
Gratet-Duplessis, 38.　The first class consists of proverbs, maxims, <i>etc.</i>, taken
textually from the Scriptures : the second of proverbs and precepts which are
only indirectly derived therefrom.　The Apophthegmata and Proverbia Ben-Sirae
are continuations of the first work.　Excellent comments on each proverb.　The
two 1660 editions are in Vol. 8 of J. Pearson's " Critici sacri " : the 1753
edition is in B. Walton's " Biblicus apparatus."　The Apophthegmata was
frequently reprinted and translated and was included by Orelli in **364.**　Duplessis
sketches the life of Drusius.　　　　　　　　　　　　　　[B.M.

444. Du Chastel (F. Anselme).　Recueil des plus notables sentences de la Bible, traduites par quatrains en manière de
proverbes, <i>etc.</i>　ff. 77.　　　　　　　　8°.　Paris, 1577.

445. Dukes (Leopold).　Rabbinische Blumenlese, enthaltend :
talmudische Sprichwörter, Sentenzen und Maximen, <i>etc.</i>
pp. viii, 333.　　　　　　　　　　8°.　Leipzig, <i>Hahn</i>, 1844.
Gratet-Duplessis, 54.　In Hebrew and German ; contains many actual proverbs
besides maxims, <i>etc.</i>　　　　　　　　　　　　　　　　[U.C.L.

446. Dukes (Leopold). Zur rabbinischen Sprachkunde, *etc.* pp. iv, 97.   8°. Wien, *Della Torre*, 1851.

Proverbs are given in Hebrew, with German translations and explanations. The bibliographical notes are very good.   [B.M.

447. Edelman (Hirsch). The path of good men, *etc.*
     8°. London, 1852.

Pp. 33-39, 149 Aphorisms of the Sages : pp. 39-51, proverbs of Arabia. [U.C.L.

448. Ehrlich (J.). Judendeutsche Sprichwörter und Redensarten.
     8°. Leiden, *Brill*, 1897.

In Der Urquell, N.F., Bd. 1, pp. 172-175. 82 proverbs with brief notes. [B.M.

449. Ehrmann (Daniel). Aus Palästina und Babylon. Eine Sammlung von Sagen . . . Sprüchwörtern . . . aus Talmud und Midrasch, *etc.* pp. xv, 309.   8°. Wien, *Hölder*, 1880.

Pp. 221-236, proverbs in German. 295 entries.   [B.M.

450. Elmslie (William Alexander Leslie). Studies in life from Jewish proverbs. pp. 288.
     6s. 8°. London, *James Clarke*, [1917].

Chapters according to subjects. Pp. 36-42, sources of Jewish proverbs. [U.C.L.

451. Finkelscherer. Das Sprüchwort in der alten jüdischen Literatur.   4°. Mainz, 1899.

In Der Israelit, Jahrgang 40, No. 22.

452. Foulché-Delbosc (R.). Proverbes judéo-espagnols.
     8°. Paris, *Picard*, 1895.

In Revue hispanique, Vol. 2, pp. 312-352. Some 1300 Jewish proverbs in Spanish. Also published separately, same date, publisher, *etc.* pp. 45.   [B.M.

453. Franck (Adolphe). Nouvelles études orientales, *etc.* pp. xxxii, 413.   8°. Paris, *Calmann Lévy*, 1896.

Pp. 157-191, sentences et proverbes du Talmud et du Midrasch. In French.   [B.M.

454. Freund (Leopold). Blüthen von den Gefilden Juda's, *etc.* pp. xiv, 150.
     8°. Budapest, *Selbstverlag des Verfassers*, 1882.

Pp. 1-31, Volkssprichwörter : pp. 32-82, Weisheit und Moral : pp. 129-131, Weltliche Klugheitsregeln. In Hebrew and German.

455. Fritsch (Theodor). Antisemiten-Katechismus . . . von Theodor Fritsch (Thomas Frey). Dreizehnte verbesserte Auflage. pp. 362.   12°. Leipzig, *Fritsch*, 1891.

Pp. 311-312, die Juden im Sprichwort. This list does not appear in some of the earlier editions.

456. Fuerstenthal (R. J.). Rabbinische Anthologie oder Sammlung von Erzählungen, Sprichwörtern, *etc.* pp. xvi, 384.
     8°. Breslau, *Friedländer*, 1834.
     Another edition.   8°. Breslau, 1854.

504 entries.

457. Galante (Abraham).   Proverbes judéo-espagnols.
8°.   Paris, Picard, 1902.

In Revue hispanique, Vol. 9, pp. 440-454.   A list of 462 proverbs of the Spanish
Jews, with explanatory notes where necessary.   [B.M.

458. Goldman (M.).   Proverbs of the sages.   Collection of proverbs, ethical precepts, from the Talmud and Midrashim,
etc. pp. 287. 4°.   New York, *Goldman & Steinberg*, 1911.

In the original, with English translations and explanatory notes.   [B.M.

459. Gressmann (Hugo).   Israels Spruchweisheit, *etc.* pp. 57.
8°.   Berlin, Curtius, 1925.

Not a collection of proverbs, but a commentary.   [B.M.

460. Gurland (Jonas).   Neue Denkmäler der jüdischen Literatur
in St. Petersburg.   Viertes Heft.   Perlen der Lehrsprüche,
enthaltend: eine Sammlung von sinnreichen Sprüchen, Sentenzen, Maximen, *etc.* pp. xvi, 51.
8°.   St. Petersburg, Ettinger, 1867.

461. Henninges (Georgius).   Proverbia: das ist: die Sprüche des
Weysen und hocherleuchten Königs Salomonis.   In kurze
einfeltige deutsche Rheimen verfasset.   ff. 90.
12°.   Magdeburg, Ross, 1575.

462. Jacobs (Joseph).   Studies in Biblical archæology.   pp. xxiv.
148.   8°.   London, *Nutt*, 1894.

Pp. 123-128, Indian origin of Proverbs 30.   [B.M.

463. Jacox (Francis).   Scripture proverbs, illustrated, annotated,
and applied.   pp. xvi, 604.
8°.   London, Hodder & Stoughton, 1874.
[B.M.

464. Jellinek (Adolph).   Der jüdische Stamm, *etc.* pp. viii, 224.
12°.   Wien, Herzfeld & Bauer, 1869.

Pp. 153-178, der jüdische Stamm in talmudischen und jüdisch-deutschen
Sprichwörtern.

465. ———: Der jüdische Stamm in nicht-jüdischen Sprichwörtern.   3 series.

8°.   Wien, Lown (1), Bermann & Altman (2-3), 1881-1885.

Second edition.   8°.   Wien, 1886-?

Proverbs from different countries concerning the Jews, explained and
illustrated.   [B.M.

466. Karrer (Ph. Jakob).   Neues vollständig-richtig-biblisches
Spruchregister, *etc.* pp. iv, 252.
8°.   Kempten, Dannheimer, 1833.

467. Kayserling (M.).   Quelques proverbes judéo-espagnols.
8°.   Paris, Picard, 1897.

In Revue hispanique, Année 4, p. 82.   23 proverbs not in Foulché-Delbosc's
collection.   [B.M.

468. Kayserling (M.). Refranes ó proverbios españoles de los Judios españoles. pp. 24. 8°. Budapest, *Posner*, 1889.

Arranged according to subject. These proverbs were also reprinted in the author's Biblioteca Española-Portugeza-Judaica, *etc.*, 1890. [U.C.L.

469. Klemperer (W..). Beiträge zur vergleichenden Gnomologie, mit besonderer Berücksichtigung der talmudischen Sprichwörter und Sentenzen. Erstes Heft. pp. 55.

8°. Berlin, *Calvary*, 1894.

Also appeared in : Allgemeine Zeitung des Judenthums, 1894.

470. Knight (William). The golden wisdom of the Apocrypha, *etc.* pp. 64.

8°. Oxford, *Blackwell*, London, *Simpkin, Marshall*, 1910.

Pp. 61-64, proverbs and sayings of the Rabbis [in English]. [B.M.

471. Kohn (Salomon). Eine Blumenlese aus dem Talmud, oder Sprüche der Rabbinen . . . Erster Theil. pp. 81.

8°. Gross-Kanizsa, *Selbstverlag des Verfassers*, 1870. [B.M.

472. Kulke (Eduard). Judendeutsche Sprichwörter aus Mähren, Böhmen und Ungarn. 8°. Leiden, *Brill*, 1896, 1897.

In Am Ur-Quell, Bd. 6, pp. 119-121, *and in* Der Urquell, N.F., Bd. 1, pp. 119-121. [B.M.

473. L——n (A——n). Sprichwörter galizischer Juden.

8°. Lunden, 1891-92.

In Am Ur-Quell, N.F., Bd. 2, pp. 66-7, 112-3, 131, 163-4, 178, 196 *et seq.* 128 proverbs. [B.M.

474. Landsberger (Artur F.). Jüdische Sprichwörter. pp. 88.

8°. Leipzig, *Wolff*, 1912.

475. Lew (Henryk). Przysłowia i anegdoty żydowskie z przeszłości Polski. fol. Warszawa, 1899.

In Kurjer Warszawski, Nr. 87, 1899. The same author, in Wisła, Tom 12, 13, gave a translation of some of the proverbs of Bernstein's Jewish collection.

476. Lewysohn (Abraham). Der Ursprung üblicher Sprichwörter.

8°. Mainz, *Le Rour*, 1858.

In Israelitische Schulbibliothek, *etc.*, 1858, pp. 92-93. 18 proverbs, with the source indicated. [B.M.

477. Lobethal (M.). Tausend jüdisch-deutsche und deutsche Redensarten zumeist in kunstlosen Reim. pp. 46.

8°. Breslau, *Selbstverlag des Herausgebers*, [1887].

478. Loewi (K.). Jüdische Sprichwörter und Redensarten. Von K. Ilöw [anagram of Löwi]. pp. 22. 8°. Prag, 1871.

479. Maiszim. Maiszim un schnokes vun e Landelwos. Pinkel No. 1. Tischre 5606. pp. 61.

8°. Leipzig, *Literarisches Museum*, 1845.

Pp. 39-49, Sprüchwörtlech. No more published.

480. Mandelstamm (L.).   Ebraisches Elementarbuch Alphabeth,
   etc. 2 tom.   8°. Wilna, *Romma*, 1849-50.
Tom. 1, pp. 290-313, 189 Sitten-Sprüche.

481. Mandl (Leopold).   Sprichwörter deutscher Juden.
                                    8°. Lunden, 1893.
In Am Ur-Quell, Bd. 4, pp. 75-76.   [B.M.

482. Mirus (Adam Erdmann).   Kurze Fragen von denen Proverbiis Sacris, *etc.* pp. 636, [24].
                              16°. Dressden, *Zimmermann*, 1716.

483. Mittelmann (A.).   Judendeutsche Sprichwörter.
                                    8°. Leiden, *Brill*, 1897.
In Der Urquell, N.F., Bd. 1, pp. 273-279. 108 proverbs with brief notes.
                                                           [B.M.

484. Muehlau (Henricus Ferdinandus).   De proverbiorum quae
   dicuntur Aguri et Lemuelis . . . origine et indole, *etc.* pp.
   xiii, 70.   8°. Lipsiae, *Hinrichs*, 1869.
                                                           [B.M.

485. Mylius (C. Fr.).   Aus Volkes Mund.   Sprichwörtliche
   Redensarten; Citate aus classischen Dichtungen, aus der
   Oper, aus der Bibel. Jüdisch-Deutsch. pp. vii, 235.
                         8°. Frankfurt a. M., *Jaeger*, 1878.

486. Nascher (Simon).   Die Sentenz bei Juden und Arabern.
   Eine vergleichende Studie. pp. 19.
                  8°. Berlin, *Stuhr'sche Buchhandlung*, 1868.
                                                           [B.M.

487. P.   Judendeutsche Sprichwörter und Redensarten.   Mit-
   geteilt von P.   8°. Leiden, *Brill*, 1897.
In Der Urquell, N.F., Bd. 1, pp. 49-50. 24 proverbs.   [B.M.

488. P. (M.).   Jüdische Sprichwörter und Redensarten aus Ost-
   Ungarn.   8°. Hamburg, 1898.
In Mitteilungen der Gesellschaft für jüdische Volkskunde, 1898, Heft 3, pp.
41-44.

489. Passy (Joseph).   Spaniolische Sprichwörter.
                                    8°. Leiden, *Brill*, 1897.
In Der Urquell, N.F., Bd. 1, pp. 205-206. 25 proverbs with French
translations.   [B.M.

490. Peters (Madison Clinton).   Wit and wisdom of the Talmud,
   etc. pp. 169.   8°. New York, *Baker & Taylor*, [1901].
A selection of axioms and maxims in English.   [B.M.

491. Pirozknikov (   ).   Idische Sprichwörter.   Vilna.

492. Placzek (B.).   Judendeutsche Sprichwörter und Redensarten. [Signed Benno, *i.e.* B. Placzek].
                                    8°. Leiden, *Brill*, 1897.
In Der Urquell, N.F., Bd. 1, pp. 271-272. 45 proverbs.   [B.M.

493. Priluzki (   ). Samelbicher far Folklor. Warsaw, 1912.
Contains a collection of 1061 Yiddish proverbs.

494. Rapaport (Samuel). Stories and sayings (translated) from
the Talmud. [1st Series]. pp. [viii], 56.
8°. London, *Valentine*, 5629—1869.
Tales and maxims from the Talmud, *etc.* [2nd Series].
pp. 165.
8°. London, *Routledge*, New York, *Dutton*, 1910.
Semitic Series. The maxims are rather moral aphorisms than proverbs. Very
readable. [B.M.

495. ——: Tales and maxims from the Midrash. pp. vii, 264.
8°. London, *Routledge*, New York, *Dutton*, 1907.
Pp. 212-214, Midrash proverbs. [U.C.L.

496. Riecke (G. A.). Salomo's Sprüche der Weisheit frei in
Reime gebracht. pp. 96.
16°. Esslingen, *Weissmann*, 1876.

497. Rio (Martinus Antonius del). Adagiala sacra Veteris et
Novi Testamenti. 2 vols. 4°. Lugduni, *Cardon*, 1612-13.
Editio secunda. 2 vols. 4°. Lugduni, *Cardon*, 1614-18.
Gratet-Duplessis, 40. A posthumous and unfinished work. Most of the sayings
included are true proverbs and the explanatory notes are full and erudite. [B.M.

498. Roberts (Joseph). Oriental illustrations of the Sacred Scriptures, collected from the customs, manners, rites, superstitions, traditions, parabolical, idiomatical, and proverbial
forms of speech . . . of the Hindoos. pp. xxiv, 619.
8°. London, *Murray*, 1835.
Second edition. pp. xvi, 612. 8°. London, *Tegg*, 1844.
Gratet-Duplessis, 52 and 60. Pp. 352-369, remarks upon the Book of Proverbs.
Other proverbs are to be found throughout the book. [U.C.L.

499. Robinsohn (Isaak). Judendeutsche Sprichwörter aus Ost-
galizien. 8°. Leiden, *Brill*, Hamburg, *Kramer*, 1898.
In Der Urquell, N.F., Bd. 2, pp. 221-222. 68 proverbs. [B.M.

500. Rubin (Salomo). Sitten-Spiegel. Enthält Weisheitssprüche sorgfältig gesammelt und gewählt aus den sinn-
reichsten Moral-Charakteristiken antiker und moderner
Psychologen, *etc.* pp. xiv, 74.
8°. Wien, *Schmidbauer & Holzwarth*, 1854.

501. Sailer (F.). Sinnsprüche aus dem Talmud und der rabbinischen Literatur. pp. vii, 89.
12°. Berlin, *Stahn*, n.d.
322 entries, in translation.

502. Schuhl (Moïse). Sentences et proverbes du Talmud et du
Midrasch, suivis du traité d'Aboth. pp. xii, 546.
8°. Paris, 1878.
Over 1300 entries, with French translations and explanations. [B.M.

503. Sprichwörter. Talmudische und rabbinische Sprichwörter.
4°. Leipzig, 1864.

In Jüdisches Volksblatt, 1864, No. 33, 37.

504. Talmud. The Talmud. Selections from the contents of that ancient book, its commentaries, teachings, poetry, and legends. . . . Translated from the original by H. Polano. pp. xi, 359.   1/6, 2/-.   8°. London, *Warne*, [1877].

Part fourth, pp. 286-299, proverbs and sayings of the Rabbis. Editions of the Talmud cannot be included in this bibliography. The last tract but one of the fourth part of the Mishnāh is the booklet of proverbs, in five chapters, called Massecheth Aboth, better known with a sixth chapter as Pirke Aboth. It is included in many prayer-books.   [U.C.L.

505. Tendlau (Abraham). Sprichwörter und Redensarten deutsch-jüdischer Vorzeit, *etc.* pp. xii, 425.
8°. Frankfurt am Main, *Keller*, 1860.

1070 entries accompanied by explanatory notes.   [B.M.

506. Torsano (Angelo Maria). Proverbia Novi ac Veteris Testamenti, *etc.* ff. [xviii], 202.

8°. Venetiis, *Gryphius*, 1563.

507. Troschel (Daniel Philipp). Salomons Moral. Die Sprüchwörter unter moralische Titel gebracht, *etc.* pp. xl, 104.
8°. Berlin, Stralsund, *Lange*, 1782.

508. Wahl (M. C.). Das Sprichwort der hebräisch-aramäischen Literatur, *etc.* pp. 181.
M.5.50.   4°. Leipzig, *Leiner*, 1871.

This is called the first book, but there was not another. Proverbs from the Bible, the Talmud, *etc.*, are compared and contrasted with English, French, German, Greek, Latin, *etc.*, proverbs.   [B.M.

509. Wallerstein (J.). Gnomen und Sprichwörter des Talmuds.
8°. Wien, *Engel*, 1865.

In Jahrbuch für Israeliten 5625, N.F., Jahrgang 11, pp. 60-83.

510. Walton (Brian). In Biblia polyglotta prolegomena. Praefatus est Io. Aug. Dathe. pp. lii, 696.
8°. Lipsiae, *sumptibus Wegandianis*, 1777.

Gratet-Duplessis, 45. Includes Drusius' work on the proverbs of the Holy Scriptures. Duplessis gives an abridged translation, " Dissertations sur les prolégomènes de Walton," *etc.* Liège, *Justel*, 1699.   [U.C.L.

511. Weissberg (Max). Sprichwörter galizischer Juden.
8°. Lunden, 1893.

In Am Ur-Quell, Bd. 4, pp. 256-257.   23 proverbs.   [B.M.

512. Yoffie (Leah Rachel). Yiddish proverbs, sayings, *etc.*, in St. Louis, Mo.   8°. Lancaster, Pa., New York, 1920.

In Journal of American Folk-Lore, Vol. 33, pp. 134-165.   420 entries, with translations.   [B.M.

513. Zehner (Joachim). Adagia sacra, *etc.* pp. [xvi], 783, [69].
4°. Lipsiae, *Schurerus*, 1601.

Gratet-Duplessis, 39. Divided into three parts. The first contains the true proverbs of the Scriptures; the second comprises moral maxims to be found throughout the various Books, and which have become more or less proverbial by use; the third contains proverbial sayings which owe their origin to the Scriptures even though not textually expressed therein. Comparisons are made with various maxims from the works of the Fathers. It includes also a section on " Germanorum adagia "—Duplessis, 552. [B.M.

See also **544n., 557, 1341,** *and under Western Asia.*

GYPSY

514. Borrow (George Henry). The Zincali; or, an account of the gypsies of Spain. First edition. 2 vols.

12°. London, *Murray*, 1841.

Second edition. 2 vols. 12°. London, 1843.

Another edition. pp. xiv, 251.

8°. London, New York, *Dent*, [1914].

Gratet-Duplessis, 893. Vol. 1 contains a few proverbs in the Gitano language and English. The 1914 edition is in Everyman's Library. [U.C.L., B.M.

515. Gerard (E.). The land beyond the forest, *etc.* 2 vols.

8°. Edinburgh, London, *Blackwood*, 1883.

Vol. 1, pp. 273-274, about 20 Roumanian proverbs from Transylvania in English. Vol. 2, pp. 102-103, about 25 Tzigane proverbs also in English. [B.M.

516. Halliday (William Reginald). Folklore studies, ancient and modern. pp. xix, 172.

7/6. 8°. London, *Methuen*, 1924.

Chapter 1, Gypsies of Turkey : pp. 45-48, Greek proverbs about gypsies.
[F.-L.S.

517. Ješina (Josef). Romani cib, oder die Zigeuner-Sprache . . . Dritte vermehrte Auflage. (1. deutsche Ausgabe.) pp. vi, 240. 8°. Leipzig, *List & Francke*, 1886.

Pp. 223-224, Einige Sprüche. Proverbs with German translations. [B.M.

518. Jimenez (Augusto). Vocabulario del dialecto jitano, *etc.* pp. 118. [Second edition].

8°. Sevilla, *Imprenta del Conciliador*, 1853.

In the appendix, pp. 106-107, are 10 proverbs in the Jitano, *i.e.* Romany, dialect, with Spanish translations. [B.M.

519. Krauss (Friedrich Saloman). Der Zigeuner im Sprichwort russischer Juden.

8°. Edinburgh, *Gypsy Lore Society*, 1908-9.

In Journal of the Gypsy Lore Society, Vol. 2, pp. 120-121. Half a dozen proverbs taken from I. Bernstein's Jüdische Sprichwörter. [B.M.

520. Leland (Charles Godfrey). The English gipsies and their language. pp. xiii, 259. 8°. London, *Trübner*, 1873.

Fourth edition. pp. xiii, 259.

8°. London, *Kegan Paul, etc.*, 1893.

This book was also published in New York in 1873. Pp. 101-108, proverbs and chance phrases; in the original, with English translations. Many of the gipsy stories and fables at the end of the book conclude with a sententious or proverbial phrase. [B.M.

521. Moeckesch (Martin Samuel). Haideblümchen. Zigeune-
rische Dichtungen und Sprichwörter, *etc.* pp. 56.
12°. Bukarest, *Thiel & Weiss*, 1873.

Pp. 51-56, proverbs with German translations.

522. Pott (August Friedrich). Die Zigeuner in Europa und
Asien. Ethnographisch-linguistische Untersuchung, vornehm-
lich ihrer Herkunft und Sprache, nach gedruckten und
ungedruckten Quellen. 2 vols.
8°. Halle, *Heynemann*, London, *Williams & Norgate*,
1844-1845.

Gratet-Duplessis, 893. Vol. 2, pp. 482-485, 35 proverbs in Romany with
German translations. Duplessis says that these proverbs are not peculiar to
the gypsies. [U.C.L.

523. Wlislocki (Heinrich von). Sprichwörter moslimischer
Zigeuner. 8°. Leiden, *Brill*, 1897.

In Der Urquell, N.F., Bd. 1, pp. 251-253. 50 proverbs with German translations.

See also **3977.**

ESPERANTO

524. Samenhof (Lazarus Ludwig). Proverbs in Esperanto and
English from Zamenhof's Proverbaro. (Translated by Mon-
tagu C. Butler). pp. 159. 32°. London, *Hill*, [1926].

Bi-lingual Series. Alphabetically arranged. [B.M.

ENGLISH

GENERAL.

525. Aesop. Aesopi fabulae explicatae. . . . Quibus adjungitur appendix necessaria continens brevem collectionem proverbiorum Anglicanorum, *etc.* pp. 139.
8°. Londini, *Pankhurst*, 1682.

Pp. 109-114, a collection of English proverbs, with their true sense and meaning fully explained.

526. Aigre (Frédéric). Méthode pratique de la langue anglaise.
. . . Anglicismes avec les Gallicismes correspondants, proverbes anglais avec les proverbes français correspondants. pp. ii, 195. 8°. Paris, *Soudier*, 1893.

527. Alfred, surnamed *the Great, King of England.* An old English miscellany. . . . Edited . . . by Richard Morris. pp. xvi, 308.
8°. London, *Early English Text Society*, 1872.

Pp. 102-138, the proverbs of Alfred, from two texts. More in the nature of moral precepts than popular proverbs. *See also* **549, 603, 642, 665.** [U.C.L.

528. ———: The proverbs of Alfred re-edited from the manuscripts by W. W. Skeat. pp. xlvi, 94.
2/6. 8°. Oxford, *Clarendon Press*, 1907.

Pp. vii-xlvi, introduction : pp. 1-52, text : pp. 53-73, notes : pp. 74-94, glossarial index. [B.M.

529. ———: The proverbs of Alfred re-edited from the manuscripts, with an introduction, notes, and glossary by Edv. Borgström, *etc.* pp. lxxix, 100. 8°. Lund, *Ohlsson*, 1908.
[B.M.

530. ———: Specimens of King Alfred's proverbs, with a Swedish translation and a glossary by L. G. Nilsson. Part 1. pp. 45.
8°. Copenhagen, *Thiele*, 1859.
An academic dissertation. [B.M.

531. Antonowicz (Julian). Grammatyka dla Polaków, *etc.* pp. [x], 144, [11].
12°. w Warszawie, *w drukarni Nadwor:*
J. K. Mci i P. K. Edu, 1788.

Pp. 141-144, Przysłowia angielskie.

531a. Apperson (G. L.). English proverbs and proverbial phrases. A historical dictionary. pp. 748.

31s. 6d. 8°. London, *Dent*, 1929.

Examples in chronological order, grouped under subject headings.

532. Arnold (Theodor). Grammatica Anglicana concentrata. . . . Neunte Auflage. 8°. Leipzig, *Züllichau*, 1797.

Contains proverbs. [Bristol Public Library.

533. ———: Grammatica Anglicana et Danica concentrata. pp. 638. 8°. Kiøbenhavn, *Mumme*, 1770.

Pp. 516-574, en samling af Engelske Ordsprog. An alphabetical list of English proverbs with Danish translations. A similar list is contained in the author's " Engelske Grammatik," 1800. [B.M.

534. Arthur (J. K.). A bouquet of brevities, *etc.* [Illustrated.] pp. v, 129, [16].

4°. London, New York, *Leadenhall Press*, 1895.

A " pretty " book, with some proverbs in English amongst other moral maxims. [B.M.

535. Bailey (Nathan). Divers proverbs with their explication and illustration. . . . Anno Domini 1721, *etc.* pp. ix, 83 + woodcuts.

8°. New Haven, Connecticut, *Yale University Press*, London, *Milford*, 1917.

[B.M.

536. Barten (John). A select collection of English and German proverbs, *etc.* pp. viii, 160, viii, 161-323. 2 pts. [in 1].

8°. Hamburg, *Kloss*, 1896.

Pp. .1-160, 4182 English proverbs : pp. 161-323, 4057 German proverbs. Equivalent proverbs in the other language are always indicated. Alphabetical arrangement. A practical book and a good collection. [B.M.

537. Beau. The beau's academy. . . . Poems, songs, letters, proverbs, *etc.* 8°. London, 1699.

538. Belcour (G.). A selection of the most popular English proverbs, familiar and idiomatic locutions, with their equivalents in French, *etc.* pp. 143.

sm. 8°. London, *Hachette*, 1888.

Is no more than it professes to be. French and English indexes.

[F.-L.S. (Stephens collection).

539. Bellezza (Paolo). Studio comparativo sui proverbi inglesi. pp. 52. 8°. Milano, *Cogliati*, 1893.

540. Benham (William Gurney). Cassell's book of quotations, proverbs, and household words, *etc.* pp. 1256.

8°. London, *etc.*, *Cassell*, 1907.

Another edition, revised. Benham's book of quotations, *etc.* pp. 1224. 8°. London, Melbourne, *Ward Lock*, 1924.

Contains about 150 pages of English proverbs arranged alphabetically, frequently with foreign equivalents underneath. [B.M.

541. Beuthnerus (A. C.). Miscellanea anglicana.

8°. Jenae, 1713.

Gratet-Duplessis, 848. Pp. 78-86, two hundred English proverbs.

542. Bodenham (John). Politeuphia. Wit's commonwealth.

12°. London, *Ling*, 1597.

Another edition.   12°. London, *Freeman*, 1707.

A collection of maxims, precepts, aphorisms, *etc.*, on all subjects. Contains a special section : " Of proverbs."   [B.M.

543. Boeddeker (K.). Altenglische Dichtungen des MS. Harl. 2253, *etc.* pp. xvi, 463.   8°. Berlin, *Weidmann*, 1878.

Pp. 285-300, Sprüchwörter Hendyng's. Text and notes.   [U.C.L.

544. Bohn (Henry George). A handbook of proverbs. Comprising an entire republication of Ray's collection of English proverbs [*q.v.*], with his additions from foreign languages, and a complete alphabetical index. *First edition.* pp. xvi, 583.   8°. London, 1855.

Another edition. pp. xvi, 583.

5/-. sm. 8vo. London, *Bell*, 1879.

Bohn's Antiquarian Library. Pp. 1-271, text of Ray : pp. 272-280, Hebrew proverbs from Ray in Hebrew and English : pp. 281-583, complete alphabet of proverbs taken from Camden, Herbert, Howell, Fuller, Ray, Trussler, and others. Reviewed in The Quarterly Review, Vol. 125, pp. 217-254.

[1879 edition, F.-L.S. (Stephens collection).

545. Bohn (Henry George). A case of plagiarism.

16°. [London, 1869].

A letter accusing Hazlitt's " English proverbs and proverbial phrases " of being a plagiarism of Bohn's " Handbook of proverbs."   [B.M.

546. Bourdillon (Francis). The voice of the people, *etc.* pp. 160.   8°. London, *R.T.S.*, [1896].

Moral essays on twenty proverbs.   [B.M.

547. Brady (John). Varieties of literature ; being, principally, selections from the portfolio of the late John Brady, arranged and adapted for publication by John Henry Brady, his son. pp. viii, 295.   8°. London, *Whittaker*, 1826.

Gratet-Duplessis, 859. Pp. 1-62, English proverbs [and expressions] with notes, not arranged in any order : pp. 285-295, index to proverbs. Rather superficial, but contains some interesting observations.   [U.C.L.

548. Breton (Nicholas). Crossing of proverbs. The second part. With certaine brief questions and answeres. By B. N. Gent. [*i.e.* N. Breton].   8°. London, *Wright*, 1616.

Gratet-Duplessis, 837. Also printed in : The works in verse and prose of Nicholas Breton, vol. 2. English proverbs and others contradicting them. Duplessis quotes an extract. The idea of these contradictory proverbs is ingenious but some items are very silly. Partly reprinted in : The Laughing Philosopher . . . by John Bull. 16°. London, 1825.   [B.M.

549. Brown (Carleton). The Maidstone text of the proverbs of Alfred. 8°. Cambridge, 1926.

In Modern Language Review, Vol. 21, pp. 249-260. [B.M.

550. Brown (Marshall). Wit and wisdom of proverbial philosophy. Odd comparisons. pp. 326.

8°. Philadelphia, *Lippincott*, 1884.

551. Budget. A budget of nursery rhymes, jingles and ditties, *etc.* pp. 28. 8°. Ribe, *Geleff*, 1867.

Pp. 16-28, proverbs. A list of 362 English proverbs. [B.M.

552. Burckhardt (G. F.). Der kleine Engländer . . . Vierte . . . Auflage. pp. iv, 274. 12°. Leipzig, *Amelang*, n.d.

Pp. 203-209, einige Sprichwörter und Anglicismen.

553. ——— and **Jost** (Isaac Marcus). Ausführliches theoretisch-praktisches Lehrbuch der englischen Sprache . . . Vierte . . . Auflage. 2 Bde. 8°. Leipzig, *Amelang*, 1852-53.

Bd. 2, pp. 21-25, proverbs. [B.M.

554. C. (M. A.). The proverbs of Chaucer, with illustrations from other sources. 8°. Aberdeen, 1893.

In Scottish Notes and Queries, Vol. 6, pp. 51-52, 69-70, 81-83, 113-115, 147-149, 178-180. Additional proverbs are sometimes given in the minor notes. [B.M.

555. Camden (William). Remaines concerning Britaine. pp. 386. 4°. London, *for J. Waterson*, 1614.

Seventh impression. pp. [viii], 557.

8°. London, *for C. Harper*, 1674.

Gratet-Duplessis, 836, commends the edition of 1674. Contains a list of proverbs, arranged alphabetically, most of which are to be found in Ray. [U.C.L.

556. Cannella Incontreras (G.). Raccolta di frasi e proverbi inglesi ed italiani. pp. viii, 67.

L.2. 16°. Palermo, *Tamburello*, 1887.

Contains some 300 proverbs.

557. Carpenter (William). Old English and Hebrew proverbs explained and illustrated. 16°. London, *Booth*, 1826.

Gratet-Duplessis, 51, 860. Contains and explains 88 English proverbs and 22 Hebrew ones. A book of very little importance. [B.M.

558. Clarke (John). Parœmiologia Anglo-Latina, *etc.* pp. [xvi], 329, [7].

8°. London, *by Felix Kyngston for Robert Mylbourne*, 1639.

Gratet-Duplessis, 838. Contains some quaint proverbs and sayings. [B.M.

E

559. Codrington (Robert). The second part of youth's behaviour, *etc.* pp. [xiv], 230, [30]. 8°. London, *for W. Lee,* 1664. *Second edition.* 2 pts. 8°. London, *for W. Lee,* 1672. The new youth's behaviour, *etc.* pp. [x], 154.
8°. London, *for Sam Keble,* 1684.

Each volume contains a section entitled : A collection of many select and excellent proverbs out of several languages, *etc.* These sections have separate title pages, and in the case of the 1672 edition, a separate pagination. The 1672 one was also published separately in 16° under its own title of : A collection of many . . . proverbs, *etc.* [B.M.

560. Comberbach (C.). Grammaire anglaise comparée aux langues flamande et allemande, *etc.* pp. 351.
8°. Bruxelles, *Greuse,* 1846.

Pp. 333-335, proverbes en Anglais les plus en usage.

61. Companion. An agreeable companion, being . . . proverbs, old sayings, customs and observations, *etc.* pp. 72.
4d. 8°. London, *Goodman,* 1742.
Quaint and amusing. [B.M.

562. Country-Man. The country-man's new commonwealth, *etc.* pp. [iv], 41, [2]. 12°. London, *Harper,* 1647.

Gratet-Duplessis, 839. Principally maxims and aphorisms rather than proverbs. [B.M.

563. Cunningham (John William). Sancho, or the proverbialist. *First edition.* pp. 181.
12°. London, *Cadell & Davies,* 1816. *Third edition.* pp. vi, 178. 12°. London, 1817.

Gratet-Duplessis, 855. A story demonstrating the falsity and misleading qualities of many proverbs. [B.M.

564. Davies (John), *of Hereford.* The scourge of folly, *etc.* pp. 264. [Signed I. D., *i.e.* J. Davies].
8°. [1611?].

Pp. 138-182, Upon English proverbs. Epigrams and verses beginning with proverbs. Also included in : The complete works of John Davies of Hereford, 1878. [B.M.

565. Democritus *Secundus.* Comes facundus in via. The fellow-traveller through city and countrey. pp. [xxxiv], 309. 2 pts. 12°. London, *for Hum. Robinson,* 1658.

Contains a large number of proverbs and sayings, particularly at pp. 19-25, 175-194, 231-239. [B.M.

566. Denham (Michael Aislabie). The Denham tracts. A collection of folklore. . . . Edited by James Hardy. 2 vols.
8°. London, 1892-1895.

Publications of the Folk-Lore Society, 29 and 35. Full of proverbs, particularly the first volume which contains those relating to some of the northern counties. Vol. 2 contains proverbs relating to the weather, the calendar, fairies, *etc.* [F.-L.S.

567. Drayton (Michael). The folk-lore of Drayton.

8°. London, 1885.

In Folk-Lore Journal, Vol. 3, pp. 88-90. Proverbs from Drayton. [F.-L.S.

568. Duschl (J.). Das Sprichwort bei Lydgate.

München, 1912.

569. Dyer (Thomas Firminger Thiselton-). Domestic folk-lore.
pp. viii, 184. 8°. London, *Cassell*, [1881].

Contains numerous proverbs scattered throughout. [B.M.

570. ——: Folk lore of Shakespeare. pp. xi, 526.

14/-. 8°. London, *Griffith*, New York, *Dutton*, [1883].

Chapter 19, pp. 416-444, proverbs quoted or alluded to by Shakespeare.
[F.-L.S. (Stephens Collection).

571. Dykes (Oswald). Moral reflexions upon select English proverbs. pp. [8], xxxvii, 280, [32]. *First edition*.

8°. London, *Sawbridge*, 1708.
English proverbs with moral reflections. *Second edition*.

8°. London, *Sawbridge*, 1709.

Third edition. 8°. London, *Sawbridge*, 1713.

Gratet-Duplessis, 846. The preface contains a discourse on the nature of
proverbs. Then follow 52 well-known proverbs with moral applications and
reflections on them. [B.M.

572. Education. The education of young ladies and gentlewomen.
. . . Whereunto is added, a collection of select and excellent
proverbs; with a table to the proverbs never before printed.

12°. London, 1680.

573. English Tutor. The English tutor . . . together with sacred
hymns and proverbs, *etc.*

6d. 12°. London, *B. Billingsley and S. Crouch*, 1682.
Fourth edition.

London, *B. Billingsley and S. Crouch*, 1698.

574. Farnaby (Thomas). Τϱοποσχηματολογία maximam partem.
Seventh edition. 8°. [London], 1683.
Fifteenth edition. pp. 28.

8°. Londini, *H. Woodfall*, 1767.

Concludes with : Adagia miscellanea, 2 pages of proverbs and sayings in
English and Latin. These are not in the edition of 1660. [B.M.

575. Festeau (Paul). Nouvelle grammaire angloise. . . Troisième
édition, *etc.* pp. [xxxvi], 350. 8°. Londres, *Wells*, 1685.

Gratet-Duplessis, 844. Pp. 263-321, a variety of English proverbs turned into
French. Some of the later editions do not contain this list of proverbs.

576. Fleay (Frederick Gard). Some folk-lore from Chaucer.

8°. London, 1879.

In Folk-Lore Record, Vol. 2, pp. 136-142, Chaucerian proverbs. [F.-L.S.

577. Foerster (Max). Das Elizabethanische Sprichwort nach Th. Draxe's Treasurie of ancient adagies, 1616.

8°. Halle, 1918.

In Anglia, Bd. 42, pp. 361-424. [U.C.L.

578. ———: Kleinere mittelenglische Texte.

8°. Halle, 1918.

In Anglia, Bd. 42, pp. 197-206, mittelenglische Sprichwörter. Text, comments, and comparisons. [U.C.L.

579. Fuller (Thomas). The history of the worthies of England : endeavoured by Thomas Fuller. *First edition.* 4 pts.

fol. London, *J. G. W. L. & W. G.*, 1662.

A new edition, with a few explanatory notes by John Nichols. 2 vols. 4°. [London], *Rivington*, 1811.

Another edition. 3 vols. 8°. London, *Tegg*, 1840.

Contains many lists of proverbs for each county. [U.C.L.

580. Gawler, *afterwards* **Ker** (John Bellenden). An essay on the archaeology of popular English phrases and nursery rhymes. pp. viii, 163.

8°. Southampton, *Fletcher*, London, *Black*, 1834.

Second edition. 2 vols.

8°. London, Southampton, *Longman*, 1835-37.

Gratet-Duplessis, 862. The unique instance of an eccentric genius going into a second edition of a lengthy effort of misplaced ingenuity. The author displays much erudition and imagination in trying to prove that most English sayings, nursery rhymes, *etc.*, are alterations and modifications of Low-German and Dutch. Reviewed in Wright's " Essays on subjects connected with literature," pp. 124-175. [B.M.

581. Gomme (*Sir* George Laurence). Dialect, proverbs and word-lore, *etc.* 8°. London, *Elliot Stock*, 1884.

Vol. 2 of the Gentleman's Magazine Library : being a classified collection of the chief contents of the Gentleman's Magazine from 1731-1868. Pp. 69-122, proverbs and proverbial phrases. [F.-L.S.

582. Green (Henry). Shakespeare and the emblem writers, *etc.* pp. xvi, 571. [Illustrated]. 8°. London, *Trübner*, 1870.

Pp. 318-345, emblems in connexion with proverbs. [B.M.

583. Greiffenhahn (Johann Elias). Wohleingerichtete englische grammatica literatorum . . . Andere . . . Auflage. pp. [xiv], 343. 8°. Jena, *Crökers*, 1741.

Pp. 335-343, a collection of English proverbs.

584. Grose (Francis). A provincial glossary, with a collection of local proverbs, and popular superstitions. *First edition.* 2 pts. 5/-. 8°. London, *Hooper*, 1787.

Second edition. 3 pts. 8°. London, *Hooper*, 1790.

Another edition, with a supplement by Pegge.
8°. London, 1814.

Gratet-Duplessis, 851. Contains local proverbs arranged under counties, with explanatory notes. A well-known source of old words and proverbs, most of which, however, are to be found either in Ray or Fielding [Wade].

[1787 edition, F.-L.S. (Stephens collection).

585. Guy-Wuarnier (E.). Idioms and proverbs intended for the use of the French and English, *etc.* pp. 64.

8°. Paris, *etc.*, *Stassin & Xavier*, 1854.

586. H. (W. J. S.). A maxim or proverb (in English) for every day in the year. Selected by W. J. S. H. pp. 27.

12°. Rugely, *James*, 1861.

Nothing more than its title implies; no notes. [B.M.

587. Haeckel (Willi). Das Sprichwort bei Chaucer. Zugleich ein Beitrag zur vergleichenden Sprichwörterkunde. pp. xii, 77.

8°. Erlangen, Leipzig, *Böhme*, 1890.

Varnhagen's Erlanger Beiträge zur englischen Philologie, Bd. 2, Heft 8. Compares Chaucer's proverbs with those from many other authorities. [U.C.L.

588. Halliwell, *afterwards* **Halliwell-Phillips** (James Orchard). A hand-book index to the works of Shakespeare, *etc.* pp. vi, 551. 8°. London, *printed by J. E. Adlard*, 1866.

Pp. 390-395, a list of the proverbs included in Shakespeare's works, with a reference to the plays from which they are taken. [B.M.

589. ———: The nursery rhymes of England, collected chiefly from oral tradition. *Second edition.* pp. xii, 259.

8°. London, *Smith*, 1843.

Fourth edition. pp. 240. 8°. London, *Smith*, 1846.

Gratet-Duplessis, 867. A charming collection of nursery rhymes, amongst which are a number of true proverbs.

Popular rhymes and nursery tales: a sequel to the nursery rhymes of England. pp. xi, 276. 8°. London, *Smith*, 1849.

[B.M.

590. Hanway (Jonas). Reflections . . . with a collection of proverbs, *etc.* 2 vols. 8°. London, *Rivington*, 1761.

The proverbs announced on the title page are a collection of moral maxims to be found at the end of vol. 1. [B.M.

591. Hastings (James). A collection of upwards of eleven hundred proverbs, wise saws, and pithy sayings . . . contributed . . . to the Art-Workmen's Industrial Exhibition, Manchester, 1865. pp. 32.

8°. Manchester, *published by the Committee*, [1865?].

English proverbs, arranged under subject headings. No notes. [B.M.

592. Hazlitt (William Carew). English proverbs and proverbial phrases, collected, . . . alphabetically arranged, and annotated, *etc.* *First edition.* pp. xxix, 505.

8°. London, *Smith*, 1869.

Another edition. pp. xxx, 580.

7/6. sm. 8°. London, *Reeves & Turner*, 1907.

An alphabetical list with explanatory notes and index.

[1907 edition, F.-L.S. (Stephens collection).

593. Hazlitt (William Carew). Offspring of thought in solitude, *etc.* pp. 384.   8°. London, *Reeves & Turner*, 1884.

Pp. 228-239, a chapter on saws.   [B.M.

594. Hendyng. For the proverbs of Hendyng, *see* **543, 605, 642, 657, 665.**

595. Henschel (F.). A collection of anglicisms, germanisms and phrases of the English and German languages, *etc.* pp. 244.

8°. Berlin, *Henschel*, 1871.

596. Herbert (George). Outlandish proverbs, selected by Mr. G[eorge] H[erbert].

8°. London, *for Humphrey Blunden*, 1640.

Jacula prudentum. Or outlandish proverbs, sentences, *etc.* Selected by George Herbert. pp. [94].

12°. London, *for T. Garthwait*, 1651.

The pagination after p. 70 is misprinted as 171, 172, *etc.*, in the 1651 edition. Pp. 1-70, Jacula prudentum : pp. 183-194 [*sic*], apothegms. These proverbs are also included in various editions of Herbert's poems, remains, works, *etc.* The 1640 edition forms part of the " Witt's recreations."   [U.C.L.

597. Heywood (John). A dialogue conteining the number in effect of all the proverbes in the Englishe tongue, *etc.*

8°. London, *Berthelet*, [1549].

Two hundred epigrammes, upon two hundred prouerbes, with a thyrde hundred, *etc.* 2 pts. 8°. [London], 1555. John Heywoodes workes. A dialogue conteyning the number of the effectuall proverbes . . . and a fifth hundred of epigrammes. Whereunto are . . . added a sixte hundred, *etc.*

4°. Londini, *Wykes*, 1566.

The proverbs of John Heywood, *etc.* pp. 6, 173.

8°. London, *Bell*, 1874.

The proverbs, epigrams, and miscellanies. . . . Edited by J. S. Farmer. pp. 466.

8°. London, *Early English Drama Society*, 1906.
[B.M., U.C.L., F.-L.S.

598. Hill (*Sir* Richard), *Bart.* Songs, carols, and other miscellaneous poems, from the Balliol MS. 354, Richard Hill's commonplace-book. Edited by Roman Dyboski. pp. lix, 198.   8°. London, 1908.

Early English Text Society, Extra Series, 101. Pp. 128-141, proverbs, verserules, and moral sentences. English and Latin.   [U.C.L.

599. Hurst (Richard Willett). 366 English proverbs, literally translated into French with many French equivalent proverbs, *etc.* pp. 31.

8°. Nice, *Imprimerie de l'Éclaireur*, 1919.
[B.M.

600. Ingleby (C. M.). The prouerbes of Syr Oracle Mar-Text. Edited from the original manuscript. 8°. Birmingham, 1882.
[Bristol Public Library.

601. K. (P.). Nomenclatura trilinguis. *Third edition.*

London, *Conyers*, 1697.

Tenth edition. pp. 102.

1/-. 8°. London, *Conyers*, [1720?].

Contains a collection of : Sentences, partly proverbial, and partly phraseo-logical. 169 entries in English and Latin. [B.M.

602. ——: The scholar's instructor, *etc.* pp. 79.

8°. London, *Conyers*, [1700?].

Pp. 36-44, proverbial sentences. 225 proverbs in English and Latin. [B.M.

603. Kellner (Leon). Altenglische Spruchweisheit. Alt- und mittelenglischen Autoren entnommen. 8°. Wien, 1898.

In Neuphilologische Abhandlungen . . . Den Theilnehmern, am 8. allg. deutschen Neuphilologentage gewidmet vom Wiener neuphilologischen Verein, 1898. A collection of maxims, proverbs, and sayings, from Chaucer, Piers Plowman, the Proverbs of Alfred, *etc.* [B.M.

Ker (John Bellenden). *See* Gawler, *afterwards* Ker.

604. King (John). The true English guide for the Germans . . . reprinted the fourth time, *etc.* pp. 431.

8°. Leipzig, *Braun*, 1740.

Eleventh edition. pp. 492. 8°. Leipzig, *Hilscher*, 1795.

Contains a section of English proverbs, with German translations and equivalents. [B.M.

605. Kneuer ( ). Die Sprichwörter Hendyngs. Nachweis ähnlicher Sprichwörter in den germanischen und romanischen Sprachen. Dissertation. Leipzig, 1901.

606. Kohl (Ida) and **Kohl** (Johann Georg). Englische Skizzen, *etc.* 3 Thle. 8°. Dresden, Leipzig, *Arnold*, 1845.

Bd. 2, pp. 159-202, Sprüchwörter : a brief commentary, with the explanation of some few proverbs : pp. 203-211, a collection of English phrases, some proverbial, with German translations. [B.M.

607. Kwang ki Chaou. Dictionary of English phrases . . . To which are added some English proverbs and a selection of Chinese proverbs and maxims, *etc.* pp. xix, 914.

8°. London, *Sampson Low*, 1881.

Pp. 797-816, English proverbs : pp. 817-825, Chinese proverbs and wise sayings, in English. [B.M.

608. Learners. For learners of French and English. Above 500 proverbs or proverbial expressions, *etc.* pp. 48.

12°. London, *Broke, etc.*, 1774.

Stirling-Maxwell, 76.

609. Lydal (Thomas). The expert English school-master. . . . Also . . . a collection of English proverbs, *etc.*

8°. London, 1701.

Second edition. 8°. London, 1702.

610. Lydgate (John). The proverbes of Lydgate. *Ends*:—Here endeth the proverbes of Lydgate upon the fall of prynces.

4°. London, *Wynkyn de Worde*, [1520?].

Gratet-Duplessis, 833. Proverbs, mostly maxims in verse, from Lydgate's "Fall of Princes." Taken from Boccaccio. Very rare. [B.M.

611. ———: Proverbys of howsholde-kepyng.

8°. London, *Early English Text Society*, 1866.

Re-edited 1903.

In Political, Religious and Love Poems, *etc.* Early English Text Society, original series 15, pp. 57-61. [B.M.

612. Mair (James Allan). A handbook of proverbs, *etc.* pp. 505. *First edition*. pp. 192. 8°. London, New York, [1873]. *Another edition*.

3/6. sm. 8°. London, New York, *Routledge*, [1874].

Pp. 21-61 of second edition, alphabet of English, Scottish, Irish, American proverbs : pp. 82-99, Shakespearian proverbs, *etc.*, giving sources : pp. 100-105, Scriptural proverbs : pp. 106-192, family mottoes : pp. 197-351, familiar quotations and index : pp. 357-383, familiar sayings and phrases in English : pp. 384-505, words and phrases from classic sources, American words and phrases, Scottish words and phrases. The second edition is greatly enlarged. The first edition was reprinted with a different title page and lacking the preface as : Proverbs and family mottoes, *etc.* pp. 192. 8°. London, *etc.*, 1891.

[Second edition, F.-L.S. (Stephens collection), B.M. (all three editions).

613. Meadmore (R.). Les idiotismes et les proverbes de la conversation anglaise. *First edition*. pp. 160.

8°. Paris, *Hachette*, 1892.

Second edition. pp. 160. 8°. Paris, *Hachette*, 1894.

A text-book for students. Each section of idioms is concluded with a list of English proverbs with French translations. [B.M.

614. Miège (Guy). Nouvelle grammaire angloise-françoise. . . . Dernière édition, *etc.* pp. 286.

8°. Rotterdam, *Beman*, 1749.

Another edition. Grammaire angloise-françoise, par Miège et Boyer, *etc.* pp. viii, 412. 8°. Paris, *Briasson*, 1767.

Contains a selection of corresponding French and English proverbs. [B.M.

615. Moralist. The moralist's medley, or a collection of proverbs, maxims, moral reflections, and descriptive passages, in prose and verse. pp. 111. 12°. London, *for E. Harding*, 1803.

Gratet-Duplessis, 853, says this has no real importance. [B.M.

616. Morgan (Aaron Augustus). The mind of Shakespeare, as exhibited in his works. pp. xxiii, 321.

8°. London, *Chapman & Hall*, 1860.

Another edition. pp. xxiii, 360.

8°. London, New York, *Routledge*, 1880.

Contains a chapter entitled : Proverbs and trite expressions introduced in the plays. [B.M.

616a. Nares (Robert). A glossary, or collection of words, phrases, . . . proverbs, *etc.*   /   4°. 1822.

617. National Proverbs. National proverbs: England. pp. 78.
              1/. 8°. London, *Palmer*, [1912].
A list of proverbs, not in any order. No notes.   [B.M.

618. Neaves (Charles), *Lord Neaves.* Songs and verses, *etc.*
pp. 70.   8°. Edinburgh, London, *Blackwood*, 1868.
Another edition. pp. viii, 176.
          8°. Edinburgh, London, *Blackwood*, 1875.
Contains : A song of proverbs. This humorous poem, containing numerous proverbs strung together, was first published in Blackwood's Magazine, 1864.
     [B.M.

619. Neumann (A.). Kurzgefasste englische Sprachlehre für Anfänger. pp. 170.   8°. Berlin, *Lüderitz*, 1833.
Pp. 151-156, English proverbs and phrases with German equivalents.

620. Northall (G. F.). English folk-rhymes, *etc.* pp. ix, 565.
          8°. London, *Kegan Paul*, 1892.
Pp. ix-xii, bibliography. Contains many proverbs.   [B.M.

621. Oppler (George Ernest). Sentences, maxims and proverbs, *etc.*, accompanied by German translations, *etc.* pp. 16.
          8°. Berlin, *Beringer*, n.d.

622. Palmer (Samuel). Moral essays on some of the most curious and significant English, Scotch and foreign proverbs. pp. xxxi, 384, [16]. sm. 8°. London, *Bonwicke, Freeman*, 1710.
Gratet-Duplessis, 847. 134 proverbs, some very uncommon, with discourses on the morals inculcated thereby. Not very interesting.
     [F.-L.S. (Stephens collection).

623. Phillips (Edward). The mysteries of love and eloquence. [The preface signed E. P., *i.e.* Edward Phillips]. 2 pts.
          8°. London, 1658.
Third edition. 2 pts.   8°. London, 1685.
Contains a list of proverbs, with comments thereon.   [B.M.

624. Preston (J.). A dictionary of English proverbs and proverbial phrases . . . by the author of " A dictionary of daily blunders," [*i.e.* J. Preston], *etc.* pp. viii, 127.
          1/-. 16°. London, *Whittaker*, [1880].
1880 proverbs arranged alphabetically by their principal words. No notes.
     [B.M.

625. Proverbiorum. Proverbiorum, hoc est sententiarum, versuum et phrasium proverbialum centuriae duae, *etc.*
          sm. 8°. Eton, [17—?].
Gratet-Duplessis, 850, says that the above collection of 200 English proverbs compared with a like number of Latin and Greek ones, forms part of an elementary Greek grammar published at Eton at the beginning of the 18th century.

626. Proverbs. Buried proverbs. Second edition, *etc.* pp. 280. 16°. London, *Simpkin, Marshall*, 1878. A key to buried proverbs. pp. 22.
16°. London, *Simpkin, Marshall*, 1878.

362 proverbs hidden in verses, and the key. [B.M.

627. ———: Proverbs and precepts for copy-lines, for the use of schools. pp. 32. 6d. sm. 8°. London, *Parker*, 1850.

An unimportant little book of proverbs and maxims with moral comments.
[B.M.

628. ———: Proverbs, from MS. Harl, 3362, of the end of the fifteenth century. 8°. London, *Smith*, 1854.

In Retrospective Review, Vol. 2, p. 309. [B.M.

629. ———: A selection of English and Scotch proverbs.
8°. Edinburgh, *Chambers*, n.d.

In Chamber's miscellany of useful and entertaining tracts, Vol. 20, No. 174.
[B.M.

630. Ray (John). A collection of English proverbs . . . with short annotations . . . By J[ohn] R[ay]. pp. [viii], 296.
8°. Cambridge, *for W. Morden*, 1670.
Second edition. pp. [viii], 414.
8°. Cambridge, *for W. Morden*, 1678.
Fifth edition. pp. xxiv, 336.
8°. London, *for G. Cowie*, 1813.

Bohn's "Handbook of proverbs," *q.v.* **21**, also includes the whole of Ray's collection. The first edition includes only English and Scotch proverbs; later ones comprise a collection of Hebrew proverbs and numerous Italian, French and Spanish ones. [B.M., U.C.L.

631. Rayner (John L.). Proverbs and maxims. Classified and arranged by John L. Rayner. pp. vii, 251.
16°. London, *Cassell, etc.*, 1910.

Pp. v-vii, introduction, including list of authorities : pp. 1-251, English proverbs and maxims arranged alphabetically by subjects.
[F.-L.S. (Stephens collection).

632. Rees (Frederick Abijah). Practical points in popular proverbs, *etc.* pp. 152.
8°. London, *Baptist Union Publication Department*, [1904].

Addresses stressing the moral side and application of various proverbs, maxims, etc. [B.M.

633. Richardson (Edward). Anglo-Belgica. The English and Netherdutch academy, *etc.* 3 pts.
12°. Amsterdam, *Swart*, 1677.

The edition of 1677 contains Pt. 2, pp. 23-39, "certain moral sayings and proverbs usefull for learning both the languages." The later editions, however, only contain half a dozen proverbs. [B.M.

634. Ronna (Antonio) and **Smith** (Léon). Guide to English and Italian conversation, *etc.* pp. viii, 383.

16°. Paris, *Hingray*, 1852.

Pp. 347-364, proverbs and idioms—Proverbi ed idiotismi. These are not included in the 1860 edition.

635. Royal Cabinet Birthday Book. Royal Cabinet birthday book of quotations and proverbs, *etc.* pp. 255.

16°. Glasgow, *Bryce*, [1884].

A kind of diary with a quotation and two or three proverbs for every day. Unimportant. [B.M.

636. S. (J. N.). Grammatica nova anglicana una cum dialogis quibusdam et proverbiis anglicanis.

8°. Jenae, *Oehrling*, 1689.

Gratet-Duplessis, 845.

637. Sadler (P.). Grammaire pratique de la langue anglaise. *Second edition.* pp. xii, 420. 8°. Paris, *Truchy*, 1856. *Twenty-fourth edition.* pp. xii, 420. 8°. Paris, 1877.

Pp. 353-355, Quelques proverbes anglais avec les proverbes français qui y répondent.

638. Sayings. Proverbial sayings and wise observations; or, something to amuse you when you have nothing to do. 1 page. Peterborough, *printed by C. Jacob*, [1820?].

A few proverbs, maxims, rules of conduct, *etc.* [B.M.

639. Siret (Pierre Louis). Éléments de la langue anglaise, *etc.* pp. 172. 8°. Paris, *Barrois*, 1814. *Another edition.* pp. 210. 8°. Paris, *Baudry*, 1861.

Contains a selection of equivalent proverbs in the English and French. These are not included in some of the earlier editions. [B.M.

640. Skeat (Walter William). Early English proverbs, chiefly of the thirteenth and fourteenth centuries, with illustrative quotations. pp. xxiv, 147 + plate.

3/6. sm. 8°. Oxford, *Clarendon Press*, 1910.

Arranged more or less chronologically under sources. Index of proverbs. [F.-L.S. (Stephens collection).

641. Smith (Léon) and **Adler-Mesnard** (Édouard). Guide to English and German conversation, *etc.* pp. xii, 367.

8°. London, *Routledge*, 1853.

Pp. 347-356, proverbs and idioms—Sprichwörter und Spracheigenheiten.

642. Solomon. The dialogue of Solomon and Saturnus, with an historical introduction by John M. Kemble. pp. vii, 326.

8°. London, *Ælfric Society*, 1848.

Contains : proverbial answers of Marcolf, the proverbs of Alfred, the proverbs of Hendyng, *etc.* [U.C.L.

643. Sporschil (J.). Kraft und Geist der englischen Sprache in Sprichwörtern, *etc.* pp. viii, 103.

12°. Leipzig, *Volckmar*, 1837.

644. Spurgeon (Charles Haddon). The salt-cellars, being a collection of proverbs, *etc.* 2 vols.

8°. London, *Passmore & Edwards*, 1889.

An alphabetical list of proverbs, with comments brief and to the point. [B.M.

645. Stone (A. T.). A book that never grows old of two thousand valuable proverbs and helpful sayings, *etc.* pp. 281.

8°. Toronto, *Bryant Press*, 1916.

A collection of moral maxims, sayings, *etc.*, in no apparent order. Of very little importance. [B.M.

645a. Taylor (Archer). Proverbia Britannica.   la. 8°.

Washington University Studies, Vol. II, Humanistic Series, pp. 409-23.

646. Taylor (Joseph). Antiquitates curiosae: the etymology of many remarkable old sayings, proverbs, and singular customs explained. *First edition.* pp. 156.   12°. London, 1818.
Second edition.   5/-. sm. 8°. London, *Allman*, 1819.

Gives the derivation of various proverbs and adages amongst other things.
[F.-L.S. (Stephens collection).

647. Tegg (William). Proverbs from far and near, *etc.* pp. iv, 124.   8°. London, *Tegg*, 1875.

An alphabetical list. [B.M.

648. Thiselton (W.). A fashionable caricature, or the proverbs of our ancestors prophetically descriptive of the most distinguished personages in the present age. pp. 29.

12°. [London?], 1792.

Gratet-Duplessis, 852. This rare little work is a satiric pamphlet in which, under the form of a collection of proverbs, the author reviews the outstanding people of his time. The initials of each person—full names are not given—are followed by a proverb designed either as a general characterisation, or to recall some special peculiarity of work or habit.

649. Thiselton (William Mathew). National anecdotes, *etc.* pp. xii, 264.

5/-. 12°. London, *for C. Cradock & W. Jay*, 1812.

Part 2, pp. 169-191, national proverbs, *etc.* English proverbs with explanations or moral reflections. [B.M.

650. Tilley (Morris Palmer). Elizabethan proverb-lore in Lyly's "Euphues," and in Pettie's "Petite Pallace." With parallels from Shakespeare. pp. x, 461.

$3.50. 8°. New York, *Macmillan*, 1927.

University of Michigan Publications in Language and Literature, Vol. 2. Reviewed in Times Literary Supplement, March 10th, 1927. The author has not sufficiently distinguished genuine proverbs from mere similes and idioms.
[B.M.

651. Townson (Thomas). The poor man's moralist, consisting of proverbs and moral sayings. By Dr. T[ownson]. pp. iv, 32.
12°. Liverpool, 1798.
Third edition. 12°. Manchester, 1799.
[B.M.

652. Tricomi (G.). A handbook of English proverbs, with their equivalents in Italian. pp. vi, 111.
8°. Catania, *Giannotta*, 1900.
An alphabetical list of over 1000 proverbs. Intended for teachers of languages.
[B.M.

653. Virendra-Nātha Vandyopādhyāya. A handbook of proverbs and sayings, *etc.* pp. ii, 56.
6 annas. 8°. Cuttack, *the Author*, 1910.
A book intended for the use of students at Indian universities. It consists of some 300 English proverbs with explanatory notes also in English. [B.M.

654. Vraja-Mohana Lāla. Dictionary of proverbs and maxims pp. ii, 123 + 2 plates. 12 annas. 8°. Balarampur, [1917].
Proverbs in English arranged alphabetically. [B.M.

655. Walker (William). Phraseologia Anglo-Latina . . . To which is added: Paroemiologia Anglo-Latina, or, a collection of English and Latin proverbs . . . By William Walker [or rather, the Paroemiologia only by him, the Phraseologia being a reprint of the work of Thomas Willis]. 2 pts.
8°. London, *Royston*, 1672.
[B.M.

656. Walz (Gotthard). Das Sprichwort bei Gower, mit besonderem Hinweis auf Quellen und Parallelen, *etc.*
Nördlingen, 1907.

657. Wells (John Edwin). A manual of the writings in Middle English, 1050-1400, [with three supplements]. pp. xv, 1247. 4 vols. 8°. New Haven, *Yale University Press*, 1916-26.
Chapter 7 (pp. 374-96, 972-78, 1063-65, 1173-74), proverbs and precepts, and monitory pieces. A valuable guide, with notes on manuscripts containing proverbs. [U.C.L.

658. Wimphen (Rachel). Multum in parvo, or English and French and French and English idioms and proverbs, *etc.* pp. 172. 1/-. 16°. Brighton, *North*, [1899].
Alphabetically arranged. [B.M.

659. Winstanley (William). The new help to discourse . . . by W[illiam] W[instanley]. pp. [xii], 311.
12°. London, 1669.
Ninth edition. pp. 162. 12°. London, 1733.
The first edition contains a list of some 20 proverbs; in the ninth about sixty are given. [B.M.

660. Wisdom. Proverbial wisdom. With preface by Blanchard Jerrold. pp. viii, 92.

8°. London, *etc.*, *Marlborough*, [1873].

Another edition. pp. viii, 92.

8°. London, *etc.*, *Marlborough*, [1877].

A preface followed by a long alphabetical list of proverbs. [B.M.

661. ———: Wisdom in miniature. . . . Third edition. pp. viii, 230. 12°. Coventry, *Luckman*, 1791.

Another edition. 12°. London, *Simpkin*, *Marshall*, 1817.

Contains a section : Short miscellaneous sentences, *etc.* Many of these are true proverbs. An edition of 1845 lacks this collection. [B.M.

662. Wren (Jenny), *pseud.* Old proverbs with new faces. pp. 120. 8°. London, *Ward & Downey*, 1893.

Inoffensive essays on 14 stale proverbs. [B.M.

663. Wright (Elizabeth Mary). Rustic speech and folk-lore. pp. xx, 341. 8°. London, *etc.*, *Milford*, 1913.

Chapter 11, pp. 158-190, popular phrases and sayings, particularly pp. 171-174 (proverbial sayings). Chapter 19, weather lore, *etc.* [F.-L.S.

664. Wright (Thomas). Essays on subjects connected with the literature, popular superstitions and history of England in the middle ages. 2 vols. 12°. London, *Smith*, 1846.

Gratet-Duplessis, 868. An excellent series of essays, most of which had previously appeared in different reviews. Vol. 1, Essay 4, pp. 124-175, on proverbs and popular sayings. This contains much interesting information on the origin of a certain number of English sayings and proverbs. [B.M.

665. ———, and **Halliwell,** *afterwards* **Halliwell-Phillips** (James Orchard). Reliquiae antiquae. Scraps from ancient manuscripts, illustrating chiefly Early English literature and the English language. 2 vols.

8°. London, *Pickering*, Berlin, *Asher*, 1841-1843.

Gratet-Duplessis, 224. Contains a number of early proverbs, chiefly old English, but with some old French and Latin. Specially notable are, the Proverbs of Hendyng, Vol. 1, pp. 109-116 and 256-257; the Proverbs of Alfred, Vol. 1, pp. 170-188; Les trente-deux folies, a proverbial poem in Anglo-French, reproduced by Duplessis, Vol. 1, p. 236; and Memorial Verses, Vol. 1, pp. 287-291. These verses, containing many rhymed proverbs, are in Latin interspersed with English. Duplessis gives three extracts from this volume. [U.C.L.

666. Zupitza (Julius). The proverbis of wysdom.

8°. Braunschweig, 1893.

In Archiv für das Studium der neueren Sprachen, Bd. 90, pp. 241-268. Proverbs in verse from a Bodleian ms. Text and notes. [B.M.

See also index at end for references to English in other sections.

LOCAL AND DIALECT.

1. NORTHUMBRIA.

667. Balfour (M. C.). County folk-lore, Vol. 4. Printed extracts, No. 6. Examples of printed folk-lore concerning Northumberland. Collected by M. C. Balfour and edited by Northcote W. Thomas. pp. xv, 180. 10/6. 8°. London, 1904.

Publications of the Folk-Lore Society, 53. Pp. 171-179, proverbs. [F.-L.S.

668. Blakeborough (Richard). Wit, character, folklore and customs of the North Riding of Yorkshire, *etc.* pp. xxi, 485.

8°. London, *Frowde*, 1898.

Pp. 210-221, some characteristic Yorkshire sayings, contributed by M. C. F. Morris : pp. 238-256, similes, proverbs, and sayings. [B.M.

669. ———— : Yorkshire toasts, proverbs, similes, and sayings. pp. 30. 4°. London, *Dennis*, 1907.

Pp. 13-29, Yorkshire sayings. [B.M.

670. Cross (H. M.). North Yorkshire dialect sayings.

8°. Newcastle upon Tyne, 1902.

In County Monthly, September, 1902, pp. 9-13. [B.M.

671. Denham (Michael Aislabie). A collection of Bishoprick [of Durham] rhymes, proverbs, and sayings, in connexion with the Border and feudal periods, *etc.* [Subscribed M. A. D., *i.e.* M. A. Denham]. 5 pts.

8°. Civ. Dunelm, [1850]-59.

With explanatory notes. The pagination of parts 1-4 is continuous. Only 50 copies printed. [B.M.

672. ———— : Folk-lore : or, a collection of local rhymes, proverbs, sayings . . . relating to Northumberland, Newcastle-on-Tyne, and Berwick-on-Tweed. pp. xii, 140. [Signed M. A. D.].

8°. Richmond, in Com. Ebor., *imprinted by J. Bell*, 1858.

50 copies printed. [B.M.

673. ———— : Folk lore ; or, manners and customs of the North of England. By M. A. D. 3 pts.

8°. Novo-Castro-sup.-Tynam, Civ. Dunelm, 1850-52.

Superstitions, sayings, customs, rhymes, proverbs, *etc.* [B.M.

674. G. (E.). Yorkshire local rhymes and sayings.

8°. London, 1878, 1881, 1883.

In Folk-Lore Record, Vol. 1, pp. 160-175 : Vol. 3, Pt. 2, pp. 174-177 : and Folk-Lore Journal, Vol. 1, pp. 164-165. [F.-L.S.

675. Gutch (Eliza), *Mrs.* County folk-lore, Vol. 2. Printed extracts, No. 4. Examples of printed folk-lore concerning the North Riding of Yorkshire, York and Ainsty. Collected and edited by Mrs. Gutch. pp. xxxix, 447.

15/-. 8°. London, 1901.

Publications of the Folk-Lore Society, 45. Section 17, pp. 429-434, proverbs. Sections 16 and 18 also contain jingles and place rhymes. [F.-L.S.

676. Gutch (Eliza), *Mrs.* County folk-lore, Vol. 6. Printed extracts, No. 8. Examples of printed folk-lore concerning the East Riding of Yorkshire. Collected and edited by Mrs. Gutch. pp. xxvii, 235.   8°. London, 1912.

Publications of the Folk-Lore Society, 69. Section 17, pp. 222-225, proverbs. Section 18 also contains some place rhymes.   [F.-L.S.

677. Harland (John) and **Wilkinson** (T. T.). Lancashire legends, traditions, pageants, sports, *etc.* pp. xxxv, 283.

4°. London, *Routledge*, Manchester, *Gent*, 1873.

Pp. 179-212, popular rhymes, proverbs, sayings and similes : pp. 213-214, chapter of proverbs, by Thomas Wilson. The latter is a satirical poem on Napoleon, each verse of which concludes with a proverb.   [B.M.

678. Meriton (George). The praise of Yorkshire ale. . . . The third edition. . . . By G[eorge] M[eriton], Gent. pp. 124.

8°. York, *for Francis Hildyard*, 1697.

Pp. 83-87, Here followeth a collection of significant and usefull proverbs, some of which are apropriated to York-shire. The proverbs are not included in the edition of 1685; they were reprinted in the Folk-Lore Record, Vol. 4, pp. 163-166.   [B.M.

679. Roper (William). Weather sayings, proverbs and prognostics, chiefly from North Lancashire. pp. 34.

8°. Lancaster, *Bell*, [1883].
[B.M.

680. Taylor (Francis Edward). The folk-speech of South Lancashire, *etc.* 2 pts.   8°. Manchester, *Heywood*, 1901.

Pt. 2, The wit and wisdom of the South Lancashire dialect, *etc.*: pp. 7-11, proverbs. Reviewed in Folk-Lore, Vol. 14.   [B.M.

681. Weeks (William Self). The Clitheroe district: proverbs and sayings, customs and legends, and much of its history. pp. 41.   4°. Clitheroe, *Advertiser & Times Co.*, [1922].

Most of the proverbs are to be found at pp. 1-12. Very readable.   [F.-L.S.

682. Yorkshire Speyks. Yorkshire speyks. 8°. Bradford, 1888.

In Yorkshire Folk-lore Journal, Vol. 1, pp. 131-133, 217-225. Local proverbs, phrases and expressions contributed by two readers.   [B.M.

2. EASTERN COUNTIES.

683. Anderson (Ruth). Scraps of English folk-lore. Suffolk (Westleton).   8°. London, 1924.

In Folk-Lore, Vol. 35, pp. 357-359, rhymes and weather proverbs.   [F.-L.S.

684. Charnock (Richard Stephen). A glossary of the Essex dialect. pp. viii, 64.   8°. London, *Trübner*, 1880.

Pp. 58-64, proverbs, sayings, *etc.*   [B.M.

685. Forby (Robert). The vocabulary of East Anglia, *etc.* 3 vols.   8°. London, 1830.

Vol. 2, pp. 416-418, popular sayings respecting the weather : pp. 426-435, proverbial sayings.   [B.M.

686. Gurdon (*Lady* Eveline Camilla). County folk-lore, Vol. 1, Printed extracts, No. 2. Suffolk. Collected and edited by Lady Eveline Camilla Gurdon. With introduction by Edward Clodd. pp. xv, 202. 8°. London, 1893.

Publications of the Folk-Lore Society, 36. Pp. 145-157, proverbs and similes. See also weather myths, pp. 160-166. [F.-L.S.

687. Gutch (Eliza), *Mrs.*, and **Peacock** (Mabel). County folk-lore, Vol. 5. Printed extracts, No. 7. Examples of printed folk-lore concerning Lincolnshire. Collected by Mrs. Gutch and Mabel Peacock. pp. xxiii, 437. 8°. London, 1908.

Publications of the Folk-Lore Society, 63. Section v, pp. 404-416, proverbs. Section vi, pp. 417-434, sayings about places. [F.-L.S.

688. Thompson (Pishey). The history and antiquities of Boston and the villages comprising the hundred of Skirbeck, in the county of Lincoln. . . . Illustrated, *etc.* pp. xxii, 824.

fol. Boston, *Noble*, 1856.

Pp. 731-736, proverbs, proverbial sayings, phrases and comparisons, *etc.*
[B.M.

3. MIDLAND AND WESTERN COUNTIES.

689. Billson (Charles James). County folk-lore, Vol. 1. Printed extracts, No. 3. Leicestershire and Rutland. Collected and edited by Charles James Billson. pp. 153.

8°. London, 1895.

Publications of the Folk-Lore Society, 37. Pp. 141-153, proverbs, place rhymes, *etc.* [F.-L.S.

690. Bridge (Joseph Cox). Cheshire proverbs and other sayings and rhymes connected with the city and county palatine of Chester, *etc.* pp. xv, 191.

10/6. 4°. Chester, *Phillipson & Golder*,
London, *Simpkin, Marshall*, 1917.

With notes and references. [B.M.

691. ———: Some Cheshire customs, proverbs and folk-lore.
8°. London, *Allen*, 1910.

In E. Barber and P. H. Ditchfield, " Memorials of old Cheshire." pp. 230-263. Pp. 246-252, proverbs and sayings. [B.M.

692. Briscoe (J. P.). Nottingham facts and fictions: being a collection of ancient local traditions, . . . proverbs, *etc.*
Nottingham, *Shepherd*, [187- ?].

Reprinted from Shepherd's Illustrated Nottingham Almanack for 1872. Pp. 14-17, some Nottingham sayings : 9 proverbs with explanations.

693. Burne (Charlotte Sophia). Shropshire folk-lore. . . . Edited by C. S. Burne from the collections of Georgina F. Jackson. pp. xi, 663 + map. 8°. London, *etc.*, *Trübner*, 1883.

Pp. 587-599, proverbs and proverbial phrases. [B.M.

F

694. Chamberlain (Edith L.), *Mrs.* A glossary of west Worcestershire words. pp. xxviii, 40.

8°. London, *Trübner*, 1882.

English Dialect Society, Series C. Original glossaries, 28. Pp. 37-38, 33 local proverbs : sayings relating to the seasons and the weather : p. 39, 18 proverbs on general subjects.   [U.C.L.

695. Evans (Arthur Benoni). Leicestershire words, phrases and proverbs, *etc.* pp. xviii, 116. *First edition.*

8°. London, *Pickering*, Leicester, *Browne*, 1848.

Another edition. pp. xxxii, 303.

10/6. 8°. London, *English Dialect Society*, 1881.

The edition of 1881 is greatly enlarged. There is a small list of proverbs with explanations at the end of the glossary.   [B.M.

696. Gloucestershire. Glossary of provincial words used in Gloucestershire, with proverbs current in that county.

8°. 1851.

[Bristol Public Library.

697. ——— : Legends, tales and songs, in the dialect of the peasantry of Gloucestershire, *etc.* pp. viii, 110.

8°. London, [1877].

P. 103, six Gloucestershire proverbs.   [B.M.

698. Hartland (Edwin Sidney). County folk-lore, Vol. 1. Printed extracts, No. 1. Gloucestershire. Edited, . . . by E. S. Hartland.   8°. London, 1892.

Publications of the Folk-Lore Society, 36. Pp. 42-44, proverbs.   [F.-L.S.

699. Hope (Robert Charles). Some Derbyshire proverbs and sayings.   8°. London, 1884.

In Folk-Lore Journal, Vol. 2, pp. 278-280.   [F.-L.S.

700. Leather (Ella Mary), *Mrs.* The folk-lore of Herefordshire, collected from oral and printed sources, *etc.* pp. xxviii, 286 + plates.

la. 8°. Hereford, *Jakeman*, London, *Sidgwick*, 1912.

Pp. 243-254, proverbs, sayings, place rhymes, *etc.*   [F.-L.S.

701. Markham (Christopher A.). The proverbs of Northamptonshire. pp. vii, 39.   8°. Northampton, *Stanton*, 1897.

With explanatory notes.   [B.M.

702. Northall (G. F.). Folk phrases of four counties (Glouc., Staff., Warw., Worc.), *etc.* pp. 43.

3/6. 8°. London, *English Dialect Society*, 1894.

Some of these phrases are proverbial.   [B.M.

703. Parker (Angelina). Oxfordshire village folk-lore (1840-1900).   8°. London, 1913.

In Folk-Lore, Vol. 24. Pp. 76-77, proverbs and sayings. See also further proverbs from Oxfordshire, Vol. 34, pp. 327-330.   [F.-L.S.

704. Smyth (John). The Berkeley manuscripts. . . . Edited by
Sir John Maclean, *etc.* 3 vols.
4°. Gloucester, *Bristol and Gloucestershire
Archæological Society*, 1883-5.
Vol. 3, pp. 22-33, Gloucestershire proverbs and phrases. [B.M.

705. Sternberg (Thomas). The dialect and folk-lore of Northamptonshire. pp. xvi, 200. 8°. London, *etc.*, *Smith*, 1851.
Stirling-Maxwell, p. 94. Pp. 190-192, Northamptonshire proverbs. [B.M.

706. West-Country. Old west-country proverbs.
8°. London, 1887.
In All the Year Round, New Series, Vol. 39, pp. 107-109. [B.M.

4. SOUTHERN COUNTIES.

707. Borlase (William Copeland). A collection of hitherto unpublished proverbs and rhymes, in the ancient Cornish language, *etc.* 8°. Truro, 1866-7.
In Journal of the Royal Institution of Cornwall, Vol. 2, pp. 7-20. [B.M.

708. Courtney (M. A.). Cornish folk-lore. 8°. London, 1887.
In Folk-Lore Journal, Vol. 5, pp. 14-61, 85-112, 177-220. Contains many
proverbs. [F.-L.S.

709. Hewett (Sarah). Nummits and crummits. Devonshire
customs, *etc.* pp. vi, 219 + frontispiece.
8°. London, *Burleigh*, 1900.
Pp. 103-122, Weather lore and wise saws. [B.M.

710. Lach-Szyrma (Wladyslaw Somerville). Cornish proverbs,
etc. pp. 4. 8°. [1883].
In Transactions of the Penzance Natural History and Antiquarian Society,
1882-1883. A brief commentary with a few examples. [B.M.

711. Nettleinghame (Frederick Thomas). Polperro proverbs and
others, *etc.* pp. 43.
1/-. 8°. Polperro, *Polperro Press*, 1926.
A collection of proverbs, rhymes, mottoes, *etc.*, used at Polperro in connection
with certain handicrafts. [B.M.

712. Pegge (Samuel). An alphabet of Kenticisms [1736] . . .
to which is added a collection of proverbs and old sayings,
which are either used in, or do relate to, the same county.
pp. 9-78. 8°. London, *Trübner*, 1876.
English Dialect Society, Series C, Original glossaries, 3, iii, edited by W. W.
Skeat. Pp. 58-78, 72 proverbs relating to the county of Kent : rearranged by
Skeat with copious notes. [U.C.L.

713. Penn (Peter). Cornish notes and queries. First series. . . .
Edited by Peter Penn. pp. 323, [15], + frontispiece.
   8°. London, *Elliot Stock*, Penzance, *Cornish Telegraph*,
                   1906.

  Notes and queries collected from the " Cornish Telegraph," where they were
first published in 1903. No more seems to have appeared. Pp. 262-272,
proverbs.   [B.M.

714. Pryce (William). Archæologia Cornu-Britannica, *etc.*
            4°. Sherborne, 1790.

  Sig. Ff.-Ff. 2, a collection of proverbs, rhymes, *etc.* In the original, with
English translations.   [B.M.

715. Sawyer (Frederick Ernest). Sussex folk-lore and customs
  connected with the seasons, *etc.* pp. 24. 8°. Lewes, 1883.
  In Sussex Archæological Collections, Vol. 33. A collection of folk-lore
notes, including many proverbs.   [B.M.

715a. ———: Sussex place rhymes and local proverbs. pp. 16.
            8°. Brighton, [188—?].

716. Thomas (Joseph), *of St. Michael's Mount*. Randigal
  rhymes, and a glossary of Cornish words. pp. xii, [3], 139
  + plate.   sm. 8°. Penzance, *Rodda*, 1895.
  Pp. 59-62, local proverbs and phrases.   [F.-L.S. (Stephens collection).

717. Udal (John Symonds). Dorsetshire folk-lore. With a fore-
  say by the late William Barnes. pp. xi, 406 + plate.
        8°. Hertford, *issued by subscription*, 1922.
  Pp. 5-9, brief discussion on proverbs in general. Chapter 10, pp. 288-306,
proverbs and proverbial sayings, arranged first under local headings, more
general ones being divided into proverbs proper and proverbial sayings. [F.-L.S.

WELSH

718. Davies (John), *of Mallwyd*. Antiquae linguae Britannicae
. . . dictionarium duplex. . . . Accesserunt adagia Britannica,
etc. 2 pts.

fol. *Londini, impensis Joan. Davies,* 1632.

Gratet-Duplessis, 874. Contains a large collection of Welsh proverbs, most
of which were reprinted by Howell, *q.v.* **91**, in his Parœmiographia, under the
title of : British or old Cambrian proverbs. [B.M.

719. Gruffydd Hiraethog. Oll synnwyr pen Kembero ygyd.
Edited by J. Gwenogvryn Evans.

8°. Bangor, *Jarvis & Foster,* London, *Dent,* 1902.

Proverbs from a ms. by Gruffyd Hiraethog, first edited by William Salesbury.
[B.M.

720. National Proverbs. National proverbs: Wales. pp. 53.

1/-. 8°. London, *Palmer,* [1920].

208 proverbs in Welsh and English. No notes. [B.M.

721. Proverbs. Welsh proverbs in English dress.

8°. Cardiff, 1882.

In The Red Dragon, September, 1822, pp. 136-137. The triads of Catwg the
Wise. [B.M.

722. Richards (Thomas). Antiquae linguae Britannicae
thesaurus, *etc.* 6/-. 8°. Bristol, *etc., Farley,* 1753.
Fourth edition. 4°. Merthyr-Tydvil, *Price,* 1839.

Contains a large collection of Welsh proverbs without translations. Mostly
taken from John Davies. [B.M., U.C.L.

723. Roberts (T. R.). The proverbs of Wales, *etc.* pp. 94.

1/6. 8°. London, *Griffiths,* 1909.

With English translations. [B.M.

724. Thomas (E. B.). Breconshire folk-lore. 8°. London, 1913.

In Folk-Lore, Vol. 24, pp. 509-511. Breconshire proverbs and sayings.
[F.-L.S.

725. Vaughan (Henry Halford). British reason in English
rhyme. pp. vi, 378. 8°. London, *Kegan Paul,* 1889.

A collection of Welsh proverbs rendered in English verse. [B.M.

See also **91.**

MANX

726. Denham (Michael Aislabie). Popular rhymes, proverbs, sayings, prophecies, etc., etc., peculiar to the Isle of Man and the Manks people. [Subscribed M. A. D., *i.e.* M. A. Denham]. pp. 17.　　　　　　8°. [Durham? 1850].

With explanatory notes. No title page.　　　　　　　　　　[B.M.

727. Harrison (William). Mona miscellany, *etc.* 2nd series.
　　　　　　　　　　　　　　　8°. Douglas, 1869, 1873.

Manx Society Publications, Vols. 16, 21. Vol. 1, pp. 1-41, Vol. 2, pp. 1-21, proverbs and sayings in Manx, with English translations and explanations. An interesting collection, the proverbs of a people in a comparatively isolated position who have developed strongly individual characteristics, but both Irish and Scotch psychology may be traced in the proverbs.　　　　[B.M.

728. Morrison (S.) and **Roeder** (C.). Manx proverbs and sayings.
　　　　　　　　　　　　　　　　　　　　　　　　1905.

729. Wood (G. W.). On the classification of proverbs and sayings of the Isle of Man.　　　　　　8°. London, 1894.

In Folk-Lore, Vol. 5, pp. 229-274. Contains a table for the classification of proverbs with many examples of each section in Manx and English, and an index of objects occurring in Manx proverbs.　　　　　　　　[F.-L.S.

SCOTTISH

730. B. (R.). Adagia Scotia; or, a collection of Scotch proverbs and proverbial phrases collected by R. B., *etc.*

12°. London, *for N. Brooke*, 1668.

731. Black (G. F.). County folk-lore, Vol. 3. Printed extracts, No. 5. Examples of printed folk-lore concerning the Orkney and Shetland Islands. Collected by G. F. Black and edited by Northcote W. Thomas. pp. xii, 277.

13/6. 8°. London, 1903.

Publications of the Folk-Lore Society, 49. Part 4, pp. 263-265, proverbs.

[F.-L.S.

732. Campbell (John Francis). Popular tales of the West Highlands, orally collected. With a translation, by J. F. Campbell. 4 vols.

8°. Edinburgh, *Edmonston & Douglas*, 1860-62.

Vol. 4, pp. 252-256, proverbs from Ossian, in Gaelic and English. [F.-L.S.

733. Chambers (Robert). Popular rhymes, fireside stories, and amusements, of Scotland, *etc.* pp. 76.

8°. Edinburgh, *Chambers*, 1842.

Another edition. pp. vii, 402.   8°. Edinburgh, 1870.

A number of these are proverbial or place rhymes.   [B.M.

734. Cheviot (Andrew). Proverbs, proverbial expressions, and popular rhymes of Scotland, *etc.* pp. xii, 434.

6/-. 8°. Paisley, London, *Gardner*, 1896.

Arranged alphabetically, with index of both local and topical sayings. The standard work on the subject.   [F.-L.S. (Stephens collection), B.M.

735. Fergusson (David). Scottish proverbs: gathered together by D. Fergusson . . . and put *ordine alphabetico* when he departed this life, anno 1598. pp. 44.

4°. Edinburgh, 1641.

Another edition. Nine hundred and forty Scottish proverbs, *etc.*   12°.   1667.

Another edition. Fergusson's Scottish proverbs from the original print of 1641, *etc.* pp. xxxix, 128.

8°. Edinburgh, London, *Blackwood*, 1924.

Gratet-Duplessis, 871. There were numerous other editions. That of 1924, besides reprinting the 911 proverbs of 1641, gives much useful information on other editions, other mss., *etc.*   [B.M.

736. Forbes (Alexander Robert). Gaelic names of beasts, birds, fishes . . . With . . . proverbs, *etc.* pp. xx, 424 + frontispiece.   12/6. 8°. Edinburgh, *Oliver & Boyd*, 1905.

Relevant proverbs and sayings are included under the different headings.
[B.M.

737. Gregor (Walter). Notes on the folk-lore of the North-East of Scotland. pp. xii, 238.   8°. London, 1881.

Folk-Lore Society, Publication 7. Contains a few proverbs, for which see index.   [F.-L.S.

738. Henderson (Andrew). Scottish proverbs . . . with an introductory essay, by W. Motherwell. pp. lxxxviii, 254.
sm. 8°. Edinburgh, *Oliver & Boyd*, London, *Longman*, 1832.
Another edition. pp. xxiii, 202.
7/6. 8°. London, *Tegg*, 1876.

Contains : Scottish proverbs arranged alphabetically by subjects, truisms, miscellaneous, weather and seasons, Scottish proverbial phrases, together with " Useful extracts from the works of Thomas Tusser : London, 1573," and a glossary.   [F.-L.S. (Stephens collection).

739. Henderson (George). The popular rhymes, sayings and proverbs of the county of Berwick, *etc.* pp. viii, 184.
8°. Newcastle-on-Tyne, *for the author*, 1856.

Chiefly place rhymes and local sayings. Contains also the rhymes and prophecies of Thomas the Rhymer.   [B.M.

740. Hislop (Alexander). The proverbs of Scotland, *etc.* pp. ix, 372.   8°. Glasgow, *Porteous & Hislop*, 1862
Third edition.   8°. Edinburgh, *Hislop*, [1870].
[U.C.L.

741. Kelly (James). A complete collection of Scotish proverbs, *etc.* pp. 400.   8°. London, *Innys*, 1721.
Another edition. pp. vi, 255.
12°. London, *Rodwell & Martin*, 1818.

Gratet-Duplessis, 873. An excellent collection of some 3000 proverbs accompanied by brief clear notes. The proverbs given are not necessarily peculiar to Scotland, but are rather those which are in use there.   [B.M.

742. Kissel (J.). Das Sprichwort bei dem mittelschottischen Dichter Sir David Lyndesay, *etc.* pp. iii, 42.
8°. Nürnberg, *Monninger*, 1892.
With full notes and many comparisons.   [B.M.

743. M. (M. L.). Proverbs. With glossary. By M. L. M. [M. L. Miln?]. pp. 211.
16°. Arbroath, *printed for private circulation*, 1895.

In English. Proverbs translated from all languages, though chiefly Scotch, arranged in alphabetical order, with a glossary.   [B.M.

744. Macdonald (T. D.). Gaelic proverbs and proverbial sayings with English translations. pp. xxi, 156.

5/-. 8°. Stirling, *Mackay*, [1926].

Contains between six and seven hundred proverbs, with explanatory notes.
[B.M.

744a. Macgillivray (Angus). Our Gaelic proverbs: a mirror of the past. 8°. Glasgow, 1928.

In Caledonian Medical Journal, Vol. 13, pp. 307-26. A great many examples given in Gaelic and English : classified according to subjects.

745. Macintosh (Donald). A collection of Gaelic proverbs and familiar phrases; accompanied with an English translation. . . . To which is added, The Way to Wealth by Dr. Franklin, *etc.* pp. x, 83. 12°. Edinburgh, *for the author*, 1785.
Another edition. pp. ii, 239.

12°. Edinburgh, *Stewart*, 1819.

A collection of Gaelic proverbs . . . based on Macintosh's collection. Edited by Alexander Nicholson. pp. xxxvi, 421.

8°. Edinburgh, London, *MacLachlan & Stewart*, 1882.
Second edition. pp. xxxvi, 421.

8°. Edinburgh, London, *MacLachlan & Stewart*, 1882.

An excellent alphabetical collection of Gaelic proverbs with translations. In the 1882 edition there are over 3900 proverbs, more than twice as many as in the first.
[U.C.L.

746. Mackay (Æneas James George). A century of Scottish proverbs and sayings . . . current in Fife, *etc.* pp. 55.

6d. 16°. Cupar-Fife, *Westwood*, [1891].

With explanatory notes.
[B.M.

747. Mackay (Charles). A dictionary of Lowland Scotch . . . and an appendix of Scottish proverbs. pp. xxxii, 398.

8°. London, *Whittaker*, 1888.

Pp. 343-382, Allan Ramsay's collection of Scottish proverbs. [B.M.

748. Maclean (Magnus). The literature of the Highlands. pp. viii, 236. 8°. London, *etc., Blackie*, 1904.
Another edition. pp. viii, 270.

8°. London, *etc., Blackie*, [1925].

Pp. 137-158, Gaelic proverbs. Begins with a sketch of the life of Donald Macintosh, the first to publish a collection of Gaelic proverbs : selections of these proverbs are given in English accompanied by excellent critical comments.
[B.M.

749. Mitchell (*Sir* Arthur). On the popular weather prognostics of Scotland. pp. 26.

8°. Edinburgh, London, *Blackwood*, [1863].

In Edinburgh New Philosophical Journal, Oct., 1863. Contains a few well-selected weather proverbs.
[B.M.

750. Muirhead (George). The birds of Berwickshire, with remarks on . . . the folk-lore, proverbs, popular rhymes and sayings connected with them. 2 vols.

8°. Edinburgh, *Douglas*, 1889-95.
[B.M.

751. National Proverbs. National proverbs: Scotland. pp. 92.
1/-. 8°. London, *Palmer*, [1913].

Scottish proverbs with a glossary. No notes. [B.M.

752. Proverbs. Historical Scottish proverbs.
la. 8°. London, Edinburgh, 1897.

In Chambers's Journal, Feb., 1897, pp. 25-28. [B.M.

753. ————: Proverbs and sayings maistly Scotch. Selected and arranged by the " People's Journal " competition editor. pp. iv, 62.
3d. 16°. Cupar-Fife, *printed by A. Westwood*, 1889.

An alphabetical list. [B.M.

754. ————: Scottish proverbs, toasts, and sentiments, *etc.* pp. 32. 32°. Glasgow, *Hamilton*, 1844.

Pp. 3-20, select Scottish proverbs.

755. Ramsay (Allan). A collection of Scots proverbs, *etc.* pp. iv, 90. 12°. Edinburgh, *Ramsay*, 1737.

Another edition. A chapbook. pp. 24.
12°. Kilmarnock, *Crawford*, 1820.

Another edition. A chapbook. pp. 24.
12°. Paisley, *Caldwell*, [1840?].

Gratet-Duplessis, 872. A very useful and interesting collection. Reviewed in the Quarterly Review, 125, pp. 217-254. [B.M.

756. Ramsay (Edward Bannerman). Reminiscences of Scottish life and character . . . Third edition, *etc.* pp. ix, 219.
8°. Edinburgh, *Edmonston & Douglas*, 1859.

Another edition. pp. 286 + frontispiece.
8°. London, *etc., Nelson*, [1910].

Contains an important chapter dealing with Scottish proverbs. First issued in this form in the third edition; a second series, dealing with the same subjects but containing additional matter, was published in 1861, and later both series were published together. [B.M.

757. Rorie (David). Stray notes on the folk-lore of Aberdeen-shire and the north-east of Scotland. 8°. London, 1914.

In Folk-Lore, Vol. 25, pp. 350-352. Local proverbs, weather sayings, *etc.*
[F.-L.S.

758. Sarauw (Christian). Specimens of Gaelic as spoken in the Isle of Skye. 8°. Halle a. S., *Niemeyer*, 1912.

In Miscellany presented to Kuno Meyer, *etc.*, pp. 36-41. 89 Gaelic proverbs, also printed in phonetics. [U.C.L.

759. Simpkins (John Ewart). County folk-lore, Vol. 7. Printed extracts, Nos. 9-11. Examples of printed folk-lore concerning Fife, with some notes on Clackmannan and Kinross-shires, *etc.* pp. xxxv, 419 + 8 plates. 8°. London, 1914.

Publications of the Folk-Lore Society, 71. Pp. 271-293, place rhymes and sayings : pp. 294-301, proverbs : pp. 347-349, local rhymes and sayings : pp. 379-381, local rhymes and sayings : pp. 413-415, proverbs. [F.-L.S.

760. Spence (John). Shetland folk-lore. pp. 255.
8°. Lerwick, *Johnson & Greig,* 1899.

Pp. 201-232, proverbs and sayings. [F.-L.S.

761. Stampoy (Pappity), *pseud.* A collection of Scotch proverbs. pp. 58. 12°. London, *printed by R. D.,* 1663.

An alphabetical list without notes. [B.M.

762. Stirling (William), *afterwards* **Stirling-Maxwell** (*Sir* William), *Bart.* The proverbial philosophy of Scotland, *etc.* pp. 20. 8°. Stirling, 1855.

Twelve copies printed. Included in pp. 1-35 of Vol. 6 of the author's Works, London, 1891. A delightful dissertation on Scottish proverbs, with many examples, and some comparisons from other countries.

[Works, F.-L.S. (Stephens collection).

See also **69, 612, 622, 629, 3644, 3857, 3860.**

IRISH.

763. Begley (Connor).   The English Irish dictionary, *etc.*   pp.
[12], 717.   4°.   Paris, *Guerin*, 1732.

Contains a number of proverbs scattered throughout, but the Irish equivalents of English proverbs are, as a rule, merely literal translations.   Some,
however, appear to be genuine Irish ones.   These are quoted by O'Rahilly, pp.
148-150.   [U.C.L.

764. Bourke (Ulick J.).   The college Irish grammar.   *First
edition.* pp. xxvii, 204.

8°.   Dublin, *O'Daly*, London, *Smith*, 1856.

Fifth edition. pp. xiv, 304.   8°.   Dublin, *Mullany*, 1868.

About 300 Irish proverbs with English translations and some equivalents
from other languages.   Some are taken from Hardiman's "Irish Minstrelsy,"
some from O'Daly's collection, and some from unspecified sources.

[U.C.L. (1868).

765. Byers (John William).   Sayings, proverbs and humour of
Ulster. pp. 66.   8°.   Belfast, *Strain*, 1904.

Concerns more the sayings, proverbial phrases, and familiar expressions,
than the true proverbs, though a number of these are included.   [B.M.

766. Concannon (Thomas) [Tomās na Concheanainn].   Mion-
chamhrādh. pp. x, 161.

1/-. 8°.   Baile ātha Cliath [Dublin], *Connradh na Gaedhilge
[Gaelic League]*, 1904.

Pp. 141-161, about 264 proverbs, source unspecified; probably in part from
Arran.   The bulk are merely copied from Bourke.   [B.M.

767. Doyle (James) [Sēamus na Dubhghaill].   Leabhar cainte,
etc. pp. vi, 172.

1/-. 8°.   Baile ātha Cliath [Dublin],
Connradh na Gaedhilge, 1901.

Gaelic League Series.   Pp. 149-172, Seàn-fhocail.   [B.M.

768. Gaelic Journal. [Anonymous, or small collections of proverbs, in various numbers of the Gaelic Journal.]
8°.   Dublin, *Gaelic League*, 1882-1909.

Vol. 2, pp. 243, 246, 272, 310, 358, 375; Vol. 3, p. 56; Vol. 4, pp. 155, 192,
207, 209, 236, 247; Vol. 5, pp. 13-14, 38-40, 71-73, 88, 139-141, 157; Vol. 6,
pp. 10, 39-40, 79, 91, 123; Vol. 7, pp. 88-89; Vol. 8, p. 180; Vol. 10, p. 30;
Vol. 12, pp. 102, 154; Vol.15, p. 109.   [U.C.L., B.M.

769. Galvin (D. J.). Proverbs and sayings from North Cork.

8°. Dublin, *Dollard*, 1895.

In the Gaelic Journal, Vol. 6, pp. 60-61, 78-79, 90-91. Irish with English translations. [U.C.L.

770. H. Rustic proverbs current in Ulster.

4°. Belfast, *Archer*, London, *Smith*, 1854.

In the Ulster Journal of Archæology, Vol. 2, pp. 126-9. 31 proverbs, compared with English or Scottish ones. The article is signed H. [B.M.

771. Hardiman (James). Irish minstrelsy. . . . Collected and edited with notes and illustrations by James Hardiman. 2 vols. 8°. London, *Robins*, 1831.

Vol. 2, pp. 397-408 : over 200 proverbs in Irish, alphabetically arranged.
[U.C.L. (with ms. translations of many proverbs).

772. Hayden (Thomas). Sean-fhocail.

8°. Dublin, *Gaelic League*, 1905-06.

In the Gaelic Journal, Vol. 14, pp. 827-831, 844-9 : Vol. 15, pp. 5-9, 19-21, 55-6, 69-71. Proverbs from South Galway. A large number of these are either identical with those current in Munster, or only differ very slightly.
[Vol. 15. U.C.L., B.M.

773. Hyde (Douglas). A few rhymed proverbs.

8°. Edinburgh, *Macleod*, London, *Nutt*, Dublin,
[*Hodges, Figgis*], 1904-05.

In the Celtic Review, Vol. 1, pp. 18-22. Irish proverbs, chiefly from Connacht, with English translations. Most of the proverbs were recovered orally. [U.C.L.

774. Joyce (Patrick Weston). English as we speak it in Ireland, *etc.* pp. x, 356.

8°. London, *Longmans*, Dublin, *Gill*, 1910.

Third edition. pp. x, 356.

8°. Dublin, *Talbot Press*, London, *Longmans*, [1920].
Pp. 105-120, proverbs. [B.M.

775. Lloyd (James) [Séamus Laoidhe]. Tonn tóime. 1915.

Pp. 105-116, 250 proverbs from Kerry.

776. ———: [Ulster proverbs contributed to the Gaelic Journal, Vols. 4, 6, 7, 12.] 8°. Dublin, *Gaelic League*, 1894-1902.

In the Gaelic Journal, Vol. 4, p. 248; Vol. 6, pp. 184-188, proverbs from Monaghan, with translations and notes, continued in Vol. 7, pp. 88-89; Vol. 12, p. 154. [U.C.L.

777. Long (William). Popular proverbs, Co. Kerry.

8°. Dublin, *Gaelic League*, 1894.

In the Gaelic Journal, Vol. 5, pp. 21-25, 37-38, 61-62, proverbs in Irish with English translations. [U.C.L.

778. Lyon (J. J.) [Seagan O'Laigin]. Sean-raidte.

8°. Dublin, *Gaelic League*, 1897-1898.

In the Gaelic Journal, Vol. 8, p. 56; Vol. 9, p. 271, proverbs from Connacht with English translations. [U.C.L.

779. MacAdam (Robert). Six hundred Gaelic proverbs collected
in Ulster. 4°. Belfast, *Archer*, 1858, 1859, 1862.
In Ulster Journal of Archæology, Vols. 6, 7, 9. With translation, and notes
where necessary; frequent comparisons are made with proverbs of other
countries. [B.M.

780. McCabe (Daniel). [Irish proverbs contributed to the Gaelic
Journal, Vols. 4, 5, 7.] 8°. Dublin, *Dollard*, 1893-97.
In the Gaelic Journal, Vol. 4, p. 236, no translation; Vol. 5, pp. 104-105,
125-126, 139, with translation; Vol. 7, p. 141, with translation. Some of these
proverbs appear to have been taken from printed sources such as Hardiman
and O'Daly. Province of origin, Munster.

[U.C.L. (Vol. 4 incomplete, lacking the first 64 pages).

781. McCarthy (P.). Proverbs—Munster.
8°. Dublin, *Gaelic League*, 1895.
In the Gaelic Journal, Vol. 5, pp. 172, 184-185; Vol. 6, pp. 9-10. Proverbs
in Irish with English translations. [U.C.L.

782. MacFinley (Conal) [Conall Mac Fhionnlaigh]. Proverbs—
Ulster. 8°. Dublin, *Gaelic League*, 1897.
In the Gaelic Journal, Vol. 8, pp. 13-14, proverbs in Irish with English
translations. [U.C.L.

783. Marstrander (Carl). Bídh Crínna.
8°. Dublin, *Hodges, Figgis*, London, *Nutt*, 1911.
In Eriu, Vol. 5, pp. 126-41. Stowe MS. 23.N.10, pp. 135-41, with translation. [U.C.L.

784. Martin (William Gregory Wood-). Traces of the elder faiths
of Ireland, *etc.* 2 vols.
la. 8°. London, *etc.*, *Longmans*, 1902.
Vol. 2, pp. 275-287, a collection of some hundreds of proverbs, in English,
especially relating to the evil eye : with commentary. For the original Irish
see the Ulster Journal of Archæology, Vols. 5 and 6. [F.-L.S.

785. Meyer (Kuno). Altirische Reimsprüche.
8°. Halle, *Niemeyer*, 1910.
In the Zeitschrift für celtische Philologie, Vol. 7, pp. 268-9, 489. Taken from
B.IV.2, H.3.18, Laud 610, Harl. 5280. [U.C.L.

786. ———: Bríathra Flainn Fina maic Ossu. From MS. 23.IV.
10 (R.I.A.), p. 5, collated with 23.D.2.
8°. Halle, *Niemeyer*, Dublin, *Hodges, Figgis*, 1910.
In Anecdota from Irish MSS. [Edited by O. J. Bergin, *etc.*] Vol. 3, pp. 10-
20. [B.M.

787. ———: The instructions of King Cormac Mac Airt. pp. xii,
62.
1/6. 8°. Dublin, *Hodges*, London, *Williams & Norgate*,
1909.
Royal Irish Academy, Todd Lecture Series, Vol. 15. With English translation. [U.C.L.

788. Meyer (Kuno). Mitteilungen aus irischen Handschriften.
Bríathra Floinn. Aus 23.N.17 (R.I.A.).
8°. Halle, *Niemeyer*, 1912.
In the Zeitschrift für celtische Philologie, Vol. 8, pp. 112.   [U.C.L.

789. ———: Mitteilungen aus irischen Handschriften. Fithels
Ratschläge an seinen Sohn. Aus 23.N.17 (R.I.A.).
8°. Halle, *Niemeyer*, 1912.
In the Zeitschrift für celtische Philologie, Vol. 8, pp. 112-13.   [U.C.L.

790. ———: Mitteilungen aus irischen Handschriften. Sprichwörtliches. Additional Brit. Mus. 30,512, fol. 33.a.2: Ferr
dála iná deabaid. *Ib.* 316.2: Oligid ecna airmitín.
8°. Halle, *Niemeyer*, 1908.
In Zeitschrift für celtische Philologie, Vol. 6, pp. 260-1.   [U.C.L.

791. ———: The triads of Ireland. pp. xv, 54.
1/6. 8°. Dublin, *Hodges*, London, *Williams & Norgate*,
1906.
Royal Irish Academy, Todd Lecture Series, Vol. 13. In the original, with
English translations.   [U.C.L.

792. Morris (Henry) [Enrí O'Muirgheasa]. Seanfhocla Uladh,
etc. pp. xvi, 320.   8°. Dublin, 1907.
Over 1600 Ulster proverbs, incorporating MacAdam's and the Gaelic Journal
collections. The bulk of these are from S.E. Ulster. A supplementary list
was published in the Journal of the County Louth Archæological Society,
Vol. 4, p. 258, 1917.

793. ———: Farney (Co. Monaghan) proverbs and sayings.
8°. Dublin, *Gaelic League*, 1898, 1902.
In the Gaelic Journal, Vol. 8, pp. 177-180, proverbs in Irish with English
translations and notes. Vol. 12, pp. 116-122.   [U.C.L.

794. National Proverbs. National proverbs. Ireland. pp. 86.
8°. London, *Palmer*, [1913].
Proverbs in English : no order or method.   [F.-L.S.

795. O'Brien (John). Sean-fhocail.
8°. Dublin, *Gaelic League*, 1906.
In the Gaelic Journal, Vol. 16, pp. 88-90, 105-106, 120-122, 136-139, 152-156,
165-167.   [B.M.

796. O'Daly (John). The Irish language miscellany, *etc.* pp.
viii, 112.   12°. Dublin, *O'Daly*, 1876.
Pp. 89-98, 190 proverbs in Irish in alphabetical order. No notes. Pp. 77-79,
wise sayings of St. Columbkill.   [B.M.

797. O'Donoghue (Teigue) [Tadhg Ó'Donnchadha]. Seanfhocail
na Muman. pp. 16.   8°. Dublin, *Gaelic League*, 1896.
In the Gaelic Journal, Vol. 7, 1896. An alphabetical list without notes.
Reprinted 1902.   [B.M.

798. O'Donoghue (Teigue). Sean-raidte, sean-ranna.

8°. Dublin, *Gaelic League*, 1896.

In the Gaelic Journal, Vol. 7, pp. 46-47, 57-59, 65-67, 104-106, Irish proverbs with English translations and notes. These proverbs are also given in the author's " Seanfhocail na Muman." [U.C.L.

799. O'Donovan (John). Cormac's instructions.

8°. Dublin, 1832-3.

In the Dublin Penny Journal, Vol. 1, pp. 213-15, 231-2. Specimens from the Book of Lecan, with translation. Reprinted in the Gaelic Journal, Vol. 1, 1883. [U.C.L. (Gaelic Journal).

800. Ō Fotharta (Domhnall). Siamsa an gheimhridh, *etc.*

8°. Baile-ata-Cliath [Dublin], *P. O'Briain*, 1892.

Pp. 99-103, 100 proverbs. [B.M.

801. O'Kelly (John). Seanfhocail.

8°. Dublin, *Gaelic League*, 1906.

In the Gaelic Journal, Vol. 16, pp. 188-190, 197-199, 230-235. [B.M.

802. O'Leary (Patrick). Sean-raidte, no sean fhocail.

8°. Dublin, *Gaelic League*, 1890, 1894.

In the Gaelic Journal, Vol. 4, pp. 41-79; Vol. 5, pp. 73-74, 88-90. Province of origin, Munster. English translations are given in some cases.

[U.C.L., B.M.

803. O'Rahilly (Thomas F.). A miscellany of Irish proverbs, collected and edited by T. F. O'Rahilly. pp. 174.

5/-. sm. 8°. Dublin, *Talbot Press*, 1922.

Irish proverbs with English translation and notes. Pp. 1-64, Mícheál Óg Ó Longáin's collection of Irish proverbs; pp. 65-78, modern Irish triads : pp. 79-124, proverbs in Irish literature : pp. 125-146, proverbial phrases in Irish literature : pp. 147-161, bibliography : pp. 162-174, indices and additional notes.

804. Proverbi. Proverbi di tutti i popoli. . . . 2. Proverbi irlandesi.

4°. Milano, *Lampato*, 1840.

For notes, *see* **2581.**

805. Proverbs. Rustic proverbs and proverbial sayings of Ulster.

8°. London, 1856.

In Chambers's Journal of popular literature, science and arts, Vol. 5, pp. 137-140. [B.M.

806. Quiggin (Edmund Crosby). A dialect of Donegal, being the speech of Meenawannia in the parish of Glenties, *etc.* pp. x, 247. 8°. Cambridge, *University Press*, 1906.

Pp. 194-195, 24 Donegal proverbs in Irish. [U.C.L.

807. Shughrue (Patrick) [Padraig Ō Siochfhradha]. Seanfhocail na Muimhneach. " An Seabhac " [*pseud.* of P. Shughrue]. pp. xii, 261.

3/6. 8°. Baile atha Cliath, Corcaigh [Dublin, Cork], *Educational Co. of Ireland*, 1926.

Gaelic proverbs and folk sayings from Munster. Reviewed in The Times Literary Supplement, Nov. 4, 1926, p. 773. [B.M.

808. Thurneysen (Rudolf). Zu irischen Handschriften und Litteraturdenkmälern. 4°. Berlin, *Weidmann*, 1912.

In Abhandlungen der Kgl. Gesellschaft der Wissenschaften zu Göttingen, Phil.-hist. Klasse, Bd. 14, No. 2. Pp. 3-11, Tecosca Cormaic und Verwandtes : pp. 11-22, Fithal's Sprüche. Critical text based on the Book of Leinster 3456, Book of Ballymote 64b, and the Yellow Book of Lecan 181d, *etc.* [B.M.

809. Ward (John). Sean-raidte.

8°. Dublin, *Gaelic League*, 1896.

In the Gaelic Journal, Vol. 7, pp. 6-7, proverbs from Donegal, with translations and notes. [U.C.L.

810. Wilde (Jane Francesca Speranza), *Lady.* Ancient cures, charms and usages of Ireland. Contributions to Irish lore. pp. xi, 256. 8°. London, *Ward & Downey*, 1890.

Pp. 244-256, remarks on Irish proverbs, followed by about seven pages of examples. [U.C.L.

See also **612, 2581.**

CHANNEL ISLES.

811. MacCulloch (*Sir* Edgar). Guernsey folk lore. . . . Edited by Edith F. Carey. pp. 616.

8°. London, Guernsey, *Stock*, 1903.

Chapter 17, pp. 509-546, proverbs, weather sayings, *etc.*, interesting not only in themselves, but also for the dialect in which they are written. [F.-L.S.

812. Messervy (Alfred). Recueil de dictons, bons mots, proverbes, etc., en patois jersiais. pp. 29. [Preface signed : A.M.S.V., *i.e.* Alfred Messervy.]

8°. Jersey, *Bureau de la " Nouvelle Chronique,"* 1900.

An alphabetical list without notes or explanations. [B.M.

G

SCANDINAVIAN.

1. GENERAL.

813. Heusler (Andreas). Sprichwörter in den eddischen Sitten-
gedichten.   la. 8°. Berlin, 1915-16.

In Zeitschrift des Vereins für Volkskunde, Jahrgang 25, pp. 108-115; Jahrgang 26, pp. 42-57.   [U.C.L.

814. Lundell (J. A.). Skandinavische Volkspoesie.—E. Sprichwörter.   la. 8°. Strassburg, *Trübner*, 1909.

Grundriss der germanischen Philologie, herausgegeben von H. Paul, Bd. 2,
Abt. 1, Lief. 6, pp. 1172-5, §§ 40-49.   [U.C.L.

815. Rosenberg (C.). Nordboernes aandsliv, *etc.* 3 bind.
            8°. Kjøbenhavn, *Danske Literaturs Fremme*, 1878-85.

Bind 2, pp. 599-604, on proverbs.   [B.M.

816. Stroembaeck (Kaspar). Nordiskt ordspråks lexikon.

1500 proverbs of Norway, Sweden, Iceland, Denmark.

2. NORWEGIAN.

817. Aalholm (N. M.). Norsk-fransk ordsamling og parleur, *etc.*
    pp. vi, 176.   sm. 8°. Christiania, *Malling*, 1861.

Pp. 167-173, Gallicismer og mundheld, *etc.:* pp. 174-176, Ordsprog.

818. Aasen (Ivar Andreas). Norske ordsprog, *etc.* pp. xxiii, 262.
                             8°. Christiania, *Werner*, 1856.
    Another edition. pp. xvi, 237.
                             8°. Christiania, *Malling*, 1881.

Norwegian proverbs with occasional notes. The later edition is arranged
alphabetically by key-words.   [B.M.

819. Sagen (Einar). A few Norwegian proverbs. [Selected by
Captain Sagen and contributed by E. E. Speight.]
                    8°. London, *Folk-Lore Society*, 1911.

In Folk-Lore, Vol. 22, pp. 213-218. In English and Norwegian. [F.-L.S.

See also **816, 868.**

3. SWEDISH.

820. Christensen (J.). Talar ni Svenska? Schwedisch-deutsches Gesprachbuch . . . Zweite verbesserte Auflage. pp. vi, 154.
8°. Leipzig, *Koch*, 1889.
Pp. 68-70, Ordspråk—Sprichwörter.

821. Djurklou (Gabriel). Ur nerikes folkspråk och folklif, *etc.*
pp. xii, 136. 8°. Örebro, *Lindh*, 1860.
Pp. 36-49, Ordspråk. [B.M.

822. Ekevall (A. F.). Gåtor och ordspråk. pp. 19.
8°. Skellefteå, *Ellverson*, 1893.
Bernstein, 980. [B.M.

823. Ekholtz (A.). Praktisches Lehr- und Hülfsbuch der schwedischen Sprache . . . Dritte . . . Auflage, *etc.* pp. 209.
8°. Lübeck, *Aschenfeldt*, 1858.
Pp. 132-142, Sprichwörter (Ordspråk).

824. Folkets Seder. Svenska folkets seder, *etc.* pp. 256.
8°. Stockholm, *Berg*, 1856.
Pp. 237-256, Svenska ordspråk.

825. Granlund (Victor). Svenska folket i sina ordspråk.
8°. Stockholm, *Riis*, 1871.
In Svenska Fornminnesföreningens Tidskrift, No. 1, pp. 27-45. [B.M.

826. Grubb (Christopher Lorenz). Penu proverbiale, *etc.*
sm. 8°. Lincopiae, *Kampe*, 1665.
Another edition. pp. [xxviii], 914, 162.
8°. Stockholm, *Wankijff*, 1678.
Gratet-Duplessis, 817. The edition of 1678 is to be preferred since it contains also a supplement to Grubb's work by L. Toerning entitled : " Veterum et novorum proverbiorum sueo-gothicorum auctarium," *etc.*, Stockholm, 1677, with its own title page and pagination. These two works should be considered as one; they are both written in Swedish and are extremely useful not only for the study of proverbs but also of the Swedish language. The proverbs are accompanied by brief explanations and quotations. [B.M.

827. Grunden (Andreas Adolphus). D. D. dissertationis de adagiis suiogothicis continuatio . . . sub praesidio . . .
Johannis Ihre, *etc.* pp. 16. 4°. Upsaliae, *Edman*, 1770.
[B.M.

828. Hildebrandsson (H. Hildebrand). Samling af bemärkelsedagar, tecken, märken, ordspråk och skrock rörande väderleken. pp. 106.
3 kronor. 8°. [Stockholm], *Kongl. Vitterhets Akademie*,
[1883].
In Antiquarisk Tidskrift för Sverige, Del. 7, Nr. 2. [B.M.

829. L——n (G. A.). Ordspråk, sanna språk. 6500 bevingade ord ur folkets mun. *Karlshamn*, 1889.

830. Ordsedher. Swenske ordsedher, eller ordsaghor.
[Stockholm], 1604.
Another edition. Swenske ordspråk, eller ordsaghor.   1636.

831. Ordspråksboken. Den svenska ordspråksboken innehållande
3160 ordspråk. pp. 98.   8°. Stockholm, *Hiertas*, 1865.
Proverbs in alphabetical order. No notes.   [B.M.

832. Prinz (Bernhard Roland). A. D. dissertatio gradualis de
adagiis suiogothicis . . . praeside . . . Johanne Ihre, *etc.*
pp. 24.   4°. Upsaliae, *Edman*, 1769.
Gratet-Duplessis, 818. A commentary in Latin.   [B.M.

833. Rabe (Casten). Elfva hundra elfva latinska och swenska
sentenser.   Göteborg, 1807.

834. Reuterdahl (H.). Gamla ordspråk på latin och swenska,
etc. pp. xix, 154.   8°. Lund, *etc.*, *Gleerup*, 1840.
1110 proverbs arranged alphabetically by the Latin followed by the Swedish.
[B.M.

835. Rhodin (Lars). Samling af swenska ordspråk, *etc.* pp.
[viii], 124.   8°. Stockholm, *Lindh*, 1807.
With correlations in other languages, English, French, Italian, Latin, and
a few notes.   [B.M.

836. Schultz (J. G.). Sex hundra svenska ordstäf.
[Stockholm], 1870.

837. Thomasson (Pehr). Gamla ordspråk med förklaringar, *etc.*
pp. 31.   30 øre. 16°. Stockholm, *Fahlstedt*, [1874].
About 30 proverbs with explanatory notes.   [B.M.

838. Toerning (L.). Veterum et novorum proverbium sueo-
gothicorum auctarium, *etc.* 8°. Stockholm, *Wankiff*, 1677.
For notes *see under* **826,** with which it was published.

839. Waldheim (L. J.). Der ächte kleine Schwede . . . Sechste
. . . Auflage. pp. iv, 124. 12°. Hamburg, *Berendsohn*, 1892.
Pp. 110-113, Swedish proverbs with German equivalents.

840. Waltman (K. H.). Lidmål. Ordspråk ock talesätt, smårim,
gåtor, *etc.*   8°. Stockholm, 1894.
In Bidrag till kånnedom om de svenska landsmalen, Bd. 13, No. 1. Pp. 10-
13, ordspråk.   [B.M.

841. Wensell (E. G.). 2000 Ordspråk samlade, alfabetiskt ord-
nade, *etc.* pp. 84.   75 öre. 12°. Gefle, *Landin*, 1863.
Proverbs in alphabetical order. No notes.   [B.M.

See also **816, 847, 888.**

4. DANISH.

842. Allen (Carl Ferdinand). Ueber Sprache und Volksthümlich-
keiten in Herzogthum Schleswig oder Südjütland, *etc.* pp.
173.   8°. Kopenhagen, *Reitzel*, 1848.
Pp. 157-160, proverbs with German translations. The book forms Heft 6 of
Krieger's Antischleswigholsteinische Fragmente, *etc.*   [B.M.

843. Andersen (J.). Der ächte kleine Däne . . . Zweite . . .
Auflage. pp. 160.   12°. Hamburg, *Berendsohn*, 1880.
Pp. 112-119, Dänische Redensarten und Sprüchwörter.

844. Balling (Christian). Ordsproglaerdom. pp. 108. 3 pts.
                            8°. Kiøbenhavn, *Schønberg*, 1877-1905.
A commentary with proverbs arranged by subjects.   [B.M.

845. Bresemann (Friedrich). Danske Ordsprog og Mundheld,
etc. pp. xvi, 294.
84 skilling. 8°. Kjøbenhavn, *Universitetsboghandler*, 1843.
Proverbs arranged in alphabetical order. No notes.   [B.M.

846. ——— and **Jones** (William). English and Danish dialogues,
etc. pp. xii, xcviii, 160.   8°. Copenhagen, *Høst*, 1844.
Another edition. pp. xiv, lxxxii, 192.
                            8°. Copenhagen, *Høst*, 1848.
Contains a selection of English and Danish proverbs.   [U.C.L.

847. Century. A century of Danish proverbs, with their English
and Scottish equivalents : to which are added a few from
Islandic [*sic*] and Swedish sources. 8°. London, [1854-5].
In Sharpe's London Magazine, New Series, Vol. 5, pp. 372-377; Vol. 6,
pp. 58-61, 81-87.   [B.M.

848. Feilberg (Henning Frederik). Fra heden, *etc.* pp. 155.
                    8°. Haderslev, *Dannevirkes Bogtrykkeri*, 1863.
Pp. 148-154, Endnu kunne moerkes følgende ordsprog.   [B.M.

849. Fenger (Peter Andreas). Ord-sprog, samlede, isoer til Skole-
Brug. pp. 58.   sm. 8°. Kjøbenhavn, *Iversen*, 1852.
Proverbs from the Scriptures and from the collections of Lolle and Syv.
                                                                   [B.M.

850. Gottleib (J. L.). Fraseologi : en Samling af danske Sœt-
ninger, *etc.* pp. 179.   8°. Kjøbenhavn, *Høst*, 1874.
Another edition. pp. 395.   8°. Kiøbenhavn, *Klein*, 1882.
The 1874 edition contains a section of proverbs at the end of the phrases,
etc. In the greatly enlarged 1882 edition, the proverbs are mingled with the
idioms, phrases, *etc.*, and arranged alphabetically by (Danish) key-words.
                                                                   [B.M.

851. Grundtvig (Nikolai Frederik Severin). Danske ordsprog og
mundheld, *etc.* pp. viii, 115.
                            8°. Kjøbenhavn, *Neitzel*, 1845.
Proverbs arranged alphabetically by the principal words. No notes. [B.M.

852. Grundtvig (Svend). Danske folkeminder, *etc.* pp. vi, 244.
8°. Kjøbenhavn, *Iversen*, 1861.

Pp. 206-218, Ordsprog og mundheld. 230 proverbs with occasional notes.
This volume forms Part 3 of the author's Gamle danske minder i folkemunde,
etc. [B.M.

852a. Hedegaard (   ). Trifulium juridicum bestaaende udi
samling af gamle danske ordsprog. 4°. Kopenhagen, 1748.

853. King (John). True English guide containing a new and
useful grammar . . . to the use of Danish gentlemen.
sm. 8°. Copenhagen, 1770.

Gratet-Duplessis, 829. Pp. 298-328, choice Danish proverbs.

854. Kjaergaard (U.). 220 danske ordsprog i 12 sange, *etc.* pp.
16. 8°. Kjøbenhavn, *Bang*, 1880.

855. Klausen (Gottlieb Ernst). Nordiske Harpentoner, eller
gnomisk Blomstersamling af danske Dichtere, *etc.* pp. xviii,
364. 8°. Altona, *Hammerich*, 1815.
Another edition. pp. xviii, 364. 8°. Altona, 1817.

Gratet-Duplessis, 830, says he does not consider this as a collection of
popular proverbs, but he includes it as it probably contains a number of rhymed
sayings and moral maxims which have become proverbial. [B.M.

856. Kok (Johannes). Danske ordsprog och talemåder fra
Sønderjylland, *etc.* pp. xi, 188.
8°. Kjøbenhavn, *Gyldendal*, 1870.

2000 proverbs, sayings, *etc.*, frequently compared with other Scandinavian
ones. Pp. x-xi, brief bibliography. [B.M.

857. Kristensen (Evald Tang). Danske Ordsprog og Mundheld,
etc. pp. 656. 8°. Kjøbenhavn, *Gyldendal*, 1890.

Proverbs, sayings, *etc.*, arranged alphabetically by key-words, with occasional
notes. [B.M.

858. Lolle (Peder). Petri Lolle vel Langlandi adagia Danica et
Latina. 8°. Hafniae, 1501.

Peder Lolles samling af danske og latinske ordsprog, *etc.* pp.
xxviii, 404. 8°. Kjøbenhavn, *Soldim*, 1828.

Östnordiska och latinska medeltidsordspråk. Peder Låles
ordspråk, *etc.* 2 pts. 8°. København, 1889-94.

Gratet-Duplessis, 825. The edition of 1501 is probably the first. The 1828
edition has a bibliography, pp. xxi-xxviii. The 1889 edition has a very
extensive commentary, and a bibliography, pp. 140-146. 1889 edition, Publication 20 of the Samfund til udgivelse af gammel nordisk litteratur. [B.M.

859. Luexdorph (Bolle Willum). Carmina. Editio secunda,
auctior. pp. xxviii, 225.
4°. Hafniae, Lipsiae, *Gyldendal*, 1784.

Pp. 122-125, Proverbia Danica Latine reddita.

860. Lundbye (H. W.). Adskillige ordsprog. 1796.
In Iris og Hebe, Vol. 4. 400 entries.

861. Mau (Jens Christian Eduard Theodor). Dansk ordsprogs-skat, *etc.* 2 vols.   8°. Kjøbenhavn, *Gad*, 1879.

Contains over 12,500 proverbs, sayings, phrases, popular expressions, *etc.*, with notes and comparisons.   [B.M.

862. Meyer (Jean). Dictionnaire des proverbes danois, traduits en françois, avec le texte en regard.   4°. Copenhague, 1757. *Another edition.* pp. 568.   4°. Copenhague, *Pripp*, 1761.

Gratet-Duplessis, 828.   Proverbs taken from the collections of Lolle, Erasmus, Syv, *etc.* Duplessis says it is very rare in France. Some Italian proverbs are also to be found scattered through the book.   Arranged alphabetically under the principal word of the Danish, with the French opposite. The edition of 1761 was published anonymously.   [B.M., 1761 *ed.*

863. Molbech (Christian). Danske ordsprog, tankesprog og riim-sprog, *etc.* pp. lx, 388.
                    8°. Kjøbenhavn, *Danske Literaturs Fremme*, 1850.

A good collection of proverbs, *etc.*, arranged alphabetically by the principal words, with notes. Pp. xxxiv-lii, bibliography.   [B.M.

864. Moller (J. P.). Folkesagn . . . fra Bornholm. pp. 59.
                    8°. Kjøbenhavn, *Eibes*, 1867.
Pp. 53-56, Ordsprog og ordspil.   [B.M.

865. Nees (Frits). Bevingede engelske Ordsprog og Talemaader med de tilsvarende dansk-norske.
                    8°. Christiania, og Kjøbenhavn, *Cammermeyer*, 1890.

A collection of proverbs, sayings, phrases, expressions, *etc.*, some 800 in all, in English and Danish.   [B.M.

866. Ordsprog. Onde ordsprog, som fordoerver Gode hoeder, *etc.* pp. [vi], 76.   12°. Kjøbenhavn, *Preusses*, 1739.

867. Ordsprogs-Bog. Ordsprogs-bog, *etc.* pp. 39.
                    sm. 8°. Kiøbenhavn, *Bing*, 1849.

868. Ottesen (M.). Deutsch-Dänisch, Norwegisch . . . Zweite Auflage, *etc.* pp. iv, 140.   16°. Berlin, *Goldschmidt*, n.d.
Pp. 136-138, einige Sprichwörter und Redensarten, *etc.*

869. Parleur. Der Franske parleur. *etc.*
                    sm. 8°. Kjovenhavn, 1827.
Gratet-Duplessis, 831. Pp. 243-297, Danish proverbs and idioms.

870. Pouch (L. Jensen). Problemata et proverbia moralia, *etc.* [By L. J. Pouch?].   [Copenhagen?], 1611.

871. Powell (Frederick York). The first nine books of the Danish history of Saxo Grammaticus. [Edited by] F. Y. Powell.
                    8°. London, *Nutt*, 1894.
Publications of the Folk-Lore Society, 33.   Introduction, pp. lxxxii-ix. Collection of old Danish proverbs in English, with references to the text of Saxo.   [F.-L.S.

872. Rasmussen (H. V.). Danske Ordsprog. Fjerde Oplag, *etc.*
pp. 27.   20 øre. 8°. Kjøbenhavn, *Gad*, 1869.
[B.M.

873. Smidth (Jens Hansen). Danske ordsprog og talemaader. . . .
Første hæfte. pp. 96.   8°. Odense, *Hempel*, 1822.
Arranged in alphabetical order, but only comprises A and B. With notes.
[B.M.

874. Sneedorff-Birch (Frederik). Tre hundrede og halvtredsind-
styve skjœmtsomme ordsprog, *etc.* pp. 92.
8°. Odense, *Miloske*, 1858.
350 proverbs with notes and a preliminary essay.   [B.M.

875. ———: Tretten Hundrede danske Ordsprog, *etc.* (Dansk
Ordsøiningslaere i Exempler . . . Første Hæfte). pp. 70.
12°. Kjøbenhavn, *Schubothe*, 1836.
1300 proverbs, with a few brief notes at the end.   [B.M.

876. Sternhagen (   ). Der kleine Däne . . . Zweite . . .
Auflage, *etc.* pp. xii, 359.
8°. Kopenhagen, *Niemeyer*, 1844.
Pp. 141-149, Einige Sprichwörter und Redensarten, welche in ihrem Aus-
drucke wesentlich vom deutschen abweichen.

877. Syv (Peder). Almindelige danske ordsproge, *etc.* 2 del.
8°. Kiøbenhafn, 1682, 1688.
Gratet-Duplessis, 827, gives the title : " Petit Syvii proverbia Danica " from
Nopitsch. The proverbs are arranged alphabetically by subjects. There is a
long introduction. Nopitsch says that Syv mentions in his preface a collection
of proverbs made by one Ludovicus Pouchius [? **870**].   [B.M.

878. ———: Peder Syvs kjernefulde Ordsprog, udsøgte og ord-
nede ved R. Nyerup. Med en fortale indeholdende bidrag
til danske ordsprogs litteratur. pp. xc, 259.
8°. Kjøbenhavn, *Cohen*, 1807.
[B.M.

879. Tode (Johann Clemens). Neue dänische Grammatik für
Deutsche. pp. 360.
8°. Kopenhagen, Leipzig, *Brummer*, 1797.
Another edition. pp. 368.
8°. Kopenhagen, Leipzig, *Brummer*, 1804.
Contains a selection of Danish proverbs with German translations.   [B.M.

880. Tuxen (Lauritz Regner). Det plattydske Folkesprog i Angel
tilligemed nogle sprogpröver. pp. [xii], 97.
8°. Kjöbenhavn, *Gyldendal*, 1857.
Pp. 68-72, Ordsprog og Mundhaeld.   [B.M.

881. Wigstroem (Eva). Folkdiktning, *etc.* 2 pts.
8°. Köbenhavn, Göteborg, *Schönberg*, 1880-81.
Pt. 1, pp. 294-299, Ordspråk och ordstäf. 120 entries.   [B.M.

882. Zepelin (Fritz de) and **Colleville** (de) *Vicomte.* Proverbes danois.   8°. Paris, 1892.

In La Tradition, Tome 6, pp. 53-57, 76-83, 121-128. 542 proverbs, translated into French. Also published separately, same date.   [B.M.

5. ICELANDIC.

883. Grettis Saga. [A review of the] Grettis Saga Asmundar sonar. Ed. R. C. Boer. (Altnordische Saga-Bibliothek, 8.) By F[rederick] Y[ork] P[owell].

8°. London, *Folk-Lore Society*, 1900.

In Folk-Lore, Vol. 11, pp. 410-412, proverbs from the saga, in English.
[F.-L.S.

884. Haldórsson (Björn). Lexicon Islandico-Latino-Danicum Björnonis Haldorsonii, *etc.* 2 vols.

4°. Havniae, *Schubothum*, 1814.

Gratet-Duplessis, 815. Contains a large number of Icelandic proverbs.
[B.M.

885. Jónsson (Fiornur). Oldislandske ordsprog og talemåder.

8°. Lund, 1914.

In Arkiv för nordiske filologi, Bd., 30 (N.F. 26), pp. 61-111, 170-217.
[U.C.L.

886. Jónsson (Guðmund). Safn af Islenzkum orðskiviðum, *etc.* pp. 423.   8°. Kaupmannahöfn, *Møller*, 1830.

A large alphabetical collection of Icelandic proverbs, maxims, adages, *etc.* The preface gives a brief bibliography.   [B.M.

887. Kaalund (Peder Erasmus Kristian). En islandsk ordsprogsamling fra 15de århundrede.

8°. København, *Møller*, 1884-91.

In Samfund til udgivelse af gammel nordisk litteratur, Publications 13, No. 7, pp. 131-184. A commentary followed by over 200 proverbs with notes. [B.M.

888. Meidinger (Heinrich). Dictionnaire étymologique et comparatif des langues teuto-gothiques . . . Traduit de l'allemand. pp. lxvi, 627.

la. 8°. Francfort-sur-le-Mein, *Meidinger*, 1833.

Vergleichendes etymologisches Wörterbuch der gothischteutonischen Mundarten. pp. xlvii, 572.

8°. Frankfurt am Main, *Meidinger*, 1833.

Second French edition. pp. lxvi, 627.

8°. Francfort s/M., *Meidinger*, 1836.

Gratet-Duplessis, 816. An extremely useful dictionary containing, at the end, Icelandic proverbs with translations, and a short list of Swedish proverbs and phrases, also with translations.   [B.M.

889. Moebius (Theodor). Malshattakvæði. Ein islandisches Gedicht des 13. Jahrhunderts, *etc.*   Halle, 1873.

889a. Poestion (Joseph Calasanz). Isländische Dichter der Neu-
zeit in Charakteristiken und übersetzten Proben ihrer Dichtung. pp. vii, 529.   M.28. la. 8°. Leipzig, 1897.
Contains a section on proverbs.

890. Schéving (Hallgrímur). Islenzskir málshættir safnadir, *etc.*
Videyar Klaustri, 1843.
Appendix. pp. 40.
          8. Reykjavík, *Reykjavikur Skóla*, 1847.
Proverbs in alphabetical order.   [B.M.

891. Vigfusson (Guðbranðr) and **Powell** (Frederick York). An
Icelandic proso reader, with notes, grammar, and glossary.
pp. viii, 559.   8°. Oxford, *Clarendon Press*, 1879.

Pp. 258-264, proverbs or sayings in Icelandic : pp. 432-433, notes (in English)
on the proverbs.   [U.C.L.

See also **816, 847.**

6. FAROE ISLES.

892. Hammershaimb (V. U.). Faerøsk anthologi. 2 pts.
          8°. København, *Møller*, 1891.
Part 1, pp. 314-321, 220 proverbs without notes or translations.   [B.M.

892a. ———: Faerøiske ordsprog. pp. 52.   la. 8°. 1851.

893. Jeaffreson (Joseph Russell). The Faröe Islands, *etc.* pp.
xiii, 272 + map and plates.
          8°. London, *Sampson Low*, 1898.
Pp. 103-105, a few Faröese proverbs translated into English.   [B.M.

FRENCH.

GENERAL.

894. Ægidius (Joannes), *Nucerinus.* Adagiorum Gallis vulgarium in . . . Latinae linguae versiculos traductio.

8°. Duaci, *apud C. Boscardum,* 1604.

Another edition. fol. 1606.

Another edition. 8°. [1610?].

Proverbes communs et belles sentences, pour familierement parler Latin et François à tout propos.

16°. Lyon, *Rigaud & Saugrain,* 1558.

Gratet-Duplessis, 232, ascribes this work to La Véprie, and calls Ægidius the translator. [B.M.

895. Ahn (Franz). Przewodnik praktyczny we francuzkiéj rozmowie potocznéj, *etc.* pp. 137.

8°. Lwów, *Stockmann,* 1850.

Pp. 134-137, French proverbs with Polish equivalents.

896. Albanese ( ). Les proverbes. Duo dialogue. ff. 3.

4°. La Haye, *Hummel,* n.d.

897. Alione (J. G.). Poésies françoises . . . composées de 1494 à 1520; publiées pour la première fois en France, *etc.* pp. 51, [118]. 8°. Paris, *Silvestre,* 1836.

Gratet-Duplessis, 233. In the following poems, Le Voyage et Conqueste de Charles huitiesme, *etc.*, and, La Conqueste de Loys douziesme, *etc.*, each verse is terminated by a proverb. [B.M.

898. Amory de Langerack (Joséphine). Les proverbes. Histoire anecdotique et morale des proverbes et dictons français. pp. 160. 8°. Lille, *Lefort,* 1860.

Second edition. pp. 168. 8°. Lille, *Lefort,* 1863.

There is a chapter on proverbs in general, followed by a list of them, with historical or explanatory notes. [B.M.

899. Arnoult (Stéphen). Proverbes anecdotiques. pp. 369.

8°. Paris, *Souverain,* 1835.

Bernstein, 125.

900. Backer (Georges de). Dictionnaire des proverbes françois
. . . par G. D. B.　　　　sm. 8°. Brusselles, *Backer*, 1710.

Gratet-Duplessis, 297. The initials G. D. B. probably indicate the Georges
de Backer who sold the book. Little more than an extract from the dictionaries
of the Académie Française, of Furetière, and of Trévoux. A list of proverbs
alphabetically arranged with brief explanations. Much better work of this
kind has been done since, but the book contains a few proverbs which are now
obsolete and difficult to find elsewhere.　　　　　　　　　　　[B.M.

901. Baecker (Louis de). De la religion du nord de la France.
avant le Christianisme. pp. xv, 353.
　　　　　　　　　　　　　　　　　　8°. Paris, *Didron*, 1854.

Pp. 269-279, proverbes populaires et croyances superstitieuses.　　[B.M.

902. Baïf (Jan Antoine de). Les mimes, enseignements et proverbes de Jan Antoine de Baïf, *etc.*
　　　　　　12°. Paris, *Patisson, chez Robert Estienne*, 1581.
Another edition.
　　　　　sm. 12°. Paris, *Patisson, chez Robert Estienne*, 1597.
Another edition. 2 tom.　　　12°. Paris, *Willem*, 1880.

Gratet Duplessis, 256. To be complete, the 1597 edition should include a
section entitled : Continuation des mimes, *etc.* Earlier editions are not considered as good as this. The work, divided into four books, consists of a series
of rhymed sestets in which the author has included most of the popular
proverbs and moral maxims of his day. Unfortunately they are distributed
without any order.　　　　　　　　　　　　　　　　　　　[B.M.

903. Barberi (J. Philippe). Petit trésor de la langue française et
de la langue italienne, *etc.* pp. 340.
　　　　　　　　　　　　　　　　　　8°. Paris, *Aillaud*, 1821.

Gratet-Duplessis, 455. Contains a considerable number of French and
Italian proverbs, of which the sense and the literal significance are clearly
explained.　　　　　　　　　　　　　　　　　　　　　　　[B.M.

904. Basset (　　). Explication morale des proverbes populaires
français, *etc.* pp. iv, 95.　　　　18°. Paris, *Colas*, 1826.

Gratet-Duplessis, 351. A book intended for children.

905. Belcour (G.). Selection of . . . French proverbs, *etc.* pp.
x, 51.　　　　　　　　　sm. 8°. London, *Stanford*, 1882.

Proverbs arranged alphabetically, followed by English equivalents. [B.M.

906. Belin (J. F.). Dictionnaire des proverbes, idiotismes, et
expressions figurées de la langue française, avec les proverbes allemands.　　　　　　8°. Penig, *Dienemann*, 1805.

Gratet-Duplessis, 335. An alphabetical list of proverbs. No notes.

907. Belleval (René de), *Marquis*. Nos pères, mœurs et coutumes
du temps passé. pp. v, 795.　　　8°. Paris, *Olmer*, 1879.

Pp. 782-788, explanation of several proverbs.

908. Bellingen (Fleury de). Premiers essais de proverbes.

La Haye, 1653.

Another edition. L'étymologie ou explication des proverbes françois, *etc.* pp. [viii], 363, 18.

sm. 8°. La Haye, *Vlacq*, 1656.

Gratet-Duplessis, 282 and 286, *q.v.* for more details. The first edition is very incomplete, the second contains 400 proverbs. The author was particularly concerned with those proverbs which have a historical interest, and some of his notes are very curious. The book had a great success, as is witnessed by the fact that a plagiarism was issued anonymously in Paris in 1665. This book, " Illustres proverbes," *q.v.*, **1001,** is a copy of Bellingen's work with some of the names changed. [B.M.

909. Benserade (Isaac de). Oeuvres, *etc.* 2 vols.

12°. Paris, *Tallemant*, 1697.

Another edition. 2 tom. 8°. Paris, *Sercy*, 1698.

Gratet-Duplessis, 279. Contains a " Ballet des proverbes, dansé per le Roy, *etc.*" This singular composition obtained a certain success at a time when allegorical ballets were very fashionable. It was also inserted at the end of an edition of the Illustres Proverbes, *q.v.*, **1001.** It was also printed separately, 4°, Paris, [*Ballard*], 1654. pp. 10. [B.M.

910. Billandeau (A. G.). Recueil des proverbes et dictons français traduits en anglais. 1903.

911. Billet (Pedro Pablo). Gramatica francesa, *etc.* pp. [xxiv], 320. sm. 8°. Madrid, *Anisson*, 1688.

Gratet-Duplessis, 504. A French grammar for the use of Spaniards. It contains a section of parallel sayings, amongst which are a number of proverbs, in both languages.

912. Bonafont (C. Ph.). Sammlung der französischen Redens-arten : Gallicismen und Sprichwörter, *etc.* pp. iv, 276.

8°. Berlin, 1831.

Sammlung französischer Redensarten . . . Nach Bonafont . . . Mit einer Sammlung technischer Ausdrücke. Vermehrte Ausgabe. Von G. F. Burguy. pp. ix, 278.

8°. Berlin, *Schneider*, 1859.

913. Bonaspes (Nicolaus). Proverbia cōmunia [written in Latin by N. B.] tā gallico : latino. atq3 teuthonica sermone noviter impssa, *etc.*

8°. Gebeñ [Geneva], *Vuygandus Koln*, [1525?].

Another edition.

8°. Lugduni, *Apud Claudium nourry : alias Le prince,*

[1525?].

Earlier edition.

8°. Parisiis, *Per Joannem Merausse*, [1514?].

Earlier edition.

8°. Paris, *M. Nicolle de la Barre*, [1510?].

Gratet-Duplessis, 232, considers J. de la Véprie as the collector and Bonaspes as an editor. [B.M.

914. Bontemps (Gerard). Nouveau recueil de pièces comiques, *etc.* [Anonymous]. pp. [vi], 251 [=351].

12°. Paris, Loyson, 1661.

Le facecieux, drolifique et comique reveil-matin, *etc.* [Anonymous]. pp. 376.   12°. Vaudemont, *Tapage*, 1715.

Another edition. La galerie des curieux. pp. vii, 232.

12°. Nice, Gay, 1873.

Gratet-Duplessis, 299. Reproductions of the " Gallerie des Curieux," par Gerard Bontemps, 8°, Paris, 1646, of which there are other editions. It contains two " Lettres des proverbes." Several such letters in proverbs, in various languages, are included in Howell's Paremiographia.   [B.M.

915. Bouchet (Emile). Maximes et proverbes tirés des chansons de geste. pp. 52.   8°. Orléans, 1893.

Separate publication of an article in Mémoires de la Société d'Agriculture, Sciences, Belles-lettres et Arts d'Orléans, Tome 31, pp. 81-130.   [B.M.

916. ———: Les proverbes dans l'épopée française.

8°. Paris, Lechevalier, 1894.

In Revue des traditions populaires, Tome 9, pp. 384-391.   [B.M.

917. Bouelles (Charles de). Caroli Bovilli Samarobrini proverbiorum vulgarium libri tres. ff. [12], 171.

sm. 8°. Parisiis, Pratensi et Roigny, 1531.

Gratet-Duplessis, 243. A rare and little-known work frequently taken for a collection of Latin proverbs, but although written in Latin it is particularly devoted to proverbial sayings used in France at the beginning of the 16th century. It contains in all 650 proverbs given also in French, though the explanations are in Latin. Duplessis quotes two brief extracts.   [B.M.

918. ———: Proverbes et dicts sententieux, avec l'interprétation d'iceux. pp. [iv, 52].

sm. 8°. Paris, Guillaume-le-Noir, 1557.

Gratet-Duplessis, p. 147 and No. 249. This is not a French translation of the preceding Latin work. It is a collection of moral maxims in French and Latin, frequently in verse, with brief explanations in French. Few of these maxims can be considered as proverbs, and none of them have been taken from the Latin collection. Duplessis thinks this book is not the work of Charles de Bouelles at all.

919. Bourdonné (Charles). Origines des proverbes français. pp. 64.   32°. Paris?, *Garnier*, 1829.

Another edition. pp. 216.   12°. Paris, [1834].

Gratet-Duplessis, 355. A book containing many faults.

920. Boutroux (L. A.). Le bouquet proverbial, ou réunion complète de tous les proverbes français, mis en chanson. pp. 9.

8°. Paris, chez les Marchands de Nouveautés, n.d.

Gratet-Duplessis, 334. A rare song composed of fifty stanzas. La Mesangère quotes two of these.

921. Boyer (Abel). The compleat French master . . . containing
. . . a collection of choice proverbs, both French and English,
etc. pp. [xiv], 255, 126. 8°. London, *Salusbury*, 1694.
Fourteenth edition. pp. 416. sm. 8°. London, 1744.
Another edition. A new French grammar, *etc.* pp. 207, 227.
8°. Rotterdam, *Beman*, 1748.
The edition of 1694 contains 50 proverbs in French and English; that of
1748 has a list of 121. [B.M.

922. Brandt (   ), *called Grierin.* Phraséologie, ou recueil de
Gallicismes, *etc.* pp. viii, 264.
8°. Berlin, Potsdam, *Stuhr*, 1842.
Gratet-Duplessis, 365. A list of French sayings with German translations.
The selection of proverbs is not very large. Elementary, and has no philo-
logical importance.

923. Bugnin (Jacques de). Le congie pris du siècle seculier.
ff. 22. sm. 4°. Vienne, *Schenck*, [1490?].
Another edition. ff. 24. 8°. [Lyon?, *Mareschal?*, 1490?].
Another edition. pp. 93.
8°. Neuchatel, *Université de Neuchatel,*
Faculté de Lettres, 1916.
Gratet-Duplessis, 235. A moral treatise in verse, composed of a number of
maxims more or less proverbial. Very rare. The introduction to the 1916
edition gives the British Museum, or Lyons copy, as being published *c.* 1495.
[B.M.

924. Burdet (   ), *Abbé.* Mazimas è proverbiis. 1860.
In Bulletin de la Société d'Agriculture, Sciences et Arts de la Lozère, 1860.

925. Caillot (Antoine). Nouveau dictionnaire proverbial, satirique
et burlesque, *etc.* pp. x, 538. 12°. Paris, *Dauvin*, 1826.
Second edition. pp. x, 538. 8°. Paris, 1829.
Gratet-Duplessis, 350. A very poor collection, without interest or importance.
[B.M.

926. Canel (Alfred). Recherches sur les jeux d'esprit, *etc.*
2 tom. 8°. Evreux, *Herissey*, 1867.
Tome 2, pp. 296-314, rhymed proverbs. [B.M.

927. Catalan (Etienne). Rime et raison ou proverbes, apoph-
thegmes, épigrammes et moralités proverbiales choisis et mis
en vers. pp. 75. 12°. Paris, *Librairie Internationale*, 1864.

928. Cato (Dionysius). Les mots dorés de Cathon en françois
et en latin, avec bons et utiles enseignemens, proverbes, *etc.*
8°. Paris, *Jehan Longis*, [n.d., but privilege dated 1530].
Another edition. 8°. Paris, *Nicholas Bonfons*, 1577.
Gratet-Duplessis, 242. Although the distiches of Cato have not been included
in the Latin section of this bibliography, they are mentioned here since the
French editions contain numerous other proverbs, sayings, *etc.* This collection
is quite different from, and less interesting than, another entitled :
Le second volume des motz dorés du grand et saige Cathon, *etc.*
8°. [n.d., but privilege dated 1533].
Full details of both these collections, with brief extracts, are given by Duplessis.
[B.M.

929. Cent Nouveaulx Proverbes. Les cent nouveaulx proverbes dorez. pp. [32].   16°. [Lyon], *Chaussard*, n.d.
Another edition.   sm. 4°. Paris, n.d.

Gratet-Duplessis, 238. Not a collection of popular proverbs, but a poem of a hundred verses of seven lines each, containing a good selection of moral maxims and useful precepts, but nothing which can really be called a proverb. The work is sometimes attributed to Gringore, but Duplessis considers this more than doubtful. The latter quotes several verses.

930. Chabod (Octave). Les proverbes français les plus usités et leurs formes italiennes correspondantes. pp. 198.
8°. Rieti, *Trinchi*, 1893.

931. Chambaud (Louis). The idioms of the French and English languages, *etc.* pp. iv, 258.   8°. London, *Nourse*, 1751.
Another edition. pp. 262.   8°. London, *Symonds*, 1793.

Concludes with a large selection of French proverbs, maxims, *etc.*, with English equivalents or translations, followed by English proverbs with French explanations and equivalents.   [B.M.

932. ———: Le trésor de la langue françoise et angloise.
8°. La Haye, *Van Cleef*, 1799.
The treasure of the French and English languages, *etc.*
2/6. 8°. London, *Vaillant*, 1786.
Another edition. pp. vi, 274.   8°. London, *Baldwin*, 1806.

Gratet-Duplessis, 332. Contains a large collection of French proverbs translated into English, but with no explanations and consequently unimportant. An edition of 1750 does not contain any proverbs, in that of 1806 there is a considerable number of them in French and English.   [B.M.

933. Chantreau (Pedro Nicolas). Arte de hablar bien Frances. . . . Nueva edición, *etc.* pp. 468.
8°. Perpiñan, *Alzine*, 1824.

Pp. 395-401, proverbios, refranes y dichos que se corresponden en ambas lenguas.

934. Codrescu (Teodor). Dialoguri francesco-romanesci, *etc.* pp. 174.   8°. Iasii, *tip. Buciumului Român*, 1851.

Pp. 156-174, idiotismes et proverbes.

935. Collection. Collection de proverbes, dictons et adages de la langue française . . . traduits en hollandais, *etc.* pp. iii, 214, xvi.   8°. Zutphen, *Someren*, 1858.

The preface is signed : De bewerker van Prof. Bischoff's " Fransche Spraakwendingen."   [B.M.

936. Collin de Plancy (Jacques Albert Simon). Dictionnaire féodal, *etc.* 2 tom.   8°. Paris, *Foulon*, 1819.

Tome 2, pp. 191-200, proverbes féodaux. Gives the origin and explanation of various French proverbs concerning feudal customs.   [B.M.

937. Comédie. La comédie des proverbes, pièce comique. pp. [xii], 164. 8°. Paris, *Targa*, 1633.

Another edition. pp. 111. 12°. Paris, *Pepingué*, 1665.

Gratet-Duplessis, 280, speaks, without details, of various editions, some earlier. Two Dutch ones (La Haye, 1654, 1655) form part of the Elzevirian collection. The author has included a very large number of popular proverbs current at the time. Sometimes attributed to Adrien de Montluc, Comte de Cramail. [B.M.

938. Corrozet (Gilles). La fleur des sentences certaines . . . enrichie de figures et de sommaire françois et italiens, propres a chacune sentence. 16°. Lyon, *De la Ville*, 1548 and 1549.

Gratet-Duplessis, 247.

939. ——: Hecatongraphie, *etc.* [Illustrated]. pp. [208]. 8°. Paris, *Janot*, 1541.

Another edition. pp. xxi, 213.

sm. 4°. [Paris], *Champion*, 1905.

Gratet-Duplessis, 244. The editions of 1541 and 1543 (*Groulleau*) are exactly the same; that of 1548 has the same illustrations without the borders, *etc.*, which were suppressed because of the format. This book contains a selection of well-chosen moral emblems, first briefly indicated, and then developed and explained in verse. There are, however, few true proverbs. [B.M.

940. Coursier (Edouard). Manuel de la conversation française et allemande, *etc.* pp. xviii, 422.

12°. Stuttgart, *Neff*, 1835.

Twenty-fourth edition. pp. xxiv, 504.

8°. Stuttgart, *Neff*, 1885.

Bernstein, 693. There is a section of French and German proverbs.

941. Crapelet (Georges Adrien). Proverbes et dictons populaires, avec les dits du mercier et des marchands, et les crieries de Paris, aux xiiie et xive siècles, publiés d'après les manuscrits de la Bibliothèque du Roi, par G.-A. Crapelet. pp. iv, 205.

la. 8°. Paris, *Crapelet*, 1831.

Gratet-Duplessis, 228. Contains amongst other things, 1) *Proverbes et dictons populaires au xiiie siècle.* This is not a commentary, but a list of proverbs found in various mss. characterising various people or places. In the original manuscripts these are not accompanied by notes, but Crapelet has added explanations.

5) *Les proverbes au Conte de Bretaigne.* These are a particular version of a proverbial poem " Les proverbes au Vilain " which was very celebrated in the 12th and 13th centuries and of which there are a number of manuscripts in the Bibliothèque du Roi (Nationale). Le Roux de Lincy in the introduction of his " Livre des proverbes français," *q.v.*, **1035,** describes several of these manuscripts, and in the appendix to Vol. 2 gives a long extract from these " proverbes au vilain," transcribed from a manuscript at Oxford. This latter version is much more interesting than the " Proverbes au Conte de Bretaigne."

6) *Les proverbes de Marcoul et de Salemons.* This is a poem of the same kind as the preceding one. It is an imaginary dialogue between Solomon and

H

a peasant, in which are included all kinds of popular sayings. There are many
widely different versions; besides the one given by Crapelet, there is another
published in Vol. 1, pp. 416-436, of Meon's " Nouveau recueil de fabliaux et
contes," 2 vols., 8°, Paris, 1823. It is difficult to give either the original date
or language of this peculiar piece; there are various Latin and German
editions of the 15th and 16th centuries. The Bertoldo series of G. C. Croce,
q.v., **2216,** are only a paraphrased imitation of this, though written in prose
and differing from it a good deal. [B.M.

942. D***, *Madame.* La bonne petite souris. Conte par Madame
D***; suivi des proverbes français. pp. 35.
16°. Troyes, *Garnier,* n.d.

Pp. 31-35, proverbes français dont on peut se servir.

943. Daelke (W.). Sammlung von französischen Sprichwörtern
und Redensarten, *etc.* pp. viii, 135. 8°. Berlin, 1854.

Stirling-Maxwell, p. 18.

944. Debonale (S.). Neue französische Grammatik für Schulen
. . . Sechste . . . Auflage. pp. xvi, 496.
8°. Hamburg, *verlegt von dem Verfasser,* 1810.

Pp. 471-473, proverbes.

945. Decotter (N.). Les proverbes français expliqués, avec leurs
équivalents en anglais—augmentés parfois de proverbes
créoles, *etc.* pp. 307. 4°. Maurice, *Esclapon,* 1920.

Arranged alphabetically by the principal words. [B.M.

946. Delamothe (G.). The French alphabet. . . . Together with
the treasure of the French tongue, *etc.* 2 pts.
8°. London, *Luke Fawne,* 1633.

Another edition. 2 pts. 8°. London, *Tho. Underhill,* 1647.

Part 2 contains a large collection of French proverbs, maxims, *etc.*, with
English equivalents or translations. [B.M.

947. Delinotte (L. Paul) and **Nolen** (Th.). Dictionnaire des
idiotismes . . . proverbes et expressions proverbiales . . . de
la langue hollandaise et de la langue française. . . . Hollan-
dais-Français. pp. 312.
8°. Amsterdam, *Maatschappy " Elsevier,"* 1891.

Dictionnaire des idiotismes . . . Français-hollandais. pp. 390.
8°. Amsterdam, 1892.
[B.M. (Pt. 1).

948. Demarteau (Servais). Le roman des proverbes en action.
Recueil de 6500 proverbes, *etc.* 2 tom.
8°. Paris, *Didier, Perrin,* [1890].

949. Denoix (V.). Recueil des gallicismes et des proverbes
français les plus usités, *etc.* pp. 176.
8°. Warszawa, *Ksiegarza,* 1859.

950. Derasmasl ( ). Proverbes et mots fantaisistes.
Paris, 1883.

951. Dict. Le dict des pays ioyeux avec les conditions des femmes, *etc.* pp. [8]. sm. 8°. [Paris?], *Leber*, [1520?].

Gratet-Duplessis, 244. Brunet gives another edition, very similar but without the " dix commandements." The " Dit des pays ioyeulx " was also printed in a " Recueil d'anciennes poèsies françaises," which bears the date 1597, but which is thought to be much more recent. This curious little poem is a collection of proverbial sayings dealing with various towns and countries and the industries and productions for which they were famed in the 16th century. It is reprinted by Duplessis. It is also reprinted by Montaiglon in Tome 5 of his " Recueil de poèsies françoises des xv⁰ et xvi⁰ siècles." [B.M.

952. Dictionnaire. Dictionnaire des Halles, *etc.*
sm. 12°. Bruxelles, *Foppens*, 1696.

Gratet-Duplessis, 293. A very rare book which is, however, only an extract from the first edition of the dictionary of the Académie Française. In it are collected a number of proverbs and sayings which were scattered throughout the large dictionary. Some of the sayings have been excluded from successive editions of the Dictionnaire de l'Académie Française. This book has been attributed to one Artaud.

953. ———: Dictionnaire des proverbes français et des façons de parler avec explication allemande, latine, et polonaise, *etc.* 2 vols. [in 1]. 8°. Warszawie, *Dufour*, 1782.

Stirling-Maxwell, p. 21.

954. ———: Dictionnaire du bas-langage, *etc.* 2 vols.
8°. Paris, *Colin*, 1808.

Gratet-Duplessis, 336. A dictionary containing a number of common sayings, including proverbs, which should not be used in polite conversation. Generally attributed to d'Hautel. [B.M.

955. ———: Dictionnaire étymologique, historique et anecdotique des proverbes et des locutions proverbiales de la langue française en rapport avec des proverbes des autres langues. pp. iv, 284. [Illustrated]. 8°. Bruxelles, *Duprez-Parent*, 1850.

Stirling-Maxwell, p. 21.

956. ———: Dictionnaire portatif des proverbes français. . . . Quatrième édition. pp. 416.
8°. Amsterdam, *Wetstein*, 1751.
[L.L.

957. ———: Le grand dictionnaire françois-latin, *etc.*
4°. [Geneva?], *Stoer*, 1606.
Another edition. 4°. Rouen, *Behourt*, 1628.
Both these editions contain an " Essay des proverbes," *etc.*, a good list of French proverbs with Latin translations. [B.M.

958. ———: Le nouveau petit dictionnaire, avec des entretiens en français et en flamand. 12°. Gand, *Goesin*, 1794.
Gratet-Duplessis, 328. Pp. 24-26, proverbes communs.

959. Dicts. Les dicts et sentences notables de divers auteurs, traduits en françois et mis par ordre alphabétique.
16°. Paris, 1560.
Gratet-Duplessis, 250. Brunet, Manuel du libraire, Vol. 2, p. 111.

960. Dorn (L. C.). Recueil de phrases, sentences et proverbes
français, *etc.* pp. 261.   8°. Nuremberg, 1857.
Bernstein, 891.

961. Dubois (   ). Dictionnaire des proverbes françois.
                                             Amsterdam, 1728.
Gratet-Duplessis, 302. Mentioned in the foreword to Panckoucke's "Dictionnaire des proverbes," 8°, Paris, 1749.

962. Dubor (Georges de). Nos vieux proverbes.
                                             8°. Paris, 1898.
In La Nouvelle Revue, Tome 115, pp. 134-138. A selection of proverbs
taken from Gruter's "Florilegium ethico-politicum," *q.v.*, **80.**   [B.M.

963. Duez (Nathanaël). Le vray et parfait guidon de la langue
françoise, *etc.*

sm. 8°.   Leyden, *Bonaventure et Abraham Elzevir*, 1643.
Another edition. pp. 848.   8°. Leyden, *Elsevier*, 1657.
Another edition. pp. [xii], 834.
                    sm. 8°. Amsterdam, *Daniel Elsevier*, 1669.
Gratet-Duplessis, 276. A French grammar for the use of Germans. Pp.
741-834, a collection of proverbs, sayings, *etc.*, some of which are expressed
in an ancient form which is not found to-day. Each proverb is translated into
German.   [B.M. (1657 edition).

Duplessis (Pierre Alexandre Gratet-). *See* Gratet-Duplessis.

964. Dupuis (Eudoxie). Vieux proverbes sur de nouveaux airs,
etc. pp. 63. [Illustrated].   4°. Paris, *Delagrave*, n.d.
Bernstein, 929.

965. E. (A. d'). Recueil de proverbes français et italiens, traduits
dans les deux langues, par A. d'E.
                    fr.2. 18°. Paris, *Henry*, 1864.
Another edition. pp. 111.   8°. Paris, *Henry*, 1872.

966. Ebert (Emil). Die Sprichwörter der altfranzösischen
Karlsagen, *etc.* pp. 52.   8°. Marburg, *Elwert*, 1884.
Pt. 23 of Stengel's Ausgaben und Abhandlungen . . . der romanischen
Philologie. Proverbs, *etc.*, from the chansons de geste, the origin indicated
in each case.   [B.M.

967. Estienne (Henri). Les premices, ou le premier livre des
proverbes epigrammatizez ou des epigrammes proverbializez,
etc. pp. [xvi], 207.   sm. 8°. [Paris?], 1594.
Gratet-Duplessis, 255. A selection of proverbs turned into epigrams. The
verse is mediocre, but there are interesting notes and comments. Very rare.
The British Museum gives the place of publication as probably Geneva. [B.M.

968. —— : Proiect du livre intitulé: De la precellence du langage françois. pp. [xxxii], 295.
                    sm. 8°. Paris, *Patisson*, 1579.
Gratet-Duplessis, 253. Pp. 161-201, recherches critiques et éclaircissements
sur quelques anciens proverbes françois. Contains much curious and interesting
information.   [B.M.

969. Fehse (Erich). Sprichwort und Sentenz bei Eustache Deschamps und Dichtern seiner Zeit. 8°. Erlangen, 1905.

In Romanische Forschungen, Bd. 19, pp. 545-594. [B.M.

970. Ferry (Dionysius). Pharos, *etc.* pp. 324.
8°. Prague, *Authoris expensis, Typis Danielis Michaeleck,*
Pp. 276-307, 626 proverbs. **1682.**

971. Fitzgerald (K.). Proverbs in French and English, *etc.* pp. 143. 32°. London, *Hill,* [1920].
Bi-Lingual Series. Corresponding proverbs, no notes. [B.M.

972. Fleuriot ( ). Recueil de proverbes français. Auswahl französischer Sprichwörter, mit deutscher Uebersetzung und Erklärung. Breslau, 1885.

973. Fries (J. G.). Proverbes et phrases proverbiales en françois et en allemand. pp. 136.
sm. 8°. Oldenburg, *etc., Saint-Jorre,* 1844.
Gratet-Duplessis, 370. Of no real importance.

974. Friesland (Carl). Französische Sprichwörter-Bibliographie. Verzeichnis der seit 1847 erschienenen Sammlungen französischer Sprichwörter. 8°. Berlin, *etc., Gronau,* 1905.
In Zeitschrift für französische Sprache und Litteratur, Bd. 28, pp. 260-287. An enlarged and improved form of two similar articles in the same periodical, Bd. 18, pp. 221-237, and Bd. 19, pp. 122-123. An excellent bibliography, containing 498 entries, of French proverbs since Duplessis. The entries are extremely brief and there are no notes, but it is a very comprehensive list, including articles from periodicals. [U.C.L.

975. ———: Zwei französische Sprichwörter. (Des Papstes Mauleselin—Die Gesandschaft von Biaron).
8°. Berlin, *Gronau,* 1896.
In Zeitschrift für französische Sprache und Litteratur, Bd. 18, pp. 238-241. [U.C.L.

976. Frisch (Johann L.). Compendium französischer Sprichwörter.
Gratet-Duplessis, 333.

977. Furetière (Antoine). Nouveau recueil des factums, *etc.* 2 vols. 12°. Amsterdam, *Desbordes,* 1694.
Another edition. 2 tom.
8°. Paris, *Poulet-Malassis et de Brode,* 1859.
Gratet-Duplessis, 292. Vol. 1 (1694), pp. 402-448, remarques sur quelques proverbes français. There are other editions of the " Factums," but this is the most complete. Furetière also made further researches on proverbs, which were first published in his " Essai d'un dictionnaire universel," 12°, Amsterdam, 1687, then in the different editions of the dictionary itself. This was soon superseded by the " Dictionnaire de Trévoux," whose first edition (1704), however, was little more than a reprint of Furetière's dictionary. The best edition :

Dictionnaire universel françois et latin, vulgairement appelé Dictionnaire de Trévoux. 8 vols. fol. Paris, 1771.
[B.M.

978. Gaidoz (Henri) and **Sébillot** (Paul Yves). Blason populaire de la France. pp. xv, 382. fr.3.50. 8°. Paris, *Cerf*, 1884.

A collection of proverbs, sayings, phrases, *etc.*, in different languages concerning France and the French. Pts. 4 and 5 deal with other French-speaking countries. Pt. 6 gives sayings dealing with the national characteristics of other countries. There is a useful list of sources at the end of each section. [B.M.

979. Garnier (Philippe). Thesaurus adagiorum Gallico-Latinorum, *etc.* pp. [xxiv], 790 [48].
    12°. Francofurti, *Sumptibus Dominici Custodi Bibliopol,* 1612.

Another edition.   12°. Francofurti, 1635.

Gratet-Duplessis, 261.   [B.M.

980. Geist. Geist der französischen Sprache, oder Sammlung von Idiotismen, Sprüchwörtern, Redensarten, *etc.*
    8°. Leipzig, *Reinicke*, 1796.

Gratet-Duplessis, 331.

981. Génie. Le génie de la langue française, ou recueil de 3200 proverbes et phrases proverbiales, avec la traduction allemande, *etc.* pp. vi, 180.   8°. Tübingen, *Osiander*, 1843.

Presumably the same as Gratet-Duplessis, 368 : Genius der französischen Sprache, *etc.*

982. Genin (François). Récréations philologiques, *etc.* 2 tom.
    8°. Paris, *Chameriot*, 1856.

Tome 2, pp. 233-252, French proverbs and sayings taken from the " Refranes " of Nuñez.   [B.M.

983. Gerbel (Nikolaus). Nationale Sprüchwörter der Franzosen.
    4°. Augsburg, 1870-71.

In Das Ausland, Jahrgang 43, Jahrgang 44, pp. 93-95, 226-229. A general study of the subject, with examples.   [B.M.

984. Giovanetti (M.). Raccolta di proverbi e frasi francesi unite alle loro corrispondenti italiane, *etc.*
    8°. Firenze, *Petrignani*, 1810.

985. Gottsched (   ). Grammaire allemande.
    8°. Strasbourg, *Koenig*, 1794.

Another edition.   8°. Strasbourg, 1800.

Gratet-Duplessis, 330. Contains French and German proverbs.

986. Grandjean (Louis Marius Eugène). Dictionnaire de locutions proverbiales, *etc.* 2 tom.
    8°. Toulon, *Municipalité de Toulon*, 1899.
    [B.M.

987. Gratet-Duplessis (Pierre Alexandre). La fleur des proverbes français, *etc.* pp. 696.   fr.2. 32°. Paris, *Passard*, 1853.

Another edition. pp. iii, 632.   32°. Paris, 1853.

About 800 proverbs are given, with comments.   [B.M.

988. Gratet-Duplessis (Pierre Alexandre). Petite encyclopédie des proverbes français . . . par Hilaire Le Gai [*pseud.* of Gratet-Duplessis]. pp. 504.

16°. Paris, *Passard*, 1860.

Reviewed in the Quarterly Review, 125, pp. 217-254.   [L.L.

989. ———: Recueil de proverbes français . . . par M. Desciseaux [*pseud.* of Gratet-Duplessis]. pp. 252.

fr.1. 16°. Paris, *Delarue*, [1864].

A collection of proverbs with explanatory notes, arranged alphabetically by key-words.   [B.M.

990. Gringore (Pierre), *dit Vaudemont. Begin:* Cy commencent les dictz et auctoritez des saiges philosophes. [Attributed to Gringoire]. pp. [16].   sm. 4°. [Lyons?, 1487?].

Gratet-Duplessis, 234. A series of quatrains containing a selection of moral maxims amongst which are a few rhymed proverbs. Very rare. [B.M.

991. ———: Notables enseignemens, adages et proverbes, *etc.*

sm. 8°. Paris, [1527].

Another edition.   8°. Lyon, n.d.

Gratet-Duplessis, 239, gives details of five other editions : that of 1528 (Paris, *Galliot*) is the most complete. One of the best and most complete collections of proverbs in use in France at that period. Duplessis reprints an 8-lined poem from it.   [B.M.

992. Gruesing (Johanna). Maximes, sentences, proverbes, etc., recueillis pour ses écolières par Johanna Grüsing. pp. 63.

16°. Nuremberg, *Korn*, n.d.

Pp. 21-63, proverbes.

993. Guichard (   ). Le danger des proverbes nationaux, conte [en vers].   12°. Paris, *Lacombe*, 1772

In La Mercure de France, avril, 1772, Vol. 1, pp. 35-37, and reprinted in the " Recueil des poésies " of the same author. Gratet-Duplessis, 318. Hécart, Bibliographie parémiologique, p. 44.   [B.M.

994. Gunzer (Simon). Dictionnaire des Gallicismes, proverbes et locutions familières de la langue française.

8°. Francfort, 1830.

Gratet-Duplessis, 358.

995. Hamel (Nicolas). A new universal French grammar. pp. vii, 284.   8°. London, *Evans*, 1796.

Another edition. pp. 392.   8°. London, *Bateman*, 1855.

Contains a brief list of French proverbs with English equivalents.   [B.M.

996. Hezel (Wilhelm Friedrich). Die Kunst, auf die möglichst geschwindeste Art französisch sprechen und schreiben zu lernen, *etc.* 4 pts.   8°. Giessen, *Mercure françois*, 1800.

Pt. 1, pp. 210-232, Sprüchwörter, Sentenzen und Maximen. 209 French proverbs with German equivalents.

997. Hezel (Wilhelm Friedrich). Die Kunst . . . oder, neues französisches Elementarwerk, *etc.* 3 pts. 8°. Giessen, 1800.

Pt. 1, 210-232.   200 French proverbs, maxims, *etc.*, with German equivalents.

998. Hircel (Kasper). Francuzka grammatyka, *etc.* pp. vi, 494.
8°. Lwów, 1840.

Another edition. pp. [vi], 652 + map.   8°. Lwów, 1849.

Contains three pages of French proverbs in the original.

999. Hofstetter (Johann Baptist). Analytisch theoretisch-practisches Lehrbuch, *etc.* pp. 183.   8°. Wien, *Grund*, 1837.

Pp. 119-138, proverbes et gallicismes.

1000. Homann (   ). Beiträge zur Kenntnis des Wortschatzes der altfranzösischen Sprichwörter.   Greifswald, 1900.

1001. Illustres Proverbes. Les illustres proverbes nouveaux et historiques, *etc.* [Anon.]   12°. Paris, *David*, 1655.

Another edition. 2 vols.   12°. Paris, *Guignard*, 1665.

Gratet-Duplessis, 286.   This work is a plagiarism of the "Étymologie" of Fleury de Bellingen, *q.v.* **908.**   [B.M.

1002. J. (A.), *amateur.* Le véritable Sancho-Panza, ou choix de proverbes, dictons, adages, *etc.* pp. 240.
fr.1. 8°. Paris, *Hachette*, 1856.

Proverbs arranged in tens under subject headings.   No notes.   [B.M.

1003. Jannet (P.) *and others.* Bibliotheca scatologica . . . par trois savants en us [P. Jannet, J. F. Payen, A. A. Veinant]. pp. xxxi, 143.   8°. Scatopolis, 5850 [=Paris, 1849].

Complément du Journal de l'amateur de livres, Tome 2.   Pp. 105-120, Memento scatoparémiologique, catalogue de sentences, proverbes, dictons, *etc.*
[B.M.

1004. Jeanrenaud (Edelbert). Recueil français pratique. . . . Alphabetical collection of phrases, idioms and proverbs in French and English. pp. 105.   12°. New York, 1875.

1005. Jeanroy (A.). Locutions populaires ou proverbiales.
8°. Paris, *Bouillon*, 1894.

In Romania, Tome 23, pp. 232-242.   [B.M.

1006. Jełowicki (Stanisław). Dykcyonarz przysłowiów francuzkich, *etc.* 2 tom.
8°. Warszawa i Krzemieniec, *Glücksberg*, 1825.

1007. Joubert (Joseph). Dictionnaire françois et latin, *etc.* pp. 1318, lv.   4°. Lyon, *Claustre*, 1710.

Another edition.   4°. Lyon, 1738.

Gratet-Duplessis, 301.   Contains a special vocabulary, with its own pagination, entitled : " Façons de parler proverbiales," *etc.*   Not to be found in all editions of Joubert's dictionary, though it is in those given above, and in that of Lyon, 1725.   It contains a number of proverbs and phrases which are not to be found elsewhere.   [B.M.

1008. Jubinal (Achille). Nouveau recueil de contes, dits, fabliaux . . . des xiiie, xive et xve siècles, *etc.* 2 tom.
8°. Paris, *Panier,* 1839-42.

Tom. 2, pp. 372-376, dictons et proverbes. The first piece is another version of the " Trente-deux folies," printed in Halliwell and Wright's " Reliquae Antiquae." All are taken from mss. in the British Museum. [B.M.

1009. Kadler (Alfred). Sprichwörter und Sentenzen der alt-französischen Artus- und Abenteuerromane, *etc.* pp. 106.
8°. Marburg, *Elwert,* 1886.

Stengel's Ausgaben und Abhandlungen . . . der romanischen Philologie, 49. [U.C.L.

1010. Kaiser (Gustav). Grammatische Bemerkungen zu franzö-sischen Sprichwörtern, sprichwörtlichen und familiären Redensarten. 4°. Köln, *Bachem,* 1874.

In Programm des Kaiser-Wilhelm-Gymnasium zu Cöln, 1873-74, pp. 3-23.

1011. Kloepper (C.). Beiträge zur Kenntnis der französischen Spruchdichtung. pp. 48.
8°. Dresden, Leipzig, *Kock,* 1905.

Neusprachliche Abhandlungen, *etc.,* Heft 14. Deals less with actual proverbs than with well-known quotations, maxims, mottoes, sayings, *etc.* [B.M.

1012. Kreibich (Johann). Die französischen Sprichwörter als Musterbeispiele für syntaktische Regeln.
8°. Prossnitz, 1895.

In 20. Jahres-Bericht der deutschen Landes-Oberrealschule zu Prossnitz, pp. 1-26.

1013. Kritzinger (Christian Wilhelm). Nouveau dictionnaire des proverbes françois-allemand, *etc.* pp. 732 + [392].
4°. Leipzig, *Richter,* 1742.

Gratet-Duplessis, 311 and 624. [London Library.

1014. Kuehne (Elsbeth). Proverbes à l'usage des familles et des écoles. pp. vi, 115. 8°. Wolfenbüttel, *Zwissler,* [1883?].

1015. Kuhff (Ph.). La France populaire. Rimes et dictons pour petits et grands. pp. iv, 151. 12°. Paris, 1878.

1016. L. (E.). La maison des jeux académiques, *etc.* pp. [viii], 300. 8°. Paris, *Loysons,* 1668.

Dedication signed " E. L." Pp. 230-235, le jeu des proverbes par personnages.

1017. Lagarde (Jules). Les proverbes. Chansons. pp. 208.
8°. Paris, *Lebailly,* 1865.

A selection of songs written round, and containing, various proverbs. [B.M.

1018. La Grue (Philippus).   Grammaire hollandoise, *etc.*
                                   8°.   Amsterdam, *Changuion*, 1762.
Another edition.   8°.   Amsterdam, *Changuion*, 1785.

Gratet-Duplessis, 322. Contains a " Recueil des plus naïves sentences proverbiales de la langue françoise." A very restricted selection translated
literally into Dutch.   [B.M.

1019. La Mesangère (Pierre de).   Dictionnaire des proverbes
français. pp. 596.   8°. Paris?, 1821.
Third edition. pp. 756.
                             8°. Paris, *etc.*, *Treuttel & Würtz*, 1823.

Gratet-Duplessis, 345. Portions of this work appeared in the " Journal des
Dames et des Modes." Popular, but contains much useful information.
Proverbs arranged by subjects.   [B.M.

1020. Lampises (Georgios D.).   Ὁδηγὸς τῆς Γαλλικῆς γλώσσης, *etc.*
pp. 10, 488.   8°. ἐν Ἀθήναις, *Κορομήλας*, 1870.

Bernstein, 4526. Pp. 448-464, French proverbs and Greek equivalents.

1021. Langlois (E.).   Anciens proverbes français.
                                              8°. Paris, *Picard*, 1899.

In Bibliothèque de l'École des Chartes, Tome 60, pp. 569-601. Nearly 800
proverbs taken from a 15th cent. ms. Occasional notes.   [B.M.

1022. Lanoue (Arthur de).   Choix de proverbes . . . français et
étrangers, *etc.* pp. 62.   8°. Paris, *Passard*, [1857?].
A list of proverbs given in French only; no notes.   [B.M.

1023. La Noue (Pierre de).   Synonyma et aequivoca gallica,
phrasibus sententiisque proverbialibus, illustrata, *etc.* pp.
513.   12°. Lugduni, *Anard*, 1618.
Another edition.   sm. 12°. Catalauni, *Dubois*, 1663.

Gratet-Duplessis, 285. Hécart, Bibliographie parémiographique, p. 78.
Phrases, sayings, proverbs, *etc.*, arranged alphabetically by subjects, with
Latin translations.   [B.M.

1024. Larchey (Lorédan).   Nos vieux proverbes. pp. xxxi, 304.
[Illustrated].
    fr.7.50. 8°. Paris, *Société anonyme de Publications*
                                              périodiques, 1886.

A collection of proverbs accompanied by explanation, moral reflections, or
illustrative anecdotes. An excellent introduction.   [B.M.

1025. La Véprie (Jean de).   Les proverbes communs. *End:* Cy
finissent les prouerbes communs qui sont en nombre enuiron
sept cens quatre vingt. [Collected by J. de La Véprie].
Black letter.   4°. [Lyon, *J. Du Pré*, 1490?].
Another edition. Black letter.   4°. [Paris?, 1495?].
Another edition. Proverbia gallicana scd'm ordinem alphabeti
reposita ab J. Egidio Nuceriensi latinis versiculis traducta.
Black letter. French and Latin.
                             8°. Trecis, *J. Lecoq*, [1519].

Another edition. Les proverbes communs. [Collected by
Jean de La Véprie: edited by A. V.]. *Reprinted from the
edition of 1539.* 8°. Paris, 1839.

Gratet-Duplessis, 232, gives many other editions. [B.M.

1026. Lebon (Jean), called *Hetropolitain.* Adages et proverbes
de Solon de Voge; par l'Hetropolitain [other name of Lebon].
Premiers livres, deux, trois et quatriesme, *etc.* pp. [360].
16°. Paris, *Bonfons,* [*circa* 1578].

Gratet-Duplessis, 252. Jean Lebon took his name of Hetropolitain from
his native village of Autreville. The fact that he lived for some time near
the Vosges probably explains the title of Solon de Voge given above. The
work begins with a preface and a rather involved essay on the nature and use
of the adage. The second book begins with a dedication dated 1576. Nopitsch,
in his "Litteratur der Sprichwörter," gives another edition, which may be
the first, with the following title :

Adages françois recueillis par J. Le Bon Hetropolitain, *etc.* pp. [116].
la. 16°. Paris, *Gauthier,* 1557.

This book of adages is the largest, best, and most interesting collection of
proverbs and popular sayings in use in France in the 16th century, that exists.
Though but a simple list of proverbs, it offers a faithful reflection of the life,
customs, manners, prejudices and opinions of its period.

Gruter reprinted in his "Florilegium ethico-politicum" a part only of
Lebon's collection; it is possible that he only knew the 1557 edition, which
Duplessis thinks to be less complete than the other. Duplessis himself, p. 154,
reprints some 40 or 50 of the proverbs.

1027. Le Duc (Jean). Proverbes en rimes, ou rimes en proverbes, *etc.* 2 pts. 12°. Paris, *Quinet,* 1665-64.

Gratet-Duplessis, 288. Very poor verse containing a number of proverbs and
sayings. [B.M.

1028. Le Duchat (Jacob). Ducatiana, *etc.* 2 vols.
sm. 8°. Amsterdam, *Humbert,* 1738.

Gratet-Duplessis, 297 and 310. Vol. 2, pp. 449-545, remarques sur quelques
proverbes françois par ordre alphabétique. These were suggested by Backer's
dictionary of proverbs, they are a mine of curious information, and fill an
important place in paremiology. [B.M.

1029. Leicht (Michele). L'Italia nei proverbi francesi.
8°. Venezia, 1882.

In L'Anteneo Veneto, Serie 5, n. 1, pp. 20-26. Proverbs gleaned from Le
Roux de Lincy's "Livre des proverbes français."

1030. Leigh (Edward). Analecta. . . . Select and choyce observations concerning the twelve first Caesars, *etc.*
8°. London, *Walbancke,* 1647.

Another edition. 8°. London, *Williams,* 1657.
Another edition. 8°. London, 1670.

Each of these editions of the observations contains at the end a selection
of French proverbs, with English translations and notes. [B.M.

1031. Leitneitz (Vincenzo). Secondo corso di lingua francese.
. . . Ventesimasettima edizione, *etc.* pp. vii, 483.
L.3. 16°. Napoli, 1884.

Pp. 272-276, 155 selected proverbs in French and Italian.

1032. Lendroy (Jacques). Parémiographe français-allemand, *etc.*
pp. [iv], 334. 8°. Francfort-sur-le-Mein, *Varrentrapp*, 1820.

Gratet-Duplessis, 343. A good collection, consisting of 1619 French proverbs,
given also in German, either in a literal translation or by corresponding
proverbs. Pp. 110-220, explanatory notes, in French, on the origin and sense
of some of these proverbs.   [B.M.

1032a. Le Petit (A.). 1192 proverbes de France, de partout et
d'ailleurs. Illustré en couleurs par A. Le Petit. Paris, 1929.

Edition limited to 550 copies.

1033. Le Picard (Philippe). La nouvelle fabrique des excellens
traits de verité . . . par Philippe d'Alcripe, sieur de Neri
[*pseud.* of Le Picard], en verbos, nouvelle édition, *etc.* pp.
[xxii], 220. ff. 126.   16°. Rouen, *Costé*, [1620?].

Another edition. pp. [xxii], 220.   12°. n.d.

Another edition. pp. xvi, 220. 16°. Paris, *Jannet*, 1853.

Gratet-Duplessis, 258. A collection of humorous anecdotes, probably parody-
ing the extravagant tales so popular at the period. Each anecdote is terminated by a rhymed saying which is frequently a popular proverb. The
language is that of the 16th century. The undated edition quoted belongs
to the middle of the 18th century : to be complete this edition should contain
1) *L'éditeur au lecteur*, 4 leaves placed between the preliminary pages and
the beginning of the work, and 2) *Additions à la nouvelle fabrique*, occupying
pp. 207-220. This book was reprinted almost wholly in : Facecieux devis et
plaisans contes par le sieur du Moulinet, comedien. Paris, *Millot*, n.d. [B.M.

1034. Le Roux (Philibert Joseph). Dictionnaire comique,
satyrique, critique, burlesque, libre et proverbiale . . . [1st
edition]. pp. 540. sm. 8°. Amsterdam, *Le Cene*, 1718.

Nouvelle édition revue, etc. pp. 668.

8°. Lion, *Les heritiers de Beringos frères*, 1735.

Another edition. 2 vols.   8°. Pampelune, 1786.

Gives authors or references, so is useful for obscure proverbs. Gratet-
Duplessis, 323, says it has no literary merit and is extremely obscene; he
gives the 1786 edition as the most complete.

[U.C.L. (1718); F.-L.S. (Stephens collection), (1735).

1035. Le Roux de Lincy (Adrien Jean Victor). Le livre des
proverbes français. Précédé d'un essai sur la philosophie de
Sancho Pança, par Ferdinand Denis. 2 tom.

12°. Paris, *Paulin*, 1842.

Second edition. 2 tom.   12°. Paris, *Delahays*, 1859.

Gratet-Duplessis, 367. Tome 1 contains Essai sur la philosophie de Sancho
Pança : Recherches sur les proverbes français : Bibliographie; and tome 2
contains French proverbs arranged in fifteen classes under subjects and
Appendice No. 1, Proverbes historiques relatifs à l'ancienne province de Champagne : Appendice No. 2, Proverbes recueillis dans les auteurs français du
xiie au xvie siècle : Appendice No. 3, Distiques de Dyonisius Cato, en Latin
et en vers français du xiie siècle : Appendice No. 4, Extrait des proverbes au
vilain, d'après . . . le manuscrit Digby, 86 Bodleian Library, *etc.:* Appendice
No. 5, Proverbes de Fraunce [*sic*] d'après un manuscrit de Cambridge du
Corpus Christi Collége : Table. A delightful book, both from the artistic and

technical points of view. The essay on Sancho Panza is rightly termed by
Le Roux de Lincy " un morceau littéraire d'une haute portée." The biblio-
graphy mentions a number of manuscripts in the Bibliothèque Royale. The
Proverbes au vilain are different from those given by Crapelet, *q.v.*, **941.**
[U.C.L.

1036. Le Roux de Lincy (Adrien Jean Victor). Proverbes.
fol. Paris, 1849.

In P. Lacroix : Moyen Âge et la Renaissance, Tome 2. An excellent essay
of twenty pages, followed by a short bibliographical list of books, all of which
are in Duplessis. It deals principally with French proverbs during the Middle
Ages, though other countries are mentioned.   [B.M.

1037. Li Muisis (Gilles). Poésies . . . publiées . . . par le baron
Kervyn de Lettenhove. 2 tom. 8°. Louvain, *Lefever,* 1882.

Tome 2, pp. 377-383, proverbs taken from the poems.   [B.M.

1038. Loisel (Antoine). Institutes coutumières, ou, manuel de
plusieurs et diverses règles, sentences, et proverbes . . . du
droict coutumier de la France. pp. 164.
8°. Paris, *Le Gras,* 1646.

Another edition. 2 tom.   8°. Paris, *Durand,* 1846.
[B.M.
See also **3825.**

1039. Loth (Johannes). Die Sprichwörter und Sentenzen der
altfranzösischen Fabliaux, nach ihrem Inhalte zusammengestellt.   4°. Greifenberg, 1895.
[B.M.

1040. Loubens (Didier). Les proverbes et locutions de la langue
française, *etc.* pp. xvii, 304.
fr.3.50. 8°. Paris, *Delagrave,* 1888.

Another edition. pp. xviii, 313.   12°. Paris, 1889.

Gives the origin and explanation of a number of French proverbs. A good
practical book containing much useful and interesting information. A brief
bibliography is given in the foreword.   [B.M.

1041. Louis (J.). Idiotismes dialogués. . . . Cinquième édition,
etc. 2 tom.   8°. Dessau, *Baumann,* 1884-1885.

Tome 1, pp. 105-111, 100 proverbs; pp. 112-118, 100 locutions proverbiales;
Tome 2, pp. 117-130, petit recueil supplémentaire de proverbes.

1042. Loyselet (Nic.). Dictionnaire françois-latin.   1617.

Concludes with : Essai des proverbes français avec l'interprétation latine.

1043. M. (G. G. D.). Pensées diverses et proverbes choisis, *etc.*
pp. [x], 306.   12°. Paris, *Mouchet,* 1712.

Gratet-Duplessis, 298. The avertissement is signed, G. G. D. M. A selection of moral maxims explained and developed, amongst which are a number
of popular proverbs.   [B.M.

1044. M. (J. V. d. N. A. D. d. l.). Bibliothèque des enfans.
pp. 342.   8°. Genève, *Dufart,* 1787.

Pp. 165-172, proverbes français dont on peut se servir.

1045. Margerie (Eugène de). Cinquante proverbes, *etc.* [13e édition]. pp. xv, 272.   16°. Paris, *Bray*, 1857.

1046. Mariette (Alphonse). French and English idioms and proverbs, *etc.* 3 vols. 8°. London, Paris, *Hachette*, 1896-97.
The notes are both useful and interesting.   [B.M.]

1047. Martel (L.). Petit recueil des proverbes français. pp. xv, 329.   8°. Paris, *Garnier*, 1883.
Twelfth edition. pp. xv, 325.   8°. Paris, [1924].
Pp. 1-86, locutions proverbiales : pp. 87-184, proverbes énonçant un fait : pp. 185-288, proverbes formant précepte.   [F.-L.S. (Stephens collection).

1048. Martin (   ). Locutions et proverbes. Origine et explications. pp. 170.   12°. Paris, 1925.

1049. Martin (Daniel). Grammatica gallica. . . . Huic acesserunt proverbia gallica, *etc.* pp. [x], 514.
    8°. Argentorati, *Zetzner*, 1632.

1050. ———: Le parlement nouveau . . . servant de dictionnaire et nomenclature aux amateurs des deux langues françoise et allemande. pp. [xvi], 813 [16].
    sm. 8°. Strasbourg, *Heritiers de Zetzner*, 1637.
Another edition. . . . Daniel Martin ou La vie à Strasbourg, *etc.* pp. 333.   8°. Strasbourg, *Staat*, 1900.
Gratet-Duplessis, 273. Contains a great number of little-known French proverbs, of some of which there are curious explanations. The proverbs are contained in the dialogues.
[1637 edition, Bibliothèque publique de Chartres; 1900 edition, B.M.

1051. Martin (Eman). Origine et explication de 200 locutions et proverbes, *etc.* pp. xi, 227.   8°. Paris, *Delagrave*, 1895.

1052. Martin (Johannes). Die proverbes au Conte de Bretaigne, *etc.* pp. 37.   8°. Erlangen, *Junge*, 1892.
The proverbs are here given with very full notes. Pp. 36-37, a brief bibliography.   [B.M.]

1053. Martin (M.). Les mots proverbiaux de M. Martin à son fils Théophile, *etc.* pp. 56.   sm. 8°.   [15—?].
Pp. 44-48, aucuns proverbes françois usités.

1054. Martinez (Francisco). Le nouveau sobrino, ou grammaire de la langue espagnole. . . . Neuvième édition, *etc.* pp. iv, 344.   8°. Bordeaux, *Laplace*, 1839.
20th edition. pp. 332.   8°. Paris, *Morizot*, 1862.
Contains a section entitled : Proverbes et sentences qui se correspondent dans les deux langues.   [B.M.]

1055. Matile (J. C. H.). Explication de quelques proverbes et locutions de la langue française.
    8°. Culemborg, *Blom & Olivierse*, 1890.
In Taalstudie, Jaargang 11, pp. 61-64, 85-87, 114-119.   [B.M.]

1056. Maupas (Charles). Les desguisez. Comédie françoise, avec l'explication des proverbes, *etc.* pp. 180, 23.

sm. 12°. Bloys, *Collas*, 1626.

Gratet-Duplessis, 271. A literal reproduction of Odet de Tournebu's comedy " Contents." Maupas has only given it a new title and added an explanation of the proverbs and proverbial phrases. This occupies the second pagination. These notes are not important, though they contain useful information on some of the proverbial sayings of the epoch. [B.M.

1057. Mazure (Ad.). Pièces inédites relatives au règne de Charles VII. pp. 19.　　　　　8°. [Poitiers, 1835].

Extrait de la Revue anglo-française. Pp. 8-13. Ballade faicte touchant la grant déception des Anglois. Each verse ends with a French proverb.

1058. Ménage (Gilles). Les origines de la langue françoise. pp. xxxviii, 845.　　　　　4°. Paris, 1650.

Another edition.　　　　　fol. Lyon, Paris, *Courbé*, 1694.

Another edition. Dictionnaire étymologique de la langue françoise, *etc.* 2 vols.　　　　fol. Paris, *Briasson*, 1750.

Gratet-Duplessis, 281. The edition of 1750 contains important additions. Ménage apparently had formed the idea of writing a " Traité étymologique des proverbes français." This project was never carried out, and it is probable that he included in his dictionary all his researches on this subject; there are at any rate a number of proverbs given, though no special list. [B.M.

1059. Menu (Henri). Quelques proverbes du xvie siècle.

8°. Paris, 1888.

In La Tradition, Tome 2, pp. 208-209. 29 proverbs from the collection of Le Bon. [B.M.

1060. Menus Propos. Les menus propos. pp. [24].

sm. 4°. [Paris], *Trepevel*, n.d.

Gratet-Duplessis, 236. This edition is believed to have been printed before 1500. Duplessis gives various others, all without dates. A curious work, consisting of a dialogue in which three characters exchange, without any connection, numbers of proverbs, quolibets, *etc.* Amongst these are some few proverbs and sayings which are not to be found elsewhere. Duplessis transcribes a page from the book.

1061. Meurier (Gabriel). La perle des similitudes, *etc.* pp [xii], 136.　　　　　4°. Malines, *Cranenbroeck*, 1583.

Gratet-Duplessis, 254. A curious and very rare book composed of a selection of 866 similitudes or comparisons, each with a moral sense, and accompanied by explanatory comments. It is also extremely interesting as a specimen of 16th century French written in the Low Countries, as it differs considerably from the French of France at that epoch. Duplessis quotes three of the similitudes. [B.M.

1062. Meyer (Paul). Proverbia magistri Serlonis.

8°. Paris, *Imprimerie Impériale*, 1868.

Part of a report by P. Meyer in : Archives des Missions scientifiques et littéraires, 2e série, Tome 5, pp. 174-183. [B.M.

1063. Miche (M. L.). La courtoisie françoise. . . . The English courtesy, *etc.* 12°. Amsterdam, *Broersz*, 1636.

Another edition. 12°. La Haye, *pour l'auteur*, 1640.

Another edition. La courtoisie francoise . . . Die französische Höflichkeit, *etc.* 16°. Francfort, *Von Sand*, 1645.

Contains several pages of proverbs, phrases, *etc.*

1064. Moisant de Brieux (Jacques). Les origines de quelques coutumes anciennes, *etc.* [*Anonymous*]. pp. [viii], 200. sm. 12°. Caen, *Cavelier*, 1672.

Another edition. 2 tom. 12°. Caen, 1874-75.

Gratet-Duplessis, 290. Contains a number of excellent and interesting observations on various proverbs and proverbial sayings. Duplessis gives details of other works by the same author, and quotes the following as forming the complement of the first.

Le divertissement de M. D. B. pp. [xxiv], 91.
sm. 12°. Caen, *Cavelier*, 1673. [B.M.

1065. Morawski (Joseph). Proverbes français antérieurs au xve siècle. pp. xxiii, 146. fr.9. 12°. Paris, *Champion*, 1925.

Les Classiques français du Moyen Âge, No. 47. The introduction contains a bibliography. The proverbs are arranged alphabetically with references to the collections in which they are to be found. With notes. [U.C.L., B.M.

1066. Morel (Fed.). Petit thrésor des mots françois. . . . Augmenté de plusieurs proverbes, dictons et manières de parler, françoises et latines. pp. 256.
8°. Rouen, *Richard l'Allemant*, 1641.

1067. Muyden (G. van). Der kleine Toussaint-Langenscheidt, *etc.* 2 Bde. 16°. Berlin, *Langenscheidt*, 1895.

Pp. 161-163, proverbes—Sprichwörter.

1068. National Proverbs. National proverbs : France. pp. 91.
1/-. 8°. London, *Palmer*, [1913].

Proverbs in French, with English translations. [B.M.

1069. Noël (François Joseph Michel) and **Carpentier** (L. J. M.). Philologie française, *etc.* 2 vols.
la. 8°. Paris, *Lenormant*, 1831.

Gratet-Duplessis, 360. Contains much interesting information on the origin, sense and application of a great number of French proverbs.

1070. Olinger ( ), *Abbé.* Nouveau dictionnaire des proverbes de la langue française . . . traduits en flamand. pp. iv, 380. 16°. Bruxelles, *Tircher*, 1855.

1071. Oudin ( ). Dictionnaire où l'on trouve toute façon de parler, à scavoir espagnol et françois. 16°.

Gratet-Duplessis, 260. Hécart, Bibliographie parémiographique, p. 49. A collection of French proverbs and sayings translated into Spanish.

1072. Oudin (Antoine). Curiosités françoises, *etc.* pp. 616.

sm. 8°. Paris, *Sommaville*, 1640.

Another edition. pp. vi, 471.   sm. 8°. Paris, 1656.

Gratet-Duplessis, 274. The second edition is much less attractive than the first, but reproduces it exactly. This work gives a lucid explanation of a large number of French proverbs and sayings whose true significance is now scarcely understood. [B.M.

1073. Oursy (Armand d'). Primer of French conversation, proverbs, *etc.* pp. 106.   16°. London, *Hachette*, 1883.

1074. P. (P. D. B. D.). Harangue en proverbes, *etc.* pp. 32.

4°. Paris, 1652.

Gratet-Duplessis, 278. Signed P. D. B. D. P. A political pamphlet belonging to the collection of satires in prose and verse known as Mazarinades. The author has expressed his thoughts by means of a large number of proverbs and popular sayings.

1075. Pachalery (A.). Thesaurus linguae Gallicae. Dictionnaire phraséologique de la langue française, *etc.* [Fasc. 1.] pp. xxvi, 176.   fr.3.50. 8°. Odessa, [1898].

Principally concerned with the explanation of proverbs and proverbial phrases. There are frequent comparisons with Latin and Russian proverbs. No more published. [B.M.

1076. Page (Remacles). 300 proverbes françois expliquez en allemand, *etc.* pp. 118.   16°. Cologne, *Demen*, 1660.

Pp. 2-37, proverbes.

1077. Panckoucke (André Joseph). Dictionnaire des proverbes françois . . . par J.P.L.N.D.L.E.F. [Panckoucke]. pp. [vi], 420.   sm. 8°. Paris, *Savoye*, 1749.

Another edition. pp. 400.

8°. Francfort, Mayence, *Varrentrapp*, 1750.

Gratet-Duplessis, 313. This is less an original work than a considerably augmented and improved edition of the dictionary of proverbs of G. de Backer, *q.v.*, **900**. It has been superseded, though it is still useful for obsolete phrases. [B.M.

1078. Pasquier (Étienne). Recherches de la France, *etc.*

fol. Paris, *Mettayer & L'Huillier*, 1596.

Another edition.   fol. Paris, *Sonnius*, 1621.

Another edition.   fol. Paris, *Guignard*, 1665.

Gratet-Duplessis, 263. Contains various chapters on proverbs. The edition of 1621 is a good one; there are various others. [B.M.

1079. Paulin (F.). Der ächte kleine Franzose . . . Fünfzehnte . . . Auflage. pp. 160.   12°. Hamburg, *Berendsohn*, 1890.

Pp. 159-160, French proverbs with German equivalents.

1080. Payne (James Bertrand de Vincheles Payen). French idioms and proverbs, *etc.* [First edition]. pp. vi, 162.

8°. London, *Nutt*, 1893.

Seventh edition. pp. 287.

8°. London, *Oxford Univ. Press*, 1924.

Sayings, idioms, proverbs, *etc.*, with English translations or equivalents, and notes where necessary. Above the average of its class. Other editions. [B.M.

I

1081. Ponge (Jules). Cent-vingt dialogues français-allemands . . . suivis d'une collection de proverbes . . . Quatrième édition, *etc*. pp. xii, 352. 8°. Leipzig, *Amelung*, 1856.

Pp. 288-338, French and German proverbs and proverbial phrases.

1082. Ponge (Jules). Cent-vingt dialogues français-allemands . . . de ponte ceci brugensis paremiarum galico et latino sermone contextarum secunda editio, *etc*. sm. 4°. *Roce*, [1500?]. *Another edition*. Sequuntur dicteria in latino et in gallico. ff. [8]. 8°. [Parisii, *Roce*, 1507].

Gratet-Duplessis, 118. A rare and curious little book. It is a selection of proverbial sayings or maxims taken from various Latin authors and translated into French, followed by a rather restricted selection of French proverbs in Latin. Duplessis thinks the former edition to be of 1500, and mentions that these proverbs are also to be found as the second part of a work entitled : Regulate de quantitate syllabarum, sm. 16°. Parisiis, *Joh. Lambert*, 1507. He also gives details of another undated edition. [B.M.

1083. Pražák (Antonín Fr.). Nejnovějsi klíč jazyka francouzského, *etc*. pp. iv, 199. 12°. v Brně, *Karafiat*, 1884.

Pp. 169-172, French proverbs and the corresponding Czech ones.

1084. Proverbes. Anciens et nouveaux proverbes, sentences, maximes, dictons : tout est bien qui finit bien, proverbe en proverbes. pp. 108. 18°. Paris, 1877.

1085. ———: Les meilleurs proverbes français et étrangers, par l'auteur de Deux Humilités Illustres, *etc*. pp. 242. 8°. Paris, Lyon, *Pélagaud*, [1865].

Notes and explanations of those which have a historical origin are given. [B.M.

1086. ———: Les notables proverbes et belles sentences de plusieurs bons autheurs . . . desquels le Latin précède le François, *etc*. 16°. Paris, *Menier*, 1602.

1087. ———: Nouveaux proverbes espagnols et français, *etc*. pp. 110. 8°. Paris, *Loyson*, 1660.

1088. ———: Proverbes choisis, explication étymologique, prose et vers. 3 pts. [in 1]. 12°. Paris, *Ribou*, 1703.

Gratet-Duplessis, 295. Rare but uninteresting. Contains some proverbs with a prose explanation taken textually from the Illustres Proverbes, *q.v.*, **1001,** and followed by a commentary in verse. This book is inserted in : Mélanges sérieux, comiques et d'érudition. 12°. Paris, 1704.

1089. ———: Proverbes, locutions proverbiales et gallicismes —Le mot propre. pp. 48. 12°. St.-Pétersbourg, *Trenké & Fusnot*, 1897.

With Russian equivalents.

1090. Proverbiana. Proverbiana, *etc*. pp. 108. 18°. Paris, *Tiger*, [1830].

Gratet-Duplessis, 357. A badly printed little book without any value or interest.

1091. Proverbs. Proverbs for learners in French and English, *etc.* 12°. London, 1774.

1092. Puce. La puce à l'oreille du bon-homme Richard, Capitaine dans la Garde non-soldée, *etc.* pp. 48.
8°. Paris, 1791.
Another edition. pp. 96. 8°. Paris, 1792.
Gratet-Duplessis, 326. A rather rare satirical pamphlet in which the author has included a number of well-known proverbs. [B.M.

1093. Quatre choses. Les quatre choses.—Cy fine le livre appelle les quatre choses. pp. [40]. sm. 4°. [Lyon?], n.d.
Another edition. 4°. [1490].
Another edition. 8°. Rouen, *Dugort*, 1556.
Gratet-Duplessis, 237. The first given is an extremely rare edition of a little-known work, which is thought to have been printed at Lyons in the last years of the 15th century. Brunet declares that a work entitled " Le quartenaire Sainct Thomas," *etc.*, sm. 8°, n.d., is the same as this. This book is not in verse, as at first sight it appears to be from its typographical arrangement. It is a collection of moral maxims, sayings and popular proverbs arranged in groups of four, either because of some supposed cabalistic value of the number, or simply as a mnemonic device. It was reprinted, with additions, in the following two works :—Instruction très bonne et très utile fait par quatrains, *etc.* 16°. Lyon, *Rigaud*, 1561; and, Questions proverbes et enseignements proffitable à un chacun, *etc.* 12°. Paris, *du Chesne et Rousset*, 1599. An Italian Riminaldo, *q.v.*, **2337,** also wrote a " Libro di quatro cose " which was translated into Spanish.

1094. ——— : Instruction tresbonne et tresutile faite par quatrains, *etc.* pp. [64]. 16°. Lyon, *Rigaud*, 1561.
Gratet-Duplessis, 251. This is a faithful and elegant reproduction, with some additions, of the " Livre des Quatre Choses." It is nearly as rare as the original edition. Amongst the additions is " La doctrine que Aristote envoya au roy Alexandre," which is composed of moral quatrains. This edition of 1561 gave rise to a later one entitled :
Questions proverbes et enseignements proffitables à un chacun, *etc.* 39 leaves. 12°. Paris, *Du Chesne et Rousset*, 1599.
This edition is typographically inferior to that of 1561, but textually the same, with one or two additions, such as the Blason des Cheveux of Mellin de Saint-Gelais. Duplessis quotes a few brief extracts from the book.

1095. Quitard (Pierre Marie). Curiosités proverbiales et bibliographiques. 8°. Paris, *Techener*, 1859.
In Bulletin du bibliophile, 1859, pp. 227-238, 441-450. [B.M.

1096. ——— : Dictionnaire étymologique, historique et anecdotique des proverbes et des locutions proverbiales de la langue française, en rapport avec des proverbes et des locutions proverbiales des autres langues. pp. xv, 701.
8°. Paris, *Bertrand*, Strasbourg, *Levrault*, 1842.
Gratet-Duplessis, 364. One of the best books on French proverbs, though the purely French ones are not sufficiently distinguished from those of foreign origin. Gives practically all the French proverbs worth knowing. [B.M.

1097. Quitard (Pierre Marie). Études . . . sur les proverbes français et le langage proverbial, *etc.* pp. xvii, 460.

8°. Paris, *Techener*, 1860.

More a commentary than a collection of proverbs, though literary and historical explanations of a large number of semi-obsolete sayings are given. Particularly important are the remarks in Chapter 11. [B.M.]

1098. Racot de Grandval (Nicolas). Almanach des proverbes pour l'année 1745 . . . par le scientifique Docteur Cartouchivandeck [By Grandval, author of the poem of Cartouche], *etc.* pp. 45. sm. 8°. Anvers, [Paris], 1745.

Second edition. pp. 45. 4°. Anvers, [Paris], 1745.

Gratet-Duplessis, 312. Barbier in his " Dictionnaire des Anonymes " indicates another edition, same date and place, which Duplessis thinks is probably the first edition with another title. A humorous work in prose and verse, amusing but without any real importance.

1099. Ranconnet (Aymar de). Tresor de la langue françoise . . . par Aymar de Ranconnet . . . revue et augmentée en ceste dernière impression de plus de la moitié, par Jean Nicot . . . avec . . . le recueil des vieux proverbes de la France, *etc.*

fol. Paris, *Douceur*, 1606.

Gratet-Duplessis, 259. The best edition of an old French-Latin dictionary; there is another good one of Rouen, 4°, 1618. The edition of 1606 contains: 1) A reprint, after the edition of Douai, 1604, of the " Proverbes communs " of Jean de La Véprie, *q.v.*, **1025,** with the Latin translation of Jean Nucerin (Gilles de Nuits). This occupies 17 pages. 2) Explication morale d'aucuns proverbes communs en la langue françoise. [B.M.]

1100. Recueil. Recueil de gallicismes, germanismes et locutions des langues française et allemande, *etc.* pp. 258.

8°. Berlin, *Henschel*, 1870.

1101. ———: Recueil des proverbes de la langue françoise, *etc.* pp. 176. 8°. Zürich, *Guesner*, 1716.

1102. Rencontres. Rencontres a tout propos, par proverbes et huictains françois tant anciens que modernes. 2 pts. [in 1].

16°. [Paris], *Groulleau*, 1554.

Gratet-Duplessis, 248, says there should be another edition, Paris, *Denis Janot*, 1542, and gives a reference to Brunet, Manuel du libraire, Vol. 4, p. 65.

1103. Renner (J. G. Friedrich). Hilfsbuch zum schnellen Erlernen der französischen Sprichwörter, *etc.* pp. 96.

8°. Quedlinburg, Leipzig, *Basse*, 1842.

1104. Robertson (Theo.). Dictionnaire idéologique. Recueil des mots, des phrases . . . et des proverbes, *etc.* pp. xxvii, 480.

8°. Paris, *Derache*, 1859.

Classified by the idea contained in them. Under " maxime," No. 496, are given over 30 correlated words. [B.M.]

1105. Roederer (A. M.), *Baron.* Comédies, proverbes, parades. 3 vols. 8°. [Dinan-sur-Meuse], 1824-26.

Gratet-Duplessis, 349. Only 100 copies published.

1106. Roland (J. F.). Dictionnaire du mauvais langage, ou recueil des expressions proverbiales . . . usitées parmi le peuple, *etc.* 8°. Lyon, *Rolland*, 1813.
Gratet-Duplessis, 339.

1107. Rosières (Raoul). Quelques proverbes français du xv⁰ siècle. 8°. Paris, *Lechevalier*, 1890.

In Revue des traditions populaires, tom. 5, No. 7. Some 15th century proverbs not to be found in the collection of Leroux de Lincy. No notes, but the place of origin is indicated in each case. [B.M.

1108. Rota (Marie). Monnaie courante de l'esprit de la conversation française, *etc.* pp. 179.
16°. Bergame, *Bolis*, 1896.

Pp. 147-166, French proverbs with Italian equivalents.

1109. Roucy (Francis de). Dictons populaires sur le temps, ou recueil des proverbes météorologiques de la France.
16°. Paris, *Plon*, 1878.
[B.M.

1110. Rozan (Charles). Petites ignorances de la conversation. Onzième édition. pp. xv, 471. 8°. Paris, *Ducrocq*, 1887.
Another edition. pp. 56. 6d. 8°. London, *Harrap*, 1909.

The 1909 edition is greatly abridged, and forms part of Harrap's Shorter French Texts. [B.M.

1111. ———: Petites ignorances historiques et littéraires. pp. iii, 551. 8°. Paris, *Quantin*, 1888.

Gives the explanation of many phrases and quotations which have passed into proverbs. Full of useful and interesting information. Of the same type as **1110**. [B.M.

1112. Ruebenkamp (Wilhelm). 1200 der gebräuchlichsten französischen Sprichwörter, *etc.* pp. 192.
8°. Zürich, *Schmidt*, 1903.

French proverbs arranged alphabetically, followed by German equivalents and notes. [B.M.

1113. Sammlung. Sammlung der besten ausgesuchtesten und gebräuchlichsten [französischen] Redensarten und Sprichwörter. 8°. Augsbourg, 1794.
Gratet-Duplessis, 329.

1114. Sébillot (Paul Yves). Le folk-lore de France. 4 tom.
8°. Paris, *Guilmoto*, 1904-07.

The proverbs are scattered throughout this work, but a good index facilitates reference. [F.-L.S.

1115. Secrétaire. Le nouveau secrétaire de la cour, ou lettres familières sur toutes sortes de sujets, *etc.* pp. [xx], 563.
8°. Paris, *Le Gras*, 1739.

Pp. 366-369, lettre en proverbes de Mademoiselle * * * à un de ses amis.

1116. Sedan (Daniel Martin). Proverbia, sententiae, *etc.* pp.
86.   12°. Argentorati, 1625.

Gratet-Duplessis, 270. Hécart, Bibliographie parémiographique, p. 71. 1111
proverbs, printed in two columns in French and German.

1117. Sermon. Sermon en proverbes, *etc.* Single sheet.
                                  fol. Beauvais, [1800?].
Another edition.   24°. Charmes, [1840?].
Another edition.   24°. Montbéliard, [1840?].
Another edition.   24°. Troyes, [1840?].
Another edition. pp. 18.   16°. Monterau, [1840?].
                                                         [B.M.

1118. Sorel (C.). La maison des jeux académiques, *etc.* pp.
xii, 288.   12°. Paris, *Loyson*, 1665.

Pp. 230-235, Le jeu des proverbes, *etc.* Contains a list of some fifty proverbs
suitable for acting.   [B.M.

1119. Souché (J. B.). Proverbes, traditions diverses, conjura-
tions, *etc.* pp. 84.   8°. Niort, 1822.

1120. Sprimont (F.). Recueil de plus de 4000 gallicismes,
idiotismes, proverbes et locutions singulières, avec la traduction russe en regard. pp. 200.
                          8°. St.-Pétersbourg, *Trenké & Fusnot*, 1872.
Bernstein, 3546.

1121. Starschedel (Albert de) and **Fries** (Georg). Nouveau dictionnaire proverbial complet, français-allemand et allemand-
français. pp. 456.   8°. Arau, *Sauerlœnder*, 1836.

Gratet-Duplessis, 362 and 763. An alphabetical list without explanations
or notes, and consequently not very important. The French section is larger
than the German.   [B.M.

1122. Stengel (E.). Die beiden Sammlungen altfranzösischer
Sprichwörter in der Oxforder Handschrift Rawlinson C.641.
                          8°. Berlin, *Gronau*, 1899.

In Zeitschrift für französische Sprache und Litteratur, Bd. 21, pp. 1-21. Full
notes.   [B.M.

1123. Tabourot (Étienne). Les bigarrures et touches du Seigneur
des Accords [É. Tabourot], *etc.* ff. [12], 216.
                                    8°. Paris, 1583.
Another edition.   12°. Paris, *Mauroy*, 1662.
Another edition. 3 vols.   Bruxelles, *Mertens*, 1866.

Gratet-Duplessis, 283, gives Guillaume as Tabourot's real name, but in the
edition of 1866 it is given as Étienne. The edition of 1662 is the best. This
book is a collection of anecdotes, jests, puns, *etc.*, and contains many proverbs.
                                                         [B.M.

1124. Tailliar (Émile). Les proverbes de Jeanneton. Chansonnette avec accompt· de piano. Paroles d'Émile Tailliar. Musique de Léopold Bougnol. pp. 3.

8°. Paris, *Carnaud*, n.d.

Bernstein, 3672.

1125. Theysbaert (Michiel). Spreekwoorden verzameld door Michiel Theysbaert. 1594.   8°. Gent, *Hoste*, 1863.

In Vaderlandsch Museum, Vijfde Deel, pp. 367-376. A collection of 69 French proverbs beginning with the letter A, with Dutch equivalents, taken from a 16th century ms.

1126. Thiollière (J. C.). Diversités littéraires, historiques et philosophiques. pp. 349.   8°. Saint-Étienne, *Boyer*, 1791.

Contains the explanation of many French proverbs and phrases.

1127. Thomas (   ). Les roses estivales recueillies des douces épines des anciens, en françois, en latin, en prose et en vers.

8°. Paris, 1624.

A little-known collection of proverbs and maxims.

1128. Tobler (Adolf). Li proverbe au vilain, *etc.* pp. xxxiii, 188.

8°. Leipzig, *Hirzel*, 1895.

A critical study, with a reprint of the proverbs, and extensive notes. [B.M.

1129. Tuet (Jean Charles François). Matinées sénonoises, ou proverbes françois, suivis de leur origine, *etc.* pp. xvi, 544.

8°. Paris, *La Rochelle*, Sens, *Tarbé*, 1789.

Abridged edition. Histoire des proverbes, *etc.* pp. 247.

12°. Paris, 1803.

Gratet-Duplessis, 325. An excellent work on the origin of 500 proverbs and sayings, together with a preliminary essay on proverbs, and a brief bibliography. It is not only full of valuable information, but is also charmingly written. Duplessis quotes a reprint of 1795.   [B.M.

1130. Ulrich (J.). Die altfranzösische Sprichwörtersammlung. Proverbes ruraux et vulgaux.   8°. Berlin, *Gronau*, 1902.

In Zeitschrift für französische Sprache und Litteratur, Bd. 24, pp. 1-35.

[U.C.L.

1131. ——: Die Sprichwörtersammlung Jehan Mielots.

8°. Berlin, *Gronau*, 1902.

In Zeitschrift für französische Sprache und Litteratur, Bd. 24, pp. 191-199. Proverbs from an old French ms.   [U.C.L.

1132. Velde (Jean van den). Bouquet printanier, *etc.* pp. [xii], 185.   sm. 8°. [Rotterdam], *Waesbergue*, 1613.

Quatrains spirituels et moraux, *etc.* pp. [7], 22 leaves.

sm. 8°. [Rotterdam], *Waesbergue*, 1613.

Gratet-Duplessis, 266, deals with these two under the same head, since they were both written for the same purpose, that of contributing to the moral advancement of youth and cultivating the memory. Both collections are composed of a choice of moral maxims in verse, amongst which are not a few rhymed proverbs. Both books are rare.

1133. Verité. La verité des proverbes, *etc.* pp. 6. 4°. 1652.

A very rare pamphlet. It is a satire against the ministers and courtiers, written in the form of proverbs.

1134. Vernon (Jean-Marie de). Le divertissement des sages, *etc.* pp. [xxiv], 708, [xx]. 8°. Paris, *Josse*, 1665. *Another edition.* Le divertissement des sages, ou discours historiques et moraux . . . par le P. Jean-Marie.
8°. Paris, 1701.

Gratet-Duplessis, 287. This book, divided into fifty-two sections, is a treatise on Christian morals, in which the author has taken as text a large number of proverbs which he explains and applies, very aptly, to religious observances.

1135. Villon (François). Ballade en proverbes.

Gratet-Duplessis, 233. This ballade is to be found in the numerous editions of the poet's collected works; Duplessis prints it on p. 125. [U.C.L.

1136. Wandelt (Oswin). Sprichwörter und Sentenzen des alt-französischen Dramas (1100-1400). Inaugural-Dissertation. pp. 75. 8°. Marburg, *Sömmering*, 1887.

Pp. 9-38, proverbs from old French plays (in old French) classified by subject, with place of origin indicated. Pp. 39-75, full notes and commentary on these proverbs, in German. [U.C.L.

1137. Watteville (Oscar de), *Baron.* Étude sur les devises personnelles et les dictons populaires, *etc.* pp. 40.
8°. Paris, *Schlaeber*, 1888.

Pp. 13-40, sayings and proverbs characterising various French families.
[B.M.

1138. Weick (Josephine). Causeries pour les enfants, *etc.* pp. viii, 112.
8°. Bielefeld, Leipzig, *Velhagen & Klasing*, 1894.

Pp. 87-95, Auswahl der gebräuchlichsten französischen Sprichwörter. 200 French proverbs with German equivalents.

1139. Weishaupt (Matthäus). Sammlung von französischen Wörtern und Redensarten, *etc.* pp. iv, 208.
8°. Kempten, *Kösel*, 1866.

Bernstein, 3999. Pp. 193-195, Sprüchwörter—Proverbes.

1140. Werneke (Otto). Sprichwörtliche und bildliche Redens-arten des Französischen. pp. 20.
4°. Merseburg, *Stollberg*, 1895.

In Dom-Gymnasium zu Merseburg, Jahresbericht 2, 1895.

1141. Wey (Francis). Remarques sur la langue française au dix-neuvième siècle, *etc.* 2 tom.
8°. Paris, *Firmin Didot*, 1845.

Gratet-Duplessis, 9. Vol. 2, pp. 248-253, des proverbes. A few remarks on the wisdom of using proverbs sparingly. [B.M.

1142. Wodroephe (John). The spared houres of a souldier in his travels, *etc.* pp. 523, [5]. la. 4°. Dort, *Waters*, 1623. *Second edition.* The marrow of the French tongue, *etc.*
fol. London, *Meighen*, 1625.

Gratet-Duplessis, 269, transcribes the whole title and gives a full list of contents. This book is a French grammar for English use, and contains : 1) Le verger des colloques recreatifs, par Gomes de Trier. See under Florio (G.), **2240**; 2) a large selection of French proverbs with English translations and brief explanations. [B.M.

1143. Zacher (J.). Altfranzösische Sprichwörter.
8°. Berlin, *Weidmann*, 1859.

In Zeitschrift für deutsches Alterthum, Bd. 11, pp. 114-144. The " Proverbia Rusticorum," French and Latin, with notes. [U.C.L.

1144. Zegerus (Tacitus Nicolaus). Proverbia Gallicana, una cum interpretatione tum Teutonica, tum Latina, *etc.*
8°. Antverpiae, *Loeus*, 1554.

Proverbs arranged alphabetically by the French, followed by the Flemish and Latin translations. [B.M.

See also index at end for references to French in other sections.

LOCAL AND DIALECT.

1. GENERAL.

1145. Combettes-Labourelie (Louis de). Roman en patois. pp. 149. 8°. Gaillac, *Dugourc*, 1878.

Pp. 113-149, proverbes patois.

1146. Favre (Léopold). Les patois de la France, *etc.* pp. viii, 168. 8°. Niort, *Favre*, 1882.

Contains a few brief lists of proverbs and sayings in patois. [B.M.

1147. Nisard (Marie Léonard Charles). Curiosités de l'étymologie française, avec l'explication de quelques proverbes et dictons populaires. pp. li, 337. 8°. Paris, *Hachette*, 1863.

This work is particularly useful for proverbs in patois. [B.M.

2. ARTOIS AND PICARDY.

(With French Flanders.)

1148. Cambrel (François de). Dictons en patois rouchi.
8°. Paris, 1892.

In La Revue du Nord, 3, No. 17. Rouchi is the patois in the old French Hainault and part of Belgian Hainault—not to be confused with Walloon.

1149. Corblet (Jules). Des dictons historiques relatifs à la Picardie. Amiens, [1851?].

In Annuaire complet de la Somme pour 1851.

1150. Corblet (Jules). Glossaire étymologique et comparatif du patois picard, *etc.* pp. 619.   8°. Paris, *Dumoulin*, 1851.

Pp. 135-209, 595-607, proverbes, maximes, et dictons picards. The proverbs are given in patois with French translations and explanations.   [B.M.

1151. Coussemaker (E. de) and **Carnel** (D.). Quelques recherches sur le dialecte flamand de France par E. de Coussemaker . . . Proverbes et locutions proverbiales chez les Flamands de France par l'Abbé D. Carnel. pp. 68.

8°. Dunkerque, *Kien*, 1859.

Pp. 56-68, proverbs.

1152. Dubois (A.). Proverbes et dictons picards, *etc.* pp. 32.

8°. Amiens, 1888.

Separate publication of an article in Mémoires de la Société des Antiquaires de Picardie, tom. 30.   [B.M.

1153. Dutailly (   ). Dictons et sobriquets populaires des Départements de l'Aisne, de l'Oise et de la Somme, par Ylliatud [anagram of Dutailly]. pp. 198.

8°. Noyon, *Tugaut*, 1887.

1154. Goedthals (François). Les proverbes anciens flamengs et françois correspondans de sentence les uns aux autres, *etc.* pp. 143.   8°. Anvers, *Plantin*, 1568.

Gratet-Duplessis, 803. A rare book containing a large number of little-known Flemish and French sayings. The Flemish proverbs are rendered, not by literal translations, but by French equivalents.   [B.M.

1155. Harou (Alfred). Les dictons de l'année.—Quelques dictons et proverbes du nord de la France et de la Belgique.

8°. Paris, 1893.

In La Tradition, tome 7, pp. 291-294.   [B.M.

1155a. ———: Le folklore de Godarville (Hainault).

8°. Anvers, 1893.

Cap. 7, pp. 85-92, proverbs.

1156. Hécart (Gabriel Antoine Joseph). Dictionnaire rouchi-français . . . Troisième édition. pp. xvi, 496, 8.

8°. Valenciennes, *Lemaitre*, 1834.

Gratet-Duplessis, 388. This book contains a few proverbs peculiar to the district round Valenciennes, together with other phrases, *etc.*, which are corrupt French. Hécart in his "Bibliographie parémiographique," p. 40, mentions a ms. collection made by him called "Augiasiana," *etc.*, 5 vols., 18°, 1824, of which there are four copies more or less complete. This latter is a collection of proverbs, *etc.*, in the Rouchi patois, and is so called because it would be a Herculean task to clean it up and sift the good from the bad.   [B.M.

1157. Ledieu (Alcius). Blason populaire de la Picardie, *etc.*

8°. Paris, 1905, *etc.*

Contains a large number of place rhymes, sayings, sobriquets, proverbs, *etc.*, relative to different parts of Picardy. *In progress?* [B.M. (Vol. 1, 1905, only).

1158. Ledieu (Alcius). Monographie d'un bourg picard, *etc.*
4 pts. 8°. Paris, *Picard*, 1890-1893.

Pp. 125-137, proverbes, comparaisons, devinettes, questions facétieuses : pp.
199-236, blason. [B.M.

1159. ———: Une poignée de dictons et sobriquets picards. pp.
32. 8°. Abbeville, *Fourdrinier*, 1890.

3. NORMANDY.

1160. Brion ( ). Proverbes en patois de La Villette. 1899.
In Bulletin des parlers normands, 3, 2.

1161. Canel (Alfred). Blason populaire de la Normandie, com-
prenant les proverbes, sobriquets et dictons, *etc.* 2 tom.
Rouen, *Lebrument*, Caen, *Le Gost-Clerisse*, 1859.

Gives the origin and explanation of numerous epithets, proverbs, sayings,
etc., concerning Normandy and the Normans. [B.M.

1162. Chrétien (L. J.). Almanach argenténois pour 1836. pp.
211. 12°. Alençon, *Poulet-Malassis*, [1835?].

Gratet-Duplessis, 390. Pp. 97-131, usages, préjugés, superstitions. Contains
a brief list of proverbs and sayings of the arrondissement of Argentan (Orne).
All well known, and not remarkable. A few copies of the article were
published separately.

1163. Decorde (J. E.). Dictionnaire du patois du pays de Bray.
pp. 140. fr.3. 8°. Paris, *etc.*, *Derache*, 1852.

Pp. 23-31, proverbes et dictons. [B.M.

1164. Du Bois (Louis). Recherches archéologiques, historiques,
biographiques et littéraires sur la Normandie. pp. xvi, 384.
8°. Paris, *Doumoulin*, 1843.

Pp. 353-359, proverbes et dictons. [B.M.

1165. Fleury (Jean). Essai sur le patois normand de la Hague.
pp. iv, 368. 8°. Paris, *Maisonneuve*, 1886.

Pp. 357-361, quelques locutions et proverbes. [B.M.

1166. ———: Littérature orale de la Basse-Normandie, *etc.* pp.
x, 396. 8°. Paris, *Maisonneuve*, 1883.

Les Littératures populaires de toutes les nations. Pp. 379-386, proverbs and
sayings. There are also other brief lists of comparisons, phrases, *etc.* [B.M.

1167. Friquassée. La friquassée crotestyllonée. [1630?].
Reprint. Genève, 1867.

Contains Norman proverbs. Very rare.

1168. Lecoeur (Jules). Esquisses du bocage normand, *etc.* pp.
[vi], 408. 8°. Condé-sur-Noireau, *Morel*, 1883.

Pp. 177-210, proverbs, sayings, local phrases, *etc.* [B.M.

1169. Levallois ( ). Sentences et proverbes en patois de
St.-Martin-de-Sallen. 1899.

In Bulletin des parlers normands, 3, 3.

1170. Plancouard (   ).   Proverbes et dictons du **Vexin**.
Paris, 1897.

1171. Pluquet (Frédéric).   Contes populaires, préjugés, patois, proverbes . . . de l'arrondissement de Bayeux.   [1e édition.]
pp. 81.   8°.   Caen, *Chalopin*, 1825.
2e édition.   pp. xiii, 163.   *Illustrated.*
8°.   Rouen, *Frère*, 1834.
Gratet-Duplessis, 389.   Pp. 109-130, proverbes, dictons, et locutions particulières.   The first edition was very incomplete; only 40 copies were printed; it includes, however, a certain number of proverbs and sayings.   Much the same list is reproduced in the author's Essai historique sur . . . Bayeux, *etc.*
1829.   [B.M.

1172. Travers (Émile).   Les Normands, la chicane et la potence d'après les dictons populaires.
8°.   Caen, *Blanc-Hardel*, Rouen, *Méterie*, 1883.
In Annuaire des cinq départements de la Normandie, 49e année, pp. 341-372.
[B.M.

1173. ———: Proverbes normands.   8°.   Paris, Amiens, 1889.
In Mémoires de la Société des Antiquaires de Picardie, Tome 30, (3e Série, Tom. 10), pp. 207-243.   [B.M.

4. BRITTANY.

1174. Brizeux (Julien Auguste Pélage).   Furnez Breiz, sagesse de Bretagne, ou recueil de proverbes bretons, *etc.*   pp. xviii, 108.   12°.   Lorient, *Gousset*, 1855.
Some 200 proverbs in Breton and French.   Included also in the author's works published, 2 tom., Paris, *Lévy*, 1860, and 4 tom., Paris, *Garnier*, [1910-1912].   [B.M.

1175. Coulabin (H.).   Dictionnaire de locutions populaires du bon pays de Rennes en Bretagne.   pp. 400.
12°.   1891.

1176. ———: Locutions populaires du bon pays de Renne-en-Bretagne.   Rennes, 1891.

1177. Ernault (E.).   Dictons et proverbes bretons.
8°.   Paris, *Rolland*, 1889.
In Mélusine, Tomes 4, 8-10.   [B.M.

1178. Hingaut (   ), *Abbé*, and **Hervé** (   ), *Abbé*.   Proverbs of Brittany.   Moses o'r Aipht'.
8°.   Edinburgh, *Macleod, etc.*, 1904-05.
In Celtic Review, Vol. 1, pp. 316-320.   Breton proverbs in English.
[U.C.L.

1179. Jobroux (L.).   Proverbes bretons.   1859.
In Bulletin de la Société archéologique du Morbihan, 1859.

1180. Kerdellec (Gabriel Marie Couffon de). Trésor des laboureurs, ou adages à l'usage des fermiers du canton de Lamballe. 2e édition. pp. 52.

12°. Saint-Brieuc, *Lemaout*, 1842.

Gratet-Duplessis, 386.

1181. Le Chef (Rodolphe). Contes, proverbes, formulettes, etc., recueillis à Bréal-sous-Montfort (Ille-et-Vilaine).

8°. Paris, *Leroux-Lechevalier*, 1895.

In Revue des traditions populaires, Tome 10, pp. 577-580. [B.M.

1182. Lecomte (Charles). Le parler dolois. Étude et glossaire de patois comparés de l'arrondissement de Saint-Malo. pp. vi, 242.   la. 8°. Paris, *Champion*, 1910.

Pp. 223-38, expressions populaires et locutions proverbiales : adages et comparaisons : proverbes et dictons. With notes and explanations. [F.-L.S.

1183. Le Goff (P.). Proverbes bretons du Haut-Vannetais, *etc.* [Collected and edited by P. Le Goff]. pp. 150.

8°. Vannes, *Lafolye*, 1909.

A large number of proverbs given in Breton, with French translations. [B.M.

1184. Milin (G.). Proverbes bretons sur les femmes. Ile de Batz.   8°. Paris, 1886.

In Revue des traditions populaires, Tom. 1, pp. 49-51. [B.M.

1185. Orain (Ad.). Proverbes et dictons de la Haute-Bretagne.

4°. Paris, *Lechevalier*, 1886-87.

In Mélusine, Tom. 3, pp. 178-182. [B.M.

1186. Sauvé (L. F.). Lavarou koz e Vreiz Izel. Dastumet ha troet e Gallek gant L. F. Salvet.—Proverbes et dictons de la Basse Bretagne, *etc.* pp. vi, 165.

8°. Paris, *Champion*, 1878.

1000 Breton proverbs with French translations, originally published in the Revue Celtique, Tom. 1-3. No notes. [B.M.

1187. Sébillot (Paul Yves). Littérature orale de la Haute-Bretagne. pp. xii, 400.   8°. Paris, *Maisonneuve*, 1881.

Les littératures populaires de toutes les nations, tome 1. Pp. 355-378, proverbes et dictons. [B.M.

1188. ———: Traditions et superstitions de la Haute-Bretagne. 2 tom.   8°. Paris, *Maisonneuve*, 1882.

Les littératures populaires de toutes les nations, tom. 9 and 10. Tom. 2, concerning animals, plants, *etc.*, contains proverbs in nearly every section. [B.M.

See also **3954.**

5. MAINE AND ANJOU.

1189. Bruneau de Tartifume (   ). Philandinopolis.   1626.

Contains : Des dicts facetieux satiriques proverbes et actions joyeuses qui ont esté et qui sont Angiers et pays d'Anjou.

1190. Dottin (Georges). Glossaire des parlers du Bas-Maine, *etc.*
pp. cxlviii, 682. fr.15. 8°. Paris, *Welter*, 1899.

Proverbs, sayings and proverbial phrases are gathered together in the index,
pp. 645-647. [B.M.

1191. Eudel (Paul). Les locutions nantaises, *etc.* pp. xxxi, 187
+ ff. 6. [Illustrated]. 8°. Nantes, *Morel*, 1884.

Contains little in the way of true proverbs, though there are a certain
number of popular phrases. [B.M.

1192. Soland (Aimé de). Proverbes et dictons rimés de l'Anjou,
etc. pp. viii, 186. 12°. Angers, *Lainé*, 1858.

This concludes with the " dicts facétieux satiriques proverbes," *etc.*, of
Bruneau de Tartifume. [B.M.

6. TOURAINE.

1193. Pineau (Léon). Le folk-lore de la Touraine. Proverbes
et dictons. 8°. Paris, *Lechevalier*, 1905.

In Revue des traditions populaires, Tom. 20, pp. 208-213. No notes or
comments. [B.M.

7. ISLE DE FRANCE.

1194. Fourtier (Alphonse). Les dictons de Seine-et-Marne. pp.
116. fr.2.50. 8°. Provins, *Lebeau*, Paris, *Dumoulin*, 1873.

8. CHAMPAGNE.

1195. Assier (Alexandre). Les archives curieuses de la Champagne et de la Brie. pp. viii, 150.
8°. Troyes, *Bouquot*, 1853.

Pp. 41-43, proverbes champenois au moyen âge. [B.M.

1196. Moiset (Charles). Dictons et sobriquets populaires . . . du
Département de l'Yonne, *etc.* pp. 26.
8°. Auxerre, *Rouillé*, 1889.

1197. Morin (Louis). Essais de folk-lore local. Proverbes et
dictons recueillis dans le Département de l'Aube. pp. 37.
8°. Troyes, *Arbouin*, 1904.

Nouvelle série. pp. 28.
8°. Troyes, *Grande Imprimerie*, 1912.

Over 2300 proverbs and sayings and phrases. [B.M.

1198. Tarbé (Louis Hardouin Prosper). Poètes de Champagne.
. . . Proverbes champenois avant le xvie siècle. [Edited by
P. Tarbé]. pp. xlviii, 176. 8°. Reims, *Regnier*, 1851.

Pp. 1-48, proverbs arranged by subjects. [B.M.
See also **1035n.**

9. BURGUNDY AND FRANCHE-COMTÉ.

1199. Beauquier (Charles). Blason populaire de Franche-Comté. Sobriquets-dictons-contes relatifs aux villages du Doubs, du Jura et de la Haute-Saône. pp. 303.

8°. Paris, *Lechevalier-Leroux*, 1897.

Place rhymes, proverbs, sayings, *etc.*, arranged alphabetically by the localities to which they refer. [B.M.

1200. Corbis (G.). Dictons populaires sur le temps.

Belfort, 1886, 1895.

In Bulletin de la Société belfortaine d'Émulation, 1886, no. 8 ; 1895, no. 14.

1201. Daguin (Arthur). Les dictons, proverbes, sobriquets concernant le Département de la Haute-Marne, *etc.* pp. 76.

8°. Langres, *Lorrette*, Chaumont, *Adonis et Roger-Lapetite*, 1893.

1202. Perron (Charles Alexandre). Proverbes de la Franche-Comté, *etc.* pp. xii, 152.

8°. Besançon, *Marion*, Paris, *Champion*, 1876.

A collection of proverbs, with notes, used in, or applied to Franche-Comté and its people. [B.M.

1203. Proverbes. Proverbes de Besançon et de la Franche-Comté.

Besançon, 1865.

In Revue littéraire de la Franche-Comté, 2.

1204. Rabiet (Eugène). Le patois de Bourberain (Côte d'Or). . . . Textes, *etc.* pp. 74.   8°. Paris, *Welter*, 1891.

Pp. 51-57, proverbes, dictons et formulettes. (82).

10. CENTRE DE LA FRANCE.

1205. Laisnel de la Salle (   ). Croyances et légendes du centre de la France, *etc.* 2 tom.   8°. Paris, *Chaix*, 1875.

Tome 2 contains various chapters on local, domestic, and weather proverbs and sayings. Under the title of "Le Berry," *etc.*, this work was reprinted as Vols. 40 and 44 of "Les littératures populaires." [B.M.

1206. Missoux (M.). Collection de proverbes patois, avec la traduction française au-dessous.

8°. Clermont-Ferrand, *Académie*, 1837.

In Annales scientifiques, littéraires et industrielles de l'Auvergne, Tom. 10, pp. 5-22. [B.M.

11. LIMOUSIN.

1207. Champeval (Jean-Baptiste). Proverbes bas-limousins, *etc.* pp. 123.   8°. Brive, *Roche*, 1886.

In Bulletin de la Société scientifique, historique et archéologique de la Corrèze, tom. 8. 626 proverbs are given.

1208. Clément-Simon (G.). Proverbes recueillis au Bas-Limousin.   8°. Montpellier, Paris, 1880.

In Revue des langues romanes, 3e série, Tome 3, pp. 84-103, Tome 4, pp. 80-89. *Also in:* Bulletin de la Société des Lettres de la Corrèze, 1880, pp. 275-299.   [B.M.

1209. Gorse (M. M.). Au bas pays de Limousin, *etc.* [Illustrated]. pp. xii, 327.   fr.6. 8°. Paris, *Leroux*, 1896.

Pp. 14-18, remarks on the use of proverbs by peasants, no examples. Various sayings and proverbs are to be found scattered throughout the book.   [B.M.

1210. Juge (J. J.). Changemens survenus dans les mœurs des habitans de Limoges, *etc.* pp. 232.
8°. Limoges, *Bargeas*, 1817.

Gratet-Duplessis, 385. A very rare book. The first edition, far less complete, appeared in 1808. Pp. 201-224, Recueil des proverbes en usage dans le Département de la Haute-Vienne (ancienne province du Limousin). These proverbs are in French, not in the Limousine patois. The list is concluded by a "Chanson de Collé," composed entirely of proverbs, which was also included in the "Philologie française" of Noël and Carpentier.

1211. Roux (J.). Prouverbes bas-lemouzis.
8°. Halle, *Niemayer*, 1882.

In Zeitschrift für romanische Philologie, Bd. 6, pp. 526-569. A large collection of proverbs in dialect with French translations and explanations.
[U.C.L., B.M.

12. POITOU.

1212. Curzon (Emm. de). Proverbes de la vie rurale.
8°. Poitiers, *Oudin*, Paris, *Derache*, 1875.

In Bulletin de la Société académique, d'Agriculture, Belles-Lettres, Sciences, et Arts de Poitiers, No. 204.

1213. Desaivre (Léo). Croyances, présages, usages, traditions diverses et proverbes, *etc.* pp. 39.
8°. Niort, *Clouzot*, 1881.

Bernstein, 815.

1214. La Chesnaye (Jehan de). Proverbes vendéens, *etc.* pp. viii, 46.   fr.2. 8°. Paris, 1906.

302 proverbs in patois with some explanatory notes.   [B.M.

1215. Lacuve (R. M.). Proverbes poitevins.
8°. Paris, *Lechevalier-Leroux*, 1894-1897.

In Revue des traditions populaires, tom. 9, 10, 12.
Published separately. pp. 7.   8°. Paris, 1895.
[B.M.

1216. Saint-Marc (   ). Traditions, proverbes et dictons poitevins.   Saint-Maixent, 1890.

Separate publication of an article in the Bulletins de la Société de Statistique, Sciences, Lettres, et Arts du Département des Deux-Sèvres, oct.-déc., 1890.

13. SAVOY.

1217. Brachet (François). Dictionnaire du patois savoyard . . .
suivi d'une collection de proverbes, *etc.* pp. 210.
8°. Albertville, *Hodoyer*, 1883.
Another edition. pp. 244. 8°. Albertville, *Hodoyer*, 1889.
Contains a list of local proverbs and sayings with French translations.
[B.M.

1218. Constantin ( ). Littérature orale de la Savoie, proverbes, devinettes, contes. Annecy, 1882.

1219. Gacy (J.). Littérature orale de la Savoie. Annecy, 1882.
Proverbs, riddles, tales, *etc.*

1220. Littérature. Littérature orale de la Savoie—Proverbes, *etc.*
pp. 32. 12°. Annecy, *Depollier*, 1882.
Pp. 9-13, proverbes savoyards (patois d'Annecy): pp. 14-18, proverbes
agricoles.

1221. Miquet (F.). Sobriquets patois et dictons des communes
de l'ancien Genèvois. Annecy, 1890.

1222. Pont (Georges). Origines du patois de la Tarentaise, *etc.*
pp. 149. 8°. Paris, *Maisonneuve*, 1872.
Pp. 73-88, proverbs and sayings in patois, with French translations. The
sayings are accompanied by explanatory notes. [B.M.

14. DAUPHINÉ.

1223. Allemand ( ). Proverbes alpins spécialement recueillis
dans la Champsaut et le Gapençais. 1884, 1885.
In Bulletin de la Société d'ét. des Hautes-Alpes, 1884, p. 369 *et seq.*; 1885,
p. 219 *et seq.*

1224. Chabrand (Jean Armand) and **Rochas D'Aiglun** (Eugène
Auguste Albert de). Patois des alpes cottiennes . . . et en
particulier du Queyras. pp. 228.
8°. Grenoble, *Maisonville*, Paris, *Champion*, 1877.
Pp. 28, 150, 154, 160 contain lists of proverbs in patois, with French
translations. [B.M.

1225. Champollion-Figeac (Jean Joseph). Nouvelles recherches
sur les patois ou idiomes vulgaires de la France, *etc.* pp. xii,
201. 12°. Paris, *Goujon*, 1809.
Gratet-Duplessis, 382. Pp. 128-130, proverbes dauphinois; not very many.
[B.M.

1226. Cochard ( ). Proverbes lyonnais.
8°. Lyon, *Barret*, Paris, *Huzard*, 1825.
In Archives historiques et statistiques du Département du Rhône, Tome 2,
pp. 343-348. Proverbs with explanations. [B.M.

K

1227. Guichard (G.). Uno pugna de prouverbes doufinens.
8°. Grenoble, *Altier*, 1889.

In Bulletin de l'Académie delphinale [de Grenoble], Série 4, Tom. 2, pp. 355-397. A selection of proverbs in patois, with explanations and translations. [B.M.

1228. Pilot-Dethorey (Jean Joseph Antoine). Proverbes dauphinois . . . usités dès les temps les plus anciens et consignés dans de vieux manuscrits antérieurs au xve siècle . . . 2e édition, *etc.* pp. 38.
75 centimes. 12°. Grenoble, *Drevet*, [1884].

A selection of proverbs and sayings, with explanatory notes. [B.M.

1229. Rivière (   ). Quelques dictons et proverbes de Saint-Maurice-de-l'Exil, Isère. 8°. Montpellier, Paris, 1897.

In Revue des langues romanes, Série 4, tom. 10, pp. 35-44. [B.M.

15. PROVENCE.

1230. Andrews (James Bruyn). Proverbes mentonnais.
la. 8°. Paris, *Leroux*, 1889.

In Revue des traditions populaires, tom. 4, nr. 5, pp. 281-282. 22 proverbs with literal French translations : also in the author's Essai du grammaire et du dialecte mentonnais, 12°, Nice, 1875, pp. 56-59. *See also* review by P. Meyer in Romania, 4e année, 1875, pp. 493-4. [B.M.

1231. Astros (d'). Discours en proverbes provençaux.
8°. Aix, *Tavernier*, 1845.

In Mémoires de l'Académie des Sciences, Agriculture, Arts et Belles-Lettres d'Aix, tom. 5, pp. 129-135. [B.M.

1232. Barjavel (C. F. Henri). Dictons et sobriquets patois . . . du Département de Vaucluse, *etc.* pp. 306.
8°. Carpentras, *Devillario*, 1849-1853.

A list, accompanied by comparison, and notes. [B.M.

1233. Brueys (Claude). Jardin deys musos provensalos, *etc.*
2 vols. sm. 12°. Aix, *David*, 1628.

Gratet-Duplessis, 376. Contains four pieces in verse called "Discours de Caramantran a baston romput," which consist of a selection of rhymed maxims, sayings, proverbs, *etc.*, strung together without any apparent connection. A very rare book, a reimpression of which was issued at Marseilles, 1843, *etc.*, as Vols. 1 and 2 of Mortreuil's Poésies provençales. Only 100 copies were published, however. The work published in 1628 was by Brueys alone, others with the same title published at later dates contain only a few poems by him, the remainder being by other authors. [B.M.

1234. Brunet (Jean). Étude de mœurs provençales par les proverbes et les dictons. 8°. Montpellier, Paris, 1884.

In Revue des langues romanes, tome 8, pp. 125 *et seq.*, Série 3, tom. 12, pp. 5-48. [B.M.

1235. Bugado. La bugado provençalo, *etc.* [By François de Bègue?]. pp. 96. 12°. n.d.

Another edition. pp. 101. 8°. Aix, 1859.

Gratet-Duplessis, 377. A very rare little collection of proverbs and sayings in Provençal, nearly always found annexed to the following book :
Lou jardin deys musos provençalos, *etc.* [By Charles Feau]. pp. 386.
sm. 12°. [Marseille], 1665.
This is not the same as the work of the same title by Claude Brueys, although it contains one or two pieces by him. The edition of 1859 forms Vol. 1 of the Bibliothèque provençale. [B.M.

1236. Cartelier ( ). Recueil de proverbes provençaux; nouvelle édition. [Par Cartelier]. pp. 52.
sm. 8°. Aix, *Adibert*, 1736.

Gratet-Duplessis, 378. A rare book containing a long list of proverbs in Provençal, most of which, however, are to be found in the general French collections.

1237. Cnyrim (Eugen). Sprichwörter, sprichwörtliche Redensarten und Sentenzen bei den provenzalischen Lyrikern. pp. 75. 8°. Marburg, *Elwert*, 1888.

Stengel's Ausgaben und Abhandlungen aus dem Gebiete der romanischen Philologie, 71. [U.C.L.

1238. Colleville (de), *Vicomte.* Proverbes niçois.
8°. Paris, 1890.

In La Tradition, tome 4, No. 12, pp. 378-379. 27 proverbs, with French translations. [B.M.

1239. Diouloufet (J. Joseph Marius). Fablos, contos, epitros et autres pouesios prouvençalos. pp. xxxix, 464, 1 plate.
8°. A-z-Ai [Aix], *Gaudibert*, 1829.

Gratet-Duplessis, 381. Contains 98 fables which are headed by, and show the application of, one or more Provençal proverbs. No author's name on the title page, but the " Epître dédicatoire " is signed Diouloufet, the Provençal form of Dieulafoy. [B.M.

1240. Garcin (Étienne). Le nouveau dictionnaire provençal-français . . . suivi de la collection la plus complète des proverbes provençaux. Par M. G. [*i.e.* É. Garcin]. pp. 385.
8°. Marseille, *Roche*, 1823.

Gratet-Duplessis, 380. There are a large number of Provençal proverbs at the end of this book, pp. 341-385, but they lack notes and explanations. Unfortunately some of the words in the proverbs are not to be found in the body of the dictionary. [B.M.

1241. Guys ( ). Marseille ancien et moderne. 8°. 1786.
Contains an essay on Marseillais and Provençal proverbs.

1242. Lacombe (François). Dictionnaire du vieux langage.

Friesland, 290. Vol. 2, pp. 76-80, proverbes provençaux et languedociens. No details available. These proverbs do not appear in the edition of 1766.

1243. La-Tour-Keyrié (A. M. de). Recueil de proverbes . . . provençaux, *etc.* pp. 120.　　　8°. Aix, *Makaire*, 1882.

Proverbs classified by subjects, preceded by a brief study of their origin, use, *etc.* They are given in Provençal, with French translations, and explanatory notes where necessary. [B.M.

1244. Lieutaud (Victor). Notes pour servir à l'histoire de Provence, *etc.* 15 (?) pts.

8°. Marseille, *Boy fils*, Aix, *Makaire*, 1873-1874.

No. 9, Proverbes topographiques provençaux. A few pages of proverbs with comments, followed by a brief bibliography. [B.M.

1245. Maas (Albert). Allerlei provenzalischer Volksglaube, nach F. Mistral's " Mirèio," *etc.* pp. 64.

8°. Berlin, *Vogt*, 1896.

Berliner Beiträge zur germanischen und romanischen Philologie, 11. Pp. 54-58, 15 proverbs, with notes in German. [B.M.

1246. Millin de Grandmaison (Aubin Louis). Essai sur la langue et la littérature provençale. pp. 51.

8°. Paris, *Sajou*, [1808?].

Pp. 49-51, Provençal proverbs with French translations. [B.M.

1247. Peretz (Bernhard). Altprovenzalische Sprichwörter, *etc.* pp. 49.　　　8°. Erlangen, *Junge*, 1887.

A separate print of an article in Romanische Forschungen, Bd. 3. [L.L.

1248. Pillet (Alfred). Die neuprovenzalischen Sprichwörter der jüngeren Cheltenhamer Liederhandschrift. pp. 130.

8°. Berlin, *Ebering*, 1897.

Romanische Studien, Heft 1. Pp. 1-84, commentary : pp. 85-126, proverbs with German translations. [B.M.

1249. Ramond (Édouard). Le livre joyeux: histoires marseillaises, galejades et proverbes de Provence. pp. 236.

12°. Paris, n.d.

1250. Recueil. Recueil de proverbes, ou sentences populaires en langue provençale. Nouvelle édition, *etc.* pp. 32.

12°. Brignoles, *Dufort*, 1821.

Bernstein, 2975.

1251. Regis de la Colombière (Marcel de). Les cris populaires de Marseille. Locutions, apostrophes, injures, expressions proverbiales, *etc.* pp. xi, 294.　　8°. Marseille, *Lebon*, 1868.

[B.M.

1252. Ricard (　　). Les proverbes de mon pays natal, ville et canton de la Ciotat.　　　　　　Marseille, 1893.

Friesland, 366.

1253. Toselli (Gioan Battista). Recuei de 3176 prouverbi, sentensa, massima, conseu, parabola, buiomot precet et diç nissart. pp. xxxi, 232. 8°. Nissa, *Cauvin-Empereur*, 1878.

[B.M.

See also **1257, 3636, 3866.**

16. CORSICA.

1254. Filippi (J. M.). Recueil de sentences et dictons usités en
Corse, *etc.* pp. 80.   12°. Paris, *Bouchy*, 1906.

1255. Mattei (Antonio). Pruverbj, detti e massime corse, *etc.*
pp. xxxi, 180.   fr.3. 16°. Paris, *Maisonneuve*, 1867.
Contains over 2000 sayings, *etc.*, of which about one-third are true proverbs.
The proverbs are in Corsican; no notes.   [B.M.

1256. Tommaseo (Niccolò). Canti popolari toscani, corsi, illyrici,
greci, *etc.* 4 vols.   8°. Venezia, *Tasso*, 1841-1842.
Gratet-Duplessis, 471. Vol. 2, pp. 363-400, contains 450 Corsican proverbs.
Most of the proverbs are in the Corsican dialect, but not very many are peculiar
to Corsica, the rest being found in various parts of Italy. Brief notes. [B.M.

17. LANGUEDOC.

1257. Boissier de Sauvages de la Croix (Pierre Augustin). Dictionnaire languedocien-françois . . . Nouvelle édition . . . Par
M. L. D. S. [*i.e.* Boissier de Sauvages]. 2 vols.
                            8. Nîmes, *Gaude*, 1785.
Another edition. 2 vols.   8°. Alais, 1820-21.
Gratet-Duplessis, 379. 1785 edition, pp. 371-395, recueil de proverbes, de
maximes et de dictons languedociens et provençaux. An edition of 1756 does
not contain the list of proverbs.   [B.M.

1258. Boucoiran (Louis). Dictionnaire analogique . . . com-
prenant . . . une collection de proverbes locaux tirés de nos
moralistes populaires. 2 tom.
                4°. Nîmes, *Imprimerie Roumieux*, 1875-1886.

1259. Burdèt (   ). Mazimas è proverbiis.   Mende, 1860.
In Bulletin de la Société d'Agriculture, Sciences et Arts de la Lozère, 1860.

1259a. Caffort (   ). Prouberbis et redits narbonneses, *etc.*
pp. 86.   8°. Narbonne, *Caillard*, 1913.
An alphabetical list of proverbs and sayings in the dialect of Narbonne.
                                            [B.M.

1260. Combes (Anacharsis). Proverbes agricoles du sud-ouest de
la France . . . 2e édition. pp. 166.   8°. Castres, *Huc*, n.d.
Bernstein, 650.

1261. Espagne (Adelphe). Proverbes et dictons populaires
recueillis à Aspiran. pp. 46.
                    8°. Montpellier, *Coulet*, 1874.
90 proverbs in dialect, with French translations and notes, preceded by a
brief essay on proverbs in general.   [B.M.

1262. F. (L. A. D.). Recueil des proverbes météorologiques et
agronomiques des Cévennois.   8°. Paris, *Huzard*, 1822.
In Annales de l'Agriculture française, série 2, tom. 19, pp. 145-180. 79
proverbs in dialect, with notes and followed by translations.   [B.M.

1263. Fayre (Christophe). Proverbes et dictons de Savièse. pp.
26.   la. 8°. Halle, 1926.
In Zeitschrift für romanische Philologie, Bd. 46.   180 proverbs in dialect,
with French translations.   [U.C.L.

1264. Fesquet (P.). Monographie du sous-dialecte languedocien
du canton de la Salle-Saint-Pierre, Gard.
                              8°. Montpellier, Paris, 1884.
In Revue des langues romanes, série 3, tome 11, pp. 63-69.   73 proverbs and
sayings.   [B.M.

1265. ———: Proverbes et dictons populaires, recueillis à
Colognac, *etc.* pp. 34.
                              8°. Montpellier, Paris, *Franck*, 1874.
Some 150 proverbs and sayings in patois, with French translations and notes.
Originally published in the Revue des langues romanes, tome 6.   [B.M.

1266. Hombres-Firmas (d'). Recueil de proverbes météorologiques et agronomiques des Cévennois . . . par M.L.A.D.F.
[=Le Chevalier d'Hombres-Firmas]. pp. 56.
                              8°. Paris, *Huzard*, 1822.
Gratet-Duplessis, 384.   An article originally published in the Annales de
l'Agriculture française, 2e série, tome 29.

1267. Laroche (Pierre). Folklore du Lauraguais, *etc.* 7 parts.
                              8°. Albi, *Nouguiès*, 1891-94.
Part 5, pp. 272-290, proverbs in patois.   On the title page the author's name
is given as P. Fagot (Pierre Laroche).   [B.M.

1268. Mazel (   ). Les mois en proverbes, dialecte cévénol.
                                                    Nîmes, 1889.
Friesland, 332.

1269. Rulman (Anne). Les proverbes du Languedoc de Rulman,
annotés et publiés par le docteur Mazel. pp. 28.
                              8°. Montpellier, *Hamelin*, 1880.
Mazel published Rulman's " Inventaire des proverbes," *in* La Revue des
langues romanes, 3e série, tome 2, pp. 42-64.

1270. Thiessing (J. B.). Eine Auswahl der gebräuchlichsten
languedocischen Sprüchwörter, reimhaften Formeln und
Redensarten.   8°.
In Archiv für neuere Sprachen, 43.

1271. Vaschalde (Henry). Dictons et sobriquets populaires du
Vivarais. pp. 16.   8°. Marseille, *Olive*, 1874.

1272. ———: Nos pères. Proverbes et maximes populaires du
Midi de la France. pp. 27.   8°. Paris, *Maisonneuve*, 1882.
Bernstein, 3839.

1273. ———: Nos pères. Proverbes et maximes populaires du
Vivarais. pp. 29.   8°. Montpellier, *Coulet*, 1875.
See also **1242.**

18. GUIENNE.

1274. Ayma (   ). Proverbes quercinois.   Cahors, 1873.

In Bulletin de la Société des études littéraires, scientifiques et artistiques du Lot, 1, 75, 134, 208, 260, 331.

1275. Bladé (Jean François). Contes et proverbes populaires recueillis en Armagnac. pp. ix, 92. 8°. Paris, *Franck*, 1867.

Pp. 61-83, proverbs.   [B.M.

1276. ———: Proverbes et devinettes populaires, recueillis dans l'Armagnac et l'Agenais, *etc.* pp. xv, 235.

8°. Paris, *Champion*, 1879.

Pp. 1-112, proverbes : pp. 113-165, supplément : pp. 166-187, proverbes tirés des manuscrits de l'abbé Daignan du Sendat. Proverbs in Gascon, with French translations.   [L.L.

1277. Buscon (L.). Recueil des proverbes patois usités dans le Département de Tarn-et-Garonne.

8°. Montauban, *Forestie*, 1873-1876.

In Bulletin archéologique . . . de la Société archéologique de Tarn-et-Garonne, tome 3, pp. 49-74; tome 4, pp. 73-88 and pp. 137-146. A large collection of proverbs in dialect with French translations. Pp. 61-63, bibliography.   [B.M.

1278. Duval (Jules). Proverbes patois en dialecte du Rouergue.

8°. Rodez, 1845.

In Mémoires de la Société des Lettres, Sciences, et Arts de l'Aveyron, 1845, pp. 437-647. 1027 proverbs are given. Also published separately, same date.

1279. Mensignac (C. de). Notice sur les superstitions, dictons, proverbes . . . de la Gironde (suite et fin). pp. 96.

8°.   1890.

1280. Menu (Henri). Proverbes et dictons populaires du Périgord.   8°. Paris, 1889.

In La Tradition, tome 3, pp. 23, 54. 27 proverbs.   [B.M.

1281. Michelet (J.). Mémoires d'un enfant.   Paris, 1867.
P. 269 *et seq.*, proverbes dans le dialecte de Montauban.

1282. Taupiac (Louis). Statistique agricole de l'arrondissement de Castelsarrasin.

Pp. 298-317, proverbes patois.

19. GASCONY.

1283. Aignan (d'). Sentences, proverbes et dictons de la Gascogne.   12°. Toulouse, *Jougla*, Auch, *Brun*, 1850.

Proverbs taken from an '' MS. pour servir a l'histoire et description de la ville d'Auch '' par M. d'Aignan, and included in : Lou parterre gascoun, *etc.*, by G. Bedout, pp. 74-84.   [B.M.

1284. Beauvais (Armand). Quelques anciens proverbes du Gers.

8°. Paris, 1889.

In La Tradition, tome 3, p. 140. 11 proverbs in dialect, with translations.

[B.M.

1285. Castet ( ), *Abbé*. Proverbes patois de la vallée de Biros, en Couserans (Ariège), *etc.* pp. 58.

8°. Foix, *Gadrat*, 1889.

Nouvelle série. 8°. Foix, 1902.

Reviewed, with a large extract from the proverbs and French translations, in the Revue des Pyrénées, tome 1, pp. 561-72.

1286. Dambielle (H.). Nos proverbes gascons. 1ère série. Les douze mois de l'année. pp. 25. 8°. Albi, 1914.

1287. Dardy (Léopold). Anthologie populaire de l'Albret, *etc.* 2 tom. 8°. Agen, *Michel et Médan*, 1891-92.

Tome 1, pp. 203-323, proverbes; also tome 2, pp. 378-379. The proverbs are given in dialect with French translations. [B.M.

1288. Foix (V.). Poésie populaire landaise, *etc.* pp. 41.

8°. Dax, *Labèque*, 1890.

Bernstein, 2619. Pp. 33-37, 43 rhymed proverbs.

1289. Voltoire ( ). Le marchand, traictant des proprietez et particularitez du commerce et negoce . . . Ensemble les motets gascons, *etc.* pp. vii, 195.

sm. 12°. Tolose, *Colomiez*, 1607.

A reprint. Lous moutets guascous deou marchan de Voltoire réimprimés sur l'édition originale.

8°. *Suivant la copie imprimée à Tolose* [reprinted 1840?].

Gratet-Duplessis, 375. 616 Gascon proverbs mostly in rhyme. The original edition is extremely rare, only two copies being known. The book is of little interest apart from the proverbs, which have a double claim to consideration, firstly as a collection of Gascon popular sayings, and secondly as specimens of a particular form of the *langue d'oc*. These proverbs are reprinted by Duplessis in his Bibliographie parémiologique, pp. 444-480; and a selection of them is given by Brunet in the " Anciens proverbes . . . recueillis par Voltoire " which he edited. [B.M.

See also **1276, 1310.**

20. BÉARN.

1290. Hatoulet (J.) and **Picot** (Auguste Émile). Proverbes béarnais, *etc.* pp. viii, 143.

8°. Paris, Leipzig, *Franck*, 1862.

Proverbs arranged alphabetically, with occasional notes. An appendix contains a few Gascon and Provençal proverbs. No translations. Béarnais is a variant of " Tolosan," the sister language of Provençal and Catalan, and common to France and Spain. [B.M.

1291. Lespy (V.). Dictons et proverbes du Béarn, *etc.* pp. xvi, 285. 8°. Pau, *Garet*, 1892.

Dictons du pays de Béarn. pp. xii, 293.

8°. Pau, *Ribaut*, 1875.

Proverbes du pays de Béarn, *etc.* pp. 109.

8°. Paris, *Maisonneuve*, 1876.

The book published in 1892 is the second, revised and combined edition of the other two. Some 700 proverbs, *etc.*, are given in patois with French translations and explanations, besides numerous place rhymes and sayings. [B.M.

BASQUE.

1292. Brunet (Pierre Gustave). Notice sur les proverbes basques, *etc.* pp. 28. 8°. Paris, *Aubry*, 1859.

Deals principally with the Basque proverbs of d'Oihenart; the 170 supplementary ones are reproduced with French translations. Useful notes are also given on various other Basque works. [B.M.

1293. Chaho (J. Augustin). Biarritz entre les Pyrénées et l'océan, *etc.* 2 pts. 8°. Bayonne, *Andreossy*, [1855].

Pt. 2, pp. 32-67, les proverbes basques. Proverbs translated into French, from the collection by Oihenart. [B.M.

1294. Dasconaguerre (J. B.). Le Golfe de Gascogne—Pays basque, *etc.* pp. 229 + map. 12°. Pau, *Menetieve*, n.d.

Pp. 197-223, 69 Basque proverbs with French translations.

1295. Duvoisin ( ). [Basque proverbs].
Pamplona, 1878-79.

In Revista Euskara, 1878-1879.

1296. Eys (W. J. van). Proverbes basques-espagnols. Refranes y sentencias comunes en Bascuence, declaradas en Romance. Reédités d'après l'Unicum de 1596, conservé à la Bibliothèque de Darmstadt. pp. [v, 64].
sm. 4°. Genève et Bâle, *Georg*, 1896.

Basque and Spanish in parallel columns. Mainly dialect of Guipuzcoa. The original, Pamplona, *Porralis de Amberes*, 1596. An essay, by J. Vinson, dealing with this book is to be found in the Revue de linguistique, tome 29, pp. 201-19. [U.C.L.

1297. Garay (Ernest de). Sentences et maximes basques.
fr. 1. [Paris, *Levy?*], 1852.

1298. Garibay y Zamálloa (Estevan de). Proverbes basques. pp. 4. 8°. [Bordeaux, 1898?].

Reprinted from **1292** and **1302**. A list of 63 Basque proverbs without translations, followed by another dozen with French translations. Printed with Spanish translations in the "Memorial histórico español," Vol. 7, pp. 627-660, 1854. [B.M.

1299. Haristoy (P.), *Abbé.* Arnauld Doyhenart et son supplément des proverbes basques. pp. 24.

8°. Bayonne, *Lamaignère*, 1892.

Contains a brief notice of d'Oihenart and a reprint of his " Atsotizen urrhenquina. Supplément des proverbes basques et traduction," of which the unique example is in the Bibliothèque Nationale. These proverbs in Basque and French are numbered from 538-706 and are supplementary to his collection of 537 proverbs entitled " Atsotizac edo Refranac." [B.M.

1300. ———: Eskualdun zuhur-hitzak. Proverbes, sentences et dictons basques, *etc.*

8°. Paris, *Bureaux de la Tradition populaire*, 1899.

In La Tradition au Pays Basque, 1899. A collection of articles by various authors published under the auspices of the Société d'Éthnographie nationale et d'Art populaire. The proverbial part occupies pp. 281-289, and contains a brief general survey of the subject; also a number of sobriquets referring to different villages, given both in the original and translated into French. [B.M.

1301. Jauregui de San Juan (Francisco). Gramera berria, *etc.* pp. xvi, 126.   8°. Buenos Aires, *Igon*, 1883.

Pp. 120-124, Basque proverbs with Spanish equivalents or translations. [B.M.

1301a. Jaurgain (Jean de). A propos de " Los refranes vascos de Sauguis," par Jean de Jaurgain, *etc.* pp. 18.

8°. Bayonne, *Lamaignère*, 1909. [B.M.

1302. Mahn (Carl August F.). Denkmaeler der baskischen Sprache, *etc.* pp. lvi, 80.

1 Thlr., 10 Sgr. 8°. Berlin, *Duemmler*, 1857.

Pp. 56-67, reprints, without translations, the Basque proverbs from the ms. of Garibay and from Oihenart. [B.M.

1303. Merkens (Heinrich). Baskische Sprichwörter.

8°. Lunden, *Kramer*, 1893.

In Am Ur-Quell, Bd. 4, pp. 60-63. Basque proverbs with German translations. [B.M.

1304. Michel (Francisque). Le pays basque, sa population, sa langue, ses mœurs, sa littérature et sa musique. pp. 547.

8°. Paris, *Firmin Didot*, London and Edinburgh,
Williams & Norgate, 1857.

Pp. 29-42, proverbs in Basque and French.   [U.C.L.

1305. Oihenart (Arnauld d'). Les proverbes basques, *etc.* 2 pts. [in 1].   sm. 8°. Paris, 1657.
Second edition. pp. lxxvi, [8], 310.

8°. Bordeaux, *Faye*, 1847.

Gratet-Duplessis, 393. The book is composed of two parts, each with its own pagination, the first being entitled : Atsotisac edo refranac—Basque adages; the second part consists of Oihenart's Basque poetry. There are 537 proverbs with literal translations into French. The book is extremely rare. The second edition has another title page in Basque. In this second edition, besides notes on Oihenart's proverbs, other Basque proverbs are given, including those of Voltoire. [B.M.

1306. Oihenart (Arnauld d'). Supplément des proverbes basques, *etc.* [Edited by V. Stempf]. pp. iv, 8, 2, 13.

8°. Bordeaux, *Destouesse*, 1894.

Reprint of Oihenart's supplementary proverbs, Nos. 538-706, with French translations. [B.M.

1307. Refranes. Refranes y dichos populares. [Collected by various people].

3 pesetas, 1 peseta to members. 8°. Vitoria, 1921.

In Anuario de la Sociedad de Eusko-Folklore, 1921, pp. 43-58. 162 Basque proverbs and sayings with Spanish translations, arranged under localities. [F.-L.S.

1308. Salguis (Bertran). Los refranes vascos de Sauguis traducidos y anotados por Julio de Urquijo é Ibarra. 2 pts.

8°. Bayonne, *Lamaignère*, 1909.

Contains : an introduction dealing with various collections of Basque proverbs; proverbs from the ms. of Bertrand de Sauguis or Salguis; and an appendix. [B.M.

1309. Vinson (Julien). Le folk-lore du pays basque. pp. xxxvii, 396.   sm. 8°. Paris, *Maisonneuve*, 1883.

Littératures populaires de toutes les nations, Vol. 15. Pp. 263-306, proverbes et dictons : 228 proverbs with French translations. Pp. 387-393, dictons sur les noms des villages de la Soule, *etc.* [B.M.

1310. Voltoire (   ). Anciens proverbes, basques et gascons, recueillis par Voltoire et mis au jour par Gustave Brunet. pp. 14.   8°. Paris, *Techener*, 1845.

Nouvelle édition, revue, augmentée, et suivie de notes et renseignements inédits. pp. 29. 8°. Bayonne, *Cazals*, 1873.

Gratet-Duplessis, 375. Proverbs in old and modern Basque and French, some in rhyme, collected from two works by Voltoire, **1289** and **1311.** Vinson says they are not really Basque (Bibliographie, 12, i). [U.C.L. (1873).

1311. ———: L'interprect ou traduction du françois, espagnol et basque. pp. [vi], 280.   obl. 16°. Lyon, *Rouyer*, n.d.

Gratet-Duplessis, 392.

SPANISH.

1. GENERAL.

1312. Abancens (Ramón). Colección de adagios, ó refranes
españoles, con una sucinta explicación, *etc*.
8°. Orense, 1861.
[B.M.

1313. Aguilar y Claramunt (Simón). El buen sentido. Colección de refranes castellanos. pp. 152.
16°. Valencia, *Ortega*, 1895.

1314. Alberti (Leonora de). Proverbs in Spanish and English.
pp. 99.   32°. London, *Hill*, [1920].
Arranged alphabetically by the Spanish. No notes.   [B.M.

1315. Alvarado (Felix Antonio de). Diálogos ingleses y españoles.
Con muchos proverbios, *etc*. pp. xliv, 615.
8°. London, *Hinchliffe*, 1718.
Another edition. pp. xxix [=xxxix], 615. 8°. Londres, 1719.
No separate collection of proverbs; some occur in dialogues 5-8.   [B.M.

1316. Arcaeus (Ferdinandus). Adagiorum ex vernacula, id est
hispana lingua, latino sermone redditorum, quinquagenae
quinque addita ad initium cuiuslibet quinquagene fabella.
8°. [Salamantice], 1533.
Gratet-Duplessis, 479.   250 Spanish proverbs followed by Latin verses. Very
rare.   [B.M.

1317. Arrom de Ayala (Cecilia Francisca Josefa). Cuentos
oraciones, advinas y refranes populares é infantiles, recogidos
por Fernán Caballero [*pseud*. of C. F. J. Arrom de Ayala].
pp. 504.   8°. Madrid, *Fortanet*, 1877.
Another edition.   8°. Leipzig, *Brockhaus*, 1878.
1878 edition is Tom. 40 of Colección de Autores españoles. Contains a large
collection of proverbs and popular sayings.   [B.M.

1318. B. y M. (D. L.). Paremiología, ó tratado expositivo de
los apotegmas proverbiales. pp. viii, 304.
8°. Valladolid, *Cuesta*, 1889.
Proverbs classified rather loosely by subject, followed by explanatory notes.
[B.M.

1319. Bastus (Joaquin). La sabiduría de las naciones. . . .
Probable origen, etimología y razón histórica de muchos proverbios, refranes, *etc.* 3 series.

8°. Barcelona, *Manero*, 1862-67.

Gives the origin, etymology, *etc.*, of some 550 proverbs. There are many
comparisons with proverbs of other countries, translated into Spanish.
[B.M. (series 1-2).

1320. Bergnes de las Casas (Antonio). Novísima gramática
inglesa. . . . Cuarta edición, *etc.* pp. 342, 46.

8°. Barcelona, *Oliveres*, Madrid, *Hernando*, 1882.

Pp. 277-286, corresponding proverbs and sayings in English and Spanish.
These proverbs are arranged alphabetically by the English; no notes.   [B.M.

1321. Bordas (Luis). Curso de temas para ejercitarse en la
lengua castellana, *etc.* pp. 142. 16°. Barña, *Mayol*, 1828.

Another edition. Colección de temas, *etc.* pp. 173.

16°. Barcelona, *Mayol*, 1857.

The later, and larger, edition is the better. It contains, pp. 145-156, after
a few brief remarks on proverbs, a selection of 83 Catalan proverbs with their
Castillian equivalents.

1322. Burke (Ulick Ralph). Sancho Panza's proverbs, *etc.* pp.
xi, 44. 8°. London, *Pickering*, 1872.

Another edition. Spanish salt, *etc.* pp. xxiv, 99.

8°. London, *Pickering*, 1877.

Third edition. Sancho Panza's proverbs, *etc.* pp. xxi, 116.

8°. London, *Pickering*, 1892.

This book contains all the proverbs to be found in Don Quixote, arranged
alphabetically by key-words, with English translations, and occasional notes
and comparisons. References are given to the various chapters of the book
where the proverbs are to be found. The third edition is much enlarged. The
introduction is worth reading.
[B.M., F.-L.S. (Stephens collection, 1877 edition).

1323. Caballero (Fermin). Nomenclatura geográfica de España,
etc. pp. xiii, 240. 12°. Madrid, *Aguado*, 1834.

Pp. 170-240, proverbios. 367 geographical proverbs.   [B.M.

1324. Caro y Cejudo (Geronimo Martin). Refranes y modos de
hablar castellanos, con los latinos que les corresponden.
[First edition.] pp. [xxiv], 417 + indices.

8°. Madrid, *Izquierdo*, 1675.

Another edition. pp. x, 446.

4°. Madrid, *Imprenta real*, 1792.

Gratet-Duplessis, 503. This is the best and most extensive collection of
Spanish proverbs which we possess. The proverbs are given in all their forms,
and are carefully compared with Latin proverbs and sayings which are equivalent to, or offer a certain analogy with, them. The Spanish proverbs are
also frequently compared amongst themselves. A most erudite work, but
concise.   [B.M.

1325. Castres (G. H. F. de). Habla V. Castellano? . . . 4.
Auflage, *etc.* pp. viii, 180. 8°. Leipzig, *Koch*, 1890.
Pp. 104-107, proverbios. Sprüchwörter.

1326. Castro (Américo). Juan de Mal Lara y su filosofía vulgar.
1926.
Included in the volume in honour of Menéndez Pidal. A critical study of
the influence of Erasmus on the Spanish Renaissance. Reviewed in " El Sol,"
10th July, 1926.

1327. Cayetano (D.). El entremés de refranes, *etc.* pp. 78.
8°. Barcelona, *Jepús*, 1883.
Contains a number of proverbs, sayings, *etc.*, from Cervantes, with Catalan
translations.

1328. Cervantes Saavedra (Miguel de). L'ingénieux chevalier
Don Quixote de la Manche. [Illustrated]. 4 vols.
12°. Paris, *Desoer*, 1821.
Gratet-Duplessis, 514. Vol. 4, pp. 401-440, proverbes et sentences tirés de
l'histoire de Don Quixote. The proverbs are arranged alphabetically by subjects
and are given both in Spanish and French. [B.M.

1329. ———: Refranes de Sancho Panza, *etc.* [Edited by Lopez
del Arco]. pp. 132. 8°. Madrid, *Lopez del Arco*, 1905.
Pp. 7-20, refranes de Sancho Panza. [B.M.

1330. ———: Sentencias de Don Quijote y agudezas de Sancho,
etc. pp. 88. sm. 8°. Madrid, *Moya y Plaza*, 1863.
Pp. 81-88, refranes. [B.M.

1331. ———: Wit and wisdom of Don Quixote. pp. xlv, 288.
8°. Boston, *Roberts*, 1882.
Selections from Don Quixote, in English, with special reference to the
proverbs. These are indexed in order to facilitate reference to them. Another
very similar book of extracts, chiefly proverbs, without the index, was published
under the same title by Appleton. 8°, New York, 1867. [B.M.

1332. Colección. Colección de coplas, de seguidillas, boleras y
tiranas. sm. 12°. Barcelona, *Roca*, n.d.
Gratet-Duplessis, 513. Pp. 305-310, coplas que concluyen en juegos de
palabras ò refranes castellanos. There are many collections of the same kind,
mostly containing the same selections; *e.g.* 2 vols., 12°, Madrid, 1816; each
contains some few specimens which are not in the others.

1333. ———: Colección de refranes, adagios y locuciones proverbiales, con sus esplicaciones é interpretaciones. pp. 237.
12°. Madrid, *Burgos*, n.d.

1334. Coll y Vehí (José). Los refranes del Quijote, ordenados
por materias y glosados por José Coll y Vehí. pp. xxv, 248.
12 rs. 8°. Barcelona, *Diario de Barcelona*, 1874.
Pp. i-xxv, an excellent preface on the proverbs in Don Quixote, including
remarks on the different meanings of " refran," " proverbio," and " adagio."
Each proverb is followed by explanatory notes, and frequently by comparisons
with others. [B.M.

1335. Collins (John). A dictionary of Spanish proverbs, *etc.*
pp. iv, 391.   la. 12°.   London, *Whittaker*, 1823.

Gratet-Duplessis, 515. A good choice of proverbs, accompanied by literal translations and explanations. The notes are rather commonplace and obvious. *Reviewed in the* Quarterly Review, 125, pp. 217-254.   [B.M.

1336. Concurso. Concurso de proverbios españoles.
4°. Madrid, 1914.

A collection of proverbs published in the " Nuevo Mundo," from August 13 to October 24, 1914.

1337. Correas (Gonzalo). Vocabulario de refranes y frases proverbiales, *etc.* pp. xiii, 633.   8°. Madrid, *Ratés*, 1906.
Another edition. pp. xvi, 661.
16 pesetas. 8°. Madrid, *Tip. de la Rev. de Archivos, etc.*, 1924.

Proverbs, phrases, *etc.*, arranged alphabetically, with notes where necessary. *See also* **1377.**   [B.M.

1338. Costa Martinez (Joaquín). Introducción a un tratado de política sacado textualmente de los refraneros, romanceros y gestas de la Península. pp. viii, 500.
8°. Madrid, *Revista de Legislación*, 1881.
Another edition. pp. viii, 500.
8°. Madrid, *Fernando Fé*, 1888.

Pp. 28-54, elementos artisticos de la poesía popular española. 1. Refranes. A commentary with numerous examples.   [B.M.

1339. Covarrubias Horozco (Sebastian de). Refranes glosados, *etc.* [With a prologue, being a study of his life and works by E. Cotarelo y Mori].   8°. Madrid, 1915, *etc.*

In Boletín de la Real Academia Española, Tomo 2, pp. 646-706; Tomo 3, pp. 98-132, 399-428, 591-604, 710-721; Tomo 4, pp. 383-396. Although marked " to be continued," the publication was not resumed in the next three volumes. Cotarelo's prologue was published separately, Madrid, 1916.   [B.M.

1340. ———: Tesoro de la lengua castellana o española, *etc.*
[First edition.]   fol. Madrid, 1611.
Another edition. 2 pts.   fol. Madrid, *Sanchez*, 1674.
Gratet-Duplessis, 502. Contains a large number of proverbs with good explanations and notes.

1341. Danon (Abraham). Proverbes judéo-espagnols de Turquie.
8°. Halle, *Niemeyer*, 1903.

In Zeitschrift für romanische Philologie, Bd. 27, pp. 72-96. 323 proverbs in Spanish with French translations and notes.   [U.C.L.

1342. Dimas Capellan. Refranes glosados, por Dimas Capellan.
4°. Toledo, *Varela*, 1510.

There is little information about this book, which might even be the same as the anonymous **1405.** It is also uncertain whether Capellan is the name, or an indication of office.

1343. Escobar (Luis de). Las quatrociẽtas respuestas a otras tantas preguntas . . . cõ quinientos proverbios de cõsejos y avisos, por manera de letania, *etc.* 2 vols.

fol. [Valladolid], *F. de Cordova*, 1545-1552.

Second edition. 2 vols.   fol. [Valladolid], 1550-1552.

Another edition. 2 vols.   12°. Envers, [1560].

500 maxims in verse, in the form of a litany. They are also included in Tom. 7 of Sbarbi, **1420,** and in Vol. 4 of Nuñez, **1386.** The author's name is given in an acrostic, not on the title page.   [B.M.

1344. Espinosa (Juan de). Diálogo en laude de las mugeres . . . compuesto por Ioan de Spinosa.   4°. Milan, *Tini*, 1580.

Full of proverbs. Reprinted in Vol. 2 of Sbarbi, **1420.** Sbarbi gives an index to the proverbs contained in Espinosa's work.   [B.M.

1345. Fajardo (Alonso Guajardo). Los proverbios morales, *etc.* pp. iv, 46 leaves.   12°. Paris, *Fouet*, 1614.

Gratet-Duplessis, 489. A series of 280 quatrains, more moral maxims than proverbs, but some are popular sayings in verse. Oudin included 50 quatrains, with a French translation, in some of the editions of **1391,** notably those of 1609 and 1659. Fajardo's book, though with its own pagination, forms part of " La doleria del sueño del mundo . . . (por Pedro Hurtado de la Vera)," *etc.*, Paris, 1614.

1346. Ferrus (   ). Nouvelle grammaire espagnole, avec un recueil de sentences et proverbes, *etc.* pp. 320.

4°. Lyon, 1704.

Pp. 268-320, corresponding proverbs in Spanish and French. The first edition lacks these proverbs.

1347. Feyjoo y Montenegro (Benito Gerónymo). Cartas eruditas y curiosas. Segunda impresión. 3 vols.

4°. Madrid, *Hierro*, 1748-51.

Nueva impresión. 5 vols.

4°. Madrid, *Imprenta real de la Gazeta*, 1777.

Gratet-Duplessis, 509. Vol. 3, Carta primera, fallibilidad de los adagios. *Reprinted in* Vol. 9 of Sbarbi, **1420.**   [B.M.

1348. Font (Ramón). Bons consells ab la traduccio castellana. pp. 164, 40. 2 parts.

8°. Gerona, *Carreras*, [1898], [Barcelona, *Jepús*], 1899.

The two parts together contain some 800 aphorisms and proverbs, more or less popular.

1349. Garay (Blasco de). Cartas de refranes de Blasco de Garay, con otras de nuevo añadidas. pp. [48].   sm. 4°. 1545.

Another edition. Dos cartas . . . le escrive por muchos refranes, *etc.*   4°. [Toledo, 1541].

Another edition with other poems. pp. [150].

sm. 16°. Anberes, *Tylenio*, 1577.

Another edition.   12°. Valencia, 1589.

Gratet-Duplessis, 481. These letters in proverbs have been reprinted in **1386, 1391, 1420** (Vol. 7), and also in Processo de cartas de amores que entre dos amantes passaran, *etc.* sm. 8°. Venetia, *Ferrariis*, 1553.

[B.M. (included in various editions).

1350. García Moreno (Melchior). Catálogo paremiológico. pp. 248 + plates.

4°. Madrid, *Soc. española de Artes gráficas*, 1918.

Primarily a catalogue of García Moreno's private collection of books of proverbs, though he mentions, without details, others which he does not possess. The entries number 480, and the book forms a very fair bibliography of Spanish proverbs.

1351. ———: Extracto de algunos juicios acerca del catálogo paremiológico de M. García Moreno. pp. 37.

8°. Madrid, *Sociedad española de Artes gráficas*, 1919.

A collection of reviews and other notices of **1350**. [B.M.

1352. Garrido (Antonio). Floresta española. . . . Cuarta edición, *etc.* pp. 335. 12°. Londres, *Boosey*, 1827.

Another edition. 12°. London, *Simpkin Marshall*, 1855.

Concludes with a few pages entitled : Refranes de la lengua española, con sus explicaciones. [B.M.

1353. Gomez (Estevan). Refranes glosados, *etc.*

sm. 8°. Valencia, *Franco*, 1602.

Another edition. sm. 8°. Barcelona, 1624.

1354. Gorgues y Lema (Juan). Lluvia de refranes.—Consejos á los forasteros en refranes españoles por medio de una carta, *etc.* pp. 32. 8°. Madrid, *Minuesa de los Rios*, 1879.

Second edition. pp. 79. 12°. Madrid, 1880.

An interesting little work written in imitation of **1349**. The second edition contains more than one letter.

1355. Guijarro (Francisco). Manual para entender y hablar el castellano. pp. 160. 8°. Valencia, *Montfort*, 1796.

Pp. 111-160, 870 proverbs, without notes.

1356. Haller (Joseph). Altspanische Sprichwörter und sprich-wörtliche Redensarten . . . in spanischer und deutscher Sprache erörtert, und verglichen mit den entsprechenden der alten Griechen und Römer, der Lateiner der späteren Zeiten, der sämmtlichen germanischen und romanischen Völker und einer Anzahl der Basken, *etc.* 2 Thle.

8°. Regensburg, *Manz*, 1883.

A very comprehensive book, giving parallels from many tongues. Theil 1 deals with 550 Spanish proverbs, accompanied by many thousand equivalents in other languages. Theil 2 is chiefly a bibliography of the proverbs, folk songs, *etc.*, of various languages. [B.M.

1357. ———: Die spanischen Sprichwörter.

fol. Leipzig, *Friederich*, 1882.

In Magazin für die Literatur des In- und Auslandes, Jahrgang 51, No. 49, pp. 677-679. A commentary, chiefly bibliographical. [B.M.

L

1358. Hay (John Milton).   Castilian days.   pp. 414.
8°. Boston, *Osgood*, 1871.

Another edition. pp. v, 414.
8°. London, *Lane*, Boston, *Mifflin*, 1897.

Pp. 267-281, proverbial philosophy. Contains numerous examples in English.
This chapter is not included in the edition of 1903.   [B.M.

1359. Huygens (Konstantyn).   Koren-Bloemen, nederlandsche
gedichten, *etc.* pp. [xxii], 1355.
4°. 's Graven-Hague, *Vlack*, 1658.

Pp. 1121-1268, Spaensche wysheit, vertaelde spreekwoorden. 1318 rhyming
proverbs in Spanish, with Dutch translations.   [B.M.

1360. Iñiguez de Medrano (Julian).   La silva curiosa.   Libro
primero. [First edition]. pp. [xxiv], 448. 8°. Paris, 1583.
No more seems to have been published.

Ditto. Corregida en esta nueva edición, y reducida a mejor
lectura por César Oudin. pp. [xvi], 328.
sm. 8°. Paris, *Orry*, 1608.

Another edition.   Madrid, 1878.

Gratet-Duplessis, 494. This collection of pieces in prose and verse contains
a number of proverbs, and various anecdotes chiefly taken from **1425**. Reprinted
in Vol. 10 of Sbarbi, **1420**.   [B.M

1361. Jimenez (Antonio).   Colección de refranes, adagios y
locuciones proverbiales, *etc.* pp. 190.
sm. 8°. Madrid, *Peralta*, 1828.

Gratet-Duplessis, 517. A good selection of the best Spanish proverbs, in
alphabetical order, with brief, clear explanations.   [B.M.

1362. Knust (Hermann).   Mittheilungen aus dem Eskurial, *etc.*
pp. 686.   8°. Tübingen, 1879.

Bibliothek des litterarischen Vereins in Stuttgart, Bd. 141. Pp. 1-65, Este
es el libro de los buen proverbios que dixeiron los phi[losophos].   [U.C.L.

1363. Koeler (Friedrich).   Sammlung spanischer Sprüchwörter,
etc. pp. 68.   8°. Leipsig, *Teubner*, 1845.

Gratet-Duplessis, 520. A good selection of 505 Spanish proverbs, with
German translations, preceded by an interesting introduction. Occasionally the
proverbs are compared with other foreign ones.   [B.M.

1364. Kotzenberg (H. W. A.).   Anleitung zur spanischen und
deutschen Umgangsprache, *etc.* pp. viii, 156.
8°. Bremen, *Heyse*, 1842.
Pp. 150-156, proverbs in both languages.

1365. Kramer (Matthias).   Grammatica et syntaxis linguae Hispanicae, *etc.* 3 vols. [in 1].
8°. Noribergae, *Ziegerus*, 1711.

Stirling-Maxwell, p. 17. Vol. 3, pp. 199-226, Hispanorum selectissima
adagia, seu proverbia quae ipsi refranes vocant.

1366. Logan (Walter MacGregor). Collection of Spanish proverbs, *etc.* pp. 71. 12°. London, *Seguin*, 1830.

Gratet-Duplessis, 518. Some 500 Spanish proverbs, with literal English translations. No notes and no order. Of little importance, since it is impossible to refer to anything. A " teacher and pupil " book. There is another title page in Spanish. [B.M.

1367. Lopez de Mendoza (Iñigo), *Marques de Santillana.* Iñigo lopez de mendoça a ruego del Rey don Juan ordeno estos refranes que dizen las viejas tras el fuego y van ordenados por el a.b.c. pp. [24]. 4°. [1500?].
Another edition. pp. [24].
4°. [Sevilla, *Cromberger*, 1508].
A facsimile of the edition of Sevilla, 1542.
8°. [Madrid, *Lacoste*, 1910].

Gratet-Duplessis, 472. There is some discussion whether the first edition given above is really earlier than that of 1508. The proverbs were reprinted in Mayans y Siscar " Origenes de la lengua española," *etc.*, 2 vols., sm. 8°, Madrid, 1737, in Vol. 1 of Sbarbi, **1420**, and in the Revue Hispanique, Vol. 25, 1911, pp. 134-219. [B.M. (various editions).

1368. ———: Los proverbios utilissimos del illustre cavallero Don Eñigo Lopez de Mendoza, *etc.* 34 leaves. [First edition?]. fol. [14—?]
Los proverbios de Yñigo lopes de Mēdoça cō su glosa.
4°. Sevilla, *Ungut aleman & Stanislao polono*, 1494.
Another edition. sm. 12°. Anvers, *Nucio*, 1594.
Another edition. Proverbios de Lopez de Mendoça, *etc.*
sm. 12°. Madrid, *Vilalpando*, 1799.

Gratet-Duplessis, 473. That of 1594 is the last of the early editions, of which there were a good many, and that of 1799 is a good fairly recent one. Composed more of aphorisms, maxims, moral reflections, *etc.*, than true proverbs.
[B.M. (various editions).

1369. Lopez de Yanguas (Hernan).
Aqui lector veras juntas
Por Hernan Lopez compuestas
Cincuenta biuas preguntas
Con otras tantas respuestas.
[Medina del Campo, *Pedro de Castro*, 1543?].
Another edition. pp. [32].
sm. 8°. Valencia, *Joan de Mey*, 1550.

Gratet-Duplessis, 484. Most of these questions and answers are true proverbial sayings. An extremely rare book. [B.M.

1370. Luna (Juan de). Diálogos familiares, *etc.* pp. 589.
12°. Paris, *Daniel*, 1619.

Gratet-Duplessis, 499, and Hécart, Bibliographie parémiographique, p. 45. Reproduced in Vol. 1 of Sbarbi, **1420**. The dialogues are given in Spanish and French, and contain numerous proverbs. They are also reproduced in Spanish and English in Oudin's " A grammar Spanish and English," *etc.*, 8°, London, 1622. [B.M.

1371. M. Proverbou spagnol, troet e verzou Brezonnec gant M***. pp. 12. 12°. [Quimper? 1760?]

Gratet-Duplessis, 511. A very rare book, containing the translation into Breton verse of 156 Spanish proverbs. Duplessis thinks it was published about the end of the 18th or the beginning of the 19th century. [B.M.

1372. M. (A.). Spaniolische Sprichwörter. (Aus Tatar Bazard-žyk in Ost-Rumelien). 8°. Leiden, *Brill*, 1897.

In Der Urquell, N.F., Bd. 1, pp. 84-86, 204-205. 40 proverbs with German translations. [B.M.

1373. M. y Ll. Refranes y adagios en castellano y catalán, *etc.* pp. 16. 4°. Barcelona, *Tasso*, 1863.

Pp. 13-16, 130 Spanish proverbs, with Catalan translations.

1374. Machado y Álvarez (Antonio). Folk-lore. Biblioteca de las tradiciones populares españolas. [Edited by A. Machado y Álvarez]. 11 tomos.
8°. Sevilla, *Álvarez, Guichot, Fé*, 1883-6.

Tom. 5, pp. 53-64, Coplas refranescas : pp. 65-71, Coplas sentenciosas : pp. 73-79, Antimonía entre un refrán y una copla. [B.M.

1375. Mallara (Juan de). La philosophia vulgar. Primera parte. *etc.* fol. Sevilla, *Diaz*, 1568.

Gratet-Duplessis, 487. No more published. An excellent and learned book, containing researches on a thousand popular proverbs. *See also* **1326.** These proverbs were reprinted at the end of various editions of **1386.** [B.M.

1376. Mar (Emanuel del). A new guide to conversation in Spanish and English, *etc.* pp. vii, 124.
3/6. 16°. London, *Wacey*, 1839.
Fourth edition. pp. viii, 179.
4/-. 8°. London, *Dulau*, 1853.

Contains a collection of proverbs and idioms in both languages. [B.M.

1377. Marín (Francisco Rodríguez). Más de 21,000 refranes castellanos no contenidos en la copiosa colección del maestro Gonzalo Correas [**1337**], *etc.* pp. l, 519.
4°. Madrid, *Revista de Archivos*, 1926.

Marín's paper, **1377b,** is given as a prologue. The proverbs were chiefly collected from country people, though some from more literary sources are included. It is doubtful whether all these are strictly proverbs. Alphabetical arrangement, with notes. *Reviewed in* El Sol, July 3rd, 1926. [B.M.

1377a. ———: Los refranes del almanaque, *etc.* pp. viii, 185.
2 pesetas. 8°. Sevilla, *Diaz*, 1896.

Spanish calendar proverbs, frequently compared with those of other countries, particularly Portugal and Italy. 750 proverbs are given arranged by months. Pp. 175-178, a list of authorities. A selection of these proverbs, without notes, was later published as : El año en refranes, Madrid, 1915. [B.M.

1377b. ——— and **Montoto y Rautenstrauch** (Luis). Discursos leídos ante la Real Academia Sevillana, *etc.* pp. 99.
8°. Sevilla, *Rasco*, 1895.

Two theses, both dealing with proverbs.

1378. Mémoires. Mémoires curieux envoyez de Madrid, *etc.*
pp. 137.   sm. 12°. Paris, *Léonard*, 1670.

Gratet-Duplessis, 501. Pp. 93-116, " Commentaire de divers proverbes et
autres façons de parler espagnolles," written in the form of a letter, dated
June 12th, 1666, and signed A. Only a few proverbs and sayings are given,
but these are some of the most remarkable and least known.

1379. Meurier (Gabriel). Coloquios familiares muy convenientes,
para . . . hablar y escribir Español y Francés. ff. 128.
                     12°. Anvers, *Waesberge*, 1568.

These dialogues are full of proverbs, maxims, *etc.*, which are distinguished
by an asterisk.   [B.M.

1380. Mez. (Nicolaus). Gramatica o instruccion española y
alemana, *etc.* ff. 67.   12°. Viena, *Rickesin*, 1667.

Ff. 6-9, Refranes españoles. A rare book.

1381. Montoto y Rautenstrauch (Luis). Un paquete de cartas,
de modismos, locuciones, frases hechas, frases proverbiales,
y frases familiares. pp. 323.
                     8°. [Madrid, Sevilla], *Fé*, 1888.

1382. Moratori (Antonio). Instrucion fundamental para aprender
el idioma español, *etc.* pp. [xxiv], 424.
                     8°. Nürnberg, *Monath*, 1723.

Bernstein, 2256. Pp. 110-127, proverbs and moral maxims in Spanish, Latin
and German.

1383. Musso y Fontes (José). Diccionario de las metáforas y
refranes de la lengua castellana. pp. 250.
                     4°. Barcelona, *Ramirez*, 1876.

Full of typographical errors which rather destroy its value.

1384. National Proverbs. National proverbs: Spain. pp. 95.
          1/-. sm. 8°. Philadelphia, *McKay*, [191—?].

A selection of proverbs in Spanish and English; no notes.
                              [F.-L.S. (Stephens collection).

1385. Nervo (Gonzalve de). Dictons et proverbes espagnols.
pp. 115.   12°. Paris, *Lévy*, 1874.

A selection of proverbs, sayings, place rhymes, *etc.*, with French translations.
No index.   [B.M.

1386. Nuñez de Guzman (Fernando). Refranes o proverbios en
romance, *etc.* ff. 142.
          5 reales. fol. Salamanca, *Juan de Canova*, 1555.

Another edition. Refranes . . . Y la Filosofia vulgar de Juan
de Mal Lara . . . las quatro cartas de Blasco de Garay, *etc.*
ff. [4], 399.   4°. Madrid, *Juan de la Cuesta*, 1619.
Another edition. Refranes o proverbios en castellano . . .
emendados por Luis de Leon. 4 vols.
                     sm. 8°. Madrid, *Repulles*, 1803-04.

Gratet-Duplessis, 486, gives various other editions. All the early editions
are rare; the best is that of 1619, since it contains not only the proverbs of

Nuñez but also the Filosofía vulgar of Mallara and the letters in proverbs of Blasco de Garay. The recent edition of 1803-04 is also a good one. Though it does not contain Mallara's work, it includes in Vol. 4 : The letters of Blasco de Garay; a series of " Refranes de Mesa," taken from a rare volume entitled " El estudioso cortesano "; a subject list of the proverbs commented on and explained in the Filosofía vulgar.

This collection of proverbs by Nuñez is one of the largest and most curious that exists. It is arranged in alphabetical order, in general without notes, though occasionally a few words of explanation are added. It contains nearly all the Portuguese proverbs and a large number of French and Italian ones. There are also some Galician proverbs.

The first edition in the British Museum contains copious ms. notes in Spanish. [B.M. (various editions).

1387. O. (K.). Colección de proverbios glosados, compuesta por K.O. pp. 81. 8°. Madrid, *Burgos*, 1834.

Stirling-Maxwell, p. 16. 52 proverbs accompanied by moral reflexions. Reprinted in Vol. 8 of **1420.** [B.M.

1388. Orbaneja y Majada (E.). El saber del pueblo, *etc.* pp. 375. 8°. Valladolid, *Pastor*, 1890.

A collection of Spanish proverbs with brief explanatory notes. These are followed by a very brief list of proverbs of other countries, in Spanish and without notes. [B.M.

1389. Ortiz del Casso (José). Colección de refranes o proverbios castellanos, con la esplicacion de los de mas difícil inteligencia, *etc.* pp. 118. 8°. Marsella, *Casa del Autor*, 1849.

Bernstein, 2421.

1390. Oudin (César). Diálogos muy apazibles escritos en lengua española y traducidos en frances, *etc.*
sm. 12°. Bruxelles, *Rutger Velpius*, 1611.

Another edition. Dialogos en español y françes, *etc.* pp. 261.
sm. 12°. Bruxelles, *Foppens*, 1643.

Gratet-Duplessis, 496. There are many editions, all equally good, of these dialogues. They contain a large number of Spanish proverbs, well interpreted and clearly explained by the translator. There was an Italian translation by Lorenzo Franciosini, *q.v.*, **2248.** [B.M.

1391. ———: Refranes o proverbios españoles, traduzidos en lengua francesa, *etc.* pp. [xiv], 187.
12°. Paris, *Orry*, 1605.

Another edition. pp. 269, 126.
12°. Brussellas, *Foppens*, 1702.

Gratet-Duplessis, 459. A good selection of proverbs well translated. Arranged alphabetically by the Spanish. There are many other editions, some of which also contain the " Cartas en refranes " of Blasco de Garay—notably the editions of 1612, 1634, 1702. The edition of 1659 contains 50 quatrains from the " Proverbios morales " of A. G. Fajardo. Oudin's collection is also included in Gruter's " Florilegium ethico-politicum," *q.v.*, **80.** [B.M., U.C.L.

1392. P. y G. (A. A.). Instrucciones económicas y políticas, dados por Sancho Panza. . . . Las da á luz D. A. A. P. y G. pp. 64. sm. 8°. Madrid, *Imprenta real*, 1791.

Gratet-Duplessis, 510. Sbarbi, who reprints this in Vol. 5 of **1420,** says Duplessis has made various mistakes; that it was published in 1791 not 1781; and that very many of these proverbs are not to be found in Don Quixote.

[B.M.

1392a. Palmireno (Lorenzo). Refranes. *See* **1420.**

1393. Percyvall (Richard). A Spanish grammar, first collected and published by Richard Percivale, Gent. Now augmented . . . by John Minsheu, *etc.* 2 pts.

fol. London, *Bollisant*, 1599.

Another edition.

fol. London, *J. Haviland, for M. Lownes*, 1623.

Contains a section of words, phrases, sentences and proverbs out of various authors, with English equivalents and literal translations. Also a brief section of true proverbs. [B.M.

1394. Perez de Gusman (Fernan). Rimas inéditas de Don Iñigo Lopez de Mendoza, Marques de Santillana, de Fernán Perez de Gusman, Señor de Batres, recogidas y anotadas por Eugenio de Ochoa. pp. xxiv, 412.

8°. Paris, *Fain y Thunot*, 1844.

Gratet-Duplessis, 519. Pp. 343-56, the proverbios of Perez de Gusman, here published for the first time; they are little more than moral quatrains. [B.M.

1395. Perez de Herrera (Christóbal). Proverbios morales y consejos christianos, *etc. First edition.* ff. [xxiv], 224.

4°. Madrid, *Sanchez*, 1618.

Another edition. pp. [xxiv], 360.

4°. Madrid, *Herederos de Francisco del Hierro*, 1733.

Gratet-Duplessis, 497. The 1733 edition is an exact copy of that of 1618. Both are equally rare. This curious work in verse consists of two parts. The first contains the " proverbios morales," moral maxims and aphorisms taken chiefly from the Scriptures and the early writers, and including very few proverbs. The second part contains 323 enigmas (in verse with their explanation in prose), moral, philosophical, natural, and most ingenious and original. The moral proverbs, not the enigmas, were reprinted in A. de Castro's Biblioteca de autores españoles, Vol. 42. [B.M. (various editions).

1396. Povius (Onophrius). Thesaurus puerilis, *etc.* pp. [xiv], 404, [8]. 12°. Valentiae, *Mey*, [1615].

Pp. 359-404, Proverbios castellanos y latinos. Some of the earlier editions do not appear to contain the proverbs.

1397. Probervios. Probervios en rimo del sabio Salamon, rey de israel, *etc.* pp. [8]. sm. 4°. [14—].

Gratet-Duplessis, 474. A free imitation of the Proverbs of Solomon. Extremely rare.

1398. Proverbs. On Spanish proverbs.

8°. London, Edinburgh, 1900.

In Chambers's Journal, Sixth Series, Vol. 3, pp. 109-111. [B.M.

1399. Proverbs. Spanish proverbs.   8°. London, 1859.

In Household Words, Vol. 19, pp. 390-393. Contains a large number of examples in English.   [B.M.

1400. Przysłowia. Przysłowia hiszpańskie.
                                   4°. w Warszawie, 1844.

In Magazyn Mód, 1844, N.3.18. Spanish proverbs translated into Polish.

1401. Puente y Úbeda (Carlos). Meteorología popular ó refranero meteorológico de la Península Ibérica. . . . 1. Climatología. pp. 279.   8°. Madrid, *Cuesta*, 1896.

1402. Ramirez y Blanco (Alejandro). Respuestas de Sanchico Panza á dos cartas . . . Primera que publica . . . Ramon Alexo de Zidra. [Anagram of Ramirez]. pp. xii, 37.
                             8°. Alcalá, *Lopez*, 1791.

Proverbs scattered throughout are gathered together in an index at the end. Reprinted by Sbarbi in Vol. 5 of **1420**.   [B.M.

1403. Refranes. Refranes.   8°. Fregenal, 1883.

In El Folklore betico-extremeño, 1883, pp. 215-216. 48 entries.

1404. ———: Refranes de la lengua castellana. 2 vols.
                        sm. 8°. Barcelona, *Rocca*, 1815.

Gratet Duplessis, 512. This collection is an extract from the Dictionary of the Spanish Academy.

1405. ———: Refranes famosissimos y provechosos glosados.
                                   4°. Burgos, 1509.

Another edition. ff. 12.
                 sm. 4°. [Burgos, *Fadrique aleman*, 1515].
Refranes glosados en los quales qualquier que con diligencia quisiere leer hallara proverbios, *etc.*
                 sm. 4°. [Burgos, *Alonzo de Melgar*, 1524].
Another edition.   4°. [Burgos?, 1530?].
Another edition.   4°. [Burgos?], 1541.
Another edition. pp. 24.   8°. Paris, *Renouard*, 1847.

Gratet-Duplessis, 475-8. These last are other editions of the first title. Duplessis reprints the 1515 edition in his "Bibliographie parémiologique," pp. 481-500. Sbarbi reprints the 1541 edition in Vol. 7 of **1420**. An excellent little collection of proverbs accompanied by moral advice.   [B.M. (various editions).

1406. ———: Refranes y avisos por via de consejos hechos por uno de Morella, *etc.* pp. [16].   sm. 8°. Valencia, 1551.

Gratet-Duplessis, 485. In verse. A selection of moral maxims including some proverbs. Very rare. Reprinted by Sbarbi in Vol. 8 of **1420**.

1407. Romero y Espinosa (L.). Dichos locales españoles.
                                   8°. Palermo, 1882.

In Archivio per lo studio delle tradizioni popolari, Vol. 1, pp. 584-587. [B.M.

1408. Rovira y Virgili (Antonio). Diccionari catalá-castellá e castellá-catalá, *etc.* pp. 840.

8°. Barcelona, *Lopez*, 1913.

Pp. 723-782, Castillian proverbs with Catalan equivalents : pp. 785-840, Catalan proverbs with Castillian equivalents.

1409. Salvá y Mallen (Pedro). Catálogo de la biblioteca de Salvà, *etc.* 2 tom. 8°. Valencia, *Ferrer de Orga*, 1872.

Pp. 195-248, Sección paremiológica. Catalogue of 139 books dealing with proverbs, moral maxims, emblems, *etc.* [B.M.]

1410. Sanchez de la Ballesta (A.). Diccionario de vocablos castellanos. . . . En el qual se declarari gran copia de refranes vulgares. Con un indice de los adagios latinos a los quales responden los castellanos. sm. 4°. Salamanca, 1587.

Gratet-Duplessis, 491. Has been superseded by later works, notably the collection of Caro y Cejudo, *q.v.*, **1324.**

1411. Santa Cruz de Dueñas (Melchior de). Libro primero (segundo) de los cien tratados, *etc.* 2 pts. [in 1].

12°. Toledo, *Ayala*, 1576.

Gratet-Duplessis, 490. A very rare work composed of moral maxims, amongst which are a number of proverbs, in verse. [B.M.]

1412. Sanz (Pedro Luis). Trezientos proverbios, consejos y avisos, *etc.* pp. [26]. 16°. [Valencia, 1545?].

Gratet-Duplessis, 480. A very rare work written in verse, and consisting of moral maxims which are not really proverbs. [B.M.]

1413. Saralegui y Medina (Manuel de). Refranero español náutico y meteorologico, *etc.* pp. 223.

8°. Barcelona, *Rieusset*, 1917.

433 proverbs with accompanying notes, and place of origin. [B.M.]

1414. Saura (Santiago Angel). Novíssim diccionari manual de las llenguas catalana-castellana, *etc.* pp. viii, 552.

8°. Barcelona, *Pujal*, 1883.

Another edition. pp. viii, 696. 8°. Barcelona, 1884.

The first edition of 1866 is the same as that of 1883. Over 3,000 Catalan proverbs with Castillian equivalents are given at the end of the first book, and a similar number of Castillian ones with Catalan equivalents, at the end of the second. [B.M.]

1415. Sbarbi (José María). Diccionario de refranes, adagios, proverbios . . . de la lengua española. Obra postuma, ordenada . . . bajo la dirección de D. Manuel José García. 2 tomos.

40 pesetas each. 8°. Madrid, *Sucesores de Hernando*, 1922.

A very large collection of proverbs, arranged alphabetically by key-words, and with explanatory notes. [B.M.]

1416. Sbarbi (José María). Doña Lucía. Novela histórica ó historia novelesca. pp. xxii, 248.

8°. Madrid, *Fuentenebro*, 1886.

The book abounds in proverbs which are not included in the dictionary of the Spanish Academy.

1417. ———: Florilegio ó ramillete alfabético de refranes y modismos comparativos, *etc.* pp. 302.

8°. Madrid, *Fuentenebro*, 1873.

Contains many proverbs amongst the sayings and comparisons, many of which have, however, become proverbial. Alphabetical arrangement by key-words. Each saying is followed by explanatory notes. [B.M.]

1418. ———: El libro de los refranes.

Madrid, *Simon y Urosa*, 1872.

Contains some 1800 proverbs, sayings, *etc.*, arranged in alphabetical order, which are not to be found in the usual collections.

1419. ———: Monografía sobre los refranes, adagios y proverbios castellanos, *etc.* pp. 412.

8°. Madrid, *Imprenta de los huérfanos*, 1891.

The standard authority on matters of Spanish paremiology. The first part contains an excellent dissertation on the origin, use and importance of proverbs, and a sermon on proverbs in Spanish and French. The second part forms a catalogue of Spanish paremiology, comprising some 600 entries. [B.M.]

1420. ———: El refranero general español, parte recopilado, y parte compuesto. 10 tom.

8°. Madrid, *Fuentenebro*, 1874-1878.

An extremely valuable work. Tomo 1, pp. 1-67, a dissertation on the character, importance and use of proverbs : pp. 69-153, **1367**: pp. 155-277, **1370**: pp. 279-293, Refranes de mesa . . . Lorenzo Palmireno, 1569.—Proverbs in alphabetical order, without notes. Tomo 2, **1344**. Tomo 3, Medicina española . . . por Iuan Sorapan de Rieros, 1616.—This contains a commentary and explanation of some 50 Spanish proverbs dealing with health and medicine. Tomo 4, **1428**. Tomo 5, pp. 1-39, **1392**: pp. 41-66, **1402**: pp. 69-159, **1426**. Tomo 6, pp. 198-291, proverbs, sayings, *etc.*, from Don Quixote, arranged in alphabetical order by the key-words. Tomo 7, pp. 1-54, **1405** (1541 edition) : pp. 55-107, **1349**: pp. 109-121, Entremes de refranes.—An interlude in dramatic form : pp. 123-166, **1387**: pp. 175-253, **1343**. Tomo 8, pp. 113-125, **1406**: pp. 127-140, proverbs taken from mss. at Madrid : pp. 141-146, a translation of **1424**: pp. 147-154, Proverbios espirituales por un religioso, *etc.* : pp. 155-201, Axiomas militares . . . por Nicolas de Castro.—Military maxims, in verse : pp. 203-248, Discurso . . . por Antonio García Gutierrez, 1862 : pp. 249-271, Discurso de Antonio Ferrer del Rio en contestacion al precedente.—These two consist of a paper on proverbs and its reply. Tomo 9, pp. 1-92, Comedia nueva . . . casarse por colosina y refranes á trompon. Manuel Vela Manzano, 1762. —Contains many proverbs : pp. 93-103. Crítica reforma de los comunes refranes . . . de El Criticon del P. Baltasar Gracian : pp. 105-128, **1347**: pp. 128-184, **1476**: pp. 185-231, **1468**. Tomo 10, **1360**. [B.M.]

1421. Sobrino (Francisco). Nouveaux dialogues espagnols expliqués en françois, contenant beaucoup de proverbes, *etc.*

8°. Bruxelles, *Foppens*, 1708.

Another edition. Dialogos nuevos en español y francés, *etc.*

8°. Brusselas, *Foppens*, 1724.

Gratet-Duplessis, 506. An elementary book of little importance. [B.M.

1422. Stein (Leopold). Untersuchungen über die proverbios morales von Santob de Carrion, *etc.* pp. 109.

8°. Berlin, *Mayer & Müller*, 1900.

[B.M.

1423. Stepney (William). The Spanish schoole-master, *etc.* pp [viii], 252. 16°. London, *Harison*, 1591.

Another edition. pp. [x], 239.

12°. London, *Harison*, 1620.

Contains a list of proverbs in Spanish and English. No notes. [B.M.

1424. Stirling (William), *afterwards* **Stirling-Maxwell** (*Sir* William), *Bart.* A few Spanish proverbs about friars. pp. 7.

sm. 4°. London, 1855-56.

Bibliographical and historical miscellanies of the Philobiblon Society, Vol. 2, item 12. A few copies printed separately. Reprinted at pp. 37-40 of Vol. 6 of the author's Works, London, 1891. These proverbs were found by Stirling, added in 16th century handwriting to a copy of Nuñez, **1386.** Translated into Spanish, they were reprinted by Sbarbi in Vol. 8 of **1420.** [B.M.

1425. Timoneda (Juan de). El sobremesa y alivio de caminantes, *etc.* 4 pts. [in 1]. sm. 8°. Çaragoça, *Guesa*, 1563.

Another edition. Alivio de caminantes, *etc.* ff. 72.

12°. Medina del Campo, *Francisco del Cauto*, 1563.

Another edition. 8°. Barcelona, 1885.

Gratet-Duplessis, 488. This work is divided into four parts, the first three of which are composed of short tales. The second, particularly, contains a number of anecdotes designed to indicate the origin of certain popular sayings. Most of these anecdotes and tales were reprinted, without naming the author, in the " Silva curiosa " of Julian Iñiguez de Medrano, *q.v.*, **1360.** Duplessis reprints four anecdotes as typical specimens. [B.M.

1426. Trigueros (Cándido Maria). Teatro español burlesco ó Quixote de los teatros, por el maestro Crispin Caramillo [*pseud.* of C. M. Trigueros], *etc.* pp. xxiv, 160.

8°. Madrid, *Imprenta de Villalpando*, 1802.

This is a burlesque of the theatre in the style of Don Quixote, and, like it, contains numerous proverbs. Included also in tomo 5 of Sbarbi, **1420:** indexed at the end. [B.M.

1427. V. (F.) and **B.** (M.). Colección de refranes y locuciones familiares de la lengua castellana con su correspondencia latina, por F. V. y M. B., *etc.* pp. [x], 509.

8°. Barcelona, *Oliveres*, 1841.

Divided into three parts, the first containing proverbs in rhyme, the second proverbs in prose, the third proverbial sayings, phrases, *etc.*, accompanied by Latin translations or equivalents.

1428. Valladares de Sotomayor (Antonio). Colección de seguidillas ó cantares, *etc.* . . . por D. A. V. D. S.

Madrid, *Franganillo*, 1799.

Contains 500-600 proverbs. Published by Sbarbi in Vol. 4 of **1420.**

1429. Valles (Pedro). Libro de refranes copilado por el ordē del
A.B.C. En el qual se cōtienen quatro mil y treziētos
refranes, *etc.*
4°. Çaragoça, *Juana Milian biuda de Diego
Hernandez*, 1549.
A facsimile printed. 4°. Madrid, *Imprenta alemana*, 1917.

Gratet-Duplessis, 482. A simple list without notes or explanations; at the
end are a few Latin proverbs. Very rare. The author's name is given in
an acrostic at the beginning. [B.M.

1430. Velázquez (Baltasar Mateo). El filosofo del aldea, *etc.*
ff. [6], 88. sm. 8°. Pamplona, *Dullort*, 1626.

Contains proverbs in various places, particularly ff. 9-10. The book is also
included in : Coleccion selecta de antiguas novelas españolas, tomo 4. [B.M.

1431. Ventura-Sabatel (Francisco). Nuevo despertador de la
infancia, *etc.* pp. 79. 16°. Granada, *Ventura*, n.d.

Bernstein, 3861. Pp. 37-43, Refranes castellanos.

1432. Verdaguer (Jacinto). Aforística. Folk-lore. pp. 92.
8°. Barcelona, *L'Avenc*, 1907.

Pp. 41-92, some 500 sayings, some literary, some popular.

1433. Vergara y Martín (Gabriel María). Algunos refranes y
modismos populares de carácter geográfico, empleados en
España con relación a Portugal. 4°. Madrid.

1434. ———: Cantares, refranes y modismos geográficos empleados en España con relacion a otros pueblos.
4°. Madrid.

1435. ———: Diccionario geográfico popular de cantares,
refranes, adagios, proverbios, *etc.* pp. 336.
4°. Madrid, *Hernando*, 1923.

A large collection of Spanish songs, proverbs and sayings, which refer to
mountains, rivers, towns, *etc.*, of Spain. [B.M.

1436. ———: Refranes y cantares geográficos de España. Con-
ferencia, *etc.* pp. 32. 8°. Madrid, *Arias*, 1906.

Presumably the numerous examples quoted were later embodied in **1435**.
[B.M.

1437. Viardot (Louis). Le petit-fils de Sancho Panza.
8°. Paris, *Renouard*, 1840.

In Babel : Publication de la Société de Gens de Lettres, Tome 1, pp. 1-56.
This Sancho, like his illustrious grandfather, continually talks in proverbs. Pp.
44-50, there is a definite collection of Spanish proverbs translated into French.
[B.M.

1438. Vidal de Valenciano (Cayetano). El entremés de refranes
¿ es de Cervantes?, *etc.* pp. 78.
8°. Barcelona, *Bastinos*, Madrid, *Fé*, 1883.

1439. Wiseman (Charles). Narcissus; or, the young man's entertaining mirror: containing a humorous descant on manners.
. . . Variously interspersed with Spanish proverbs. . . . Taken
from the Spanish Galatéo of Don Lucas Gracian de Antisco,
etc. pp. xi, [4], 252.   12°. London, *Bew*, 1778.

Contains numerous proverbs, in Spanish with English translations, scattered
throughout.   [B.M.

1440. Yriarte (Juan de). Obras sueltas, *etc.* 2 vols.
                                        4°. Madrid, 1774.

Gratet-Duplessis, 508. Vol. 2, pp. 1-224, Refranes castellanos, traducidos en
verso latino. An excellent selection of proverbs, arranged alphabetically, turned
into Latin.   [B.M.

*See also index at end for references to Spanish in other
sections.*

LOCAL AND DIALECT.

1. GALICIA.

1441. Saco y Arce (Juan A.). Gramática gallega. pp. 313.
                                        8°. Lugo, *Soto*, 1868.

Pp. 263-282, Refranes gallegos. An alphabetical list of proverbs taken from
Murguia's Historia de Galicia.   [B.M.

See also **1386.**

2. ASTURIAS.

1442. Canella Secades (Fermin). Estudios asturianos, *etc.* pp.
286.   8°. Oviedo, *Brid*, 1886.

Pp. 278-284, an alphabetical list, without notes, of Asturian proverbs. [B.M.

1443. F. (J. F.). La olla asturiana. Librito curioso y entre-
tenido. pp. 146.   16°. Madrid, *Hernandez*, 1874.

Pp. 7-18, refranes : pp. 19-20, refranes pa los llabraóres (agricolas).   [B.M.

3. CATALONIA

(including Roussillon).

1444. Amat (Juan Carlos). Quatre cents aforismes catalans, *etc.*
pp. 32.   16°. Barcelona, *Nogués*, 1647.
Another edition.
            Cervera, *Imp. de la Pontifica y Real Universitat*, 1805.

Gratet-Duplessis, 522. Other editions. This rare collection is formed of a
series of moral distiches, which for the most part are true proverbs rhymed.
                                                                [B.M.

1445. Bergnes (E.). Collecció de proverbis, maximes, y adagis
catalans, *etc.* pp. 34.   8°. Perpinyá, *Julia*, 1882.

Some 400 proverbs, *etc.*, adapted to the dialect of Roussillon.

1446. Bofarull (Manuel de). Proverbis arabes extrets d'un manuscrit català del sigle xiv, *etc.* pp. 16.
4°. Barcelona, *L'Avenç*, 1891.

Some 400 aphorisms and proverbs, which form the basis of the " Aforismes e
proverbis " of Bulbena y Tusell, *q.v.*, **1448.**

1447. Bonsenyor (Jahuda). Llibre de paraules e dits de savis e
filosofs, los proverbis de Salomo, lo llibre de Cato, fets
estampar . . . par En Gabriel Llabres y Quintana. pp. xxxix,
148.   8°. Palma de Mallorca, *J. Colomar y Salas*, 1889.
[B.M.

1448. Bulbena y Tusell (Antoni). Aforismes e proverbis his-
torichs e tradicionals . . . d'en Antoni Tallander [*pseud.* of
Bulbena y Tusell], *etc.* pp. 112.
8°. Barcelona, *Viladot & Cuesta*, [1900].

One of the largest collections of Catalan sayings.

1449. ———: Assaig de bibliografía paremiológica catalana, *etc.*
pp. viii, 103.   8°. Barcelona, *Babra*, 1915.

An excellent bibliography of Catalan proverbs, written in Catalan, and
arranged alphabetically. The appendix contains phrases from Seneca, and from
a French philosopher translated into Catalan, also a list of those Catalan plays
which have a proverb for their title, *etc.* Many of the entries concern moral
maxims or literary phrases rather than true proverbs.   [B.M.

1450. Cervera (Guylem de). Les proverbes de Guylem de Cervera, poème catalan du xiiie siècle.   8°. Paris, 1886.

In Romania, tome 15, pp. 25-110. Maxims or proverbial sentences owing
much to the Proverbs of Solomon, in Catalan verse.   [U.C.L.

1451. Cortils y Vieta (Joseph). Ethología de Blánes. pp. 201, v.
12 rals. 8°. Barcelona, *Verdaguer*, 1886.

Biblioteca popular de la Associació d'Excursions Catalana, 3. Pp. 177-185,
proverbs, sometimes compared with variants from other parts of Spain. [B.M.

1452. D. y M. Diccionario catalán-castellano, *etc.* pp. 962.
12°. Barcelona, *Roger*, 1847.

An appendix contains a collection of 450 Catalan sayings with Castillian
equivalents. This appendix was later published separately under the title :
Refranes catalanes, *etc.* pp. 27. 12°. Barcelona, *Timbre Imperial*, 1887.

1453. Diccionario. Diccionario castellano-catalán y catalán-
castellano. 2 vols.   16°. Reus, 1836-39.

Gratet-Duplessis, 523. At the end of Vol. 2 is a fairly long list of Catalan
proverbs in Spanish.

1454. Dites. Dites y refrans que s'usen en el poble de Sant
Hilari y sa rodalía.   fol. 1914.

In La Estivada, No. 73.

1455. Esteve y Segui (Josep). Paremiología comarcana.
4°. Manresa, *Imp. de S. Josep*, 1907-1913.

In Buttleti del Centre Escursionista de la comarca de Bages, from No. 14,
1907, till the end of 1913.

1456. Farnés (Sebastià). Assaig de paremiologiá catalana comparada. Vol. 1, pp. 320. 8°. Barcelona, *Thomas*, 1913.

No more published. An excellent collection of Catalan proverbs in all their variants, frequently with Spanish, French, Italian or Latin equivalents.

1457. Font (Ramón). Refráns de la llengua catalana, *etc.* pp. 147. 8°. Barcelona, *Jepús*, 1900.

Some 2400 proverbs, more or less popular, with notes.

1458. G. (J.). Meteorologia popular.
4°. Manresa, *Imp. de S. Josep*, 1911.

In Buttleti del Centre Escursionista de la comarca de Bages, 1911, No. 48 *et seq.*

1459. Genis (Salvador). Refranes catalanes con sus equivalentes en castellano, *etc.* pp. 438. 8°. Gerona, *Torres*, 1883.

1460. ——— : Vocabulari català-castellà. pp. 245.
8°. Barcelona, *Horta*, 1910.

Pp. 219-245, 400 Catalan proverbs with Castillian equivalents.

1461. Lang (Peter). Eigenartige kastilianische und katalonische Sprüchwoerter, *etc.* pp. 11.
4°. Barcelona, *Tipografia del " Bazar del Norte,"* 1900.

Contains some 300 sayings which were also published with German translations in the same author's " Katalonische Volkslieder," *etc.* 1910.

1462. Llagostera y Sala (Francesch). Aforística catalana ó sía col·lecció de refranis populars catalans. . . . Segona edició. pp. 48. 8°. Barcelona, *Verdaguer*, 1883.

These aphorisms and sayings were first published in the periodical " Lo Gay Saber," 1883, Nos. 20 and 21. Some 1500 sayings are given. [B.M.

1463. Llibre. Lo llibre de tres. pp. 17.
8°. Barcelona, *Serra e Russell*, 1907.

Recull de textes Catalans antichs, Vol. 3. A selection of triads of the 14th century.

1464. Miró (Oleguer). Calendari folk-loric de la comarca de Bages. 4°. Manresa, *Imp. de S. Josep*, 1909.

In Buttleti del Centre Escursionista de la comarca de Bages for 1909. Proverbial sayings for saints' days and festivals.

1465. Pépratx (Justin). Ramellets de proverbis, maximas, refrans y adagis catalans, *etc.* pp. 165.
la. 8°. Perpinyá, *Latrobe*, 1880.

Proverbs, maxims, *etc.*, in verse, with French translations. There is an appendix of rural maxims also, in Catalan and French, but not in verse. [B.M.

1466. Saglietti (Hermenegild Vila). Refrans . . . y Catalunya!!!, *etc.* pp. 58. 4°. Gerona, *Torres*, [1902].

At the end some fifty Catalan proverbs with Spanish translations are given.

1467. Serra y Boldu (Valeri). Calendari folk-lóric d'Urgell. pp.
348.   8°. [Barcelona, *Seix & Barral*, 1915].
This contains a large number of sayings, proverbs, *etc.*, chiefly concerning
festivals or saints' days.

1468. X. y F. (J. A.). Diccionario de refranes catalanes, y castellanos . . . por D. J. A. X. y F. pp. 125.
                                32°. Barcelona, *Sauri*, 1831.
Over 500 proverbs in Catalan and Spanish. Reprinted in Vol. 9 of Sbarbi,
1420.

See also **30, 1321, 1327, 1373, 1408, 1414, 3701, 3856, 3867,
3905.**

4. BALEARIC ISLES.

1469. Boatella (Damián) and **Bosch** (Matiás). Frases, dichos y
refranes. Enseñanza práctica del castellano en los Baleares.
. . . Sexta edición. pp. 258.   8°. Palma, *Gelabert*, 1889.
Pp. 223-258, some 900 proverbs in the Majorcan dialect, with Spanish equivalents.

1470. Burguera (Miguel). De adagis pueris valde utilibus, *etc.*
pp. 39.   16°. Palma, *Guasp*, 1817.
Pp. 25-39, 176 popular adages with Latin translations.

1471. Figuera (Antoni). Diccionari mallorquí-castellá, *etc.* pp.
614.   fol. Palma, *Trias*, 1840.
Pp. 598-614, a collection of 746 Majorcan adages and sayings, with Castillian
equivalents.

1472. Louis Salvator, *Archduke of Austria*. Die Balearen in
Wort und Bild geschildert. 7 Bde.
                                fol. Leipzig, *Brockhaus*, 1869-91.
Bd. 2, pp. 305-312, Mallorquinische Sprüchwörter, 187 proverbs in the dialect,
with German translations : Bd. 6, pp. 135-141, 176 proverbs of Minorca, with
translations.   [B.M.

1473. Lull (Ramón). Liber de mille proverbiis, *etc.* pp. [xxvi],
183.   8°. Palmae Majoricarum, *Cerda & Antich*, 1746.
Maxims with Latin translations.   [B.M.

1474. Soler (Julio). Refranes e idiotismos. Gramática de la
lengua menorquina. pp. 128. 16°. Mahon, *Fábregues*, 1858.
Pp. 108-112, Minorcan proverbs and sayings with their Castillian equivalents.

5. VALENCIA.

1475. Martí y Gadea (Joaquím). Adages y refranys. pp. 425.
An interesting collection of over a thousand Valencian sayings.

1476. Ros (Carlos). Rondalla de rondalles, a imitacio del cuento de cuentos . . . treta á llum per Carlos Ros. pp. 91. *First edition.*   sm. 8°. Valencia, *Monfort*, 1769.
Another edition. pp. 76.
                                          sm. 8°. Valencia, *Monfort*, 1820.
Gratet-Duplessis, 525. This curious work, written in the Valencian dialect, was composed expressly to contain all the proverbs and popular sayings in use in Valencia. It is beginning to be rare. Reprinted in Vol. 9 of Sbarbi, **1420.**
                                                                      [B.M.

1477. ———: Tratat de adages y refranys valencians, . . . Segona impressiò.   sm. 8°. Valencia, *Cabrera*, 1733.
Another edition. pp. 48.   8°. Valencia, *Garcia*, 1736.
Another edition. pp. 133.   sm. 8°. Valencia, *Estévan*, 1788.
Gratet-Duplessis, 524. A large collection of proverbs in alphabetical order, with some observations on the Valencian dialect, and a useful preface. A large number of the proverbs in this collection are the same as some old Provençal and Languedoc ones, not only in idea, but also in expression and language.   [B.M.

6. MURCIA.

1478. Fuentes y Ponte (Javier). Murcia que se fué. pp. xix, 439. 8°. Madrid, *Biblioteca de Instrucción y Recreo*, 1872.
According to Sbarbi, 250, this book contains many proverbs.

7. ANDALUSIA.

1479. Marin (Francisco Rodríguez). Cien refranes andaluces de meteorologia, cronologia, agricultura, y economia rural, *etc.* pp. 32. *First edition.*   4°. Sevilla, 1885.
2nd edition.   4°. Sevilla, *Rasco*, 1894.
Proverbs frequently compared with those of other languages.

1480. ———: Mil trescientas comparaciones populares andaluzas, *etc.* pp. xix, 118.   8°. Sevilla, *Diaz*, 1899.
An original collection, with a good preface.   [B.M.

M

PORTUGUESE.

1481. Alberti (Leonora de). Proverbs in Portuguese and English.
pp. 103. 32°. London, *Hill*, [1920].
Bi-lingual Series. Proverbs arranged alphabetically by the Portuguese, with English translations or equivalents opposite. No notes. [B.M.

1482. Aleixo *de Sancto Antonio.* Philosophia moral tirada de algūs prouerbios ou adagios. pp. [xiv], 295, [40].
4°. Coimbra, *Diego Gomez de Loureiro*, 1640.

1483. Bellermann (Christian Friedrich). Portugiesische Volkslieder und Romanzen, *etc.* pp. xii, 284.
8°. Leipzig, *Engelmann*, 1864.
Pp. 244-261, calendar and other proverbs, with German translations. [B.M.

1484. Bluteau (Rafael). Vocabulario portuguez e latino, *etc.* 8 tom.
fol. Coimbra, *Real Collegio des Artes da Companhia de Jesu*, 1712-1721.
Supplemento ao vocabulario portuguez e latino. 2 pts.
fol. Lisboa Occidental, *Officina da Musica*, 1727-28.
Gratet-Duplessis, p. 317. This may be usefully consulted for Portuguese proverbs. [B.M.

1485. Braga (Theophilo). O povo Portuguez, *etc.* 2 vols.
8°. Lisboa, *Libraria Ferreira*, 1885.
Many proverbs are scattered throughout the two volumes, and may be found from the analytical index. [B.M.

1486. Branner (John C.). Proverbs from the Portuguese.
8°. San Francisco, 1893.
In Overland Monthly, Second Series, Vol. 21, pp. 501-503. [B.M.

1487. Cunha de Pina Manique (Francisco Antonio). Ensaio phraseologico, ou collecção de phrases metaphoricas, . . . proverbios e anexins da lingua portugueza. pp. 127.
8°. Lisboa, *Typographia da-Nação*, 1856.
A dictionary of Portuguese sayings, phrases, proverbs, expressions, *etc.*
[B.M.

1488. Delicado (Antonio). Adagios portuguezes reduzidos a lugares communs. pp. [xi], 190.
sm. 4°. Lisboa, *Rosa*, 1651.
Gratet-Duplessis, 528. Very rare in this original edition. Brunet says it was reprinted : 8°, Lisbon, 1785. Proverbs arranged alphabetically under subject headings; no notes. [B.M.

1489. Dictos. Dictos diversos postos por orden de alfabeto, *etc.*
8°. Evora, *Andr. de Burgos*, 1555.
Gratet-Duplessis, 527. A rare book known in Portugal as the " Dictos da Freira."

1490. Folqman (Carlos). Portugeese en nederduitse spraakkonst, *etc.* pp. 118. 8°. Lisboa, *Impressão Regia*, 1804.
Pp. 113-118, Collecção de varios proverbios hollandezes e portuguezes. [B.M.

1491. Joven. Contos moraes seguidos de maximas, adagios e anecdotas . . . Por um joven. pp. 16.
12°. Nova-Goa, *Imprensa nacional*, 1862.
Pp. 14-15, adagios.

1492. Luz Soares (Mathias da). Maximas, conselhos moraes, . . . e proverbios. . . . Segunda edição. pp. ix, 323.
8°. Porto, *Chardron*, 1890.
Pp. 296-313, Sentenças breves, adagios e proverbios, *etc.*

1493. Pereira (Bento). Florilegio dos modos de fallar, e adagios da lingua portuguesa, *etc.* pp. 124, 39.
fol. Lisboa, *Craesbeeck*, 1655.
Prosodia in vocabularium trilingue. . . . Quarta editione, *etc.*
fol. Ulyssipone, *Craesbeeck*, 1669.
Prosodia in vocabularium bilingue. . . . Nona editio, *etc.* pp. [vi], 970, 128, 125.
fol. Eborae, *Typographia Academica*, 1732.
The " Florilegio," which was incorporated in later editions of the " Prosodia," contains a long alphabetical list of Portuguese proverbs with the corresponding Latin ones. [B.M.

1494. Perestrello da Camaro (Paulo). Collecção de proverbios, adagios, rifaos . . . da lingoa portugueza. pp. vi, 288.
8°. Rio de Janeiro, *Laemmert*, 1848.
Stirling-Maxwell, p. 69. Proverbs alphabetically arranged, with some explanatory notes. [B.M.

1495. Philosophia. Philosophia popular em proverbios. pp. 64.
8°. Lisboa, 1882.
Biblioteca do povo e das escolas, edited by D. Corazzi, Vol. 35.

1496. Pires (Antonio Thomaz). Folk-lore alentejano, 23. . . . Florilegio de proverbios, adagios, *etc.* 4°. 1888.
In Revista do Minho, No. 2.

1497. ———: Proverbios e adagios portuguezes.
8°. Palermo, 1884.
In Archivio per lo studio delle tradizioni popolari, Vol. 3, pp. 450-452.

1498. Rolland (Francisco). Adagios, proverbios, rifaós e anexins
da lingua Portugueza. . . . Por F[rancisco] R[olland]
I[mpressor] L[ivreiro] E[m] L[isboa]. pp. 341.
8°. Lisboa, Typografia Rollandiana, 1780.

Another edition. pp. 150.   4°. Lisboa, 1841.

Gratet-Duplessis, 529. A large and excellent collection of proverbs, many of
which are peculiar to Portugal. Alphabetical arrangement by key-words; no
notes.   B.M.

1499. Vieyra (Antonio). A new Portuguese grammar. *First (?)*
edition. pp. vi, 376.   8°. London, *Nourse*, 1768.

Tenth edition. pp. viii, 391.
8°. London, Collingwood, 1827.

Each edition contains a section of Portuguese proverbs with English translations.   [B.M.

See also **1386, 1433, 3681, 3807.**

AZORES.

1500. Lang (Henry R.). Tradições populares açorianas.
8°. Halle, Niemayer, 1889.

In Zeitschrift für romanische Philologie, Bd. 13. Pp. 425-426, adagios.
[U.C.L.

ALSACE-LORRAINE AND VOSGES.

1501. Adam (Lucien). Les patois lorrains. pp. li, 459.
8°. Nancy, *Grosjean-Maupin*, Paris, *Maisonneuve*, 1881.
Pp. 381-398, agricultural and calendar proverbs. [B.M.

1502. Alsaticus (J. R.). Elsässischer Sprichwörterschatz. Acht-hundert Sprichwörter und sprichwörtliche Redensarten aus dem Elsass, *etc.* pp. 63. 8°. Strassburg, *Bull*, 1883.
Bernstein, 70.

1503. Clarac (E.). Proverbes et curiosités du dialecte de Stras-bourg. pp. 8, 170. fr.1. 8°. [Paris], *Didier*, [1908].
Phrases, proverbs, sayings, *etc.*, arranged alphabetically, with French trans-lations and explanatory notes. [B.M.

1504. Geiler (Johann) *von Kaisersberg*. 496 Sprichwörter und sprichwörtliche Redensarten aus den Schriften Geilers von Kaisersberg, gesammelt von August Stöber.
8°. Mülhausen, *Rissler*, 1868.
In Alsatia, 1862-1867, pp. 131-162. [B.M.

1505. Haillant (Nicolas) and **Virtel** (Albert). Choix de proverbes et dictons, patois de Damas . . . Vosges. pp. 36.
8°. Épinal et Damas, *Les auteurs*, Paris, *Bouillon*, 1902.
180 proverbs and sayings, without translations, but with occasional notes.
[B.M.

1506. Lambs (August). Ein Dutzend elsässischer Sprichwörter aus Geyler's Schriften. pp. 40. 8°. Strassburg, *Heitz*, 1890.
Schriften des protestantischen liberalen Vereins in Elsass-Lothringen, 32.
Illustrations, *etc.*, of 12 proverbs. [B.M.

1507. Lerond (H.). Lothringische Sammelmappe. 7 Bde.
8°. Forbach, *Hupfer*, Metz, *Even*, 1890-97.
Bd. 1, pp. 75-97, Sprüche und sprüchwörtliche Redensarten. Bd. 2, pp. 15-27, Lothringische Bauernregeln.

1508. Moscherosch (Johann Michael). Sprichwörter und sprich-wörtliche Redensarten aus Johann Michael Moscherosch's Schriften. Mit Erläuterungen von August Stöber.
8°. Colmar, *Barth*, 1873.
In Alsatia, Neue Reihenfolge, 1868-1872, pp. 319-338. [B.M.

1509. Muendel (Curt). Haussprüche . . . im Elsass, *etc.* pp. 76.   8°. Strassburg, *Schmidt*, 1883.

Inscriptions and sayings from houses in Alsace.   [B.M.

1510. Oberlin (Jéremie Jacques). Essai sur le patois lorrain des environs du comté du Ban de la Roche, fief royal d'Alsace. pp. [vi], 287.   8°. Strasbourg, *Stein*, 1775.

Pp. 153-154, proverbes. (28.)   [B.M.

1511. Pauli (Johann). Das Buch Schimpff und Ernst, *etc.* 2 Thle.   fol. Strassburg, Franckfurt, 1533-56.

Another edition.   fol. Augspurg, 1535.

Another edition.   8°. Stuttgart, 1866.

Les propos de la table, *etc.* [Selections from Schimpff und Ernst]. pp. xvi, 231.   4°. Paris, 1866.

Many other editions. The book contains a number of old proverbs.   [B.M.

1512. Rathgeber (Julius). Elsässische Sprichwörter und sprichwörtliche Redensarten.   8°. Strassburg, *Heitz*, 1890-93.

In Jahrbuch für Geschichte, Sprache und Litteratur Elsass-Lothringens, herausgegeben von dem historisch-litterarischen Zweigverein des Vogesen-Clubs, Jahrgang 6, pp. 138-143; Jahrgang 7, pp. 141-145; Jahrgang 8, pp. 81-84; Jahrgang 9, pp. 98-101.

1513. Redensarten. Strassburger Redensarten, *etc.*   8°. Strassburg, *Heitz*, 1895.

In Jahrbuch für Geschichte, Sprache und Litteratur Elsass-Lothringens, Jahrgang 11, pp. 110-131.

1514. Richard (   ). Contes populaires, traditions, croyances, superstitions, proverbes et dictons applicables à des villes de la Lorraine.   Remiremont, 1835.

Second edition.   Remiremont, 1848.

Friesland, 463.

1515. Spieser (J.). Sprachproben aus dem Münsterthale. Münsterthäler Sprachproben. Sprichwörter.   8°. Strassburg, *Heitz*, 1886, 1890.

Two articles in Jahrbuch für Geschichte, Sprache und Litteratur Elsass-Lothringens, Jahrgang 2, pp. 166-169, and Jahrgang 6, pp. 144-153. 201 proverbs.

1516. ———: Zillinger Sprachproben. Sprichwörter und Kinderlieder in der Mundart des Dorfes Zillingen bei Pfalzburg.   8°. Strassburg, *Heitz*, 1889.

In Jahrbuch für Geschichte, Sprache und Litteratur Elsass-Lothringens, Jahrgang 5, pp. 133-140. Pp. 134-139, proverbs (120).

1517. Stoeber (August). Elsässisches Volksbüchlein, *etc.* pp. 116.   8°. Strassburg, *Schuler*, 1842.

Pp. 63-69, Bauernregeln, Haussprüche, Sprichwörter. (47.)   [B.M.

1518. Stoeber (August). Sprichwörter und sprichwörtliche Redensarten im Elsass, *etc.* 8°. Mülhausen, *Rissler*, 1850-51.

In Neujahrs-Stollen auf 1850, pp 28-30. *In* Alsatia (continuation of same periodical), 1851, pp. 25-29. [B.M.

1519. Stoeber (Daniel Ehrenfried). Neujahrsbüchlein in Elsasser Mundart vom Vetter Daniel [*i.e.* D. E. Stöber]. pp. vi, 32.
8°. Strassburg, *Schuler*, 1824.
Bernstein, 2337. Pp. 16-23, Sprichwörter.

1520. Zéliqzon (Léon). Lothringische Mundarten, *etc.* pp. 109.
4°. Metz, *Scriba*, 1889.
Pp. 45-50, proverbs with French translations. This book forms Ergänzungs-Heft zum Jahrbuch der Gesellschaft für lothringische Geschichte und Altertumskunde, 1. [B.M.

GERMAN.

GENERAL.

1521. A. B. C. A. B. C. und Lese-Büchlein für Jung und Alt in gereimtem Sprichwort und Wahrwort, *etc.* pp. 82.
8°. Heilbronn, *Güldig*, 1862.

1522. Abel (Joachim Gottvald). Beitrag zu einer Geschichte der Sprichwörter. 8°. Leipzig, *Jacobi*, 1750.
Gratet-Duplessis, 632.

1523. Abraham (P.), *a Santa Clara* [Ulrich Megerle]. Abrahamisches Parömiakon. Oder: die Sprichwörter . . . des P. Abraham a St. Clara . . . von K. F. W. Wander. pp. xxv, 412. 8°. Breslau, *Kohn*, 1838.
Over 3000 sayings, *etc.*, are given. [B.M.

1524. ———: Sprichwörter und sprichwörtliche Redensarten bei P. Abraham a S. Clara, zusammengestellt von Friedrich Lauchert. pp. 42. 8°. Bonn, *Hanstein*, 1893.

1525. Agricola (Johann), *of Eisleben.* Drihundert gemene Sprikwörde, *etc.* 8°. Magdeburg, 1528.
Another edition. 8°. Eisleben, 1548.
Another edition. pp. 350. 8°. Wittemberg, *Krafft*, 1592.
Gratet-Duplessis, 537. The first edition is the most rare, and is written in Plattdeutsch. There are many others, all written in ordinary German. The edition of 1592, printed after that of 1534, contains 750 proverbs. Agricola, whose German name was Schnitter, was born at Eisleben, and is not the same as Agricola of Spremberg. Since the work of Bebelius, *q.v.*, **1533,** only gave Latin translations, Agricola's collection may be considered the first of its kind. *See also* **1656, 1657, 1712, 1789a.** [B.M. (1529 and 1548 editions).

1526. Agricola (Johann), *of Spremberg.* Kurtze reglen . . . durch Joh[ann] Agr[icola]. 16° *or* 24°. Spremberg, 1601.
Gratet-Duplessis, 540. The author of these moral or proverbial maxims in verse is not to be confused with Agricola of Eisleben whose contemporary he was. Nopitsch thinks there is an earlier edition of this book.

1527. Anstaedt (P.). Eine Auswahl deutscher Sprichwörter erklärt und evangelisirt, *etc.* pp. 110.
18°. Gettysburg, 1853.
Stirling-Maxwell, p. 5.

1528. Appelmann (J. C.). Sprüchwörter Sitten- und Lehr-Sprüche aus den alten griechischen und römischen Schrift-stellern gezogen und in deutsche Verse übersetzt. pp. [xiv], 270. sm. 8°. Frankfurt und Leipzig, 1754.

Stirling-Maxwell, p. 6.

1529. Bahder (Carl von). Die deutsche Philologie im Grundriss. pp. xvi, 456. 8°. Paderborn, *Schöningh*, 1883.

Pp. 292-301, Sprichwörter. [B.M.

1530. Banck (Otto). Literarisches Bilderbuch, *etc.* 3 Bde. 8°. Leipzig, *Kummer*, 1866.

Bd. 2, pp. 198-212, Zur Literatur der Sprichwörter. Von verschiedenen Verfassern.

1531. Barnabe (Stephan). Teutsche und italienische Discours, samt etlichen Proverbien, Historien und Fabeln, *etc.* 8°. Wien, 1660.

Another edition. pp. 228. 8°. München, *Rauch*, 1682.

Gratet-Duplessis, 425.

1532. Basedow (Johann Bernhard). Des Elementarwerks erster (-dritter) Band, *etc.* 5 pts. 8° and obl. 4°. Dessau, *Crusius*, 1774.

Third edition. pp. xvi, 1020, xv. 8°. Stuttgart, *Verlags-Bureau*, 1849.

Bd. 2, Buch 5, contains a section : Lehren in Sprüchwörtern. [B.M.

1533. Bauer-Czarnomski (Francis). Proverbs in German and English. pp. 113. 32°. London, *Hill*, [1920].

Proverbs arranged alphabetically by the German, with English translations or equivalents opposite. [B.M.

1534. Bebel (Heinrich). Bebeliana, *etc.* Argentorati, 1508.

Another edition. 4°. [Argentorati, *Schurerius*, 1512].

Another edition. 4°. Parrhysiis, *Nicolai de Pratis*, 1516.

Gratet-Duplessis, 532. German proverbs in Latin with brief explanations. There were many other editions : that of Paris, 1516, given above is a good one. This is generally regarded as the oldest published collection of German proverbs. Duplessis gives further details of Bebel and quotes a few of the proverbs. [B.M. (1512 edition).

1535. ———: Heinrich Bebel's Proverbia Germanica. Bearbeitet von W. H. D. Suringar. pp. lvi, 615. 8°. Leiden, *Brill*, 1879.

Contains the complete text, followed by comparisons of each proverb with those of different languages. The origin is indicated in each case. [B.M.

1536. Bechstein (Ludwig). Arabesken. pp. 203. sm. 8°. Stuttgart, *Halberger*, 1832.

Pp. 84-102, Von einigen alten deutschen Sprüchwörtern. [B.M.

1537. Beer (Johann Christoph). Historische Zeitvertreibung bestehend in siebenhundert auserlesenen und anmuthigen Geschichten, *etc.* pp. [xiv], 987, [37].

8°. Augsburg, Innsbrugg, *Wolff*, 1761.

Amongst other things, this book contains the explanation of a number of proverbs. [B.M.

1538. Beiche (Eduard). Eine Blumenlese geographisch-historischer Sprüchwörter und Reime, oder Notizen zur Landes- und Völkerkunde der Vergangenheit.

4°. [Magdeburg?], 1873.

In Blätter für Handel, Gewerbe und sociales Leben (Beiblatt zur Magdeburgischen Zeitung), Nos. 28-30.

1539. Beispielssprichwort. Der apologische oder Beispielssprichwort. 4°. Leipzig, *Brockhaus*, 1864.

In Blätter für literarische Unterhaltung, 1864, pp. 148-149. [B.M.

1540. Berger (Johann Wilhelm). Stromateus academicus, seu dissertationes varii argumenti. 4°. Wolfenbüttel, 1720.

Another edition. pp. [xxx], 1054, [78].

4°. Lipsiae, *Jacobi*, 1745.

Gratet-Duplessis, 605. Contains a dissertation entitled " De philosophia vulgi," which treats of proverbs in general, and the superiority of German proverbs in particular.

1541. Bergmann (Joseph). Deutsche Sprichwörter und Redensarten.

Articles under this title appeared in the following : Deutsche Volks-Zeitung, 1888, Nr. 3-17; Karlsbader Wochenblatt, 1888, Nr. 21-24, 26, 28, 30, 32; Unterhaltungs-Blatt zur Freitags-Nummer der Oesterreichischen Volkszeitung, 1892, 1894, 1895, 1897.

1542. Berkenmeyer (Paul Ludolph). Curieuser Antiquarius. 2 Theile. 12°. Hamburg, 1720.

In French. Le curieux antiquaire, *etc.* 3 vols.

8°. Leide, *Pierre van der As*, 1729.

Gratet-Duplessis, 604. Contains : Sprichwörter von Ländern und Städten. [B.M. (French translation).

1543. Bessel (Christian Georg von). Neuer politischer Glücks-Schmied . . . mit auserlesenen Sprichwörtern, *etc.*

12°. Franckfurt, *Naumann*, 1681.

Another edition. pp. [xxx], 558.

12°. Franckfurt, *Liebezeit*, 1697.

[B.M.

1544. Binder (Wilhelm). Sprichwörterschatz der deutschen Nation, *etc.* pp. xiv, 224. 8°. Stuttgart, *Schaber*, 1873.

4234 entries.

1545. Birlinger (Anton). Kleine Beiträge. 6. Sprichwörter und sprichwörtliche Redensarten. 8°. Wien, *Gerold*, 1871.

In Germania, 16. Jahrgang (Neue Reihe, 4. Jahrgang), pp. 86-88. [B.M.

1546. ———: Sprichwörter teutsche von der Mitte disz Jahrhunderts 1746. 8°. Bonn, *Haustein*, 1888.

In Alemannia, Jahrgang 16, pp. 241-242. [B.M.

1547. ———: Sprichwörter und Sprüche.
8°. Wien, *Gerold*, 1870.

In Germania, 15. Jahrgang (Neue Reihe, 3. Jahrgang), pp. 102-104. [B.M.

1548. Bluemner (Hugo). Der bildliche Ausdruck in den Reden des Fürsten Bismarck. pp. vi, 198.
8°. Leipzig, *Hirzel*, 1891.

Pp. 182-186, proverbs used by Bismarck. [B.M.

1549. Blum (Joachim Christian). Deutsches Sprichwörterbuch. 2 pts. [in 1]. 8°. Leipsig, *Weygand*, 1780-82.

Gratet-Duplessis, 655. 766 proverbs carefully and clearly explained. Classified by subjects. [B.M.

1550. Blumenthal (Clara). Eine Auswahl deutscher Sprichwörter mit den englischen Aequivalenten, *etc*. pp. 39.
1/-. 16°. London, *Nutt* [1910].

Arranged alphabetically in two sections, German with English opposite, and English with German opposite. No notes. [B.M.

1551. Bock (Johann Georg). Idioticon Prussicum, oder, Entwurf eines preussischen Wörterbuches, *etc*. pp. [viii], 86.
8°. Königsberg, *Woltersdorf*, 1759.
[B.M.

1552. Borchardt (Wilhelm). Die sprichwörtlichen Redensarten im deutschen Volksmund, *etc*. pp. xvi, 478.
8°. Leipzig, *Brockhaus*, 1888.
Third edition. Neubearbeitet von G. Wustmann. pp. x, 534.
M.7. 8°. Leipzig, 1894.
Sixth edition. Neu-bearbeitet von G. Schoppe. pp. x, 518.
M.13.50. 8°. Leipzig, 1925.

1132 proverbial phrases explained and frequently compared with those of other nations. The second edition contains 1277 entries. [B.M. (1888 edition).

1553. Braun (J. M.). Bibliothek des Frohsinns. . . . Viertes und fünftes Bändchen. (Sechs Tausend deutsche Sprüchwörter und Redensarten). pp. viii, 240.
8°. Stuttgart, *Köhler*, 1840.

Proverbs arranged alphabetically by the principal words.
[F.-L.S. (Stephens collection).

1554. Bruder. Der lustige Bruder. Ein Sammlung der besten Räthsel, Sprichwörter, *etc*. *Second edition.*
16°. Altona, 1806.

Gratet-Duplessis, 731.

1555. Buettner (Johann). Predigten über Sprichwörter, *etc.*
Koburg, 1806.

1556. Busch (Moritz). Deutscher Volkshumor. pp. 349.
8°. Leipzig, *Grunow*, 1877.
Pp. 133-148, Komische Redensarten und Sprichwörter, Appositionen und Priameln.

1557. Buschmann (J.). Deutsches Lesebuch. . . . 5. Auflage.
pp. xii, 361.   8°. Trier, *Lintz*, 1885.
Pp. 356-361, Sprichwörter.

1558. Carisch (Otto). Grammatische Formenlehre der deutschen und rhätoromanischen Sprache, *etc.* pp. viii, 102.
8°. Chur, *Hitz*, 1851.
Another edition. pp. viii, 214.   8°. Chur, *Hitz*, 1852.
Pp. 100-101 (1851 edition), Sprichwörter und Lehren der Erfahrung. 34 German proverbs.   [B.M.

1559. Castelli (J. F.). Lebensklugheit in Haselnüssen. Eine Sammlung von tausend Sprichwörtern, *etc.* pp. ii, 215.
12°. Wien, 1825.

1560. Clauert (Hans). Der werkliche Hanns Clauert. . . . Ist recht neu gedruckt. pp. 144.   8°. [1650?].
Pp. 91-144, Red-Arten und Sprüchwörter. Some 700 proverbs.   [B.M.

1561. Complementier-Büchlein. Complementier-Büchlein . . . Nebst einem Anhang unterschiedlicher Redens-Arten auch etlicher gewöhnlicher Sprichwörter und üblichen Reimen. Gedruckt in disem Jahr. pp. 111.   sm. 8°. n.d.
Another edition. ff. 48.   sm. 8°. Nürnberg, *Kramern*, 1667.

1562. Cott, *Lehrer.* Deutsche und französische Sprichwörter vergleichend zusammengestellt.   4°. Gotha, 1854.
In Programm des Herzoglichen Realgymnasiums zu Gotha, 1854, pp. 1-14.

1563. Curti (Fidel). Lebensweisheit in deutschen Sprichwörtern, Sprüchen und Sentenzen. . . . 3. Auflage. pp. viii, 468, ix.
8°. Zürich, *Schmidt*, 1881.

1564. ——— : Spruch und Sprichwort als Freund und Führer, *etc.* pp. 130, v.   8°. St. Gallen, *Wirth*, 1884.

1565. Darbaris (Demetrios). Γραμματικὴ Γερμανικὴ ἀκριβεστάτη, *etc.* pp. [xvii], 479.   8°. Βιενῆ, [1785].
Pp. 435-445, German proverbs with modern Greek equivalents.   [B.M.

1566. Deuringer (Johann Georg). Deuringer'sches neues A. B. C. für Jung und Alt. Oder: kurze gesammelte Grundsätze, Ansichten, Bilder, Sprüchwörter und Lebensregeln, *etc.* pp. iv, 116.   8°. Augsburg, *Wirth*, 1840.

1567. Deuringer (Johann Georg). Neugefasste Edelsteine. Eine Sammlung von biblischen und andern weisen Denksprüchen, *etc.* pp. 272.   8°. Augsburg, *Kohler*, 1847.

Pp. 261-272, Zugabe einer kleinen Sammlung in Versen abgefasster Sprüchwörter, *etc.*

1568. Deutsch. Deutsch, Deutscher und Deutschland im Sprichwort. (Probe aus Wanders deutschem Sprichwörter-Lexikon).   8°. Leipzig, *Fritsch*, 1869.

In Deutscher Sprachwart, Bd. 4, pp. 82-86.   [B.M.]

1569. Distler (Carl). Sprichwörter in Wort und Bild, ein unzerreissbares Bilderbuch für artige Kinder, *etc.* ff. 8.
    4°. Stuttgart, *Hänselmann*, n.d.

1570. Dove (N. R.). Politisches Sprichwörterbrevier, *etc.* pp. xl, 256.   8°. Leipzig, *Wigand*, 1872.

Contains 1206 proverbs, with explanatory notes.   [B.M.]

1571. Ebeling (Max). Blicke in vergessene Winkel, *etc.* 2 Bde.
    8°. Leipzig, *Böhme*, 1889.

Bd. 2, pp. 320-330, Sprichwörter und Scherzreden.   [B.M.]

1572. Eckart (Rudolf). Der Lehrer im Sprichwort.
    fol. Aachen, 1893.

In Rheinisch-Westfälische Schulzeitung, 16. Jahrgang, Nr. 52.

1573. ———: Stand und Beruf im Volksmund. Eine Sammlung von Sprichwörtern, *etc.* pp. 248.
    8°. Göttingen, *Wunder*, 1900.

3560 proverbs without notes, arranged alphabetically under the principal word.   [B.M.]

1574. Egenolff (Christian). Sibent-halbhüdert Sprichwörter, *etc.*
    8°. Franckfurt, 1532.

Another edition.   4°. Frankfurt a. M., 1548.

1575. Einsiedel (Johannes). Parochus jovialis, das ist: geistliche Kurzweil für melancholisches und langweiliges Gemüth . . . Vierte, vermehrte Auflage. 3 Bde.
    8°. Augsburg, *Rieger*, 1869, 1882, 1870.

Bd. 1, pp. 339-344, Hundert kurzweilige Sprüchwörter, darunter manche regula pastoralis.

1576. Eiselein (J.). Die Sprichwörter und Sinnreden des deutschen Volkes in alter und neuer Zeit, *etc. First* (?) *edition.*
    8°. Donaueschingen, *im literarischen Verlage*, 1838.

Another edition. pp. lii, 675.
    8°. Freiburg, *Wagner*, 1840.

Gratet-Duplessis, 769. Pp. i-lii, Einleitung : pp. 1-660, proverbs arranged alphabetically under their key-words. An excellent collection, giving the origin of each proverb. There are references to early authors and some comparisons with foreign proverbs.   [U.C.L.]

1577. Eisenlohr (Theodor). Deutsche Volksschule und deutsches Sprichwort, *etc.* pp. 15. 8°. Stuttgart, *Aue*, 1862.
A brief essay on German proverbs. [B.M.

1578. Entstehung. Entstehung altdeutscher Sprüchwörter, in kleinen Erzählungen vorgetragen. pp. [xvi], 400.
8°. Leipsig, *Breitkopf*, 1793.
Gratet-Duplessis, 685. This work is attributed to J. G. Schulz by Nopitsch, 76.

1579. Eriksen (G. L. V.). Deutsche Edelsteine. Eine Sammlung von Idiotismen und Germanismen; von eigentlichen, uneigentlichen und sprichwörterlichen Ausdrücken und Redensarten, *etc.* pp. 34. 8°. Kopenhagen, 1847.

1580. Erklärung. Erklärung der vornehmsten teutschen Sprichwörter. Nach ihrem Ursprung und wahrem Verstande. pp. [xxii], 120. Leipzig, 1748.
Explanatory notes on 28 German proverbs.

1581. Eyering (Eucharius). Proverbiorum copia. Etlich viel hundert lateinischer und teutscher schöner und lieblicher Sprichwörter, *etc.* 3 Theile.
8°. Eissleben, *Typis Grosianis*, 1601-1603.
Gratet-Duplessis, 551. Arranged in alphabetical order. The explanations which accompany the proverbs are given in very mediocre verse. The book contains a few illustrations. [B.M.

1582. Faust (Johann Heinrich). Das, was wir lieben im Rahmen des Sprüchwortes. Humor, Witz und Satire über die Töchter Eva's. Frauen und Jungfrauen gewidmet und den Männern empfohlen. pp. 80. 12°. Cöln, *Heyn*, [1880].

1583. Faustmann (K.). Aus tiefem Brunnen. Das deutsche Sprichwort. Mit Beitrag: Lebensweisheit der deutschen Sprichwörter. 8°. Freiburg, 1920.

1584. Feldbausch (Peter Anton). Denksprüche und Sprüchwörter. . . . 2. Auflage. pp. 147.
12°. Speyer, *Bregenzer*, 1865.

1585. Firmery (J.). De perusitatis in lingua Germanica proverbialibus formulis, *etc.* pp. 117.
8°. Rhedonibus, *Oberthur*, 1886.

1586. Fischart (Johann), *called Mentzer.* Bewärung und Erklärung des úralten gemeynen Sprüchwörts, *etc.* [ff. 40].
sm. 8°. [Strasburg?], 1584.
[B.M.

1587. Fischer (C. C. G.). Collectio proverbiorum et sententiarum notabilium, *etc.* pp. viii, 248. 8°. Halle, *Hendel*, 1805.
Gratet-Duplessis, 728.

1588. Franck (J.). Die deutschen Sprüchwörter und sprüchwörtlichen Redensarten über das Geflügel seit den ältesten
Zeiten, *etc.* 4°. Berlin, 1861-2.

In Tauben- und Hühnerzeitung, Jahrgänge 6 and 7.

1589. ———: Die Sprichwörtersammlung des Friedrich Peters.
[**1715**]. 4°. Nürnberg, 1866.

In Anzeiger für Kunde der deutschen Vorzeit, Neue Folge, 1866, Nos. 11-12.
[B.M.

1590. ———: Zur Quellenkunde des deutschen Sprichworts.
8°. Braunschweig, 1867.

In Archiv für das Studium der neueren Sprachen, Bd. 40, pp. 45-142, Bd. 41,
pp. 125-148. [B.M.

1591. Franck (Sebastian). Erste namenlose Sprichwörtersammlung vom Jahre 1532 . . . herausgegeben von Friedrich
Latendorf. pp. vii, 367. 8°. Poesneck, *Latendorf*, 1876.

Contains the explanation of 663 proverbs. Theil 2, pp. 234-367, Sachliche,
sprachliche und literargeschichtliche Erörterungen. [B.M.

1592. ———: Sprüchwörter, Erzählungen und Fabeln der
Deutschen. Herausgegeben und erläutert von Bernhard
Guttenstein. pp. 226.
12°. Frankfurt a. M., *Bronner*, 1831.
[B.M.

1593. ———: Sprichwörter, schöne, weise, herrliche Clugreden,
und Hoffsprüch, *etc.* (Ander Theyl, . . . von Everardo
Tappio und Antonio Tunicio zusamen gebracht, *etc.*). 2 vols.
4°. Franckenfurt am Meyn, *Egenolph*, [1541].

Another edition. Franckenfurt am Meyn, 1582.

Gratet-Duplessis, 541. An edition published at Zürich about 1545 has the
proverbs arranged in alphabetical order, and is written in the German of
Switzerland. This collection of proverbs on all subjects and from all languages
with its notes and explanations, obtained a great success when first published.
It is not common, even in Germany, in spite of its many editions. Extracts
from it are given in **1592**. [B.M.

1594. ———: Sprichwörter, schöne, weise Klugreden, *etc.* [Com-
piled by S. Franck]. ff. 4, 181.
4°. Francfort, *Egenholff*, 1548.

Another edition.
sm. 8°. Franckfort am Meyn, *Egenholff*, 1560.

Gratet-Duplessis, 544, treats this as purely anonymous, and says that though
it has a title remarkably like that of Sebastian Franck's collection, it contains
only a selection of proverbs taken from various authors such as Erasmus,
Seneca, Tunicius, Franck, *etc.* He mentions, without details, various other
editions, including one of 1601, but says it is still fairly rare. A good collection, with excellent notes.
[B.M. (1548 and various other editions) : U.C.L. (1560 edition).

1595. Freund (Leonhard). Deutsche Treue in Sprüchen und
Sprichwörtern. 8°. Leipzig, *Fritsch*, 1869.

In Deutscher Sprachwart, 1869, Bd. 4, pp. 340-348. [B.M.

1596. Freund (Leonhard). Treue und Untreue in deutschen Sprüchen und Sprichwörtern. pp. 38.

8°. Leipzig, *Pfau*, 1886.

Second edition. Die Treue im Spiegel der Sprüchweisheit. 1. Deutsche Sprüche und Sprichwörter, *etc.* pp. 49.

8°. Leipzig, *Kössling*, 1892.

Heft 1 of Volksweisheit und Weltklugheit. [B.M.

1597. Freydank. Proverbia eloquentis Freydangks innumeres in se utilitates complectentia. pp. [72].

4°. [Lipsiae?, 1500?].

Another edition. Der Freydank nuve, *etc.* + woodcuts.

4°. [Strassburg], *Gruninger*, 1508.

Another edition. 8°. Berlin, 1877.

Gratet-Duplessis, 533. This is not a collection of proverbs, but a selection of moral maxims in verse, known as "Bescheidenheit." It is supposed to have been written about the middle of the 13th century, and is important as a specimen of early German literature. The edition of 1500 has a Latin paraphrase. [B.M. (various editions).

1598. Friedreich (J. B.). Geschichte des Räthsels. pp. viii, 248.

8°. Dresden, *Kuntze*, 1860.

Pp. 54-58, Sprichworträthsel. [B.M.

1599. Friedrich, *Dr.* Zweikämpfe zwischen Sprichwörtern.

8°. Berlin, 1886.

In Central-Organ für die Interessen des Realschulwesens, Jahrgang 14, pp. 853-858.

1600. Frischbier (Hermann). Preussische Sprichwörter und volksthümliche Redensarten, *etc.* pp. 103.

8°. Königsberg, *Nürmberger*, 1864.

Another edition. pp. xiii, 322.

M.3. 8°. Berlin, *Enslin*, 1865.

1601. ———: Preussische Sprichwörter. . . . Zweite Sammlung, *etc.* pp. xii, 264. 8°. Berlin, *Enslin*, 1876.

A collection of over 3000 proverbs and sayings, with notes. [B.M.

1602. Fritsch (Ahasuerus). Verwerfung einiger bösen üblichen Sprichwörter. 8°. 1687.

Gratet-Duplessis, 575.

1603. Fünfhundert. Fünfhundert deutsche Sprichwörter und kurze Lehren in alphabetischer Ordnung, *etc.*

16°. Magdeburg, 1785.

Gratet-Duplessis, 663.

1604. Gabriel (H.) and **Suprian** (K.). Goldener Hausschatz, *etc.* pp. viii, 392.

8°. Bielefeld, Leipzig, *Velhagen & Klasing*, 1881.

Pp. 375-389 Sprichwörter (Nach der Sammlung von Simrock).

1605. Gedankenforscher. Der scherzhafte Gedankenforscher. Eine räthzelhafftäuschende Belustigung mit Sprichwörtern.

8°. Altona, 1696.

Gratet-Duplessis, 693.

1606. Geerling (Carl F. A.). Der deutsche Aufsatz. . . . 11. Stufe. Achte Auflage. pp. 206.

8°. Leipzig, *Gestewitz*, 1892.

Pp. 134-144, Sprichwörter, Begriffsentwickelungen.

1607. Gerber (Gustav). Die Sprache als Kunst. 2 Bde.

8°. Bromberg, *Mittler*, 1871-1874.

Bd. 2, Hälfte 2, pp. 166-182, Das Sprüchwört. A commentary. [B.M.

1608. Gerberus (Christian). Unerkannte Sünden der Welt.

8°. Dresden, 1703.

Another edition. 8°. Dresden, 1725.

Gratet-Duplessis, 584.

1609. Gerlingius (Joannes). Sylloge adagiorum aliquot Des. Erasmi aliorumque. . . . Germanico idiomate expressorum.

4°. Lugd. Bat., 1649.

1610. Goedeke (Karl). Grundrisz zur Geschichte der deutschen Dichtung. Aus den Quellen. . . . Zweiter Band. Das Reformationszeitalter. pp. iv, 600.

8°. Dresden, *Ehlermann*, 1886.

Pp. 3-19, German proverbs, *etc.*, at the time of the Reformation, with bibliography. [U.C.L.

1611. Goltz (Bogumil). Zur Geschichte und Charakteristik des deutschen Genius. . . . Zweite Auflage von: Die Deutschen. 2 Bde. 8°. Berlin, *Janke*, 1864.

Bd. 1, pp. 31-33, Die deutschen Sprüchwörter und Redensarten.

1612. Gomolcky (Daniel). Der Heller gilt am meisten wo er geschlagen ist . . . über tausend der gleichen Sprüchwörter, *etc.* [ff. 28]. 8°. 1734.

1613. Gossel (J.). Sprichwörtliche Redensarten mit ihren Erklärungen. pp. 104. 8°. Berlin, *Stubenrauch*, 1880.

1614. Gottsched (Johann Christoph). Grundlegung einer deutschen Sprachkunst . . . bey dieser dritten Auflage merklich vermehret. pp. [xxviii], 678, [xviii].

8°. Leipzig, *Breitkopf*, 1752.

Pp. 509-528, Von den Kern- und Gleichnissreden, ingleichen den Sprüchwörtern der deutschen Sprache. This, apparently, is not included in the edition of 1748.

1615. Greif (Carl). Der Erzähler, oder: das Buch für lange Winterabende, *etc.* pp. 388.

8°. Grimma, *Verlags-Comptoirs*, n.d.

Pp. 21-25, Modernisirte Sprichwörter.

N

1616. Grossen (Albrecht). Schöne lustige Sprichwörter und Sentenzen der alten weisen Heiden in deutsche Reimen gebracht.
8°. Francfort, 1593.
Gratet-Duplessis, 549.

1617. Gryphius (Christoph). Der teutschen Rätzel-Weisheit. Erster aus Rätzeln, Sprüchwörtern und Fabeln bestehenden Theil, *etc.* Breslau, 1692.

1618. Guenther (Friedrich Joachim). Entwürfe zu Vorträgen und Aufsätzen über 100 Sprichwörter, *etc.* pp. xii, 450.
8°. Eisleben, *Reichardt*, 1861.
Explanations and illustrations of 100 proverbs and 100 sayings of Schiller.
[B.M.

1619. H. (G.). Das Sprichwort und die Prediger.
4°. Leipzig, *Brockhaus*, 1863.
In Unterhaltungen am häuslichen Herd, Vierte Folge, Bd. 1, pp. 373-375.
[B.M.

1620. Haehl (Emanuel). Pädagogische Sprichwörter. pp. iv, 61. 8°. Stuttgart, *Blum & Vogel*, 1857.
821 entries. There are frequent comparisons with proverbs of other languages.
[B.M.

1621. Haerlin (Heinrich). Sprüchwort und Gottes Wort. Deutsche Sprüchwörter mit Bibelsprüchen und kurzen Erklärungen und Erzählungen. pp. vi, 146.
8°. Stuttgart, *Steinkopf*, 1851.

1622. Handbüchlein. Handbüchlein oder Vorzeichnüs etzlicher feiner und fürnehmer Sprüchlein, *etc.* [ff. 15].
4°. Dreszden, *Bergen von Lübeck*, 1588.
A very rare book, containing proverbial sayings in the form of triads.

1622a. Handschin (Ch. H.). Das Sprichwort bei Hans Sachs.
Madison, 1904.

1623. Harsdörfer (Georg Philipp). Frauenzimmer-Gesprächspielen. 8 Theile.
obl. 8°. Nürnberg, *Wolffgang End Tern*, 1642-49.
Gratet-Duplessis, 561. Theil 2, pp. 309-416, contains a German comedy entirely composed of proverbs and proverbial sayings. Theil 2 is of the second edition. [B.M. (second edition of Theil 2).

1624. Hartmann, *Pfarrer.* Wie das Volk spricht: fränkische Sprichwörter und sprichwörtliche Redensarten, *etc.*
8°. Stuttgart, *Kohlhammer*, 1890.
In Würtembergische Vierteljahrshefte für Landesgeschichte, Jahrgang 12, 1889, pp. 70-75. 201 entries. [B.M.

1625. Hassler (Ludwig Anton). Moralischer Gebrauch der Sprichwörter. 1819.
Gratet-Duplessis, 749. *In* Constanzer Archiv für Pastoralconferenzen, 1819.

1626. Hecker (Oskar). Die italienische Umgangssprache in systematischer Anordnung, *etc.* pp. xi, 312.

8°. Braunschweig, *Westermann*, 1897.

Pp. 243-254, German proverbs with Italian equivalents : pp. 254-257, Italian proverbs, without German equivalents : pp. 257-258, German proverbs without Italian equivalents.

1627. Hegewald, *Dr.* Aus den Papieren eines deutschen Patrioten. pp. vii, 131. 8°. Karlsruhe, *Creuzbauer*, 1868.

Pp. 69-76, Die Sprichwörter der Deutschen erklärt und auf ihren Ursprung zurückgeführt.

1628. Heineccius (J. G.). Vermischte Anmerkungen und rechtslichen Gutachten. 4°. Berlin, 1742.

Gratet-Duplessis, 622. Contains : Vom Nutzen der Sprichwörter in der Rechtsgelehrsamkeit, *etc.*

1629. Hermann (Johann). Sprichworte und Denksprüche für unsre Schule gesammelt. 8°. Wien, *Gerold*, 1862.

In 3. Jahresbericht der öffentlichen Knaben-Hauptschule des k. k. Schulrathes Hermann in der inneren Stadt Wien, 1861-1862, pp. 20-50.

1630. Hertz (K.). Worte der Weisen aus allen Völkern und Zeiten, *etc.* pp. viii, 370. 8°. Stuttgart, *Kröner*, [1886].

1910 quotations, sayings, maxims, *etc.*, from many sources, in German. A large number of these are proverbs. [B.M.

1631. Herzog (H.). Beispielssprichwörter. pp. iv, 70.

8°. Aarau, *Sauerländer*, 1882.

1366 entries.

1632. ——: Deutsche Sprichwörter, *etc.* pp. iv, 171.

8°. Aarau, *Sauerländer*, 1882.

1633. ——: Das Sprichwort in der Volksschule. pp. viii, 264.

8°. Basel, *Bahnmaier*, 1868.

Gives the explanation of numerous proverbs. [B.M.

1634. Hess ( ). Ueber den Ursprung einiger deutschen Sprüchwörter und sprüchwörtlichen Redensarten. 4°. 1862.

In Allgemeines Nassauisches Schulblatt, Jahrgang 13, Hälfte 2, No. 33.

1635. Hetzel (S.). Wie der Deutsche spricht . . . Ausdrücke, Redensarten, Sprichwörter und Citate . . . gesammelt und erläutert. pp. viii, 355. 8°. Leipzig, *Grunow*, 1896.

Arranged alphabetically by the principal words. [B.M.

1636. Heusler (J. A.). Luther's Sprichwörter aus seinen Schriften gesammelt, *etc.* pp. viii, 160. 8°. Leipzig, *Barth*, 1824.

478 entries.

1637. Hildebrand (Rudolf). Gesammelte Aufsätze und Vorträge zur deutschen Philologie, *etc.* pp. viii, 335.

8°. Leipzig, *Teubner*, 1890.

Pp. 154-162, Etwas vom Sprichwort in der Schule. A commentary. [B.M.

1638. Hilka (Alfons).   Beiträge zur Fabel- und Sprichwörter-
Literatur des Mittelalters.   pp. 38.

8°.   Breslau, *Aderholz*, 1914.

1639. Hoeck (Johann Carl).   Miscellen.   pp. viii, 438.

8°.   Gmünd, *Ritter*, 1815.

Pp. 233-236, Zur Geschichte der Sprüchwörter.

1640. Hoffmann (August Heinrich), *von Fallersleben*.   Spenden
zur deutschen Litteraturgeschichte . . . Erstes Bändchen :
Aphorismen und Sprichwörter aus dem 16. und 17. Jahrhundert, meist politischen Inhalts.   pp. 154.

sm. 8°.   Leipsig, *Engelmann*, 1844.

Gratet-Duplessis, 777.   A curious work, formed of extracts from rare, for-
gotten, or unknown books.   It contains a large number of moral or political
proverbs from various German paremiographers.   [B.M.

1641. Hub (Ignaz).   Die komische und humoristische Literatur
der deutschen Prosaisten des sechzehnten Jahrhunderts, *etc.*
2 pts.   8°.   Nürnberg, *Ebner*, 1856-7.

The first part includes Geiler von Kaisersberg, Joh. Pauli, T. Murner,
Luther, von Hutten, Seb. Franck, Joh. Agricola, Erasmus, A. Musculus, J.
Westphal and C. Spangenberg.   The second part relates more to generalities
than proverbs.   The accounts of the lives and works of the worthies noticed
are useful.   [B.M.

1642. Huber (Friedrich).   Erklärungen deutscher Sprichwörter
. . . Dritte . . . Auflage.   pp. 32.

8°.   Weinheim, *Ackermann*, 1911.

1643. Huebener (Friedrich).   Sprichwörter für Kinder von sechs
bis neun Jahren in Fabeln und kleinen Erzählungen, *etc.*
pp. 87.   8°.   Stendal, *Franzen & Grosse*, 1859.

1644. Kainis, *Dr.*   Die Derbheiten im Reden des Volkes.   pp.
156.   12°.   Leipzig, *Literatur-Bureau*, [1880?].

Proverbs arranged alphabetically by principal words.   [B.M.

1645. Kellner (L.).   Ausgewählte Musterstücke, Sätze, Sprüchwörter, Räthsel und Gedichte für Volkschulen, *etc.*   14.
Auflage.   pp. viii, 85.   8°.   Erfurt, *Otto*, 1863.

1646. Kern.   Der Kern auserlesener Sprichwörter.

8°.   Francfort, Leipsig, 1718.

Gratet-Duplessis, 600.

1647. Kieser (Eberhard).   Thesauri philopolitici, oder politisches
Schatz-Kästleins zweyten Buchs, erster (-funffter) Theil.   In
welchem zwey und fünffzig schöner Sprüchwörter . . . em-
blematischer Weise . . . in Figuren . . . fürgestellt. . . . Durch
J. L. G[ottfried K. Lieboldt, H. Kornmann] . . . an Tag
geben durch E. Kieser.

obl. 4°.   Franckfurt am Mayn, *Kiesern*, 1627-30.

Proverbs, mottoes, emblems, *etc.*, of different places.   Thle. 1 and 5 contain
the proverbs.   [B.M.

1648. Kirmes-Büchlein. Kirmes-Büchlein, enthält eine Sammlung der besten teutschen Trinklieder mit leichten Melodieen
im Volkstone, Sprüchwörter, *etc.* pp. xx, 189.
12°. Frohburg, [1800?].

Pp. 150-158, Sprüchwörter zu Kirmesspielen. 200 entries. [B.M.

1649. Klapper (Joseph). Die Sprichwörter der Freidankpre-
digten . . . Ein Beitrag zur Geschichte des ostmitteldeutschen
Sprichworts und seiner lateinischen Quellen. pp. 112.
8°. Breslau, Marcus, 1927.
[B.M.

1650. Kocher (Christianus Fridericus). Manualis scholastici pars
posterior, *etc.* pp. 118, 70, [17].
8°. Stutgardia, Müllerus, 1722.

Contains : Proverbia Latino-Germanica soluta et metrica.

1651. Koerte (Friedrich Heinrich Wilhelm). Die Sprichwörter
und sprichwörtlichen Redensarten der Deutschen, *etc.* pp.
xl, 567. la. 8°. Leipzig, Brockhaus, 1837.
Second edition. pp. xxxii, 579.
8°. Leipzig, Brockhaus, 1861.

Gratet-Duplessis, 766. The introduction contains interesting observations on the
nature and character of proverbs, with brief German bibliographical indications.
Then follow 7202 proverbs, arranged alphabetically by their key-words, accompanied where necessary by brief but sufficient explanations. The book is
concluded by two appendices, one containing a list of 142 drinking proverbs
and sayings, without explanations, the other containing 256 sayings concerning
agriculture, the calendar, *etc.*, with brief notes on this type of proverb. [B.M.

1652. Kradolfer (J.). Der Volksglaube im Spiegel des deutschen
Sprichworts, *etc.* pp. 51. 12°. Bremen, *Bruns*, [1880].
Schriften der nordwestdeutschen Protestantenvereine, 3. [B.M.

1652a. Kriegk (Georg Ludwig). Schriften zur allgemeinen Erd-
kunde. pp. x, 370. 8°. Leipzig, *Engelmann*, 1840.
Pp. 101-109, Geographische Sprichwörter und Redeweisen. Proverbs in
German concerning different places. [B.M.

1653. Kuechle (Georg). Dichterwort und Sprichwort nach ihrem
ethischen Gehalt erläutert. 2 Hefte.
8°. Augsburg, Berlin, Preyss (Heft 1),
Zilessen (Heft 2), 1884, 1889.

1654. Kueffner (Georg M.). Die Deutschen in Sprichwort, *etc.*
pp. iv, 93. 8°. Heidelberg, Winter, 1899.
Proverbs in all languages concerning the Germans.

1655. Lassenius (Johannes). Sinnlicher Zeitvertreiber ange-
wiesen in einigen der besten und nach-dencklichsten teutschen
Sprich-Wörter, *etc*. pp. 358. 12°. Jehna, *Schrödter*, 1664.
Another edition. Zinryke tydverdryver, *etc*. pp. [x], 244.
12°. Amsterdam, *Wetekamp & Eleveld*, 1760.
Gratet-Duplessis, 619. [B.M.

1656. Latendorf (Friedrich). Agricola's [of Eisleben] Sprichwörter, ihr hochdeutscher Ursprung und ihr Einfluss auf die
deutschen und niederländischen Sammler, nebst kritischen
Bemerkungen über die Sprichwörter und Sprichwörtersammlungen der Gegenwart. pp. 252.
8°. Schwerin, *Bärensprung*, 1862.
[B.M.

1657. ———: Die Ausgabe der Sprichwörter Agricola's v. J.
1548. 4°. Nürnberg, 1866.
In Anzeiger für Kunde der deutschen Vorzeit, Neue Folge, Jahrgang 13,
1866, columns 207-210. Another brief article by the same author on Agricola's
proverbs is to be found in No. 2 of the same periodical, 1868. [B.M.

1658. ———: Lessing's Name und der öffentliche Missbrauch
desselben im neuen deutschen Reich, *etc*. pp. 60.
8°. München, Leipzig, *Heinrichs*, 1886.
Contains a number of proverbs from the collections of S. Franck, Agricola,
etc. [B.M.

1659. ———: Unbekannte Sprüche und Sprichwörter des sechzehnten Jahrhunderts. 8°. Leipsig, *Teubner*, 1867.
In Neue Jahrbücher für Philologie und Pedagogik, Zweite Abteilung, 1867,
pp. 263-269. [B.M.

1660. Lauchert (Friedrich). Sprichwörter und sprichwörtliche
Redensarten bei P. Abraham a S. Clara.
8°. Bonn, *Hanstein*, 1892.
In Alemannia, Jahrgang 20, pp. 213-254. [B.M.

1661. Laurentius (G.). Apophthegmata, oder scharfsinnige
Reden, Sprichwörter und Geschichten, *etc*.
8°. Dresden, 1705.
Gratet-Duplessis, 586.

1662. Leben. Alte teutsche zu vorsichtigen Leben und vernehm-
lichen Reden dienende Sprichwörter. 8°. Helmstadt, 1674.
Gratet-Duplessis, 570. In alphabetical order, without notes or explanations.

1663. Le Bourgeois (Marcel). Deutsche und französische sprichwörtliche Redensarten, *etc*. pp. 62.
8°. Leipzig, *Violet*, 1891.

1664. Lehmann (Christoph). Altdeutsche Reime und Sprüche,
etc. pp. vii, 201. 8°. Berlin, *Duncker*, 1890.
Selections of proverbs, sayings, *etc*., from **1665**. [B.M.

1665. Lehmann (Christoph). Florilegium politicum. Politischer Blumengarten, *etc.* pp. [xvi], 947.

8°. [Frankfort?], *impensis authoris*, 1630.

Another edition. 4 pts.

12°. Franckfort, *Schönwetter*, 1662.

Christoph Lehmann's Blumengarten frisch ausgejätet, auf-geharkt und umzäunt von einem Liebhaber alter deutscher Sprache und Weisheit. pp. xiv, 191.

8°. Berlin, *Duncker*, 1879.

Gratet-Duplessis, 559. An excellent compilation of proverbs, precepts, maxims, *etc.*, taken from many writers. The first edition is incomplete and lacks a commentary. There are many other editions, that of Francfort, 1662, being the most complete. Nopitsch mentions two other editions of the same date, one of Giessen and the other of Amsterdam, but without giving details. Hoffmann von Fallersleben gives numerous extracts from this work in **1640**.

[B.M.

1666. Leinweber (Heinrich). Die Weisheit auf der Gasse. Neue Sprichwörter-Sammlung, nebst Zusammenstellung und kurzer Erklärung sprichwörtlicher Redensarten. pp. xv, 232.

8°. Paderborn, *Schöningh*, 1897.

3. Auflage.   8°. Paderborn, 1922.

1667. Leistner (Ernst). Des deutschen Landwirths Sprüchwort-buch, *etc.*   Leipzig, 1876.

1668. Lévy (Antoine). Germanismen, Gallicismen und Sprich-wörter, *etc.* pp. 172.   8°. Paris, Leipzig, *Soudier*, 1889.

1669. ———: Méthode pratique de la langue allemande. . . . Troisième partie; idiotismes et proverbes, *etc.* pp. viii, 206.

8°. Paris, *Soudier*, 1888.

Corresponding proverbs in German and French.

1670. Lier (E.). Deutsche Sprichwörter. Durch Beispiele erläutert und zum Verständnis gebracht, *etc.* pp. iv, 31.

8°. Langensalza, *Gressler*, 1883.

1671. Lloyd (Joseph Henry). Idioms of the German language, together with the proverbs, *etc.* pp. vi, 198.

8°. London, Edinburgh, *Williams & Norgate*, 1875.

Pp. 98-155, proverbs. An alphabetical list of German proverbs with English equivalents or translations, also equivalents from many other languages.

[B.M.

1671a. Loebe (M.). Altdeutsche Sinnsprüche in Reimen gesam-melt. pp. 164.   1883.

1672. Loewe (Heinrich). Deutsch-Englische Phraseologie in systematischer Ordnung, *etc.* pp. xi, 222.

M.2. 8°. Berlin, *Langenscheidt*, 1877.

Pp. 152-157, Deutsche und englische Sprichwörter.   [B.M.

1673. Lohrengel (W.).   Altes Gold.   Deutsche Sprichwörter und
Redensarten, nebst einem Anhange, *etc.* pp. vii, 83.
16°.   Clausthal, *Grossen*, 1860.
An alphabetical list.   [B.M.

1674. Losert (Walter).   Heitere Gedanken.   Eine Auslese
bekannter Sprichwörter in moderner Beleuchtung. pp. 32.
16°.   Wien, *Dietl*, [1911].

1674a. Luther (Martin).   Luthers Sprichwörtersammlung.   Nach
seiner Handschrift herausgegeben von L. Thiele.
Weimar, 1900.

1675. Maass (Carl).   Ueber Metapher und Allegorie im deutschen
Sprichwort, *etc.* pp. 23.   4°.   Dresden, *Ramming*, 1891.

1676. Mader (Joseph).   Vermischte Aufsätze aus der Moral,
Staatskunst und Staatenkunde.   8°.   Prag, 1788.
Gratet-Duplessis, 669.   No. 6 contains : Von Sprichwörtern.

1677. Maître.   Le maître de la langue allemande, . . . composée
sur le modèle . . . de Gottsched, *etc.* pp. xxiv, 576.
8°.   Strasbourg, *Konig*, 1766.
Fourth edition.   Le maître allemand, *etc.* pp. xxiv, 552.
8°.   Strasbourg, *Konig*, 1763.
Eighteenth edition. pp. viii, 472.
8°.   Paris, Strasbourg, *Konig*, 1823.
Contains a section of " Germanismes et proverbes," with French translations.   First edition published 1754.   [B.M.

1678. Marbach (Gotthard Oswald).   Sprichwörter und Sprüchreden der Deutschen.   [Anonymous.] pp. 131.
8°.   Leipsig, *Wigand*, 1842.
Another edition.   Leipzig, 1847.
Gratet-Duplessis, 772.   Nos. 28 and 29 of the Deutsche Volksbücher published by G. O. Marbach.   A long list of proverbs, sayings, *etc.*, not in any
order.   No notes.   [B.M.

1678a. Mauvillon (J.).   Dramatische Sprüchwörter.   Beytrag zum
gesellschaftlichen Vergnügen in Deutschland.   2 Theile.
Leipzig, 1785.

1679. May (Johann Friedrich).   De proverbiorum Germanicorum
collectoribus praefatus, *etc.* pp. 8.
4°.   [Lipsiae, *ex officina Breitkopfia*, 1756].
A brief commentary on certain collectors of German proverbs.   [B.M.

1680. ———— : De sapientia proverbiali veterum Germanorum,
exemplis illustrata. pp. 12.
4°.   Lipsiae, *Breitkopf*, 1756.
Gratet-Duplessis, 531.   A rare book, containing observations on the nature
and influence of proverbs, with a close examination of some German ones.

1681. May (Johann Friedrich). Progymnasma de proverbiorum germanicorum collectoribus.   4°. Lipsiae, 1754.
Gratet-Duplessis, 530.

1682. ———: Specimen sapientiae proverbialis apud Germanos circa artes atque scientias.
             4°. Lipsiae, *ex officina Breitkopfia*, 1760.
Gratet-Duplessis, 643. Also published under the title : " Prolusio de sapientia proverbiali."

1683. Meinau (Carolina). Aufklärende Erzählungen über bekannte Sprüchwörter für Knaben und Maedchen, *etc.* pp. x, 286.   8°. Noerdlingen, *Beck*, n.d.

1684. Mejsner (Ernst). Einhundert drey und dreysig gotteslästerliche, gottlose, schändliche und schädliche, auch unanständige und theils falsche teutsche Sprichwörter, *etc.* pp. [xvi], 143.   8°. Jena, *Bielcke*, 1705.
Gratet-Duplessis, 585. According to Nopitsch, this is a pseudonymous work whose real author is J. E. Michaelis, the theologian. Comments on 133 blasphemous and pernicious proverbs.   [B.M.

1685. Mercker (G.). Deutsche-französische Sprichwörter und Redensarten, *etc.* pp. 46.   12°. Osterode, *Sorge*, 1850.

1686. Mereau (Friedrich Ernst Carl). Taschenbuch der deutschen Vorzeit auf das Jahr 1794. pp. [vi], 276.
           16°. Nürnberg, Jena, *Schneider-Weigel*, 1794.
Gratet-Duplessis, 686. Pp. 272-274, Sprichwörter aus der frühern Zeit : pp. 274-276, Denksprüche aus der frühern Zeit.

1686a. Merguin (F. J. H.). Teutsch-französische, französischteutsche Sprichwörter.   1828.

1687. Meyer (Gerhard). Etliche 100 gemeiner deutscher Sprichwörter.   8°. Augsbourg, 1568.
Gratet-Duplessis, 545. A list only, without notes.

1688. Meyer (Johann Jakob). Hortulus adagiorum Germanicolatinorum.   12°. Basileae, 1677.
Gratet-Duplessis, 571, 172.

1689. Meyer (Jürgen Bona). Probleme der Lebensweisheit. pp. vi, 369.
        8°. Berlin, *Allgemeiner Verein für deutsche Literatur*, 1887.
Pp. 1-33, Erziehungsweisheit im Sprichwort. This article had previously appeared in : Die Gegenwart, Bd. 6, 1874.   [B.M.

1690. Mieg (Johann Friedrich). Ueber das Studium der Sprache, *etc.*   8°. Frankfurt am Main, *Esslinger*, 1782.
Gratet-Duplessis, 658. Pp. 162-203, Ueber die Volksweisheit in Sprüchwörtern.

1691. Mone (Franz Joseph). Quellen und Forschungen zur Geschichte der teutschen Litteratur und Sprache . . . Erster Band, *etc.* pp. vii, 568.

8°. Aachen, Leipzig, *Mayer*, 1830.

No more published. Pp. 186-214, Zur Litteratur und Geschichte der Sprüch-wörter. [B.M.

1692. Morel (A.) and **Gérimont** (Éduard). La morale universelle. L'esprit des Allemands. Pensées, maximes, sentences, et proverbes, *etc.* pp. 346. 8°. Paris, *Hachette*, n.d.

1693. Muellenhoff (Carl Victor) und **Scherer** (Wilhelm). Denk-mäler deutscher Poesie und Prosa aus dem viii-xii. Jahrhundert. pp. xxxiv, 548. 8°. Berlin, *Weidmann*, 1864.

3rd edition. 2 Bde. 8°. Berlin, *Weidmann*, 1892.

Contains a section of German and Latin proverbs. [B.M.

1694. Mueller (Johann Georg). Unterhaltungen mit Serena. 2 Bde. 8°. Winterthur, *Steiner*, 1793-1803.

Gratet-Duplessis, 723. Bd. 1, pp. 235-237, Arabische Sprüchwörter : Bd. 2, pp. 169-179, Sprüchwörter : pp. 250-267, Sprüche von der göttlichen Vorsehung.

1695. Murner (Thomas). Schreiben an den Herausgeber, einige Spracherklärung enthaltend, nebst Anhang einiger veralteten Sprüchwörter. [Anonymous]. 8°. Leipzig, *Weygand*, 1779.

Gratet-Duplessis, 654. *In* Deutsches Museum, 1779, pp. 446-453. Proverbs taken from Murner's Schelmenzunft. [B.M.

1696. Nachlassenschaft. Nachlassenschaft, oder Abhandlung über Sprichwörter. 8°. Brême, 1787.

Gratet-Duplessis, 665.

1697. Naht (A.). Deutsch-russisch. Handbuch zur Erlernung der russischen Sprache. . . . 3. Auflage, *etc.* pp. iv, 308.

8°. Berlin, *Goldschmidt*, 1897.

Pp. 288-296, proverbs and phrases in German and Russian. There was a fourth edition, same date and place. [B.M.

1698. Naumann (H.). Germanische Sprüchweisheit, *etc.* pp. 71. 8°. Jena, 1926.

1699. Neander (Michael). Ethica veterum latinorum sapientum.
8°. Basileæ, 1585.

Gratet-Duplessis, 548. Contains : Germanorum veterum sapientia, sive proverbia Germanica. These proverbs were also republished under the title : Michael Neanders deutsche Sprichwörter. Herausgegeben . . . von Friedrich Latendorf. pp. 58. 12°. Schwerin, *Bärensprung*, 1864. [B.M. (1864 edition).

1700. Nehm (Wilhelm). Methodisches Handbuch für den Unter-richt in den deutschen Stylübungen, *etc.* pp. xi, 436.

Essen, *Bädeker*, 1838.

Pp. 283-309, German proverbs which can serve as a theme for exercises in style.

1701. Nemo. Historische Sprüchwörter und Verwandtes.
8°. Glogau, *Flemming*, 1864.
In Schlesische Provinzialblätter, Neue Folge, Bd. 3, pp. 28-30. [B.M.

1702. Neus (J.). Weisheitsregeln aus den gebräuchlichsten Sprichwörtern der Deutschen. . . . 2. Ausgabe.
Lindau, 1834.

1703. Nieden (Johannes). Deutsche Gedichte, nebst einem Anhange von Sprüchen und Sprichwörtern zum Auswendiglernen. . . . Dritte Auflage. pp. 192.
8°. Leipzig, *Lindner*, 1898.
Pp. 181-187, Sprichwörter, alphabetisch nach den Stichworten geordnet. 216 entries.

1704. Nieter (Christoph Georg Heinrich). Erklärung und Berichtigung einiger Sprichwörter. pp. 191.
8°. Halberstadt, *Gross*, 1798.
Gratet-Duplessis, 704.

1705. Nissl (Joseph). Lebens-Schule, in einer Sammlung von Sprüchwörtern, Denk- und Sittensprüchen. 3 pts.
8°. München, 1806.
Gratet-Duplessis, 732.

1706. Olorinus (Johannes). Joh. Olorini geistliche und weltliche Sprichwörter, *etc.* 8°. Magdeburg, 1606.
Gratet-Duplessis, 555. Also published, at the same date, under the title of Joh. Olorini Varisci paroemiologia germanica.

1706a. Oschilewski (W. G.). Deutsche Sprichwörter. Ausgewählt von W. G. Oschilewski. Mit 15 Zeichnungen von J. L. Gampp. M.4. 8°. Jena, *Diederichs*, 1924.

1707. Otto (Emil). Kleines deutsch-französisches Gesprächbuch . . . 55. . . . Auflage, *etc.* pp. 196.
16°. Strasbourg, *Schultz*, 1883.
Pp. 184-191, German and French proverbs.

1708. Ottow (A. M.). Beiträge zur Sprichwörterliteratur.
4°. Nürnberg, 1868.
In Anzeiger für Kunde der deutschen Vorzeit, Neue Folge, 1868, No. 6.
[B.M.

1709. ———: Der Einfluss der ältesten niederländischen Sprichwörtersammlung auf die ältern deutschen Sprichwörtersammlungen. 4°. Nürnberg, 1865.
In Anzeiger für Kunde der deutschen Vorzeit, Neue Folge, 1865, No. 1.
[B.M.

1710. ———: Luther'sche Sprichwörtersammlung.
4°. Leipzig, 1869.
In Deutscher Sprachwart, Bd. 4, No. 15. [B.M.

1711. Ottow (A. M.). Sprichwörter und sprichwörtliche Redensarten aus: Andreae Gryphii Seug-Amme, oder untreues
Gesind, Lust-Spiel. Bresslau, 1663. 4°. Leipzig, 1872.

In Deutscher Sprachwart, Bd. 6, No. 17. [B.M.

1712. Passavant (Ludwig von). Verantwortung: der Schmach
und Lesterschrifft so Johannes Agricola Eyssleben genant im
büchlin ausslegung Teütscher Sprüchwort, *etc.*

4°. [Strasburg?, 1530?].

Another edition. L. v. Passavant gegen Agricola's Sprichwörter. In wortgetreuem Abdruck herausgegeben und erläutert von Friedrich Latendorf, *etc.* pp. 34.

4°. Berlin, *Calvary*, 1873.

[B.M.

1713. Paulus (H. G.). Allgemeines Lesebuch, für den Bürger
und Landmann. . . . Neueste Auflage. pp. xviii, 594.

8°. Bamberg, Würzburg, *Goebhardt*, 1812.

Pp. 1-15, Vorübungen des Verstandes durch Sprüchwörter als Sittensprüche
und Klugheitslehren.

1714. Peroch (Sigismondo). Grammatica tedesca, *etc.* pp. viii,
182. 8°. Vienna, *etc.*, *Hartleben*, n.d.

Die Kunst der Polyglottie, Theil 54. Pp. 180-182, Proverbi—Sprichwörter.

[B.M.

1715. Peters (Friedrich). Der teutschen Weissheit, *etc.*

8°. Hamburg, *Ohr*, 1605.

Gratet-Duplessis, 554. This is one of the largest and most complete collections of German proverbs. It is arranged alphabetically, and does not contain
proverbial sayings. There are not many explanations. Hoffmann von Fallersleben quotes a few maxims in verse from this in his " Spenden zur deutschen
Litteraturgeschichte. *See also* **1589.** [B.M.

1716. Peugeot (Pierre). L'esprit allemand d'après la langue et
les proverbes, *etc.* pp. xxiv, 93. 8°. Paris, *Giraud*, 1885.

1304 proverbs.

1717. Pirrone-Giancontieri (Francesco). Raccolta di proverbi e
modi di dire tedeschi e italiani. pp. 113.

la. 16°. Palermo, *Clausen*, 1889.

Pitrè, 3135. The proverbs are divided into three parts, in the first are those
which correspond literally, in the second those which partly resemble each other
in form, in the third those which are equivalent in sense. Arranged alphabetically under the Italian. Some notes.

1718. Pizanski (G. C.). Erläuterung einiger preussischen Sprüchwörter. . . . Herausgegeben von G. C. P[izanski]. pp. 8.

4°. Königsberg, 1760.

Gratet-Duplessis, 789. Nopitsch, 242, declares the author to be Pizanski.
The book gives the explanation of 23 German proverbs used in Prussia. [B.M.

1719. Plaut (M.). Deutsches Land und Volk im Volksmund. Eine Sammlung von Sprichwörtern, *etc.* pp. 120.

8°. Breslau, *Hirt*, 1897.

Proverbs, sayings, phrases, *etc.*, concerning the Germans, the different provinces of Germany, Austria-Hungary, Holland and Belgium. Pp. 6-9, bibliography. [B.M.

1720. Preime (August). Erklärung deutscher Redensarten. pp. 18. 4°. Cassel, *Jungklaus*, 1875.

Proverbial phrases rather than proverbs. [B.M.

1721. Proverbs. [Two collections of German proverbs].

Annaburg, 1577.

Gratet-Duplessis, 547, and Hoffmann von Fallersleben, Spenden der deutsche Litteraturgeschichte, p. 149, indicate two collections of German proverbs in alphabetical order. Neither collection has a title, and both were printed at Annaburg in 1577. The first appears to be a list from some manuscript work on proverbs which has not been found. It is a folio of 70 leaves, on the last of which is printed : Gedruckt zur Annaburg, im Churf. Sachssis. Hofflager, den 8 aprilis 1577 Jar, durch Gimel Bergen.

The second, of 14 leaves only, begins : Volgen etliche gemeine Sprichwörter, ohne Auslegung, and ends : Gedruckt zur Annaburg, im 1577 Jar.

The only known copies of these two collections are at Dresden in the Royal Library.

1721a. Pusch (K.). Ueber Sebastian Francks Sprichwörter-sammlung vom Jahr 1541. pp. 42.

4°. Hildburghausen, 1894.

1722. Quick (Robert Herbert). Essentials of German. With poetry and proverbs, *etc.* pp. vi, 166.

8°. London, *Longmans*, 1882, [1881].

Pp. 113-135, proverbs in German with English translations and equivalents, and exercises or variations on them. [B.M.

1723. R. (D. C. A.). Moralische Sprichwörter der Deutschen, *etc.* 8°. Halberstadt, 1822.

In verse. [B.M.

1724. Rabener (Gottlieb Wilhelm). Satiren, *etc.* 5 Bde.

8°. Carlsruhe, *Schmieder*, 1777.

Sämmtliche Werke, *etc.* 4 Bde.

8°. Stuttgart, *Scheible*, 1839.

Gratet-Duplessis, 651. Contains a section entitled : Antons Pansa von Mancha Abhandlung von Sprüchwörtern, *etc.* [B.M.

1724a. ———: Fortgesetzte Abhandlungen von Sprüchwörtern, wie solche zu verstehen und zu gebrauchen sind.

8°. Frankfurt, 1774.

1725. Ramann (Sylvester Jakob). Moralischer Unterricht in Sprichwörtern, *etc.* 6 Bde. 8°. Erfurt, *Keyser*, 1789-1800.

Another edition. 8°. Altenbourg, 1801-1802.

Gratet-Duplessis, 675. The complete work containing the explanation of about 180 proverbs appeared in six successive parts at Erfurt from 1789-1800. There were later editions of the separate parts.

1726. Ramann (Sylvester Jakob). Neue Sammlung von Sprichwörtern, *etc.* 4 pts.
8°. Altenburg, *Rinck & Schnuphase*, 1801-1804.

Gratet-Duplessis, 726. This is to be distinguished from the last entry, which
was primarily destined for children, while this is intended for adults.

1727. ———: Predigten über Sprüchwörter. 4 Bde.
8°. Erfurt, *Henning*, 1799-1801.

1728. Rasch (Johann). Vier stuck. Nichts wehrt. 270 Nützliche feine viertailige lehrpuncten der alten Weisen, *etc.*
4°. München, *Berg*, 1589

Gratet-Duplessis, 237. A book somewhat similar to the " Livre des quatre
choses." [B.M.

1729. Reinsberg-Düringsfeld (Ida von), *Baroness*. Das Sprichwort als Kosmopolit. 3 Bde. sm. 8°. Leipsig, *Fries*, 1863.

Bd. 1, Das Sprichwort als Philosoph. Bd. 2, Das Sprichwort als Praktikus.
Bd. 3, Das Sprichwort als Humorist. Mostly German proverbs, but followed
by those of other countries in German. [U.C.L.

1730. Richard (August Victor). Licht und Schatten, *etc.* pp.
xxxii, 432. 8°. Leipzig, *Teubner*, 1861.

Pp. 377-395, Sprüchwörter aus dem xvi. Jahrhundert. [B.M.

1731. Richter (Albert). Deutsche Redensarten. Sprachlich und
kulturgeschichtlich erläutert. pp. 158.
8°. Leipzig, *Richter*, 1889.
Second edition. pp. 190. 8°. Leipzig, *Richter*, 1893.

1732. Richter (Ludwig). Die deutschen Sprichwörter und
Sprüchreden. Mit Illustrationen von Ludwig Richter, *etc.*
pp. 131. 12°. Leipzig, *Weigand*, 1876.

1733. Rose (D. C. A.). Moralische Sprichwörter der Deutschen.
8°. Halberstadt, *Vogler*, 1822.
Second edition. Potsdam, 1833.
[B.M.

1734. Rosental (Francesc' Antonio). Esercizii di traduzione dal
tedesco in italiano. . . . Questi esercizii racchiudono . . .
massime morali; sentenze; proverbi, *etc.* pp. 64.
8°. Milano, *Ubicini*, 1844.

1735. Sager (Otto). Tiller's von Tscherlow [*pseud.* of O. Sager]
philosophische Abhandlung von den bekanntesten Sprichwörtern der alten Deutschen. pp. [xxxviii], 248.
8°. Augsburg, *Rieger*, 1777.
Gratet-Duplessis, 652. A moral satire after the style of Rabener. [B.M.

1736. Sailer (Johann Michael von). Die Weisheit auf der Gasse, *etc.* pp. xvi, 404. 8°. Augsburg, 1810.
Deutsches Sprichwörter- und Sprüchebuch. . . . 1. Sprich-
wörterbuch: Die Weisheit auf der Gasse. . . . 2. Sprüchebuch: Goldkörner der Weisheit und Tugend-Sprüche mit und
ohne Glosse. Zweyte . . . Auflage. [J. M. S. . . . gesammelte Werke . . . Theil 20]. 8°. Grätz, 1819.
Sprüche mit und ohne Glosse. . . . Zweyte verbesserte Ausgabe. pp. 80. 8°. 1821.
Die Weisheit auf der Gasse. . . . Sprüche mit und ohne
Glosse, *etc.* 2 Bde. 16°. Salzbach, *Seidel*, 1843.
Gratet-Duplessis, 734. [B.M.

1737. Sammlung. Sammlung der ausgesuchtesten und gebräuchlichsten Redensarten und Sprichwörter.
8°. Augsburg, 1794.
Gratet-Duplessis, 687.

1737a. Sanders (D.). Zitatenlexikon. Sammlung von über 12,000
Zitaten, Sprichwörtern und sprichwörtlichen Redensarten und
Sentenzen. 4. Auflage. pp. 712. 8°. Leipzig, 1922.

1738. Sandvoss (Franz). So spricht das Volk. Volksthümliche
Redensarten. pp. vi, 70. 12°. Berlin, *Schotte*, 1860.
Second edition. pp. vi, 70. 12°. Berlin, 1861.
Arranged alphabetically by the principal words. Some notes. [B.M.

1739. ———: Spreu. Erste (-Fünfte) Hampfel, ausgeworfen
von Xanthippus [*pseud.* of F. Sandvoss]. 5 pts.
8°. Rom, *Loescher*, München, *Straub*, 1879-85.
Hampfel 5, pp. 16-31, Zu Sprichwörtern und Redensarten. [B.M.

1740. ———: Sprichwörter aus Burkhard Waldis mit einem
Anhänge: zur Kritik des Kurzischen B. Waldis und einem
Verzeichniss von Melanchthon gebrauchter Sprichwörter, pp.
159. 8°. Friedland, *Richter*, 1866.

1741. Saphir (M. G.). Humoristische Abende. . . . Fünfte verbesserte Auflage. pp. 228. 12°. Dresden, *Kaufmann*, n.d.
Pp. 199-221, Marinirte Redensarten und Sprichwörter, nebst Betrachtungen
über Dilletantismus und Stroh.

1742. Schatzkästlein. Schatzkästlein altdeutscher Sprichworte
und Redensarten, *etc.* pp. 32.
8°. Wien, *Verfasser des Landfreundes*, 1819.

1743. Schellhorn (Andreas). Teutsche Sprichwörter. . . . Nebst
einem Anhänge von Sprichwörtern und Denksprüchen in
lateinischen Versen, *etc.* pp. [xii], 160, 56.
8°. Nuremberg, *in der Steinischen Buchhandlung*, 1797.
Gratet-Duplessis, 702. With explanatory notes. [B.M.

1744. Schoch (Johann Georg). Neu-erbaueter poetischer Lust u. Blumen-Garten. . . . Vier Hundert Denk-Spruchen, Sprüch-Wörtern, Retzeln, *etc.* 16°. Leipzig, *Kirchner*, 1660.

1745. Schottelius (Justus Georgius). Ausführliche Arbeit von der deutschen Hauptsprache, *etc.* pp. 1466 + preliminary pages and indices. 4°. Braunschweig, *Zilligern*, 1663.

Gratet-Duplessis, 567. Buch 5, Tractat 3, pp. 1101-1146, a collection of about 2000 German proverbs, chiefly taken from the collections of Franck and Agricola. Not much order; no explanations. [B.M.

1746. Schrader (Friedrich). Ein Tausend deutsche Sprichwörter. [Or, under the following title] : Frid. Schraderi alte deutsche Sprichwörter. 8°. Helmstadt, 1688.

Gratet-Duplessis, 576.

1747. Schrader (H.). Der Bilderschmuck der deutschen Sprache in tausenden volkstümlichen Redensarten. 5. Auflage. 8°. Weimar, 1896.

1748. Schreiben. Schreiben an den Herausgeber, einige Sprach-erklärungen enthaltend, nebst Anhang einiger veralteten Sprüchwörter. 8°. Leipzig, *Weygand*, 1779.

In Deutsches Museum, 1779, Bd. 2, pp. 446-453. [B.M.

1749. Schuetze (R.). Deutsche Sprichwörter erläutert von R. S[chütze]. pp. 31. 12°. Barmen, *Klein*, n.d.

Groschen-Bibliothek für das deutsche Volk, No. 59.

1749a. Schulz (J.). Telegraph auf der Bahn des Lebens, oder : 200 der gangbarsten und vorzüglichsten deutschen Sprich-wörter in ihrem Geiste dargestellt und auf das praktische Leben angewendet. pp. xii, 356. 8°. Wien, 1841.

1750. Schulze (Carl). Ausdrücke für Sprichwort. 8°. Leipzig, *Weidmann*, 1851.

In Zeitschrift für deutsches Alterthum, Bd. 8, pp. 376-384. [U.C.L.

1751. ——— : Die biblischen Sprichwörter der deutschen Sprache. pp. 202. 8°. Göttingen, *Vandenhoeck & Ruprecht*, 1860.

Biblical proverbs, their use, variations, *etc.*, in German speech and literature. [B.M.

1752. Schwalm (Johann Heinrich). Schwälmer Wees. Das Schwälmer Leben im eigenen Sprichwort, *etc.* pp. iii, 66. 8°. Kassel, *Scheel*, 1913.

1753. Schwann (Mathieu). Sinn und Unsinn deutscher Sprich-wörter. fol. Frankfurt, 1897.

In Frankfurter Zeitung und Handelsblatt, 1897, Nr. 335.

1754. Schweitzer (Charles). Sprichwörter und sprichwörtliche Redensarten bei H. Sachs. 8°. Nürnberg, *Raw*, 1894.

In Hans Sachs-Forschungen . . . Herausgegeben von A. L. Stiefel, 1894, pp. 353-381. [B.M.

1755. Seiler (Friedrich). Das deutsche Sprichwort. pp. viii, 77.
8°. Strassburg, *Grübner*, 1918.

Grundriss der deutschen Volkskunde, Bd. 2. An excellent little book treating of German proverbs, both original and borrowed from other nations, their origin, development, *etc.* A good list of characteristic proverbs is given at the end. A brief bibliography is given after each chapter; there are many references to articles in little-known periodicals. [B.M.

1756. ———: Deutsche Sprichwörterkunde. pp. x, 457.
8°. München, *Beck*, 1922.

Handbuch des deutschen Unterrichts, *etc.* Bd. 4, Theil 3. A survey of the origin, importance, exterior and interior forms, *etc.*, of German proverbs.
[U.C.L.

1757. Serz (Georg Thomas). Teutsche Idiotismen, Provin-zialismen, Volksausdrücke, sprüchwörtliche . . . Redensarten, *etc.* pp. 184. 8°. Nürnberg, *Schneider & Weigel*, 1797.

Gratet-Duplessis, 695. [B.M.

1758. Siebenkees, *Dr.* Teutsche Sprichwörter mit Erläuterungen, *etc.* [Edited by Dr. Siebenkees]. pp. [xiv], 135.
8°. Nürnberg, *Bauer- und Mann'schen*
Buchhandlung, 1790.

Gratet-Duplessis, 676. A useful book, carefully edited.

1759. Simon (Ch. F. L.). Nützliche und unterhaltende Beleh-rungen für die Jugend. . . . Wohlfeilere Ausgabe. 3 Bde.
8°. Leipzig, *Lehnhold*, 1839.

Bd. 2, pp. 1-80, Sprichwörter und sprichwörtliche Redensarten.

1760. Simrock (Carl Joseph). Die deutschen Sprichwörter, . . .
Vierte Auflage. pp. v, 677.
8°. Frankfurt a. M., *Winter*, n.d.

Another edition. pp. v, 677. 8°. Basel, *Schwabe*, [1888].

This book also forms Bd. 5 of Simrock's Die deutschen Volksbücher, pub-lished at Basel, *Schwabe*, n.d., M.2, and at Frankfurt a. M., *Brönner*, 1846. It is a simple list of proverbs arranged alphabetically by key-words; no notes.
[U.C.L. (n.d. edition), B.M. (1888 edition).

1761. Spanutius (Hermann Justus). Teutsch-Orthographisches Schreib-Conversation-Zeitungs- und Sprüch-Wörter-Lexicon, *etc.* 8°. Leipzig, *Förster*, 1720.

Dritter Theil, pp. 495-634, Sprüchwörter-Lexicon. Darinnen nebst vielen bekannten teutsch- und lateinischen Sprüchwörtern auch sehr artige Redens-arten enthalten.

1762. Spindler (Wilhelm), *junior.* Sammlung von circa 400 der gediegensten Sinn- und Trinksprüche und kernigen Sprüch-wörtern ausgewählt. . . . Zweite vermehrte Auflage. pp. vi, 74. 12.° Stuttgart, n.d.

1763. Sprichwoerter. Alte Sprichwörter. 4°. Munich, 1820.
Gratet-Duplessis, 756. *In* Flora, No. 72, 1820.

o

1764. Sprichwoerter. Alte Teutsche zu vorsichtigem Leben und annehmlichen Reden dienende Sprichwörter. pp. 95.

8°. Helmstädt, *Müller*, 1674.

Gratet-Duplessis, 570. Proverbs arranged alphabetically. No notes. [B.M.

1765. ———: Bekannte Sprichwörter und Sprüche.

8°. Hildesheim, 1654.

Gratet-Duplessis, 565.

1766. ———: Deutsche Sprichwörter als Materialien zu Aufsatz- und Diktando-Uebungen und Hausaufgaben, *etc.* 10 pts.

8°. Würzburg, *Staudinger*, 1875-89.

Bernstein, 3508. 861 entries.

1767. ———: Die deutschen Sprichwörter gesammelt. pp. v, 591. sm. 8°. Frankfurt am Main, *Brönner*, 1846.

Gratet-Duplessis, 779. Contains an alphabetical list of 12,396 proverbs, and is perhaps the largest of the German collections. No explanations.

1768. ———: Sprichwörter von Alten und Jetzigen in Gebrauch gehabt. 8°. Francfort, 1600.

Gratet-Duplessis, 550.

1769. ———: Sprichwörter zur Belehrung für's Leben. Als Manuscript gedruckt. pp. 32. 4°.

Bernstein, 3505.

1770. ———: 1000 Sprichwörter. So spricht das Volk! 1000 Witze und Wahrheiten. pp. 20. 8°. Leipzig, *Minde*, 1888.

Bernstein, 3540.

1771. ———: Ein tausend teutsch Sprichwörter.

8°. Francfort, 1568.

Gratet-Duplessis, 546.

1772. Sprichwort. Das deutsche Sprichwort im Dienste des Religionsunterrichts in der Volksschule, *etc.* pp. 211.

8°. Würzburg, *Staudinger*, 1882.

Bernstein, 3499. 240 entries.

1773. Sprueche. Tausend Sprüche. pp. 192.

16°. Halle, *Fricke*, 1880.

Apophthegms and proverbs in alphabetical order.

1774. Spruechwoerter. Drei Hundert deutsche Sprüchwörter und Denksprüche neue und alte, *etc.* pp. 16.

8°. Reutlingen, *Fleischhauer & Spohn*, 1859.

A simple list without notes of any kind. [B.M.

1775. ———: Sprüchwörter, Citate, Räthsel und Charaden zur bildlichen Darstellung, *etc.* pp. 63.

16°. Dresden, *Jaenicke*, n.d.

Bernstein, 3558.

1776. Spruechwoerter. Sprüchwörter und sonderbare Einfälle berühmeter Gelehrten und Künstler. pp. 215.

16°. Prag, *Herrl*, 1794.

Bernstein, 3665.

1777. Spruech-Woerterspiel. Allegorisches Sprüch-Wörterspiel, *etc.* [Illustrated]. 8°. Leipzig, 1797.

Gratet-Duplessis, 697.

1778. ———: Neues allegorisches Sprüchwörterspiel, *etc.* [Illustrated]. 12°. Leipzig, 1798.

Gratet-Duplessis, 705, says this may well be only another edition of the preceding book.

1779. St. (J. J.). Goldkörner. 1000 Sprichwörter, . . . gesammelt von J. J. St., herausgegeben von M. F. Wendt. pp. 124. 8°. Leipzig, *Jackowitz*, 1863.

A thousand proverbs, sayings, aphorisms, *etc.*, grouped more or less by subject. [B.M.

1780. Stammbuch. Stammbuch des Studenten. pp. vi, 230.

8°. Stuttgart, *Spemann*, n.d.

Bernstein, 3574. Pp. 236-238, Sprichwörtlich. Proverbs on German students and universities.

1781. Steiger (Karl). Pretiosen deutscher Sprichwörter, mit Variationen, *etc.* pp. iv, 490.

8°. St.-Gallen, *Scheitlin & Zollikoffer*, 1843.

2. Auflage. St. Gallen, 1865.

Gratet-Duplessis, 774. A collection of 365 proverbs chosen principally for their moral tendency or practical utility, and accompanied by brief comments. The book is both useful and agreeable to read. [B.M.

1782. Steiner (Josef). Sprichwörter und Sprüche als Uebungsstoff für den Unterricht in der deutschen Rechtschreibung, *etc.* pp. xiv, 91. 8°. Wien, *Hölder*, 1882.

1783. Steinhaeuser (C.). Merk- und Uebungssätze aus dem Sprichwörterschatze, *etc.* pp. x, 171.

8°. Langensalza, *Beyer*, 1876.

1784. Stengel (C. L.). Ueber ein altdeutsches Sprichwörterbuch. sm. 8°. Berlin, *Haude & Spener*, 1790.

Gratet-Duplessis, 678. *In* Berliner Monatsschrift, Bd. 16, pp. 263-273. An article concerning Franck's Sprichwörter, **1594.** [B.M.

1785. Stern (Eduard). Neue Sprichwörter. 1818.

Gratet-Duplessis, 747. *In* Der Freimüthige, Nos. 122-132.

1786. Stickel (G.). Die Natur und Bedeutung des Sprichworts. 8°. Breslau, Berlin, *Trewendt*, 1892.

In Deutsche Revue über das gesamte nationale Leben der Gegenwart, 1892, pp. 223-232, 346-356. A commentary on German proverbs. [B.M.

1787. Stiehr (Carl Friedrich). 466 einzeilige deutsche Sprichwörter biblischen Inhalts, *etc.* pp. 23.
16°. Glogau, *Flemming*, 1835.

1787a. Strackerjan (L.). 1000 deutsche Sprüche.
8°. Bremen, 1876.

1788. Straub (Joseph Wendelin). Vergleichung sinnverwandter
Sprichwörter in Aufsätzen zum Schulgebrauche, *etc.* pp.
viii, 95. 8°. Leipzig, *Brandstetter*, 1859.
[B.M.

1789. Struve (Christian August). Erklärung teutscher Sprichwörter in Rücksicht auf Erziehung und Behandlung der
Kinder. 2 pts. 8°. Glogau, *Günther*, 1798-1799.
Gratet-Duplessis, 703. The first part contains the explanation of 52 proverbs,
the second of 42.

1789a. Suringar (Willem Hendrik Dominicus). Ioannis Glan-
dorpii monasteriensis disticha . . . quae . . . Agricolae proverbiis conversa esse ostendit editor W. H. D. Suringar.
2 pts. 8°. Lugduni-Batavorum, *Brill*, 1874-76.
[B.M.

1790. Susan (S.). Sammlung Wörter, Sprichwörter und Redensarten. . . . Zweite erweiterte Auflage. pp. iv, 86.
8°. Groningen, *Noordhoff & Smit*, 1876.

1791. Sutor (Andreas). Latinum chaos, *etc.* pp. [xviii], 1099,
[21]. 8°. Augspurg, *Gruber*, 1716.
Der hundert-augige blinde Argos und zwey-gsichtige Janus,
oder : Latinum chaos der andere Bettl-Hasen, *etc.* pp. [xii],
1037. 8°. Augspurg, *Rieger*, 1740.
Maxims, sentences, emblems, proverbs, apophthegms, *etc.*, of all sorts.
[B.M.

1792. Tappius (Eberhardus). Germanicorum adagiorum cum
Latinis ac Graecis collatorum, centuriae septem. ff. 244,
[20].
8°. Ex libera Argentina, *in aedibus Vuendelini Rihelii*,
1539.
Another edition. ff. 244, [20].
8°. Argentorati, *per Wendelium Rihelium*, 1545.
Gratet-Duplessis, 539. [B.M.

1793. Taschenbuch. Taschenbuch für muntre Tischgesellschaften
. . . vermehrte Auflage. pp. 200. 16°. 1795.
Pp. 56-74, Sammlung dramatischer und anderer Sprüchwörter (300).

1794. Thirring-Waisbecker (Irene). Zur Volkskunde der Hienzen.
3. Mundartliches. 4°. Budapest, 1896.
In Ethnologische Mitteilungen aus Ungarn, Bd. 5, pp. 98-104. Pp. 98-101,
proverbs and phrases. [B.M.

1795. Thomaszik (E.). Sprichwörter und Lebensregeln nebst kleinen Erzählungen und Anekdoten. . . . Erste Sammlung— Zweite Auflage. pp. 50. 8°. Cassel, *im Selbstverlage*, 1877.

1796. Trenkler (Robert). 6275 deutsche Sprichwörter und Redensarten. pp. 211. 8°. München, *Medler*, 1884.

1797. Trinius (Johann Anton). Schrift- und vernunftmässige Betrachtungen über einiger Sprichwörter und derer Missbrauch, *etc.* pp. 270. 8°. Leipsig, *Jacobi*, 1750.

Gratet-Duplessis, 633. At the end of the preface is Abel's work " Beitrag zu einer Geschichte der Sprichwörter," *q.v.*, **1522.**

1798. Troppmann (Johann Adolf). 403 Denksprüche, Gedichte und Sprüchwörter. . . . Zweite Auflage. pp. xx, 90.
12°. Donauwörth, *Auer*, 1877.

1799. Uhle (Carl). Die gangbarsten Sprichwörter sammt kurzen Erläuterungen. . . . Zweite Ausgabe. pp. 92.
8°. Wien, *Pichler's Witwe & Sohn*, 1855.

1800. Untersuchung. Untersuchung der vornehmsten teutschen Sprichwörter. . . . Erster Stuck. pp. 120. 8°. Leipsig, 1725.

Gratet-Duplessis, 612. The editions of Leipsig 1746 and 1748 are the same as this with a different title page. This first part of a work which was never continued ; contains excellent observations on 28 proverbs.

1801. Urbas (Wilhelm). Die Sprichwörter und ihre Entstehung.
8°. Leipzig, *Günther*, 1876.

In Neue Monatshefte für Dichtkunst und Kritik, Bd. 4, pp. 501-513.

1802. Venedey (Jacob). Die Deutschen und Franzosen nach dem Geiste ihrer Sprache und Sprichwörter. pp. x, 176.
sm. 8°. Heidelberg, *Winter*, 1842.

Gratet-Duplessis, 366 and 773. A comparative study of German and French proverbs containing interesting observations and ideas. Duplessis, however, says the author is not always correct about the French proverbs, particularly when he quotes some as being peculiar to France which are really general or of foreign origin. [B.M.

1803. Vogl (Johann N.). Fruchtkörner aus deutschem Grund und Boden. Ein Volksbüchlein. pp. 110.
12°. Wien, *Adolph*, Leipzig, *Cnobloch*, 1830.

Contains 400 rhymed proverbs.

1804. Voigt (Ernst). Florilegium Gottingense.
8°. Erlangen, *Deichert*, 1887.

In Romanische Forschungen, Bd. 3, 281-314. Reprinted from a 14th century ms. [B.M.

1805. ——— : Ueber die ältesten Sprichwörtersammlungen des deutschen Mittelalters. 8°. Berlin, *Weidmann*, 1886.

In Zeitschrift für deutsches Alterthum, Bd. 30. Pp. 260-280, a description of, with many quotations from, some of the earlier collections of proverbs.
[U.C.L.

1806. Voss (Christoph). Wiederlegte Entschuldigungen der Sünden. Darin allerley Arten des Selbstbetruges . . . Ausflüchte, falsche Axiomata, Sprüch-Wörter, *etc.* 2 Thle.

4°. Hamburg, *Hertel*, 1735-36.

1807. Wachler (Ludwig). Auszug aus Seb. Franck's Sprichwörtern. 8°. Leipzig, *Barth*, 1818.

Gratet-Duplessis, 745. *In* Philomathie von Freunden der Wissenschaft und Kunst, Bd. 1, pp. 239-247. [B.M.

1808. Wackernagel (Carl Heinrich Wilhelm). Deutsches Lesebuch. 2. Ausgabe. 4 Thle.

8°. Basel, *Schweighauserische Buchhandlung*, 1839.

Gratet-Duplessis, 813. A certain number of proverbs are to be found in different places throughout this work. Discontinued after p. 490 of Th. 4. There are also later editions. [B.M.

1809. Waechter (Oskar). Altes Gold in deutschen Sprüchwörtern. pp. 216. 8°. Stuttgart, *Spemann*, n.d.

Arranged alphabetically.

1810. ———: Sprichwörter und Sinnsprüche der Deutschen in neuer Auswahl. pp. viii, 392.

8°. Gütersloh, *Bertelsmann*, 1888.

1811. Wagener (Samuel Christoph). Sprüchwörter-Lexicon, mit kurzen Erläuterungen, *etc.* pp. iv, 210.

8°. Quedlinburg, *Basse*, 1813.

Gratet-Duplessis, 736. Contains more than four thousand proverbs and sayings arranged alphabetically. [B.M.

1812. Wagner (Friedrich Ludwig). Neues Handbuch für die Jugend in Bürgerschulen, *etc.* 8°. Frankfurt a. M., 1799. *Another edition.* 8°. Frankfurt am Main, *Guilhauman*, 1819.

Gratet-Duplessis, 711. Contains: Sittensprüche, Sprichwörter und Räthsel.

1813. Wagner (J.). Sprichwörter, deren Erklärung als Musterbeispiele zu deutschen Aufsätzen. . . . Zweite . . . Auflage. pp. 111. 8°. Paderborn, *Esser*, 1899.

1814. Wahl (M. C.). Das Sprichwort der neueren Sprachen. Ein vergleichend phraseologischer Beitrag zur deutschen Literatur. pp. 86. M.2. 8°. Erfurt, *Keyser*, 1877.

A commentary, with many examples, on German proverbs compared with English, French and Italian. [B.M.

1814a. ———: Das Sprichwort innerhalb der Phraseologie der neueren Sprachen. pp. 32. 4°. Erfurt, 1877.

1815. ———: Wahrheiten mit und ohne Hülle. 2 vols.

8°. Jena, *Voigt*, 1800.

1816. Wahr- und Spruechworte. Wahr- und Sprüchworte. Aus dem Buche der Gesetze der Weisheit auf der Gasse.
4°. Brunn, *Winiker*, 1844.

In Jurende's Vaterländische Pilger, Jahrgang 31, pp. 99-106. Contains 315 German proverbs, and 96 of other countries, translated into German.

1817. Waldfreund (J. E.). Sprichwörtlich angewendete Vornamen und damit verbundene Kinderreime.
8°. Nürnberg, 1856.

In Die deutschen Mundarten, Jahrgang 3, pp. 314-317. [B.M.

1818. Wander (Karl Friedrich Wilhelm). Allgemeiner Sprichwörterschatz, *etc.* pp. xxii, 210.
8°. Hirschberg, *Zimmer*, 1836.
Another edition. 8°. Leipsig, 1838.

Gratet-Duplessis, 767. This is announced as Book 1, but it is the only one which was published. A general survey of German proverbs, their use, abuse, origin and importance. Pp. 196-208, bibliography. [B.M.

1819. ———: Deutsch, Deutscher und Deutschland im Sprichwort.
4°. Leipzig, 1869.

In Deutscher Sprachwart, Bd. 4, Nr. 6. [B.M.

1820. ———: Deutsches Sprichwörter-Lexikon, *etc.* 5 Bde.
la. 8°. Leipzig, *Brockhaus*, 1867 [1863], -1880.

Each volume contains a preface, a list of authorities, and proverbs arranged in alphabetical order by key-words. Explanatory notes, comparisons, *etc.*, are frequently given. A most important and comprehensive work. [B.M.

1821. ———: Nüsse für Kinder. . . in einer Sammlung neuer Sprichwörter, *etc.* pp. 40. 12°. Hirschberg, *Zimmer*, 1835.

Gratet-Duplessis, 762.

1822. ———: Scheidemünze . . . oder, 5000 neue deutsche Sprichwörter, *etc.* 2 vols.
16°. Hirschberg, *Nesener, Zimmer*, 1831-35.

Gratet-Duplessis, 760.

1823. ———: Der Sprichwörtergarten. Oder, kurze und fassliche Erklärung von 500 Sprichwörtern, *etc.* pp. xviii, 300.
16°. Breslau, *Kohn*, 1838.

Gratet-Duplessis, 764.

1824. ———: Weihnachtsnüsse, oder 500 neue Sprichwörter. . . . Dritte . . . Auflage. pp. 32.
12°. Hirschberg, *Nesener*, 1832.

Gratet-Duplessis, 761.

1825. Weber (Carl Julius). Demokritos, oder hinterlassene Papiere eines lachenden Philosophen, *etc.*
12°. Stuttgart, *Rieger*, 1863.

Another edition of Demokritos forms a supplement to Weber's " Sämmtliche Werke." Includes an essay : Ueber komische Sprüchwörter, a commentary with numerous examples from different languages. [B.M.

1826. Weingaertner (Theodor). Katechismus in Sprüchwörtern, *etc.* pp. 104. 8°. Erfurt, *Villaret*, 1855.

1827. Weinreiter (Victorin). Sammlung von 500 Sprüchwörtern, Denksprüchen und Redensarten in deutscher und lateinischer Sprache, *etc.* pp. xviii, 140. 8°. Grätz, *Kienreich*, 1826.

1828. Weisheit. Die Weisheit auf der Gasse. Deutsche Sprichwörter religiösen und sittlichen Inhaltes, *etc.* pp. 243.
8°. Gotha, *Perthes*, 1892.
Bernstein, 4000.

1829. ———: Die Weisheit meiner Mutter; ein Sprichwörterbüchlein für Kinder. pp. xii, 67.
8°. Hamburg, *Heubel*, [1855].
Stirling-Maxwell, p. 104.

1830. ———: Weisheit und Witz in altdeutschen Reimen und Sprüchen. Gesammelt vom Herausgeber von '' Altdeutscher Witz und Verstand.'' pp. 182. 8°. Berlin, *Enslin*, 1881.
Bernstein, 4003.

1831. Weiss (Carl Theodor). Sprichwort und Lebensklugheit aus dem xviii. Jahrhundert.
8°. Freiburg i. B., *Fehsenfeld*, 1899.
In Alemannia, Jahrgang 27, pp. 124-152. 323 entries. [B.M.

1832. Werfer (Albert). Blüthen und Früchte . . . Mit vier illuminirten Bildern. pp. 206. 12°. Tübingen, *Fues*, 1864.
Pp. 149-176, Denksprüche und Sprüchwörter.

1833. Wider (Philipp Ehrenreich). Evangelische Reise- und Sprüchwörter-Postill, in welcher auf alle Sonn-, hohe Fest- und Apostel-Tage . . . ein anmuthiges Sprüchwort zum Eingang eingeführet, darnach auf folgende Text Erklärung, *etc.* pp. 819, 150. 8°. Nürnberg, *Endters*, 1725.

1834. Willesky (J. H.). Betrachtung der so bekannten, als zum Theil angebrachten, zum Theil gottlosen Sprichwörter.
8°. Leipsig, 1744.
Gratet-Duplessis, 626.

1835. Windel (Rudolf). Zur Würdigung der Sprichwörtersammlung des Johann Agricola. 8°. Leipzig, *Teubner*, 1897.
In Zeitschrift für den deutschen Unterricht, Jahrgang 11, pp. 643-653.
[B.M.

1836. Winkler (Paul). Gute Gedanken, oder 3000 deutsche Sprichwörter. 12°. Görlitz, 1685.
Gratet-Duplessis, 573. Praised by Morhof in his '' Polyhistor literarius.''

1837. Wippo, *Presbyter.* Proverbia Wiponis . . . ad Henricum Chuonradi imperatoris filium.

These moral proverbs in rhyme are to be found in the following books :—
Fabricius (J. A.). Bibliotheca Latina, *etc.* Tom. 1.
8°. Hamburgi, 1734.

Martene (E.) and Durand (U.). Veterum scriptorum . . . collectio, *etc.* Tom. 9. fol. Parisiis, 1738.

Pertz (G. H.). Monumenta Germaniae historica, *etc.* Tom. 13. fol. Hannoverae, 1854.

Pertz (G. H.). Scriptores rerum Germanicarum . . . Wippo.
8°. Hannoveriae, 1853.
[B.M.

1838. Wittstock (Albert). Reim-Spruchbuch der deutschen Volksweisheit. pp. v, 111. 8°. Leipzig, *Wigand*, 1899.

Contains German rhymed proverbs, maxims, *etc.*

1839. Witz. Altdeutscher Witz und Verstand. Reime und Sprüche aus dem sechzehnten und siebenzehnten Jahrhunderte. . . . Fünfte Auflage. pp. x, 218.
16°. Bielefeld und Leipzig, *Velhagen & Klasing*, 1880.

1840. Wunderlich (G.). Deutsche Sprichwörter volksthümlich erklärt und gruppiert, *etc.* 3 Bde.
8°. Langensalza, *Gressler*, 1881.

1841. ———: Sprichwörtliche und bildliche Redensarten, *etc.* pp. viii, 155. 8°. Langensalza, *Gressler*, 1882.

1842. Wurst (Caspar). Auswahl deutscher Sprichwörter, *etc.* pp. vi, 56. 8°. Freiburg, 1841.

1843. Wurzbach (Constant von), *von Tannenberg.* Historische Wörter, Sprichwörter und Redensarten. *First edition.*
8°. Prag, *Kober*, 1863 [1862, 63].

Second edition. pp. xvi, 428.
8°. Hamburg, Leipzig, *Richter*, [1866].

The proverbs, phrases, *etc.*, here explained and illustrated are principally, though not entirely, German. [B.M.

1844. Wushmann (G.). Die sprichwörtlichen Redensarten im deutschen Volksmunde erläutert. [2. Auflage.]
8°. Leipzig, 1894.

1845. Zacher (Julius). Die deutschen Sprichwörtersammlungen, nebst Beiträgen zur Charakteristik der Meusebachschen Bibliothek. Eine bibliographische Skizze. pp. 55.
8°. Leipzig, *Weigel*, 1852.

A bibliography of the German books of proverbs in the Royal Library of Berlin. [B.M.

1846. Zarnack (August). Deutsche Sprichwörter, *etc.* pp. xvi, 380. 8°. Berlin, 1821.

Gratet-Duplessis, 758. Contains over 1100 proverbs.

1847. Zarnack (August).　Sophronia.　Oder Unterredungen, Erzählungen und dramatische Spiele über deutsche Sprichwörter . . . Zweite Auflage.　pp. vii, iv, 213.

8°.　Leipzig, *Krappe*, n.d.

1847a. Zincgref (J. W.).　Der Teutschen scharpfsinnige kluge Spruch Apothegmata genant.　pp. xl, 452, xlii.

8°.　Strassburg, *Richel*, 1538.

Teutsche Apothythegmata. . . . Durch I. L. Weidnern.　pp. xxiv, 322, 96, 449.

12°.　Amsterdam, *bey L. Elzevier*, 1653.

Scharfsinnige Sprüche der Teutschen. . . . In Auswahl von B. F. Guttenstein.　　　　　　　　　　Mannheim, 1835.

1848. Zingerle (Ignaz Vincenz).　Die deutschen Sprichwörter im Mittelalter, *etc.*　pp. 199.

2 fl. 30 km.　8°.　Wien, *Braunmüller*, 1864.

Proverbs arranged alphabetically by key-words.　The original collection is indicated in each case.　A useful book for specialists.　　　　　[B.M.

See also index at end for references to German in other sections.

LOW COUNTRIES.

1. GENERAL.

1849. Eckart (Rudolf). Niederdeutsche Sprichwörter und volkstümliche Redensarten, *etc.* pp. viii, 586.
la. 8°. Braunschweig, *Appelhaus & Pfenningstorff*, 1893.

Proverbs arranged alphabetically under key-words. German translations of
words and phrases are given where necessary. No notes. Pp. vii-viii, a useful
bibliography of Low German proverbs. [B.M.

1850. Eichwald (Karl). Niederdeutsche Sprichwörter und
Redensarten, *etc.* pp. 92. 12°. Leipzig, *Hübner*, 1860.
Fifth edition. pp. 92. 8°. Bremen, *Haake*, 1881.

Stirling-Maxwell, p. 25. 2096 proverbs arranged alphabetically by key-words.
No notes. [B.M.

1851. Hoefer (Albert). Ueber apologische oder Beispiels-Sprich-
wörter im Niederdeutschen. 8°. Berlin, *Schulze*, 1844.

In Germania, Bd. 6, pp. 95-106. [B.M.

1852. Hoffmann (August Heinrich), *von Fallersleben.* Findlinge.
Zur Geschichte deutscher Sprache und Dichtung. Erstes
Heft. pp. viii, 496. 8°. Leipzig, *Engelmann*, 1860.

Pp. 79-85, Niederdeutsche Sprichwörter, 1539 : pp. 434-463, Sprüche des 16.
und 17. Jahrhunderts. [B.M.

1853. Hoffmann (F. L.). Proverbes de la Basse Allemagne, en
rapport avec les spots wallons. 8°. Liège, 1862.

In Bulletin de la Société liégeoise de Littérature wallonne, Année 5, 1861,
Pt. 2, pp. 17-25. [B.M.

1854. Luebben (A.). Niederdeutsche Sprichwörter.
8°. Nürnberg, *Ebner*, Nördlingen, *Beck*, 1855-59.

In Die deutschen Mundarten, Jahrgang 2-6. A collection of nearly 800
proverbs, which appeared at intervals in the above periodical. The editor,
G. Carl Frommann, adds philological notes to each article. [B.M.

1855. Niclas (Hendrik). Proverbia HN. The proverbes of
H[endrik] N[iclas]. . . . Translated out of base-almayne.
ff. 46. 8°. [Amsterdam? 1575].

Not popular proverbs, but moral maxims and aphorisms. [B.M.

1856. Nordduetsche Bu'rn. So spröäken de norddütsche Bu'rn.
Röädensarten, Sprüchwüö'r, Bu'rröäthsel, *etc.* pp. 200.
8°. Berlin, *Schlingmann*, 1870.
1484 proverbs, proverbial phrases, *etc.*, in alphabetical order. [B.M.

1857. Schroeder (C.). Über hundert niederdeutsche Sprichwörter,
gesammelt aus mittelniederdeutschen und mittelnieder-
ländischen Dichtungen. 8°.
In Archiv für neuere Sprachen, 44, pp. 337-344.

1858. Tunicius (Antonius). Tunnicius. Die älteste niederdeutsche Sprichwörtersammlung, von Antonius Tunnicius,
gesammelt und in lateinische Verse übersetzt. Herausgegeben mit hochdeutscher Uebersetzung, Anmerkungen und
Wörterbuch von Hoffmann von Fallersleben. pp. 224.
8°. Berlin, *Oppenheim*, 1870.
1362 proverbs in Low German and Latin, followed by the same in High
German. [U.C.L.

2. FRISIAN.

1859. Bendsen (Bende). Die nordfriesische Sprache nach der
Moringer Mundart, *etc.* pp. xxvi, 479.
8°. Leiden, *Brill*, 1860.
Pp. 416-444, proverbs, proverbial phrases, idioms, *etc.* [B.M.

1860. Clement (K. J.). Der Lappenkorb von Gabe Schneider
aus Westfrisland, *etc.* pp. vi, 347.
8°. Leipzig, *Engelmann*, [1846].
Pp. 294-316, Nordfrisische Sinnsprüche oder Sprichwörter.

1861. Dirksen (Carl). Ostfriesische Sprichwörter, *etc.* 2 parts.
8°. Ruhrort, *Andreae*, 1889-91.
Contains some 500 proverbs and proverbial sayings accompanied by explanatory notes. [B.M. (Part 1 is second edition).

1862. Dykstra (Waling). Uit Friesland's volksleven van vroeger
en later, *etc.* 2 vols.
8°. Leeuwarden, *Suringar*, [1892-96].
Vol. 2, pp. 144-146, Spreekwoorden : Vol. 2, pp. 277-427, Spreekwoorden en
gezegden, *etc.* Arranged alphabetically with explanatory notes. [B.M.

1863. Hoeufft (Jacob Henrik). Taalkundige aanmerkingen op
eenige oud-friesche spreekwoorden. 8°. Breda, 1812.
Second edition. pp. viii, 234, 148.
8°. Breda, *van Bergen*, 1815.
Gratet-Duplessis, 798. Grammatical notes on old Frisian proverbs. 39 of
these proverbs with Dutch and English translations were reprinted in the
periodical " Janus," published at Edinburgh in 1826. [B.M.

1864. Johansen (Christian). Die nordfriesische Sprache, *etc.* pp. viii, 286.   8°.   Kiel, *Akademische Buchhandlung*, 1862.
Pp. 190-192, Sprichwörter, Redensarten und Reime.   With German translations.   [B.M.

1865. Kern (W. G.) and **Willms** (W. J.). Ostfriesland, wie es denkt und spricht. Eine Sammlung der gangbarsten ostfriesischen Sprichwörter und Redensarten, *etc.* pp. xvi, 137.
8°. Norden, *Soltau*, 1869.
[B.M.

1866. Mechlenburg (Lor. Friedrich). Friesische Sprichwörter.
8°. Leipzig, *Weidmann*, 1851.
In Zeitschrift für deutsches Alterthum, Bd. 8, pp. 350-376.   Nearly 400 proverbs in dialect with German translations.   [U.C.L.

1867. Nissen (M.). De freske findling, dat sen freške sprékkwurde önt karkirdinge, *etc.* 3 vols.
8°. Stedesand, *Selbstverlage des Verfassers*, 1873-75.
Proverbs from different parts of Friesland, with English translations.

1868. Posthumus (R.). Eene lijst en korte opheldering van eenige friesche woorden, spreekwijzen en spreekwoorden.
8°. Leeuwarden, *Suringar*, 1837-46.
In Die Vrije Fries, Deel 1-4.

1869. Sprenger (R.). Zu den ostfriesischen Sprichwörtern.
8°. Hamburg, 1897.
In Korrespondenzblatt des Vereins für niederdeutsche Sprachforschung, Jahrgang 1896-1897, pp. 75-76.   [B.M.

1869a. Tannen (Karl). Dichtungen un spreekwoorden up syn Moermerlander Oostvrees. pp. vii, 358.
8°. Leer, *Neemann*, 1892.

1870. Wassenbergh (E.). Verhandeling over de eigennaamen der Friesen, *etc.* pp. 94.   8°. Franeker, *Lomars*, 1774.
Pp. 85-94, Toelage van eenige oude friesische spreekwoorden.
[Bristol Reference Library.

3. DUTCH, BELGIAN, AND FLEMISH.

1871. Adagia. Adagia quaedam ac carmina magis obvia ex optimis quibusdam auctoribus, *etc.*   8°. Brugis, 1727.

1872. Adagiorum. Adagiorum maxime vulgarium thesaurus, *etc.*
8°. Aldenardae, [1747].
Perhaps a later edition of the last entry.

1873. Alof. Spreekwoordenboek voor scholen en huisgezinnen. pp. 71.   sm. 8°. Alkmaar, *Coster*, 1861.
Contains 50 proverbs explained and illustrated.   [B.M.

1874. Andriessoon (S.). Duytsche adagia ofte spreecwoorden, *etc.* pp. 103.   8°. Antwerpen, *Alssens*, 1550.
Gratet-Duplessis, 802.

1874a. B. (W.). Verhandeling over de spreekwoorden. Zij zijn allen geene koks, die lange messen dragen; en De kleederen maken den man. Door W. B. Gevolgd van eenig mengel-werk in proza en poëzie.   Rotterdam, 1833.

1875. Bilderdijk (Willem). Nieuwe taal- en dichtkundige ver-scheidenheden. 4 vols.
        8°. Rotterdam, *Immerzeel*, 1824-25.
Vol. 2, pp. 201-209; Vol. 3, pp. 183-198; Vol. 4, pp. 193-208; Proeve, by wege van uittreksel uit eene verklaring van meedere spreekwoorden en spreekwijzen.
[B.M.

1876. Bogaert (P.). Toegepaste spreekwoorden, een boek voor het volk. pp. 112.   8°. Gent, *Dooselaere*, 1852.
Stirling-Maxwell, p. 9. A commentary on practical proverbs with many examples.   [B.M.

1877. Bolland (Gerardus Johannes Petrus Josephus). De boeken der spreuken uit der leerzaal van zuivere rede. pp. 237.
        8°. Leiden, *Adriani*, 1915.
Contains over a thousand sayings.   [B.M.

1878. Braakenburg (D.). Verzameling van nederland'sche spreek-woorden, *etc.*   8°. Haarlem, *Bohn*, 1828.

1879. Brune (Johan de). Nieuwe wijn in oude leêrzacken, *etc.* pp. [xxiv], 496, [8]. 12°. Middelburgh, *Z. Roman*, [1636].
Proverbs arranged under subject headings, no notes.   [B.M.

1880. C. (A.). Adagiorum maxime vulgarium thesaurus, *etc.* pp. 56.   12°. Gandavi, *Meyer*, n.d.
Flemish and Latin.

1881. Cock (Alfons de). Spreekwoorden en zegswijzen, afkomstig van oude gebruiken en volkszeden.   Gent, *Hoste*, 1902.
Second edition. pp. x, 426.   8°. Gent, 1908.
Over 500 proverbs and sayings explained and illustrated. Pp. 375-386, list of authorities.   [B.M.

1882. ———: Spreekwoorden, zegswijzen en uitdrukkingen op volksgeloof berustend. . . . 1. pp. viii, 240.
        8°. Antwerpen, *etc.*, *De Sikkel*, *etc.*, 1920.
Proverbs, phrases, expressions, *etc.*, founded on superstitions and beliefs.
[B.M.

1883. Dale (J. H. van). Spreekwoorden en spreekwordelijke uit-drukkingen toegelicht en verklaard. . . . Met 12 geleurde platen. pp. 94. sm. 4°. Leiden, *Noothoven van Goor*, n.d.

1884. Dekker (K. J.). Nederlandsche spreekwoorden. . . . . Met zes gekleurde plaatjes. pp. [46].
12°. Schiedam, *Roelants*, [1860?].
Little stories illustrating some dozen proverbs. [B.M.

1885. Enchyridion. Enchyridion scholasticum, in quo Flandrorum vernaculo idiomati celebres paroemiae et orationes . . . redduntur. 4°. [Winnoxbergen], 1553.

1886. Eyk (J. P. Sprenger van). Handleiding . . . van onze vaderlandsche spreekwoorden . . . bijzonder aan de scheepvaart en het scheepsleven, het dierenrijk en het landleven. 5 parts. 8°. Rotterdam, *Baalen*, 1844.
This is presumably the book indicated by Gratet-Duplessis, 797. It contains a large selection of proverbs, sayings, *etc.*, arranged under subject headings and accompanied by explanatory notes. [B.M.

1887. Fleischauer (Johann Friedrich). Vollständige holländische Sprachlehre für Deutsche. . . Zweite Auflage. pp. xxiv, 384.
8°. Amsterdam, *Diederichs*, Leipzig, *Vogel*, 1834.
Pp. 249-266, Dutch proverbs with the corresponding German ones.

1888. Fokke (Arend). Verzameling van eenige, hier te lande gebruikelijke spreekwoorden, *etc.*
8°. Amsterdam, *Saakes*, 1810.
6 proverbs, with explanations and illustrations. [B.M.

1888a. Folqman (Carlos). Grammatica Hollandeza, *etc.* pp. [xii], 127. 8°. Lisboa, *Galmann*, 1742.
Another edition. Portugeese en nederduitse spraakkonst. .. . Grammatica hollandeza, *etc.* pp. 118.
8°. Lisboa, *Impressão Regia*, 1804.
Contains : Collecção de varios proverbios hollandezes e portuguezes. [B.M.

1889. Gales (G. J.). Twee redevoeringen of zoogenaamde voorlezingen, veelal in hollandsche spreekwoorden, *etc.* [By G. J. Gales?]. pp. viii, 46.
8°. Amsterdam, *Wijnands*, 1795.

1890. Graaf (M. H. de). Luimige en ernstige gedachten.
8°. Utrecht, *Bosch*, 1838.
Pp. 69-130, Spreekwoorden.

1891. Guikema (H.). Vijftig (Tweede vijftigtal) Ieerzame verhalen, ontleend uit de nederlandsche spreekwoorden, *etc.* 2 vols. sm. 8°. Groningen, *Scholtens*, 1842-43.

1892. Haek (D.). Die Kunst, die holländische Sprache, *etc.* pp. viii, 182. 8°. Wien, *etc.*, *Hartleben*, n.d.
Die Kunst der Polyglottie, Th. 40. Pp. 106-107, some 40 proverbs in Dutch and German. [B.M.

1893. Hall (C. van). De nederlandsche spreekwoorden, tot het regt betrekkelijk. Amsterdam, 1853.

1894. Handt-Boecxken. Handt-boecxken van Epictetus. . . .Als oock mede 't Mergh van de nederlandtsche spreeckwoorden: waer in H. L. Spiegels by-spraecks almanack, *etc.* 3 deel.
sm. 8°. Amsterdam, *Van den Bergh*, 1660.
Bernstein, 1408.

1895. Harrebomée (Pieter Jakob). Spreekwoordenboek der nederlandsche taal, *etc.* 3 dln.
8°. Utrecht, *Kemink*, 1853-1870.

A large collection of proverbs arranged alphabetically by key-words. Full notes. Deel 3, pp. 446-469, gives a list of authorities. [B.M.

1896. Heeres (G.). Populaire voorlezing, verzameld uit spreekwoorden, spreuken, dagelijksche gezegden. pp. 29.
8°. Kampen, *Van Hulst*, [1880].

1897. Heigmans (S. E.). Nederlandsche spreekwoorden in tweeregelige hebreeuwsche versen.
8°. Amsterdam, *Levisson*, 1867-70.

1898. Hoffmann (August Heinrich) *von Fallersleben.* Altniederländische Sprichwörter, nach der ältesten Sammlung. Gesprächbüchlein, romanisch und flämisch. Herausgegeben von Hoffmann von Fallersleben. pp. 99.
8°. Hannover, *Rümpler*, 1854.

In Flemish and Latin, arranged alphabetically under the Flemish. Pp. 1-50, proverbs. *In* Horae Belgicae, Pt. 9. [U.C.L.

1899. Hollaender. Der beredte Holländer, *etc.* pp. 159.
12°. Bern, *Heuberger*, 1890.

Pp. 157-159, Dutch proverbs with German equivalents.

1900. Horning (H. A.). Spreuken en spreekwoorden op het godsdienstig leven toegepast. . . . Tweede druk. pp. 164.
8°. Amsterdam, *Bekker*, 1889.

1901. Hornstra (P.). Voedsel voor verstaand en hart, uit spreekwoorden en spreuken afgeleid, *etc.*
sm. 8°. Sneek, *Holtkamp*, 1832.

1902. Hulst (N. van der). Luim en ernst of verklaring en uitbreiding van eenige vaderlandsche spreekwoorden, *etc.* 2 st.
8°. Rotterdam, *Cornel*, 1823.

1903. Idinau (Donaes). Lot van wiisheyd ende goed geluck; op drije hondert ghemeyne sprekvvoorden, *etc.* pp. 307.
obl. 16°. Antvverpen, *Plantin*, 1606.
Proverbs and sayings in rhyme. [B.M.

1904. J. (A. D.). Bijdragen tot de kennis der nederduitsche spreekwoorden.

8°. Rotterdam, *Wijnhoven Hendriksen*, 1840.

In Taalkundig magazijn, *etc.*, Deel 3, pp. 81-128 and 457-499. Contains a bibliography, and explanatory notes on proverbs, *etc.* [B.M.

1905. Jager (Arie de). Bijdragen tot de kennis der nederduitsche spreekwoorden.

8°. Rotterdam, *Wijnhoven Hendriksen*, 1840.

In Taalkundig Magazijn, 1840, Derde Deel, pp. 81-128. Pp. 86-96, bibliography. [B.M.

1906. Jagt (J. A. Manus van der). Levenswijsheid, *etc.* pp. xii, 167. 8°. Rotterdam, *Jagt*, 1871.

Another edition. pp. xii, 167.

8°. Utrecht, *Hendriksen*, 1873.

Proverbs, sayings, *etc.*, principally from the Bible, arranged by subjects. [B.M.

1907. Jong (Willem de). Lessen en wenken aan nederlandsche spreekwoorden ontleend, *etc.* pp. 236.

8°. Tiel, *Mijs*, [1873].

Stories, *etc.*, illustrating proverbs. [B.M.

1908. Koning (L.). Schetsen ter herinnering en oefening.

sm. 8°. [1833].

Contains Verzameling van honderd veertig spreekwoorden opgehelderd.

1909. Kuyper (G.). Éléments de la grammaire néerlandaise. . . . Nouvelle édition, *etc.* pp. 199. 8°. La Haye, *Nijhoff*, 1870.

Pp. 185-187, equivalent proverbs in French and Dutch.

1910. Laurillard (E.). Bijbel en volkstaal. Opgave en toelichting van spreuken of gezegden in de volkstaal, aan den Bijbel ontleend, *etc.* pp. 136. 8°. Amsterdam, *Centen*, 1875.

1911. Loehr (J. A. C.). Voedsel voor het kinderlijk verstand, bestaande in gesprekken . . . spreekwoorden, *etc.*

sm. 8°. Leyden, *Du Mortier*, 1804.

Second edition. sm. 8°. Leyden, 1832.

1912. Lossius (K. F.). Tafereelen uit het daaglijksche leven, benevens eenige spreekwoorden, *etc.* [By K. F. Lossius?].

sm. 8°. Amsterdam, *Van Vliet und Van der Hey*, 1802.

Second edition. sm. 8°. Amsterdam, 1817.

1913. Lublink (Joannes). Verhandeling over verscheidene onderwerpen, *etc.* 3 vols. 8°. Amsterdam, 1788.

Another edition. 2 dln. 8°. Rotterdam, *Immerzeel*, 1823.

Contains Verhandeling over de spreekwoorden.

P

1914. Magazijn. Magazijn van spreekwoorden en zedenspreuken, *etc.* 3 deelen.   8°.   Amsterdam, *Van Vliet,* 1800-02.
Bernstein, 2028.

1915. Martinet (J. F.).   Oorspronglyke nederlandsche logogryphen, of de verzameling van vaderlandsche spreekwoorden, *etc.*   sm. 8°.   Amsterdam, *Van Vliet,* n.d.

1916. ———: Verzameling van vaderlandsche spreekwoorden, opgelderd, *etc. First edition.*
                 sm. 8°.   Amsterdam, *Allart,* 1796.
Third edition.   8°.   Leyden, *Du Mortier,* 1829
Gratet-Duplessis, 799.

1917. Meijer (Gerrit Johan).   Oude nederlandsche spreuken en spreekwoorden, *etc.* pp. x, 123.
                 8°.   Groningen, *Oomkens,* 1836.
A reprint of the proverbs from the Ghemeene duytsche spreekwoorden, *etc.*, 1550, and from Goedthals' Proverbes anciens flamengs et françois, 1568.   [B.M.

1918. Meyer (G. J.).   Oude nederlandsche Spreuchen en Spreekwoorden.   8°.   Groningen, 1836.
Gratet-Duplessis, 812.

1919. Moerbeek (Adam Abrahamzz van).   Neue vollkommene holländische Sprachlehre, *etc.* pp. x, 324.
                 8°.   Leipzig, *Junius,* 1791.
Another edition. pp. x, 324.   8°.   Leipzig, 1804.
Pp. 239-272, Sammlung einiger holländischen Redensarten und Sprüchwörter. Dutch proverbs with German equivalents and translations.   [B.M.

1920. Molema (H.).   Nederduitsche spreekwoorden.
                 8°.   Utrecht, *Van der Post,* 1862-63.
In De Taalgids, jaargang 4 and 5, 1862-63.   A commentary and a long list of proverbs, with notes.   [B.M.

1921. National Proverbs. National proverbs: Holland. pp. 78.
             1/-.   8°.   London, *Palmer,* [1915].
Proverbs in English only; no notes.   [B.M.

1922. Nijenborgh (Johan van).   De weeck-wercken, *etc.* pp. [viii], 352.   4°.   Groningen, *Cöllen,* 1657.
Contains numerous proverbs scattered throughout.   [B.M.

1923. Pagenstecher (Alexander Arnold).   Sylloge dissertationum, *etc.* pp. [xii], 724 and index.
             12°.   Bremae, *Saurman,* 1713.
Gratet-Duplessis, 808.   Pp. 483-522, Ad paroemias Belgicas.   [B.M.

1924. Pan (J.).   Drenthsche woorden en spreekwijzen.
                        [*c.* 1850.]

1925. Proverbia. Incipiunt Proverbia Seriosa in theutonice prima, deinde in latino, *etc. Sig.* A—c.

4°. Bois-le-Duc, 1487.

Another edition. Sig. A—c.

sm. 4°. [Cologne, *Heinrich Quentell*, 1488].

Gratet-Duplessis, 801. The first edition given above is thought to be from a German press of the 15th century. Duplessis gives further details about these and another edition; these editions are given by Hain in his Repertorium Bibliographicum, tome 2, pt. 2, pp. 162-163. Extremely rare. *See also* **1948-9.**

[B.M.

1926. Raadt (J. Th. de). Les sobriquets des communes belges.

Bruxelles, 1904.

1927. Raven (T.). Toegepaste spreekwoorden, gezegden en voorvallen, *etc.* sm. 8°. Groningen, *Folkers*, 1853.

1928. Reddingius (W. G.). Hollandsche spreekwoorden, opgehelderd door leerzame voorbeelden.

sm. 8°. Groningen, *Zuidema*, 1814.

1929. Rijn (C. J. van). Spreekwoorden, spreuken en uitdrukkingen . . . verklaard in het Hollands en met de engelse equivalenten, *etc.* pp. 56. 8°. Kaapstad, [1919].

Contains more idioms than proverbs. [B.M.

1930. Roodhuyzen (H. G.). Lessen van levenswijsheid, geput uit eenige nederlandsche spreekwoorden, *etc.* pp. 176.

8°. Amsterdam, *Hassels*, [1860].

[B.M.

1931. Ruyter (B.). Der ächte kleine Holländer, *etc.* pp. 159.

12°. Hamburg, *Berendsohn*, 1888.

Pp. 135-137, Dutch proverbs with German equivalents.

1932. Sancho-Pança. De antwerpsche Sancho-Pança. Verzameling van ongeveer 700 spreekwoorden. . . . Almanach voor 1849. sm. 8°. Antwerpen, *Buschmann*, 1849.

Second edition. sm. 8°. Antwerpen, 1850.

1933. Sandwijk (G. van). Spreekwoorden aanschouwelijk voorgesteld en verklaard . . . met 48 plaatjes.

4°. Purm, *Schuitemaker*, [1852].

1934. Sartorius (Johannes). Adagia a Joanne Sartorio in Batavicum sermonem proprie ac eleganter conversa.

12°. Antverpiae, *Loeus*, 1561.

Another edition. Adagiorum chiliades tres, *etc.* pp. 634, [39]. sm. 8°. Amstelodami, *Ravesteinius*, 1670.

Gratet-Duplessis, 805, says the 1561 edition is probably the first, and mentions another of 1656. As the author has not only given a literal translation of the Greek and Latin proverbs herein, but also compared them with Flemish equivalents which gave the same meaning in a different form, the work is best placed here. The notes given are clear and useful. [B.M.

1935. Scheltema (Paulus Cornelis). Verzameling van spreekwoorden, gezegden en anekdoten, *etc.* 2 stukje.
　　8°.　Franeker, Leeuwarden, *Ypma* (1. stuk),
　　　　　　　　　Schierbeck (2. stuk), 1826-31.
Proverbs, phrases, anecdotes, *etc.*, explained and illustrated.　　[B.M.

1936. Schoock (Martin). Tractatus de turffis, ceu cespitibus
bituminosis, *etc.* pp. [viii], 256.
　　　　　　　　12°. Groningae, *Cöllenus*, 1658.
Caput 20, pp. 167-173, Notantur varia Belgarum proverbia, turffas respicientia.
　　　　　　　　　　　　　　　　　　　　　　　[B.M.

1937. Schrant (Jan Matthias). Oud-neêrlandsch rijm en onrijm,
etc. pp. viii, 278.　　　　　8°. Leiden, *Hoek*, 1851.
Pp. 275-278, Ghemeene duytsche spreekwoorden. About 50 proverbs without
notes or explanations.　　　　　　　　　　　　　[B.M.

1938. Schuetze (Johann Friedrich). Apologische Sprichwörter
der niederländischen Volksprache.　sm. 8°. Weimar, 1800.
Gratet-Duplessis, 810. *In* Wieland's neue deutscher Merkur, October, 1800.
　　　　　　　　　　　　　　　　　　　　　　　[U.C.L.

1939. Smits (W.). Proverbia vulgatae editionis versione Belgica,
etc.　　　　　　　　　　　　Antverpiae, 1746.

1940. Spaan (Gerrit van). Lyste van rariteten, *etc.* 2 deel.
　　16°. Arabien, midden op de Zand-Zee, *Zeg-Waardt*, n.d.
Deel 2, Lyste van spreekwoorden, op verscheyde voorvallen toepasselijk, *etc.*

1941. Spraakleer. Nieuwe nederlandsche spraakleer, *etc.* pp. ix,
479.　　　　　　　　8°. Nijmegen, *Haspels*, 1846.
Pp. 406-437, Over de spreekwoorden. A small collection of Dutch proverbs,
with explanatory notes on their origin.

1942. Spreckwoorden. Gemeene duytsche spreckwoorden: adagia
oft proverbia ghenoemt, *etc.*
　　　　　　　sm. 8°. Campen, *Warnersen*, n.d.

1943. Spreeckwoorden. Seer schoone spreeckwoorden, oft proverbia, in Franchoys ende Duytsch, *etc.*
　　　　　　　12°. Tantwerpen, *Hans de Laet*, 1549.
Arranged alphabetically by the French.　　　　　　　[B.M.

1944. Sprichwörter. Flammische und französische Sprichwörter.　　　　　　　　8°. Antwerp, 1568.

1945. Stoett (F. A.). Nederlandsche Sprukwoorden, spreek-
wijzen, *etc.* pp. xvi, 744.　　8°. Zutphen, *Thieme*, 1901.
Another edition. 2 deel.　　　　8°. Zutphen, 1924-25.
Over 2000 proverbs, expressions and common phrases, with explanatory notes
　　　　　　　　　　　　　　　　　　　　　　　[B.M.

1946. Studeerkamer. De boere studeerkamer of rariteyt-kraam der zotten en zottinen, *etc.* 2 vols.

sm. 8°. 'sGravenhage, Van Os, 1765-67.

Dutch proverbs with humorous explanations. According to an old catalogue the author is F. L. Kersteman.

1947. Suringar (Willem Hendrik Dominicus). Erasmus over nederlandsche spreekwoorden, *etc.* pp. civ, 595.

4°. Utrecht, Kemink, 1873.

Pp. xv-civ, bibliography of authorities. Compares and contrasts the Dutch proverbs of the Adagia with others of the same period.   [B.M.

1948. ———: Glossarium van de oud-Hollandsche en midden-eeuwsch Latijnsche woorden, voorkomende in de Proverbia Communia [**1925**], *etc.* pp. xix, 86. 8°. Leyden, *Brill*, 1865.
[B.M.

1949. ———: Over de Proverbia Communia, ook Proverbia Seriosa geheeten, de oudste verzameling van nederlandsche spreekwoorden [**1925**], *etc.* pp. 131. 4°. Leyden, 1862-63.

1950. Susan (S.). Sammlung Wörter, Sprichwörter und Redensarten . . . Zweite . . . Auflage. pp. iv, 86.

8°. Groningen, Noordhoff & Smit, 1876.

1952. Teirlinck (Is.). Le folklore flamand. pp. 165.

8°. Bruxelles, Rozez, 18—?

Bibliothèque belge des connaissances modernes. Pp. 33-5, proverbes, locutions, dictons populaires dans lesquels intervient le nom de Dieu : pp. 94-7, proverbes, dictons, locutions se rapportant au diable.   [F.-L.S.

1953. Tratsaert (Jan). National proverbs: Belgium. Compiled by Jan Tratsaert. pp. 79.

1/-. sm. 8°. London, Palmer, [1915].

Section 1, pp. 7-61, Belgian sayings in Flemish. Section 2, pp. 63-79, Belgian sayings in French. No notes.   [F.-L.S. (Stephens collection).

1954. Tuinman (Carolus). De oorsprong en uitlegging van . . . nederduitsche spreekwoorden, *etc.* 2 deel.

4°. Middelburg, Schryver, 1720-1727.

Presumably Gratet-Duplessis, 809.   [B.M.

1955. ———: Zedenzangen, over een groot gedeelte der nederlandsche spreekwoorden, *etc.* pp. [vi], 115.

sm. 8°. Leiden, Langerak, 1720.

Proverbs in verse, with music.

1956. Venne (Adriaen van de). Tafereel van de belacchende werelt, *etc.* pp. [xii], 280.

4°. 'sGravenhage, voor den Autheur, 1635.

Contains many proverbs.   [B.M.

1957. Verdam (Jakob). De geschiedenis der nederlandsche taal, *etc.* pp. xvi, 224. 8°. Leeuwarden, *Suringar*, 1890.
Second edition. pp. xiii, 306.

8°. Dordrecht, *Revers*, 1902.

Contains a section on proverbs entitled : De spreekwoordenschat onzer taal.
[B.M.

1958. Verklaring. Verklaring van een vijfentwintigtal vader-landsche spreekwoorden, *etc.*

sm. 8°. Amsterdam, *Van Munster*, 1848.

1959. Verstegen (Richardus). De gazette van nieuwe-maren. . . . Door R[ichardus] V[erstegen].

sm. 8°. T'Hantwerpen, *Verdussen*, 1618.

Pp. 101-123, Wederlegginghe van eenige valsche, ende onbequame neder-lantsche spreek-woorden.

1960. ———: Medicamenten teghen de melancolie. . . . Door R[ichardus] V[erstegen].

sm. 8°. Antvverpen, *Aertssens*, 1633.

Pp. 67-94, 20 valsche, ydele, ende onstichtighe nederlantsche spreeck-woorden.

1961. Vervliet (J. B.). Volkswijsheid in beeld en schrift, *etc.* pp. 26. 8°. Brecht, *Braeckmans*, 1894.

1962. Verzameling. Verzameling van spreekwoorden en zegs-wijzen, opgehelderd en toegepast, *etc.*

sm. 8°. Sneek, *Smallenburg*, 1822.

1963. Vos (J. G. R.). Engelsch-nederlandsche idiomatische uit-drukkingen en spreekwoorden, *etc.* pp. 232.

8°. 's-Gravenhage, *Ijkema*, 1892.

1964. Willems (Jan Frans). Keur van nederduitsche Spreek-woorden, *etc.* pp. x, 73.

8°. Antwerpen, *Schoesetters*, 1824.

Gratet-Duplessis, 811. Proverbs and sayings classified by subject. [B.M.

1965. ———: Oude rymspreuken. 8°. Gent, *Gyselynck*, 1837.

Gratet-Duplessis, 813. *In* Belgisch Museum, Vol. 1, pp. 99-136. Oude rym-spreuken. [B.M.

1966. Zeeman (Catharinus Florandinus). Nederlandsche spreek-woorden, spreekwijzen . . . aan den Bijbel ontleend. pp. viii, 538. 8°. Dordrecht, *Revers*, 1877.
Second edition. pp. viii, 538.

8°. Dordrecht, *Revers*, 1888.

Arranged alphabetically with notes. There is a list of authorities in the preface. [B.M.

1967. Zegerus (Tacitus Nicolaus). Proverbia teutonica latinate
donata, *etc.*   8°. Antverpiae, *Loëus*, 1558.
Another edition.   8°. Antverpiae, 1563.
Another edition. [pp. 120].   sm. 8°. Antverpiae, 1571.
Stirling-Maxwell, p. 107. Proverbs arranged alphabetically by the Flemish.
The origin is indicated in most cases, and occasionally a Greek as well as a
Latin equivalent is given. There is a brief preface on proverbs, adages,
enigmas, *etc.*   [B.M.

1968. Zieman (Adolf). Altdeutsches Lesebuch, Sprüche aus dem
xiii. Jahrhundert.   Quedlinburg, Leipsig, 1838.
Gratet-Duplessis, 813, 2. Pp. 213-334, proverbs of the Netherlands.

1969. Zutphen (A. van). Vaderlandsche spreekwoorden, *etc.*
pp. viii, 93. 2 st.
                    sm. 8°. Gorinchem, *Noorduyn*, 1821-1823.

4. LOCAL.

1970. Groesser (H.). Rommelzoo, Antwerpsche spreekwoorden
en pittige volksgezegden.   Antwerpen, 1897.

1971. Harrebomée (Pieter Jakob). Utrechtsche spreekwoorden.
                            8°. Utrecht, *Bosch*, 1864-65.
In Utrechtsen Volks-Almanak voor 1864 and 1865.

1972. Jongeneel (J.). Een zuid-limburgsch taaleigen, *etc.* pp.
xxvii, 120. 3 stuk.   8°. Heerlen, *Weyerhorst*, 1884.
Pp. 83-86, Spreekwijzen. Pp. 87-96, Spreekwoorden. Proverbs with Dutch
translations.   [B.M.

1973. Welters (H.). Feesten, zeden, gebruiken en spreekwoorden
in Limburg. pp. 120.   8°. Venloo, *Uyttenbroeck*, [1877].
Pp. 77-118, Spreekwoorden en Spreekwijzen in Limburg, *etc.*

5. LUXEMBURG.

1974. Dicks (E.). Die luxemburger Sprichwörter und sprichwörtlichen Redensarten, *etc.* 2 Th.
                        8°. Luxemburg, *Buck*, 1857-1858.

6. WALLOON.

1975. Alexandre (A. J.). Li p'tit corti aux proverbes wallons.
                            8°. Lüttich, 1863.
Separate publication of an article in the Bulletin de la Société liègeoise de
Littérature wallonne, tome 4, pp. 661-701. This forms a supplement to **1978.**

1976. Cambrésier (R. L. J.). Dictionnaire wallon-françois, ou
recueil de mots et de proverbes françois, *etc.* pp. 197.
                    sm. 8°. Liège, *Bassompierre*, 1787.
Gratet-Duplessis, 387. In spite of the title, it does not contain many proverbs.
                                                                    [B.M.

1977. Comhaire (Ch. J.). Le folk-lore du pays de Liège. Proverbes et sentences populaires. la. 8°. Paris, *Leroux*, 1889.

In Revue des traditions populaires, 4e année, tome 4, pp. 594-599. Proverbs, frequently in rhyme, in dialect with French translations. No notes. [B.M.

1978. Dejardin (Joseph). Dictionnaire des spots ou proverbes wallons . . . précédé d'une étude sur les proverbes par J. Stecker. pp. viii, 628. 8°. Liège, *etc.*, 1863.
Another edition. 2 tom. 1891-2.

2232 proverbs with literal French translations, explanations, and quotations. The book also contains a poem in proverbs in Walloon and French, by A. J. Alexandre [**1975**]. [B.M.

1979. Detrische (L.). Recueil de spots, expressions, termes, axiomes, dictons et proverbes wallons en dialecte de Stavelot, par un vieux Stavelotain [L. Detrische]. pp. 116.
fr.1. 8°. Liège, *Bouché*, 1901.

Sayings, expressions, *etc.*, arranged alphabetically by key-words. No notes. [B.M.

1980. Harou (Alfred). Les mines et les mineurs—xvi. Proverbes liégeois. 8°. Paris, 1891.

In Revue des traditions populaires, tome 6, pp. 485 *et seq.* [B.M.

1981. Siermon. Siermon en proverbes pa l' curé d' Lambusaut, en 1747. fol. Bruxelles, 1895.

In Li Marmite. Gazette Wallonne, No. 41. A humorous article in the form of a sermon, containing a large number of proverbs in the Walloon dialect.

1982. Zéliqzon (Léon). Aus der Wallonie, *etc.* pp. 28.
4°. Metz, *Lothringer Zeitung*, 1893.

Pp. 12-16, proverbs with French translations and occasional notes in German. [B.M.

See also index at end for Low Country proverbs in other sections.

GERMAN, LOCAL AND DIALECT.

1. GENERAL.

1983. Firmenich Richartz (Johannes Matthias). Germaniens Völkerstimmen, Sammlung der deutschen Mundarten, in Dichtungen, *etc.* 3 Bde.
8°. Berlin, *Schlesinger*, [1843-54[66]].

Gratet-Duplessis, 775. Contains a large number of proverbs in different German dialects. There are separate lists of these proverbs in most of the sections. [B.M.

1984. Hoefer (Edmund). Wie das Volk spricht. *First edition.* pp. 48. 8°. Stuttgart, *Krabbe*, 1855.
Seventh edition. pp. viii, 220. 16°. Stuttgart, 1873.
Ninth edition. pp. iv, 227. 12°. Stuttgart, *Kröner*, 1885.

The second edition (1856) contains 665 proverbs in different German dialects, with place of origin briefly indicated. The seventh edition contains over 2000, and also has occasional notes. [B.M.

2. PLATTDEUTSCH (GENERAL)

(*i.e.* Low German within the boundaries of modern Germany).

1985. Guenther (I. C. F.). Plattdeutsche Redensarten und Sprichwörter, eine Fortsetzung zu der Sammlung von J. Mussaeus in Jahrbüchern 5, p. 120. pp. 198-201.
8°. [1847?].
An extract from an unknown book or periodical.

1986. Haupt (Moriz). Fiv unn twintig Sprekwoerder. pp. 6.
sm. 4°. 1850.
Bernstein, 1441. Very rare.

1987. ———: Twe unn föftig Sprekwörd, *etc.* [ff. 28].
16°. 1850.
Bernstein, 1442. Very rare.

1988. Latendorf (Friedrich). Ueber die sprichwörtliche Anwendung von Vornamen im Plattdeutschen.
8°. Nürnberg, *Ebner*, 1856.
In Die deutschen Mundarten, Jahrgang 3, pp. 1-8. On pp. 370-374 two lists of additions are to be found, one by the author of the above, the other by Fr. Woeste. [B.M.

1989. Marahrens (August). Grammatik der plattdeutschen Sprache, *etc.* pp. 126.
8°. Altona, *auf Kosten des Verfassers*, 1858.
Pp. 95-98, Plattdütsche Sprüchwörd. [B.M.

1990. Raabe (H. F. W.). Allgemeines plattdeutsches Volksbuch, *etc.* pp. xiv, 242.
sm. 8°. Wismar, Ludwigsluft, *Hinstorff*, 1854.
Lists of proverbs are given in various places. [B.M.

1991. Schambach (Georg). Die Familie im Spiegel plattdeutscher Sprichwörter. 4°. Bremen, 1855.
In Bremer Sonntagsblatt, Jahrgang 3, No. 4, pp. 28-29. [B.M.

1992. Schroeder (Wilhelm). Jan Peik de noorddütsche Spassmaker. . . . Mit 23 Holzschnitt-Illustrationen. pp. xiii, 216.
8°. Berlin, *Janke*, [1875].
Pp. 196-216, Plattdütsche Sprüchwörder uut ohle un nee Boöker un uutn Dagessnack tosamensöcht un nah't A.B.C. tosamenstellet. [B.M.

1993. ———: De plattdutsche Sprüchwörder-Schatz, *etc.* pp. 70. 16°. Leipzig, *Reclam*, n.d.

1994. Sprueckwoerder. Pladdusche Sprückwörder.
8°. Leipsig, 1590.
Gratet-Duplessis, 780.

1994a. Wagenfeld (K.). Volksmund. Plattdeutsche Sprichwörter und Redensarten.

3. OLDENBURG AND BREMEN.

1995. Folkskarakter. Oldenburger Folkskarakter und Sprichwörter. 4°. Leipzig, *Fritsch*, 1869.
In Deutscher Sprachwart, Bd. 4, pp. 30-31. [B.M.

1996. Goldschmidt (J.). Der Oldenburger in Sprache und
Sprüchwort, *etc.* pp. 164. 8°. Oldenburg, *Schulz*, 1847.
There is also a special section, pp. 157-164, giving a list of Oldenburg
proverbs. This book is Theil 3 of the author's " Kleine Lebensbilder." [B.M.

1997. Koester (Friedrich). Alterthümer, Geschichten und Sagen
der Herzogthümer Bremen und Verden . . . Zweiter Abdruck.
pp. viii, 271. 8°. Stade, *Pockwitz*, 1856.
Pp. 250-255, Volksthümliche Sprüchwörter und Redensarten.

1998. Mindermann (Marie). Plattdeutsche Gedichte in bre-
mischer Mundart, *etc.* pp. viii, 148.
4°. Bremen, *Geisler*, 1860.
Pp. 115-147, Sprichwörter und Redeweisen. 679 entries. [B.M.

4. WESTPHALIA.

1999. Ausdrücke. Witzige Ausdrücke und Sprichwörter des west-
phälischen Volks. Dortmund, 1800.
Gratet-Duplessis, 794. In Westphälischer Anzeiger, pp. 667 *et seq.*

2000. Bahlmann (P.). Alt-Münsterische Bauern-Praktik. Eine
Sammlung münsterländischer Sprichwörter und Erfahrungs-
sätze, *etc.* pp. 32. 8°. Münster, *Regensberg*, 1896.
200 proverbs, *etc.*

2001. ———: Münsterische Lieder und Sprichwörter in plattdeutscher Sprache, *etc.* pp. lx, 159.
8°. Münster, *Regensberg*, 1896.
Pp. 77-156, Sprichwörter und Redensarten. 1068 entries.

2002. Geschichten. Münsterische Geschichten, Sagen und
Legenden, nebst einem Anhänge von Volksliedern und
Sprüchwörtern. pp. 307. 8°. Münster, *Coppenrath*, 1825.
Pp. 295-302, Sprüchwörter.

2003. Lyra (F. W.). Plattdeutsche Briefe . . . mit besonderer
Rücksicht auf Sprichwörter und eigenthümliche Redensarten
des Landvolks in Westphalen. pp. xviii, 204.
8°. Osnabrück, *Verlag des Herausgebers*, 1845.
Another edition. 8°. Osnabrück, *Rackhorst*, 1856.
[B.M.

2004. Mielck (W. H.). Sprichwörter aus Westfalen.
8°. Hamburg, 1884.
In Korrespondenzblatt des Vereins für niederdeutsche Sprachforschung, Jahrgang 1884, Heft 9, pp. 88-89. 54 entries. [B.M.

2005. Pruemer (Carl). Westfälische Volksweisheit. Plattdeutsche Sprichwörter, Redensarten, Volkslieder und Reime. pp. [vi], 91. 8°. Barmen, *Moellenhoff*, 1881.

2006. Regenhardt (C.). Mundartliches aus dem Münsterlande. 8°. Nördlingen, 1859.

In Die deutschen Mundarten, Jahrgang 6, pp. 423-428. Pp. 424-428, Volkssprüche und Sprichwörter. [B.M.

2007. Sprichwoerter. Plattdeutsche (münsterländische) Sprichwörter—Spreuken en Spreukwoorden. 8°. Braunschweig, *Westermann*, 1871.

In Archiv für das Studium der neueren Sprachen und Literaturen, 26. Jahrgang, Bd. 48, pp. 363-365. 21 Low German, 14 Dutch, proverbs. [B.M.

2008. Walter (Fritz). Plattdeutsche Sprichwörter und sprichwörtliche Redensarten aus der Stadt Recklinghausen, *etc.* pp. 36. 8°. Recklinghausen, *Alby*, 1896.

In Zeitschrift der Vereine für Orts- und Heimathskunde im Vest Recklinghausen, 1896.

5. BRUNSWICK AND ALTMARK.

2009. Beck (H.). Niederdeutsche Spruchweisheit aus Nordsteimke (Braunschweig). 8°. Berlin, *Asher*, 1898-1899.

In Zeitschrift des Vereins für Volkskunde, Jhg. 8, pp. 301-304; Jhg. 9, pp. 81-83. [B.M.

2010. Danneil (Johann Friedrich). Wörterbuch der altmärkisch-plattdeutschen Mundart. pp. x, 299. 8°. Salzwedel, *Schmidt*, 1859.

Pp. 205-207, under the heading : Sprëkwort, and pp. 275-279, under the heading : Språkwôr, many proverbs are given, with German translations. [B.M.

2011. Schambach (Georg). Die plattdeutschen Sprichwörter der Fürstenthümer Göttingen und Grubenhagen, *etc.* pp. 91. 8°. Göttingen, *Vandenhoek & Ruprecht*, 1851.

Niederdeutsche Sprichwörter der Fürstenthümer Göttingen und Grubenhagen. . . . Zweite Sammlung. pp. viii, 190. 8°. Göttingen, 1863.

With notes and explanations. [U.C.L.

2012. Schwerin (Fritz). Der Altmärker. Eine Reihe Sprüchwörter, plattdeutsch auf altmärkische Manier ausgelegt, nebst einigen plattdeutschen Gedichten. pp. xiii, 198. 8°. Neuhaldensleben, *Eyraud*, [1859].

[B.M.

6. HOLSTEIN.

2013. Diermissen (J.). Ut de Musskist. Plattdeutsche Reime, Sprüche und Geschichtchen für Jung und Alt aus Nord-albingien. pp. 80. 8°. Kiel, *Homann*, 1862.
[B.M.

2014. Idioticon. Holsteinisches Idioticon, *etc.* 4 pts.
8°. Hamburg, Altona, 1800-1806.
Gratet-Duplessis, 787. A collection of anecdotes, proverbs, sayings, songs, *etc.*, of Holstein.

2015. Staecker (N.). Sprichwörter und Redearten [*sic*] aus Drage in Stapelholm.
8°. Lunden in Holstein, Hamburg, 1893.
In Am Ur-Quell, Bd. 4, pp. 257-258. 20 entries.   [B.M.

7. MECKLENBURG.

2016. Ruhestunden. Bützowsche Ruhestunden, gesucht im Mecklenburgschen, *etc.* 24 Thle.
8°. Bützow, *Fritze*, 1761-1766.
According to Wander, the author's name is E. J. F. Mantzel. Theil 5, pp. 30-40; Theil 6, pp. 69-79; Theil 13, pp. 49-56; Theil 18, pp. 14-21; Theil 20, pp. 26-33; Theil 24, pp. 51-66, Proverbs.

2017. Wossidlo (Richard). Der typische Gebrauch der Vornamen in meklenburger Platt. A. Vornamen in Sprichwörtern und sprichwörtlichen Redensarten. 8°. Hamburg, *Soltau*, 1884.
In Korrespondenzblatt des Vereins für niederdeutsche Sprachforschung, Jahr-gang 1884, Heft 9, No. 6.   [B.M.

See also **3670, 3702, 3952.**

8. POMERANIA.

2018. Haken (J. Ch. Ludwig). Sprichwörter der plattdeutschen Mundart in Hinterpommern. 8°. Stettin, *Leich*, 1806.
Gratet-Duplessis, 781. *In* Koch's Eurynone, *etc.*, Heft 1.

2019. Knoop (Otto). Plattdeutsche Sprüchwörter aus Hinter-pommern. 8°. Hamburg, 1885.
In Korrespondenzblatt des Vereins für niederdeutsche Sprachforschung, Jahr-gang 1885, Heft 10, pp. 52-59. 300 proverbs.   [B.M.

2020. ———: Plattdeutsches aus Hinterpommern. 3 pts.
4°. Posen, *Decker*, 1890.
Erste Sammlung : Sprüchwörter und Redensarten, pp. 25.   [B.M.

9. BRANDENBURG.

2021. Engelien (August) and **Lahn** (W.). Der Volksmund in der Mark Brandenburg. Sagen, . . . Sprichwörter und Gebräuche, *etc.* pp. viii, 285. 8°. Berlin, *Schultze*, 1868.
Pp. 213-224, 167 proverbs and proverbial phrases.   [B.M.

2022. Haase (K. Eduard). Sprichwörter und Redensarten aus der Grafschaft Ruppin und Umgegend. 8°. Berlin, 1892.

In Zeitschrift des Vereins für Volkskunde, Jahrgang 2, pp. 437-440. 67 entries. [U.C.L.

10. EAST PRUSSIA.

2023. Sembrzycki (Johannes). Ostpreussische Sprichwörter, Volksreime und Provinzialismen. 8°. Hamburg, 1891-92.

In Am Ur-Quell, Bde. 2 and 3. 360 entries.

11. RHINELAND.

2024. Dirksen (Carl). Meidericher Sprichwörter, sprichwörtliche Redensarten und Reimsprüche, *etc.* Meiderich, 1890. *Second edition.* pp. 56. 8°. Königsberg, *Hartung*, 1893.

2025. ———: Volkstümliches aus Meiderich (Niederrhein), *etc.* pp. 58. 8°. Bonn, *Handstein*, 1895.

Pp. 51-58, Meidericher Sprichwörter. 80 entries.

2026. Fischbach (P. J.) and **Giese** (J. van der). Dürener Volksthum, *etc.* pp. xxiv, 180. 8°. Düren, *Knoll*, 1880.

Pp. 1-61, Redensarten und Sprichwörter.

2027. Gierlichs (Hubert). Sprichwörter aus der Eifel.
8°. Bonn, 1896.

In Rheinische Geschichtsblätter, 1896, pp. 278-279, 334-337. [B.M.

2028. Gloch (J. Ph.). Lieder und Sprüche aus dem Elsenzthale, *etc.* pp. 63. 8°. Bonn, *Hanstein*, 1897.

Pp. 52-63, Allerlei Sprüche für Alt und Jung. 185 entries.

2029. Haupt (Herman). Oberrheinische Sprichwörter und Redensarten des ausgehenden 15. Jahrhunderts.
8°. Halle a. S., *Buchhandlung des Waisenhauses*, 1896.

In Zeitschrift für deutsche Philologie, Bd. 29, pp. 109-110. 23 entries.
[U.C.L.

2030. Hoenig (Fritz). Sprichwörter und Redensarten in kölnischer Mundart. pp. 168. 8°. Köln, *Neubner*, 1895. Nachtrag (Als Manuscript gedruckt). pp. 13.
8°. Koln, 1895.

Another edition. pp. 167. 8°. Köln, *Kreuter*, 1912.

An alphabetical list. [B.M.

2031. Joerres (P.). Sparren, Spähne und Splitter von Sprache, Sprüchen und Spielen aufgelesen im Ahrthal. pp. 42.
8°. Ahrweiler, *Plachner*, 1888.

Pp. 19-27, Sprüche. 85 entries. [B.M

2032. Laven (Ph.). Gedichte in trierischer Mundart, *etc.* pp. xxxvii, 291.   12°. Trier, *Lintz*, 1858.

Pp. 174-198, Gereimd Drierisch Sprichwöhrder (149).   [B.M.

2033. Maurmann (Emil). Grammatik der Mundart von Mülheim a. d. Ruhr. pp. vii, 108.

8°. Leipzig, *Breitkopf & Härtel*, 1898.

Sammlung kurzer Grammatiken deutscher Mundarten, Bd. 4. Pp. 81-83, Sprichwörter, sprichwörtliche Redensarten, *etc.* 28 proverbs in dialect, with German translations.   [B.M.

2034. Moersch. Wie se te Mörsch stechlen, optrekken, dor de Blumm spreken on achter heröm kallen. pp. 22.

8°. Meurs, *Dolle*, 1846.

Contains 485 proverbs of Meurs.   [B.M.

2035. Petsch (Robert). Kölnische Sprichwörter und Kinder-reime.   fol. München, 1899.

In Beilage zur Allgemeinen Zeitung, Jahrgang 1899, Nr. 123.

2036. Reifferscheid (A.). Kölner Volksgespräche und Sprich-wörter.   Hamm, 1876.

2037. Roettsches (H.). Die Krefelder Mundart, *etc.*

8°. Halle, *Buchhandlung des Waisenhauses*, 1877.

In Die deutschen Mundarten, Bd. 7 (N.F., Bd. 1), pp. 36-91. Pp. 77-86, Sprichwörter und Redensarten. 245 entries.   [B.M.

2038. Schmitz (J. H.). Sitten und Sagen, Lieder, Sprüchwörter und Räthsel des Eifler Volkes, *etc.* 2 Bde.

8°. Trier, *Lintz*, 1856-58.

Bd. 1, pp. 165-202, Sprüchwörter.   [B.M.

2039. Schmitz (Wilhelm). Die Misch-Mundart in den Kreisen Geldern . . . Kempen . . . Aachen . . . Krefeld, *etc.* pp. 211.

8°. Dülken, *Kugelmeier*, [1893].

Pp. 75-93, Sprichwörter, sprichwörtliche und bildliche Redensarten.   [B.M.

2040. Schollen (M.). Aachener Sprichwörter und Redensarten.

8°. Aachen, *Benrath & Vogelgesang*, 1886.

Second edition. pp. xi, 228.   8°. Aachen, *La Ruelle*, 1913.

In Zeitschrift des Aachener Geschichtsvereins, *etc.*, Bd. 8, pp. 158-208. Over 1000 proverbs and sayings. There is a brief list of authorities at the beginning. The second edition is presumably a separate publication.   [B.M.

2041. ———: Volksthümliches aus Aachen, *etc.* pp. vi, 78.

16°. Aachen, *Jacobi*, 1881.

Pp. 28-30, Wetter-, Gesundheits-, und Rechts-Regeln; pp. 33-50, 290 Sprüch-wörter und Redensarten.

2042. Spee (J.). Volksthümliches vom Niederrhein. 2 pts.

8°. Köln, *Roemke*, 1875.

Pt. 1, pp. 21-27; Pt. 2, pp. 37-48, Sprüchwörter.

2043. Sprichwoerter. Sprichwörter und alte Volks- und Kinderlieder in kölnischer Mundart. pp. 65.

12°. Köln, *Stauff*, n.d.

Pp. 1-25, Kölnische Sprichwörter und sprichwörtliche Redensarten.

2044. Wegeler (Julius). Coblenz in seiner Mundart, etc. pp.
viii, 256. 8°. Coblenz, *Hergt*, 1876.

Pp. 97-102, einige Sprichwörter und Redensarten. Arranged alphabetically.
[B.M.

2045. Weitz (Wilhelm). Klänge der Heimath, oder Sammlung
auserlesener Gedichte in der Aachener Volkssprache, *etc.*
pp. 120. 8°. Aachen, *Cremer*, n.d.

Pp. 85-92, Sprichwörter in Reimen.

2046. Weyden (Ernst). Cöln's Vorzeit, *etc.* pp. xii, 308.

8°. Cöln am Rhein, *Schmitz*, 1826.

Pp. 296-300, Cölnische Sprüchworte und sprüchwörtliche Ausdrücke. [B.M.

2047. ———: Kölns Legenden, Sagen . . . Anekdoten, Sprichwörter, u.s.w. Köln, 1839-40.

12. HESSE AND NASSAU.

2048. Curtze (Ludwig). Volksüberlieferungen aus dem Fürsten-
thum Waldeck, *etc.* pp. xiv, 518.

8°. Arolsen, *Speyer*, 1860.

Pp. 305-366, Sprichwörter : 624 entries. Pp. 311-312, brief bibliography.
[B.M.

2049. Eckart (Rudolf). Aus Kurhessen: Schilderungen, Dichtungen, Sprichwörter, Anekdoten und Sagen, *etc.* pp. 202.

8°. Cassel, *Gotthelft*, 1917.

Contains some few proverbs. [B.M.

2050. Kehrein (Joseph). Volkssprache und Volkssitte im Herzogthum Nassau, *etc.* 2 Bde. 8°. Weilburg, *Lanz*, 1860-62.

Bd. 2, pp. 28-29, Sprichwörter und sprichwörtliche Redensarten : pp. 105-112,
Räthsel, Sprichwörter, Volkswitze. Bd. 2 was also published separately in
1891 under the title : Volksthümliches aus Nassau, *etc.* [B.M.

2051. Kuenzel (Heinrich). Geschichte von Hessen, *etc.* pp.
xvi, 661. 8°. Friedberg, *Scriba*, 1856.

Second edition. Grossherzogthum Hessen, *etc.* pp. xiii, 786.

8°. Giessen, *Roth*, 1893.

The second edition contains, pp. 423-430, Alte hessische Sprichwörter und
sprichwörtliche Redensarten : pp. 594-595, Idiotismen und charakterische sprichwörtliche Redensarten der Provinz Starkenburg. The first edition contains
only the latter of these lists. [B.M.

2052. Muelhause (Elard). Die Urreligion des deutschen Volkes
in hessischen Sitten, Sagen, Redensarten, Sprüchwörtern und
Namen. pp. 357. 8°. Cassel, *Fischer*, 1860.

No special list of proverbs. [B.M.

2053. Muenz (P. J.). Taufnamen als Gattungsnamen in sprichwörtlichen Redensarten Nassaus. 4°. Wiesbaden, 1870.

In Annalen des Vereins für nassauische Alterthumskunde und Geschichtsforschung, Bd. 10, pp. 89-112. [B.M.

2054. Nebel (Ernst Ludwig Wilhelm). Alte Sprüchwörter der Hessen, geschichtlich erläutert.

8°. Marburg, Cassel, *Krieger*, 1824.

In Die Vorzeit, 1824, pp. 174-198. Comments on 12 proverbs. [B.M.

2055. Pistor (J.). Sprichwörter und sprichwörtliche Redensarten aus Wigand Lauzes hessischer Chronik.

8°. Leipzig, 1891.

In Zeitschrift für Volkskunde, Bd. 3, pp. 146-147. [B.M.

2056. Quilling (Paul). Schrulle un Flause von hiwwe, driwwe un drause. . . . 2. Auflage. pp. viii, 136.

8°. Frankfurt am Main, *Fey*, 1884.

Pp. 33-35, Sachsenhäuser Sprüchwörter und Redensarten.

2057. Stoltze (Friedrich). Vermischte Schriften. . . . Dritte Auflage. pp. xxii, 383 + 1 plate.

12°. Frankfurt am Main, *Keller*, 1896.

Pp. 342-383, Frankfurt in seinen Sprüchwörtern und Redensarten.

13. THURINGIA.

2058. Reinwald (W. F. H.). Hennebergisches Idiotikon, *etc.* 2 Thle. 8°. Berlin, Stettin, *Nicolai*, 1793-1801.

Theil 1, pp. 112-114, Hennebergische Sprüchwörter. [B.M.

2059. Schleicher (August). Volkstümliches aus Sonneberg im Meininger Oberlande. pp. xxv, 158.

8°. Weimar, *Böhlau*, 1858.

Pp. 80-86, Sprichworte, sprichwörtliche Redensarten und verwandtes. In dialect, with occasional notes. [B.M.

2060. Spiess (Balthasar). Henneberger Mundart . . . Sprichwörter und Volkssprüche. 8°. Nürnberg, 1855.

In Die deutschen Mundarten, Jahrgang 2, pp. 407-416. [B.M.

2061. ———: Volksthümliches aus dem Fränkisch-Hennebergischen, *etc.* pp. xvi, 216. 8°. Wien, *Braumüller*, 1869.

Pp. 38-62, 831 Sprichwörter und Redensarten. [B.M.

2062. Sprichwoerter. Jenaische Sprichwörter. Nach einer Handschrift des xvii. Jahrhunderts.

8°. Weimar, *Landes-Industrie-Comptoirs*, 1817.

In Curiositäten der physisch-literarisch-artistisch-historischen Vor- und Mitwelt, Bd. 6, pp. 226-236. [B.M.

2063. Wagner (Carl). Sprichwörter und Redensarten in Rudolstadt und dessen nächster Umgegend, *etc.*

8°. Rudolstadt, *Mitzlaff*, 1882.

14. SOUTH GERMAN AND AUSTRIAN.

2064. Bergmann (Joseph). Einleitung zu Schmeller's cimbrischen Wörterbuche. 8°. Wien, 1855.

In Sitzungsberichte der philosophisch-historischen Classe der kaiserlichen Akademie der Wissenschaften, Bd. 15, 1855, pp. 60-159. Pp. 144-145, Einige Sprichwörter, welche der Herausgeber in Asiago sammelte. [B.M.

2065. Birlinger (Anton). So sprechen die Schwaben. pp. 136. 12°. Berlin, *Dümmler*, 1868.

A collection of proverbs, weather sayings, phrases, house-rhymes, *etc.*, with occasional brief notes. [B.M.

2066. Doederlein (Johann Alexander). Antiquitates gentilismi Nordgaviensis, *etc.* pp. 128. 4°. Regenspurg, *Geissart*, 1734.

Gratet-Duplessis, 788. A commentary on the paganism of the ancient inhabitants of Nordgau, after their proverbs, customs, old documents, *etc.*
[B.M.

2067. Gerhard (Laurentius). Brevis Bavariae geographia. . . . Cum appendice adagiorum. pp. 165. 8°. Wirceburgi, *Thein*, 1844.

Gratet-Duplessis, 785. Pp. 115-165, Appendix selectorum adagiorum Latino-Germanicorum, *etc.*

2068. Hofmann ( ). Johanesminne und deutsche Sprichwörter aus Handschriften der Schwabacher Kirchen-Bibliothek.

8°. München, *Akademische Buchdruckerei*, 1870.

In Sitzungsberichte der königl. bayer. Akademie der Wissenschaften zu München, Jahrgang 1870, Bd. 2, pp. 15-38. A commentary with examples.
[B.M.

2069. Kaehn (Johannes). Gedichte in Rieser Mundart. . . . 3. . . . Auflage. pp. xi, 124. 12°. Nördlingen, *Beck*, 1894.

Pp. 100-109, Sprichwörter und Redensarten im Rieser Gewand.

2069a. Laemmle (A.). Der Volksmund in Schwaben. Schwäbische Lebensweisheit und Spruchkunst in Sprichwörtern, Redensarten und Reimsprüchen. 1924.

2070. Leoprechting (Carl von), *Baron*. Aus dem Lechrain, zur deutschen Sitten- und Sagenkunde. pp. xii, 296, 16.

8°. München, *Literarisch-artistische Anstalt*, 1855.

Pp. 290-296, Sprüchwörter und Redensarten. [B.M.

2071. Mayer (Thomas). Baierische Sprichwörter, mit Erklärung, *etc.* 2 pts. 8°. München, *Lentener*, 1812.

Gratet-Duplessis, 783.

2072. Michel. Der schwäbische Michel als Allerwelts-Spassmacher. . . . Nebst einem Anhang von schwäbischen Sprüchwörtern und Redensarten mit ihrer Erklärung. pp. 283.

16°. Stuttgart, *Fischhaber*, [1870].

Pp. 253-283, Schwäbische Redensarten und Sprüchwörter. [B.M.

Q

2073. Nefflen (J.). Der Vetter aus Schwaben, *etc.*   1840.
J. Nefflen's Werke. Revidierte Ausgabe seiner Volksbücher:
" Der Vetter aus Schwaben," und " Der Orgelmacher von
Freudenthal," *etc.* pp. xvi, 316.

8°. Stuttgart, *Lutz*, 1888.

Contains a section : Erklärung schwäbischer Redensarten. Nach Stich-
wörtern alphabetisch geordnet.   [B.M.

2074. Peter, *Lehrer.* Sprüchwörter und Redensarten aus der
Gegend von Waldsee, *etc.*   4°. Ulm, *Ebner*, 1891.

In Ulm Oberschwaben. Mitteilungen des Vereins für Kunst und Altherthum
in Ulm und Oberschwaben, Heft 2, pp. 22-24.

2075. Pfeiffer (Friedrich W.). Volksthümliche Sprichwörter und
Redensarten aus Franken.   8°. Nürnberg, 1859.

In Die deutschen Mundarten, Jahrgang 6, pp. 161-170, 314-330, 462-469.
[B.M.

2075a. Reiser (Karl). Sagen, Gebräuche und Sprichwörter des
Allgäus. pp. 1329. 2 Bde.   M.33. 8°. Kempten, 1895.

2076. Ruedel (K.). Sprichwörtliches aus Franken.

8°. Nürnberg, 1856.

In Die deutschen Mundarten, Jahrgang 3, pp. 352-360.   [B.M.

2077. Sartorius (Johann Baptist). Die Mundart der Stadt Würzburg. pp. iv, 234.   8°. Würzburg, *Stahel*, 1862.

Pp. 153-187, Sprüchwörter und Redensarten. In alphabetical order, with
notes.   [B.M.

2078. Schmeller (Johann Andreas). Die Mundarten Bayerns
grammatisch dargestellt, *etc.* pp. xii, [12], 586 + map.

8°. München, *Thienemann*, 1821.

Pp. 509-512, Sprichwörter.   [B.M.

2079. Schmid (Johann Christoph von). Schwäbisches Wörterbuch. . . . *First edition.* pp. xvi, 630.

8°. Stuttgart, *Schweizerbart*, 1831.

Second edition. pp. xvi, 630.   8°. Stuttgart, 1844.

Contains a section entitled : Schwäbische Sprichwörter, Redensarten, Sprüche.
[B.M.

2080. Schoenwerth (Friedrich X. von). Sprichwörter des Volkes
der Oberpfalz in der Mundart.   8°. Stadtamhof, *Mayr*, 1874.

In Verhandlungen des historischen Vereins von Oberpfalz und Regensburg,
Bd. 29, pp. iii-lx, 1-86. A commentary, followed by a list of 1385 proverbs.
[B.M.

2081. Schwaben-Spiegel. Schwaben-Spiegel aus alter und neuer
Zeit. pp. 184.   8°. Stuttgart, *Vogler & Beinhauer*, 1870.

Pp. 37-41, Die Schwaben im Sprichwort. This collection is not in many
other editions of the Schwaben-Spiegel.

2082. Sprichwoerter. Einige ulmische Sprichwörter.   1787.

Gratet-Duplessis, 792. *In* Korresp. von und für Deutschland, 1787, No. 13.

2083. Sprichwoerter. Sprichwörter auch sprichwörtliche . . .
Redensarten . . . besonders des gemeinen Volks in Schwaben.
1789.

Gratet-Duplessis, 793. *In* Hausleutners Schwäbisches Archiv, 1789, No. 3,
pp. 339 *et seq.*

2084. Stengel (A.). Beitrag zur Kenntnis der Mundart an der
schwäbischen Retzat und mittleren Altmühl.
8°. Halle, 1877.

In Die deutschen Mundarten, Bd. 7, pp. 389-410. Pp. 408-410, Sprichwörtliche Redensarten. [B.M.

2085. Taschenbuch. Taschenbuch für die Jugend . . . nebst einem
Anhänge baierischer Sprichwörter. pp. 38.
sm. 8°. München, 1820.

Gratet-Duplessis, 784.

2086. Tschinkel (Wilhelm). Sprichwörter und sprichwörtliche
Redensarten im Gottscheer Volksmunde. 8°. Wien, 1906.

In Zeitschrift für österreichische Volkskunde, Jahrgang 12, pp. 138-148.
[B.M.

2087. Unseld (Wilhelm). Schwäbische Sprichwörter und Redensarten gesammelt in Stuttgart, Tübingen, Ulm und Blau-
beuren. 8°. Heidelberg, *Winter*, 1900.

In Zeitschrift für hochdeutsche Mundarten, Jahrgang 1, pp. 98-104. 202
proverbs.

2088. Westenrieder (Lorenz von). Beschreibung der Haupt- und
Residenzstadt München, *etc.* pp. [xviii], 429, [9] + plan.
8°. München, *Strobl*, 1782.

Pp. 323-327, Provincialismen und Sprüchwörter. [B.M.

2089. Woeste (Friedrich). Apologische Sprichwörter in Mundarten des märkischen Suderlandes.
8°. Nürnberg, *Ebner*, 1856.

In Die deutschen Mundarten, Jahrgang 3, pp. 253-264. [B.M.

2090. ———: Stehende oder sprichwörtliche Vergleiche aus der
Grafschaft Mark. 8°. Nördlingen, 1858.

Bernstein, 4088. *In* Die deutschen Mundarten, Jahrgang 5, 1858, pp. 57-66,
and 161-172. [B.M.

2091. Wurth (Johann). Proben der niederösterreichischen Mundart, *etc.* 8°. Nürnberg, 1856.

In Die deutschen Mundarten, Jahrgang 3, pp. 387-391. Pp. 389-391, 60
proverbs. [B.M.

2092. ———: Sprichwörter und Redensarten. Aus dem Munde
des Volkes in Niederösterreich, *etc.* 8°. Wien, 1862.

In Wiener Schulkalender für das Jahr 1862. Some 300 entries.

2093. Zaupser (Andreas). Versuch eines baierischen und ober-
pfälzischen Idiotikons, *etc.* (Nachlese . . . Erste Abtheilung,
etc.). 2 vols. 8°. München, *Lentner*, 1789.

Vol. 1, pp. 89-93, Baierische und oberpfälzische Sprüchwörter. Vol. 2, pp.
48-51, Noch einige in Baiern und der obern Pfalz gewöhnliche Sprüchwörter.
[B.M.

15. SAXONY.

2094. Bergmann (Joseph). Deutsche Sprichwörter und Redensarten des Erzgebirges.   8°. 1887.
In Erzgebirgs-Zeitung, Nr. 11-12.

2095. Freytag (Ernst Richard). Sachsens geschichtlich-geo-
graphische Sprichwörter und geflügelte Worte, *etc.* pp. vi,
94.   8°. Leipzig, *Wunderlich*, 1898.

2096. Goepeert (Ernst). Die Mundart des sächsischen Erzgebirges, *etc.* pp. viii, 119.   8°. Leipzig, *Veit*, 1878.
Pp. 93-95, Sprichwörter : pp. 95-102, sprichwörtliche Redensarten.   [B.M.

2097. Haase (K. Eduard). Sprichwörter aus der Grafschaft Hohn-
stein.   8°. Lunden, 1892, 1894.
In Am Ur-Quell, Bd. 3, pp. 165-166, and Bd. 5, pp. 255-257.   [B.M.

2098. Haltrich (Josef). Zur Volkskunde der Siebenbürger Sachsen. In neuer Bearbeitung herausgegeben von I. Wolff.
                              la. 8°. Wien, *Graeser*, 1885.
Pp. 341-406, Sprichwörter, sprichwörtliche Redensarten, *etc.* Classified by
subjects; many examples.   [F.-L.S.

2099. Koehler (Johann August Ernst). Volksbrauch, Aber-
glauben, Sagen und andere Ueberlieferungen im Voigtlande,
etc. pp. vi, 652.   8°. Leipzig, *Fleischer*, 1867.
Pp. 337-348, Bauernregeln, Sprichwörter und sprichwörtliche Redensarten,
Räthsel.   [B.M.

2100. Kriebitzsch (Carl Theodor). Siebensachen zu den stilisti-
schen Uebungen der Schule, *etc.* pp. viii, 267.
                              8°. Berlin, *Stubenrauch*, 1867.
Pp. 30-112, proverbs and proverbial phrases.

2100a. Schlauch (G.). Sachsen im Sprichwort.   M.3. 1905.

16. OBER- UND NIEDER-LAUSITZ.

(Lusatian Wends.)

2101. Altmann (Julius). Die Sprichwörter der lausitzischen
Serben.   8°. Bautzen, *Schmaler*, 1857.
In Jahrbücher für slawische Literatur, *etc.*, Bd. 2, pp. 34-52. A commen-
tary containing a large number of examples.   [B.M.

2102. Buk (Jakub). 1000 serbskich přisłowow a přisłownych pra-
jidmow. pp. 60.   8°. Budyšinje, 1862.
Bernstein, 445.

2103. Haupt (Leopold) and **Schmaler** (Johann Ernst). Pjesnički
hornych a delnych Łužiskich Serbow. . . . Volkslieder der
Wenden in der Ober- und Nieder-Lausitz, *etc.* [Illustrated].
2 vols.   la. 4°. Grimma, *Gebhart*, 1841-1843.
Gratet-Duplessis, 882. Vol. 2, pp. 188-206, Wendische Sprichwörter (199)
with German translations.

2104. Klix (F. F.). Oberlausitzer Sprichwörter und sprichwörtliche Redensarten. 4°. 1869.
In Bautzener Nachrichten, 1869.

2105. Wehle (Jan Radyserb). Sprichwörter und sprichwörtliche
Redensarten der oberlausitzer Wenden, *etc.* pp. xiv, 314.
8°. Bautzen, Freiberg i. S., 1902.

17. SILESIA.

2106. Arvin ( ). Zu den schlesischen Sprichwörtern und
Redensarten. 8°. Glogau, *Flemming*, 1882.
In Schlesische Provinzialblätter, Neue Folge, Bd. 1, pp. 567-570.

2107. Langer (Ernst). Sprüchwörter-Chronik, enthaltend über
1000 schlesische Sprichwörter und Redensarten, *etc.* pp. 39.
8°. Wüstegiersdorf, *Jacob*, 1879.
Proverbs arranged alphabetically; no notes. [B.M.

2108. Peter (Anton). Volksthümliches aus Österreichisch-
Schlesien, *etc.* pp. xiv, 458.
8°. Troppau, *Selbstverlage des Verfassers*, 1865.
Pp. 443-454, Sprichworte, sprichwörtliche Redensarten und Verwandtes.
[B.M.

2109. Pfeiffer (Friedrich). Breslauische Sprichwörter.
8°. Nürnberg, 1856.
In Die deutschen Mundarten, Jahrgang 3, pp. 241-253, 408-419. [B.M.

2110. Robinson (Michel). Curieuse Sammlung von Tausend in
Schlesien gewöhnlichen Sprichwörtern und Redensarten.
8°. Leyden, *Peter von der Linden*, 1726.
Gratet-Duplessis, 791, thinks this may well be the same as the anonymous
2111.

2110a. Rother (K.). Die schlesischen Sprichwörter und Redensarten. pp. xvi, 476. M.25. 4°. Breslau, 1928.
A collection of over 20,000 proverbs.

2111. Sammlung. Sammlung von Tausend schlesischen Sprichwörtern. 8°. Breslau, 1725.
Gratet-Duplessis, 790.

2112. Strusche (H.). Schlesische Sprüchwörter, Redensarten und
Ausdrücke. 8°. Breslau, *Trewendt*, 1866.
In Schlesische Provinzialblätter, Neue Folge, Jahrgang 5, pp. 428-429.
[B.M.

2113. Trull (Ernst). Oall'rhand Schnötzla. Gedichte und
Sprüche in schlesischer Mundart und schlesische Sprüchwörter. pp. 228, xxvi. 8°. Freudenthal, *Krommer*, [1911].

2114. Walde (Philo vom). Schlesien in Sage und Brauch, *etc.*
pp. xii, 160.   8°. Berlin, *Senff*, [1883].

Pp. 155-157, some 50 proverbs.   [B.M.

2115. Wander (Carl Friedrich Wilhelm). Sammlung schlesischer
Sprichwörter.   8°. Glogau, *Flemming*, 1862.

In Schlesische Provinzialblätter, Neue Folge, Bd. 1, pp. 287-291, 680-685.

[B.M.

SWISS.

2116. Amateur. Recueil de morceaux choisis en vers et en prose, en patois, . . . Recueillis par un amateur. pp. viii, 212, lx.
12°. Lausanne, *Corbaz*, 1842.

Gratet-Duplessis, 383. Contains principally 59 " Proverbes en patois vaudois ou roman " with French translation. At various other places in the book there are other small collections of proverbs from French Switzerland; most of these are taken from the French, and very few can be considered peculiar to Switzerland. [B.M.

2117. Aucourt (d'). Chants et dictons ajoulots.
8°. Zürich, 1898.

In Schweizerisches Archiv für Volkskunde, Bd. 2, pp. 152-158. [F.-L.S.

2118. Bridel (Philippe Syriach). Glossaire du patois de la Suisse Romande. . . . Avec . . . une collection de proverbes, *etc.*
pp. xiii, 547. 8°. Lausanne, *Bridel*, 1866.

Mémoires et documents publiés par la Société d'Histoire de la Suisse Romande, Tome 21. Pp. 530-544, proverbs. [B.M.

2119. Chenaux (J.) and **Cornu** (J.). Una panerâ de revi fribordzey. Proverbes patois du canton de Fribourg et spécialement de la Gruyère, recueillis par J. Chenaux, et suivis de comparaisons et rapprochements par J. Cornu.
8°. Paris, *Vieweg*, 1877.

In Romania, 6e année, pp. 76-114. Pp. 85-86, list of authorities. [U.C.L.

2120. Courthion (L.). Dictons et devinettes en usage au val de Bagnes. 8°. Zürich, 1898.

In Schweizerisches Archiv für Volkskunde, Jahrgang 2, pp. 240-244.
[F.-L.S.

2121. Gilliéron (Jules). Patois de la Commune de Vionnaz (Bas Valais), *etc.* pp. 196 + map. 8°. Paris, *Vieweg*, 1880.

Bibliothèque de l'École des Hautes Études, fasc. 40. Pp. 119-128, proverbs. Many of the proverbs are similar to those published by J. Chenaux and J. Cornu in Romania, Tome 6. [B.M.

2122. Hoermann (Ludwig von). Haussprüche aus den Alpen.
pp. xxiv, 201. 32°. Leipzig, *Liebeskind*, 1890.
[B.M.

2123. Keller (Walter). Indovinelli, proverbi, filastrocche e canti popolari ticinesi. la. 8°. Basel, 1928.

In Schweizerisches Archiv für Volkskunde, Bd. 28, pp. 106-18. 102 examples : Ticinese dialect and Italian translation in parallel columns.

[F.-L.S.

2124. Kirchhofer (Melchior). Wahrheit und Dichtung. Sammlung schweizerischer Sprüchwörter, *etc.* pp. viii, 366.

8°. Zürich, *Orell, Füssli*, 1824.

Proverbs classified by subject. Explanatory notes are given to the first section of historical proverbs. [B.M.

2125. Leonhardi (G.). Sprachliche Mittheilungen.

4°. Schaffhausen, 1858-60.

Various articles in Die Schweiz, Jahrgang 1-3.

2126. ———: xii Sprichwörter religiösen und moralischen Inhalts, die in Brusio und Poschiavo gebräuchlich sind.

8°. Schaffhausen, 1858.

In Die Schweiz, Jahrgang 1, p. 234.

2127. Patois. Le patois neuchâtelois. Recueil de dictons et de morceaux en prose et en vers. Neuchâtel, 1896.

2128. Rueb (J. A.). Sprüchwörter und Redensarten. Aus dem Frickthal und Hauensteinschen. 4°. Schaffhausen, 1859.

In Die Schweiz, Jahrgang 2, p. 184. 50 entries.

2129. Schild (Franz Joseph). Der Grossatti aus dem Leberberg, *etc.* 2 Bde.

16°. Biel, *Steinheil*, Grenchen, *Selbstverlag des Verfassers*, 1864-73.

Bd. 1, pp. 56-119, Bd. 2, pp. 19-62, proverbs, sayings, weather rules, *etc.*, with occasional notes. [B.M. (Bd. 1).

2130. Schmid (Th.). Sprichwörter und Redensarten (Aargau).

4°. Schaffhausen, 1860.

In Die Schweiz, Jahrgang 3, p. 144. 22 entries.

2131. Singer (S.). Alte schweizerische Sprichwörter. pp. 33.

8°. Basel, 1916.

2132. Sprichwörter. Schweizerische Sprichwörter und Redensarten. 4°. Schaffhausen, 1858.

In Die Schweiz, Jahrgang 1. 147 proverbs contributed by various people.

2133. Sulzer (Felix). Schweizerische Sprichwörter und Redensarten. Kanton Schaffhausen. 4°. Schaffhausen, 1859.

In Die Schweiz, Jahrgang 2, p. 168. 55 entries.

2134. Sutermeister (Otto). Die schweizerischen Sprichwörter der Gegenwart in ausgewählter Sammlung. pp. xi, 152.

8°. Aarau, *Christen*, 1869.

[B.M.

2135. Tobler (Titus). Appenzellischer Sprachschatz. Eine Sammlung appenzellischer Wörter, Redensarten, Sprichwörter, Räthsel, Anekdoten, *etc.* pp. lviii, 464.

8°. Zürich, *Orell, Füssli*, 1837.

No separate list of proverbs. [B.M.

2136. Tscheinen (M.). Walliser Sprichwörter. Aus einem Manuskript von M. Tscheinen in Grächen.

8°. Zürich, *Cotti*, 1897.

In Schweizerisches Archiv für Volkskunde, Jahrgang 1, p. 162. 10 proverbs.

[F.-L.S.

TYROLESE.

2137. Hauser (Christian). Sprüche und sprichwörtliche Redensarten aus Paznaun. 8°. Berlin, *Asher*, 1897.

In Zeitschrift des Vereins für Volkskunde, Jahrgang 7, pp. 199-202.

[U.C.L.

2138. Hoermann (Ludwig von). Mythologische Beiträge aus Wälschtirol, mit einem Anhange wälschtirolische Sprichwörter, *etc.* 8°. Innsbruck, *Wagner*, 1870.

Also with the title of "Contribuzioni mitologiche del Tirolo italiano, con un' appendice di proverbi e canti popolari italo-tirolesi." *In* Zeitschrift des Ferdinandeums für Tirol und Vorarlberg. . . . Dritte Folge, pp. 209-244.

2139. ———: Volkstümliche Sprichwörter und Redensarten aus den Alpenlanden, *etc.* pp. xxi, 165.

32°. Stuttgart, Berlin, *Cotta*, 1913.

A good and interesting little book, principally dealing with Tirol. [B.M.

2140. Menghin (Alois). Aus dem deutschen Südtirol, *etc.* pp. 171. 8°. Meran, *Plant*, 1884.

Pp. 152-157, Sprüche, Regeln, Redensarten und Namen. [B.M.

2141. Waldfreund (J. E.). Einige Sprichwörter und Redensarten, im Unterinnthal gesammelt. 8°. Nördlingen, 1859.

In Die deutschen Mundarten, Jahrgang 6, pp. 33-39. [B.M.

RHAETO-ROMANIC AND LADIN VALLEYS.

2142. Alton (Giovanni). Proverbi, tradizioni ed aneddoti delle valli ladine orientali, con versione italiana. pp. 146.

8°. Innsbruck, *Wagner*, 1881.

Pp. 22-54, 452 Ladin proverbs classified as in Giusti's book, with modifications. There are proverbs both in the dialect of Gardena and that of Fassa, as well as more general ones; each is accompanied by an Italian translation. There are a few brief notes, chiefly philological. [B.M.

2143. Andeer (P. Justus). Ueber Ursprung und Geschichte der rhaeto-romanischen Sprache. pp. viii, 138.

8°. Chur, *Hitz*, 1862.

Pp. 52-54, Rhaeto-Romanic proverbs compared with Spanish and Italian ones. [B.M.

2144. Boehmer (Eduard). Churwälsche Sprichwörter.

8°. Strassburg, *Trübner*, 1876.

In the author's Romanische Studien, Bd. 2, pp. 157-209. In all, some 500 proverbs with German translations. [B.M.

2145. Brentari (Ottone). Guida storico-alpina di Belluno, Feltre, Primiero, Agordo, Zoldo. pp. viii, 406.

L.5. 16°. Bassano, *Sante Pozzato*, 1887.

P. 114, proverbs of Primiero on rain, snow and thunder, taken from an article by Fortunato Fratini, *q.v.*, **2153** : p. 247, proverbs of Livinallongo (Ladino).

2146. Buehler (J. A.). Collecziun de proverbis rhaeto-romanschs. pp. 93. 8°. Cuera, *Casanova*, 1888.

In Annalas della Sociedad Rhaeto-Romanscha, Ann. 3, pp. 3-93. A large collection arranged alphabetically, without notes. [B.M.

2147. C. (M.). Reglas da moralitat a prudienscha cun proverbis, las amprimas en prosa, ils auters en riema . . . tras M. C. pp. 18. 8°. Coira, 1812.

91 moral rules followed by as many maxims or proverbs in rhyme. These are sometimes attributed to Matthias Conradi. [B.M.

2148. Cavalli (Jacopo). Reliquie ladine, raccolte in Muggia d'Istria, *etc.* pp. 208. 8°. Trieste, *Caprin*, 1893.

Pp. 150-162, 226 proverbs and sayings.

2149. Condrau (Placidus).   Cudisch instructiv pella giuventegna catolica, *etc.*   2 części.   8°.   Mustér, *Condrau*, 1857.

Część 1, pp. 164-169, 160 proverbs.   [B.M.

2150. Conradi (Matthias).   Praktische   deutsch-romanische Grammatik, *etc.*   pp. xiv, 176.
                              8°.   Zürich, *Orell, Füssli*, 1820.

Pp. 83-85, einige Sprichwörter in versen.   [B.M.

2151. Cudasch.   Prüm cudasch da scuola per ils infaunts nel Chantun Grischun, *etc.*   pp. 294.
                              8°.   Coira, *S. Benedict*, 1833.

Pp. 292-294, Massimas mixtas in cuorts proverbis (35).

2152. Decurtins (Caspar).   Rätoromanische Chrestomathie, *etc.*
   In progress.   8°.   Erlangen, *Junge*, 1888, *etc.*

Bd. 2, pp. 161-169 : Bd. 4, pp. 1005-1014 : Bd. 6, pp. 1-3 : Bd. 9, pp. 283-288 : Bd. 10, pp. 683-697, 1099-1104 : Bd. 11, pp. 167-176, 246-252.   [B.M.

2153. Fratini (Fortunato).   Le valli di Primiero e di Canal S.
   Bovo.   Trento, *Ditta Sottochiesa*, 1885.

In Annuario degli Alpinisti Tridentini, An. 11.   Proverbs of Primiero on snow, rain and thunder.   These were reprinted by Brentari in his " Guida storico-alpina di Belluno, *etc.*," *q.v.*, **2145.**

2154. Guidotti (T.).   Collecziun da proverbis rhaeto-romanschs.
                              8°.   Palermo, 1891-92.

In Archivio per lo studio delle tradizioni popolari, Vols. 10 and 11.   783 entries.

2155. Heinrich (Giachem).   Il pitschen lectur, *etc.*   pp. 81.
                              12°.   Cuoira, *Sutter*, 1845.

Pp. 78-81, Alchüns proverbis romauntschs (48).   [B.M.

2156. Lectura.   Amprima lectura par la giuventegna da scola e'gl Cantun Grischun, *etc.*   pp. 288.   8°.   Cuêra, *Barmier*, 1834.

Pp. 286-288, Doctrinas maschadadas par uffonts en curtas sententias.   35 proverbs.

2157. Pasqualigo (Christoforo).   Proverbi di Primiero.
                              8°.   Palermo, 1885.

In Archivio per lo studio delle tradizioni popolari, Vol. 4, pp. 253-258.   47 proverbs.   [B.M.

2158. Proverbi.   Proverbi.
             60 kl.   8°.   Dispruk, *Union dei Ladins*, 1915.

In L Kalënder ladin per l ann 1915, *etc.*, pp. 83-85, 123-124.   [B.M.
   See also Italian, Local (Trentino, Venezia, Friuli, Istria).

ITALIAN.

GENERAL.

2159. A. and **C.** Frasario, ossia raccolta e spiegazione di voci, frasi eleganti e proverbi; con appendice di componimenti varii pubblicati per cura di A. e C. pp. 104.
L.0.75. 16°. Torino, Roux e Favale, 1878.

2160. Abbecedario. Abbecedario con una raccolta di massime, proverbi, e favole morali. 8°. Milano, *Marelli*, 1786.
Another edition. 8°. Milano, *Agnelli*, 1822.

Pitrè, 2394-96. There are several works with this or a similar title, mostly for the use of schools.

2161. Abbicì. Abbicì dei fanciulli, con una raccolta di massime, proverbi, favole morali, aneddoti, ed esempi.
16°. Modena, Rossi, 1867.

2162. Adimari (Alessandro). Sonetto in proverbi.
8°. Londra [Lucca e Pisa], 1775.
[B.M.

2163. Ajello (Luigi). Massimi e proverbii morali, raccolti ed ordinati da un' uomo di garbu, *etc.* pp. 32.
16°. Mazzara, Ajello, 1854.

736 maxims and proverbs arranged under arbitrary subject headings. Order not alphabetic. Another edition, spoken of on the back of the title page as possibly forthcoming, was never published.

2164. Alberti (Leonora de). Proverbs in Italian and English, *etc.* pp. 103. 32°. London, *Hill*, [1920].

Proverbs arranged alphabetically by the Italian, with English translations and equivalents on the opposite page. No notes. [B.M.

2165. Albitès (Felice Coën). Bussola per lo studio pratico della lingua italiana . . . contenente idiotismi, proverbi, *etc.* pp. 299. 8°. Londra, *etc., Treuttel, Wurtz, etc.*, 1831.

Pp. 11-55, idiotismi e proverbi. With French equivalents. [B.M.

2166. Alfabeti. Tre alfabeti esemplari de' sapienti filosofi antichi, ne' quali si contengono molti documenti, sentenze, proverbi, *etc.* pp. [24]. 12°. Ferrara, *Baldini*, 1588.
Three series of proverbs, *etc.*, in verse.

2167. Alfabeto. L'alfabeto moderno nello quale con bellissimi proverbi si dimostra il viver d'hoggi, *etc.* pp. [viii].

12°. n.d.

Stirling Cat., 3.

2168. Alfani (Augusto). Proverbi e modi proverbiali scelti ed annotati da A. Alfani. pp. xvi, 327.

L.1. 8°. Torino, *Tipografia Salesiana*, 1882.

Second edition. 60 centesimi. 24°. [Torino?], 1890.

Biblioteca della Gioventù italiana, Vol. 157. Proverbs classified by subjects, with explanatory notes. Illustrations of some 30 proverbs conclude the book.

[B.M.

2169. ———: Scene e ritratti. Dialoghi in lingua e modi proverbiali parlati. pp. 228. 8°. Firenze, *Cellini*, 1870.

2170. Almanacco. Almanacco dei giuochi di conversazione per ogni classe di persone ed età per l'anno bisestile 1872. pp. 160. 50 centesimi. sm. 16°. Venezia, Trieste,

Coen, [1872?].

Contains 150 Italian and 138 Venetian proverbs.

2171. ———: Almanacco proverbiale per l'anno 1868. pp. 160.

75 centesimi. 16°. Bergamo, *Sonzogni*, 1867.

Pitrè, 2425.

2172. Altieri (Ferdinando). Gramatica inglese per gl'Italiani. . . . In questa nuova edizione molto accresciuta, *etc.* pp. iv, 332. 8°. Livorno, *Fantechi*, 1754.

Pp. 321-326, Italian and English proverbs : pp. 327-328, sententious sayings, also in Italian and English. The 1750 edition of this book does not contain the proverbs.

2173. Armonia. Armonia con suavi accenti del novo fior di virtu. Raccolto da diversi autori. Nel quale si contiene per ordine d'alfabeto, molti proverbi, sententie, motti e documenti morali. Con molti amaestramenti, *etc.* pp. 12.

12°. Modona [end of 16th century].

Another edition. 12°. Lucca, *Bertini*, 1826.

Also in Giornale di Erudizione, Vol. 3, Nos. 7 and 8, 1891, p. 116. Pitrè gives five other editions. [B.M. (1826 edition).

2174. Azzocchi (Tommaso). Vocabolario domestico della lingua italiana. . . . Seconda edizione . . . con aggiunta di una raccolta di . . . proverbi. pp. xi, 204.

8°. Roma, *Monaldi*, 1846.

Pp. 185-end, proverbs in alphabetical order with some Latin comparisons and some notes.

2175. B. (G.). Proverbi e massime di G. Dr. B. pp. 8.

8°. Mantova, *Eridi Segna*, 1871.

2176. Baccini (Giuseppe). Gente allegra Iddio l'ajuta ovvero proverbi, burle, aneddoti e curiosità letterarie, *etc.* pp. 255.
32°. Firenze, *Salani*, 1887.

Pp. 9-32, 36 proverbial phrases taken from the works of various authors.

2177. Baldini (Vittorio). Selva di varie sententie, proverbi, documenti, e detti notabili di V. Baldini, *etc.* ff. 6.
12°. Vicenza, *Perin Libraro e Giorgio Greco compagni*, 1585.

2178. Bambagiuoli (Graziolo). Trattato delle volgari sentenze sopra le virtù morali, *etc.* pp. xii, 42.
8°. Modena, *Eredi Soliani*, 1821.
Another edition. Modena, 1865.

2179. Banchieri (P. Adriano). Novella di Cacasenno, *etc.*
See **2216.**

2180. ———: Il scacciasonno, . . . curiosita copiosa di novelle, rime, motti, proverbi, ecc. con variati ragionamenti comici. [By Camillo Scaliggeri della Fratta, *pseud.* Banchieri].
8°. Bologna, *Magnani*, 1623.
Another edition. pp. 94.   12°. Venetia, *Salvadori*, 1637.

2181. ———: Trastulli della villa . . . dove si leggono novelle, moteggi, sentenze, proverbi, essempi, paradossi. . . . Curiosità drammatica di Camillo Scaliggeri della Fratta.
[*First edition?*].   sm. 8°. Venezia, 1617.
Another edition. pp. [8], 416.
sm. 8°. Bologna, *Mascheroni*, 1627.
Another edition. pp. [16], 336. 8°. Venetia, *Giuliani*, 1627.

Gratet-Duplessis, 423. Pitrè, 2455, shows differences in the Bologna edition. A collection of anecdotes, *etc.*, of all kinds. There are very few proverbs, but the book is worth including for the sake of some observations on the origin and value of certain proverbial sayings which, possibly, are not to be found elsewhere. Written in several Italian dialects. A rare book.

2182. Barbieri (Giuseppe). Opere, Vol. 1. Sermoni. Terza edizione con aggiunte. pp. [xii], 186.
8°. Firenze, *Tipografia Chiari*, 1828.

Pp. 131-136, proverbi. The eighteenth discourse is almost entirely composed of proverbs.

2183. Barosso (Pier Antonio). Proverbj e detti proverbiali . . . con gli equivalenti latini. pp. 90.
8°. Torino, *Presso l'Editore*, 1837.

The proverbs are arranged alphabetically by the Italian, with the Latin equivalents beneath. No notes.   [B.M.

2184. Barra (Giovanni). Barra Giovanni. L'anno del divertimento, cioè proverbi, racconti e moralità secondo i giorni dell'anno, raccolti dal suddetto e pubblicati per cura di Lorenzo Vacca. 2 vols.
    sm. 8°. Napoli, *Tipografia San Giorgio de' Genovesi*, 1864.

2185. Barthe (H.) and **Dujob** (C.). Proverbi italiani, *etc.* pp. 104.   32°. Angers, n.d.

2186. Belisario da Cingoli. Barzeleta de Messer Faustino da Terdosio in laude de la pecunia e le autorita de Salomone in frotola de Belisario da Cinguli. Con alquanti sonetti artificiosi, opra nova. ff. 8.   8°. Venezia, *Zopino*, [15—].
A collection of proverbs, belonging to the first half of the 16th century.

2187. Beltrame (Oreste). Proverbi-stornelli. 4°. Torino, 1888.
In Il Giovedì, Anno 1, Nos. 27, 29, 30, 45, 46, 50. 60 proverbs.

2187a. Bembo (Pietro). Motti inediti e sconosciuti di M. Pietro Bembo, pubblicati e illustrati con introduzione da Vittorio Cian. pp. 107.   L.2. 8°. Venezia, *Merlo*, 1888.
Cian studies the authenticity and particular characteristics of these motti. At the foot of p. 24 are notes of great interest for comparative paremiology.

2188. Bencivenni (Ildebrando). Cento proverbi del nonno illustrati con brevissime favolette, dialoghi e racconti morali, *etc.* pp. 112.   la. 8°. Firenze, 1874.
Another edition, enlarged. Proverbi illustrati, *etc.* pp. 146.
   L.1. 16°. Torino, *Ufficio del giornale Il Maestro elementare italiano*, 1878.
Another edition. Cento proverbi del nonno, *etc.* pp. 111.
   L.0.40. 16°. Firenze, *Salani*, 1893.
A proverb is placed at the head of each tale and repeated at the end.

2189. Berruti (Giuseppe). Aforismi e proverbi dedicati alla gioventù. pp. 80.   L.1. 16°. Torino, *Bersezio*, 1874.

2190. Bertoldo Trilogy. *See* **2216.**

2191. Biancardi (Sebastiano). Raccolta di proverbii, parabole, sentenze . . . cavati dalla Sacra Scrittura, tradotti in verso endecasillabo.   8°. Venetia, 1740.
Gratet-Duplessis, 444.

2192. Bissi (Benedetto). Proverbj, motti, e sentenze ad uso ed istruzione del popolo. pp. 140.   8°. *Orcesi*, 1805.
The proverbs, *etc.*, are paraphrased in Italian verse. From the preface, pp. 3-7, it would seem that Bissi is the author.

2193. Bondi (Clementino). Saggio di sentenze e proverbi, epigrammi ed apologhi serî e scherzevoli. pp. 64.
    8°. Milano, *Stella*, 1817.

2194. Buoni (Tomaso). Lettere argute . . . piena di proverbi e sentenze morali per ammaestramenti della vita. pp. xxii, 304.   12°. Venetia, *Guarisco*, 1603.

2195. ————: Nuovo thesoro degli proverbi italiani. . . . Ove con brieve espositione si mostra l'origine e l'uso accomodato loro: distinto in sei capi. pp. [xl], 398.

4°. Venetia, *Ciotti*, 1604.

Another edition. pp. [xl], 398.

8°. Venetia, *Giunta, Ciotti*, 1610.

Gratet-Duplessis, 416, quotes considerable extracts from the book. Pp. 1-7 contain a discourse on the excellence of proverbs. The proverbs are explained and illustrated with anecdotes and commentaries.   [B.M. (1610 edition).

2196. ————: Seconda parte del thesoro del gli proverbii italiani. . . . In cui si dichiara l'origine, et uso loro, con espositione delle cose naturali, delle historie et favole, *etc.* pp. [xxiv], 376.   sm. 8°. Venetia, *Ciotti*, 1606.

Pitrè, 2513, gives this as sm. 4°. Gratet-Duplessis, 416.   [B.M.

2197. Buontempone, *Dr.* Evviva. Raccolta di brindisi per tutte le occasioni, *etc.* pp. 128.

12°. Trieste, *Tipografia italiana*, 1864.

Pp. 119-126, proverbs. Other editions of this were published, notably one with the name of the author as Prof. Giovale : Napoli, 1888, and another, with many alterations, as :

Raccolta di brindisi, sonetti, proverbi e poesie per tutte le occasioni . . . per cura di Armando Dominicis. pp. 126. sm. 16°. Firenze, *Salani*, 1892. Pp. 89-99, 156 proverbs.

2198. Caglià-Ferro (Antonino). I proverbi illustrati. Tesoro di lingua e di popolare sapienza, *etc.* pp. xvi, 296.

8°. Messina, *Tipografia dell' Avvenire*, 1883.

Proverbs in alphabetical order with explanations.

2199. Calleri (Celestino). Il paradiso dei bambini. [Illustrated]. pp. 222.   8°. Milano, *Agnelli*, 1886.

Contains some 80 proverbs.

2200. Cantù (Ignazio). Sanità e industria, racconti di un medico di villagio, *etc.* pp. 160.

16°. Milano, *Tamburini e Valdoni*, 1843.

Cap. 5, Letture popolari : i proverbi, *etc.*

2201. Capecelatro (Enrichetta). Proverbii dichiarati ai fanciulli per mezzo di racconti. pp. 226. 16°. Roma, *Voghera*, 1879.

Second edition. pp. 172.   8°. Milano, *Carrara*, 1880.

2202. Capra (Luigi). Sapienza volgare. Sentenze proverbiali popolari, illustrate da osservazione e racconti. Parte prima.

2ª edizione. pp. iv, 116.   16°. Torino, *Speirani*, 1890.

Pp. i-iv, Sapienza volgare. 34 proverbs, 17 of which were previously published in various numbers of Il Giovedì.

2203. Carcano (D. Francesco). Capitoli piacevoli d' autore occulto, la prima volta pubblicati.

4°. Utrecht [Milano?], 1785.

Pitrè, 2537. Pp. 1-21, De' proverbi. This is also, presumably, the book referred to by Gratet-Duplessis, 448, and Pitrè, 6080.

2204. Castagna (Niccola). I proverbi dell' Ariosto, tratti dal poema e illustrati da N. Castagna. pp. 46.

L.1. 8°. Ferrara, *Taddei*, 1877.

63 proverbs.

2205. Castro (Giovanni de). Proverbi italiani, illustrati a cura di G. de Castro, con un discorso di Niccolò Tommaseo. pp. xi, 238. 8°. Milano, *Sanvito*, 1858.

38 proverbs explained and illustrated by various authors, preceded by a brief essay on proverbs in general. [B.M.

2206. Chwatal (A. R.). Proverbi e sentenze morali raccolti e tradotti. Italienische Sprüche gesammelt und übersetzt. pp. 79. 8°. Magdeburg, *Faber*, 1887.

2207. Collana. Collana di racconti, proverbii, sentenze e detti ameni ed istruttivi. 7ª edizione, con aggiunte. pp. 128.

L.0.20. 16°. Udine, *Patronato*, 1885.

Nona edizione, con nuove aggiunte. pp. 156.

20 centesimi. 24°. Venezia, *Cordella*, 1890.

2208. Cornazano (Antonio). Antonii Cornazani, Placentini, novi poetae facetissimi : quod de proverbiorum origine inscribitur ; *etc.* pp. [4], lviii.

4°. Mti [Milani], per *Petrum martirem de Mantegatiis*, 1503.

Another edition. 4°. Milano, *Gerardo da Ponte*, n.d.

Gratet-Duplessis, 395. Contains 9 Italian proverbs and 1 Latin, described in elegiac Latin verse. Four of these proverbs are reproduced in the same author's Proverbi in facetie. Very rare. [B.M. (1503 edition).

2209. ———— : Proverbi in facetie.

8°. Venetia, *Bindoni*, 1518.

Another edition. [48 leaves].

8°. Venetia, *Nicolo Zopino de Aristotile*, 1525.

Another edition. pp. x, 164.

12°. Parigi, *Didot maggiore*, 1812.

Another edition. Proverbs in jests, *etc.* pp. xxiii, 216.

12°. [Paris], *Liseux*, 1888.

Gratet-Duplessis, 395, and Pitrè, 2595-2618, both give many other editions. 1518 is the first edition, and 1525 the best. Duplessis gives the 1812 one as the best of the later editions. The book is a collection of extremely free and licentious tales, each headed by a proverb which serves as text. Duplessis gives half a page to the question of the Pontifical privilege supposed to have been given to this book. [B.M. (various editions).

R

2210. Costo (Tomaso). Il fuggilozio di Tomaso Costo diviso in otto giornate, *etc.*   8°.   Napoli, *Carlino et Ant. Pace*, 1596.
Another edition.   12°.   Venetia, *Pittoni*, 1688.

Gratet-Duplessis, 412, speaks of an edition of 1600 as the earliest then known. This book is a collection of tales, anecdotes, jests, *etc.*, containing at the end a table of all the sentences and proverbs to be found in the work. Duplessis gives more detailed information.   [B.M. (various editions).

2211. Cowper (Frederick Augustus Grant).   Italian folk tales and folk songs. pp. viii, 165.
          8°.   Chicago, Illinois, *University of Chicago Press*, [1923].
University of Chicago Italian Series. Pp. 107-112, proverbs. 120 entries, without either notes or translations.   [F.-L.S.

2212. Crecchio (Alessandro da).   Scelta di proverbi morali italiani, *etc.* pp. 47.   12°.   Roma, *Monaldi*, 1863.
Another edition. pp. 48.
                    16°.   Bovino, *Tipografia Diocesana*, 1873.
1190 proverbs, arranged alphabetically.

2213. Crivelli (Giuseppe).   Un po' di tutto di tutti per tutti, ovvero scelta raccolta di adagi, proverbi, motti, sentenze, massime, *etc.* pp. 136.
                    L.2.50.   32°.   Pavia, *Marelli*, 1878.
Pitrè, 2644, also mentions an edition of 1877.

2214. Croce (Giulio Cesare).   Selva di esperienza nella quale si sentono mille e tanti proverbi, *etc.* pp. [30].
                    12°.   Bologna, *Cochi*, 1618.
Another edition.   8°.   Bologna, 1628.
A collection of proverbs, in alphabetical order.   [B.M. (1628 edition).

2215. ———— : Il tre, *etc.*   Bologna, *Benacci*, 1614.
Another edition.   [4 leaves].
                    sm. 8°.   Bologna, Trevigi, *Righettini*, 1627.
Gratet-Duplessis, 422. Pitrè gives various other editions. A book of proverbs, maxims, familiar sayings, *etc.*, concerning or including the number " three."

2216. ———— and **Banchieri** (P. Adriano).   Le sottilissime astutie di Bertoldo, *etc.* pp. [79].
                    12°.   Firenze, Pistoia, [1600?].
Another edition. pp. 48.   16°.   Venezia, 1838.
Le piacevoli et ridiculose semplicità di Bertoldino, *etc.* pp. 56.   8°.   Bologna, *Verdi*, 1608.
Another edition. pp. 64.
                    8°.   Lucca, *Marescandoli*, [1825?].
Novella di Cacasenno . . . dal sign. Camillo Scaliggeri dalla Fratta [*pseud.* of Banchieri], *etc.*   12°.   Bologna, [1750?].
Another edition. pp. 48.   8°.   Todi, [1830?].
Gratet-Duplessis, 442. The first two works are by Croce, the third by

Banchieri : all have been translated into many languages. The principal characters talk in proverbs and apophthegms, after the manner of Sancho Panza : the third is the least interesting of the three, and the least rich in proverbs. The Lucca edition contains all three. [B.M. (various editions).

Bertoldo con Bertoldino e Cacasenno, in ottava rima, con argomenti, allegorie, ed annotazioni. [Illustrated]. pp. 346, 128. 4°. Bologna, *Della Volpe*, 1736.

Another edition. 3 vols. 12°. Bologna, 1741.

Another edition. 3 vols.
18°. Bologna, *Fratelli Masi*, 1822.

Gratet-Duplessis, 442. The best editions are those of 1736 and 1741, the latter having a translation into Bolognese dialect. This poem is a poetic paraphrase of the "Bertoldo trilogy," and composed by a society of Bolognese men of letters. It is accompanied by full and interesting notes (by Dr. Barrotti) on the numerous proverbs found in the work. It is chiefly by reason of these notes that the poem has a place in this bibliography. Duplessis gives full information on this poem. [B.M. (1736 and various editions).

2217. Dalmedico (Angelo). Della fratellanza dei popoli nelle tradizioni comuni, *etc.* pp. 48. 8°. Venezia, *Cecchini*, 1881.

Pp. 44-48, similar proverbs in various Italian dialects, French, English and German. [B.M.

2218. Dialogo. Dialogo nel quale si contengono varii discorsi, di molte belle cose e massimamente de proverbi, de risposte pronte et altre cose simili. . . . D'incerto autore. ff. 30.
8°. Padova, *Perchacino*, 1561.

Gratet-Duplessis, 407. Mentioned by Gamba in his "Delle novelle italiane in prosa," p. 141. Contains discussions on various proverbs. [B.M.

2219. Domenichi (Lodovico). Facecies, et motz subtilz, d'aucuns excellens espritz et tresnobles seigneurs. En françois et en italien. 64 leaves.
sm. 8°. Lyon, *Grandjon*, 1559.

Another edition. pp. 205. 16°. Lyon, *Rigaud*, 1597.

French and Italian in two columns. The last four leaves are "motz subtilz," or proverbs. [B.M. (1559 edition).

2220. Doni (Antonfrancesco). I marmi del Doni, Academico Peregrino. 4 parts. 4°. Vinegia, *Marcolini*, 1552.

Another edition. 2 vols. 8°. Firenze, *Barbèra*, 1863.

Dialogues, *etc.*, containing many proverbs, ancient and modern. [B.M.

2221. ——— : La zucca del Doni. [Illustrated]. 4 vols.
8°. [Vinegia, *Marcolini*, 1551-1552].

Another edition. 8°. Venetia, *Bissuccio*, 1607.

Gratet-Duplessis, 404. Not a book of proverbs, but many are given in it at the foot of various anecdotes, and the book is useful as showing the meaning of a number of early Italian proverbs. There were many editions, and a Spanish translation in the same year as the original. Duplessis gives long notes. [B.M. (1551 edition).

2222. Du Bois de Gomicourt (Jacques). Sentenze e proverbi
italiani cavati da diversi autori . . . portati in francese, *etc.*
pp. xiv, 206.
         8°. Roma, *per M. Eriole a spese di F. Pesaretti*, 1679.
Another edition, in French. pp. [vi], 199.
            8°. Lyon, *Boudet*, 1702.
Gratet-Duplessis, 438. In alphabetical order by the Italian. Particularly
full of those with a moral teaching. No notes.   [B.M. (1679 edition).

2223. Duez (Nathanael). Le guidon de la langue italienne. Avec
. . . une guirlande de proverbes, *etc.* pp. 286.
         8°. Leyden, *Elsevier*, 1641.
Another edition. pp. 256.   8°. Amsterdam, 1670.
The garland of proverbs is the well-known letter in proverbs of Arsiccio
Intronato [*q.v.* under Vignali (A.)].   [B.M. (1670 edition).

2224. Dulcis (Catharinus). Italicae exercitationes, *etc.* pp. 208.
         12°. Patavii, *Bertellius*, 1613.
Pp. 6-10, Aurearum sententiarum centuria una : pp. 129-208, Proverbia
Italica, Latino idiomati data.

2225. ——— : Schola Italica. . . . Editio altera, *etc.* pp. 124,
799.   8°. Francoforti, *Musculus*, 1616.
Another edition.   8°. Francofurti, 1620.
Pp. 185-205, Scholae Italicae renovatae selectissimarum sententiarum centuriae v. An alphabetical list of proverbs, maxims, *etc.*   [B.M.

2226. Eco d'Italia. L'eco d'Italia. Eine Sammlung italienischer
und deutscher Gespräche und Redensarten . . . sowie auch
der gebräuchlichsten Idiotismen und Sprichwörter, *etc* pp.
151.   8°. Pesth, 1844.
Another edition. pp. 151.   8°. Leipzig, *Haendel*, n.d.
Gratet-Duplessis, 460. An elementary book, possibly useful to students, but
without any literary importance. Pp. 28-31, Proverbi italiani—Italienische
Sprichwörter.

2227. F. (A.). Frasario comparato italiano francese . . . Coll'
aggiunta di cento proverbi. pp. 64.
      80 centesimi. 8°. Mantova, *Mondovì*, 1890.
Pp. 60-64, proverbs with French translations.

2228. Fabricius (Johann). Elementa linguae italicae, *etc.*
         12°. Altorfi, 1688.
Gratet-Duplessis, 436. Pp. 166-188, Ghirlanda di varii fioretti e proverbi
italiani.

2229. Fabritii (Aloyse Cynthio degli). Libro della origine delli
volgari proverbi.
     fol. Venezia, *Maestro Bernadino e Matho
de i Vitali fratelli*, 1526.
Gratet-Duplessis, 396. A similar work to Cornazano's; the author explains
in a series of extremely free tales, written in verse, the origin of 45 proverbs.
A very rare book. For further details see Duplessis and Pitrè (2686). [B.M.

2230. Fanfani (Pietro). Prima centuria di proverbi e motti italiani d'origine greca e latina. pp. 126. *First edition.*
L.1. 8°. Firenze, *Direzione delle Letture di Famiglia*, 1878.

Another edition. Cento proverbi e motti d'origine greca e latina. pp. 64. 8°. Milano, 1906.

These proverbs were also published in various periodicals. [B.M.

2231. ———: Proverbi illustrati. Firenze, 1854.

In L'Industriale, 1854.

———: Firenze, 1880.

In Letture di Famiglia, Nos. 26, 28-30.

2232. Fano (Giovanni Pietro Rodolfo). Proverbia italica et latina. . . . His accesserunt nonnullae sententiae et in calce cujusque litterae phrases proverbiales. pp. 395.
8°. Pisauri, *Concordia*, 1615.

Gratet-Duplessis, 419. Pitrè (2756) says the author's name is possibly Giovanni Pietro Rodolfi *of Fano.*

2233. Feri (Michele). Nuovo metodo breve, curioso, e facile per imparare . . . la lingua franzese. . . . Terza edizione, *etc.*
pp. 365. 8°. Venise, *Pavin*, 1707.

Pp. 255-286, Recueil de proverbes. Italian proverbs with French equivalents.

2234. Ferrara (Mario). Per la storia del proverbio nel secolo xvi. Frate Benedetto da Firenze e la sua "Divisio Proverbiosa."
pp. iv, 20. Lucca, *Tip. Editrice Lucchese*, 1925.

2235. Filippi (D. A.). Italienische Sprachlehre . . . Zwölfte . . . Original-Auflage. pp. x, 580. 8°. Wien, *Heubner*, 1829.

Pp. 363-385, einige der vorzüglichsten italienischen Sprichwörter und sprichwörtlichen Redensarten. Italian proverbs with German equivalents.

2236. ———: Le nouveau maître italien. . . . Troisième édition. *etc.* pp. xxiv, 501. 8°. Vienne, *Camesina*, 1805.

Pp. 277-286, proverbes les plus remarquables de la langue italienne.

2237. Filippi (P. A. de). Praktischer Lehrgang . . . der italienischen Sprache, *etc.* pp. 198.
8°. Wien, *Jasper*, 1846.

Bernstein, 1111. Pp. 79-116, Italian proverbs and proverbial phrases with German equivalents.

2238. Fiori (Annibale). Manuale di conversazione italiana e tedesca. . . . Sesta edizione, *etc.* pp. xxii, 488.
8°. Stu'tgart, *Neff*, 1887.

Pp. 286-300, Italian and German proverbs.

2239. Florio (Giovanni). Florio his first fructes: which yeelde familiar speech, merie proverbes, wittie sentences, and golden sayings, *etc.* ff. 163.

4°. London, *for Thomas Woodcocke*, 1578.

Gratet-Duplessis, 421. Chap. 18, sentences divine and profane. Chap. 19, proverbs Italian and English. [B.M.

2240. ———: Le verger des colloques recreatifs . . . en langue françoise et italienne, par Gomes de Trier, gentilhomme malinois. pp. [viii], 249, 6. 4°. Amsterdam, 1623.

Gratet-Duplessis, 421, thinks this is probably a mere translation of Florio's "First fructes." Pitrè, 2780, also includes it under Florio. The twelve dialogues of which it is composed were also included in Wodroephe's "Spared houres of a souldier in his travels." In any case, it contains a great number of Italian proverbs.

2241. ———: Florio's second frutes, . . . to which is annexed his Gardine of Recreation yeelding six thousand Italian proverbs. 4°. London, *Woodcock*, 1591.

Gratet-Duplessis, 411. The "Second Frutes" alone does not contain any special list of proverbs, though a number are quoted in one of the dialogues, pp. 95-105. [B.M.

2242. ———: Giardino de ricreatione, nel quale crescono fronde, fiori e frutte vaghe, leggiadre e soaui, sotto nome di sei miglia proverbii, *etc.* 4°. Londra, *Woodcock*, 1591.

Gratet-Duplessis, 411. 6150 Italian proverbs arranged alphabetically without notes. This is really the second part of Florio's "Second Frutes," and is the Gardine of Recreation mentioned in the title. [B.M.

2243. ———: Le jardin de récréation, auquel croissent rameaux, fleurs et fruicts . . . sous le nom de six mille proverbes, et plaisantes rencontres françoises, recueillies et triées par Gomes de Trier. 4°. Amsterdam, *Ravesteyn*, 1611.

Gratet-Duplessis, 265, says this is an unacknowledged translation of the last entry. It is therefore in reality an Italian collection, though included by Duplessis among the French.

2244. ———: Vocabolario italiano ed inglese. . . . Whereunto is added a dictionary English and Italian . . . by Giovanni Torriano. fol. London, 1659.

Another edition. fol. London, *Sawbridge*, 1688-7.

Gratet-Duplessis, 427. The book concludes with "An appendix of some few choice Italian proverbs with the English to them." [B.M.

2245. Fornasari-Verce (A. J. de). Cours théorique et pratique de la langue italienne, *etc.* pp. viii, 508. *Second edition.*

8°. Vienne, *Volke*, 1826.

Fourth edition. pp. vi, 376. 8°. Vienne, *Volke*, 1843.

Contains a selection of Italian proverbs translated into French.

2246. Franceschi (Enrico Luigi). In città e in campagna. *Third edition.* pp. xxvi, 588. 8°. Torino, *Giuseppe*, 1874. *Eighth edition.* pp. xxiv, 639.

la. 16°. Torino, *Giuseppe*, n.d.

Dialogo 34 is on proverbs, of which 44 are given. This dialogue does not occur in the first edition. [B.M.

2247. Franceschi (Giulio). Proverbi e modi proverbiali italiani. pp. 380. 8°. Milano, 1908, [1907].

[B.M.

2248. Franciosini (Lorenzo). Grammatica spagnuola ed italiana, in questa seconda impressione arricchita . . . alla quale . . . ha l'autore aggiuntovi otto dialoghi castigliani e toscani, con mille detti politici e morali, *etc.* 2 vols.

8°. Roma, *Stamperia del R. Cam. Apostolica*, 1638.

Another edition. 2 pts. 8°. Genevra, 1707.

Another edition of the dialogues. Dialogos apazibles, compuestos en Castellano, y traduzidos en Toscano.

sm. 8°. Geneva, *Chouet*, 1687.

Gratet-Duplessis, 426. The dialogues contain many Spanish proverbs with explanatory notes showing where they differ from the Italian ones. The " political and moral sayings " at the end of the dialogues also contain many maxims and proverbs in Italian and Spanish. There is a French translation of these dialogues by Cesar Oudin, *q.v.*, **1390.** They are not included in the edition of 1624; there were many separate editions of them. [B.M.

2249. Frencia (Giuseppe). Espressioni naturali e familiari . . . con un' aggiunta in fine di proverbi e detti arguti, *etc.* pp. 416. 8°. Torino, *Reycends e Soffietti*, 1792.

This edition is also to be found dated 1793.

2250. Freund (Leonhard). Aus der italienischen Spruchweisheit. Parömiologische Skizzen.

8°. Leipzig, *Frankenstein & Wagner*, 1892.

In Zeitschrift für Volkskunde, Bd. 4, pp. 172-174, 215-217, 265-269, 314-326, 377-386. [B.M.

2251. Fumagalli (Giuseppe). Bibliografia paremiologica italiana, *etc.* 8°. Palermo, *Lauriel*, 1887.

Originally published in the Archivio delle tradizioni popolari, Vols. 5 and 6. A good bibliography comprising 408 entries. Revised and continued up till 1889 in the Archivio delle tradizioni popolari, Vol. 10. Some few copies of this were published separately.

2252. Garnier (Philippe). Quatro dialogi. . . . Ultima editione, *etc.* pp. 232. 8°. [Lyons], *Giouan di Tornes*, 1627.

Pp. 179-227, an alphabetical list of proverbs. [B.M.

2253. Gatti (G. M.). and **Grünwald** (V.). Piccola raccolta di proverbi italiani comparati coi corrispondenti tedeschi, *etc.* pp. 69. 16°. Livorno, *Belforte*, 1892.

650 proverbs, Italian on one page and German on the other. Many of these were previously published in different numbers of " La lingua tedesca."

2254. Ghedini Bortolotti (Fanny). Proverbi spiegati al popolo.
First edition. pp. 175. 8°. Milano, *Agnelli*, 1863.
Second edition. pp. 152. 16°. Milano, *Treves*, 1869.
Proverbs of a moral or educational character.

2255. Gialongo (Vincenzo). Saggio di proverbi illustrati in verso.
pp. 13. 8°. Palermo, *Bizzarrilli*, 1878.

2256. Giani (Leopoldo Carlo Massimiliano). Sapienza italiana in
bocca alemanna . . . Italienische Sprichwörter, *etc.* pp. viii,
359. 8°. Stoccarda, *Neff*, 1876.
1882 entries. Italian and German. [B.M.

2257. Giannone (Vicenzo). La scuola di comuneglia, ossia pro-
verbi e sentenze morali, *etc.*
L.1.20. 16°. Milano, *Agnelli*, 1878.
Second edition, enlarged. pp. 191. 16°. Milano, 1889.
Pp. 13-64, 855 proverbs, including maxims and phrases.

2258. Giovanetti, *Abate.* Raccolta di proverbi e frasi francesi
uniti alle loro correspondenti italiane, *etc.* pp. 176.
8°. Firenze, 1810.
Gratet-Duplessis, 453.

2259. Giovannetti (Pietro). Massime e proverbi di un eremita.
. . . 2ª edizione con aggiunta.
Napoli, *Tip. del Tintorello*, [1886].

2260. Gloria (Andrea). Volgare illustre nel 1100 e proverbi volgari del 1200. pp. 89. 8°. Venezia, *Antonelli*, 1885.
Pitrè, 2835. 178 proverbs of Geremia da Montagnone in vulgar *pavano* of the
second half of the 13th century. They were also published in the " Atti del
R. Istituto Veneto di Scienze, Lettere ed Arti," tomo 3, serie 6, disp. 2.

2261. Gradi (Temistocle). Proverbi e modi di dire dichiarati con
racconti, *etc.* pp. 108. 12°. Firenze, *etc.*, *Paravia*, 1869.
Pp. 7-73, explanations and illustrations of various proverbs, *etc.* [B.M.

2262. Guicciardini (Lodovico). Detti et fatti piacevoli, *etc.*
8°. Venetia, 1685
L'hore di recreatione, *etc.* 8°. Anversa, 1583.
Another edition, Italian-French-German.
obl. 12°. Cölln, 1624.
English translation. The garden of pleasure, *etc.*
8°. London, 1573.
" L'hore di recreatione " differs very little from " Detti e fatti piacevoli.'
Both contain a selection of proverbs and maxims from Piovano and Boccaccio;
translations are given in the English version. Numerous other editions. [B.M.

2263. Humières (d'). Recueil des proverbes italiens.
Paris, 1800.

2264. Jagemann (Christian Joseph). Italiänische Sprachlehre . . . Dritte . . Auflage. pp. xvi, 552.

8°. Leipzig, *Vogel*, 1811.

Pp. 510-521, proverbi e modi proverbiali.

2265. Juliani (   ), *Sieur.* La nomenclature et les dialogues familiers. . . . Les proverbes divertissans, *etc.* 2 pts.

sm. 8°. Paris, 1641.

Another edition. La nomenclature, dialogues, proverbes et heures de récréation, *etc.* 2 pts.   12°. Paris, 1648.

Another edition. La nomenclature, et les dialogues familiers, *etc.* 2 pts.   12°. Paris, *Loyson*, 1668.

Gratet-Duplessis, 428. It is not certain if this is the correct title of the 1641 edition : Duplessis merely mentions it as an earlier edition, without giving details. Part 2 : Les proverbes divertissans, *etc.*, contains a large number of Italian and French proverbs, which Duplessis considers without merit or unimportant.   [B.M.

2266. Kornmann (Heinrich). Enucleatae questiones complectentes perjucundum tractatum de virginum statu ac jure, *etc.*

sm. 12°. Norimbergae, *Ziegerus*, 1679.

Another edition. Tractatus de virginitate, virginum statu et jure, *etc.*   12°. Norimbergae, *Ziegerus*, 1706.

Gratet-Duplessis, 434. Forms Part 4 of Kornmann's Opera curiosa. Contains a number of proverbial sayings in Latin, on the women of various Italian towns, under the title : " De variis virginum, in variis Italiae locis, dotibus et vitiis externis." Duplessis reproduces the proverbs in full, p. 267. This work was also republished with two others, under the title : Sybilla Trig-Andriana, *etc.* sm. 8°. Coloniae, 1765.   [B.M.

2267. Kradolfer (J.). Das italienische Sprichwort und seine Beziehungen zum deutschen, *etc.*

8°. Berlin, *Dümmler*, 1877.

In Zeitschrift für Völkerpsychologie und Sprachwissenschaft, Bd. 9, pp. 185-271.   [B.M., U.C.L.

2268. Landini Ruffino (Elena). Fiori e spine. Proverbi illustrati per fanciulli. pp. 112.   8°. Roma, *etc.*, *Páravia*, 1886.

33 entries. Bernstein, 1824. Pitrè, 3256, calls the authoress Ruffino Landini.

2270. Lena (Francesco). Saggio di proverbi o detti sententiosi italiani e latini, raccolti da diversi autori. pp. [xii], 528.

sm. 12°. Lucca, *Paci*, 1674.

Second edition. Proverbi italiani e latini, *etc.* pp. 666.

12°. Bologna, *Longhi*, 1694.

Gratet-Duplessis, 433. A large collection of Italian proverbs arranged alphabetically and accompanied, not by translations, but by equivalent Latin sentences or proverbs. An excellent, though rare and little-known book.   [B.M.

2271. Lizio-Bruno (L.). Da un piu lungo scritto intorno ai popolari proverbi.   4°. Napoli, *De Angelis*, 1873.

In La Scuola Italica, *etc.*, Anno 1, No. 7, pp. 76-77.

2272. Logan (Walter Macgregor). Raccolta di proverbi italiani. . . . Collection of Italian proverbs, with a literal translation into English, *etc.* pp. 59. 12°. London, 1830.
Stirling-Maxwell, 55. [B.M.

2273. Lorenzo, *da Volturino, Minorite.* La scienza pratica. Dizionario di proverbi e sentenze, *etc.* pp. 701.
4°. Quaracchi, *Bonaventura*, 1894.
Arranged alphabetically by the principal words. [B.M.

2274. Luciani (Tomaso). Raccolta di proverbi e modi di dire.
1889.
In Pro patria nostra, fasc. 7.

2275. Mandalari (Mario). I proverbi del Bandello. pp. 206, ii, 8. 8°. Catania, *Giannotta*, 1900.
A collection of maxims, sayings and proverbs from the novels of Matteo Bandello, collected and commented on by M. Mandalari. [B.M.

2276. Manuzio (Paolo). Phrases italicae in singolis Pauli Manuti: parœmiis, scolasticis, *etc.* pp. 232.
sm. 8°. Venetiis, *Rosco*, 1603.
Gratet-Duplessis, 413. Pitrè and Duplessis differ somewhat in their spelling of the title.

2277. Marinoni (Pietro). Sylva proverbiorum et sententiarum, *etc.* Patavii, *Frambotto*, 1675.
Another edition. pp. 48. 16°. Bassani, *Remondini*, 1694.
Contains Italian and Latin proverbs.

2278. Marzano (G. B.). Proverbi in uso nel Mandamento di Laureana di Borrello. pp. 156.
8°. Monteleone, *Raho*, 1895.
Bernstein, 2100.

2279. Ménage (Gilles). Le origini della lingua italiana, compilate dal signor Egidio Menagio, gentiluomo francese. Colla giunta de' modi di dire italiani, raccolti, e dichiarati dal medesimo. *First edition.*
4°. Parigi, *Marbre-Cramoisi*, 1669.
Another edition. pp. [viii], 519, 34, [25].
fol. Geneva, *Chouët*, 1685.
Gratet-Duplessis, 435. The Modi di dire, pp. 1-34, contain the explanation of some of the more remarkable Italian proverbs. This edition is more complete than the first. [U.C.L. (1685 edition), B.M.

2280. Menghini (Mario). Antichi proverbi in rima. pp. 15.
8°. Bologna, *Fava e Garagnani*, 1891.
Taken from two old manuscripts.

2281. Merbury (Charles). A briefe discourse of royall monarchie. . . . A collection of Italian proverbs, *etc.*
4°. London, *Vautrollier*, 1581.
A large collection of proverbs with occasional translations. [B.M.

2282. Migne de Marolles (   ). Lettre au sujet du livre intitulé: Origine delle volgari proverbi di Aloyse Cynthio degli Fabritii, Vinegia, 1526.   Paris, 1856.

Reprinted from L'Esprit des Journaux, septembre, 1780, pp. 213-226. [B.M.

2283. Mitelli (Giuseppe Maria). Proverbi figurati, *etc.* 48 plates.
                                          fol.   Bologna, 1678.
Proverbi gia figurati e misteriosi.   Viterbo, 1678.

Gratet-Duplessis, 431. Illustrated proverbs. There are other collections of the same sort by the same author. A rare book.

2284. Monosinius (Angelus). Floris italicae linguae libri novem . . . ubi . . . conferuntur plus mille proverbia et explicantur. In quatuor ultimis enodatae sunt pro uberiori copia ad tres adagiorum chiliades, *etc.* pp. xx, 434, 62.
                  4°. Venetiis, *apud Jo. Guerilium*, 1604.

Gratet-Duplessis, 415. A rare and interesting book, said by Duplessis to be the most important treatise on their proverbs which the Italians possess. Italian, or more particularly Tuscan, proverbs compared and contrasted with Greek and Latin ones. Duplessis gives full notes and a long extract in order to show the scope of the book. There are other editions, the first being a sm. 8°, n.d., bearing the name of Henri Estienne.   [B.M.

2285. Morandi (Felicita). I proverbi della zia. pp. 81.
             12°. Milano, *Le Prime Letture*, 1872.
Fourth edition. pp. 151.   8°. Milano, *Carrara*, [1885].

2286. Mueller (Wilhelm). Egeria, raccolta di poesie italiane popolari, cominciata da Guglielmo Müller, . . . terminata e pubblicata da O. L. B. Wolff. pp. xviii, 262, + 8 of music.
             8°. Lipsiæ, *Fleischer*, 1829.

Gratet-Duplessis, 457. A collection of popular poems, songs, *etc.*, in various Italian dialects, which would be greatly improved by fuller notes. Pp. 113-117, proverbi italiani; p. 222, proverbi piemontesi; p. 227, proverbi sardi; p. 245, Adagi siciliani. Also, La nuova tramutazione delle canzon de proverbi, composta da me Paolo Britti, *q.v.* **2407.** This last item is reprinted by Duplessis, pp. 278-280.   [B.M.

2287. Muelmann (Johann). Raccolta d' ingeniosissimi proverbi e sentenze, *etc.* pp. 114.   12°. Lipsiæ, *Voigt*, 1678.

Gratet-Duplessis, 432, says it is an alphabetical list of small importance.
                                               [B.M.

2288. National Proverbs. National proverbs: Italy. pp. 91.
             1/-. 8°. London, *Palmer*, [1913].
Proverbs in Italian with English translations. No notes.   [F.-L.S.

2289. Ninni (A. P.). Ribruscolando. pp. 190.
             12°. Venezia, *Longhi e Montanari*, 1890.
Bernstein, 2351. Pp. 17-28, 111-121, Proverbi.

2290. Novati (Francesco). Le serie alfabetiche proverbiali e gli alfabeti disposti nella letteratura italiana de' primi tre secoli.

8°. Torino, 1890, 1891.

In Giornale storico della Letteratura italiana, Anno 8, Vol. 15, pp. 337-401; and Anno 9, Vol. 18, pp. 104-147. Vol. 15 contains a long general introduction, and Vol. 18 the texts. [B.M.

2291. Ogobbio (Carlo Gabrielli d'). Insalata mescolanza, *etc.* pp. [vi], 376. 4°. Bracciano, *Fei*, 1621.

Contains many Italian proverbs.

2292. Opera. Opera quale contiene le diece tavole de proverbi, sententie, detti, e modi di parlare, *etc.* [36 leaves].

sm. 8°. Turino, *per Martino Cravoto*, 1535.

Another edition. 8°. Roma, *Antonio d'Asola*, 1536.

Gratet-Duplessis, 399. A rare and curious little volume. Some of the proverbs are accompanied by brief explanations. [B.M.

2293. Operetta. Operetta nella quale si contengono proverbii, sententie, detti, et modi di ragionare, *etc.* [24 leaves].

8°. [Venice, 1530?].

Another edition. 8°. San Polo, 1546.

Gratet-Duplessis, 398, quotes two verses from the back of the title page. An alphabetical list of proverbs, unimportant philologically, but interesting since it shows what proverbs were current in Italy at the beginning of the 16th century. Amongst them are several which are not to be found in more recent collections. Pitrè, 3063, *etc.*, regards this merely as another edition of **2292,** but Duplessis treats them separately, though admitting that the Opera embodies a great deal of the Operetta. [B.M.

2294. Origine. Origine dei proverbi e varietà. Almanacco per l'anno 1822. pp. 126. 12°. Milano, *Pirola*, [1821].

2295. Orlandi (Venerio). Il giovinetto filologo. pp. 183.

L.1.50. sm. 8°. Torino, *Loescher*, 1879.

Second edition, enlarged. pp. xi, 168.

L.2. 16°. Città di Castello, *Lapi*, 1889.

Illustrates 156 proverbs and sayings.

2296. P. (G. A.). Cinquanta sentenze proverbiali recate in versi italiani. pp. 16. 8°. Venezia, *Merlo*, 1869.

Bernstein, 3369.

2297. Paravicino (Pietro). Choice proverbs and dialogues in Italian and English, *etc.* 4°. London, 1660.

Another edition. 2 pts. 8°. London, 1666.

A readable and interesting booklet throwing much light on contemporary habits. [B.M.

2298. Pardini (Angelo). Novelle e proverbi illustrati. pp. 196.

L.1.25. 16°. Milano, *Trevisini*, 1883.

Another edition. pp. 190. 8°. Milano, *Trevisini*, 1891.

2299. Pasetti (Antonio Maria). Proverbi notabili, sentenze gravi, documenti morali, et detti singolari . . . accommodati in rime. pp. 586. sm. 12°. Ferrara, *Baldini*, 1610.

Gratet-Duplessis, 417, calls this a moral poem containing nearly all the popular proverbs and maxims in use in Italy. Fumagalli, however, says it is of no importance for parœmiology. [B.M.

2300. Pasquarelli (Michele). Inchiesta psicologica traverso ai proverbi. Napoli, 1892.

In L'Anomalo, Febbraio-Marzo, 1892.

2301. Passarini (Ludovico). Modi di dire proverbiali e motti popolari italiani, *etc.* [By Pico Luri di Vassano, anagram of L. Passarini]. 8°. Firenze, 1873.

In La Unità della Lingua, Anno 4, Nos. 14, 15, 17-20. [B.M.

2302. ———: Saggio di modi di dire proverbiali e di motti popolari italiani, spiegati e commentati da Pico Luri di Vassano. pp. iv, 355. L.3.50. 8°. Roma, *Sinimberghi*, 1872.
Another edition. pp. viii, 629.
L.12. la. 8°. Roma, *Tip. Tiberina*, 1875.

The later edition is much fuller than the first. Pitrè, 3089-96, gives in each case a list of the principal headings. A continuation of these proverbial sayings was published in Il Propugnatore, Tom. 12-16, 18. Gives the explanation of many obscure proverbs. [B.M.

2303. Pavanello (Michele). Proverbi, riboboli, e detti proverbiali, *etc.* pp. xii, 72, 72, 72.
8°. Vicenza, *Rossi*, 1794-1796.

Gratet-Duplessis, 451. The aim of the author was to instil, by means of proverbs, a number of moral ideas into the heads of children. There are 437 of these sayings, accompanied by appropriate passages from the poets or the philosophers. [B.M.

2304. Pazzaglia (Gio. Antonio). Ingresso al viridario proverbiale, *etc.* pp. 398. 8°. Hannovera, *Freytag*, 1702.

Gratet-Duplessis, 439. Proverbs with German translations.

2305. Pellegrini (Antonio). La guida dell' uomo nel mondo, tracciata da una collezione alfabetica di proverbi classificati per ordine di materie, *etc.* 4 vols.
8°. Padova, *Tip. Liviana*, 1846-47.

2306. Pera (Francesco). Cento proverbi italiani commentati . . . e illustrati con figure, *etc.* pp. xii, 160.
8°. Firenze, *Bemporad*, 1899.

Bernstein, 4615.

2307. Pescetti (Orlando). Proverbi italiani. *First edition.*
Venetia, 1598.

Another edition. Proverbi italiani, raccolti, e ridotti sotto a certi capi, e luoghi communi per ordine d'alfabeto, *etc.* pp. [22], 286. 12 °. Venetia, *Spineda*, 1629.

Gratet-Duplessis, 414. Arranged under subjects. Pitrè, 3108-17, gives many other editions, but that of 1603 quoted by Duplessis and later ones are better arranged and fuller than the first. This book was republished almost wholly, in the " Florilegium ethico-politicum " of Gruter, *q.v.* **80.** An excellent collection, with notes explaining the meaning of some obscure proverbs, but with no indication of origin, *etc.* [1629 edition, F.-L.S. (Stephens collection).

2308. Pescetti (Orlando). Proverbi italiani e latini. *First Edition.*
12°. Verona, *F. dalle Donne*, 1602.

Another edition. Proverbi italiani, e latini, per uso de' fanciulli, che imparan grammatica, raccolti, *etc.* pp. [92].
12°. Venetia, *Spineda*, 1629.

Another edition. pp. 92. 12°. Trevigi, *Righettini*, 1673.
Gratet-Duplessis, p. 245. [1629 edition, F.-L.S. (Stephens collection).

2309. Petrarca (Francesco). Sentenze, massime e proverbj estratti dalle rime di Messer Francesco Petrarca, con annotazioni di E[mmanuele] C[estari]. pp. 40.
16°. Venezia, *Clementi*, 1838.
[B.M.

2310. Picchianti (Francesco). Proverbi italiani ordinati e illustrati da Francesco D'Ambra [*pseud.* of F. Picchianti]. pp. 459. 16°. Firenze, *Salani*, 1886.

Proverbs, mostly taken from such collections as Giusti's and Pasqualigo's, either Italian or italianised : classified by subjects. The " Proverbi attiladi novi et belli," *etc.*, *q.v.* **2319,** are given in an appendix. There are occasional notes. [B.M.

2311. Pitrè (Giuseppe). Bibliografia delle tradizioni popolari d'Italia. . . . Con tre indici speciali. pp. xx, 603.
4°. Torino, Palermo, *Clausen*, 1894.

Pp. 177-257, bibliography of Italian proverbs. Later additions are also to be found in Varia, pp. 506-517, and Appendix, pp. 464-475. A most valuable and scholarly work containing over 1000 entries concerning proverbs. [U.C.L.

2312. Pizzigoni (Carlo). Petit recueil de proverbes italiens avec leurs correspondants français, *etc.* pp. 173.
16°. Milano, *Guigoni*, 1868.

2313. Poggiali (Cristoforo). Proverbi, motti e sentenze ad uso ed istruzione del popolo. Centurie xxiv. *First edition.*
12°. Piacenza, *Orcesi*, 1805.
Another edition. pp. 192. L.1. 16°. Codogno, *Cairo*, 1881.
In rhyme.

2314. ———: Scelta di motti, sentenze e proverbi. pp. 112.
16°. Parma, *Paganino*, 1830.
Bernstein, 2624. 1000 entries.

2315. Polesi (Giacomo). Dictionnaire des idiotismes italiens-français et français-italiens, contenant tous les proverbes, *etc.* 2 tom. 8°. Paris, *Baudry*, 1829.
[B.M.

2316. Polidori (Gaetano). Moderna conversazione in diciotto dialoghi. . . . Con una scelta di proverbi, *etc.* pp. 10, 89.
8°. Londra, *Nardini e Dulau*, 1802.

Pp. 79-89, Italian and French proverbs and proverbial phrases.

2317. Proverbi. Alcuni proverbi e modi proverbiali dichiarati. pp. 63. L.2.50. 8°. Babilonia [Naples], 1873.

26 proverbs and proverbial phrases illustrated by a Neapolitan.

2318. ———: I proverbi. Treviso, *Priuli*, 1876.

In L'Archivio domestico, Anno 1, No. 18. An article on the wisdom of popular proverbs. Also reprinted in La Scuola popolare degli adulti, Treviso, 1878.

2319. ———: Proverbi attiladi novi et belli, *etc.* ff. [6].
8°. Venetia, 1586.

Appears also as appendix to **2310.** Reprinted by G. Romagnoli in : Due Opuscoli rarissimi del secolo xvi. 8°. Bologna, 1865. [B.M

2320. ———: I proverbi del buon contadino. Almanacco pel 1832. 12°. Milano, *Silvestri*, [1832?].
Pitrè, 2888.

2321. ———: Proverbi, motti e sentenze ad uso ed istruzione del popolo. 8°. Piacenza, 1805

Gratet-Duplessis, 452. This is probably the same book as Pitrè 6136, which has the same title and is published in Milano, n.d.

2322. ———: I proverbi, ossia le massime e sentenze proverbiali e giornali per l'anno 1804-1808. 4 tom.
8°. Milano, [1808?].
Pitrè, 2895.

2323. ———: Proverbi pei contadini in quattro classi divisi, *etc.*
pp. 30. 8°. Venezia, *Graziosi*, 1790.
Bernstein, 2810.

2324. ———: Proverbi scelti, *etc.* pp. 63.
8°. Milano, *Sonzogno*, 1878.
Biblioteca del Popolo, Vol. 47.

2325. ———: Proverbi, sentenze e canzonette italiani . . . fondata sopra la Sacra Scrittura e i SS. Padri. 2ª edizione corretta e accresciuta. 8°. Palermo, 1738.
Pitrè, 3188.

2326. ———: I proverbi. Strenna pel 1873. Raccolta di 200 tra' migliori proverbi italiani. Anno 1. pp. 11.
30 centesimi. 8°. Napoli, *de Angelis*, 1872.
Anno 2. pp. 11.
50 centesimi. 8°. Napoli, *de Angelis*, 1874.
Pitrè, 2896, 2897.

2327. Proverbi. Proverbi utilissimi et sententiosi, *etc.* pp. 8.
16°. Milano, *Girardone*, n.d.
Gratet-Duplessis, 397.   Very rare.

2328. Proverbii. Proverbii e sentenze ad istruzione del popolo.
pp. 64.   32°. Monza, *Corbetta*, 1843.
Pitrè, 6135.

2329. ———: Proverbii, sententiosi detti e modi di parlare che
oggidi nella commun lingua si usano.
sm. 8°. Roma, *Asola*, n.d.
Another edition, probably later.   8°. Roma, *Blado*, 1536.
Gratet-Duplessis, 401.   Very rare.

2330. Raccolta. Raccolta di massime e proverbi per uso dei
fanciulli. pp. 35.   16°. Livorno, *Mazzajoli*, 1858.
Bernstein, 2920.

2331. ———: Raccolta di proverbi e detti sentenziosi. pp. 120.
32°. Ancona, *Sartori*, [1830].
Bernstein, 2922.

2332. ———: Raccolta di proverbi italiani, *etc.* pp. 22.
16°. [Firenze, *Salani*, 1892].
136 proverbs in alphabetical order, followed by 32 moral maxims.

2333. ———: Raccolta di proverbi, massime, sentenze. Cosa e
meglio? pp. 8.   8°. Cuneo, *Isoardi*, 1885.
Pitrè, 3210.   Each of these proverbs contains the idea of something which
is better than, or preferable to, something else.

2334. Rafaelli (Filippo), *Marchese.* Illustrazione di un antico
codice inedito di proverbi. pp. 11.   16°. Bologna, 1885.
Bernstein, 4652.

2334a. Rampoldi (G.).   I proverbi e le sentenze proverbiali.
Third edition. pp. 562.   8°. Milano, 1852.

2335. Reponse. Bonne reponse a tous propos. Livre . . . auquel
est contenu grand nombre de proverbes et sentences joyeuses
. . . traduit de l'italien en françois.
16°. Paris, *Angelier*, 1547.
Another edition. pp. 164.   12°. Rouen, *Le Villain*, 1610.
Gratet-Duplessis, 402.   Pitrè, 2492-2500.   Italian proverbs with French translations in alphabetical order.   Both bibliographies quote other editions.   No
notes or explanations.

2336. Ricciardi (Giuseppe). Saggio intorno ai proverbi ed osservazioni morali, *etc.* pp. 73.
L.1. sm. 16°. Milano, *Battezzati*, 1881.
Was first published as part of the author's Etica Nuova, in all its editions
from 1863 onwards.

2337. Riminaldo (Orazio). Libra di quattro cose.

Gratet-Duplessis, 505 and p. 130. There are no details of the original of this book available, but it is a collection of maxims and proverbs grouped by fours like the Livre des Quatre Choses, Gratet-Duplessis, 237; it is, however, quite a different book. It was translated into Spanish and published under the title : Destierro de ignorancia, etc. ff. 33. 12°. Barcelona, *Baresson*, 1592. This translation is to be found at the end of many editions of Gracian Dantisco's " Galateo español," which was a free translation of the " Galateo " of Giovanni de la Casa. A good edition is : Galateo español . . . el destierro de ignorancia, etc. pp. viii, 234, 71. 8°. Barcelona, *Piferrer*, 1796.   [B.M.

2338. Ritio (Darinel). Li nomi et cognomi di tutte le provintie et città, et più particolarmente di tutte quelle dell' Italia, etc. ff. [4].   8°.   1585.

Very rare. Proverbial sobriquets. Reprinted by G. Romagnoli in : Due opuscoli rarissimi del secolo xvi. 8°. Bologna, 1685.   [B.M.

2339. Salvini (Antonio Maria). Discorsi accademici, . . . Tomo 11.   Bologna, *Nobili*, 1722.

Another edition. Tomo 3.   4°. Venezia, *Pasinelli*, 1735.

Another edition. Tomo 6.   4°. Napoli, *Orsino*, 1786.

Gratet-Duplessis, 441. One of the discourses, pp. 108-13 in 1735 edition, is entitled " Sopra alcuni proverbi," where the author searches for Greek equivalents of certain Italian proverbs and sayings. This discourse is not included in the edition of 1695.   [B.M.

2340. Scelta. Scelta di proverbi. pp. 90.

                              8°. Milano, *Visaj*, 1831.
Pitrè, 6146.

2341. Schiavo da Bari. I proverbi del Schiavo da Bari ad ammaestrare uno giovine, etc. pp. [viii]. 4°.   n.d.

Another edition. Proverbii. Incominanzo li proverbi de lo Schiavo de Baro, etc. pp. [viii].   4°.   [*circa* 1500].

Another edition. Dottrina del Schiavo di Bari. . . . 2ª edizione.   16°. Bologna, 1863.

A great number of these proverbs were also printed under the title : El savio romano, etc. 4°. n.d.

2342. Serdonati (Francesco). Proverbi inediti, etc. pp. 20.
                              4°. Padova, *Penada*, 1873.

2343. Soave (Francesco). Abbecedario con una raccolta di massime, proverbi e favolette morali, etc. pp. 47.
                              8°. Venezia, *Martini*, 1809.
Pp. 14-17, Massime e proverbi morali.

2344. Sprichwoerter. Italienische Sprichwörter.
                              4°. Bremen, 1858.
In Bremer Sonntagsblatt, 1858, Nr. 14.   [B.M.

2345. Strafforello (Gustavo). Curiosità ed amenità letterarie, etc. pp. xx, 230.   L.3. 8°. Firenze, *Niccolai*, 1889.
Pp. 101-108, Dei proverbi; pp. 126-132, Filosofia dei proverbi russi.
s

2346. Tenca (Carlo). Prose e poesie scelte. 2 vols.
L.10. 8°. Milano, Hoepli, 1888.

Vol. 2, pp. 121-172, proverbi toscani, veneziani, e lombardi. Articles from the " Crepuscolo " à propos of the collections of Giusti, Dalmedico and Samarini. [B.M.

2347. Tiscornia (Francesco). Dei proverbii, ossia della filosofia del popolo: saggio. pp. 32.
30 centesimi. 16°. Roma, Tip. alle Terme
Diocleziane, 1885.

2348. Torriano (Giovanni). The Italian revived, etc. 2 pts.
8°. London, for T. Martyn, 1673.
Another edition. 2 pts.
8°. London, for R. Chiswell, etc., 1689.

Pt. 1, pp. 147-160, 234 Italian proverbs with English translations. [B.M.

2349. ———: Piazza universale di proverbi italiani: or, a common place of Italian proverbs and proverbial phrases, etc. pp. [xx], 338, 242, 115.
fol. London, printed by F. & T. W. for the Author.
[Opposite title page: Imprimatur Robert
L'Estrange], 1666.

Pitrè, 3328. Presumably this is the book indicated by Duplessis, 427. It includes the " Lettera piacevole in proverbi dell'Arsiccio Intronato " [q.v. under Vignali (A.)]. After the Piazza, comes " The proverbial phrases digested in alphabetical order," etc. The whole book is a monument of industry, and abounds in parœmiological and philological interest. [B.M.

2350. ———: Select Italian proverbs, the most significant, etc.
pp. 100. 12°. Cambridge, Daniel, 1642.
Another edition. pp. [viii], 98.
12°. Cambridge, Martin & Ridley, 1649.

Gratet-Duplessis, 424. A curious and rare little book containing a choice of the best Italian proverbs, translated literally into English, and occasionally accompanied by brief, clear notes. Alphabetical arrangement. [B.M.

2351. U. (G.). Voci e maniere di dire proverbiali spiegate da G. U. 12°. Torino, 1878.
Pitrè, 3337.

2352. Varchi (Benedetto). L'Hercolano, dialogo di Messer Bene-detto Varchi nel quale si ragiona delle lingue, etc.
4°. Firenze, Giunti, 1570.
Another edition. Riveduta e illustrata da P. dal Rio. pp. xvi, 750. 8°. Firenze, 1846.

Both Pitrè, 3356-60, and Duplessis, 405, give many other editions. This work contains many curious and interesting observations on languages in general and Italian in particular; incidentally it explains the sense and origin of a great number of proverbs and sayings. [B.M.

2353. Veneroni (Giovanni di). Italiänisch-französisch- und teutsche Grammatica, oder Sprach-Meister, *etc.* pp. [xii], 464. 8°. Franckfurt, Leipzig, *Andrea*, 1713. *Another edition.* pp. 488.
8°. Franckfurt, Leipzig, *Andrea*, 1779.

Contains a list of Italian proverbs with French and German translations or equivalents. The same author's " Maître italien " and " Complete Italian master " also contain lists of proverbs, with French and English translations respectively. [B.M.

2354. Vezù (Antonio). Scielta di nomi, verbi, avverbi, proverbii . . . cavata dall' opere de D. Pietro Marinoni, *etc.*
8°. Bassano, *Remondini*, n.d.

Pp. 81-139, proverbi sacri, proverbi historici, proverbi poetici.

2355. Vienna (Carlo). Florilegio di proloquj, e proverbi italiani, *etc.* pp. 39. L.1. 8°. Belluno, *Tissi*, 1852.

2356. Vignali (Antonio). Alcune lettere amorose ; una dell' Arsiccio Intronato [*pseud.* of Vignali] in proverbj, e l'altre di Alessandro Marzi, *etc.* pp. 24. 4°. Siena, *Bonetti*, 1538.
Another edition. Alcune lettere piacevoli una dell' Arsiccio Intronato, *etc.* pp. 23. 4°. Siena, *Bonetti*, 1571.
Another edition. pp. viii, 54. 16°. Napoli, *Ferrante*, 1864.

Gratet-Duplessis, 408. A letter almost entirely composed of proverbs, interesting and curious but of no real importance. It was also reprinted by Gotti, *q.v.* **2476,** and by several others. [B.M.

2357. Vitalini (Carlo). L'educatore di sè stesso . . . con accurata raccolta di oltre a duecento proverbi, sentenze e detti diversi. pp. [11], 120. 8°. Milano, *Guglielmini*, 1869.

2358. Vocabolario. Vocabolario italiano e latino . . . nei quali si contengono . . . proverbj, *etc.* 2 vols.
4°. Roma, *Roisecco*, 1763.
Pitrè, 3391.

2359. Zappi (Vincenzo). Proverbi in azione, *etc.* pp. viii, 176.
8°. Codogno, *Cairo*, 1881.
Bernstein, 4168.

See also index at end for references to Italian in other sections.

LOCAL AND DIALECT.

1. PIEDMONT.

2360. Azeglio (E. d'). Studi di un ignorante sul dialetto piemontese. pp. 207.
8°. Torino, *Unione tipografico-editrice,* 1886.

Pp. 47-125, proverbs, sayings and proverbial phrases of Piedmont.

2361. Ball (E. A. Reynolds-). Unknown Italy—Piedmont and the Piedmontese. pp. xi, 254. la. 8°. London, *Black*, 1927.
Chapter 2 (pp. 15-20), proverbs and weather-lore.

2362. Canziani (Estella). Piedmontese proverbs in dispraise of woman. 8°. London, 1913.
In Folk-lore, Vol. 24, pp. 91-96. With English translations. See also p. 216, a few Piedmontese calendar and weather sayings in English. [F.-L.S.

2363. ———— and **Rohde** (Eleanour). Piedmont. pp. viii, 204 + 50 plates. la. 8°. London, *Chatto & Windus*, 1913.
Pp. 78-79, Balme weather proverbs in English; pp. 139-140, proverbs in Piedmontese and English. [F.-L.S.

2364. Fernow (C. L.). Piemontesische Sprichwörter.
Zürich, 1808.
In Römische Studien, 3.

2365. Ferraro (Giuseppe). Nuova raccolta di proverbi o detti popolari monferrini. 8°. Palermo, 1886.
In Archivio per lo studio delle tradizioni popolari, Vol. 5, pp. 413-438. [B.M.

2366. ————: Superstizioni, usi, e proverbi monferrini, raccolti ed illustrati da Giuseppe Ferraro. pp. 103.
8°. Palermo, *Lauriel*, 1886.
Curiosità popolari tradizionali, publicate per cura di Giuseppe Pitrè, Vol. 3. Pp. 45-103, proverbs from Monferrato with a few explanatory notes. [U.C.L.

2367. Jachino (Giovanni). Varietà tradizionali e dialettali alessandrine, *etc.* pp. 179.
L.2. 8°. Alessandria, *Jacquemod*, 1889.
Parte 2; v, some 60 proverbs.

2368. Manzone (Beniamino). Norme per raccogliere i proverbi piemontesi. pp. 3. sm. fol. Bra, 1884.

2369. Pipino (Maurizio). Grammatica piemontese.
8°. Torino, *Stamperia reale*, 1783.
Gratet-Duplessis, 464. Pp. 153-197, Raccolta di proverbi e modi proverbiali piemontesi, *etc.* Most of these proverbs are accompanied by Italian translations and brief notes; few of them are peculiar to Piedmont. [B.M.

2370. Rosa (Ugo). Glossario storico popolare piemontese. Dichiarazione di ccx voci, motti locali e locuzioni proverbiali di origine storica. pp. 118.
L.2. 16°. Torino, *Clausen*, 1889.
Pitrè, 3253.

2371. Seves (Filippo). La donna e il matrimonio nei proverbi piemontesi, *etc.* pp. 22. la. 16°. Pinerolo, *Zanetti*, 1893.
108 proverbs collected in the valleys of Pinerolo.

2372. Seves (Filippo).   Proverbi piemontesi.

8°.   Palermo, Torino, 1894.

In Archivio per lo studio delle tradizioni popolari, Vol. 13, pp. 505-518. Also published separately.

[B.M.

See also **2286.**

2. LOMBARDY.

2373. Bolla (Bartolomeo).   Nova novorum novissima, *etc.*

12°.   *Stampatus in Stampatura Stampatorum*, 1670.

Gratet-Duplessis, 429. This forms the second part, with its own title page but with a single continuous pagination, of : Antonius de Arena . . . ad suos compagnones, *etc.* Bolla's work runs from pp. 107-191. It contains, pp. 121-129, Dicta excellentissima de omnibus Italiae nationibus, *etc.*, a series of proverbial sayings characterising different places, and : Versus Bergamasci de Italiae civitatibus.

[B.M.

2374. ———— :   Thesaurus proverbiorum Italico-Bergamascorum rarissimorum et garbatissimorum, *etc.* pp. [140].

8°.   Francofurti, *in officina Bergamascorum,*
apud Ioannem Saurium, 1605.   [Reprinted 1890?].

Gratet-Duplessis, 461. Nopitsch, p. 278, also mentions, without other details, an edition of 1604, 4°, *in officina Bergamascorum.* Proverbs in alphabetical order, each phrase with a Latin translation.

[B.M.

2376. F. (L.).   Mille e settantaquattro proverbi milanesi, *etc.*
pp. 60.   12°.   Milano, *Cioffi,* 1858.

Bernstein, 2812.

2377. Foresti (Lorenzo).   Vocabolario piacentino italiano. Terza edizione, *etc.* pp. xviii, 752. 16°.   Piacenza, *Solari,* 1882.

Pp. 715-752, proverbi piacentini illustrati. These proverbs are frequently compared with others. This section is not in the edition of 1836.

2378. Fumagalli (Giuseppe).   Bartolomeo Bolla da Bergamo e il thesaurus proverbiorum italico-bergamascorum.   pp. 27 [=37].   8°.   Milano, *Tip. Bortolotti,* 1893.

Pitrè, 6094. A study of Bolla's Thesaurus disproving various errors.

2379. Oh Che Rid.   Oh che rid i proverbi Milanes. pp. 31.

12°.   Novara, *Crotti,* 1843.

Verse, in which are included many proverbs : in the Milanese dialect.

2380. Ostiani (Luigi Francesco Fè d').   I proverbi e modi di dire storici e bresciani, *etc.* pp. 16.

40 centesimi. 16°.   Brescia, *Bersi,* 1879.

2381. Pellandini (Vittore).   Proverbi ticinesi raccolti in Arbedo.

8°.   Palermo, Torino, 1898.

In Archivio per lo studio delle tradizioni popolari, Vol. 17, pp. 451-455.

[B.M.

2382. Proverbi.   I proverbi de Meneghin per chi viv in del 1849.

12°.   Milan, 1849.

Pitrè, 2889.

2383. Proverbi. I proverbi milanes. pp. 54.

sm. 16°. Monscia, *Corbetta*, [1840?].

Pitrè, 2894. The proverbs are connected by 140 sextets in the Milanese
dialect.

2384. Raccolta. Raccolta di proverbi milanes, sestinn, e dialogo
di Don Nasone, classicista, con Don Kyrieleison romanticista,
terzine.   16°. Milano, *Vallardi*, 1820.

Gratet-Duplessis, 465. Proverbs in verse, giving a good specimen of Milanese
dialect, and a fairly complete list of the proverbs in use in that part of Lom-
bardy.

2385. Restelli (Eugenio). I proverbi milanesi raccolti, ordinati e
spiegati, *etc.* pp. 243.

L. 1.80. 16°. Milano, *Brigola*, [1885].

Pitrè, 3230. About 2500 proverbs, sayings and phrases, *etc.*

2386. Rosa (Gabriele). Documenti storici, *etc.* pp. 84.

L.1. 12°. Bergamo, *Mazzoleni*, 1850.

Second edition. Dialetti, costumi e tradizioni delle di Bergamo e di Brescia, *etc.* pp. 253.

L.4. 8°. Bergamo, *Pagnoncelli*, 1857.

Terza edizione. pp. 389.   8°. Brescia, *Fiori*, 1870.

Pitrè, 5283-5285. Contains a list of proverbs. The second and third editions
are preferable to the first, as they are much enlarged.   [B.M.

2387. Rotta (Paolo). Raccolta di frasi, proverbi e traslati in
dialetto milanese, *etc.* pp. 163.

8°. Milano, *Riformatorio Patronato*, 1893.

Aggiunta alla raccolta di frasi, proverbi e traslati, *etc.* pp. 48.

8°. Milano, *Riformatorio Patronato*, 1898.

Bernstein, 4662.

2388. Samarini (Bonifacio). Proverbi lombardi raccolti ed illustrati. pp. 464.   8°. Milano, *Guglielmi*, 1858.

Another edition. pp. 464.   8°. Milano, *Brigola*, 1870.

Follows Giusti's scheme of arrangement. Contains 3500 proverbs, but not all
these are truly Lombard. There are many notes and explanations, some clear
and appropriate, others the reverse. An interesting collection, but not as accu-
rate and trustworthy as it should be. Some of the proverbs were later published under the title : " Una manata di proverbi lombardi," in the Strenna
del Orfano. 8°. Como, 1877.   [B.M.

2389. Tiraboschi (Antonio). Proverbi bergamaschi: agricoltura,
economia rurale.   8°. Palermo, 1882.

In Archivio delle tradizioni popolari, Vol. 1, pp. 588-593.

2390. ——— : Raccolta di proverbi bergamaschi, *etc.* pp. 170.

L.2. 16°. Bergamo, *Bolis*, 1875.

Proverbs arranged alphabetically under subjects, with Italian translations
and notes.   [U.C.L.

2391. Vocabolario. Vocabolario bresciano e toscano, compilato
per facilitare . . . il ritrovamenti de' vocaboli, modi di dire e
proverbj toscani a quelli corrispondenti. pp. xliv, 600.

8°. Brescia, *Pianta*, 1759.

Gratet-Duplessis, 463. Contains many proverbial sayings in dialect, with
Italian translations and brief explanations. Melzi, in his " Opere anonime e
pseudonime," asserts that this is really the work of Bartolomeo Pellizzari, in
spite of the fact that it appears to be by some Brescian students. [B.M.

2392. Z. (A.). Aforismi, sentenze, massime, frizzi del paesano
del Mincio. pp. 22. 16°. Mantova, *Eredi Segna*, 1877.

See also **2346.**

3. TRENTINO.

2393. Beltrami (Giovan Pietro). Cento proverbi volgari trentini,
parafrasati e ridotti alla lingua ed al genio maccaronico,
italiano e latino, *etc.* pp. 37.

8°. Trento, *Manauni*, [1870].

2394. Bolognini (Nepomuceno). Proverbi topici tridentini.

8°. Palermo, 1883.

In Archivio per lo studio delle tradizioni popolari, Vol. 2, pp. 132-133. [B.M.

2395. ———: Saggio di proverbi e modi proverbiali tridentini.
pp. 52. 16°. Rovereto, *Tipografia Roveretano*, 1882.

Reprinted from the 8° Annuario della Società degli Alpinisti Tridenti, 1881-
1882.

2396. Lumbroso (Alberto). Napoleone I° nei modi di dire del
Trentino. 8°. Palermo, Torino, 1898.

In Archivio per lo studio delle tradizioni popolari, Vol. 17, pp. 352-353. [B.M.

2397. Zenatti (Albino) and **Zenatti** (Oddone). Una centuria di
proverbi trentini. pp. 16.

8°. Venezia, *Stab. dell'Emporio*, 1884.

See also **2426.**

4. VENEZIA.

2398. Api. Api e vespe. Milano, 1847.

This contains 67 Venetian proverbs put into verse by G. Capparozzo, P.
Canal, G. Veludo, L. Carrer, B. Montanari, and A. R. Z. They were republished by P. Ferrato.

2399. Balladoro (Arrigo). Due centurie di proverbi veronesi.

8°. Torino, 1906.

In Archivio per lo studio delle tradizioni popolari, Vol. 23, pp. 172-183. [B.M.

2400. ———: Folk-lore veronese: proverbi. pp. 176.

8°. Verona, *Franchini*, 1896.

2401. Balladoro (Arrigo). Un mazzetto di proverbi veronesi.
8°. Catania, 1926.

In Il Folklore Italiano, anno primo, fasc. 4, dicembre, 1925, pp. 400-416. Veronese proverbs in alphabetical order, many taken from a manuscript in the Biblioteca Comunale of Verona. [U.C.L.

2402. ———: Proverbi veronesi inediti. Verona, 1904.

2403. Barozzi (Nicolò). Latisana e il suo distretto. Notizie storiche statistiche ed industriali. pp. 82.
8°. Venezia, *Tipografia del Commercio*, 1858.
Chapter 7 contains some proverbs.

2404. Bastanzi (Giambattista). Le superstizioni delle Alpi Venete, con una lettera aperta al Prof. Paolo Mantegazza. pp. 79, [4], 212. 8°. Treviso, *Zoppelli*, 1888.
Pp. 147-154, Proverbi : pp. 154-155, Proverbi Cadorini : pp. 155-156, Proverbi di Livinallongo.

2405. Bianchi (Giovanni). Proverbi e modi proverbiali veneti, *etc.* pp. vii, 303. 8°. Milano, *Rebeschini*, 1901.
Classified by subjects arranged alphabetically; occasional explanatory notes and comparisons with Latin equivalents. [B.M.

2406. Brentari (Ottone). Guida storico-alpina di Bassano, Sette Comuni, Canale di Brenta, Marostica, Possagno. pp. viii, 314. 16°. Bassano, *Sante Pozzato*, 1885.
P. 154, 24 proverbs of Sette Comuni.

2407. Britti (Paolo). La nuova tramutatione della canzon de' proverbij. pp. [8].
sm. 8°. Venetia, *Domenico Louisa*, [1625].
Another edition. 8°. Venezia, *Righettini*, 1629.
Gratet-Duplessis, 462. Reprinted in the " Egeria " of Mueller e Wolf, **2286** (Gratet-Duplessis, 457), and also in Duplessis, pp. 278-280. [B.M. (1625 edition).

2408. Coletti (Ferdinando) and **Fanzago** (Filippo). Proverbi veneti, *etc.* 3 series. 12°. Padova, *Sicca*, 1855-57.
Extract from Raccoglitore, Pubblicazione annuale della Società d'Incoreggiamento nella Provincia di Padova, Anno 5-7. The first series deals with agricultural and meteorological, the second with hygienic, and the third with economic, Venetian proverbs. Accompanied by notes, and sometimes by illustrations. The first two series are anonymous, but the names are given in the third. There is a useful list of authorities. [B.M.

2409. Conti (Giovanni). Dizionario di alcune frasi, modi avverbiali, detti e proverbi più comuni usati generalmente nel dialetto veneto, coi termini corrispondenti toscani. pp. 27.
4°. Vicenza, *Burato*, 1871.

2410. Dalmedico (Angelo). Proverbi veneziani, raccolti da Angelo Dalmedico e raffrontati con quelli di Salomone e co' francesi, *etc.* pp. 125. L.2.50. 8°. Venezia, *Antonelli*, 1857.
Some 900 proverbs and proverbial phrases. Collected in Venice in 1841. Arranged alphabetically, with occasional notes. [B.M.

2411. Fapanni (Francesco). I proverbi del Trivigiano. pp. 24.
8°. Venezia, *Cecchini*, 1872.

2412. Giovanni, *Cieco Veneto*. Proverbi et ammaestramenti nouamente composti per Giovanni Cieco Veneto.
8°. Venetia, *Bindoni*, 1547.

Gratet-Duplessis, 403. There appears to be another edition, undated, but probably of 1530. This booklet, written in verse, is extremely rare. Duplessis quotes one of the curious poems of which it is composed.

2413. Guernieri (Angelo). Saggio di proverbi bellunesi. pp. 11.
8°. Belluno, *Guernieri*, 1878.

Reprinted from La Provincia di Belluno, 1878, Nos. 36, 37, 40.

2414. Lamberti (Antonio). Proverbi veneziani, *etc.* pp. 95.
16°. Venezia, *Molinari*, 1824.

Pp. 7-22, 91 proverbs. [B.M.

2415. Leoni (Carlo). Proverbi veneti. Libro pegli operai, n. 3.
8°. Venezia, *Naratovich*, 1866.

2416. Libretto. Libretto copioso di bellissimi proverbii, motti et sententie. . . . Accommodati per ordine di alfabeto. pp. [50]. 8°. [Venice, 1550?].

Gratet-Duplessis, 400. A rare and practically unknown book which was probably printed in Venice about the middle of the 16th century. An alphabetical list of proverbs, many of them in the Venetian dialect, and concluding with moral precepts in verse. Duplessis quotes some of these. [B.M.

2417. Marson (Luigi). Guida di Vittorio e suo distretto.
16°. Treviso, *Zoppelli*, [1889].

Pp. 103-152, a brief essay on proverbs, followed by proverbs in use in Vittorio.

2418. Mazzucchi (Pio). Proverbi popolari del Polesine.
8°. Palermo, 1890.

In Archivio per lo studio delle tradizioni popolari, Vol. 9, pp. 163-168, 542-548. 278 proverbs of the province of Rovigo. Also published separately. [B.M.

2419. Morpurgo (Salomone). [Proverbi veneziani antichi].
8°. Roma, n.d.

In Giornale di Filologia romanza, Vol. 4, No. 4, pp. 204-206. Proverbs written in Venice in the middle of the 14th century. They occur in notes at the foot of the page. [B.M.

2420. Musatti (Cesare). Duecento proverbi veneziani, *etc.* pp. 34. 16°. Venezia, *Merlo*, 1891.
[B.M.

2421. ———: Maldicenze nazionali e internazionali in proverbi veneziani di 4 secoli fa. 8°. Palermo, Torino, 1899.

In Archivio per lo studio delle tradizioni popolari, Vol. 18, pp. 174-175.
[B.M.

2422. ———: Modi di dire popolari veneziani.
8°. Palermo, Torino, 1899.

In Archivio per lo studio delle tradizioni popolari, Vol. 18, pp. 54-56. [B.M.

2423. Musatti (Cesare).   Proverbi veneziani.
8°.   Venezia, *Successore Fontana*, 1893.

In L'Ateneo Veneto, Serie 17, Vol. 2, Fasc. 4-6, pp. 250-266.   261 proverbs, mostly unpublished before this date.   Giusti-Capponi classification.

2424. ———— : Dei proverbi veneziani (a proposito di una recente pubblicazione) con 2 dozzine di proverbi nuovi.   pp. 11.
Venezia, 1902.

2425. Ninni (A. P.).   Materiali per un vocabolario della lingua rusticana del contado di Treviso, *etc.*   2 tom.
12°.   Venezia, *Longhi e Montanari*, 1891.

Bernstein, 2352.   Pp. 101-120, 167-187, proverbi, detti e aforismi.

2426. Pasqualigo (Cristoforo).   Raccolta di proverbi veneti, *etc.* 3 vols.   sm. 16°.   Venezia, *Tip. del Commercio*, 1857-58. Terza edizione, accresciuta, dei proverbi delle Alpi Carniche, del Trentino e dei tedeschi dei Sette Comuni vicentini.   pp. viii, 372.   8°.   Treviso, *Zoppelli*, 1882.

Proverbs classified like those of Giusti with some modifications.   Very useful for students of dialect.   [B.M.

2427. Wolf (Adolf).   Volksdichtungen aus Venezien.
Wien, 1863.

In Österreichische Wochenschrift, 1, p. 129.

2428. Zanardelli (Tito).   Saggi folklorici in dialetto di Badi, *etc.* pp. 89.   8°.   Bologna, *Zanichelli*, 1910.

Pp. 59-60, detti sui paesi : pp. 61-64, proverbi.   [B.M.

See also index at end for references to Venezia in other sections.

5. FRIULI.

2429. Almanacco.   Almanacco del Dottor Vatri per l'anno 1860. Anno iv.   Udine, *Tipografia Zavagna*, 1859.

Pp. 135-141, some proverbs of Friuli, and some Tuscan proverbs compared with some of Friuli.

2430. Joppi (Vicenzo).   Testi inediti friulani dei secoli xiv e xix.
8°.   Roma, *etc.*, 1878.

In Archivio glottologico italiano, Vol. 4.   Includes 27 Friuli proverbs, arranged in alphabetical order.

2431. Ostermann (Valentino).   Proverbi friulani, *etc.*   pp. 307.
L.3.   16°.   Udine, *Doretti*, 1876.

Some 5000 proverbs.

2432. ———— : Superstizioni, pregiudizi e credenze popolari relativi alla cosmografia, geografia fisica e meteorologia, *etc.*   pp. 81.
8°.   Udine, *Doretti*, 1891.

Bernstein, 2423.   Pp. 20-29, Proverbi friulani relativi alla luna : pp. 29-33, Proverbi che pronosticano l'andamento delle stagioni.

2433. Proverbi. Proverbi friulani. Udine, 1856.

In Annatore friulano, Anno 4, Nos. 17-24, 37.

See also **3649.**

6. ISTRIA.

2434. C. (Luigi). Saggio di alcuni proverbi rovignesi.
Rovigno, *Coana*, 1861.

In L'Aurora, strenna di Rovigno, pp. 160-178.

2435. Cassani (Angelo C.). Saggio di proverbi triestini. pp. x,
109. Soldi 60. 8°. Trieste, *Coen*, 1860.

Alphabetical arrangement under subject headings. 323 proverbs and 136
proverbial sayings, many of which, however, are real proverbs, explained and
illustrated. [B.M.

2436. Combi (Carlo A.). Istria. Studi storici e politici. pp.
xlv, 318. L.5. 8°. Milano, *Rebeschini*, 1886.

Pp. 143-149, dei proverbi istriani. A brief selection of proverbs, with notes.
[B.M.

2437. Czink (Ludwig) and **Körösi** (Alexander). Italienische
Sprüche und Lieder aus Fiume.
8°. Kolozsvar, *Közmüvelödés*, 1892.

In Ethnologische Mitteilungen aus Ungarn, Bd. 2, Heft 9-10. 204 proverbs
and sayings, besides children's rhymes, songs, *etc.* There are a few brief
notes in German. [B.M.

2438. Ive (Antonio). Saggi di dialetto rovignese, *etc.* pp. 78.
8°. Trieste, *Lloyd Austro-Ungarico*, 1888.

Pp. 19-53, proverbi. [B.M.

2439. Luciani (Tomaso). Tradizioni popolari albonesi. pp. xi,
103. la. 8°. Capodistria, *Cobol & Priora*, 1892.

A large collection of proverbs, maxims, phrases, *etc.*, used by the people of
Albona.

2440. Proverbi. Dei proverbi istriani. Trieste, *Coen*, 1859.

In Porta Orientale, An. 3, pp. 232-241.

2441. Saggi. Saggi di proverbi rovignesi. Rovigno.

In L'Aurora, An. 1, pp. 160-168.

See also **303, 2148, 2602, 2675.**

7. LIGURIA.

2442. Mazzetto. Un mazzetto di proverbi. 8°. Firenze, 1873.

In L'Unità della lingua, Anno 4, pp. 163-168, 248-255. Proverbs collected
in the neighbourhood of Spezia. [B.M.

2443. Staglieno (Marcello). Proverbi genovesi con i corrispondenti in latino ed in diversi dialetti d'Italia, etc. pp. [vii],
208. L.2.50. 8°. Genova, *Garbarino*, 1869.

665 proverbs in alphabetical order, without notes, but rich in comparisons
with other dialects, *etc.* Some of these are slightly inaccurate. [B.M.

8. EMILIA.

2444. Bagli (Giuseppe Gaspare). Saggio di studi su i proverbi, i pregiudizî e la poesia popolare in Romagna. pp. 55.

la. 8°. Bologna, *Fava e Garagnani*, 1886.

In Atti e Memorie della R. Deputazione di Storia Patria per le Provincie di Romagna, Serie 3, Vol. 3, Fasc. 5 e 6. Some 200 proverbs divided into 34 sections, and occasionally illustrated by superstitions or peasant beliefs. [B.M.

2445. ———: Nuovo saggio di studi su i proverbi, gli usi, i pregiudizî e la poesia popolare in Romagna. pp. 80.

8°. Bologna, *Fava e Garagnani*, 1886.

In Atti e Memorie della R. Deputazione di Storia Patria per le Provincie di Romagna, Serie 3, Vol. 4, Fasc. 4-6. Pp. 10-24 [of the article], proverbs and sayings in the Romagna dialect : pp. 76-79, bibliography of Romagna folk-lore and dialect. [B.M.

2446. Brianzi (Luigi). Breve raccolta di parole, frasi, proverbi, voci di paragone e d'arti e mestieri, in bolognese, italiano e francese, *etc.* pp. 48.

16°. Milano, *Presso l'Autore*, Bologna. *Zanichelli*, n.d.

The proverbs, *etc.*, are arranged in three columns, one for each language, and there is a fourth blank column for equivalents in any other language desired.

Second edition. Breve raccolta . . . in milanese, italiano e francese. 16°. Milano, *Dumolard*, 1883.

First Disp., pp. 1-16. Pitrè, 2507, does not know if this was ever completed.

2447. Buini (Giuseppe Maria). 'L dsgazi d' Bertuldin dalla Zena miss in rima. . . . Con le osservazioni, e spiegazioni dei vocabili o termini Bolognesi, *etc.* pp. [viii], 136.

4°. Bologna, *Pisani*, [1736].

Proverbs and proverbial phrases scattered throughout the book, with Italian translations.

2448. Coronedi-Berti (Carolina). Proverbi Bolognesi. Agricoltura, meteorologia. 8°. Palermo, 1882.

Pitrè, 2620. *In* Archivio per lo studio delle tradizioni popolari, Vol. 1, pp. 116-119. 37 proverbs are here illustrated. [B.M.

2449. Emmanueli (Antonio). L'alta valle del Taro e il suo dialetto, *etc.* pp. vii, 377. 8°. Borgotaro, *Cavanna*, 1886.

Parte 2, pp. 371-377, proverbs. [B.M.

2450. Ferraro (Giuseppe). Tradizioni ed usi popolari ferraresi. 8°. Palermo, 1886.

In Archivio per lo studio delle tradizioni popolari, Vol. 5, pp. 268-287. Pp. 279-281, proverbi. [B.M.

2451. Lumbroso (Alberto). Proverbi e modi riminesi. 8°. Palermo, 1897.

In Archivio per lo studio delle tradizioni popolari, Vol. 16, p. 136. [B.ᴹ.

2452. Morri (Antonio). Manuale domestico-tecnologico di voci, modi, proverbi, riboboli, idiotismi della Romagna e loro corrispondente italiano, *etc.* pp. [viii], 957.

8°. Persiceto, *Giambattistelli e Brugnoli*, 1863.

Another edition, anonymous. 16°. Persiceto, 1865.

Presumably Pitrè, 2981, is a later edition of Pitrè, 3042.

2453. Placucci (Michele). Usi e pregiudizi dei contadini della Romagna. pp. xix, 215. *First edition.* pp. 176, 3, 8.

8°. Forlì, *Barbiani*, 1818.

Another edition. pp. xix, 215. 8°. Palermo, *Lauriel*, 1885.

Curiosità popolari tradizionali, publicate per cura di Giuseppe Pitrè, Vol. 1. Pp. 178-183, some proverbs of the Romagna in dialect, with Italian translations and notes. [U.C.L. (1885 edition).

2454. Ptagulò *di Ferrara.* Ptagulò d' Frara, l, dialugh in frares pr al lunari dl. ann 1850, *etc.* 16°. Frara, 1849.

Contains : Zzent pruverbi fraris. [Bristol Public Library.

2455. Rognoni (Carlo). Raccolta di proverbii agrari e meteorologici del Parmigiano. *First edition.* Parma, *Grazioli*, 1866 *Second edition.* pp. 38.

50 centesimi. la. 8°. Parma, *Ferrari*, 1881.

2456. Strolgament. Strolgament dil strell, pr. l'ann. 1838 . . . e a dì pr. dì divers proverbi paisan. pp. 80.

sm. 16°. Parma, *Carmignen*, [1837?].

2457. Ungarelli (Gaspare). Proverbi bolognesi: agricoltura, economia rurale. 8°. Palermo, 1891.

In Archivio delle tradizioni popolari, Vol. 10, pp. 157-160. 36 proverbs. 20 copies were published separately, pp. 4. 8° (*Clausen*), same place and date of publication.

2458. ———: Proverbi bolognesi: meteorologia, stagioni, tempi dell'anno. 8°. Palermo, 1891.

In Archivio delle tradizioni popolari, Vol. 10, pp. 390-396. A few copies were published separately. 76 proverbs under all the months of the year except July and October.

2459. ———: Saggio di una raccolta di proverbi in dialetto bolognese, *etc.* pp. 88.

la. 8°. Bologna, *Fava e Garagnani*, 1892.

Proverbs, mostly collected orally, with notes and comments. Republished from : Atti e Memorie della R. Deputazione di Storia Patria per le Provincie di Romagna, Serie 3, Vol. 10.

9. TUSCANY.

2460. Appel (Carlo). Laudi cortonesi del secolo xiii, edite da Guido Mazzoni, con un' appendice " I proverbi di Gharzo " di Carlo Appel. pp. 140.

8°. Bologna, *Fava e Garagnani*, 1890.

Pp. 113-138, Appendice. I proverbi di Gharzo.

2461. Baldovini (Francesco). Chi la sorte ha nemica usi l'ingegno, *etc.* pp. [iv], 212. 8°. Firenze, *Moücke*, 1743.

Another edition. 8°. Firenze, 1763.

Contains the explanation of many Tuscan sayings and proverbs to be found in the work. [B.M. (1763 edition).

2462. Benelli (Gustavo). Raccolta di proverbi, massime morali, aneddoti, ed altro. pp. 173.

8°. Firenze, *Carnesecchi*, 1876.

Pp. 5-81, some little-known proverbs in alphabetical order, in Italian-Tuscan, frequently with Latin, French and German equivalents. Some of them are phrases and proverbial sayings : pp. 83-150, 429 moral maxims. [B.M.

2463. Bianchini (E. Giuseppe). Modi proverbiali e motti popolari toscani, *etc.* pp. 155.

L.1.50. 8°. Reggio nell'Emilia, *Stab. tip. lit. degli Artigianelli*, 1888.

Second edition. pp. xii, 124. 8°. Livorno, *Giusti*, 1900.

2464. Bini (Silvestro). Prime letture per le bambine della sezione inferiore della prima classe elementare.

30 centesimi. 16°. Roma, *Paravia, etc.*, 1883.

Pp. 16-18, some Tuscan proverbs.

2465. Dani (Francesco). Satire, dettati e gerghi della città di Firenze. pp. 128. 16°. Firenze, *Salani*, 1886.

Contains various proverbs of Florence, particularly pp. 21-24. [B.M.

2466. Fa per Tutti. Fa per tutti. Piccola strenna per l'anno 1870. . . . Arrichita di una serie di massime e proverbi presi da buoni autori, *etc.* pp. 206.

12°. Roma, *Pallotta*, [1869?].

Pp. 126-134, Tuscan proverbs.

2467. Faborni (Giovanni Valentino). Proverbi toscani pei contadini, in quattro classi divisi. Perugia, 1786

Pitrè, 2740.

2468. Fanfani (Pietro). Diporti filologici. Dialoghi di Pietro Fanfani. pp. xv, 203.

4°. Napoli, *Stamperia del Vaglio*, 1858.

No. 10, pp. 150-172, contains more than 100 Tuscan proverbs not in Giusti's collection or in Gotti's " Aggiunta."

2469. Fiacchi (Luigi). Dei proverbi toscani, lezione . . . con la dichiarazione de' proverbi di Gio. Maria Cecchi, *etc.* pp. 30.
4°. Firenze, *Piatti*, 1818.
Second edition. pp. 103. 8°. Firenze, *Piatti*, 1820.
Third edition. pp. 154. 8°. Milano, *Silvestri*, 1838.

Gratet-Duplessis, 394. Read before the Accademia della Crusca in 1813, and published in Vol. 1 of its "Atti." Also published as part of Cecchi's "L'Assiuolo," 8°. Milano, 1863. The Lezione is an excellent short commentary on proverbs and their use, and the Dichiarazione gives an explanation of 64 proverbs and proverbial sayings. Duplessis gives further details and quotes from Fiacchi. [B.M.

2470. Fidelissimi (Giovanni Battista). Il giardino morale . . . nel quale in rime et versi lirici toscani si contengono detti, proverbi, *etc.* pp. 56. 4°. Bologna, *Rebaldini*, 1622.
Another edition. ff. 38. 8°. Bologna, *Bonardo*, n.d.

Gratet-Duplessis, 420. Scarcely a book of proverbs, but contains a number of popular sayings, in verse, in the midst of the moral maxims. Very rare. [B.M.

2471. Giuliani (Giambattista). Delizie del parlare toscano. Lettere e ricreazioni. . . . Quarta edizione, *etc.* 2 vols.
16°. Firenze, *Successori Le Monnier*, 1880.
Vol. 1, Lettera 49 is on proverbs. [B.M.

2472. Giuliari (Giovanni Battista Carlo). Nuova serie di proverbi toscani esposti in rima per ordine d'alfabeto da un codice della Capitolare Biblioteca.
8°. Verona, *Tip. Vescovile Vincenti e Franchi*, 1867.

Pp. 17-27, the proverbs of Gharzo, after a 15th c. ms. These were republished, with many changes, by Giuliari in Il Propugnatore, Nuova Serie, Vol. 3, Parte 1. Bologna, 1890.

2473. Giusti (Giuseppe). Raccolta di proverbi toscani con illustrazioni cavata dai manoscritti di Giuseppe Giusti, ed ora ampliata ed ordinata. pp. xii, 423.
16°. Firenze, *Le Monnier*, 1853.

Arranged alphabetically under subjects, with notes. Pitrè gives all the headings of the classification employed, which was frequently adopted for other collections of proverbs. [U.C.L.

2474. ———: Aggiunta ai proverbi toscani di Giuseppe Giusti. [Anonymous]. 16°. Siena, 1854.

2475. ———: Raccolta di proverbi toscani nuovamente ampliata da quella di G. Giusti e pubblicata da Gino Capponi. pp. iv, xxvii, 489. 8°. Firenze, *Le Monnier*, 1871.
Another edition. pp. xxix, 489. 8°. Firenze, *Salani*, [1911].

Capponi's enlargement includes not only Giusti's original work but also the "Aggiunta" of Gotti, *q.v.* **2476,** besides other proverbs. [U.C.L.

2476. Gotti (Aurelio). Aggiunta ai proverbi toscani di G. Giusti, compilata per cura di Aurelio Gotti e corredata d'un indice generale dei proverbi contenuti nelle due raccolte. pp. iv, 135.   8°. Firenze, *Le Monnier*, 1855.

Pitrè, 2826. Giusti's Raccolta, together with this Aggiunta, were republished by Capponi, *q.v.* **2475**. Gotti includes the letter in proverbs of Antonio Vignali, *q.v.* **2356**.   [B.M.

2477. Illustrazione. L'illustrazione nazionale, . . . pel 1867, *etc.* pp. 160.   la. 16°. Firenze, Torino, *Cassone*, 1866.

P. 29, 28 agricultural proverbs of Tuscany.   [B.M.

2478. Lastri (Marco). Proverbi toscani dei contadini. [By Marco Lastri. *In* Corso di agricoltura pratica].
                          Firenze, *Pagani*, 1787-1790.
Another edition. Proverbi pei contadini, in quattro classi divisi, *etc.* pp. 30.   8°. Venezia, 1790.

Most of these proverbs were used and reproduced by Fapanni. The Corso di agricoltura was also republished, 5 vols., Firenze, 1801-1803.

2479. Lippi (Lorenzo). Il malmantile racquistato. Poema di Perlone Zipoli [*pseud.* of Lorenzo Lippi]. Con le note di Puccio Lamoni [*pseud.* of Paolo Minucci], *etc.* pp. xvi, 545, [12].   4°. Firenze, *Taglini*, 1688.
Another edition. 4 vols.   4°. Prato, *Vannini*, 1815.
Another edition.   8°. Milano, 1889.

Gratet-Duplessis, 430. Contains various Tuscan proverbs in the poem. The edition of 1815 is better, as it contains more notes on proverbs. The rare first edition appeared in 12° in 1676; a Florentine edition of 1750, on which the 1815 one is founded, is recommended by Duplessis for its accuracy and its commentaries.   [U.C.L.

2480. Lunario. Lunario per i contadini della Toscana per l'anno 1783, *etc.* pp. 136.   12°. Firenze, *Buonaiuti*, [1783?].

Pp. 128-129, Proverbi de contadini per regola di loro arte. This collection is probably by M. Lastri.

2481. Minà-Palumbo (Francesco). Proverbi agrarj toscani.
                          Palermo, 1854.

In L'Empedocle, Vol. 4, pp. 268-292, 445-453. 475 proverbs with notes and French and Sicilian equivalents to many of them.

2482. ——— : Proverbi siciliani e toscani sulla viticoltura. *See* **2559.**

2483. Moniglia (Giovanni Andrea). Delle poesie drammatiche, *etc.* 3 vols. 4°. Firenze, *Stamperia di S.A.S.*, 1689-1690.
Another edition. 3 vols.   sm. 8°. Firenze, 1698.

Gratet-Duplessis, 437. At the end of Part 3 is a " Dichiarzione dei proverbi e vocaboli degli abitanti del contado e della plebe fiorentina." This list, though not long, contains useful information which it would be difficult to find elsewhere.   [B.M.

2484. Morandi (Luigi). I proverbi del Giusti. [By Omega, *pseud.* of Morandi]. Città di Castello, 1885.

In the Antologia critica, pp. 195-198. This article also appeared in all the successive editions of the Antologia, at least until 1890.

2485. Nieri (Idelfonso). Dei modi proverbiali toscani e specialmente lucchesi, *etc.* pp. 84. 8°. Lucca, *Giusti*, 1893.

Pp. 3-34, Discorso : pp. 35-84, Modi proverbiali ; about 1200 arranged in alphabetical order. Also published in : Atti della Reale Accademia Lucchese, Vol. 27, pp. 53-136. [B.M.

2486. ———: Proverbi toscani specialmente lucchesi, *etc.* pp. 177. 8°. Lucca, *Giusti*, 1894.

Another large collection of proverbs, preceded by an introduction. Also published in : Atti della Reale Accademia Lucchese, Vol. 27, pp. 183-359. [B.M.

2487. Palagi (Giuseppe). Due proverbi storici toscani, *etc.* pp. 39. sm. fol. Firenze, *Le Monnier*, 1876.
[B.M.

2488. Paoli (Sebastiano). Modi di dire toscani ricercati nella loro origine. pp. [viii], 360. 4°. Venezia, *Occhi*, 1740. *Another edition.* pp. 368. 8°. Venezia, 1761.

Gratet-Duplessis, 443. Interesting and erudite information on Tuscan proverbs. [B.M.

2489. Pino (Callisto). Saggio di proverbi toscani, *etc.* pp. [iv], 144. L.1.50. 8°. Empoli, *Traversari*, 1876. *Seconda edizione* [really the fifth]. pp. 256.
L.2. 16°. Torino, *Scioldo*, 1879.

This work was also published in various periodicals. Only ten proverbs are dealt with, illustrated and explained. [B.M. (1876 edition).

2490. Proverbs. Tuscan proverbs. 8°. London, *Parker*, 1857.

In Fraser's Magazine, Vol. 55, pp. 18-28. Article giving numerous examples in Italian and English. [B.M.

2491. Raccolta. Nuova raccolta di xxiv proverbi toscani rappresentati in figure, *etc.* fol. Firenze, *Cellai*, 1826.

Principally a series of coloured plates.

2492. Serdonati (Francesco). Proverbi fiorentini . . . aggiuntivi alcuni veneti in versi rimati. pp. 23.
8°. Padova, *Salmin*, 1871.

Pitrè, 3280-3283, gives various editions and full details. The proverbs are taken from a ms. of Serdonati, " Origine di tutti i proverbii fiorentini," in the Biblioteca Magliabechiana in Florence. Accompanied by explanatory notes. [B.M.

2493. Teglia (Francesco del). Lezione preliminare della nuova etica volgare tolta da proverbi toscani. pp. [9], xxv.
4°. Firenze, *Nestenus & Borghini*, 1714.

T

2494. Tigri (Giuseppe). Proverbi toscani sulla coltivazione delle selve. 8°. Palermo, 1889.

In Archivio delle tradizioni popolari, Vol. 8, pp. 297-298.

2495. Veglie. Le veglie della nonna presso il canto del fuoco. pp. 23. 24°. [Firenze, *Saloni*, 1873].

1. Motti e sentenze : 4. Proverbi e motti toscani rimati. Some of these proverbs are paraphrased in verse.

2496. Zannoni (G. B.). Saggio di scherzi comici, *etc.*
Firenze, *Stamperia del Giglio*, 1825.
Another edition. pp. 538. 8°. Milano, *Silvestri*, 1850.

Pitrè, 3409, 3410, also mentions an earlier edition of Firenze, 1819. This work contains many proverbs and sayings of the Florentine people, and it has been largely used by the two Düringsfelds and the continuers of Giusti, for their collections. [B.M.

See also index at end for references to Tuscan in other sections.

10. UMBRIA.

2497. Morandi (Luigi). Saggio di proverbi umbri, raccolti ed illustrati. pp. 26. 8°. Sanseverino-Marche, *Corradetti*, 1869.

Reprinted from L'Umbria e le Marche. 269 proverbs. [B.M.

11. MARCHES.

2498. Castellani (Luigi). Tradizioni popolari della provincia di Macerata. pp. 40. 8°. Foligno, *Sgariglia*, 1885.

Pp. 19-23, 47 proverbs. This booklet was also republished as Part 4 of the Scritti di Luigi Castellani, 16°. Città di Castello, *Lapi*, 1889.

2499. Ciavarini-Doni (Ivo). Proverbi marchigiani. pp. xxxv, 246. 8°. Ancona, *Tipografia del Commercio*, 1883.

The proverbs are divided into 29 categories according to their import, and each category is preceded by brief remarks on the nature of the proverbs.

2500. Conti (Egidio). Saggio di proverbi dialettali metaurensi. pp. 16. 8°. Cagli, *Balloni*, 1898.

44 proverbs, with Italian translations and explanations, preceded by a brief study of dialect proverbs generally. [B.M.

2501. Gianandrea (Antonio). Calendario popolare marchigiano.
8°. Arcevia, 1890.

In Nuova Rivista Misena, *etc.* An. 1 e 2, 1888-1889, Nos. 4-15. Marche calendar and weather proverbs for each month of the year, accompanied by songs, descriptions of local customs, *etc.* Some 400 proverbs in all.

2502. ——— : Proverbi agrarî marchigiani illustrati.
Ancona, 1885.

In L'Agricolture della provincia di Ancona, Nos. 1-3.

2503. Gianandrea (Antonio). Proverbi marchigiani: città, paesi, nazioni. 8°. Palermo, 1882.

In Archivio per lo studio delle tradizioni popolari, Vol. 1, pp. 99-115. 180 proverbs. [B.M.

See also **3929.**

2504. Marcoaldi (Oreste). Guida e statistica della città e comune di Fabriano. pp. 327.

8°. Fabriano, *Crocetti*, 1873.

Pp. 214-224, Alcuni proverbi contadineschi sull'agricoltura e sulla meteorologia del territorio fabrianese.

2505. Pigorini-Beri (Caterina). I proverbi e i modi proverbiali nell' Appennino marchigiano. 8°. Roma, 1881.

In Nuova Antologia, Seconda Serie, Vol. 27, pp. 265-290. [B.M.

2506. Rondini (Druso). Canti popolari marchigiani, *etc.* pp. 80.

8°. Palermo, *Tip. del Giornale di Sicilia*, 1889.

Contains 60 proverbs.

12. ROME.

2507. Besso (Marco). Roma nei proverbi e nei modi di dire. pp. viii, 184. L.5. 8°. Roma, *Loescher*, 1889.

Another edition. Roma e il Papa nei proverbi e nei modi di dire. Nuova edizione illustrata. pp. xliii, 336.

4°. Roma, *Loescher*, 1904.

Appendix 2, Bibliografia. There are proverbs from all nations and in all languages taken from 96 different authorities. An excellent and valuable work. [B.M.

2508. Mueller (Wilhelm). Rom, Römer und Römerinnen, *etc.* 2 Bde. 8°. Berlin, *Duncker und Humblot*, 1820.

Bernstein, 2287. Bd. 1, pp. 81-82; Bd. 2, pp. 220-225, proverbs. [B.M.

2509. Rom. Rom im Sprichwort. Wien, 1871.

In Neue Wiener Tageblatt, No. 167, *and in* Reichenburger Zeitung, No. 143.

2510. Zanazzo (Luigi). Proverbi romaneschi. pp. 202. L.1.50. sm. 16°. Roma, *Perino di Cerroni e Solaro*, 1886.

Nearly 2000 proverbs of Rome arranged by Giusti's classification, modified. Calendar proverbs from this collection were later published in a periodical. For details see Pitrè, 3402-3407.

See also **225.**

13. ABRUZZI.

2511. Finamore (Gennaro). Proverbi abruzzesi.

8°. Erlangen, 1901.

In Romanische Forschungen, Bd. 11, pp. 122-200, 567-622. [B.M.

2512. ———: Vocabolario dell' uso abruzzese. pp. vii, 337.

L.5. 8°. Lanciano, *Carabba*, 1880.

Pp. 241-262, proverbi raccolti della viva voce del popolo. Arranged alphabetically under subject headings. The second edition does not contain this list. [B.M.

2513. Nino (Antonio de).   Proverbi abruzzesi raccolti e illustrati.   pp. 128.   8°.   Aquila, *Forcella*, 1877.

A collection of some hundreds of proverbs, in Italian, arranged under thirty arbitrary headings.

2514. ———— : Vizi e virtù delle donne in alcuni proverbi abruzzesi.   8°.   Torino, *Bocca*, 1892.

In Archivio di Psichiatria, Vol. 13, Fasc. 1, pp. 113-114.   About 9 proverbs, with Italian translations and comments.   [B.M.

2515. Savini (Giuseppe).   Sul dialetto teramano, *etc.*   pp. 343.
                                  8°.   Ancona, *Civelli*, 1879.

Pp. 112-224, frasi e modi di dire : pp. 225-296, proverbii, ditterii e boci di paragone.   The proverbs are arranged in Giusti's order, and are compared with Tuscan ones.

14. CAMPANIA.

2516. Angelis (Enrico de).   Pochi proverbi raccolti in Meta di Sorrento.   fol.   Napoli, 1887.

In Giambattista Basile, Anno 5, Num. 12.

2517. Castagna (Niccola).   Proverbi italiani raccolti e illustrati.   pp. 180.   *First edition*.

                      L.1.80.   16°.   Napoli, *Metitiero*, 1866.
Third edition.   pp. 376.   L.2.   16°.   Napoli, *Nobile*, 1869.

1452 Neapolitan proverbs, classified by subject, Italianised, with notes.   The second (pp. 367, 1868) and third editions, very similar, are better than the first as being greatly enlarged and containing indices.   [B.M. (second edition).

2518. Chiurazzi (Luigi).   Proverbie napolitane.
                    Napoli, *Stamperia de lo Progresso*, 1875-1877.
In Lo Spassatiempo, *etc.*, Anno 1-3.   Some 800 proverbs in all.

2519. ———— : Smorfia Napoletana, . . . con . . . una raccolta di proverbi tutti napoletani. . . . Seconda edizione, con molte aggiunte.   pp. 256.   L.2.   16°.   Napoli, *Chiurazzi*, 1876.
Pp. 219-239, some 600 proverbs in alphabetical order.

2520. Croce (Benedetto).   Proverbi trimembri napoletani.
                                            Napoli, 1883.

Pitrè, 2645. *In* Giambattista Basile, Anno 1, No. 9, pp. 66-67. 45 proverbs, which, with another 10, were republished by V. Imbriani in the '' Posile-cheata di Pompeo Sarnelli,'' 1885.

2521. Galiani (Ferdinand).   Vocabolario delle parole del dialetto napolitano, *etc.* [Continued by F. Azzareti and F. Mazzarella-Farao].   2 vols.   12°.   Napoli, *Porcelli*, 1789.

Gratet-Duplessis, 467.   Vol. 2, pp. 213-292, L'eccellenza della lingua napoletana con la maggioranza alla toscana, *etc.* This dissertation, notably pp. 271 *et seq.*, contains many Neapolitan proverbs and proverbial sayings.   [U.C.L.

2522. Gerning (Johann Isaac von), *Baron*. Reise durch Oester-
reich und Italien. 3 Thle.
8°. Franckfurt am Main, *Wilmanns*, 1802.
Gratet-Duplessis, 466. Vol. 1 contains a brief list of " Neapolitanische
Sprichwörter." [B.M.

2523. Giordano (Arturo). Proverbi del popolo napolitano.
Napoli, 1888.
In La Revista, Anno 11, Nos. 7-8. From an unpublished work entitled
" Datte e mutte napoletane."

2524. Pitrè (Giuseppe). Proverbi napoletani.
8°. Palermo, 1883, 1884.
In Archivio per lo studio delle tradizioni popolari, Vol. 2, pp. 593-597 : Vol.
3, pp. 287-290. 217 proverbs. [B.M.

2525. Wentrup, *Dr.* Neapolitanische Sprüchwörter.
8°. Braunschweig, *Westermann*, 1858.
In Archiv für das Studium der neueren Sprachen, Bd. 23, pp. 206-08. 93
entries in the Neapolitan dialect. [B.M.

15. APULIA.

2526. Carlo (Cosimo de). Proverbi dialettali del Leccese, *etc.*
pp. 283. L.3. 8°. Trani, *Vecchi*, 1907.
Proverbs explained and illustrated, arranged under subject headings. [B.M.

2527. Casetti (Antonio C.). Un gruzzolo di proverbi leccesi. pp.
31. 16°. Lecce, *Tipografia Garibaldi*, 1873.
280 Lecce proverbs, with a few Neapolitan ones. The author wished to show
that some proverbs are directly contradicted by others, and that though many
proverbs are the same in meaning in all languages yet the forms of expression
vary ; to this end he quotes some 16 English, French, Spanish and German
examples.

2528. La Sorsa (Saverio). La sapienza popolare nei proverbi
pugliesi. Bari, 1922.

2529. Pasqualigo (Cristoforo). Centocinquantadue proverbi tro-
iani, *etc.* pp. 10. 8°. [Treviso?], 1882.

16. BASILICATA.

2530. Pasquarelli (Michele). Pagina di psicologia di un paese di
Basilicata. pp. 22. 8°. Napoli, *Tocco*, 1892.
Pitrè, 6125, 6126. 380 proverbs of Basilicata, in Italian, which formed the
basis of a collection later published in the Archivio per lo studio delle tradizioni
popolari, Vol. 11, 1892 ; Vol. 12, 1893, under the title : Proverbi e frasi nel
dialetto di Marsico Nuovo (Basilicata). 25 copies were published separately.

17. CALABRIA.

2531. Capialbi (Vito). Proverbii calabresi (spigolature).

Monteleone, 1889.

In La Calabria, Anno 11, No. 3, pp. 5-6 (=21-22). 22 Calabrian proverbs, with Italian translations.

2532. Cardamone (Raffaele). Proverbi calabresi.

Firenze, 1865.

In La Civiltà Italiana, Anno 1, No. 10, pp. 156-57. 75 proverbs and 7 other proverbial phrases.

2533. Corso (D.). I detti dell' antico, ossia raccolta di proverbii calabresi.   Monteleone, 1890.

In La Calabria, Anno 3, Nos. 2 and 3. 38 agricultural and weather proverbs, with Italian translations.

2534. Mandalari (Francesco Maria). Proverbi calabro-reggini. Studio filologico.   4°. Napoli, *Jovene*, 1874.

In La Scuola Italica, Anno 2, No. 20; 2º semestre, Nos. 2, 4, 7, 9, 13, 16. A study, more philological than paremiological, on 76 proverbs. Pitrè, 2975-77, gives full details of these and other proverbs published in different periodicals.

2535. Morosi (Giuseppe). Dialetti romaici del mandamento di Bova in Calabria.   8°. Torino, *Loescher*, 1878.

In Archivio glottologico italiano, Vol. 4, pp. 89-95, 132 proverbs in dialect with Italian translations.   [B.M.

2536. ———: Studi sui dialetti greci della Terra d'Otranto, *etc.* pp. viii, 214.   L.8. 4°. Lecce, *Tip. Salentina*, 1870.

Pp. 77-79, proverbi di Martano e Calimera.   [B.M.

2537. Pasquale (Luigi de). Raccolta di favole calabresi, novelle, superstizioni e proverbi. pp. 29.

8°. Monteleone, *Raho*, 1893.

Contains 79 proverbs.

2538. ———: Raccolta di proverbi calabri. 8°. Palermo, 1890.

In Archivio per lo studio delle tradizioni popolari, Vol. 9, pp. 50-56, 217-222. 305 proverbs.   [B.M.

2539. Polito (F.). Proverbii calabresi raccolti a Nicotera.

4°. Monteleone, 1890.

In La Calabria, Anno 2, Nos. 9 and 10. 80 proverbs with a literal translation into Italian.

2540. Presterà (Carlo Massinissa). Proverbii in uso nel Monteleonese.   4°. Monteleone, 1888, 1889.

In La Calabria, Anno 1, Nos. 2-4; Anno 2, Nos. 5-11. In all, 582 proverbs with Italian translations.

2541. Severini (Vincenzo). Raccolta di proverbî moranesi. pp. 78.   8°. Castrovillari, 1889.

Another edition.   Castrovillari, *Patitucci*, 1893.

18. SICILY.

2542. Abecedario. Abecedario ad uso delle scuole lancastriane o di mutuo insegnamento in Sicilia, *etc.* pp. 122.
12°. Palermo, *Virzì*, 1860.
Another edition. pp. 168.   24°. Palermo, *Mauro*, 1874.

Earlier editions exist, of which no bibliographical details are available. Pp. 87-9 (in 1860 edition), pp. 115-8 (in 1874 edition), 59 Sicilian proverbs and proverbial phrases, with Italian equivalents.

2543. Bondice (Vicenzo). Raccolta di proverbi siciliani in ottave, *etc.* pp. 64. 2 pts. [in 1].   8°. Catania, *Pastore*, 1845.
[B.M.

2544. Bono (Michele del).   Dizionario siciliano-italiano-latino, *etc.* 3 vols.   4°. Palermo, *Gramignani*, 1751-1804.
Second edition. 4 vols.   4°. Palermo, *Abbate*, 1783-1785.

Pitrè, 2682, 2683. Contains many proverbs which are gathered together in various indices. Pitrè gives full details. The first edition is the best.   [B.M.

2545. Caglià-Ferro (Antonino).   Nomenclatura familiare siculo-italica, seguita da una breve fraseologia. pp. xx, 119.
8°. Messina, *Capra*, 1840.

Pp. 99-114, some Sicilian proverbs with Italian translations and equivalents are included amongst figurative phrases, *etc.* : pp. 61-96 contain figurative phrases and proverbial sayings, *etc.*, taken from the best Italian authors.
[B.M.

2546. Castagnola (Michele).   Fraseologia siculo-toscano. pp. 458.   8°. Catania, *Galatola*, 1863.

About 800 proverbs, phrases, *etc.*, in the Catanian dialect; not always corresponding, however, with the Tuscan ones placed opposite.   [B.M.

2547. Catania (Paolo).   Canzoni morali sopra i motti siciliani. 7 vols.   16°. Palermo, *Colicchia* (Vols. 1, 3-7),
Bisagni (Vol. 2), 1652-1663.

Tavola alfabetica di tutti i motti cavati dal' otto libri di canzoni con l'agiunta di altri 300 poste appresso composte dal medesmo autore. Tomo 8, date in luce dal Dottor Gioanbattista del Giudice. pp. 214, 152 + frontispiece.
sm. 8°. Palermo, *Colicchia*, 1663.

In the eight volumes given above, Catania collected and paraphrased, in Sicilian octaves, some 3500 Sicilian proverbs and proverbial phrases. Pitrè, 2549-50, states that this edition of Vol. 1 is not the only one, and gives some brief indications of another. Vol. 8, pp. 1-214, alphabetical table; pp. 1-151, of the second pagination, contain the other 300 sayings. Arrangement, one proverb and one poem to the page.

2548. Crane (Thomas Frederick).   Sicilian proverbs.
8°. Philadelphia, *Lippincott*, 1885.

In Lippincott's Magazine, New Series, Vol. 9, No. 51, pp. 309-313. A brief article on Sicilian proverbs with many examples, given in English, and sometimes compared with those of other countries. A readable article, but comparatively unimportant.   [B.M.

2549. Giorgi (Paolo). Nozze Cristiani-Marchesini. pp. 12.
8°. [Lucca, *Giusti*, 1892].
29 Sicilian proverbs collected in Castroreale.

2550. Giovanni (Gaetano di). Diciotto proverbi canaresani.
8°. Palermo, 1889.
In Archivio per lo studio delle tradizioni popolari, Vol. 8, pp. 49-56. With a
bibliography of 7 authors. [B.M.

2551. ———: Origine di alcuni proverbi, motti e modi proverbiali
castelterminesi. 8°. Palermo, 1885.
In Archivio per lo studio delle tradizioni popolari, Vol. 4, pp. 103-126. 20
proverbs with their explanatory traditions. [B.M.

2552. Grisanti (Cristoforo). Usi, credenze, proverbi e racconti
popolari di Isnello, *etc.* pp. 250.
L.3. sm. 8°. Palermo, *Reber*, 1899.
Section 3z, pp. 169-187, maxims and proverbs in the dialect of Isnello and
in ordinary Italian, followed by a section on proverbial and figurative phrases.
[F.-L.S.

2553. Guizzino (Celestino). I primi passi al comporre, *etc.* pp.
64. 50 centesimi. 16°. Palermo, *Amenta*, 1872.
Pp. 49-52, 47 Sicilian proverbs and sayings followed by the same number of
Italian ones.

2554. La Via Bonelli (Mariano). Proverbi nicosiani di Sicilia.
(Nuova raccolta di proverbi, *etc.*) 8°. Palermo, 1886.
In Archivio per lo studio delle tradizioni popolari, Vol. 5, pp. 68-74, 549-555.
Proverbs in the dialect of Nicosia, with Italian translations. [B.M.

2555. Longo (Agatino). Proverbi e modi di dire siciliani.
Firenze, 1864.
In Il Borghini, An. 2. 334 proverbs and proverbial sayings in the dialect of
Catania, with a literal Italian translation.

2556. Macaluso Storaci (Sebastiano). Nuovo vocabolario
siciliano-italiano e italiano-siciliano . . . contenente . . . i proverbi d'uso più comune, con aggiunte e correzioni. pp. xvi,
352, 44. 4°. Siracusa, *Norcia*, 1875.
Some hundred proverbs scattered throughout the book, but distinct by reason
of their block capitals. An interesting work with a good introduction. [B.M.

2557. Mangia (A.). Raccolta di proverbi siciliani.
Palermo, 1912.

2558. Minà-Palumbo (Francesco). Apicultura. Istruzioni per
gli agricoltori siciliani. Palermo, 1855.
In L'Empedocle, Vol. 5, pp. 26-50, 172-185. Section 4 contains Sicilian
proverbs on bees.

2559. ———: Proverbi siciliani e toscani sulla viticoltura.
8°. Palermo, 1865.
In Giornale di agricoltura, industria e commercio, Vol. 4, pp. 255-284. A
comparison of Sicilian and Tuscan proverbs on vine culture.

2560. Minà-Palumbo (Francesco). Studi agrarii sulla campagna settentrionale delle Madonie. . . . Proverbi agrarii, *etc.* pp. 298. 8°. Palermo, *Lauriel*, 1854.

Reprinted from the Annali di agricoltura siciliana, Serie Seconda, Vol. 1.

2561. Percolla (Vincenzo). Piccola fraseologia italiana . . . con l'aggiunta di molti proverbi siciliani dichiarati. pp. iv, 681. la. 16°. Catania, *Battiato*, 1889.

Contains many proverbs in Italian and Sicilian.

2562. Pitrè (Giuseppe). Alterazione di alcuni proverbi in Sicilia. 8°. Palermo, 1894.

In Archivio per lo studio delle tradizioni popolari, Vol. 13, pp. 149-152.
[B.M.

2563. ———: Blasone popolare siciliano. Proverbi inediti, *etc.* pp. 15. 8°. Palermo, *Tip. del Giornale di Sicilia*, 1891.

These proverbs are not included in the author's "Proverbi siciliani." Separate issue of an article in : Archivio per lo studio delle tradizioni popolari, Vol. 10, pp. 195-203.

2564. ———: Proverbi e canti popolari siciliani illustrati. pp. 43. 8°. Palermo, *Giornale di Sicilia*, 1869.

Bernstein, 2596. Only 206 copies issued.

2565. ———: Proverbi, motti e scongiuri del popolo siciliano. Raccolti ed illustrati da G. Pitrè. pp. ix, 441. L.7. 8°. Torino, *Clausen*, 1910.

Biblioteca delle tradizioni popolari siciliane, Vol. 23. Contains over a thousand proverbs not included in **2566.** Good from the point of view of both paremiology and folk-lore. Pp. 3-252, proverbs arranged under subjects; pp. 252-441, proverbial sayings, comparisons, threats, charms, *etc.* [F.-L.S.

2566. ———: Proverbi siciliani raccolti e confrontati con quelli degli dialetti d'Italia, *etc.* 4 vols. L.20. 16°. Palermo, *Lauriel*, 1880.

Pitrè, 3143. This work forms Vols. 8-11 of the "Biblioteca delle tradizioni popolari siciliane," edited by Pitrè. Vol. 1, pp. xlvii-lviii, Bibliography of Sicilian proverbs : pp. lix-lxx, bibliography of Italian proverbs in dialect : pp. lxxi-ccxxxiv, a long study on proverbs in general. Each Sicilian proverb is followed by its variants in 36 different dialects. There are also references to Biblical and classical proverbs. Altogether 30,000 proverbs, the classic book on the subject. The author occupied the Chair of Folk-lore at the University of Palermo. [B.M.

2567. ———: Proverbi siciliani spiegati dal popolo e illustrati. 8°. Palermo, *Natale*, 1874.

In Nuove Effemeridi siciliane, Serie 2, Vol. 1, pp. 103-109.

2568. ———: Sopra i proverbi. 8°. Palermo, *Giliberti*, 1863.

In La Favilla, Serie Seconda, Anno Primo, Nos. 1, 4, 8, 9. In all 182 Sicilian proverbs compared with Tuscan ones, with notes.

2569. Proverbi. Proverbi e canzoni siciliane. pp. 79. 12°. Messina, *Pappalardo*, 1829.

Pp. 5-28, Sicilian proverbs in verse. [U.C.L.

2570. Rapisarda (Santo). Raccolta di proverbj siciliani ridutti in canzuni. 4 vols.

    16°. Catania, *Università degli Studi, etc.*, 1824-1842.

Another edition. pp. viii, 277, xxx.

A proverb stands at the head of each poem.

      L.1.25. 16°. Catania, *Giannotta*, 1881.

                [B.M.

2571. Roccella (Remigio). Poesie e prose nella lingua parlata piazzese. pp. 192.

      L.2.40. 8°. Caltagirone, *Mantelli*, 1877.

Pp. 173-183, 235 " Proverbi Piazzesi."

2572. Salomone-Marino (Salvatore). Aneddoti, proverbi e motteggi illustrati da novellette popolari siciliane.

             8°. Palermo, 1883-84.

In Archivio per lo studio delle tradizioni popolari, Vol. 2, pp. 545-562; Vol. 3, pp. 89-96, 255-272, 569-580.   [B.M.

2573. ———: La omnipotenza dei proverbi dimostrata da una novelletta popolare siciliana.   8°. Palermo, 1891.

In Archivio per lo studio delle tradizioni popolari, Vol. 10, pp. 228-234. [B.M.

2574. Satta (Gio. Antonio Maria). Motti e concetti siciliani colla corrispondenza alla Sacra Bibbia, *etc.* pp. xii, 119.

        4°. Palermo, *Gagliani*, 1789.

718 proverbs, sayings and phrases arranged under subject headings and compared with excerpts from the Bible.

2575. Scarcella (Vincenzo). Adagi, motti, proverbi e modi proverbiali siciliani . . . con la corrispondenza dei latini, degli italiani, del testo biblico e delle sentenze dei filosofi e classici antichi. pp. 178. 8°. Messina, *Stamperia Fiumara*, 1846.

1500 proverbs and proverbial sayings in alphabetical order. The quotations from other texts, particularly the Latin, are frequently incorrect.   [B.M.

2576. Veneziano (Antonio). Raccolta di proverbij siciliani in ottava rima.   8°. Palermo, *Maringo*, 1628.

Latin translation. Siculorum proverbiorum, Sicularumque cantionum Latina traductio. pp. 192.

          12°. Messanae, 1744.

Another edition.   8°. Messina, *Rosano*, 1779.

Gratet-Duplessis, 468-469. Pitrè, 3371-3376, gives other editions.   [B.M.

2577. Vigo (Lionardi). Canti popolari siciliani, *etc.* pp. 372.

       8°. Catania, *Galatola*, 1857.

Pp. 355-370, proverbii.   [B.M.

See also **2286, 2481, 3659, 3767, 3795, 3994.**

19. MALTA.

2578. Sandreczki (C.). Die maltesische Mundart.

8°. Leipzig, 1879.

In Zeitschrift der deutschen morgenländischen Gesellschaft, Bd. 33, pp. 225-247. Pp. 226-247, Maltesische Sprüchwörter und Sprüche. 101 proverbs from Vassalli with German translations.   [B.M.

2579. Vassalli (Michel Antonio). Motti, aforismi, e proverbii maltesi, *etc.* pp. viii, 93.

8°. Malta, *stampato per l'autore*, 1828.

Gratet-Duplessis, 88. 863 proverbs arranged alphabetically in Maltese characters with Italian translations. Some of the illustrations are in Arabic. Reviewed in Journal des savants, avril, 1829.   [U.C.L.

20. SARDINIA.

2580. Delius (Nicolaus). Sardinische Sprichwörter.

4°. Bremen, 1858.

In Bremer Sonntagsblatt, 1858, Nr. 14. Proverbs, with German translations.
                                                                     [B.M.

2581. Proverbi. Proverbi di tutti i popoli. 1. Proverbi della Sardegna settentrionale. 2. Proverbi irlandesi.

4°. Milano, *Lampato*, 1840.

In L'Album, 1840, pp. 50-51, 117-118. 60 Sardinian proverbs taken from the mss. of Spano. 80 Irish ones republished from the Dublin Penny Journal, 1832-33. All are followed by an Italian translation.

2582. Spano (Giovanni). Proverbii sardi trasportati in lingua italiana, *etc.* pp. xvi, 92.

la. 8°. Cagliari, *Tip. Nazionale*, 1852.

Another edition. Proverbi sardi trasportati in lingua italiana, *etc.* pp. 414.   16°. Cagliari, *Tip. del Commercio*, 1871.

The later edition has 500 more proverbs than the first; altogether it contains just under 3000. The proverbs are nearly all in the Sardinian dialect, arranged alphabetically by their key-words. All have Italian translations, and most of them are compared with examples from the Hebrew, Latin, Greek, Arabic, *etc.* A useful book for students of Mediterranean dialects, not only from the paremiographical point of view, but because it preserves specimens of an interesting language. The 1852 edition was also published as part of the author's : Vocabolario Sardo-Italiano.   [B.M.

See also **2286.**

BALKAN.

1. JUGO-SLAV.

2583. Appendini (Francesco Maria). Grammatica della lingua illirica. . . . Edizione seconda. pp. xvii, 335.
8°. Ragusa, *Martecchini*, 1828.
Third edition. pp. 390. 8°. Ragusa, 1838.
Contains a section entitled Proverbii illirici. The proverbs have Italian translations and occasional brief explanatory notes. [B.M.

2584. Berilo. Pervo berilo za slovenske šole v c. k. austrijanskih deželah. pp. 156.
8°. na Dunaju, *v ces. kralj. založbi šolskih bukev*, 1863.
Pp. 73-74 and 136, Pregovori.

2585. Berlić (Ignaz Alois). Grammatik der illirischen Sprache. . . . 2. Auflage. pp. xviii, 384. 8°. Agram, 1842.
Third edition. pp. xv, 412. 8°. Agram, *Suppan*, 1850.
Contains a section of Illyrian and German proverbs. [B.M.

2587. Daničić (G.). Poslovice na svijet izdao. pp. xviii, 160.
8°. u Zagrebu, *Župan*, 1871.
5935 entries.

2588. Dobrowský (Josef). Slovanka, *etc.* 2 tom.
8°. Prag, *Herrl*, 1814-15.
Tom. 2, pp. 67-94, Serbian proverbs from the collection of Muškatiroić, with German translations. [B.M.

2590. Dragoni (S.). Narodne poslovice i rečenice.
fol. Mostar, 1884.
In Novi Hercegovački Bosiljak, God. 1, Br. 19, and God. 2, Br. 5.

2591. Ferić (Juro). G. Ferrichii Rhacusani fabulae ab illyricis adagiis desumptae. pp. 143.
8°. Rhacusae, *Trevisani*, 1794.
32 Illyrian proverbs, followed by Latin fables.

2593. Forster (Riccardo). Proverbi popolari dalmati.
Zara, 1889 and 1891.
In La Domenica, An. 2, No. 14; An. 4, No. 6. Communicated by Riccardo Forster.

2594. Forster (Riccardo). Tradizioni popolari dalmate. Proverbi meteorologici: santi, mesi e giorni.

10 soldi. fol. Zara, *Artale*, 1891.

In Il Dalmata, giornale politico, economico, letterario, Anno 26, Nos. 91-93. 11 proverbs of Zara, with many variants taken from different Italian collections.

2595. Frankl (Ludwig August). Gusle. Serbische National-lieder. pp. xxiv, 126. 8°. Wien, *Wenedikt*, 1852.

Pp. 121-126, Serbian proverbs translated into German. [B.M.

2596. Froehlich (Rudolph A.). Kurze theoretisch-praktische Taschen-Grammatik der serbischen Sprache. *Second edition*. pp. 232. 12°. Wien, *Wenedikt*, 1870.

Contains a section of Serbian proverbs with German translations. [B.M.

2597. ———: Theoretisch-praktische Taschen-Grammatik . . . der illirischen Sprache . . . Zweite . . . Auflage, *etc.* pp. lxviii, 83. 8°. Wien, *Wenedikt*, 1850.

Pp. 43-49, proverbs with German translations. [B.M.

2598. Gilferding (A. Th.). Старинный сборникъ сербскихъ пословицъ, *etc.* 8°. С.-Петербургъ, 1869.

In Записки Императорскаго Русскаго Географическаго Общества, по Отдѣленію Этнографіи,

Tom. 2, pp. 115-224. 3565 entries in alphabetical order. [B.M.

2599. Hanuš (Igňać Jan). Bibliotheka slovanského příslovnictví. Svazek 1. Literatura příslovnictví slovanského a německého, či předchůdcové Fr. Lad. Čelakovského v "Mudroslovi národu slovanského v příslovích." Uspořádal Dr. Igň. Jan Hanuš. pp. [x], 147. 8°. v Praze, *Nakladem spisovatelovým*, 1853.

Contains many bibliographical notes concerning principally books of Slavonic proverbs. [B.M.

2600. Hess (Emil). Говорите ли српски. Serbo-kroatisch-deutsches Gesprächbuch, *etc.* pp. viii, 155. 8°. Leipzig, *Koch*, 1892.

Pp. 103-105, proverbs. [B.M.

2601. Ilić (Luka). Narodni slavonski običaji, *etc.* pp. 316. 8°. u Zagrebu, *Suppan*, 1846.

Pp. 243-252, 271 proverbs in alphabetical order. [B.M.

2602. Ive (Antonio). L'antico dialetto di Veglia. 8°. Roma, *etc.*, *Loescher*, 1886.

In Archivio glottologico italiano, Vol. 9, p. 141. 21 sayings and proverbs quoted. [B.M.

2603. Janežić (Anton). Cvetje slovanskega naroda, *etc.* pp. viii, 96. 12°. v Celovcu, *Kleinmayr*, 1852.

Pp. 85-91, Prislovice in pregovori. [B.M.

2604. Janežić (Anton). Praktischer Unterricht in der slovenischen Sprache . . . Zweite . . . Auflage. pp. 228.
8°. Klagenfurt, *Sigmund*, 1850.
Pp. 157-159, einige Sprichwörter.

2605. Kapetanovitć-Ljubušak (Mehmed), *Beg*. Narodno blago, *etc.* pp. 460. 8°. u Sarajevu, *Troškom vlastnika*, 1887.
More than 5000 proverbs. Reviewed in Mélusine, Tome 4, Col. 73-76.
[B.M.

2606. Karadzić (Vuk Stefanović). Народне српске пословице, *etc.* pp. l, [10], 362, [16].
Another edition. pp. liii, 388.
8°. на Цетињу, *Народна Штампарија,* 1836.
8°. у Бечу, *Јерменски,* 1849.
[B.M.

2608. ———: Serbische Sprichwörter in serbischer Sprache.
Wien, *Volke*, 1836.

2609. ———: Volksmärchen der Serben, *etc.* pp. xii, 345.
8°. Berlin, *Reimer*, 1854.
Pp. 271-345, Sprichwörter. [B.M.

2610. Kasumović (Ivan). Hrvatske i srpske narodne poslovice spram grčkih i rimskih poslovicâ i krilaticâ.
8°. u Zagrebu, *Jugoslavenska Akademija*, 1911, 1912.
In Rad Jugoslavenske Akademije znanosti i umjetnosti, knjiga 189, pp. 116-276; and knjiga 191, pp. 68-264. A commentary, followed by a large collection of proverbs and sayings compared with Greek and Latin ones. [B.M.

2611. Kocbek (Fran.). Pregovori, prilike in reki. pp. iv, 95.
8°. v Ljubljani, *Trstenjak*, 1887.
Contains about 3000 proverbs and a bibliography.

2612. Korajac (Vilim). Filozofija hrvatsko-srbskih narodnih poslovica. pp. 134. 8°. u Osieku, *Selzer*, 1876.
[B.M.

2613. Krauss (Friedrich S.). Sreća. Glück und Schicksal im Volksglauben der Süd-Slaven, *etc.* pp. 197.
8°. Wien, *Hölder*, 1886.
Pp. 177-188, Glückssprichwörter, 46 proverbs in the original and with German translations. This is a separate publication of an article in Mittheilungen der anthropologischen Gesellschaft in Wien, Bd. 16 (N.F., Bd. 6).

2614. Krek (Gregor). Einleitung in die slavische Literaturgeschichte, *etc.* pp. vi, 336.
8°. Graz, *Leuschner & Lubensky*, 1874.
Second edition. pp. xi, 887. 8°. Graz, 1887.
There is a section entitled Sprichwörter, Aberglaube, Zaubersprüche und Räthsel, which contains bibliographical and other notes on proverbs. [B.M.

2615. Křížek (Vácslav). Anthologie jihoslovanská, *etc.* pp. xiv, 344. 8°. v Praze, *Storch*, 1863.

Pp. 68-69, 146-147, 232-233, Serb and Slovene proverbs, *etc.* [B.M.

2616. Marković (Fr.). Etički sadržaj naših narodnih poslovica, *etc.* 8°. u Zagrebu, *Hartmann*, 1889.

In Rad Jugoslavenske Akademije Znanosti i Umjetnosti, Knjiga 96. Razredi filologicko-historički i filosofičko -juridički, 25, pp. 167-227. A commentary. [B.M.

2617. Metelko (Franz Seraph). Lehrgebäude der slowenischen Sprache, *etc.* pp. xxxvi, 296. 8°. Laibach, *Eger*, 1825.

Pp. 275-280, Proverbs of Carniola with German translations. [B.M.

2618. Muegge (Maximilian A.). Serbian folk songs, fairy tales and proverbs. (Fairy tales and proverbs . . . translated from Miss Karadžić's [translation of V. S. Karadžić's] Volksmärchen der Serben). pp. 167.

3/6. sm. 8°. London, *Drane*, [1917].

Pp. 145-152, proverbs in English. [F.-L.S. (Stephens collection).

2619. Muka (Ernst). Hornjoserbske Iudowe pešnje, *etc.* pp. 11. 8°. [w Budyšinje, *Monse*, 1887].

Bernstein, 2281. Reprint of an article from some periodical. Pp. 6-11, Serbske narodne přislowa, *etc.*

2620. Muškatiroić (Ivan). Pričte iliti po prostomu poslovice.

Wien, 1787.

Another edition. 12°. Budin, 1807.

In Serbian characters. The book referred to in Bernstein, 873, is presumably the same as that included by Stuckey Lean, p. 104. [Bristol Public Library.

2621. Pečnik (Carl Joseph). Praktisches Lehrbuch der slovenischen Sprache, *etc.* pp. 191.

sm. 8°. Wien, *Hartleben*, [1890].

Die Kunst der Polyglottie, 31. Pp. 105-106, 24 proverbs with German translations. [B.M.

2622. Plohl Herdvigov (Rikardo Ferdinando). Hrvatske narodne pjesme i pripoviedke u Vrbovcu, *etc.* 3 tom.

12°. u Varaždinu, *Platzer*, 1868-76.

Tom. 2, pp. 80-96, Nekolikho hrvatskih narodnih poslovica, izraza i rieči.

2623. Popović (Marko Miljanov). Примјери чојства и јунаштва. pp. 103. 8°. Београд, 1901.

[B.M.

2624. Poslovice. Narodne poslovice. 8°. u Zagrebu, 1850, 51, 61.

In Bosanski Prijatelj, Svezak 1-3. 863 entries.

2625. ———: Narodne poslovice i rečenice.

fol. Mostar, 1884, 1885.

In Novi Hercegovački Bosiljak, God. 1, Br. 2, and God. 2, Br. 1.

2626. Primiz (Janes Nep.).   Deutsch-slovenisches Lesebuch, *etc.* pp. 147.   8°.   v Nemshkim Gradzu, *Milerzi*, 1813.

Pp. 79-86, Sprichwörter—Prigóvori.

2627. Proverbs. Servian proverbs.   8°.   London, 1855.

In Fraser's Magazine, Vol. 51, pp. 517-526.   An article containing numerous examples in English.   [B.M.

2628. Sabalich (G.).   Ricreazioni dialettali.

4°.   Zara, *Woditzka*, 1891.

In Zara, *etc.*, Anno 1, Nos. 39-42.   In No. 39, an article on proverbs and particularly on dialect proverbs.   In Nos. 40-42, a collection of Dalmatian proverbs and proverbial sayings and comparisons with some Venetian ones. Published collectively as :

Saggio di voci, modi e proverbi nella parlata popolare zaratina. pp. 54.
la. 8°.   Zara, 1892.

2629. Slaveikov (Petko Rachev). Български притчи или пословици и характерни думи. 2 pts.

8°.   Пловдив, *Единство,* 1889.
                                                                                    [B.M.

2630. Sprichwörter. Bosnische Sprichwörter.   fol.   Wien, 1887.

In Die Presse, Jahrgang 40, No. 354, 24th December, 1887.

2631. Stojanović (Mijat).   Šala i zbilja, *etc.* pp. iv, 254.

12°.   u Senju, *Luster*, 1879.

Pp. 144-187, Narodne poslovice.

2632. ———— : Sbirka narodnih poslovicah, riečih i izrazah.   pp. 271.   8°.   u Zagrebu, *Jakić*, 1886.

Arranged alphabetically by the principal words, with brief notes.   [B.M.

2633. Svillić (M.).   Narodne poslovice i rečenice.

fol.   Mostar, 1884.

In Hercegovački Bosiljak, God. 2, Br. 17.

2634. Turner (K. Amy).   National proverbs : Serbia. pp. 91.

1/-. sm. 8°.   London, *Palmer*, [1915].

Serbian proverbs translated into English.   No notes, only a list.

[F.-L.S. (Stephens collection).

2635. Urbas (Wilhelm).   Sprichwörter der Slowenen.

4°.   Wien, Prag, *Tempsky*, 1897.

In Zeitschrift für österreichische Volkskunde, Jahrgang 3, pp. 334-342. 301 proverbs translated into German.   [B.M.

2636. Urlić (Ivan).   Narodne poslovice.   fol.   Mostar, 1884.

In Hercegovački Bosiljak, God. 2, Br. 1.

2637. Velimirović (Nikolaj).   Serbia in light and darkness, *etc.* pp. xii, 147 + plates.   8°.   London, *etc.*, *Longmans*, 1916.

Pp. 105-130, fragments of Serbian national wisdom.   A collection of proverbs, maxims, sayings, aphorisms, *etc.*, in English.   [B.M.

See also under Istria, and **3798, 3799, 3851, 3985.**

2. ALBANIAN.

2640. Camardo (Demetrio). Appendice al saggio di grammato-
logia comparata sulla lingua albanese. pp. lviii, 268.
8°. Prato, *Alberghetti*, 1866.
Pp. 54-60, proverbs in Albanian with Italian translations.

2641. Dozon (Louis Auguste Henri). Manuel de la langue chkipe
ou albanaise, *etc.* 2 pts. 8°. Paris, *Leroux*, 1878.
Part 1, pp. 122-126, 59 proverbs with French translations. [B.M.

2642. Hahn (Johann Georg von). Albanesische Studien, *etc.*
3 Hefte. 4°. Jena, *Mauke*, 1854.
Heft 2, pp. 151-157, toskische Sprichwörter, Redensarten und Sentenzen.
138 proverbs with German translations. [B.M.

2643. Mitkos (E.). ᾿Αλβανικὴ μέλισσα, *etc.* pp. 11 + 233 + 12.
8°. Alexandria, 1878.
Pp. 9-33, 490 Albanian proverbs with corresponding Greek ones.

2644. Pisko (Julius). Kurzgefasstes Handbuch der nordalbanesi-
schen Sprache. pp. iv, 165. 8°. Wien, *Hölder*, 1896.
Pp. 163-165, Albanesische Redensarten und Sprichwörter. A few proverbs
with German translations. [B.M.

2645. Rada (Girolamo de). Proverbe t' Arbëres = Proverbi
albanesi. 8°. Corigliano, *Tip. letteraria*, 1883-1884.
Pitrè, 2698-2700. *In* Fiàmuri Arbërit, La Bandiera dell' Albania, *etc.*,
Anno 1, Nos. 3, 4, 6. In all, 38 proverbs with Italian translations. [B.M.

3. BULGARIAN.

2646. Altmann (Julius). Die Sprichwörter der Bulgaren.
8°. Bautzen, *Schmaler*, 1853.
In Jahrbücher für slawische Literatur, 1853, pp. 1-10. Proverbs are quoted
in German. [B.M.

2647. Baerlein (Henry). The shade of the Balkans: being a
collection of Bulgarian folk-songs and proverbs [compiled by
P. R. Slaveikov] . . . rendered into English [by H. Bernard,
pseud. of H. Baerlein], *etc.* pp. 328.
7/6. 8°. London, *Nutt*, 1904.
Pp. 225-232, 101 proverbs translated into English.
[F.-L.S. (Stephens collection).

2648. Cholakov (Vasili). Българскый народенъ сборникъ.
[Edited by V. Cholakov]. pp. 356, xii.
8°. [Болградъ, 1872.]
Pp. 125-246, 3300 proverbs and proverbial sayings in alphabetical order.
[B.M.

2649. Karavelov (Lyuben). Памятники народнаго быта болгаръ,
etc. pp. 324. 8°. Москва, *Андерсъ*, 1861.
Pp. 1-157, Пословицы и поговорки. Pp. 158-172, Примѣчанія къ
пословицамъ. 3000 entries. [B.M.

U

2650. Krachtoglus (A. K.). Συλλογὴ τῶν ἐν Βάρνῃ καὶ τοῖς πέριξ αὐτῆς ἐν χρήσει δημώδων παροιμιῶν. pp. 32.

8°. ἐν Ἀθήναις, Κούβελος καὶ Τρίμης, 1880.

Bernstein, 1764.

2651. Slaveikov (Petko Rachev). Български притчи или пословици, *etc.* 2 v. 8°: Пловдив, София, 1889-97.

Arranged alphabetically. [B.M.

ROUMANIAN.

2652. Barcianu (Sav'a Popovici). Theoretisch-praktische Grammatik der romänischen Sprache, *etc.* pp. vi, 384.

8°. Hermannstadt, *Steinhaussen*, 1858.

Third edition.   8°. Hermannstadt, *Schmiedicke*, 1871.

1858 edition, pp. 325-334, proverbs with German translations. The third edition only contains a brief list without translations.   [B.M.

2653. Codrescu (Teodoru). Dialoguri francesco-romanesci. . . . Editia a treia. pp. 174.   8°. Iasii, 1851.

Pp. 156-174, Idiotismes et proverbes.

2654. Dumitrescu (Al.). Galicisme, proverbe, maxime, barbarisme.   Bucuresci, *Muller*, 1894.

2655. Franzos (Carl Emil). Vom Don zur Donau, *etc.* 2 Bde.

8°. Leipzig, *Dunker & Humblot*, 1878, 1877.

Bd. 1, pp. 295-333, Rumänische Sprichwörter. A commentary with numerous examples in German.   [B.M.

2656. Gaster (Moses). Chrestomathie roumaine, *etc.* 2 tom.

8°. Leipzig, *Brockhaus*, Bucuresči, *Socecŭ*, 1891.

Tom. 2, pp. 372-376, Proverbe şi zicătorĭ. A list of proverbs from Pann's Povestea vorbii.   [B.M.

2657. ———: Literatura populară romăna. pp. xii, 605.

8°. Bucureşti, *Haimann*, 1883.

Pp. 197-223, proverbs.   [B.M.

2658. Gerrard (E.). The land beyond the forest, *etc.* *See* **515.**

2659. Haltrich (Josef). Zur Culturgeschichte der Sachsen in Siebenbürgen, *etc.* pp. 38.

8°. Hermannstadt, *Steinhaussen*, 1867.

Pp. 27-31, Sprichwörter, bildliche Redensarten, Regeln der Bauernpraktik.

2660. ———: Zur Volkskunde der Siebenbürger Sachsen, *etc.* pp. xvi, 535.   8°. Wien, *Graeser*, 1885.

Pp. 91-102, Die Tierwelt in Sprichwort und Redensart : pp. 341-406, Sprichwörter, sprichwörtliche Redensarten, *etc.*: pp. 407-492, Deutsche Inschriften aus Siebenbürgen. The proverbs are given in dialect, with German translations.   [B.M.

2661. Hintescu (J. C.). Proverbele românilorú, *etc.* pp. viii, 210. 12°. Sibiu, *Closius*, 1877.

2662. Ispirescu (P.). Dicătorĭ populare.

8°. Bucurescĭ, 1883-84.

In Revista pentru Storie, Archeologie şi Filologie, Vol. 1, pp. 224-235, 450-460 : Vol. 3, pp. 144-163. Over 1500 proverbs. [B.M.

2663. Kaindl (Raimund Friedrich). Die Huzulen, *etc.* pp. iv, 129 + plate. 8°. Wien, *Hölder*, 1894.

Pp. 120-125, 56 proverbs with German translations. [B.M.

2664. Pann (Anton). Culegere de proverburi sau Povestea vorbiĭ. pp. 192. 8°. 1847.

Another edition. 3 pts. 8°. Bucuresci, 1852-53.

Another edition. pp. viii, 179 + portrait.

8°. Bucuresci, *Cucu*, 1889.

The edition of 1852-53 is in Cyrillic characters. A selection of these proverbs is contained in M. Gaster's Chrestomathie roumaine. [B.M.

2665. Papahagi (Perikle). Sammlung aromunischer Sprichwörter und Rätsel. 8°. Leipzig, *Barth*, 1895.

In Zweiter Jahresbericht des Instituts für rumänische Sprache zu Leipzig, 1895. Pp. 147-192, 384 proverbs with German translations, and occasional notes or comparisons with proverbs of other languages. [B.M.

2666. Petricelcu-Hasdeu (Bogdanŭ). Legende şi basmele Romaniloru, *etc.* pp. xxi, 180.

12°. Bucurescĭ, *Typographia Laboratorilor Romani*, 1872.

Pp. 164-180, Proverbĭ.

2667. Reinsberg-Düringsfeld (Otto von), *Baron.* Die Sprichwörter der Romänen im Vergleich zu denen anderen romanischen Völker. 8°. Leipzig, *Brockhaus*, 1865.

In Jahrbuch für romanische und englische Literateur, Bd. 6, pp. 173-195.

[B.M.

2668. Schuller (Johann Carl). Aus der Walachei. Romänische Gedichte und Sprichwörter, *etc.* 8°. Hermannstadt, 1851.

Third edition. pp. 55.

8°. Hermannstadt, *Steinhaussen*, 1852.

Contains a large collection of proverbs in German, with occasional notes or comparisons with other languages. [B.M.

2669. Schuster (Friedrich Wilhelm). Siebenbürgisch-sächsische Volkslieder, Sprichwörter, Räthsel, *etc.* pp. xxiv, 556.

8°. Hermannstadt, *Steinhaussen*, 1865.

Pp. 147-258, Sprichwörter (zum grössten Theil aus Mühlbach und Schässburg, dann aus Sächsisch-Regen, Bistritz, Marpod, Braler und Kronstadt). 1131 proverbs. [B.M.

2670. Teodorescu (G. Dem.). Cercetărĭ asupra proverbelorŭ române . . . Ştudiŭ criticŭ şi bibliograficŭ. pp. 107.

    8°. Bucuresčĭ, *Noua typographia Laboratorilor Romani*, 1877.

A commentary with some examples. [B.M.

2671. Valentineanu (I. G.). Gugetărĭ, maxime, proverbe, anecdote. Bucuresci, 1890.

2672. Vizoly (E. Z.). Sprichwörter des rumänischen Volkes, *etc.* pp. 80. 8°. Panscova, *Wittigschlager*, 1883.

1000 entries translated into German.

2673. Wechsler (Théophile). Praktisches Lehrbuch der rumänischen Sprache, *etc.* pp. viii, 184.

    8°. Wien, *Hartleben*, [1890].

Die Kunst der Polyglottie, Th. 21. Pp. 138-142, Sprichwörter-Sammlung. Roumanian proverbs with German translations. [B.M.

2674. Weigand (Gustav). Die Aromunen, *etc.* pp. xviii, 383. 2 Bde. 8°. Leipzig, *Barth*, 1895, 94.

Bd. 2, pp. 276-279, Sprichwörter und sprichwörtliche Redensarten. 25 proverbs in the original and with German translations. [B.M.

2675. Zanne (Juliu A.). Proverbele Românilor din România, Basarabia, Bucovina, Ungaria, Istria şi Macedonia, *etc.* *In progress.* 8°. Bucaresci, *Socecŭ*, 1895, *etc.*

A huge collection, forming 9 vols. to date, of Roumanian proverbs, maxims, idioms, phrases, *etc.*, arranged alphabetically. Full notes. Proverbs of other languages are frequently given in comparison. There is a bibliography of authors quoted, and a Roumanian-French glossary. [B.M.

See also **515 n., 934, 3168.**

HUNGARIAN.

2676. Almásy János). Magyar közmondások gyüjteménye különös tekintettel az életbölcseségre és a nevelésre, *etc.* pp. 379.　frt.1.　8°.　Budapest, *Franklin-Társulat,* 1890.

Pp. 16-19, bibliography. Over 600 proverbs arranged under subject headings. [B.M.

2677. Bloch (Móricz). Baronyai Decsi János és Kis-Viczay Péter közmondásai. Ballagi Mór R. Tagtól A. M. Tud [*i.e.* by M. Bloch]. pp. 15.

8°. Budapest, *Am. Tud. Akadémia Könyvkiadóhivatala,* 1882.

In the Academy's series, Értekezések a nyelv és széptudományi osztály köréböl, köt. x, szam. 5. A brief article on the collections of proverbs made by the above writers. [B.M.

2678. ——— : Magyar példabeszédek, közmondások és szójárások gyüjteménye, *etc.* pp. xxviii, 462. 2 kötet.

　　　　　　　　　　　　　　8°. Szarvason, *Réthy,* 1850.

Second edition.　　　　　　　Pest, *Heckenast,* 1855.

Stirling-Maxwell, p. 6. Bernstein, 157-8. 8313 proverbs and sayings arranged alphabetically by key-words, frequently accompanied by notes and comparisons with proverbs of other countries. [B.M.

2679. Buenker (J. R.). Heanzische Sprichwörter.

　　　　　　　　　　　　　8°. Budapest, *Boruth,* 1894.

In Ethnologische Mitteilungen aus Ungarn, Bd. 3, pp. 287-291. 100 proverbs in dialect. [B.M.

2680. Dugonics (András). Magyar példa beszédek és jeles mondások, *etc.* 2 rész.　　　　8°. Szegeden, 1820.

Gratet-Duplessis, 878. With full notes. [B.M.

2681. Erdélyi (János). Magyar Közmondások Könyve, *etc.* pp. iv, 462.

　　　　20 frt., 20 kr. 8°. Pesten, *Kisfaludy Társaság,* 1851.

Stirling-Maxwell, p. 31. 9000 Magyar proverbs arranged alphabetically, followed by a commentary. [B.M.

2682. Faludi (Ferencz). Faludi F. Költeményes Maradványi, *etc.* 2 köt.　　　　8°. Györött, *Strajbig,* 1786-87.

Vol. 2, pp. 117-144, Magyar közmondások. An alphabetical list without notes. [B.M.

310

2683. Fauvin (Léon). Études sur la langue magyare, *etc.* pp. 300. 8°. Pesth, *Rosenberg,* 1870.
Pp. 279-281, 25 Hungarian proverbs with French translations.

2684. Füredi (Ignác). Ungarisch-deutsche Gespräche, *etc.* pp. 352. 12°. Budapest, *Méhner,* n.d.
Pp. 182-315, proverbs and phrases in Hungarian and German.

2685. Garay (János). Magyar és német beszelgetesek kézikönyvf . . . Handbuch ungarisch - deutscher Gespräche. *Fourth edition.* pp. xvi, 320. 8°. Pesten, *Heckenast,* 1851.
Twelfth edition. pp. xvi, 300.
8°. Budapest, *Franklin-Verein,* 1895.
Contains a section of Hungarian and German proverbs and proverbial phrases. [B.M.

2686. Kis-Viczay (Péter). Selectiora adagia latino-hungarica, *etc. pp.* [xxxii], 552.
12°. Bartphae, *Typis civitatis,* 1713.

2687. Kovács (Pál). Magyar példa, és közmondási. pp. 235.
sm. 8°. Győrben, *Streibig,* 1794.
Bernstein, 1762.

2688. Margalits (Ede). Bácskai közmondások és szólásmódok. pp. 45. sm. 8°. Baján, 1877.

2689. ———: Magyar közmondások és közmondásszerü szólások, *etc.* pp. vii, 770. 8°. Budapest, *Kokai,* [1896].
Proverbs arranged alphabetically by the principal words; no notes. A large collection. B.M.

2690. Proverbia. Proverbia metrico-rhythmica, *etc.* pp. 58.
50 kr. 8°. Budapest, [1889].
Proverbs arranged alphabetically by the Latin, followed by the Hungarian. [B.M.

2691. Rauck (Melchior). Der ungarische Sprachmeister, . . . von Meliboeo [*pseud.* of Melchior Rauck].
8°. Pressburg, *Landerer,* 1774.
Gratet-Duplessis, 879. Pp. 196-212, Hungarian proverbs. Earlier editions do not contain the proverbs.

2692. Schlandt (Heinrich). Deutsch-magyarisches Sprichwörter-Lexikon, *etc.* pp. 393. 8°. Kronstadt, *Kerschner,* 1913.
Arranged alphabetically by the German, with the Hungarian opposite. No notes. [B.M.

2693. Schröer (Karl Julius). Versuch einer Darstellung der deutschen Mundarten des ungrischen Berglandes mit Sprachproben und Erläuterungen. pp. 253-436 + map.
8°. Wien, *K. K. Hof- und Staatsdruckerei,* 1863.
In Sitzungsberichte der phil.-hist. Classe der kais. Akademie der Wissenschaften, Bd. 44, pp. 378-380, Sprichwörter und Redensarten aus Metzenseifen (36). [B.M.

2694. Sirisaka (Andor).   Magyar közmondások könyve, *etc.* **pp.**
lxx, 279.   frt.2.   8°.   Pécsett, *Engel*, 1890.
A long introduction, containing, pp. xlvi-lv, a bibliography, followed by a
large collection of proverbs in alphabetical order, with some brief notes. [B.M.

2695. Stockinger (Julius).   Ungarische Sprichwörter in deutscher
Sprache, *etc.*   1. Stufe.   pp. 36.
                                 sm. 8°.   Wien, *Hartleben*, [1919].

2696. Szabó (Román).   Válogatott közmondások, *etc.*   pp. 70.
                                          8°.   Miskolcon, 1856.

2697. Szent-Páli (Stephanus).   Grammatica Hungarica, *etc.*
                                 8°.   Cibinii, *Hochmeister*, 1795.
Gratet-Duplessis, 880.   Pp. 283-302, Adagia in Transylvaniae principatu
inter Hungaros vigentia, eaque Hungarico-latina.

2698. Szirmay (Antal).   Hungaria in parabolis, sive commentarii
in adagia et dicteria Hungarorum, *etc.*   pp. [xvi], 160.
                                          8°.   Budae, 1804.
Gratet-Duplessis, 881.   [B.M.

2699. Takács (Emerico).   L'Arte di diventare un perfetto
ungherese . . . con una parte pratica, contenente i . . . proverbi, *etc.*   pp. 75.   8°.   Verona, *Zanchi*, [*c.* 1860].
Pp. 57-63, proverbs with Italian translations.

CZECH.

2700. Bartoš (František). Česká čítanka pro druhou třídu škol
středních. Druhé, poopravené vydání. pp. 203.
8°. v Brně, *Winiker*, 1886.
Bernstein, 184. Pp. 21, 109, 126, 150, 191, proverbs.

2701. ———: Česká čítanka pro první třídu škol středních.
Vydání třetí, nezměněné. pp. 203.
8°. v Praze, *Urbánek*, 1883.
Bernstein, 183. Pp. 16-17, 87-88, 138-139, 179-180, 183, proverbs.

2702. ———: Lid a národ, *etc*. pp. 337.
12°. ve Velkém Meziříčí, *Šašek*, 1885.
Bernstein, 185. Pp. 327-337, Pes v zrcadle našich přísloví a pořekadel.

2703. ———: Moravská přísloví a pořekadla.
8°. v Praze, *Šimáček*, 1896.
In Český Lid, Ročník 5, pp. 417-422, 541-546. [B.M.

2703a. Bernolák (Antonius). Grammatica slavica, *etc*. pp. xvi,
312. 8°. Posonii, *Landerer*, 1790.
Bernstein, 272. Pp. 284-312, Porekadla slowenské—Adagia slavica.

2704. Březina (Josef). Hláskování spojené se psáním, *etc*. pp.
x, 107. 8°. v Kolíně, *Bayer*, 1880.
Bernstein, 392. P. 94, Přísloví.

2705. Brunclík (Josef). Obrazy z písemnictví Českého, *etc*. pp.
125. 8°. Mladá Boleslav, *Vačlen*, 1893.
Bernstein, 413. Pp. 70-71, proverbs, *etc*.

2706. Carro (Jean de). Proverbes bohèmes. 12°. Prague, 1841.
Bernstein, 515. *In* Almanach de Carlsbad, Année 11, pp. 136-149.

2707. Čelakovský (František Ladislav). Česká čítací kniha pro
druhou třídu nižšiho gymnasia. Vydání šesté. pp. [viii],
289. 8°. v Praze, *Tempský*, 1875.
Eighth edition. pp. 249. 8°. v Praze, *Tempský*, 1884.
Each edition contains two small sections entitled respectively : Přísloví o
domovu a vlasti, and Pravidla opatrnosti v národních příslovích. [B.M.

2708. Červenka (Matěj). Přislowi česká. (Ze starého rukopisu).
8°. v Praze, *Calve*, 1829.

In Časopis společnosti wlastenského Museum w Čechách. Třeti ročni běh. Swazek čtwrtý, pp. 39-73. Červenka is the author of the old ms. [B.M.

2709. Čupr (František). Böhmisches Lesebuch . . . Zweite umgeänderte Auflage. pp. viii, 268.
8°. Prag, *André*, 1852.

Bernstein, 729. This book forms Theil 2 of " Böhmisches Elementarwerk." Pp. 113-114, Přísloví česká : pp. 146-147, Pořekadla česká : pp. 158-159, Přísloví všeslovanská.

2710. Dobrowský (Josef). Sammlung böhmischer Sprichwörter.
8°. 1804.
Gratet-Duplessis, 877.

2710a. Dobšinský (Pavel). Sbierka slovenských porekadiel a jim podružných viet. 8°. vo Viedni, *Matica Slovenská*, 1870.

In Sborník slovenských národnich piesni, *etc.*, Swäzok 1, pp. 83-107. 1174 entries.

2711. Doležal (Pavel). Grammatica Slavico-Bohemica, *etc.* pp. xxviii, 321. 8°. Posonii, *Typis Roverianis*, 1746.

Gratet-Duplessis, 876. Pp. 272-321, proverbs followed by metaphorical phrases and Cato's distiches in Bohemian, with Latin translations. [B.M.

2712. Encyklopedie. Encyklopedie humoru a vtipu, *etc.*
8°. v Praze, *Vilimek*, n.d.
Bernstein, 990. Svazek 7, Sešit 7, 8, pp. 221-231, humorous proverbs.

2713. Flajšhans (Václav). Česká přísloví, *etc.* 2 vols.
4°. v Praze, *Šimáček*, 1911-13.

A large collection of proverbs and phrases arranged alphabetically by the principal words. The introduction contains a bibliography. [B.M.

2714. Flaška (Smil) *z Pardubic.* Der neue Rath, . . . des Herrn Smil von Pardubic, *etc.* pp. viii, 85.
sm. 8°. Leipzig, *Weigel*, 1855.

Bernstein, 3427. Pp. 75-85, Altböhmische Sprüche und Sprüchwörter.
[B.M.

2715. Hrubý (Karel). Sbírka přísloví, pořekadel a průpovědí, kterých užívá náš lid rolnický. pp. 39.
8°. v Praze, *Otto*, 1880.
Bernstein, 1546.

2716. Hulakovský (J. E.). Česká přísloví s příslovími v moderních a klassických jazycích srovnává J. E. Hulakovský. [Příloha ku Kroku 3]. pp. 95.
8°. [v Praze, *Šimáček*, 1889?].
Bernstein, 1551. In Krok, Ročník 3-5, 1889-1891.

2717. Hykeš (Vácslav). Zlatá zrna, čili Schránka přísloví, *etc.* pp. 48. 8°. v Praze, *Otto*, 1874.
Bernstein, 1555.

2718. Jahelka (Boh.). Přísloví a pořekadla na Hořicku.
8°. v Hořicích, *Redakčni Komitet*, 1895.
In Národopisný Sborník okresu Hořického, 1895, pp. 116-126.

2719. Jireček (Josef). Anthologie z literatury české, *etc.* 3 pts.
8°. v Praze, 1860, 58, 61.
Another edition. 3 pts. 8°. v Praze, *Tempský*, 1879-1881.
Svazek 1 contains a small section entitled : " z přísloví "; Svazek 3, a slightly larger one entitled : " Přísloví a pořekadla." [B.M.

2720. Komenský (Jan Amos). Didaktika, *etc.* pp. xx, 268.
8°. v Praze, *u Řiwnáče*, 1849.
Bernstein, 1742. Pp. 198-268, Maudrost starých předků za zrcadlo **wystawená** potomkům.

2721. Kopecký (Jan). Pravidla moudrosti a opatrnosti, kteráž z " Mudroslovi " Fr. L. Čelakovského mládeži české vybral J. Kopecký. pp. 93. 12°. v Praze, *Urbánek*, 1875.
Bernstein, 1747. Pp. 9-66, Česká přísloví : pp. 67-93, Česká pořekadla.

2722. Kosina (Jan) and **Bartoš** (František). Malá Slovesnosť . . . Vydání třetí. pp. 340. 8°. v Brně, *Winiker*, 1883.
Bernstein, 1757. Pp. 223-226, Přísloví, Gnoma, Epigram.

2723. Kueffer (Wilhelm). Sprichwörter und Redensarten in Gründner Mundart. Aus Merény (Wagendrüssel).
8°. Budapest, *Vörösmarty Buchdruckerei*, 1897.
In Ethnologische Mitteilungen aus Ungarn, Bd. 5, 1896, pp. 207-210. 153 proverbs. Zips proverbs, a German dialect in Czecho-Slovakia. [B.M.

2724. Liblínský (Jan Slawibor). Česká přislowi a pořekadla, *etc.* pp. xxx, 236. 16°. v Praze, *Hess*, 1848.

2725. Macháček (Simeon Karel). Böhmische Chrestomathie für Deutsche, *etc.* pp. 271, 125.
8°. Prag, *Kronberger & Weber*, 1830.
Pp. 5-10, Sprichwörter der Böhmen : pp. 10-18, Denksprüche **und kürzere** Aufsätze. In Czech, with a few words and remarks in German. [B.M.

2726. Mojžíš (Antonín). České dítě, *etc.* pp. viii, 120.
4°. v Praze, *Hynek*, 1889.
Bernstein, 2233. Pp. 103-116, proverbs and sayings.

2727. Novák (J. V.) and **Vorovka** (Karel). Kniha moudrosti. Sborník aforismi a sentencí pædagogických. pp. viii, 324.
8°. v Praze, *Bursik & Kohout*, 1892.
Bernstein, 2369. Contains many proverbs.

2728. Palice (Antonín). Šlechetnosť v rouše příkladů veršem i prosou se sbírkou přísloví a průpovědí, *etc.* pp. 172.
12°. v Praze, 1884.
Bernstein, 2464. Pp. 155-172, Sbírka přísloví a průpovědí.

2729. Peck (Eduard). Valašské národní písně a říkadla s nápěvy do textu vřaděnými. pp. 116.   8°. v Brně, 1884.

Bernstein, 2520. Some proverbs are in the Moravian dialect.

2730. Petrů (Vácslav). Čítanka pro nižší třídy středních škol. 2 část.   8°. v Praze, *Kober*, 1887.

Bernstein, 2555. Část' 1, pp. 56, 114-115; Část' 2, pp. 17, 126-127, proverbs and sayings.

2731. ———: Proprava k české stilistice, *etc.* pp. 144, 128.
8°. v Praze, *Urbánek*, 1876.

Bernstein, 2554. Oddíl 2, pp. 78-86, Přísloví.

2732. Podstránský (Josef). Kytka z průpovídek a z přisloví pořádkem katechismu, *etc.* pp. iv, 62.
8°. v Praze, *Rohlíček*, 1858.

2733. Prasek (V.). Praktický pravopis s mluvničkou a cvičné úlohy z přísloví a pořekadel pro školu, *etc.* pp. 104.
8°. v Olomouci, *Žákovský*, 1874.

Bernstein, 2678.

2734. Přísloví. Vtipná i žertovná přísloví a pořekadla slovanská.
4°. v Praze a ve Vídni, *Kober & Markgraf*, 1860.

In Obecné Listy, Ročník první, 1860, Čís. 2, 5, 6, 10. In each of these numbers there is a brief list of proverbs, principally Czech, though including a few Polish, Russian, Serb, *etc.*, in translation.   [B.M.

2735. Procházka (J.). Prostonárodní říkadla. pp. 48.
12°. v Praze, *Bačkovský*, 1890.

Bernstein, 2695.

2736. Průpowjdky. Průpowjdky.   4°.   1839.

Bernstein, 2831. *In* Česká Wčela, Číslo 38, 39, 44, 47, 76, 102. Czech proverbs and sayings.

2737. Rozum (Jan Vácslav). Ezop, mudrc v otroctvi, *etc.* pp. 64.   12°. v Praze, 1850.

Bernstein, 3082. Each section of the book is headed : Czech proverb.

2738. ———: Mravo-učeni z přísloví Českoslovanských, *etc.* pp. x, 100.   16°. v Praze, *Pospíšil*, 1851.

Bernstein, 3083.

2739. ———: Slovanské bájesloví, *etc.* pp. 22.
16°. v Praze, 1857.

Bernstein, 3084.

2740. Rybička (Antonín). Pravidla, přísloví a povědění, vztahující se k správě veřejné a obecni i k právu občanskému a trestnímu, *etc.* pp. 275.
8°. v Praze, *Jednota právnická*, 1872.

Bernstein, 3104. 4232 entries.

2741. Skopalík (František). Památky obce Záhlinic, *etc.* 2 část.
8°. v Brně, *Tiskem mor. akc. knihtiskárny*, 1884-85.

Bernstein, 3422. Pp. 47-63, Obyčeje a zvyky i pořekadla při výročních slávnostech, *etc.*

2742. Srnec (Jakub). Dicteria seu proverbia Bohemica, ad phrasim Latinorum accommodata, *etc.* pp. [xvi], 224, [18].
8°. Pragae, *Nigrinus*, 1582.
Bernstein, 3569.

2743. ——— and **Horný** (František Ondřej). Českých příslowi zbjrka, *etc.* pp. xv, 96.
12°. v Praze, *Herrle*, 1804.

2744. Stárek (Jan Nepomuk). Moudrost na ulici v příslovích a pořekadlech národa Českého, *etc.* pp. 178.
8°. v Praze, 1881.
Bernstein, 3515.

2745. Šťastný (Jan), *and others.* Čítanka pro školy obecné, *etc.*
6 pts. 8°. v Praze, *Cis. král. školní knihosklad*, 1890-2.

Bernstein, 3577. Pt. 3, pp. 6, 11-12; Pt. 4, pp. 4-6, 9-12; Pt. 5, p. 7; Pt. 6, pp. 4-5, proverbs.

2746. Sychra (Mathias Jos.). Versuch einer böhmischen Phraseologie, *etc.* 2 vol. 8°. Brünn, *Trassler*, 1821.

Bernstein, 3654. Contains a large number of proverbs with German translations.

2747. Vojtíšek (Carl A.). Der kleine Čeche. . . . *Fifth edition.*
pp. 160. 16°. Wien, *Wenedikt*, 1873.
Sixth edition. pp. 160. 16°. Brünn, *Karafiat*, [1882].

There is an additional title page as follows : " Neuer unfehlbarer Schlüssel zur schnellen Erlernung der böhmischen Sprache." The book contains a section : Redensarten und Sprichwörter, die von den deutschen verschieden sind. In Czech and German. [B.M.]

2748. Wenzig (Joseph). Westslavischer Märchenschatz, *etc.*
8°. Leipzig, *Lorck*, 1857.
Pp. 302-309, Bohemian proverbs in German. [B.M.]

2748a. Záturecký (Adolf Petr). Slovenská přísloví, pořekadla a úsloví. pp. vi, 389.
la. 8°. v Praze, *Česká Akademie Cisaře Františka Josefa*, 1896.
Slovak proverbs and sayings classified by subjects, with notes. [B.M.]

2748b. ———: Slovenské porekadla.
8°. v Praze, *Šimáček*, 1894.
In Český Lid, 3, pp. 385-392. [B.M.]

2749. Ziak (Vincenz Paul). Böhmische Sprachlehre für Deutsche . . . Dritte . . . Auflage. pp. 456.
8°. Brünn, *Winiker*, 1849.
Pp. 338-347, einige Redensarten und Sprichwörter, die von den deutschen abweichen. [B.M.]

See also **1083, 3731, 3799, 3832.**

POLISH AND KASZUB

2750. Adalberg (Samuel). Liber proverbiorum polonicorum, *etc.*
pp. xviii, 805. 8°. Varsaviae, *Skiwski*, 1889-94.

Polish proverbs arranged alphabetically by key-words. Pp. 1-31, bibliography. [B.M.

2751. Adamowicz (Alexander). Praktische polnische Grammatik
für Teutsche, *etc.* pp. iv, 230.
sm. 8°. Wien, Prag, *Schönfeld*, 1796.

Bernstein, 4219. Pp. 176-181, polnische Sprüchwörter. Polish proverbs and German equivalents.

2752. Anczyc (Władysław Ludwik). 1. Książeczka dla wiejskich
dziatek które już elementarz skończyły. Ułożona przez
Kazimierza Góralczyka [*pseud.* of W. L. Anczyc]. pp. 201.
12°. w Lublinie, *Arct*, 1862.

Bernstein, 1315. Pp. 109-114, Przypowieści staropolskie : pp. 139-145, Przysłowia.

2753. Antoniewicz (Karol). Czytanie postępowe, *etc.* pp. 133.
8°. Leszno i Gniezno, *Günther*, 1848.

Bernstein, 107. The author's name is given only on the cover. Pp. 128-133, 159 proverbs.

2754. Baranowski (J. J.). Anglo-Polish lexicon. 2 pts.
12°. Warsaw, *Lesman & Swiszczowski*, 1883.

Bernstein, 165. Part 2, pp. 64-78, English and Polish proverbs, *etc.*

2755. Bartoszewicz (Kazimierz). Księgi humoru polskiego, *etc.*
4 tom. 8°. Petersburg, *Grendyszyński*, 1897.

Tom. 1, pp. 305-22, proverbs, *etc.* [B.M.

2756. Bartoszewicz (Zygmunt). Wypisy Polskie dla użytku
młodzieży płci żeńskiej prozą i wierszem, *etc.* pp. 165.
12°. Wilno, *Glücksberg*, 1836.

Bernstein, 191. Pp. 44-47, Przysłowia.

2757. Bauer-Czarnomski (Francis). Proverbs in Polish and English. pp. 103. 32°. London, *Hill*, [1920].

Proverbs arranged alphabetically by the Polish. No notes. [B.M.

318

2758. Błazewski (Marcin). Setnik przypowieści uciesznych 1608.
Wydał Dr. Wilhelm Bruchnalski. pp. xi, 117.
8°. Kraków, *Nakładem Akademii Umiejętności*, 1897.
100 fables in verse, each headed by a proverb. [B.M.

2759. Boczyłowicz (Jakób). Orator politicus, álbo wymowny
polityk, *etc.* pp. [xiv], 572, [28].
sm. 8°. Thorunii, *Lauret*, 1699.
Bernstein, 2406. Pp. 292-318, Wymownego polityká przysłowia, which
contains Latin proverbs, maxims, *etc.*, as well as the Polish ones.

2760. Bretholz (Uscher). Über unbekannte und wenig bekannte
polnische Dichter des xvii. Jahrhunderts. 1. Theil, *etc.* pp.
97. 8°. Krakau, *Verlag des Verfassers*, 1897.
Pp. 70-71, calendar proverbs in Polish from Thomas Ormiński. [B.M.

2761. Brueckner (Alexander), *Polish Philologist.* Przyczynki do
dziejów przysłowi polskich. 8°. Warszawa, 1896.
In Wisła, Tom. 10, pp. 600-619.

2762. ———: Przysłowia, *etc.* 8°. Warszawa, *Cotta*, 1895.
In Ateneum, 1895, Tom. 3, pp. 157-184, 278-310, 531-575. A commentary.
[B.M.

2763. Brzozowski (Franciszek Korab). Przysłowia polskie. pp.
xviii, 191. 4°. Kraków, *Słomski*, 1896.
Proverbs arranged alphabetically by key-words, with occasional notes, and
indications of origin. [B.M.

2764. Čelakovský (František Ladislav). Všeslovanské počáteční
čtení, *etc.* pp. 242.
8°. v Praze, *Syny Bohumila Haase*, 1850.
Bernstein, 567. Pp. 5-9, Polish proverbs.

2765. Cenôva (Stanjislav Florjan). Skôrb Kaszébskosłovjnskjè
môvé. [With 2 supplements]. Nos. 1-13.
8°. Svjecé, *Hauffe*, 1866-68.
Pp. 1-25, Pjrszi tésąc kaszébsko-słovjnskjch gôdk. [B.M.

2766. Chimani (Leopold). Przewodnik dla nauczycieli w domach
ochrony, *etc.* pp. 348. 8°. Warszawa, *Rymarska*, 1841.
Bernstein, 597. Pp. 272-297, Przysłowia, zdania moralne, *etc.*

2767. Chociszewski (Józef). Polak uczący się po niemiecku, *etc.*
pp. 192. 12°. Poznań, *Księgarnia Katolicka*, 1893.
Bernstein, 598. Pp. 187-190, Przysłowia : Sprichwörter.

2768. Cinciała (Andrzej). Przysłowia, przypowieści i ciekawsze
zwroty językowe ludu polskiego na Śląsku w księstwie Cieszyń-
skiém, *etc.* pp. 47.
8°. Cieszyń, *Nakładem autora*, 1885.
948 entries in alphabetical order. [B.M.

2769. Czeczot (Jan). Piosnki wieśniacze, *etc.* pp. xxxiv, 134.
8°. Wilno, *Zawadzki*, 1846.

Bernstein, 2582. Pp. 106-123, proverbs.

2770. Derdowski (Jarosz). Nórcyk kaszubści abo koruszk i jedna maca jedrnyj prowde, *etc.* pp. 17.
8°. w Winonie w Nórtowyj Ameryce, *Derdowści*, 1897.

Bernstein, 4345. Contains a collection of proverbs.

2771. Donatus (Aelius). Aelii Donati vetustissimi grammatici elementa, una cum explicatione Polonica, *etc.*
8°. Cracoviae, 1764.

Another edition. pp. 72.
sm. 8°. Cracoviae, *Stachowicz*, 1786.

Another edition. pp. 80, [xvi]. sm. 8°. Posnaniae, 1797.
Contains a list of Polish proverbs with Latin equivalents. [B.M.

2772. Dygasiński (Adolf). Wypisy Polskie, *etc.* 2 pts.
8°. Warszawa, *Lesman*, 1881-82.

Bernstein, 940-941.

2773. Ehrenberg (G.). Wykład bajek Krasickiego, *etc.* pp.
276. 8°. Kraków, *Uniwersytet Jagielloński*, 1871.

Bernstein, 963. Pp. 223-228, Zdania i przysłowia wyjęte z bajek Krasickiego.

2774. Elementa. Elementa puerilis institutionis. pp. 63.
sm. 8°. [Czenstochowa], *Typis Clari Montis Częstochoviensis*, 1854.

Bernstein, 986. Pp. 60-62, Polish proverbs with Latin equivalents.

2775. Ernesti (Johannes). Pohlnisches Handbüchlein, darinnen nebst denen Stammvieldeutenden Sprüchwörtern auch allerhand täglich vorfallende Redensarten enthalten, *etc.*
8°. Schweidniss, *Okeln*, 1689.

Gratet-Duplessis, 891.

2776. Fedorowski (Michał). Lud okolic Żarek, Siewierza i Pilicy, *etc.* 2 tom. 8°. Warszawa, *Arct*, 1888-89.

Bernstein, 1084. Tom. 2, pp. 347-389, Przysłowia, zagadki i zabobony.

2777. Fredro (Andrzej Maksymilian). Przysłowia Mów Potocznych, albo przestrogi obyczáiowe, rádne, woienne, . . . Przez wiernego Oyczyznie Anonyma [*i.e.* A. M. Fredro]. . . . Wtore drukowánie. 4°. [w Krakowie, *Lukasz Kupisz*, 1659].
Another edition. pp. 86. 4°. Sanok, *Pollak*, 1855.
Another edition. 2 tom.
16°. Paryż, *Księgarnia Luxemburgska*, [1867].

Polish proverbs, *etc.* The 1855 edition contains some 900 entries, and forms Ser. 1, Zesz 23 and 24, of the Biblioteka Polska. Many other editions.
[B.M.

2778. Gargulski (Stanisław).   Wypisy z pisarzów Polskich, *etc.*
pp. iv, 312.   8°. Warszawa, *Nakład autora*, 1880.
Bernstein, 1238.   Pp. 140-147, Przysłowia.

2779. Gloger (Zygmunt).   Skarbczyk, *etc.* pp. 80.
8°. Warszawa, *Prószyński*, 1885.
Abridged edition. Skarbczyk [II], *etc.* pp. 76.
8°. Warszawa, 1891.
Bernstein, 1298-99.   Contains a list of nearly 500 proverbs, *etc.*

2780. Godzina czytania.   Godzina czytania, *etc.* pp. 258.
8°. Żytomiérz, *Kwiatkowski*, 1860.
Bernstein, 1304.   Pp. 251-258, Przysłowia i przypowieści Polskie.

2781. Grabowski (Ambrozy).   Krótkie przypowieści dawnych
Polaków, *etc.* pp. vi, 146.
8°. w Krakowie, *Grabowski*, [1819].
Pp. 54-55, Przysłowia staro-polskie z dziełka pod tyt. Kolęda dziecinna na
r. 1775.   Some 15 proverbs.   [B.M.

2782. Grajnert (Józef).   Podarunek dla ludu naszego. . . .
Napisał Łukasz Mrówka [*pseud.* of Grajnert]. 3 pts.
gr.20. 8°. Warszawa, 1862-63.
Bernstein, 2276.   Pt. 2, pp. 29-31; Pt. 3, pp. 55-56, proverbs, *etc.*   [B.M.

2783. Gregorowicz (Jan Kanty).   Książeczki obrazowe, przez
Janka z Bielca [*pseud.* of Gregorowicz]. 3 pts.
12°. Warszawa, *Nowolecki*, 1862-63.
Bernstein, 1592.   Pt. 2, pp. 72-73, and Pt. 3, pp. 82-85, Przysłowia i
przypowieści.

2784. Hoff (Bogumil).   Lud Cieszyński, *etc.* pp. 74 + frontispiece. [Illustrated].   4°. Warszawa, *Arct*, 1888.
Pp. 67-69, Przysłowia—an alphabetical list.   [B.M.

2785. Hoffmanowa (Klementyna) *z Tańskich.*   Encyklopedya
doręczyna . . . przez autorkę pamietki po dobréj Matce [Hof-
manowa z Tańskich]. 2 tom.
8°. Warszawa, *Orgelbrand*, 1851.
Bernstein, 991.   Tom. 2, pp. 34-49, proverbs.

2786. Hora (F. A.).   Rukovět' konversace Česko-Polské, *etc.*
pp. 127.   8°. Praga, *Storch*, 1887.
Bernstein, 1537.   Pp. 115-121, Přisloví a polonismy.

2787. Horain (Juljan).   Chwile stracone, *etc.* pp. 160.
8°. Wilno, *Zawadzki*, 1857.
Bernstein, 1538.   Pp. 129-146, Fizyologja przysłów.

2788. Jachowicz (Stanisław).   Kalendarzyk dla dzieci . . . na
rok 1848. pp. 44.   16°. Warszawa, *Strąbski*, 1848.
Bernstein, 1579.   Pp. 38-40, Przysłowia wyjaśnione.

x

2789. Jachowicz (Stanisław). Książka dla rzemieślnika. pp. [vi], 132. 8°. Warszawa, *Gazeta Codzienna*, 1855.

Bernstein, 1580. Pp. 33-43, rhymed proverbs : pp. 69-80, Przysłowia.

[B.M.

2790. ———: Pamiątka dła Eryczka, *etc.* 4 tom. 8°. Warszawa, *Unger*, 1846-47.

Bernstein, 1578. Contains various sections of proverbs.

2791. Jachowiczowa (Antonina). Przewodnik dla wieku dziecinnego na cały rok. Przez Antoninę J. . . . pp. 148.

sm. 8°. Warszawa, *Merzbach*, 1839.

Pp. 113-118, Przysłowia.

2792. Jeske (August). Mała stylistyka zawierająca materyały i wskazówki metodyczne. . . . Część 1, *etc.* pp. vii, 96, ii. 8°. Warszawa, w Lublinie, *Arct*, 1876.

Bernstein, 1608. Pp. 90-92, 44 proverbs.

2793. Kalendarz. Kalendarz Domowy, *etc.* 8°. Warszawa, *Glückberg*, 1868, 1869, 1870.

Bernstein, 1644, 1645, 1648. Each year contains about ten pages of proverbs.

2794. Kamiński (Mścisław). Przysłowia ludu nadwilejskiego. 8°. Warszawa, *Gebethner i Wolff*, 1866.

In Biblioteka Warszawska, Tom. 4, pp. 302-312. [B.M.

2795. Kampmann (C. F.). Grammatik der polnischen Sprache. . . . Zweite, verbesserte Ausgabe, *etc.* pp. xiv, 96, 62. 8°. Breslau, *Hirt*, 1863.

Pp. 89-96, Sprichwörter und kurze Sätze. 300 proverbs in Polish. [B.M.

2796. Karłowicz (Jan). Przyczynek do zbioru przysłów, piosenek, ucinków i przypowieści, *etc.* pp. 31. 8°. [Kraków], *Nakładem autora*, 1879.

Bernstein, 1667.

2797. Knapski (Grzegorz). Idiotismi Polonici, seu voces polonicae . . . per Thesaurum Polono Latinum, *etc.*

12°. [Kalisz], 1682.

Another edition. pp. 259.

12°. Vilnae, *Typis Acad. Soc. Iesu*, 1687.

Arranged alphabetically, with Latin translations. [B.M.

2798. ———: Thesauri Polono latino graeci . . . tomus tertius. Continens adagia Polonica, *etc.* pp. 1388.

4°. Cracoviae, *Caesarius*, 1632.

Gratet-Duplessis, 890. There are other editions of the other two books of the Thesaurus, but this is the only one of Vol. 3, which alone is concerned with proverbs. There is a long preface in Latin concerning proverbs in general, and tracing the general scheme of the book. Then follow over 3000 proverbs in Polish accompanied by Latin and Greek equivalents, and numerous quotations, chiefly from the Scriptures. [B.M.

2799. Kolberg (Henryk Oskar). Chełmskie. Obraz etnograficzny, *etc.* 2 tom.

8°. Kraków, *Uniwersytet Jagielloński*, 1890-91.

Tom. 2, pp. 72-79, Przysłowia i zdania przysłowiowe. [B.M.

2800. ———: Lud. Jego zwyczaje, sposób życia, mowa, podania, przysłowia, *etc.* 23 Ser.

8°. Warszawa, *Jaworski*, 1865-90.

Contains many proverbs, particularly Ser. 3, pp. 197-203; Ser. 8, pp. 247-289; and Ser. 17, pp. 166-178. [B.M.

2801. Kopczyński (Onufry). Grammatyka dlá szkół narodowych, *etc.* pp. 109, 265. 8°. 1783.

Another edition. Grammatyka języka Polskiego, *etc.* pp. 267, [16]. 8°. w Warszawie, *u Piiarów*, 1817.

Contains a section of Polish proverbs. [B.M.

2802. Kraków (Paulina). Proza i poezya polska. . . . Cześć 1. pp. xvi, 328. 8°. Warszawa, *Kowalewski*, 1860.

Bernstein, 1768. Pp. 326-328, Przysłowia.

2803. Książka. Książka do czytania, *etc.* pp. 179.

sm. 8°. w Wiedniu, *W c. k. składzie książek szkolnych*, 1857.

Bernstein, 1791. Pp. 169-179, Przysłowia i zdania moralne.

2804. ———: Druga Książka do czytania dla szkól ludowych. pp. 228 + map.

8°. we Lwowie, *Zakład Narodowy imienia Ossolińskich*, 1888.

Bernstein, 1792. Pp. 170-188, Przysłowia.

2805. Kuryłowicz (Stefan). Der kleine Pole, oder kurze Bemerkungen über die Wörter der polnischen Sprache, *etc.* pp. 128. 12°. Wien, *Gerold*, 1833.

Pp. 81-105, Polish and German proverbs.

2806. Langie (Karol). Świętojanka. Noworocznik, *etc.* pp. 132. 12°. w Krakowie, 1843.

Bernstein, 1827. Pp. 126-132, Gminne wróżebne przypowieści o zmianach powietrza w ciągu roku.

2807. Legatowicz (Ignacy Piotr). Apoftegmata to jest prawdy . . . maksymy . . . przysłowia, *etc.* pp. 84. 16°. Wilno, *Nakładem autora*, 1854.

Bernstein, 1878. 772 entries.

2808. Łepkowski (Józef). Przegląd krakowskich tradycyj, legend, nabożeństw, zwyczajów, przysłow i właściwości. pp. 68. 8°. Kraków, *Kirchmayer*, 1866.

[B.M.

2809. Lieder (Franciszek). Zadania do grammatyki niemieckiéj zastosowane, *etc.* pp. 246.

8°. Warszawa, *Wróblewski*, 1837.

Bernstein, 1939. Pp. 188-191, Przysłowia—Sprichwörter.

2810. Lipiński (Tymoteusz). Przysłowia i przypowieści od nazw panujących. 8°. Warszawa, *Gazeta Codzienna*, 1856.

In Biblioteka Warszawska, 1856, Tom. 1, pp. 57-66. [B.M.

2811. ———: Przysłowia i wyrażenia od gór i rzek. pp. 10.

8°. [Warsaw, 1853?].

Reprinted from Biblioteka Warszawska, 1853, Tom. 2, pp. 53-61. [B.M.

2812. ———: [Begins] Przysłowia i wyrażenia od miast i wsi. Zebrał Tymoteusz Lipiński. pp. 39.

8°. [Warsaw, 1852].

262 proverbs and phrases, in alphabetical order, with notes. A brief bibliography is given in the list of abbreviations at the end. No title page. Reprinted from Biblioteka Warszawska, 1852, Tom. 4, pp. 236-274. [B.M.

2813. Lompa (Józef). Przysłowia i mowy potoczne ludu polskiego. w Śląsku, *etc.* pp. 36.

8°. w Bochni, *Wawrzyniec Pisz*, 1858.

Proverbs in alphabetical order; no notes. [B.M.

2814. Łukaszewski (Kaswery F. A. E.). Przyjaciel dzieci. . . . Trzecie poprawione wydanie. pp. vi, 337.

8°. Berlin, *Mittler*, 1861.

Another edition. pp. vi, 336. 8°. Berlin, 1864.

Another edition. pp. xii, 334. 8°. w Berlinie, 1870.

Contains two sections entitled : Zdania moralne i przysłowia, and Niektóre zdania i przysłowia. [B.M.

2815. Łyskowski (Ignacy). Pieśni gminne i przysłowia ludu polskiego, *etc.* pp. vii, 66.

8°. Brodnica, *Nakładem wydawcy*, 1854.

Pp. 53-66, Przysłowia. An alphabetical list. [B.M.

2816. Łyskowski (Maksymilian). Wypisy z pisarzów polskich, *etc.* pp. 288, 64. 8°. Warsawa, *Unger*, 1850.

Bernstein, 2015. Pp. 34-45, proverbs and adages.

2817. Maciejowski (Wacław Aleksander). Pamiętniki o dziejach, piśmiennictwie i prawodawstwie Słowian, *etc.* 2 pts.

8°. w Peterzburgu i w Lipsku, *Eggers i Hinrichs*, 1839.

Pt. 2, pp. 79-84, Uczoność, mądrość, przysłowia. A commentary. [B.M.

2818. ———: Piśmiennictwo Polskie, *etc.* 3 tom.

8°. Warszawa, *Orgelbrand*, 1851-52.

Tom. 1, pp. 142-154, Historyczny rozwój przysłowiów ludu. [B.M.

2819. Manasevich (Boris). Die Kunst die polnische Sprache . . . zu erlernen, *etc.* pp. xii, 180.

8°. Wien, *etc.*, *Hartleben*, [1887].

Pp. 140-142, Polnische Sprichwörter. Polskie przysłowia. Proverbs with German translations. [B.M.

2820. Marewicz (Wincenty Ignacy). Przysłowia i maxymy. pp. [66]. 16°. w Warszawie, 1788.

Bernstein, 2075.

2821. Mecherzyński (Karol). Wypisy polskie, . . . Wydanie drugie. pp. 485. 8°. w Krakowie, *Himmelblau*, 1875. *Another edition.* pp. 479.

8°. w Krakowie, *Himmelblau*, 1877.

Contains four or five pages dealing with proverbs. [B.M.

2822. Milczewski (Oktaw). Практическій учебникъ польскаго языка, *etc.* pp. 90. 8°. С.-Петербургъ, 1864 [1863].

Bernstein, 2203. Pp. 83-85, 34 Polish proverbs with Russian translations.

2823. Minasowicz (Józef Epifaniusz). Zbiór rytmów Polskich, *etc.* pp. 282. 4°. w Warszawie, 1756.

Bernstein, 2213. Pp. 204-213, Przysłowia, *etc.* 138 entries.

2824. Moneta (Johann). Enchiridion Polonicum.

8°. Thorn, 1722.

Polnische Grammatik . . . vermehrt . . . von Daniel Vogel. Achte Auflage. pp. xiv, 769. 8°. Breslau, *Korn*, 1805. *Ninth edition.* pp. xiv, 769. 8°. Breslau, 1809.

Gratet-Duplessis, 892. Contains : " Polnische deutsche erklärte Sprüchwörter," a collection of several hundred Polish proverbs in alphabetical order, with German translations or equivalents. [B.M.

2825. Nadmorski ( ). Kaszuby i Kociewie, *etc.* pp. 167.

8°. Poznań, *Dziennik Poznański*, 1892.

Pp. 143-150, Zagadki i przysłowia, *etc.* [B.M.

2826. Opowiadania. Opowiadania z pism polskich wyjęte, *etc.* pp. 393. 8°. Warszawa, *Kowalewski*, 1859.

Bernstein, 2401. Pp. 75-81, Przysłowia polskie, *etc.*

2827. Orda (Napoleon). Grammaire analytique et pratique de la langue polonaise, *etc.* pp. 443. 8°. Paris, *Martinet*, 1856.

Pp. 396-419, Polonismes et proverbes. In Polish with French translations. [B.M.

2828. Paulík (Josef). Učebnice jazyka polského se vzłáštním zřením k výslovnosti, *etc.* pp. 111.

8°. v Praze, *Bačkovský*, 1891 [?1892].

Bernstein, 2506. Pp. 97-101, Przysłowia narodowe.

2829. Perły Humoru. Perły humoru polskiego. 3 tom.

8°. Kraków, *Bartoszewicz*, 1884-86.

Proverbs, *etc.*, are to be found in Tom. 1, pp. 1-2, 244-249, 292-299; Tom. 2, pp. 11-16, 84-96.

2830. Petrow (Alexander). Lud ziemi Dobrzyńskiéj, *etc.*
8°. Kraków, *Uniwersytet Jagiellonski*, 1878.

In Zbiór wiadomości do Antropologii krajowéj wydawany staraniem Komisyi antropologicznej Akademii Umiejętności w Krakowie, Tom. 2, pp. (1)-(182) : pp. (174)-(178), 284 proverbs in alphabetical order. [B.M.

2831. Pleszczyński (Adolf). Bojarzy międzyrzeccy, *etc.* pp. 226, 11, 4 + map. 8°. Warszawa, *Arct*, 1892.

Bernstein, 2612. Pp. 157-170, proverbs.

2832 Przysłowia. Przysłowia i zdania moralne, dowcipne lub krytyczne, *etc.* pp. 112.
8°. Warszawa, *Nowakowski*, 1851.

Bernstein, 2890.

2833. ———: Starodawne przysłowia dla ochronek. pp. 84.
12°. Poznań, *Jan Konstanty Żupański*, 1862.

Polish proverbs, including many calendar ones. [B.M.

2834. Radwański (Jan). Część mądrości ksiąg polskich. pp. 227.
8°. Krakow, "*Czas,*" 1857.

Contains various proverbs. [B.M.

2835. Rostafiński (Józef). Legenda o Filipie z Konopi. pp. 13.
8°. w Krakowie, *Kluczycki*, 1884.

Bernstein, 3073. Gives an explanation of the origin of various proverbs.

2836. Rymarkiewicz (Jan). Wzory prozy, *etc.* 3 vols.
8°. Poznań, *Żupański*, 1874.

Another edition. 3 vols. 8°. Poznań, 1860, 1856.

Contains a section entitled : Adagia i sentencye czyli przysłowia i zdania moralne. [B.M.

2837. Rysiński (Salomon). Proverbiorum polonicorum . . . centuriae decem et octo.
sm. 4°. Lubecae ad Chronum, *Kmita*, 1618.

Another edition. Przypowieści Polskie, *etc.* pp. 82.
4°. [Cracow], 1634.

These proverbs are also reproduced from an edition of 1629 in Wójcicki's " Biblioteka starożytna pisarzy polskich," Tom. 2, pp. 97-204. The proverbs are arranged in alphabetical order with frequent Latin translations. [B.M.

2838. ———: Przypowieści polskie, *etc.*
4°. w Krakowie, 1619.
Another edition. 4°. w Krakowie, 1620.
Another edition. 8°. Lublin, *Wirowski*, 1629.

This long list of Polish proverbs with occasional Latin equivalents is also included in Tom. 2 of K. W. Wójcicki's Biblioteka starożytna, 1843 and 1854. [B.M.

2839. S. (H.). Wybór rozrywek dla różnego wieku płci obojej, . . . Żebrany przez H. S. 2 części.
12°. Warszawa, *Jaworski*, 1853.

Bernstein, 4149. Część 1, pp. 4-6; Część 2, 61-66. and 168-172, proverbs.

2840. Seredyński (Władysław) and **Dzieduszycka** (Anastazya), *Countess*. Wypisy, przykłady i wzory form prozy i poezyi polskiej, *etc.* pp. v, 882, viii.
8°. Warszawa, *Gebethner i Spółka*, 1881.
Pp. 471-475, Przysłowia historyczne : pp. 475-479, Zdania, myśli, ziarnka mądrości. [B.M.

2841. Sk. (H.). Literatura dla młodzieży płci obojej ze wzorowych pisarzy polskich zebrana przez H. Sk. 2 części.
12°. Warszawa, *Jaworski*, 1862.
Bernstein, 1956. Część 1, pp. 4-6; Część 2, pp. 61-66 and 168-172 deal with proverbs.

2842. Skarbek (Fryderyk), *Count*. Sanszopansiana. pp. 32.
sm. 8°. w Wrocławiu, *Schletter*, 1840.
Explains a few proverbs in a humorous style. [B.M.

2843. Staszyc (Franciszek). Kalendarz ludowy illustrowany na rok 1862. Ułożony przez Franka z Wielkopolski [F. Staszyc], *etc.* pp. xxvi, 96. 8°. Warszawa, *Glückberg*, 1862.
Pp. 40-42, Przysłowia gospodarskie i przygodne. [B.M.

2844. Stopka (Andrzej). Materyały do etnografi Podhala . . . Część 1, *etc.*
8°. w Krakowie, *Akademija Umiejętności*, 1898.
Contains a section of proverbs. This article was published in Tom. 3 of '' Materyały antropologiczne archeologiczne i etnograficzne '' of the Akademija Umiejętności. [B.M.

2845. Suchorowski (Michael). Theoretisch-praktische Anleitung zum gründlichen Unterricht in der polnischen Sprache, *etc.* pp. [xii], 346. 8°. Lemberg, *Piller*, 1829.
Bernstein, 3630. Pp. 234-238, Polish proverbs and German equivalents.

2846. Świętek (Jan). Lud Nadrabski, *etc.* pp. ix, 728.
8°. w Krakowie, *Akademija Umiejętności*, 1893.
Pp. 664-686, Przysłowia i przymówki. 812 entries in alphabetical order. No notes. [B.M.

2847. Sz. (M.). Kalendarz do zrywania na rok 1897. Z następującą treścią: anegdoty-aforyzmy i przysłowia . . . Zebrał i ułożył M. Sz. 16°. w Płocku, *Kempner*, 1897.
Bernstein, 1649.

2849. Tetzner (Franz). Die Slovinzen und Lebakaschuben, *etc.* pp. viii, 272. 8°. Berlin, *Felber*, 1899.
In Beiträge zur Volks- und Völkerkunde, Bd. 8. Pp. 248-251, proverbs. [B.M.

2850. Trembecki (Henryk). Neueste unfehlbare Methode zur schnellsten Erlernung der polnischen Sprache . . . Zweite vermehrte Auflage. pp. 158. 16°. Wien, *Wenedikt*, 1862.
Pp. 130-136, Polish proverbs with German translations.

2851. Trusiewicz (Ignacy). Kwiaty i owoce. pp. iv, 321.
8°. Kijów, *Uniwersytecka Drukarnia*, 1870.

Pp. 128-142, Przysłowia od nazwisk szlacheckich. Proverbs arranged alphabetically with explanations and illustrations. [B.M.

2852. Weryha-Darowski (Aleksander). Historya jednego rozdziału do przyszłej księgi przysłów polskich. pp. 8.
8°. [Kijów, *Metzger*, 1867].
Bernstein, 4024.

2853. ———: Jeden rozdział do przyszłej xięgi przysłow polskich obejmujący nazwiska rodzin szlacheckich a innych, *etc.* pp. viii, 85.   8°. Kijów, *Drukarnia uniwersytecka*, 1867.
Bernstein, 3081.   The dedication is signed A. W. D.

2854. ———: Przysłowia polskie odnoszace się do nazwisk szlacheckich i miejscowości, *etc.* pp. xiii, 219.
8°. Poznań, *Żupański*, 1874.

Proverbs arranged in two series, with notes. There is a short list of provincial proverbs at the end. Reviewed in Biblioteka Warszawska, 1874, pp. 337-346. [B.M.

2855. Wicherkiewicz (Władysław). Methode Gaspey-Otto-Sauer. Polnische Konversations-Grammatik, *etc.* pp. viii, 485.
8°. Heidelberg, *Groos*, 1892.
Bernstein, 4031.   Pp. 388-395, 100 proverbs with German translations.

2856. Wierzbowski (Teodor). Wypisy Polskie, *etc.* pp. xiii, 600.
8°. Варшава, 1884.
Bernstein, 4052.   Pp. 554, 562, 570, 580-581, Polish, Russian, *etc.*, proverbs.

2857. Wisłocki (W. S.). Пословицы и поговорки, *etc.* pp. 138.
8°. С.-Петербургъ, 1868.
Bernstein, 2665.

2858. Wiszniewski (Michał). Historya literatury polskiéj. 10 tom.   8°. Kraków, *Gieszkowski*, 1840-57.
Tom. 1, pp. 230-238, Filozofia tkwiąca w przypowiastkach i przysłowiach.
[B.M.

2859. Wójcicki (Kazimierz Władysław). Historyczne przysłowia.
8°. Warszawa, *Dzwonkowski*, 1864.
In Noworocznik (Kalendarz) illustrowany dla Polek, 1864, pp. 52-62. [B.M.

2860. ———: Kalendarz ludowy.   4°. Warszawa, 1863.
In Jozefa Ungra Kalendarz Warszawski, 1863, pp. 96-105.

2861. ———: Obrazy starodawne. 2 tom.
8°. Warszawa, *Sennewald*, 1843.
Tom. 1, pp. 1-16, Przysłowia zmarłe. [B.M.

2862. ———: O niektórych przysłowiach narodowych.
8°. w Warszawie, *Glücksberg*, 1827.
In Dziennik Warszawski, Tom. 7, 9. Gives explanations of 67 proverbs.
[B.M.

2863. **Wójcicki** (Kazimierz Władysław). Przysłowia Kaszubskie.
8°. Warszawa, *Gazeta Codzienna*, 1856.
In Biblioteka Warszawska, Tom. 2, pp. 105-114. [B.M.

2864. ———: Przysłowia narodowe, *etc.* 3 tom.
sm. 8°. w Warszawie, *Hugues & Kermen*, 1830.
Proverbs, *etc.*, with explanations and illustrations. [B.M.

2865. ———: Przysłowia narodowe. 4°. Warszawa, 1861.
In Jana Jaworskiego Kalendarz astronomiczno-gospodarski, 1861, pp. 126-131.

2866. ———: Przysłowia polskie czyli nauka starych a rozumnych
naszych ludzi. (Staraniem redakcyi Biblioteki Warszawskiej.)
pp. 28. sm. 8°. Warszawa, 1862.
Bernstein, 4104.

2867. ———: Starożytne przypowieści z xv, xvi i xvii wieku.
pp. vi, 236. 8°. Warszawa, *Nakładem autora*, 1836.
Contains some 800 entries. [B.M.

2868. ———: Słówko o przysłowiach polskich.
4°. Warszawa, 1853.
In Jósefa Unger Kalendarz Warszawski, 1853, pp. 12-14.

2869. ———: Zarysy domowe. 4 tom.
8°. w Warszawie, *Chmielewski*, 1842.
Tom. 2, pp. 39-54, Chłopskie przysłowia. [B.M.

2870. ———: Zmarłe przysłowia. 8°. Warszawa, 1842.
In Biblioteka Warszawska, Tom. 4, 1842, pp. 225-235. [B.M.

2871. **Woyna** (Johann Carl von Jaśienicá). Kleiner Lustgarten
worinn gerade Gänge zur polnischen Sprache angewiesen
werden, *etc.* pp. 336. 16°. Danzig, *Schreiber*, 1762.
Another edition. pp. 336. 12°. Danzig, *Schreiber*, 1769.
Pp. 241-278, Polish and German proverbs in alphabetical order. [B.M.

2872. **Wurzbach** (Constant von) *von Tannenburg*. Die Sprichwörter der Polen, . . . Zweite . . . Ausgabe. pp. xv, 355.
8°. Wien, *Pfautsch & Voss*, 1852.
Stirling-Maxwell, p. 106. Historical Polish proverbs arranged chronologically, considered with regard to Lithuanian, Ruthenian, Serbian and
Slovene characteristics. The proverbs are given in German and Polish with
German notes. Pp. x-xv, bibliography. [B.M.

2873. **Wybór.** Wybór wyjątków ze znakomitszych autorów Polskich, *etc.* pp. 160. 8°. Wilno, *Manes i Zymel*, 1830.
Bernstein, 4753. Pp. 5-11, proverbs.

2874. **Wypisy.** Nowe wypisy polskie, *etc.* 2 pts.
8°. w Lesznie i Gnieźnie, *Günther*, 1841, 1838.
Część 1, pp. 220-225; Część 2, pp. 283-288, proverbs, maxims and sayings.
[B.M.

2875. Wypisy. Wypisy polskie dla klas niższych c. k. szkół gimnazyalnych i realnych. Wydanie piąte. 4 tom.

8°. we Lwowie, *Zakład narodowy imienia Ossolińskich*, 1882, 1878-1880.

Bernstein, 4152. Tom 1, pp. 251-260; Tom 2, pp. 337-346; Tom 3, pp. 332-339 and 465-471; Tom 4, pp. 304-309 and 462-467, proverbs, maxims, sayings, *etc.*

2876. ———: Wypisy polskie z celniejszych pisarzów zebrane, dla użytku szkół powiatowych. pp. [vii], 207.

8°. Wilno, *Glücksberg*, 1831.

Bernstein, 4151. Pp. 23-31, Wyjątki z przysłów Salomona Rysinskiego.

2877. Zbiór. Zbiór przygadek, przysłow i t. d. wyjętych z 2ᶜʰ dziełek dawnych: Facecyje Polskie, *etc.* pp. 29.

8°. Kraków, *Czas*, 1857.

Bernstein, 4176.

2878. Zeglicki (Arnolf Kazimierz). Adagia polonica selectioribus tam patria, quam Latina, eruditione insignium authorum sententiis illustrata, *etc. First edition.* pp. 192.

8°. Varsaviae, 1735.

Adagia, ex celeberrimis scriptoribus tam Latinis, quam Polonicis . . . collecta. Editio secunda, *etc.* pp. 309.

8°. Varsaviae, 1751.

Adages and proverbs in Polish and Latin, in alphabetical order.   [B.M.

2879. Ziarnko. Ziarnko soli. Pogadanka przyrodnicza. pp. ii, 55.   8°. Warszawa, *Gebethner i Wolff*, 1884.

Bernstein, 4197. Pp. 46-55, Przysłowia i przypowieści o soli.

2880. Zienkowicz (Leon). Lacha z Lachow [*pseud.* of L. Zienkowicz] malowniczy podarek ludowy, *etc.* pp. iv, 261.

sm. 8°. Lipsk, *Brockhaus*, 1865.

Pp. 197-214, Mądrość narodowa w przysłowiach.   [B.M.

2881. Żmigrodzki (Michał). Folklore polonais. 1. Cracovie et ses environs. 8. Les proverbes.   8°. Paris, 1896.

In La Tradition, Tome 8, pp. 202-204. 66 Polish proverbs in French.

[B.M.

See also **2885, 3743-5, 3777, 3799.**

LITHUANIAN

2882. Becker (Friedrich). Der Kleine Littauer, *etc.* pp. viii, 218.   8°. Tilsit, *Selbstverlag*, 1866.

Bernstein, 219. Pp. 199-210, 200 Lithuanian proverbs with German translations.

2883. Bezzenberger (Adalbert). Litauische Forschungen, *etc.* pp. xiii, 206 + 7.   8°. Göttingen, *Peppmüller*, 1882.

Pp. 50-55, Sprichwörter und sprichwörtliche Redensarten. Occasional German notes and translations. [B.M.

2884. Davainis-Silvestraitis (Meczius). Patarles ir dainos, *etc.* pp. 30.   12°. Tilżeje, *Otto von Mauderode*, 1889.

A booklet containing maxims and proverbs. [B.M.

2885. Jucewicz (Ludwik Adam). Przysłowia ludu Litewskiego, *etc.* pp. vii, 125.   12°. Wilno, *Marcinowski*, 1840.

44 proverbs given in Lithuanian and Polish, with explanations in Polish. [B.M.

2886. Kraszewski (Józef Ignacy). Litwa, *etc.* 2 vols.   8°. Warszawa, *Strąbski*, 1847-50.

Vol. 1, pp. 353-408, Przysłowia litewskie. 403 proverbs. [B.M.

2887. Lepner (Theodorus). Der preusche Littauer, *etc.* pp. 152.   sm. 8°. Danzig, *Rüdiger*, 1744.

Pp. 116-118, some proverbs with German translations. [B.M.

2888. Mulevičius (P.). Patarlēs ir išminties grudeliai.
Chicago, *Draugas*, 1917.

2889. Schleicher (August). Handbuch der litauischen Sprache. 2 vols.   8°. Prag, *Calve*, 1856-57.

Bd. 2, pp. 73-104, proverbs in Lithuanian only. [U.C.L.

2890. Tetzner (Franz). Zur Sprichwörterkunde bei Deutschen und Litauern.   4°. Braunschweig, 1903.

In Globus, Bd. 84, pp. 61-63. A comparative study of 50 Lithuanian and German proverbs. [B.M.

LETTISH

2891. Altmann (Julius). Beiträge zum Sprichwörter- und Räthselschatz der Letten, *etc.* 8°. Bautzen, *Schmaler*, 1854.
In Jahrbücher für slawische Literatur, 1854, pp. 153-252. [B.M.

2892. Elberwelts (Kahrlis Gattarts). Lihgfmibas grahmata, *etc.* pp. 232. 8°. Jelgawâ, [Mittau], *Steffenhagen*, 1804.
Bernstein, 982. Pp. 77-84, 183 proverbs.

2893. Stender (Gotthard Friedrich). Neue vollständigere lettische Grammatik, *etc.* pp. [xiv], 164, 220.
8°. Braunschweig, *Waisenhaus*, 1761.
Second edition. Lettische Grammatik, *etc.* pp. 312.
8°. Mitau, *Steffenhagen*, 1783.
The first edition contains, pp. 186-197, Lettische Sprüchwörter; the second contains, pp. 240-258, Catalogus proverbiorum, proverbs in Lett and German. [B.M.

2894. Treuland (Theodor J.). Матеріалы по этнографіи латышскаго племени, *etc.* pp. x, 224. 4°. Москва, *Архиповъ*, 1881.
Труды Этнографическаго Отдѣла, Книга 6. Pp. 1-38, 209-212, Lett proverbs and adages with Russian translations. [B.M.

LIVONIAN

2895. Sjögren (Andreas Johan). Livische Grammatik, *etc.* pp. civ, 408. 4°. St. Petersburg, *Eggers*, 1861.
Pp. 363-365, 37 proverbs and riddles with German translations. Forms Bd. 2, Thl. 1, of Sjögren's Gesammelte Schriften. [B.M.

ESTHONIAN

2896. Hupel (August Wilhelm). Ehstnische Sprachlehre, *etc.*
pp. [xii], 536. 8°. Riga, Leipzig, *Hartknoch*, 1780.

Pp. 103-119, Ehstnische Sprüchwörter. Proverbs arranged in alphabetical
order, with German translations. [B.M.

2897. Koerber (K.). Kleine ehstnische Hand-Grammatik, *etc.*
pp. 96. 8°. Dorpat, *Karow*, 1867.

Pp. 77-85, Esthonian proverbs with German translations. [B.M.

2898. Volkslieder. Volkslieder. [Edited by J. G. von Herder].
2 Th. 8°. Leipsig, *Weygand*, 1778-1779.

Gratet-Duplessis, 824. Th. 2, pp. 85 *et seq.*, Esthnische Sprichwörter.
Only 10 proverbs are given; in German. [B.M.

2899. Wiedemann (Ferdinand Johann). Aus dem inneren und
äusseren Leben der Ehsten, *etc.* pp. vi, 495.
1 Rub. 90 Cop. 8°. St. Petersburg, *Eggers*, 1876.

Pp. 1-211, Sprichwörter und sprichwörtliche Redensarten, *etc.*, pp. 211-240,
Umschreibende . . . Redensarten: pp. 240-257, Sprichwörtliche Vergleichungen.
German translations are given. [B.M.

FINNISH AND LAPP

2900. Ahlquist (August Engelbrekt). Walittuja Suomen kansan sananlaskuja, *etc.* pp. ix, 152.

8°. Helsingissä, *Edlund*, 1869.

Over 2700 proverbs arranged alphabetically. [B.M.

2901. Buch (Max). Die Wotjäken, *etc.* pp. 185.

4°. Helsingfors, *Finnische Literatur Gesellschaft*, 1882.

Separate publication of an article in : Acta Soc. Scient. Fenn., Tom. 12. Pp. 103-104, Sprichwörter. 9 proverbs in the original, with German translations. [B.M.

2902. Donner (Otto). Lieder der Lappen, *etc.* pp. 164.

8°. Helsingfors, *Druckerei der Finnischen Litteratur Gesellschaft*, 1876.

Pp. 17-18, Sadneva jasak. Sprichwörter. 20 proverbs with German translations. [B.M.

2903. Friis (Jens Andreas). Lappiske sprogprøver, *etc.* pp. vi, 157. 8°. Christiania, *Cappelen*, 1856.

Pp. 113-116, proverbs in Lapp and Norwegian. [B.M.

2904. Gottlund (Carl Axel). De proverbiis Fennicis dissertatio [*Praes.* J. Tranér], *etc.* pp. [x], 39.

4°. Upsaliae, *Zeipel & Palmblad*, 1818.

Gratet-Duplessis, 822. Pp. 29-39, 100 Finnish proverbs or proverbial sayings, with Latin translations and comparisons. [B.M.

2905. Lönnrot (Elias). Suomen kansan sananlaskuja. pp. ix, 576. 8°. Helsingissä, *Simelius*, 1842.

Suomalaisen Kirjallisuuden Seuran Toimituksia, Osa 4. Proverbs in alphabetical order. Preface signed by author. [B.M.

2906. Poestion (Joseph Calasanz). Lappländische Märchen, Volkssagen, Räthsel und Sprichwörter, *etc.* pp. x, 274.

M.6. 8°. Wien, *Gerold*, 1886.

Pp. 271-274, Sprichwörter und sprichwörtliche Redensarten. Lapp proverbs translated into German. [B.M.

2907. Přislovi. Finska přjslowj. 1839.

In Česká Wčela, Číslo 20, 21, 24. Dne 8, 12, 22. Finnish proverbs translated into Czech.

2908. Schultz (Georg Julius). Jenseits der Scheeren, oder: der Geist Finnlands . . . von Dr. Bertram [*pseud.* of G. J. Schultz]. pp. 75. 8°. Leipzig, *Breitkopf und Härtel*, 1854.

Pp. 37-75, Finnish proverbs in German. [B.M.

2909. Sederholm (   ). Finnische Sprüchwörter und Gnomen, *etc.*   4°. Mitau, *Reyher*, 1845.

Gratet-Duplessis, 823. *In* Sendungen der Kurländischen Gesellschaft für Literatur und Kunst. Bd. 2, pp. 7-10, 135 Finnish proverbs in German.

2910. Sjögren (Andreas Johan). Ueber die finnische Sprache und ihre Literatur. pp. viii, 70.
8°. St. Petersburg, *Gretsch*, [1821].

Pp. 65-70, Finnish proverbs with German translations. [B.M.

2911. Strahlmann (Johann). Finnische Sprachlehre für Finnen und Nicht-Finnen. pp. v, 252, [11].
8°. St. Petersburg, *Iversen*, 1816.

Gratet-Duplessis, 821. Pp. 223-228, 76 Finnish proverbs with German translations. [B.M.

2912. Tammerlinus (Laurentius Petrus). Liber proverbiorum Fennicorum, *etc.*   8°. Aboæ, 1702.

Gratet-Duplessis, 820. Very rare.

2913. Ujfalvy (Károly Jenö). Essai de grammaire vêpse ou tchoude du nord, *etc.* pp. 128.   8°. Paris, *Leroux*, 1875.

Pp. 52-55, proverbes tchoudes ou vêpses. In the original, with French translations. [B.M.

2914. Wichmann (Yrjö). Wotjakische Sprachproben. Im Auftrage der Finnisch-Ugrischen Gesellschaft. Gesammelt und herausgegeben von Yrjö Wichmann. 2 vols.
6 fmk. 8°. Helsingfors, *Druckerei der Finnischen Litteratur Gesellschaft*, 1901.

Vol. 2, pp. 1-9, proverbs in four Votyak dialects, and in German. [F.-L.S.

SLAV

GENERAL.

2915. Brueckner (Alexander). Zur slavischen Parömiographie.
8°. Berlin, *Weidmann*, 1896.
In Archiv für slavische Philologie, Bd. 18, pp. 193-205. [B.M.

2916. Čelakovský (František Ladislav). Mudrosloví národu slovanského ve příslovích, *etc. First edition.* pp. 644.
8°. v Praze, *Řivnáč*, 1852.
Another edition. pp. xv, 783. 8°. v Praze, *Hynek*, 1891-3.
The preface mentions a number of other collections of Slav proverbs. Czech compared with other Slav proverbs. [B.M.

2917. Jungmann (Josef). Slowesnost aneb Náuka o wýmluwnosti básnické i řečnické se sbírkau příkladů newázané i wázané řeči. *Second edition.* pp. xxx, 836.
8°. v Praze, *Kronberger a Riwnáč*, 1845.
Třetí wydání, *etc.* pp. xix, 834.
8°. v Praze, *Kronberger a Riwnáč*, 1846.
Pp. 171-177, Czech, Russian, Polish and Serbian proverbs translated into Czech. [B.M.

2918. Krek (Gregor). Einleitung in die slavische Literaturgeschichte, *etc.* pp. vii, 336.
8°. Graz, *Leuschner & Lubensky*, 1874.
Another edition. pp. xi, 887.
8°. Graz, *Leuschner & Lubensky*, 1887.
Contains a few pages dealing with proverbs and gives a list of the principal Slav collections. [B.M.

2919. Sinapius (Daniel). Daniele Sinapiuse Neoforum Latino-slovenicum, *etc.* pp. 80.
8°. v Praze, *Česká Akademie Cisaře Františka Josefa*, 1908.
This book forms Skup. 2, Čís 11, of the Sbírka pramenův, *etc.*, of the Česká Akademie Císaře Františka Josefa. In Latin and Czech. [B.M.

RUSSIAN

GENERAL.

2920. Ablamsky (Nikolai Danilovich).   Азбука русской грамоты
для домашняго обученія дѣтей письму, *etc.* pp. 32.
4°. Кіевъ, Фроницкевичъ, 1890.
Bernstein, 9. Pp. 17-18, proverbs.

2921. Adamides (A. I.).   Новѣйшій учебникъ къ теоретическому
и практическому изученію русскаго языка, . . . Переводъ для
грековъ, *etc.* pp. ii, 496, [4], 99.   8°. Одесса, 1879.
Pp. 433-435, proverbs in Russian with Greek translations.

2922. Aleksandrov (F.).   Russian and English idiomatic phrases
and dialogues, *etc.* pp. viii, 136.
8°. London, Thimm, 1891.
Pp. 130-133, Russian proverbs with English equivalents.   [B.M.

2923. Altmann (Julius).   Die provinciellen Sprichwörter der
Russen.   8°. Bautzen, *Schmaler*, 1853.
In Jahrbücher für slawische Literatur, Jahrgang 1853, pp. 65-135. A com-
mentary with numerous examples in German.   [B.M.

2924. ———: Die Sprichwörter der Russen die einen allgemeinen
Charakter haben, *etc.*   8°. Bautzen, *Schmaler*, 1855.
In Jahrbücher für slawische Literatur, Jahrgang 1855, pp. 377-528. A com-
mentary.   [B.M.

2925. ———: Über die Sprichwörter der Russen.
fol. Berlin, 1854.
In Magazin für die Literatur des Auslandes, 1854, Nos. 90-92.   [B.M.

2926. Amszejewicz (A.).   Русско-нѣмецкій букварь съ образ-
чиками письма, *etc.* pp. 94.
8°. Варшава, Бресляуеръ, 1881.
Bernstein, 90. Pp. 88-91, proverbs.

2927. Andriyashev (A.).   Книга для первоначальнаго чтенія въ
сельскихъ и городскихъ приходскихъ и народныхъ учи-
лищахъ, *etc.* Часть 2. pp. iv., 226.
8°. Кіевъ, Университетская Типографія, 1880.
Bernstein, 100. Pp. 24-25, proverbs.

2928. Anofriev (N.).   Сборникъ старыхъ пословицъ военнаго быта. pp. 16.

8°. въ Варшавѣ, *Шкарадзинскій и Комп*, [1898].

Bernstein, 4232.   Contains 286 military proverbs in alphabetical order.

2929. Arkhangelsky (A.).   Село Давшино, Ярославской губерніи, Пошехонскаго уѣзда.   8°. Санктпетербургъ, 1854.

In Этнографическій сборникъ, издаваемый Императорскимъ Русскимъ Географическимъ Обществомъ, Выпускъ 2. Pp. 61-75, proverbs and sayings.   [В.М.

2930. Azbuka.   Азбука и уроки изъ исторіи Ветхаго и Новаго Завѣта съ картинами. pp. 101.   8°. Москва, 1862.

Bernstein, 137.   Pp. 22-26, Краткія Изреченія.

2931. Basistov (P.).   Для чтенія и разсказа, *etc.* pp. 368.

8°. Москва, *Салаевъ*, 1883.

Bernstein, 197.   16th edition of the 1st course.   Pp. 333-339, proverbs.

2932. Bauer-Czarnomski (Francis).   Proverbs in Russian and English, *etc.* pp. 103.   32°. London, *Hill*, [1920].

Proverbs arranged alphabetically by the Russian with English translations or equivalents opposite.   [В.М.

2933. Blinov (Nikolai N.).   Пчелка. Сборникъ стихотвореній, пословицъ и загадокъ. pp. 78, ii.

12°. Москва, *Мамонтовъ*, 1873.

Another edition. pp. 52.   8°. Вятка, *Куклинъ*, 1884.

Bernstein, 320.

2934. Bogdanovich (Ippolit Fedorovich).   Русскія пословицы, *etc.* 3 pts.

8°. St. Petersburg, *Academia Imperialis*, 1785.

Another edition. 3 pts.   1787.

Gratet-Duplessis, 885.   Russian rhymed proverbs.   [В.М.

2935. Bogišić (Valtazar).   Publication et enquête de proverbes en Russie.   8°. Paris, *Rolland*, 1901.

In Mélusine, tome 10, col. 129-141.   [В.М.

2936. Bomby.   Бомбы и картечи умной глупой рѣчи!! ... Вып. 1. pp. 100.   12°. Одесса, *Бродскій*, [n.d.].

Bernstein, 346.   Pp. 97-100, proverbs, sayings, *etc.*

2937. Borisovsky (A.).   Примѣты, обычаи и пословицы въ пяти волостяхъ Нижегородскаго уѣзда.

Нижній-Новгородъ, *Типографія Нижегородскаго Губернскаго Правленія*, 1870, 1875.

Bernstein, 357. *In* Нижегородскій Сборникъ, Vol. 3, pp. 197-224; Vol. 5, pp. 257-276.

2938. Borovikovsky (L.). Народни пословицы.
12°. С.-Петербургъ, Поляковъ, 1841.
In Ластôвка, 1841, pp. 317-330. 82 entries.

2939. Bukharev (I.). Книга для обученія русскому чтенію и письму, <i>etc. Third edition.</i> pp. 354, [12].
8°. Москва, Орловъ, 1869.
Bernstein, 423. Pp. 160-161, Пословицы.

2940. Buslaev (Theodor Ivanovich). Историческіе очерки русской народной словесности и искусства, <i>etc.</i> 2 vols.
4°. Санктпетербургъ, Товарищество „ Общественная Польза,“ 1861.
Vol. 1, pp. 78-136, Русскій быть и пословицы. [B.M.

2941. ———: Русскія пословицы и поговорка, <i>etc.</i> pp. [iv], 204.
8°. Москва, Семенъ, 1854.
In Архивъ историко-юридическихъ свѣдѣній, Кн. 2, Полов. 2.
[B.M.

2942. Catharine II., <i>Empress of Russia.</i> Bibliothek der Grossfürsten Alexander und Konstantin. Von I[hrer] K[ayserlichen] M[ajestät] d[er] K[ayserin] a[ller] R[eussen], <i>i.e.</i> Catharine II.]. 2 pts.
8°. Berlin und Stettin, Nicolai, 1784.
Pt. 2, pp. 105-130, Auswahl russischer Sprüchwörter.

2943. Choix. Choix de sentences et de proverbes russes.
fol. Paris, 1852.
In Le Magasin pittoresque, 20e année, p. 215. 30 Russian proverbs translated into French. [B.M.

2945. Dal' (Vladimir Ivanovich). Пословицы русскаго народа, <i>etc.</i> pp. xl, 1095, 6.
8°. Москва, Университетская Типографія, 1862.
Another edition. 4 vols.
8°. С.-Петербургъ, 1904.
The fullest collection of Russian proverbs. [B.M., L.L.

2946. Depolovich (P.). Пословицы, притчи и басни. [Collected by П. Д., <i>i.e.,</i> P. Depolovich]. pp. 51.
8°. St. Petersburg, 1902
[B.M.

2947. Dikarev (M. A.). Воронежскій этнографическій сборникъ, <i>etc.</i> pp. 314.
8°. Воронежъ, Типо-Литографія Губернскаго Правленія, 1891.
Pp. 69-286, proverbs, <i>etc.</i>

2948. Dimitriewicz (Nikolaus). Russisches Lesebuch, <i>etc.</i> pp. 265, [v], 36. 8°. Lemberg, <i>Im Selbstverlage,</i> 1891.
Pp. 260-265, Русскія пословицы. 220 entries. [B.M.

2949. Dobrovolsky (Vasily Nikolaevich). Смоленскій этнографическій сборникъ. 3 часть.

8°. С.-Петербургъ, *Худековъ*, 1894.

Часть 3, Пословицы. [B.M.

2950. Dobrowský (Josef). Slavin. Beiträge zur Kenntniss der
slawischen Literatur, *etc.* pp. 479 + 3 tables.

8°. Prag, *Herrlsche Buchhandlung*, 1808.

Second edition. pp. 496. 8°. Prag, *Mayregg*, 1834.

Contains a list of 100 Russian proverbs in Roman characters, followed by
German translations. [B.M.

2951. Dolmatov (K.). Русскія пословицы и поговорка, *etc.* pp.
40. 12°. С.-Петербургъ, *Котоминъ*, 1882.

Русскія пословицы . . . безплатно прилагаемое ко всѣмъ его
альбомамъ русскихъ и малороссійскихъ узоровъ. pp. 4.

4°. [Спб., *Стасюлевичъ*, 1883].

Bernstein, 879-80.

2952. Efimenko (Petr Savvich). Матеріалы по этнографіи
русскаго населенія Архангельской губерніи. Часть 2,
Народная словесность, *etc.* pp. x, 276.

4°. Москва, *Архиповъ*, 1878.

Pp. 243-250, Пословицы и поговорки. *In* Труды Этнографическаго
Отдѣла Императорскаго Общества Любителей Естествознанія, *etc.*
Кн. 5, Вып. 2.

2953. Elemens. Elemens de la langue russe. *First edition.* pp.
[xiv], 368.

8°. Saint-Pétersbourg, *Imprimerie de l'Académie
Impériale des Sciences*, 1791.

Second edition. pp. [xii], 668.

8°. Saint-Pétersbourg, *ditto*, 1791.

Fourth edition. 8°. Saint-Pétersbourg, *ditto*, 1805.

Gratet-Duplessis, 887. Contains Proverbes et sentences russes. 214 proverbs
accompanied by literal French translations. Duplessis has reprinted these
proverbs, in French, pp. 501-506 of his bibliography. [B.M.

2954. Ermakov (N. Ya). Пословицы русскаго народа. pp. 48.

8°. С.-Петербургъ, *Корнатовскій*, 1894.

Sayings, *etc.*, with notes. [B.M.

2955. Evstafiev (Petr Vasil'evich). Древняя русская литература,
etc. 2 pts. 8°. С.-Петербургъ, *Полубояриновъ*, 1901.

Pt. 1, pp. 59-63, Пословицы. [B.M.

2956. ———: Приложеніе къ выпуску 1-му древней русской
литературы, *etc.* pp. 203.

8°. С.-Петербургъ, *Русская Художественная
Типографія*, 1877.

Bernstein, 1060. Pp. 166-182, Русскія народныя пословицы.

2957. Evstignyeev (Misha). Алмазы свѣтлаго ума и шутки въ анекдотахъ, *etc.* pp. 176, vi [=iv].

12°. Москва, *Абрамовъ*, 1880.

Bernstein, 1061. Pp. 67-86, Посповицы, поговорки и присловія.

2958. Fin (Samuel Josef). Талмудъ Лашонъ Руссія, *etc.* pp. 160. 4°. Вильно, *Роммъ и Зимелъ Типографъ*, 1847.

Bernstein, 4406. Pp. 108-112, Пословицы.

2959. Fuchs (Paul). Russische Conversations-Grammatik zum Schul- und Privatunterricht. pp. vi, 365.

8°. Heidelberg, *Gross*, 1871.

Pp. 337-346, Sprichwörter und der russischen Sprache eigenthümliche Aus-drücke. Russian proverbs with German equivalents. [B.M.

2960. Galakhov (Aleksandr Pavlovich). Исторія русской словес-ности, древней и новой, *etc.* 2 vols.

8°. Санктпетербургъ, *Тип. Морскаго Министерства*, 1863-75.

Another edition. 2 vols.

8°. Санктпетербургъ, *Тип. Морскаго Министерства*, 1880.

Vol. 1 contains a section of proverbs. [B.M.

2961. Gebhard (W. H. D.). Сборникъ самыхъ употребительныхъ русскихъ и имъ соотвѣтствующихъ нѣмецкихъ пословицъ и поговорокъ, *etc.* pp. 68. 8°. Libau, *Niemann*, 1887.

638 proverbs and proverbial phrases in Russian and German. [B.M.

2962. Gints (E. G.). Свѣтильники міровоззрѣнія или родникъ благополучія въ пословицахъ, *etc.* pp. 18.

8°. Варшава, *Ковалевскій*, 1890.

Bernstein, 1288.

2963. Glagolevsky (P.). Синтаксисъ языка русскихъ пословицъ, *etc.* pp. 48. 8°. С.-Петербургъ, *Исаковъ*, 1873.

Bernstein, 1294.

2964. Gol'dgardt-Landau (G. M.). Русскія пословицы, *etc.* pp. 180, xxxvi. 1 R. 50 K. 8°. Одесса, [1888?].

1475 Russian proverbs arranged alphabetically, followed by French and German equivalents. [B.M.

2965. Gol'shukh (I.). Пословицы, *etc.* pp. 103.

8°. Казань, *Типографія Императорскаго Университета*, 1887.

700 proverbs and sayings in Russian, with equivalents in French and Ger-man, followed by another 300 Latin ones with Russian equivalents. [B.M.

2966. Gorbunov-Posadov (I.). Земля-Кормилица, *etc.* pp. 135, vii. 8°. Москва, *Сытинъ*, 1890.

Another edition. pp. 135, vii.

8°. Москва, *Сытинъ*, 1898.

Contains brief lists of proverbs on various pages. [B.M.

2967. Gruszecki (B.). Первоначальное знакомство съ русскимъ языкомъ для польскихъ дѣтей, *etc.* pp. ii, 46, 4.

8°. Warszawa, *Jaworski*, 1867.

Bernstein, 1361. Pp. 15-18, Народныя русскія пословицы—Przysłowia narodowe ruskie.

2968. ――――: Русская грамота со статьями для чтенія составлена. pp. 126, xviii, viii.

8°. Варшава, *Тип. Варшавскаго Учебнаго Округа*, 1886.

Bernstein, 1362. Pp. 112-117, Народныя русскія пословицы.

2969. Gurvich (Boris). Kriminalistische Gedanken und Anschauungen in den Sprichwörtern des russischen Volkes. (Mittel-Russland). 8°. Leipzig, *Frankenstein und Wagner*, 1891.

In Zeitschrift für Volkskunde, Bd. 3, pp. 343-346, 382-385, 421-425. [B.M.

2970. Hupel (August Wilhelm). (Nordische Miscellaneen). Ueber den Nationalkarakter der Russen, *etc.* 17 vols.

8°. Riga, *Hartknoch*, 1781-91.

Stuck 1, pp. 1-23, Sprüchwörter und Stellen aus russischen Autoren zum Exponieren. In Russian and German. Stuck 8, pp. 232-256, Russische Sprüchwörter. A commentary on Russian proverbs, followed by a brief list of them, in German. [B.M.

2971. Illyustrov (Iakinth I.). Юридическія пословицы и поговорки русскаго народа, *etc.* pp. 72, iv.

8°. Москва, *Чичеринъ*, 1885.
[B.M.

2972. ――――: Жизнь русскаго народа въ его пословицахъ. pp. xcviii, 469. 3 R. 50 K. 8°. St. Petersburg, 1910.

Another edition. St. Petersburg, 1915.

[B.M. (1910 edition), L.L. (1915 edition).

2973. Ivanov (Sergyei). Сибилла. Искусство узнавать будущее, *etc.* pp. 394. 8°. Москва, 1884.

Bernstein, 1574. Pp. 95, 97-98, 99, 101-112, proverbs.

2974. Ivashchenko (P. S.). Религіозный культъ Южно-Русскаго народа въ его пословицахъ, *etc.* 8°. Кіевъ, *Фрицъ*, 1875.

In Записки Юго-западнаго Отдѣла Императорскаго Русскаго Географическаго Общества, Томъ 2, pp. 71-108.

2975. Kasinova (Evdoksija). Manuel de la conversation russe. . . . Tome premier. pp. 196.

8°. Odessa, *Sadovsky*, 1860.

Bernstein, 1671. Pp. 194-196, proverbes—Пословицы.

2976. Khrestomatiya. Русская хрестоматія для учениковъ двухъ низшихъ классовъ, *etc.* pp. ii, 192.

8°. Москва, *Университетская Типографія*, 1869.

Bernstein, 603. Pp. 50-53, Пословицы.

2977. Khudyakov (Ivan Aleksandrovich). Русская книжка, *etc.*
pp. 170, ii.   8°. С.-Петербургъ, *Бакстъ,* 1863.
Bernstein, 611. Pp. 13-15, Пословицы.

2978. Kiesewetter (J. O. K. Ch.). Ueber Sprichwörter überhaupt, nebst einer Auswahl russischer Sprichwörter.
8°. Berlin, *Maurer,* 1796.
Gratet-Duplessis, 886. *In* Berlinisches Archiv der Zeit und ihres Geschmacks,
Sept., 1796, pp. 243-248. 54 Russian proverbs are given in German.   [B.M.

2979. Knyazhevich (Dmitry). Полное собраніе русскихъ пословицъ и поговорокъ, *etc.* pp. vii, 31, 296.
8°. Санктпетербургъ, *Край,* 1822.
Bernstein, 3441, states that the preface of this anonymous book is signed
D. K., *i.e.*, Dmitri Knyazhevich. 5365 entries. This is Gratet-Duplessis, 888.

2980. Koltsov (A. N.). Русскія пословицы.
8°. Санктпетербургъ, 1861.
In Воронежская Бесѣда на 1861-й годъ, pp. i-xx.

2981. Kondaraki (V. Kh.). Учебникъ для первоначальнаго само-
образованія. pp. 192, iii.   8°. Москва, *Чичеринъ,* 1883.
Bernstein, 1744. Pp. 16-19, Russian proverbs.

2982. Kovanko (Semen). Старинная пословица во вѣкъ не сло-
мится, *etc.* pp. 88.
8°. Харьковъ, *Университетская Типографія,* 1848.
Bernstein, 2652.

2983. Kurganov (Nikolai). Письмовникъ, содержащій въ себѣ
науку Россійскаго языка со многимъ присовокупленіемъ
разнаго учебнаго и полезнозабавнаго вещесловія, *etc.* 2
vols.
8°. Санктпетербургъ, *Тип. Императорской*
Академіи Наукъ, 1790.
Another edition. 2 vols.   8°. Москва, *Степановъ,* 1837.
Bernstein, 1799-1803. Vol. 1 contains a selection of proverbs.

2984. Long (James). On Russian proverbs, *etc.* pp. 21.
8°. [London, 1876].
In Transactions of the Royal Society of Literature, Vol. 11, Part 2, New
Series. A commentary with numerous examples in English.   [U.C.L.

2985. Manasevich (Boris). Russicismen. Russische Redens-
arten und Sprichwörter mit gegenüberstehender deutscher
Uebersetzung. pp. 48.   12°. Leipzig, *Gerhard,* 1881.
[B.M.

2986. Mandelkern (Solomon). Историческая хрестоматія по русской словесности, *etc.* pp. xii, 488.
8°. Hannover, *Hahn,* 1891.
Pp. 49-54, Sprichwörter—(Пословицы).   [B.M.

2987. Mandelkern (Solomon). Русское Эхо. Бесѣды, пословицы и поговорки изъ русской жизни, *etc.* pp. 158, 84.

8°. Leipzig, *Violet*, 1888.
[B.M.]

2988. Masson (Paul). Le Tsar dans le proverbe russe.

8°. Paris, 1889, 1894.

In Revue des traditions populaires, Vol. 4, p. 91, and Vol. 9, pp. 694-701. Russian proverbs in French, concerning the Tsar. [B.M.]

2989. Melnikova (Aleksandra). Пословицы и поговорки въ стихахъ. pp. 222.

32°. въ Кіевѣ и Харьковѣ, *Югансонъ*, [1894].
Bernstein, 2148.

2990. Meri-Khovi. Сборникъ пословицъ, поговорокъ, примѣтъ и проч., *etc.* pp. iii, 252.

8°. Санктпетербургъ, *Губернская Типографія,* 1882.
Bernstein, 2164.

2991. Mikhelson (Morits Il'ich). Русская мысль и рѣчь, *etc.* 2 vols. 8°. St. Petersburg, 1902-3.
[B.M.]

2992. Morachevsky (G. M.). Характеристики образцовъ литературы для начальнаго изученія словесности. pp. 179.

8°. Кіевъ, *Даваденко,* 1884.
Bernstein, 2251. Pp. 168-172, proverbs.

2993. Nadezhdin (P.). Пособіе для практическихъ занятій по русскому, *etc.* pp ii, v, v, 305, 53.

8°. Тифлисъ, *Михельсонъ,* 1877.
Bernstein, 2310. Pp. 177-183, Пословицы.

2994. National Proverbs. National proverbs : Russia. pp. 79.

1/-. sm. 8°. Philadelphia, *McKay*, [191—?].

National Proverbs Series. Russian proverbs translated into English. A brief list : no notes. [F.-L.S. (Stephens collection).

2995. Nikolenko (M.). Пособіе для практическихъ занятій при первоначальномъ изученіи русскаго языка, *etc.* Книга 1-я, 6-е изд. pp. xvi, 216. 8°. Санктпетербургъ, 1883.
Bernstein, 2349. Pp. 159-160, 171-173, Пословицы и поговорки.

2996. Nosovich (I. I.). Бѣлорусскія пословицы и поговорки. Сборникъ Н. Н. [*sic*] Носовича. Coll. 160.

4°. Санктпетербургъ, *въ Типографіи Имп.*

Академіи Наукъ, 1853.

In Памятники и образцы народнаго языка и словесности. Изданіе 2. Отдѣленія . . . Академіи Наукъ, Томъ 1.

2997. ——— : Сборникъ бѣлорусскихъ пословицъ.

8°. С.-Петербургъ, 1867.

In Записки Императорскаго Русскаго Географическаго Общества, по Отдѣленю Этнографіи, Томъ первый, pp. 251-482. [B.M.]

2998. Orlov (M. A.). Курсъ исторіи русской литературы, *etc.*
2 pts. 8°. С.-Петербургъ, *Добродѣевъ*, 1884-85.
Another edition. 2 pts. 8°. С.-Петербургъ, 1885-90.
Pt. 1 contains two pages of proverbs and sayings. [B.M.

2999. Ostroumie. Русское народное остроуміе. Сборникъ характерныхъ комическихъ пословицъ, поговорокъ, *etc.* pp. 69, ii.
8°. Казань, *Ключниковъ*, 1883.
Bernstein, 2426.

3000. Ovsyannikov (Ya.). Женщина. Изреченія и мысли извѣстныхъ писателей и русскія пословицы. pp. 30.
16°. Москва, *Кольчугинъ*, 1894.
Another edition. pp. 46. 16°. Москва, *Сытинъ*, 1896.
Bernstein, 4606-7.

3001. Pilet (Raymond). La Russie en proverbes. pp. 29.
sm. 8°. Paris, *Leroux*, 1905.
Bibliothèque slave Elzévirienne, tome 15. Proverbs in French, classified : no notes. [F.-L.S.

3002. Pinkerton (Robert). Russia ; or, miscellaneous observations on the past and present state of that country, *etc.* pp.
[8], 486. 8°. London, *Seeley*, 1833.
Pp. 349-356, Russian proverbs translated into English. [B.M.

3003. Pogovorki. Новыя русскія поговорки и присказки. 4 vols.
16°. Москва, *Семенъ*, 1852-58.
Bernstein, 2625. 1547 entries.

3004. Porfir'ev (Ivan Yakovlevich). Исторія русской словесности, *etc.* pp. 724, iv. 2 vols.
8°. Казань, *Тип. Императорскаго Университета,*
1886-91.
Vol. 1, pp. 164-170, Русскія пословицы. [B.M.

3005. Poslovitsui. Пословицы и поговорки Галицкой и Угорской Руси. pp. 138. 8°. С.-Петербургъ, *Майковъ*, 1868.
In Записки Императорскаго Русскаго Географическаго Общества, по Отдѣленію Этнографіи, Т. 2, 1868.

3006. ———: Пословицы на каждый день, *etc.* pp. 72.
12°. Москва, *Сытинъ*, 1887.
Another edition. pp. 80.
12°. С.-Петербургъ, *Евдокимовъ*, 1887.
Bernstein, 2657-8.

3007. Proverbs. Russian proverbs.
8°. London, *Murray*, 1875.
In The Quarterly Review, Vol. 139, pp. 493-525. An informative essay with numerous examples in English. [B.M.

3008. R. (P.). Бытъ русскаго народа въ его пословицахъ. П. P. pp. 16. 8°. Москва, *Катковъ*, 1859.
Bernstein, 476.

3009. Rodde (Jacob). Russische Sprachlehre. . . . 2. Auflage.
3 pts. 8°. Riga, *Hartknoch*, 1778.
3. Auflage. 8°. Riga, *Hartknoch*, 1784.
Pt. 2, Russian proverbs with German equivalents. [B.M.

3010. Sakharov (I.). Сказанія русскаго народа, *etc.* 2 vols.
fol. Санктпетербургъ, 1841-49.
Another edition. 2 vols.
8°. С.-Петербургъ, *Суворинъ*, 1885.
Bernstein, 3115-6. Vol. 1 contains a collection of proverbs.

3011. Schiller (Johann Christoph Friedrich von). Schiller's Demetrius . . . Herausgegeben von Gustav Kettner, *etc.* pp. lxx, 312. 8°. Weimar, *Goethe-Gesellschaft*, 1894.
Pp. 258-259, Russische Sprichwörter. 21 proverbs translated into German.
[B.M.

3012. Segal (Louis). Russian proverbs and their English equivalents. pp. vi, 63.
16°. London, *Kegan Paul*, New York, *Dutton*, [1917].
Arranged in alphabetical order; no notes. In Russian characters, with English translations or equivalents. [B.M.

3013. Sergyeev (Aleksyei). Русскія пословицы и поговорки въ лицахъ. pp. [vii], 168.
8°. С.-Петербургъ, *Печатано въ Военной Типографіи,*
1830.
Bernstein, 2667.

3014. Shafranov (S.). Русскія народныя пословицы и пѣсни, *etc.* pp. iii, 135. 8°. Полтава, *Пигуренко*, 1884.
Bernstein, 3659. Pp. 1-38, Русскія пословицы. 100 Russian proverbs with Latin, French, and German parallels.

3015. Shafranov (S.) and **Nikolich** (I.). Русская хрестоматія для употребленія, *etc.* 2 часть. 8°. Ревель, *Клугъ*, 1872-80.
Bernstein, 3659. Часть 1, pp. 362-371; Часть 2, pp. 216-223, Пословицы.

3016. Shatokhin (L.). Употребительнѣйшія бытовыя русскія пословицы. pp. 30. 12°. Кіевъ, *Давиденко*, 1876.
Bernstein, 3662.

3017. Shimellovich (Movshei). Грамматика россійскаго языка, *etc.* pp. [vi], 136. 4°. Вильно, *Зымель и Манесъ*, 1824.
Bernstein, 4719. Pp. 91-93, 56 Russian proverbs with Hebrew translations.

3018. Sichler (Léon). Proverbes et dictons russes sur la Russie et ses habitants. 8°. Paris, *Leroux*, 1889.
In Revue des traditions populaires, 4e année, tome 4, pp. 91-96. Russian proverbs and sayings in French. [B.M.

3019. Sidoratsky (Vasily Petrovich). Petit manuel de langue russe, *etc.* pp. 15.   25 centimes. 32°. Paris, [1893].

Pp. 12-14, proverbs. P. 14, traduction de ces proverbes. An edition of 1895 contains about three proverbs only.

3020. Sirot (I. M.). Параллели. Библейскіе тексты и отраженіе. . . . Выпускъ 1. Изреченія и притчи Ветхаго Завѣта въ сопоставленіи съ русскими народными пословицами и поговорками. pp. 117.   8°. Одесса, *Шпенцеръ,* 1897.

Bernstein, 3416. 553 entries.

3021. Snegirev (Ivan Mikhailovich).   Рускіе въ своихъ пословицахъ, *etc.* 4 vols.

Москва, *Университетская Типографія,* 1831-34.

Presumably the one indicated by Duplessis, 889. Bernstein, 3433, says this also gives proverbs in many Slav and other languages, including Greek and Latin.   [B.M.

3022. ———: Русскія народныя пословицы, *etc.* pp. xlv, 503.
        8°. Москва, *въ Университетской Типографіи,* 1848.

The introduction contains a bibliography. The proverbs, sayings, *etc.*, are arranged alphabetically; there are a few brief notes. Parallels from English and many other languages given.   [B.M.

3023. Sobranie. Собраніе пословицъ и поговорокъ русскаго народа, *etc.* pp. v, 290.
        12°. Санктпетербургъ, *Императорская*
                                Академія Наукъ, 1862.

Bernstein, 3442.

3024. ———: Собраніе 4291. Древнихъ россійскихъ пословицъ. pp. 320.
        8°. Москва, *при Императорскомъ Московскомъ*
                                        Университетъ, 1770.

Another edition. pp. 203.
        8°. Москва, *Компанія Типографическая,* 1787.

Gratet-Duplessis, 883.

3025. Stolpyansky (N. P.) and **Abaza** (K. K.).   Книга для начальнаго чтенія въ войскахъ, *etc.* pp. [vi], 144.
        8°. С.-Петербургъ, *Типографія Дома Призрѣнія*
                                Малолѣтныхъ Бѣдныхъ, 1871.

Bernstein, 3619. Contains numerous brief lists of proverbs.

3026. Tappe (August Wilhelm). Neues russisches Elementar-Lesebuch . . . zweiter Theil der theoretisch-praktischen russischen Sprachlehre. . . . Achte unveränderte Auflage. pp. 11, 119.   8°. St. Petersburg, *etc.*, *Simonsen,* 1835.

Pp. 2-23, Правила, правоучительныя изреченія и пословицы. With German translations.   [B.M.

3027. Timofeev (Konstantin).   Пособіе при изученіи исторіи
русской словесности, *etc.*
8°.   С.-Петербургъ, *Траншель,* 1869.
Another edition.   pp. 216.
8°.   С.-Петербургъ, *Ѳедоровъ,* 1873.
Pp. 31-35, Русскія пословицы.   [B.M.

3028. Timoshenko (Ivan Eleazarovich).   Литературные первои-
сточники и прототипы трехъ-сотъ русскихъ пословицъ и
поговорокъ, *etc.* pp. xxv, 170.   8°. Кіевъ, *Барскій,* 1897.
[B.M.

3029. Trapitsuin (I.).   Народный нравоучитель или собраніе
русскихъ пословицъ.   Изданіе второе. pp. 117.
8°.   Ярославль, *Фалькъ,* 1870.
Bernstein, 3741.   109 rhymed proverbs, with full notes.

3030. Verkhovskaya (O.).   Сборникъ русскихъ пословицъ съ
картинками. pp. 143.   8°.   С.-Петербургъ, *Бенке,* 1883.
Bernstein, 4016.

3031. Vladimirov (P. V.).   Введеніе въ исторію русской словесности, *etc.* pp. vi, 276.   8°.   Кіевъ, *Завадзкій,* 1896.
Pp. 132-137, Русскія народныя пословицы.   [B.M.

3032. Vodovozov (Vasily Ivanovich).   Древняя русская литература, *etc.* pp. iv, 350.
8°.   Санктпетербургъ, *Глазуновъ,* 1872.
Pp. 76-104, Народныя сказки и пословицы.   [B.M.

3033. ——: Русская азбука, *etc.* pp. iii, 105.
8°.   С.-Петербургъ, *Котоминъ,* 1879.
Bernstein, 4082.   Contains numerous short lists of proverbs.

3034. Volzhensky (S. V.).   Руководство для первоначальнаго
обученія чтенію и письму. . . . Изданіе третіе, *etc.* pp. 112.
8°.   Москва, *Коммиссіонеръ,* 1874.
Bernstein, 4116.   Pp. 100-105, Пословицы.

3035. Voskresensky (V.).   Русская народная поэзія, *etc.* pp. v,
iv, 339.   8°.   С.-Петербургъ, *Семья и Школа,* 1881.
Bernstein, 4127.   Pp. 322-331, Пословицы.

3036. Zander (Ivan Ya.).   Начатки русскаго языка, *etc.* 3 част.
8°.   Рига, *Götschel,* 1869.
Часть 2, Anthologie russischer Sprüchwörter und Russismen, *etc.* Russian
and German.   [B.M.

See also **1089, 1697, 2345, 2856, 3745, 3799, 3820, 3893.** For
Siberian *see* Northern and Central Asiatic.

LOCAL AND DIALECT.
1. LITTLE RUSSIAN.

3037. A. Przysłowia Rusi. 8°. Wilno, *Glücksberg*, 1844.
In Athenæum, tome 3, pp. 204-216. An alphabetical list. [B.M.

3038. Barącz (Sadok). Bajki, fraszki, podania, przysłowia i
piesni na Rusi. pp. 248.
8°. Tarnopol, *by the Author*, 1866.
Another edition. pp. 271.
8°. Lwów, *Wajdowiczowa*, 1886.
Contains a brief alphabetical list of proverbs. [B.M.

3039. Chubinsky (P. P.). Труды Этнографическо-Статистической
Экспедици въ Западно-Русскій край. . . . Томъ первый, *etc.*
pp. xxx, 467. 8°. С.-Петербургъ, 1872.
Pp. 229-304, Пословицы. [B.M.

3040. Dragomanov (Mikhail Petrovich). Малорусскія народныя
преданія и разсказы, *etc.* pp. xxv, 432.
8°. Кіевъ, *Фрицъ*, 1876.
Pp. 376-381, Приказки. [B.M.

3041. G . . . (M.). Ужинок рідного пола вистачиній працеу
М. Г. . . . pp. iv, 371. 8°. Москва, *Каткоŷ*, 1857.
Pp. 327-352, Прислоŷки і примоŷки. [B.M.

3042. Gattsuk (Mikola). Украінска абéтка. pp. vi, 117.
4°. Москва, [1861].
Bernstein, 1225. Pp. 55-60, ПрислоꝆки і примоꝆки.

3043. Holovatsky (Ivan B. Th.). Вѣнок русинам на обжинки. 2
tom. 12°. у Вѣдни, *Чер. О. О. Мехитаристовъ*, 1846-47.
Bernstein, 1309. Tome 2, pp. 240-254, gives the explanation of various
proverbs connected with domestic economy.

3044. Hrinchenko (Boris Dmitrovich). Этнографическіе матеріалы, *etc.* 2 tom.
8°. Черниговъ, *Тип. Губернскаго Земства*, 1895-1899.
Tom. 1, pp. 231-247 : Tom. 2, pp. 302-310, proverbs. [B.M.

3045. Ilkievich (Grigory). Галицкіи приповѣдки и загадки. pp.
vi, 124.
8°. у Вѣдни, *Черепками О. О. Мехитаристовъ*, 1841.
Bernstein, 1565. Pp. 1-118, Приповѣдки.

3046. Kolberg (Henryk Oskar). Pokucie, *etc.* 4 tom.
8°. Kraków, *Uniwersytet Jagielloński*, 1882-89.
Tom. 3, pp. 179-198, 661 proverbs.

3047. Komarov (M.). Нова збирка народнихъ малоруськихъ прыказокъ, *etc.* pp. x, 124.

sm. 8°. Одесса, *Фесенко,* 1890.

Bernstein, 1741. Pp. 1-102, proverbs, *etc.* Includes a bibliography.

3048. Lewicki (Joseph). Grammatik der ruthenischen oder kleinrussischen Sprache in Galizien, *etc.* 2 pts.

8°. Przemysl, *Griech. kath. bischöfliche Buchdruckerey,* 1834.

Pp. 201-210, in Galizien gebräuchliche Sprichwörter. Proverbs with German translations. [B.M.

3049. Lutskay (Michael). Grammatica Slavo-Ruthena, *etc.* pp. xvi, 176.

8°. Budae, *Typis regiae Universitatis Pestensis,* 1830.

Pp. 158-166, Adagia Ruthenica. Ruthenian proverbs with German translations.

3050. Manzhura (I. I.). Сказки, пословицы и т. п., *etc.* pp. 194, vii.

8°. Харьковъ, 1890.

Bernstein, 2069. *In* Сборникъ Харьковскаго Историко-Филологическаго Общества, Томъ 2, Вып. 2. Pp. 161-173, 400 proverbs and sayings.

3051. Marcinkowski (Antoni). Lud ukraiński przez Antoniego Nowosielskiego [*pseud.* of Marcinkowski]. 2 tom.

8°. Wilno, *Glücksberg,* 1857.

Tom. 2, pp. 231-261, Przysłowia. An alphabetical list of proverbs, without notes. [B.M.

3052. ———: Przysłowia Ukraińskie. [Article signed: A. Nowosielski]. 8°. Wilno, *Zawadzki,* 1879.

Bernstein, 2374. *In* Upominek Wileński, 1879, pp. 183-197.

3053. Markovich (O. V.). Українські приказки, прислівъя ... спорудив М. Номис. [*pseud.* of Simonenko]. pp. vii, 304, xvii. 8°. С.-Петербург, *Тибленъ и Кулишъ,* 1864.

14,339 entries. [B.M.

3054. Pavlovsky (Aleksyei Pavlovich). Грамматика малороссійскаго нарѣчія, *etc.* pp. vi, 114.

8°. Санктпетербургъ, *Плавильщиковъ,* 1818.

Pp. 78-86, phrases, proverbs, sayings, *etc.* [B.M.

3055. Pichler (Carl Wladimir). Kurzgefasste russinische Sprachlehre. pp. 35. 8°. Lemberg, *Stengel,* 1849.

Pp. 24-28, Sprichwörter. There are German translations of certain words, but not of the whole of the proverbs. [B.M.

3056. Pogovorki. Поговорки и пословицы употребляемыя въ Волынской губерніи.

8°. Санктпетербургъ, *Головинъ,* 1864.

In Этнографическій Сборникъ издаваемый Императорскимъ Русскимъ Географическимъ Обществомъ, Выпускъ 6, pp. 77-82. 179 entries. [B.M.

3057. Poslovitsui. Пословицы и поговорки Галицкой и Угорской Руси. 8°. С.-Петербургъ, 1869.

In Записки Императорскаго Русскаго Географическаго Общества, по Отдѣленію Этнографіи, Томь 2, pp. 225-362. [B.M.

3058. Pripovyedki. Галицко-Русскіи приповѣдки. 8°. Wien, *Braumüller*, 1851.

In Slavische Bibliothek oder Beiträge zur slavischen Philologie und Geschichte, Bd. 1, pp. 264-266. [B.M.

3059. Prusinowski (Jan). Przysłowia Ukraińskie w piosnkach. 8°. Warszawa, *Gazeta Polska*, 1862-63.

In Biblioteka Warszawska, 1862, Vol. 4, pp. 440-443; 1863, Vol. 1, pp. 456-460; Vol. 3, pp. 56-60. [B.M.

3060. Romanov (E.). Бѣлорусскій сборникъ, *etc. In progress.* 8°. Кіевъ, *Кульженко*, Витебскъ, *Малкинъ*, 1886, *etc.*

Vol. 1, pp. 290-316, Пословицы, *etc.* 757 entries. [B.M.

3061. Rudchenko (Ivan Yakovlevich). Чумацкія народныя пѣсни. pp. vii, xiii, 257. 8°. Кіевъ, *Фрицъ*, 1874.

Pp. 245-57, Словарь рѣже употребляемыхъ словъ, съ пословицами къ Чумацкому быту. [B.M.

3062. Rulikowski (Edward). Zapiski etnograficzne z Ukrainy. 8°. Kraków, *Uniwersytet Jagielloński*, 1879.

In Zbiór wiadomości do Antropologii krajowej, Tom. 3, pp. (62-166). Pp. (152-164), Przysłowia. 516 entries. [B.M.

3063. Russe. Der kleine Russe, *etc.* pp. 139. 8°. St. Petersburg, *Kurth*, Braunschweig, *Leibrock*, 1844.

Bernstein, 4666. Pp. 132-139, Auswahl von Russicismen und Sprichwörtern.

3064. Shishatsky-Illich (Aleksandr). Сборникъ Малороссійскихъ пословицъ и поговорокъ. pp. 97. 8°. Черниговъ, *Губернская Типографія*, 1857.

A large alphabetical list. [B.M.

3065. Smirnitsky (V. N.). Малороссійскія пословицы и поговорки. Собранныя В. Н. С. 8°. Харьковъ, 1834.

3066. Sumtsov (Nikolai Thedorovich). Опытъ историческаго изученія малорусскихъ пословицъ. pp. 11. 8°. Харьковъ, 1896.

Bernstein, 3634.

3067. Wójcicki (Kazimierz Władysław). Stare gawędy i obrazy. 4 tom. 12°. Warszawa, *Sennewald*, 1840.

Tom. 2, pp. 237-276, O przysłowiach historycznych i rolniczych ludu w Polsce i na Rusi, *etc.* [B.M.

3068. Zakrevsky (Nikolai). Старосвѣтскій Бандуриста, *etc.* 2 pts. 8°. Москва, 1860-61.

Bernstein, 4162. Pp. 141-242, proverbs, *etc.*

3069. Zgarsky (Evgeny Ya.). Народная русская философія, *etc.*
pp. 96. 8°. Коломыя, *Бѣлоусъ*, 1873.
Bernstein, 4195.

2. WHITE RUSSIAN.

3070. Bulgakovsky (Dmitry Gavrilovich). Пинчуки. Этнографическій сборникъ. Пѣсни, загадки, пословицы, *etc.* pp. vi,
200. 8°. С.-Петербургъ, *Безобразовъ*, 1890.
Bernstein, 450. Pp. 176-178, Пословицы и поговорки. 65 entries.

3071. Dybowski (Władysław). Przysłowia Białoruskie z powiatu
Nowogródzkiego. pp. [23].
8°. w Krakowie, *w druk. Universytetu Jagiellońskiego*, 1881.
Bernstein, 938.

3072. Kamiński (Mścisław). Przysłowia ludu nadwilejskiego.
8°. Warszawa, *Gebethner i Wolff*, 1866.
In Biblioteka Warszawska, Tom. 4, pp. 302-312. 199 entries, with notes.
[B.M.

3073. Kolberg (Henryk Oskar). Zwyczaje i obrzędy weselne z
Polesia, *etc.* pp. 38.
8°. Kraków, *Uniwersytet Jagielloński*, 1889.
Pp. 37-38, Zdania i przysłowia od Pińska. 31 White Russian proverbs.

3074. Lyatsky (Evgeny A.). Нѣсколько замѣчаній къ вопросу
о пословицахъ и поговоркахъ. I-V. pp. 38.
8°. Санктпетербургъ, *Императорская Академія
Наукъ*, 1897.
In Извѣстія Отдѣленія Русскаго Языка и Словесности Императорской Академіи Наукъ, Т. 2, Кн. 3, pp. 745 *et seq.* [B.M.

3075. ————: Матеріалы для изученія творчества и быта Бѣлоруссовъ. I. Пословицы, поговорки, загадки. pp. viii, 63.
8°. Москва, *Университетская Типографія*, 1898.
Bernstein, 4524. 2022 entries.

3076. Nosovich (I. I.). Бѣлорусскія пословицы, *etc.*
8°. С.-Петербургъ, 1869.
In Записки Императорскаго Русскаго Географическаго Общества, по Отдѣленію Этнографіи, Томъ 2, pp. 363-371. [B.M.

3077. ————: Бѣлорусскія пословицы и поговорки.
4°. Санктпетербургъ, 1852.
In Памятники и образцы народнаго языка и словесности.
Изданіе 11-го, col. 33-80. 988 entries.

3078. Nosovich (I. I.). Сборникъ бѣлорусскихъ пословицъ. pp. vi, 232. 8°. Санктпетербургъ, *Императорская Академія Наукъ*, 1874.

In Сборникъ Отдѣленія Русскаго Языка и Словесности Императорской Академіи Наукъ, Томъ 12, № 2. [B.M.

3079. Poslovitsui. Посповицы и поговорки. 8°. Вильна, 1866.

In Сборникъ памятниковъ народнаго творчества въ Сѣверозападномъ Краѣ. Изданіе Редакціи Виленскаго Вѣстника, pp. 287-294.

3080. Radchenko (Zinaida). Гомельскія народныя пѣсни, *etc.* pp. xiii, 265. 8°. С.-Петербургъ, *Безобразовъ*, 1888.

In Записки Императорскаго Русскаго Географическаго Общества, по Отдѣленію Этнографіи, Томь 13, Вып. 2. Pp. 246-249, over 80 proverbs. [B.M.

3081. Shein (Pavel Vasil'evich). Матеріалы для изученія быта и языка русскаго населенія Сѣверо-Западнаго Края, *etc.* 2 tom. 8°. Санктпетербургъ, *Императорская Академія Наукъ*, 1887-93.

Tom. 2, pp. 472-484, Пословицы и поговорки. 195 entries. [B.M.

3082. Tyszkiewicz (Eustachy). Opisanie powiatu borysowskiego, *etc.* pp. iii, 446, 43, iv. 8°. Wilno, *Marcinowski*, 1847.

Pp. 411-438, Przysłowia ludu znad Berezyny, *etc.* [B.M.

z

GEORGIAN

3083. Sakhokia (Th.). Les proverbes géorgiens. pp. 34.
8°. Paris, *Lechevalier*, 1902-03.

In Revue des traditions populaires, tome 17, pp. 547-565, and tome 18, pp. 119-133. A selection of over 800 Georgian proverbs in French, with occasional notes. Arranged under subject headings. [B.M.

3084. Schiefner (Franz Anton von). Tschetschenzische Studien. pp. viii, 72.
4°. St. Petersburg, *K. Akademie der Wissenschaften*, 1864.

In Mémoires de l'Académie Impériale des Sciences de St.-Pétersbourg, 7e série, Tome 7, No. 5. P. 41, K'iciniś—Sprüchwörter. 17 proverbs in the original, with German translations. [B.M.

3085. Seidlitz (N. von). Grusinische Sprichwörter.
4°. Stuttgart, 1889.

In Das Ausland, Jahrgang 62, pp. 256-257. In German. [B.M.

3086. Tsagareli (Aleksandr Antonovich). Мингрельскіе этюды, *etc.* 2 pts. 8°. С.-Петербургъ, *Академія Наукъ*, 1880.

Pt. 1, pp. 81-86, Пословицы, *etc.* [B.M.

AZERBAIJANIAN

3086a. Seinally (Ch.). Azerbaidschan atalar sözi. Azerbaid-schanische Sprichwörter und Redensarten. pp. xxix, 234.
8°. Baku, 1926.

WESTERN ASIATIC

GENERAL.

3087. Agnellini (Timoteo). Proverbii utili e virtuosi in lingua araba, persiana e turca, gran parte in versi, con la loro ispiegatione in lingua latina et italiana, *etc.* pp. 84.
sm. 8°. Padova, *Stamperia del Seminario*, 1688.

Gratet-Duplessis, 71. Collection of a number of moral maxims, including some proverbs. A book of little importance. [B.M.

3088. Benas (Baron Louis). Semitic proverbs.
8°. London, *Longman*, Liverpool, *Marples*, 1869.

In Proceedings of the Literary and Philosophical Society of Liverpool, 1868-9, pp. 228-245. [B.M.

3089. Boyajian (Zabelle C.). Wit and wisdom from the Near East. 8°. London, 1922.

In Contemporary Review, Vol. 122, pp. 744-749. [B.M.

3090. Clouston (William Alexander). Book of wise sayings selected largely from Eastern sources. pp. viii, 134.
8°. London, *Hutchinson*, 1893.
[B.M.

3091. Dombay (Franz Lorenz von). Popular-Philosophie der Araber, Perser und Türken, *etc.* pp. 277.
8°. Agram, *Bischöff*, 1795.

Gratet-Duplessis, 77. Pp. 161-176, Sprüchwörter. Proverbs from all three languages translated into German. [B.M.

3092. Duchenoud (Charles). Recueil d'adages et de pensées détachées empruntés . . . aux langues orientales, *etc.* pp. 281. 8°. Paris, *Challamel*, 1867.

3093. Galland (Antoine). Les paroles remarquables, les bons-mots et les maximes des Orientaux, *etc.* pp. [xvi], 344 + 17 leaves. 12°. La Haye, *Van Dole*, 1694.

Another edition. Orientaliana, *etc.* Amsterdam, 1730.

Gratet-Duplessis, 72. Not a collection of proverbs; but amongst the maxims which occupy the second half of the book there are a number of true proverbs. In French. [B.M.

3094. Khazînat. Khazînat al-amsâl, *etc.* [Edited by Maulavi Turâb 'Ali]. 8°. Cawnpore, 1853.

An alphabetical collection of proverbs in Arabic, Persian, and Hindustani. Edited with a preface in Hindustani, marginal notes in Persian, and an interlineary translation in the latter language to the Arabic portion of the collection.

3095. Lennep (Henry J. van). Bible lands, their modern customs and manners, *etc.* 2 pts.

8°. London, *Murray*, 1875.

Pt. 2, pp. 813-816, Oriental proverbs, *etc.* In English. [B.M.

3096. Long (James). Eastern proverbs and emblems, illustrating old truths. pp. xv, 280.

6/6. 8°. London, *Trübner*, 1881.

Trübner's Oriental Series. Limited to proverbs illustrating moral and religious subjects, in English only, but taken from many languages. Notes and full references. [F.-L.S. (Stephens collection).

3097. ———: Scripture truth in oriental dress, *etc.* pp. viii, 269. 8°. Calcutta, *Thacker, Spink*, 1871.

Pp. 217-263, Oriental proverbs and similes illustrating Holy Writ. In English. [B.M.

3098. Nilaratna Sarman, *called* **Haldar.** The bohoodurson . . . being a choice collection of proverbs and morals in the English, Latin, Bengalee, Sanscrit, Persian, and Arabic languages. pp. 4, 147. 8°. Serampore, 1826.

[B.M.

3099. Paultre des Ormes (Charles). La morale primitive, ou pensées, maximes, proverbes et sentences des Orientaux. 2 pts. 16°. Paris, *Passard*, [1857?].

Gratet-Duplessis, 27. Moral maxims with a few proverbs. In French.

[B.M.

3100. Rehatsek (E.). Some parallel proverbs in English, Arabic, and Persian. 8°. Bombay, 1878.

In Journal of the Bombay branch of the Royal Asiatic Society, Vol. 14, pp. 86-116. Also issued as a separate publication. [B.M.

3101. Rhasis (D.). Analecta (une collection de sentences, proverbes et extraits de poésie en Arabe, Persan, et Turc, *etc.*). pp. 84.

8°. Constantinople, *Imprimerie du Journal " Constantinoupolis,"* 1889.

[B.M.

3102. Seidel (A.). Anthologie aus der asiatischen Volkslitteratur. pp. xiv, 396. 8°. Weimar, *Felber*, 1898.

Beiträge zur Volks- und Völkerkunde, Bd. 7. Contains many brief lists of proverbs of various Asiatic races. The proverbs are translated into German.

[B.M.

3103. Wilson (Charles Thomas). Peasant life in the Holy Land, *etc.* pp. x, 321 + plates. la. 8°. London, *Murray*, 1906. Chap. 16, pp. 302-314, proverbs. [B.M.

ANCIENT
(Assyrian, Babylonian, Aramaic).

3104. Jaeger (Martin). Assyrische Räthsel und Sprüchwörter. 8°. Leipzig, *Hinrich*, 1894.

In Delitzsch and Haupt's Beiträge zur Assyriologie, Bd. 2, pp. 274-305. [B.M.

3105. Langdon (S.). Babylonian proverbs. 8°. Chicago, 1912.

In American Journal of Semitic Languages and Literatures, Vol. 28, pp. 217-243. [B.M.

3106. Lewin (Moses). Aramäische Sprichwörter und Volks-sprüche, *etc.* pp. 90, xii. 8°. Berlin, *Itzkowski*, 1895.

Proverbs in the original with German translations. Pp. 7-11, bibliography. [B.M.

MEDIÆVAL AND MODERN.

1. ARABIC.

3107. Abu Al-Kasim Ibn Sadīrah. Cours pratique de langue arabe, *etc.* pp. xii, 290. 8°. Alger, *Jourdan*, 1891.

Pp. 256-262, proverbes rimés. With transliterations and French translations. [B.M.

3108. ——— : Dialogues français-arabes, *etc.* pp. vii, 370. 8°. Alger, *Jourdan*, 1877.

Another edition. pp. viii, 370. 12°. Alger, *Jourdan*, 1892.

Pp. 307-312, proverbes. With transliterations and French translations. [B.M.

3109. Abū Madyan Ibn Ḥammād Ibn Muḥammad, *Al-Fāsī.* Ebu Medini Mauri Fessani sententiae quaedam Arabicae . . . Edidit ac Latine vertit Franciscus de Dombay. pp. 72. 8°. Vindobonae, *Roetzel*, 1805.

Gratet-Duplessis, 78. 340 entries. [B.M.

3110. Ahmad Ibn Muhammed, *called* al-Maidani. Meidanii ali-quot proverbia arabica, cum interpretatione latina edidit . . . Christianus Maximilianus Habicht. 4°. Vratislaviae, *Typis Universitatis*, 1826.

Latin version first, followed by the Arabic. [B.M.

3111. ——— : Meidanii proverbiorum Arabicorum pars. Latine vertit et notis illustravit Henricus Albertus Schultens, *etc.* pp. xvi, 314, 8.

4°. Lugduni Batavorum, *sumptibus auctoris*, 1795.

Gratet-Duplessis, 75. Posthumous work of Schultens, finished and published by Schroeder. Schultens had formed the project of publishing integrally the collection of 6000 Arabic proverbs made by Meydany, but the work was cut short by his death and does not go beyond the 454th proverb. The commentary is carefully done and gives a good lucid extract of the rather verbose notes which Meydany joined to his collection. [B.M.

3112. ———: Selecta quaedam Arabum adagia . . . latine versa, *etc.* [By E. F. C. Rosenmüller]. pp. 28.
4°. Lipsiae, *Breitkopf & Hartel,* [1796].
With transliterations, and Latin translations and notes. [B.M.

3113. ———: Specimen proverbiorum Meidanii. Ex versione Pocockiana, edidit H. A. Schultens. pp. x, 55.
4°. Londini, *Richardson,* 1773.
Gratet-Duplessis, 75. This contains an interesting preface, reproduced in **3111,** and 120 proverbs with Latin explanations and translations. [B.M.
See also **3132, 3152.**

3114. 'Alī Ibn Abī Tālib, *Caliph.* Ali's hundert Sprüche, arabisch und persisch paraphrasirt von Reschideddin Watwat, nebst einem doppelten Anhänge arabischer Sprüche herausgegeben, . . . von M. Heinrich Leberecht Fleischer. pp. vii, 136.
4°. Leipzig, *Vogel,* 1837.
With German translations. [U.C.L.

3115. ———: Apothegms of Alee. . . . [The Arabic text] with an early Persic paraphrase and an English translation by William Yule. 4°. Edinburgh, 1832.
42 entries. Another English translation, known as Sentences of Ali, *etc.,* was made by Simon Ockley, London, 1717. [B.M.

3116. ———: Sententiae . . . Latine vertit . . . Cornelius van Waenen. pp. xvi, 428.
4°. Oxonii, *Typographeo Clarendoniano,* 1804.
These apophthegms were also included in Tscherning's Deutscher Gedichte Frühling. [B.M.

3117. Amthor (Eduard). Klänge aus Osten enthaltend neun Makamen des Hamadani, *etc.* pp. xii, 215.
8°. Leipzig, *Engelmann,* 1841.
Pp. 205-210, ein A.B.C. von Sprüchwörtern verschiedenen Inhalts. In German. [B.M.

3118. Barthélemy (L.). Cent proverbes arabes recueillis en Syrie. 8°. Paris, 1890.
In Revue de Linguistique, Tome 23, pp. 349-368. Transliterated and with French translations and notes. [B.M.

3119. Bāsim, *the Smith.* Bâsim le forgeron . . . accompagné d'une traduction et d'un glossaire par le comte Carlo de Landberg, *etc.* 8°. Leyde, 1888.
Pp. 61-87, Table des proverbes et dictons qui se rencontrent dans ce volume. 59 proverbs with French translations. [B.M.

3120. Bauer (L.). Arabische Sprichwörter. 8°. Leipzig, 1899.
In Zeitschrift des deutschen Palaestina-Vereins, Bd. 21, pp. 129-148. 205 proverbs collected in Jerusalem, transliterated and with German translations and notes. [B.M.

3121. Berndt (Johann Carl). Abdelkader, . . . Nebst einem Anhange von . . . Gebräuche, Sprüchwörter, Redensarten, *etc.* pp. 262. 8°. Berlin, *Nicolai*, 1840.
Pp. 229-260, Anhang, enthaltend Erklärungen verschiedener Sitten und Gebräuche, Redensarten, *etc.* [B.M.

3122. Burckhardt (John Lewis). Arabic proverbs, *etc.* pp. viii, 232. la. 4°. London, *Murray*, 1830.

Another edition. pp. vii, 283.
8°. London, *Quaritch*, 1875.

German translation. pp. xii, 396. 8°. Weimar, 1834.
Gratet-Duplessis, 80. An excellent collection of 782 Arabic proverbs used in Egypt, with English translations and explanations. Amongst the information to be found in this book is a study of a certain caste of women called Ghowázy, which has been translated by Duplessis and reprinted as an appendix, pp. 439-443, of his Bibliographie parémiologique. Reviewed in the Journal des Savans, 1832; also in the Quarterly Review, 125, pp. 215-254.
[B.M.

3123. Burton (*Sir* Richard Francis) and **Drake** (Charles Frederick Tyrwhitt). Unexplored Syria, *etc.* 2 vols.
8°. London, *Tinsley*, 1872.

Vol. 1, pp. 263-294, Proverbia communia syriaca. 187 proverbs with English translations and notes. These proverbs, with a foreword, were published in the Journal of the Royal Asiatic Society, Vol. 5, pp. 338-366. [B.M.

3124. Caise (Albert). Equivalents de quelques dictons et pro-verbes arabes. 8°. Alger, *Bouyer*, 1889.
In La Revue algérienne, littéraire, artistique et mondaine, Année 2, Nos. 32, 33.

3125. Chassebœuf de Volney (Constantin François), *Count.* Simplification des langues orientales, *etc.* pp. 136.
8°. Paris, *Imprimerie de la République*, an iii [=1795].
Gratet-Duplessis, 76. Pp. 121-135, proverbes arabes. 43 proverbs in the original with transliterations and French translations. [B.M.

3126. Daumas (Melchior Joseph Eugène). La vie arabe, *etc.* pp. xv, 590. 8°. Paris, *Michel Lévy*, 1869.
Pp. 473-503, proverbes et sentences. With numerous examples. [B.M.

3127. Diez (Heinrich Friedrich von). Denkwürdigkeiten von Asien, *etc.* 2 Thle. 8°. Berlin, *Nicolai*, 1811-15.
Theil 1, pp. 4-29, and Bd. 2, pp. 71-100, Vierhundert Sprüche aus dem Arabischen. Theil 2, pp. 458-463, Aussprüche des Propheten und Sprüchwörter aus dem Arabischen. [B.M.

3128. Doumani (Joseph) and **Dubois** (L. M.). Proverbes et fables traduits de l'Arabe, *etc.* pp. 111.
8°. Paris, *Saint-Paul*, 1899.

3129. Durand (A.) and **Cheikho** (L.). Elementa grammaticae Arabicae, *etc.* 2 pts.

8°. Beryti, *Patrum Societatis Jesu*, 1896-97.

Pt. 2, pp. 217-241, proverbia. With Latin translations. [B.M.

3130. Einsler (Lydia). Arabische Sprichwörter, *etc.*

8°. Leipzig, 1896.

In Zeitschrift des deutschen Palästina-Vereins, Bd. 19, pp. 65-101. 206 proverbs in the original with transliterations, German translations and notes.

[B.M.

3131. Erpenius (Thomas). Selecta quaedam ex sententiis proverbiisque Arabicis . . . cum versione Latina . . . et accessione centum proverbiorum mere [*sic*] Arabicorum, *etc.* pp. 64.

4°. Hardervici, *Mooien*, 1775.

[B.M.

3132. Freytag (Georg Wilhelm). Arabum proverbia, vocalibus instruxit, Latine vertit, commentario illustravit, . . . G. W. Freytag. 3 tom.

la. 8°. Bonnae ad Rhenum, *A. Marcus*, 1838-43.

Gratet-Duplessis, 81. Tom. 1-2, Meydany's proverbs, collected, with Latin translations, and notes : Tom. 3, partie 1, pp. 1-552, Proverbia sententiaeque proverbiales : pp. 553-606, Dies inter Arabes pugnis celebres : pp. 607-665, Facete ingeniosque dicta : partie 2, pp. 1-220, Commentatio de proverbiis Arabicis a Meidanio collectis et explicatis : pp. 221-520, Indices, corrigenda et addenda. An extraordinarily rich and full collection of Arabic proverbs. Duplessis gives a brief extract from the preface. Reviewed in Jahrbücher der Litteratur, No. 113, 1846. [U.C.L.

3133. Gerschovius (Jacobus). Centuria locmannica proverbiorum Arabicorum distichis latinis expressorum.

8°. Gryphiswaldae, 1635.

Gratet-Duplessis, 68.

3134. Green (Arthur Octavius). A collection of modern Arabic stories, *etc.* 2 pts. 8°. Cairo, 1886.

Another edition. 2 pts.

8°. Oxford, *Clarendon Press*, 1909.

Pt. 2 closes with proverbs and idioms. [B.M.

3135. Handjéri (Alexandre). Proverbes et adages arabes, traduits par le prince Alexandre Handjéri. 8°. Paris, 1859.

In Revue orientale et américaine, Tome 2, pp. 329 *et seq.*

3136. Harfouch (Joseph). Le drogman arabe, *etc.* pp. xvi, 354.

12°. Beyrouth, *Imprimerie Catholique*, 1894.

Pp. 311-399, Arabismes et proverbes. Transliterated and with French translations. [B.M.

3137. Herbin (Auguste François Julien). Développemens des principes de la langue arabe moderne, *etc.* pp. vii, 254 + tables. 4°. Paris, *Baudouin*, an xi [=1803].

Pp. 199-220, Proverbes arabes. With French translations. [B.M.

3138. Hetzel (Wilhelm Friedrich). Anweisung zur arabischen Sprache, *etc.* 2 Bde. 8°. Leipzig, *Böhme*, 1784-85.

Bd. 1, pp. 3-104, Ausführliche grammatische Erklärung auserlesener arabischer Sprichwörter. Arabic proverbs with German translations and comments.

3139. ———: Erleichterte arabische Grammatik, *etc.* pp. [14] 104, 48. 8°. Jena, *Fickelscherr*, 1776.

Pt. 2, pp. 1-5, Proverbia Arabica. The same proverbs as are contained in **3138.** In the original. [B.M.

3140. Husain Ibn 'Alī, *called* al-Ṭughrā'ī. L'élégie du Togra i . . . traduit de l'arabe par P. Vattier. pp. 80.
8°. Paris, *Estienne*, 1660.
Latin edition. 8°. Lugd. Batav., *Elzevir*, 1629.

Gratet-Duplessis, 70. Pp. 65-80, les perles des proverbes . . . de Gali, fils d'Abutalib, *etc.* Not common proverbs, but celebrated and popular maxims. [B.M.

3141. Huxley (Henry Minor). Syrian songs, proverbs and stories, *etc.* 8°. New Haven, 1902.

In Journal of the American Oriental Society, Vol. 23, pp. 175-288. Pp. 223-234, proverbs. In the original with transliterations, English translations and occasional notes. The article contains a full bibliography. [B.M.

3142. Jewett (James Richard). Arabic proverbs and proverbial phrases, *etc.* 8°. New Haven, 1893.

In Journal of the American Oriental Society, Vol. 15, pp. 28-120. 289 proverbs in Arabic, in transliteration, and in English translation with notes. Pp. 31-32, list of authorities. A few proverbs contributed by the same writer are to be found in the same journal, Vol. 13, pp. cxxix-cxxxii. [B.M.

3143. Kāsim Ibn Salām. Libri proverbiorum Abi 'Obaid Elqasimi, filii Salami Elchuzzami. . . . Latine vertit et annotationibus instruxit Ernestus Bertheau.
8°. Gottingae, *Dieterich*, 1836.
[B.M.

3144. Kustantin Ilyās Khūrī. Arabic manual. . . . Third edition, *etc.* pp. 416. 8°. [Beirut], 1885.

Pp. 414-416, English and Arabic proverbs. 50 entries. [B.M.

3145. Landberg (Carlo von), *Count.* Proverbes et dictons du peuple arabe. . . . Vol. 1. Proverbes et dictons de la province de Syrie, Section de Saydà. pp. xlviii, 458.
8°. Leide, *Brill*, Paris, *Maisonneuve*, 1883.

247 proverbs and glossary, with French translations, explanations, and notes. A valuable book. [B.M.

3146. Machuel (Louis). Méthode pour l'étude de l'arabe parlé. *Second edition.* pp. xvi, 364. 8°. Alger, *Jourdan*, 1875.
Fourth edition. pp. xvi, 455. 8°. Alger, *Jourdan*, 1887.

Contains a list of Arabic proverbs with French translations. [B.M.

3147. Mahmūd Ibn 'Umar, *Al-Zamakhsharī.* Anthologia senten-
tiarum Arabicarum. Cum scholiis Zamachsjarii. Edidit . . .
H. A. Schultens. pp. 171. 4°. Lugduni Batavorum, 1772.
Arabic and Latin.

Samachshari's Goldene Halsbänder . . . arabisch und deutsch
von Joseph von Hammer. pp. 54, 55.   8°. Wien, 1835.
Samachsharis Goldne Halsbänder, von neuem übersetzt . . .
von G. Weil.   12°. Stuttgart, 1836.
Les colliers d'or. . . . Texte arabe suivi d'une traduction . . .
et d'un commentaire philologique par C. Barbier de Meynard.
8°. Paris, 1876.
[B.M.

3148. Mejdoub Ben Kalafat. Choix de fables de La Fontaine, de
Florian, de Fénélon, *etc.* pp. xiv, 175.
8°. Constantine, *Leca*, 1890.
Second edition. 8°. Constantine, 1900.
Pp. 149-160, Dictons populaires. 102 proverbs in the original.

Meydany. *See* Ahmad Ibn Muhammed, *called* al-Maidani,
3110-3113.

3149. Muhammad Ayyad El-Tantavy. Traité de la langue arabe
vulgaire, *etc.* pp. xxv, 231.   8°. Leipsic, *Vogel*, 1848.
Bernstein, 3676. Pp. 110-133, proverbes. With French translations.

3150. National Proverbs. National proverbs. Arabia. pp. 76.
1/-. 8°. London, *Palmer*, [1913].
Proverbs in English; no notes.   [F.-L.S.

3151. Neuphal (Georges). Guide de conversation en deux langues,
arabe et française. pp. 527.
16°. Beyrout, *Imprimerie Catholique*, 1868.
Third edition.   Beyrout, 1876.
Contains a list of proverbs with French equivalents.   [B.M.

3152. Reiske (Johann Jacob). Sammlung einiger arabischen
Sprüchwörter, *etc.* pp. 31.   4°. Leipzig, *Löper*, 1758.
Gratet-Duplessis, 75. Proverbs from Meydany's collection.

3153. Rosenmüller (Ernst Friedrich Carl). Institutiones ad
fundamenta linguae Arabicae, *etc.* pp. xii, 446.
4°. Lipsiae, *Barth*, 1818.
Gratet-Duplessis, 79. Pp. 367 *et seq.*, selectae quaedam Arabum sententiae.
With Latin translations. These were also reproduced in Orelli's " Opuscula
Graecorum," *etc.*, Tome 2, pp. 515-520.   [B.M.

Samachshari. *See* Mahmūd Ibn 'Umar, *Al-Zamakhsharī.*

3154. Scaliger (Joseph Juste) and **Erpenius** (Thomas). Proverbiorum Arabicorum centuriae duae, . . . cum interpretatione Latina, *etc. First edition.*

4°. Leidae, *in officina Raphelengiana*, 1614.
Editio secunda, priore emendatior. pp. [xvi], 134.
sm. 8°. Lugduni Batavorum, *Maire*, 1623.

Gratet-Duplessis, 67. Proverbs in Arabic and Latin with notes; a good selection. These proverbs were frequently reprinted at the end of the Arabic Grammar of Erpenius. [U.C.L.

3155. Sennertus (Andreas). Centuria proverbiorum Arabicorum, juxta cum interpretatione latina, *etc.* ff. 12.

4°. Wittebergae, *Fincelius*, 1658.
Gratet-Duplessis, 69.

3156. Singer (*Mrs.* A. P.). Arabic proverbs, *etc.* pp. xii, 76, 15.
8°. Cairo, *Diemer*, 1913.

169 proverbs given first in transliteration with English translations and notes, then in Arabic. [B.M.

3157. Socin (Albert). Arabische Sprichwörter und Redensarten, *etc.* pp. x, 41, 14. 4°. Tübingen, *Laupp*, 1878.

574 proverbs given first in German translation, then in Arabic text. [B.M.

3158. Sulaimān Ibn Ya'kūb, *al-Shāmī al-Sālihānī, called* Salomon Negri. Arabum philosophia popularis . . . a Jacobo Salomone Damasceno dictata, interpretatus est Fridericus Rostgaard; edidit . . . Joannes Christianus Kallius. pp. [xxiv], 192.

8°. Hafniae, *Hopffner*, 1764.

Gratet-Duplessis, 73. A well-chosen collection of 545 Arab proverbs, accompanied by a Latin translation and explanatory notes. [B.M.

3159. Tallquist (Knut Leonard). Arabische Sprichwörter und Spiele, *etc.* pp. 152. 8°. Helsingfors, *Erben*, 1897.

Also published 1897, in Öfversigt af Finska Vetenskaps-Societetens Förhandlingar, 39. 200 proverbs with transliterations, German translations and notes. [B.M.

3160. Wahrmund (Adolf). Praktisches Handbuch der neu-arabischen Sprache, *etc.* 3 Thle.

8°. Giessen, *Ricker*, 1861.
Third edition. 3 Thle. 8°. Giessen, *Ricker*, 1886.

Contains a section entitled Sprüche und Sprüchwörter. 200 proverbs in the original. [B.M.

3161. Weston (Stephen). Moral aphorisms in Arabic, and a Persian commentary in verse, translated from the originals, *etc.* pp. xxix, 127. 8°. London, 1805.

3162. Wolff (Philipp). Arabischer Dragoman . . . Dritte . . . Auflage. pp. vi, 369. 8°. Leipzig, *Brockhaus*, 1883.

Pp. 347-349, Sprichwörter. With transliterations, and German translations. Not contained in the edition of 1857. [B.M.

3163. Yahuda (A. S.). Yemenische Sprichwörter aus Sanaa.

8°. Strassburg, 1911.

In Zeitschrift für Assyriologie, Bd. 26, pp. 345-358. 30 proverbs with German translations and notes. [B.M.

See also index at end for references to Arabic in other sections.

2. ARMENIAN.

3164. Bayan (G.). Armenian proverbs and sayings, *etc.* pp. 58.

12°. Venice, *Academy of St. Lazarus*, 1889.

Proverbs in Armenian, with English translations. The book was also published in French in 1888. [B.M.

3165. Berger (Wilhelm). Beiträge zur armenischen Folk-lore Uneditierte Redensarten und Sprichwörter aus Türkisch-Armenien, *etc.* pp. 8. sm. 8°. Kolozsvar, London.

3166. Joannissiany (Abgar). Armenische Sprichwörter.

4°. Augsburg, 1871.

In Das Ausland, Jahrgang 44, pp. 403-405. A list of proverbs in German. [B.M.

3167. Lankau (Johann M.). Armenische Sprichwörter.

8°. Wien, *Hartleben*, 1897.

In Deutsche Rundschau für Geographie und Statistik, Jahrgang 19, pp. 266-268. Armenian proverbs translated into German. [B.M.

3168. Wlislocki (Heinrich von). Märchen und Sagen der Buko-winaer und Siebenbürger Armenier, *etc.* pp. viii, 188.

8°. Hamburg, *Richter*, 1891.

Pp. 175-183, Anhang : Sprichwörter. Armenian proverbs with German translations. [B.M.

3. IRANIAN

(Persian and Afghan).

3169. 'Abd Al-Latīf Khān, *Iṣfahānī*. Anglo-Persian idioms, containing proverbs, *etc.* pp. 224. 8°. [Bombay?], 1896.

Pp. 171-184, proverbs and quotations from prose and poetry. In the original, with English translations. [B.M.

3170. Brugsch (Heinrich). Die Muse in Teheran. pp. xvi, 128.

8°. Frankfurt a. O., *Trowitzsch*, [1886].

Pp. 121-128, Sprüchwörter. A few Persian rhyming proverbs translated into German. [B.M.

3171. Darmesteter (James). Chants populaires des Afghans.

2 pts. 8°. Paris, *Imprimerie Nationale*, 1888-90.

Pp. 235-240, proverbes. The French translation of 60 proverbs, which are given in the original in the second part. [B.M.

3172. Dombay (Franz Lorenz von). Grammatica linguae Persicae, *etc.* pp. 114. 8°. Vindobonae, *Camesina,* 1804.
Gratet-Duplessis, 65. Pp. 84-101, Sententiae Persicae. With Latin translations. [B.M.

3173. Huart (Cl.). Grammaire élémentaire de la langue persane, *etc.* pp. 150. 8°. Paris, *Leroux,* 1899.
Bernstein, 4480. Pp. 130-146, proverbes. With French translations.

3174. Jamshedjī Bejajī Kāngā and **Pestanjī Kāvajī Kāngā.** Hints on the study of Persian . . . Second edition, *etc.* pp. viii, 252. Bombay, *Education Society's Press,* 1889.
Sixth edition.
Bombay, *Education Society's Steam Press,* 1898.
Contains a selection of proverbs with English translations. In the sixth edition moral maxims are substituted for the proverbs. [B.M.

3175. Karam 'Alī Raḥīm Nānjiāni. A collection of select Persian proverbs and familiar sayings, with their English and Gujarâti equivalents. 3 pts. 6 annas. 8°. Bombay, 1882.
Another edition. 8°. Bombay, 1886.
The later edition also contains Hindustani equivalents. [B.M., L.L.

3176. Palmer (E. H.). The Jávídán Khirad; or, the proverbial philosophy of ancient Persia. 8°. London, 1869.
In The Student and Intellectual Observer, Vol. 2, pp. 168-180. A general account of the book followed by a selection of maxims from it. [B.M.

3177. Phillott (Douglas Craven). Common saws and proverbs collected . . . in Southern Persia. pp. [36].
4°. Calcutta, 1906.
In Memoirs of the Asiatic Society of Bengal, Vol. 1, No. 15, pp. 301-337. 358 proverbs not in Roebuck's collection, with English translations. [U.C.L.

3178. Roebuck (Thomas). A collection of proverbs, and proverbial phrases, in the Persian and Hindoostanee languages, *etc.* [Begun by W. Hunter. Edited, with additions, by H. H. Wilson]. pp. xxxi, 406, 397.
4°. Calcutta, *Hindoostanee Press,* 1824.
Gratet-Duplessis, 59. Pp. i-xxxi, Introduction : pp. 1-406, Persian proverbs : pp. 1-397, Hindoostanee proverbs. An excellent book, but unfortunately lacking an index. Each proverb is accompanied by a literal translation, and explanatory notes where necessary. [U.C.L.

3179. Sykes (Ella C.). Persian folklore. 8°. London, 1901.
In Folk-Lore, Vol. 12, pp. 278-280, Persian proverbs and saws in English. [F.-L.S.

3180. Warner (Levinus). Proverbiorum et sententiarum persicarum centuria, *etc.* pp. [8], 44.
4°. Lugduni Batavorum, *Maire,* 1644.
Another edition. 4°. Lugduni Batavorum, 1648.
Gratet-Duplessis, 64. With Latin translations and notes. [B.M.

See also index at end for references to Persian in other sections.

4. TURKISH.

3181. Ahmad Midhat. Osmanli proverbs . . . with English translations . . . by E. J. Davis. pp. viii, 401 + appendix.
8°. London, [1898].

Transliterations and translations of a book of Turkish proverbs published
about twenty years previously. The Turkish original is given as an appendix.
No index. [B.M.

3182. Clodius (Johann Christian). Compendiosum lexicon Latino-
Turcico-Germanicum, *etc.* 3 pts.
8°. Lipsiae, *Deer*, 1730-29.

Gratet-Duplessis, 83. Pt. 3, pp. 180-188, Proverbia turcica. With transliterations and Latin translations. [B.M.

3183. De Courdemanche (Jean Adolphe). Mille et un proverbes
turcs, *etc.* pp. vii, 122. 8°. Paris, *Leroux*, 1878.

Pp. 109-115, Bibliographie. [B.M.

3184. Démétriades (Jean D.). Proverbes turcs-français.
8°. Constantinople, *Eb-uz-zia*, 1888.

353 proverbs with French translations.

3185. Desjardins (P. A.). Les bas-fonds de Constantinople par
Paul de Regla [*pseud.* of P. A. Desjardins]. Troisième
édition. pp. xviii, 400. 8°. Paris, *Tresse & Stock*, 1892.

Pp. 383-391, Maximes et proverbes musulmans. Proverbs translated into
French. [B.M.

3186. Dictionary. A pocket dictionary of the English, Armenian
and Turkish languages. 3 vols.
12°. Venice, *Press of the Armenian College
of S. Lazarus*, 1843.

Vol. 3 contains an appendix of 180 Turkish proverbs with English translations. [B.M.

3187. Donado (Giovanni Battista). Della letteratura de' Turchi,
etc. pp. [ix], 140, 8. 12°. Venetia, *Poletti*, 1688.

Pp. 97-101, Traduttione d'alcuni proverbi, overo detti in Turchesco. [B.M.

3188. Durūbi. Durūbi amsāli-osmanīje. [Second edition].
Stambul, 1287 [= 1870].

3189. Fink (Ludwig M.). Türkischer Dragoman, *etc.* pp. vi,
162. 8°. Leipzig, *Brockhaus*, 1872.

Second edition. pp. vi, 200.
8°. Leipzig, *Brockhaus*, 1879.

Concludes with a brief list of proverbs transliterated and with German translations. [B.M.

3190. Fleischer (H. F.). Der türkische Selbstlehrer. pp. 146.
4°. Wien, 1853.

With an appendix of phrases, proverbs, conversation and vocabulary.

3191. Hifzî. Hifzî Zurûb i amsâl. 8°. Constantinople, 1846.
[Bristol Reference Library.

3192. Jaubert (Pierre Amédée Emilien Probe), *Count.* Eléments
de la grammaire turke, *etc.* pp. vii, 150 [+ about 30 litho-
graphed pages]. 4°. Paris, *Imprimerie Royale*, 1823.
Second edition. 8°. Paris, *Firmin Didot*, 1833.

Gratet-Duplessis, 85. Gives a selection of Turkish proverbs with French
translations.
[U.C.L.

3193. Loebel (D. Theophil). Deutsch-türkisches Wörterbuch
. . . Zweite . . . Auflage. pp. 334.
16°. Constantinopel, *Keil*, Leipzig, *Wagner*, 1894.
Third edition. pp. 334.
8°. Constantinopel, *Keil*, Leipzig, *Wagner*, 1896.

Pp. 296-300, Auswahl türkischer Sprichwörter. Turkish proverbs transcribed,
with German translations. [B.M.

3194. Megiser (Hieronymus). Institutionum linguae Turcicae,
etc. 8°. Lipsiae, 1612.

Pp. 142-167, Duae centuriae proverbiorum et sententiarum, *etc.* Transliterated, with Latin translations. [B.M.

3195. Merx (Ernst Otto Adalbert). Türkische Sprichwörter ins
Deutsche übersetzt. pp. 82.
12°. Venedig, *Armenische Druckerei*, 1877.
2. Ausgabe. 12°. Venedig, 1893.

355 entries, the Turkish printed in Armenian characters. [B.M.

3196. Murād Damar. Türkdsche söjlemisiniz?, *etc.* pp. viii,
208. 8°. Leipzig, *Koch*, 1882.

Pp. 56-58, Türkische Sprichwörter und Redensarten. Transcribed, with
German translations. [B.M.

3197. Ostroumov (Nikolai Petrovich). Сарты. Этнографическіе
матеріалы, *etc.* 3 pts. 8°. Ташкентъ, 1890-95.

Pt. 3, pp. 1-137, proverbs, sayings, *etc.*

3198. Piqueré (P. J.). Grammatik der türkisch-osmanischen
Umgangsprache, *etc.* pp. 344.
12°. Wien, *Wenedikt*, 1870.

Pp. 287-303, Sprichwörter. 140 proverbs in Turkish with transliterations
and German translations. [B.M.

3199. Preindl (Joseph de). Grammaire turque, *etc.* pp. xii,
591. 8°. Berlin, 1791.

Pp. 155-162, Des proverbes turques, traduits tant qu'il était possible mot par
mot. [B.M.

3200. Proverbes. Proverbes turcs traduits en français. pp. 59.
16°. Venise, *Imprimerie Arménienne*, 1875.
Another edition. pp. 59.
16°. Venise, *Imprimerie Arménienne*, 1881.

Probably a French translation of the " Turkish proverbs translated into
English " and the " Türkische Sprichwörter " of A. Merx, **3195,** also printed
at the Armenian monastery.

3201. Proverbi. Proverbi popolari turchi scritti con lettere armene e tradotti in italiano. pp. 60.

393 entries.   16°. Venezia, *S. Lazzaro*, 1879.

3202. ———: Proverbi turchi.   8°. Palermo, 1889.

In Archivio per lo Studio dei Tradizioni popolari, Vol. 8, pp. 26-28, 174-176. 140 proverbs translated into Italian. Although the article is marked " Continua," a further instalment was not given.   [B.M.

3203. Proverbs. Turkish proverbs translated into English, *etc.* pp. 33.

L.1.   12°.   Venice, *Armenian Monastery of S. Lazarus*, 1844.

Another edition. pp. 37.

50 centesimi. 12°.   Venice, *Armenian Monastery of S. Lazarus*, 1880.

The 1844 edition contains 180, the 1880 edition 192, Turkish proverbs in the original accompanied by English translations.   [B.M.

3204. Raccolta. Raccolta curiosissima d'adaggj turcheschi trasportati dal proprio idioma nell' italiano e latino, dalli giovani di lingua sotto il bailaggio . . . Gio. Battista Donado. pp. 87, [8].   8°. Venezia, *Poletti*, 1688.

Gratet-Duplessis, 82. In four columns : Latin, Italian, paraphrase, Turkish.   [B.M.

3205. Recueil. Recueil de proverbes et de contes traduits du turc en français.   8°. Smyrne, 1848.

3206. Sandreczki (E.).   Türkische Sprüchwörter und einige Weisheitssprüche.   la. 8°. Augsburg, *Gotta*, 1872.

In Das Ausland, 1872, No. 51, pp. 1201-1207.   [B.M.

3207. Sprichwoerter. Osmanische Sprichwörter, herausgegeben durch die K.k. orientalische Akademie in Wien, *etc.* [Under the direction of Ottokar Maria von Schlechta-Wssehrd]. pp. xii, 180.   8°. Wien, *K.k. orientalische Akademie*, 1865.

In French, German, and Turkish, with transcriptions and literal translations. 500 entries.   [B.M.

3208. Vámbéry (Ármin).   Cagataische Sprachstudien, *etc.* pp. viii, 358.   8°. Leipzig, *Brockhaus*, 1867.

Pp. 45-48, Einige özbegische Sprüchwörter. 112 entries in the original with German translations.   [B.M.

3209. Wells (Charles).   The literature of the Turks, *etc.* pp. xix, 272.   8°. London, *Quaritch*, 1891.

Pp. 1-10, Turkish proverbs and sayings. Followed by Turkish aphorisms. In the original, with transliterations and English translations.   [B.M.

3210. Wickerhauser (Moriz).   Wegweiser zum Verständniss der türkischen Sprache, *etc.*

8°. Wien, *K.k. Hof- und Staatsdruckerei*, 1853.

Pp. 1-10, Einige Sprichwörter und gleichnissweise Beden. In German, Turkish originals follow.   [B.M.

See also index at end for references to Turkish in other sections.

NORTHERN AND CENTRAL ASIATIC

3211. Altmann (Julius). Sprichwörter der krimschen Tartaren.
8°. Leipzig, *Brockhaus*, 1855.

In Blätter für literarische Unterhaltung, Jahrgang 1855, No. 4, pp. 67-70.
A commentary with numerous examples in German. [B.M.

3212. Bergé (Adolph P.). Татарскія пословицы.
4°. Тифлисъ, 1871.

In Сборникъ свѣдѣній о Кавказѣ, Томъ 1, pp. 334-336. 80 Tartar proverbs in Russian.

3213. K. (V.). Сборникъ Киргизскихъ пословицъ, *etc.* pp. ii, 153. 8°. Orenburg, *Жариновъ*, 1899.
[B.M.

3214. Kalashev (A.). Татарскіе тексты, *etc.*
8°. Тифлисъ, 1894.

In Сборникъ матеріаловъ для описанія мѣстностей и племенъ Кавказа, 1894, Pt. 2, pp. 37-71. Pp. 51-53 and pp. 61-65, 69 Tartar proverbs in Russian.

3215. Kalashev (N. D.). Пословицы ширванскихъ Татаръ, *etc.*
8°. Тифлисъ, 1898.

In Сборникъ матеріаловъ для описанія мѣстностей и племенъ Кавказа, 1898, Pt. 3, pp. 1-211, 1982 Tartar proverbs in Russian.

3216. Le Coq (Albert von). Sprichwörter und Lieder aus der Gegend von Turfan, *etc.* pp. iv, 100. fol. Leipzig, 1911.

Baessler Archiv, Beiheft 1. Pp. 6-47, 312 proverbs in the original, with transcriptions, German translations, and notes. [B.M.

3217. Makhmudbekov (   ). Татарская народная словесность въ Закавказьѣ. 8°. Тифлисъ, 1894.

In Сборникъ матеріаловъ для описанія мѣстностей и племенъ Кавказа, 1894, Pt. 2, pp. 227-325. Pp. 286-325, 481 Tartar proverbs in Russian.

3218. Ostroumov (Nikolai Petrovich). Пословицы туземнаго населенія Туркестанскаго края, *etc.* pp. vi, 48.
8°. Ташкентъ, *Каменскій*, 1895.

Bernstein, 2428. 492 proverbs accompanied by Russian translations.

3219. Vámbéry (Ármin). Sittenbilder aus dem Morgenlände. pp. 317. 8°. Berlin, *Hofmann*, 1876. *Second edition.* pp. 317. 8°. Berlin, *Hofmann*, 1877. *Another edition.* Obrazy obyczajowe ze Wschodu. pp. iii, 454. 8°. w Warszawie, *Kaufman*, 1880.

In the German editions : pp. 289-308, Osmanische Sprüche (530) : pp. 309-310, Oezbegische Sprüche (36) : pp. 311-312, Kazanisch-Tartarische Sprüche (42) : pp. 313-317, Altaische Sprüche. In German. [B.M.

3220. Whymant (Neville J.). Mongolian proverbs: a study in the Kalmuck colloquial. 8°. London, 1926.

In Journal of the Royal Asiatic Society for 1926, pp. 257-267. [B.M.

INDIAN

GENERAL.

3221. Cassidy (James). A chapter on Indian proverbs.
8°. London, 1905.
In Westminster Review, Vol. 164, pp. 445-449. [B.M.

3222. Chaube (Ramgharib). On some proverbial sayings of the
Hindus of Northern India. 8°. Bombay, 1901.
In Journal of the Anthropological Society of Bombay, Vol. 5, pp. 340-345.
[B.M.

3223. Guiterman (Arthur). Betel nuts, *etc.* pp. 48 + frontis-
piece. 12°. San Francisco, New York, *Elder*, [1907].
Proverbs and sayings from Hindustan translated and rhymed in English.
[B.M.

3224. Isvarī Dāsa. Domestic manners and customs of the
Hindoos of Northern India, *etc.* pp. vi, 270.
8°. Benares, *Medical Hall Press*, 1860.
Second edition. pp. xi, 280.
8°. Benares, *Lazarus*, London, *Trübner*, 1866.
Contains a chapter of proverbs with English translations and notes. [B.M.

3225. Long (James). Oriental proverbs and their uses, in
sociology, ethnology, philology, and education. pp. 16.
8°. [1875?].
Ditto. 8°. London, *Trübner*, 1876.
In Transactions of the International Congress of Orientalists, Vol. 2, pp.
380-95. A general survey of the subject. [B.M.

3226. ———: Oriental proverbs in their relations to folk-lore,
history, sociology, *etc.* 8°. London, *Trübner*, 1875.
In Journal of the Royal Asiatic Society, New Series, Vol. 7, pp. 339-352. A
commentary with various examples. Pp. 351-352, desiderata on Indian proverbs.
[U.C.L.

3227. Risley (*Sir* Herbert Hope). The people of India. pp. xvi,
289, clxxxix + plates.
8°. Calcutta, *Thacker, Spink*, London, *Thacker*, 1908.
Second edition. pp. xxxii, 472 + plates.
8°. Calcutta, *etc.*, *Thacker*, 1915.
Contains a bibliography of proverbs. Chap. 3 and Appendix 1, Caste in proverbs and popular sayings. Chap. 3 is a general survey with many examples;
the appendix consists of the proverbs themselves classified under the castes with
which they are concerned. [U.C.L.

ANCIENT
(Sanskrit).

3228. Akhila-Chandra Chattopādhyāya. The student's companion: a compendious handbook containing numerous familiar proverbs in English and Sanskrit, *etc.* pp. vi, 235.
Rs.1.4. 8°. Calcutta, *the author*, 1908.

Pp. 1-19, English proverbs with Bengali or Sanskrit equivalents : pp. 204-214, Sanskrit proverbs and proverbial quotations.   [B.M.

3229. Arnold (*Sir* Edwin). Indian poetry, *etc.* pp. 270.
7/6. 8°. London, *Trübner*, 1881.
Another edition. 2 pts.
8°. London, *Kegan Paul, etc.*, 1915.

Trübner's Oriental Series. Contains a selection in English from the metrical Sanskrit proverbs and maxims of the Hitopadesa.   [U.C.L.

3230. Benfey (   ). Chrestomathie sanscrite. Leipzig, 1853.
Contains proverbs.

3231. Chalapati Rāu. Sanskrit proverbs. pp. 96.
8 annas. 8°. Ellore, *Manjuvani Press*, 1907.
In Sanskrit. 489 entries.   [B.M.

3232. Formichi (C.). La sapienza dell' antica India nei suoi proverbi.   Roma, 1921.
In Nuova Antologia, Vol. 214, pp. 53-63.

3233. Nilaratna Sarman, *called* **Hāldār.** The kobita-rutnakur, or collection of Sungskrit proverbs . . . translated into Bengalee and English. . . . Second edition. pp. 166.
8°. Serampore, 1830.

203 proverbs with explanatory notes. The first edition was privately printed, and did not contain the translations.   [B.M.

3234. Wilkins (*Sir* Charles). Fables and proverbs from the Sanskrit, being the Hitopadesa translated. pp. 277.
8°. London, New York, *Routledge*, 1885.
In English.   [F.-L.S. (Stephens Collection).

NORTH-WEST.
1. PASHTO.

3235. Raverty (Henry George). The Pushto manual, *etc.* pp. 245.   8°. London, *Allen*, 1880.
Another edition. pp. 257.   8°. London, *Allen*, 1890.

Pp. 172-176, Wise saws and sayings. In the original, with English translations.   [B.M.

3236. Thorburn (Septimus Smet). Bannú; or, our Afghán frontier. pp. x, 480 + map. 8°. London, *Trübner*, 1876.

Pp. 231-473, a large collection of proverbs, given first in English translations, then in the original.   [B.M.

2. KASHMIRI.

3237. Knowles (James Hinton). A dictionary of Kashmiri proverbs and sayings, *etc.* pp. viii, 263.

8°. Bombay, *Education Society's Press*, 1885.

In Roman characters, with English translations and notes. [B.M.

3. PANJABI.

3238. Gaṅgā Rāma, *Rāi Bahādur.* Punjab agricultural proverbs and their scientific significance, *etc.* pp. 37.

fol. Lahore, [1920].

Contains a large number of proverbs, chiefly from Maconachie's collection, with English translations. [B.M.

3239. Maconachie (J. Robert). Selected agricultural proverbs of the Panjab, *etc.* 8°. Delhi, 1890.
Another edition. 1905.

3240. Punjabee. Short essays on social and Indian subjects, by Punjabee. pp. 173. 8°. Calcutta, *Central Press*, 1869.

Pp. 144-148, Panjab proverbial philosophy. A general study containing a few examples in English. [B.M.

3241. Temple (*Sir* Richard Carnac). Some Panjabi and other proverbs. 8°. London, 1883.

In The Folk-Lore Journal, Vol. 1, pp. 175-184. Proverbs chiefly collected and translated from a " Grammar of the Panjabi language," 1851, and Roebuck's " Collection of proverbs and proverbial phrases in the Persian and Hindoostanee languages," 1824. [F.-L.S.

3242. Usborne (Charles Frederick). Panjabi lyrics and proverbs, *etc.* pp. vi, 65.

8°. Lahore, *Civil and Military Gazette Press*, 1905.

Pp. 46-65, proverbs in English. [B.M.

3243. Wilson (J.). Grammar and dictionary of Western Panjabi, *etc.* 6 pts. 8°. Lahore, *Punjab Government Press*, 1899.

Bernstein, 4246. Pt. 4, proverbs and sayings current in the Shahpur district. Transcribed and with English translations.

4. MARWARI.

3244. Adams (Archibald), *Lieut.-Colonel.* The western Rajputana states, *etc.* pp. xi, 455 + plates. Second edition.

8°. London, *Junior Army and Navy Stores*, 1900.

Pp. 96-97, Marwari proverbs with English translations. [R.A.I.

3245. Lālchandra (Vidyā Bhāshkar). Marwari weather proverbs.

8°. London, 1892.

In Journal of the Royal Asiatic Society, 1892, pp. 253-257. [U.C.L.

5. SINDHI.

3246. Gangadhar Govind Sāpkar. Handbook of Sindhi proverbs.
Karachi, 1895.

3247. Rochirām Gajumal. A handbook of Sindhi proverbs, with
English renderings and equivalent sayings. pp. 324.
1 rupee. 8°. Karachi, *Commissioner's Press*, 1895.
Second edition. pp. 128.
Rs.1/12. 8°. Hyderabad, *Premier Printing Press*, [1920].
[B.M.

NORTH
(Hindi, Hindustani, Urdu).

3248. Chhanū Lāla Gupta. Bunch of proverbs. . . . With their
equivalents in Urdu, some in Hindi and Persian. . . . New
edition. pp. 60.
12°. Delhi, *Imperial Medical Hall Press*, 1892.
[B.M.

3249. Fallon (S. W.). A dictionary of Hindustani proverbs, *etc.*
pp. iii, 320. 8°. Benares, *Lazarus*, London, *Trübner*, 1886.
Lacks an index. Over 12,500 proverbs, transcribed and with English notes
and translations. [B.M.

3250. Gangādatta Upreti. Proverbs and folklore of Kumaun and
Garhwal, *etc.* pp. iv, ix, viii, 413.
8°. Lodiana, *Lodiana Mission Press*, 1894.
A large number of proverbs with transcriptions, English translations and
notes. [R.A.I.

3251. Johnson (W. F.). Hindi proverbs with English translation, *etc.* pp. 307. 12°. Allahabad, 1898.
[B.M.

3252. Lallū Lāl, *Kavi.* The new cyclopædia Hindoostanica of
wit; containing . . . humorous stories, in the Persian and
Nagree characters; interspersed with appropriate proverbs,
etc. 8°. Calcutta, *India Gazette Press*, 1810.
Gratet-Duplessis, 58. [B.M.

3253. Mādhava Nārāyana. Makhzan-ul-mahawrat. . . . Containing English proverbs, with their equivalents in Hindustani. *First edition.* pp. 56. 8°. [Delhi, 1885].
Another edition. pp. 48.
4 annas. 8°. Delhi, *Imperial Book Depot Press*, 1903.
The title page of the first edition is in Hindustani only. [B.M.

3254. Morris (J.). English proverbs with Hindustani parallels.
pp. 123. *First edition.*
16°. Lahore, *Sham-ul-Hind Press*, 1896.
Fourth edition. pp. 125, iii.
32°. Lahore, *Shams-ul-Hind Press*, 1898.
[B.M.
736 entries.

3255. Prabhúdása Dása. Proverbs Hindi, Urdú and Persian, *etc.*
pp. 58. 8°. Allahabad, *Mission Press*, 1870.
Alphabetically arranged. No translation. [B.M.

3256. Ram Dayal Bhargava. A treasury of English proverbs . . .
with their Hindustani equivalents. ff. 37.
8°. Cawnpore, *Lala Hira Lal & Badri Pershad*, 1889.
Bernstein, 2939.

3257. Roebuck (Thomas). A collection of proverbs . . . in the
Persian and Hindoostanee languages.
Pp. 1-397, Hindoostanee proverbs. *See* **3178.**

3258. Shamser Singh. A book of proverbs Urdu-English, *etc.*
pp. 65. 8°. Lahore, *Shamser Singh*.
462 entries. [B.M.

3259. Sukhadevaprasáda. A manual of English proverbs, . . .
equivalents in Persian, Urdu and Hindi, *etc.* pp. 31.
4 annas. 8°. Agra, *Moon Press*, 1896.
100 proverbs. [B.M.

3260. Tagliabue (Camillo). Proverbi, detti e leggende indostani,
etc. pp. vii, 254. 8°. Roma, 1899.
Bernstein, 4720.

3261. Temple (*Sir* Richard Carnac). North Indian proverbs.
8°. London, 1885.
In Folk-Lore Journal, Vol. 3, pp. 16-44. Proverbs which are not in Fallon's
"Dictionary of Hindustání Proverbs," with English translations. Divided into
Persian, Urdú, Hindí, and Panjabí proverbs. [F.-L.S.

3262. Wazír Aḥmad. 1000 English proverbs with Urdu equivalents. pp. 52. 3 annas. 16°. Bareilly, [1892]
No notes. [B.M.

NORTH-EAST.
1. BIHARI.

3263. Christian (John). Behar proverbs, *etc.* pp. lvii, 256.
8°. London, *Kegan Paul*, 1891.
Trübner's Oriental Series. 506 proverbs classified by subject, with English
translations and notes. Good introduction; the whole book is a mine of folk-
lore. [B.M.

2. BENGALI.

3264. Khanai Lal Ghoshal. A collection of Bengali and Hindi
proverbs with annotations. pp. 138.
8°. Calcutta, *Kanai Lall Ghoshal*, 1890.
Bernstein, 1637.

3265. Lewin (Thomas Herbert). Hill proverbs of the Chittagong hill tracts. pp. ii, 30.

fol. Calcutta, *Bengal Secretariat Press*, 1873.

Proverbs in the original, with English translations and occasional comparisons with other proverbs. [B.M.

3266. Long (James). Bengali proverbs. pp. 21.

8°. [Calcutta, 1851].

176 proverbs in the original, with English translations and notes. [B.M.

3267. ———: Popular Bengali proverbs, *etc.* pp. 7.

8°. Calcutta, *Newman*, 1868.

Read before the Bengal Social Science Association. In English. [B.M.

3268. Mitra (Sarat Chandra). On some proverbs from the Tāngāil sub-division in the district of Mymensingh in Eastern Bengal.

8°. Bombay, *British India Press*, London, *Luzac*, 1918.

In Journal of the Anthropological Society of Bombay, Vol. 11, pp. 120-169. Proverbs in the original, with translation. [F.-L.S.

3269. Morton (William). A collection of proverbs, Bengali and Sanskrit, with their translation and application in English. pp. viii, 160. 8°. Calcutta, *Baptist Mission Press*, 1832.

873 entries. [B.M.

3270. Prabodhaprakāsa Sena Gupta. Dictionary of proverbs. pp. 245. 12°. Calcutta, *Queen Press*, 1899.

Bengali and English. [B.M.

3271. Pravāda Málá. Prabad Mala, or, the wit and wisdom of Bengali ryots and women, *etc.* [Collected by J. Long?]. pp. 70. 8°. Calcutta, "*Englishman*" *Press*, 1869.

Reprinted from the Englishman's Weekly Journal. A collection, in English, of 2358 Bengali proverbs. [B.M.

3272. Proverbs. Proverbs of Europe and Asia. Translated into the Bengali language, *etc.* 8'. Calcutta, 1869.

3273. ———: Two thousand Bengali proverbs illustrating native life and feeling. pp. 138. 8°. Calcutta, *Bose*, 1868.

Bernstein, 2828. 2358 proverbs in the original.

3274. Upendrakrīshna Vandyopādhyāya. A handbook of proverbs: English and Bengali. . . New edition. pp. 163.

12°. Calcutta, *Guru Das Chatterjee*, 1891.

589 entries. [B.M.

See also **3228.**

3. ASSAMESE.

3275. **Gurdon** (Phillip Richard). Some Assamese proverbs. Compiled and annotated by Captain P. R. Gurdon. pp. xxiv, 98.
2 rupees. la. 8°. Shillong, *Assam Secretariat
Printing Office*, 1896.

Second edition. pp. iii, 118.
1 rupee : 1/6. Shillong, *Assam Secretariat
Printing Office*, 1903.

Proverbs classified according to their character, and given in Assamese, transliterated, and in English. [F.-L.S.

4. ORIYA.

3276. **De** (B. N.). A breif [*sic*] collection of ancient caste proverbs [in Oriya]. pp. 38.
12°. Balasore, *Utkal Press*, 1904.
With transliterations, English translations and explanatory notes. [B.M.

WEST.

1. BOMBAY (GENERAL).

3277. **Gupte** (B. A.). Folklore in caste proverbs (Bombay Pre-
sidency). pp. 12. la. 8°. Calcutta, 1917.
In Journal and Proceedings of the Asiatic Society of Bengal (N.S.), Vol. 13.
[F.-L.S.

2. GUJARATI.

3278. **Javeri** (Mahāsukha Chunīlāla), *Shah*. Proverbs, Gujarati
and English . . . by M[ahāsukha] Ch[unīlāla Javeri] Shah.
pp. 40. 2 annas. 16°. Ahmedabad, *G.G. Press*, 1892.
[B.M.

3279. **Kārbhārī** (Bhagu Fathchand). Gujarati proverbs with
their English equivalents. pp. 39.
4 annas. 8°. Ahmedabad, *Vijaya Pravartak Press*, 1898.
These proverbs are also given at the end of the author's Gujarati-English
dictionary, 1899. [B.M.

3280. **Mehta** (Damubhai Dayabhai). Gujerati proverbs, . . .
with an essay on proverbs. pp. 3, 385.
8°. Ahmedabad, *Aryodaya Press*, Baroda,
Veerkshetra Mudralaya, 1893.

3281. **Nānjiāni** (Karam 'Alī Rahīm). Kutchi proverbs in Gujarāti
characters. As. 1.3. [188—?].

3282. **Narottama** (Desai). A collection of Gujarati proverbs with
their English equivalents. pp. 106.
12 annas. 8°. Bombay, " *Tatra-Vivechaka* " Press, 1900.
[B.M.

3283. Patel (Manilāl Dolatrām).   The Gujarati-English proverbs. [Second edition].   pp. 16.
12°. Ahmedabad, *Gujarati Printing Press*, 1901.
[B.M.

3284. Petit (Jamsetjee).   Collection of Gujarāti proverbs.
Bombay,

3285. Proverbs. The Gujerati proverbs. pp. 106.
12°. Bombay, 1868.
Original only.   [Malan Collection.

3. MARATHI.

3286. Chhatre (Narayan Damodar).   Marāthi practical proverbs.
Poona, 1871.

3287. Deshprānde (Ganesh Nārāyan).   A dictionary of Marāthi proverbs.   Pocna, 1900.

3288. Manwaring (Alfred).   Marathi proverbs, *etc.* pp. x, 271.
8°. Oxford, *Clarendon Press*, 1899.
Reviewed in Folk-Lore, Vol. 11, pp. 98-99.   1910 proverbs carefully selected, with English translations and notes.   [B.M.

SOUTHERN (DRAVIDIAN).

1. TAMIL.

3289. Asbury (Robert O. D.).   A collection of Tamil proverbs . . . with their parallels in English, etc., and copious notes, *etc.*
8°. Madras, *S.P.C.K.*, 1887.

3290. Athivira-Ramen. The proverbs, or sententious sayings, of Athivira-Ramen.   4°. Madras, 1835.
In Oriental Historical Manuscripts in the Tamil language : translated . . . by William Taylor, Vol. 2, Appendix, pp. 21-24. In English.   [B.M.

3291. Chelva-Kesavarāya-Mudaliyār. Parallel proverbs. Tamil and English, and English and Tamil. pp. 123.
8 annas. 8°. Madras, *Naicher*, 1900.
Second edition. pp. 234.
1 rupee. 8°. Madras, *S.P.C.K.*, 1903.
[B.M.

3292. Haeghen (Philip van der).   Maximes populaires de l'Inde méridionale, *etc.* pp. 39.
8°. Paris, *etc., Bohné & Schultz*, 1858.
100 Tamil proverbs and maxims, with translations, explanatory notes, and frequent comparisons with the proverbs of other languages.   [B.M.

3293. Jensen (Herman). A classified collection of Tamil proverbs, with translations, explanations and indices. pp. xxiv, 499.
8°. Madras, *Methodist Episcopal Publishing House*, London, *Trübner*, 1897.

3644 entries. Contains index of first word of each proverb, and also index of non-initial words from the body of the proverbs. Very valuable, but text of the proverbs has to be established by reference to Lazarus, Percival and Winslow's Lexicon. Alphabetical arrangement, and index to English headings in front. Also issued, same date with different title page, in Trübner's Oriental Series. [B.M.

3294. Kristnaswamy Sastry (A.). A collection of choice Tamil proverbs with their parallels in English and other languages. pp. 48. 8°. Coimbatore, *Venkataramaniah*, 1889.

Bernstein, 1782. 460 proverbs with English translations.

3295. Lazarus (John). A dictionary of Tamil proverbs, with an introduction and hints in English on their meaning and application. pp. xxv, 662. 8°. Madras, *Albinion Press*, 1894.

9417 proverbs in the original with English explanations. Very valuable preface. Some of the applications are open to question. [B.M.

3296. Natêsá Sâstrî (S. M.), *Pandit.* Folklore in southern India. 2 pts. Bombay, *Education Society's Press*, 1884-86.

Full of proverbs and references to proverbs. *Reviewed* in Academy, No. 741, 1886 : Athenæum, No. 3065, 1886 : and Folk-Lore Journal, Vol. 4, pp. 267-9.

3297. Percival (Peter). Tamil proverbs with their English translation. . . . *1st edition.* pp. xi, 573. 1842.
2nd edition. pp. xi, 573.
8°. Madras, *Dinavartamani Press*, 1874.
3rd edition, 1st English issue. 8°. London, 1875.

The first edition contains about 1900 proverbs, the second 6156. Alphabetical arrangement. [B.M.

3298. Rāmasvāmi Aiyangār. Parallel proverbs in Tamil and English. pp. 39.
2 annas. 8°. Madras, *Indian Printers Agency*, 1905.
348 entries. [B.M.

3299. Roberts (Sydney Gordon). Tamil proverbs: a key to the language and to the mind of the people.
8°. London, *Asiatic Review, Ltd.*, 1920.

In Journal of the East India Association, New Series, Vol. 11, pp. 178-208. Many examples, in Tamil with translations. [U.C.L.

3300. ——— : Tamil proverbs as essential to correct conversation and to full comprehension of the language.

In 17th International Congress of Orientalists, Section VIa, 2. Summary only; full paper to appear in Bulletin of the School of Oriental Studies, London.

3301. Sabhāpati Mudaliyār. Selected Tamil proverbs with appropriate English version, *etc.* pp. 204.

8 annas. 8°. Madras, *Havelock Press*, 1898.

1288 entries. [B.M.

3302. Satya Nesan (P.). Handbook of Tamil proverbs and phrases. 1888.

3303. Teacher. Tamil proverbs with their English equivalents . . . by an experienced teacher. pp. 12.

9 pies. 8°. Madras, *Memorial Press*, 1893.

154 entries. [B.M.

3304. Vēnkatasāmi Aiyar. Five hundred instructive Tamil proverbs with their English equivalents, *etc.* pp. 49.

2 annas. 8°. Madras, *Venkatachalam & Co.*, 1907. [B.M.

3305. Winslow (Miron). A comprehensive Tamil and English dictionary. 4°. Madras, 1862.

Contains very many proverbs as illustrations, and will never be superseded. [B.M.

2. MALAYALAM.

3306. Gundert (H.). One thousand Malayalam proverbs, *etc.* [Second edition]. pp. 67.

12°. Mangalore, *Basel Mission Press*, 1868.

The first edition, published by the Tellicherry Mission Press in 1857, has no English.

3307. Paulinus, *a Sancto Bartholomaeo.* Centum adagia Malabarica, *etc.* pp. 12. 4°. Romae, *Fulgonius*, 1791.

Gratet-Duplessis, 61. Malabar proverbs with Latin translations. [B.M.

3308. Proverbs. One thousand Malayalam proverbs. pp. 67.

12°. Mangalore, 1868.

Original only. [Malan Collection.

3309. ———: Twelve hundred Malayalam proverbs.

Mangalore, *Basel Mission Press*, [18—?].

3310. ———: A wreath of Malayalam proverbs, *etc.* pp. 40.

3 annas. 16°. Mangalore, *Basel Mission Press*, 1906.

332 proverbs with English equivalents. [B.M.

3. KANARESE.

3311. Aiman (Shadrach) and **Narasimha Rāu.** Popular Canarese proverbs. pp. 22.

2 annas. 12°. Mangalore, *Basel Mission Press*, 1894.

150 proverbs in Canarese with English translations. [B.M.

3312. Buehler (M.). 100 Badaga Sprüchwörter.
                                                8°. Leipzig, 1853.

In Zeitschrift der deutschen morgenländischen Gesellschaft, Bd. 7, pp. 381-389. With German translations.   [B.M.

3313. Edwardes (Stephen Meredyth). Some Kanarese proverbs relating to castes in Southern India.   8°. Bombay, 1905.

In Journal of the Anthropological Society of Bombay, Vol. 7, pp. 321-330.
                                                                  [B.M.

3314. Hanamanta Gōvinda Jōsi. Samati-Sangraha, or a collection of Canarese proverbs, with their English equivalents, *etc.*
pp. 52.   4 annas. 8°. Belgaum, 1894.
Second edition.   6 annas. 8°. Belgaum, 1906.

The second edition contains 1292 entries.   [B.M.

3315. Narasimha Rāu. A handbook of Canarese proverbs, *etc.*
pp. 84.   16°. Madras, *S.P.C.K. Press, Vepery,* 1906.

Proverbs in Canarese with English equivalents and an English index. [B.M.

3316. Proverbs. One thousand Canarese proverbs. pp. 56.
                    12°. Mangalore, *Stolz & Hirner,* 1874.

Original only.   [Malan Collection.

3317. ———: Three hundred Canarese proverbs, *etc.* pp. 32.
              16°. Mangalore, *Basel Mission book and tract
                              depository,* 1903.

Proverbs in Canarese with English equivalents.   [B.M.

3318. Sikhs. History of the Sikhs; or, translation of the Sikkhán de Ráj di Vikhiá. . . . Translated and edited by Henry Court pp. lxxxiv, 239.
              8°. Lahore, *Civil and Military Gazette Press,* 1888.

Pp. 136-141, proverbs. 26 proverbs in English, with explanatory notes.
                                                                  [B.M.

3319. Stolz (C.). Die Weisheit auf der Gasse in Indien. Kanaresische Sprichwörter.   8°. St. Gallen, 1890-1.

In Mittheilungen der Ostschweizerischen geogr.-commerc. Gesellschaft in St. Gallen, 1890-91, pp. 57-60.

4. TELUGU.

3320. Carr (Mark William). A collection of Telugu proverbs . . . together with some Sanskrit proverbs. (A supplement to the collection, *etc.*). 2 pts.
              8°. Madras, *C.K.S.,* London, *Trübner,* 1868.

A selection of Telugu proverbs, *etc.* pp. 178.
              8°. Madras, *Ramaswamy Sastrulu,* 1922.

2700 Telugu proverbs and nearly 500 Sanskrit ones, with English translations and notes. The Selection of 1922 contains 1185 proverbs, taken principally from the bigger collection, with the addition of some others. [U.C.L.

3321. Narasimha Āchāryulu (A.). Vakyamanjari. A collection of Telugu idioms, colloquial expressions and proverbs, *etc.* pp. 88.   8 annas.   12°.   Madras, *Kalaratnakaram Press*, 1882.

With English translations.   1236 entries.   [B.M.

5. OTHER.

3322. Brigel (J.).   A grammar of the Tulu language.   pp. iv, 139. iv [=6].   8°.   Mangalore, *Stolz*, 1872.

Pp. 134-139, Tulu proverbs.   [B.M.

3323. Neilgherry. The tribes inhabiting the Neilgherry hills, . . . from the rough notes of a German missionary.   Edited by a friend.   Second enlarged edition.   pp. 154.
         sm. 6°.   Mangalore, *Basel Mission Press*, 1864.

Pp. 91-98, proverbs in English.   [R.A.I.

3324. Veil (F.).   Sprichwörter und Räthsel aus dem Kurgland.
                                   8°.   Aarau, 1890.

In Fernschau.   Jahrbuch der mittelschweizen geogr-commer. Gesellschaft in Aarau, Bd. 4, pp. 40-45.   120 proverbs in German from Coorg.   [B.M.

3325. ———: [800 Kurgische Sprichwörter].
                 Mangalur, *Baseler Missionspresse*, 1885.

Mentioned by the author, in last entry, as having been published, but title not given.

SINHALESE.

3326. Emerson (James), *afterwards* **Tennent** (*Sir* James Emerson). Christianity in Ceylon, *etc.* pp. xv, 348. [Illustrated]. 8°. London, *Murray*, 1850.

Pp. 346-348, Singhalese proverbs in English. [U.C.L.

3327. Knox (Robert). An historical relation of the land of Ceylon, in the East Indies, *etc.* pp. [22], 189.
fol. London, *Chiswell*, 1681.

Another edition. 8°. Glasgow, *MacLehose*, 1911.

Chap. 9, " Of their lawes and language," contains a list of fifteen proverbs, some in the original with English translations, and some in English only.
[B.M.

3328. Mendis (Nicholas). A number of Sinhalese and European proverbs, *etc.* pp. 74.
1 rupee. 8°. Colombo, *Fonseka*, 1890.

Pp. 1-31, 259 Sinhalese proverbs with English translations : pp. 57-70, 125 European proverbs with Sinhalese translations. [B.M.

3329. Zoysa (Louis de). Specimens of Sinhalese proverbs.
8°. Colombo, 1871-73.

In Journal of the Ceylon branch of the Royal Asiatic Society, 1870-71, pp. 134-148 : 1871-72, pp. 25-32. 166 proverbs with English translations and notes where necessary. [B.M.

BURMESE, MANIPURI

3330. Cust (Robert). Hill proverbs. ff. 20.   8°.

Bernstein, 1508. 186 proverbs in Burmese and English.

3331. Gray (James). Ancient proverbs and maxims from Burmese sources, *etc.* pp. xi, 179.

               8°. London, *Trübner*, 1886.

Trübner's Oriental Series. A good collection, with interesting footnotes.

                       [B.M.

3332. Judson (Adoniram). Burmese-English dictionary. Revised and enlarged by Robert C. Stevenson. pp. vii, 6, 4, 1188.

          8°. Rangoon, *Printed by the Superintendent,*
                   Government Printing, Burma, 1893.

Another edition. pp. iii, 1123.

        8°. Rangoon, *American Baptist Mission Press,* 1914.

Concludes with a selection of proverbs and sayings in the original, with English translations. The edition of 1883 is the first to contain this separate list.   [B.M.

3333. Macdougal (J.). Proverbs, idioms and meanings, with Burmese equivalents. pp. 92.

             8°. Mandalay, *Irriwaddi Press,* 1917.

English proverbs with brief explanatory notes and Burmese equivalents.

                       [B.M.

3334. Milne (*Mrs.* Leslie). The home of an Eastern clan. A study of the Palaungs of the Shan States. pp. viii, 428.

        8°. Oxford, *Clarendon Press,* 1924.

Pp. 371-376, proverbs in English.   [U.C.L.

3335. Primrose (Arthur John). A Manipuri grammar, *etc.* pp. 100.   8°. Shillong, *Assam Secretariat Press,* 1888.

Pp. 91-95, Manipuri proverbs. In the original, with transcriptions and English translations.   [B.M.

3336. Wince (H. J.). Manipuri proverbs.   8°. London, 1911.

In Folk-Lore, Vol. 22, pp. 473-475. Twenty proverbs with exact translations, and the nearest English equivalent.

FAR EAST

1. CHINESE.

3337. Aubazac (Louis). Proverbes de la langue cantonnaise, *etc.*
pp. iv, 176. 12°. Hongkong, *Imprimerie de Nazareth*, 1918.

1228 proverbs in the original, with transliterations and French translations.
[B.M.

3338. Brown (Brian). The wisdom of the Chinese; their philosophy in sayings and proverbs, *etc.* pp. 201 + frontispiece.
8°. New York, *Brentano*, [1921].

Issued in England with a different title page in 1922. Chiefly moral
precepts; pp. 171-179, proverbs and maxims. In English. [B.M.

3339. Ch'en Chi T'ung. Les Chinois peints par eux-mêmes. Par
le colonel Tcheng-Ki-Tong [Ch'en Chi-T'ung]. pp. x, 291.
8°. Paris, *Calmann Lévy*, 1884.

Translated into English 1884, also into German. Contains a chapter of
proverbs and maxims. [B.M.

3340. Cibot, *Père.* Mémoires concernant l'histoire . . . des
Chinois; par les missionnaires de Pe-kin.
4°. Paris, *Nyon*, 1784.

Gratet-Duplessis, 56. Vol. 10, pp. 144-178, Pensées, maximes et proverbes,
extraits et traduits de divers livres chinois, par M. Cibot. See particularly
pp. 157 *et seq.* In French. [B.M.

3341. Courcy (de), *Marquis.* L'Empire du milieu, *etc.* pp.
xi, 692. 8°. Paris, *Didier*, 1867.

Pp 391-393, 20 Chinese proverbs translated into French. [B.M.

3342. Davis (*Sir* John Francis), *Bart.* Chinese novels translated
from the originals: to which are added proverbs and moral
maxims, *etc.* pp. 250. la. 8°. London, *Murray*, 1822.

Gratet-Duplessis, 57. Pp. 225-250, 126 proverbs translated into English.
No notes. [B.M.

3343. ——— : Chinese proverbs and moral maxims.
4°. New York, 1863.

In The Philobiblion, Vol. 2, pp. 84-87. 85 entries in English. [B.M.

3344. ——— : Hien wun shoo. Chinese moral maxims, with a
free and verbal translation, *etc.* pp. viii, 199.
8°. London, *Murray*, Macao, China,
Company's Press, 1823.

200 entries. Another edition, consisting of the English versions only, was
published in 1910 as No. 36 of Gowan's International Library. [B.M.

3345. Dialogi. Dialogi latino-sinenses. Ho-Kien, 1864.
Pp. 85-88, proverbs.

3346. Doolittle (Justus). Social life of the Chinese, *etc.* [Illustrated]. 2 vols. 8°. New York, *Harper*, 1867.
Vol. 2, pp. 268-272, proverbs and book phrases. In English. [B.M.

3347. ———: Vocabulary and hand-book of the Chinese language, *etc.* 2 vols.
4°. Foochow, China, *etc.*, *Rozario, Marcal*, 1872.
Vol. 2 contains a large number of different lists of proverbs with English translations. [B.M.

3348. Giles (Herbert Allen). Gems of Chinese literature. pp. xv, 254. 8°. London, *Quaritch*, Shanghai, *Kelly & Walsh*, 1884.
Pp. 243-249, proverbs in English. [B.M.

3349. ———: A history of Chinese literature. pp. viii, 448.
8°. London, *Heinemann*, 1901.
Pp. 436-439, some Chinese proverbs in English. [B.M.

3350. Gonçalves (Joachimo Affonso). Arte China constante de alphabeto e grammatica, *etc.* pp. viii, 500, 46.
4°. Macao, *Real Collegio de S. Jose*, 1829.
Pp. 308-326, Proverbios. Chinese proverbs with Portuguese translations. [B.M.

3351. Hao Ch'iu Chuan. Hau Kiou Choaan, or, the pleasing history, *etc.* [Translated by J. Wilkinson]. 4 vols.
8°. London, *Dodsley*, 1761.
Vol. 3, pp. 181-267, a collection of Chinese proverbs and apophthegms. In English with notes, and parallels from other languages. A good and characteristic selection, though the proverbs have lost conciseness in translation. Translated into German, 1766. [B.M.

3352. Hisa (Michitaro). Some Japanized Chinese proverbs.
8°. Boston, 1896.
In Journal of American Folk-Lore, Vol. 9, pp. 132-138. [B.M.

3353. Jenings (Forster H.). The proverbial philosophy of Confucius. Quotations from the Chinese classics for each day in the year, *etc.* pp. ix, 120.
New York, London, *Putnam*, 1895.
In English. [B.M.

3354. Klaproth (Heinrich Julius von). Chrestomathie Mandchou, *etc.* pp. xi, 273. 8°. [Paris], *Imprimerie Royale*, 1828.
Pp. 5-23, Collection de proverbes chinois traduits en Mandchou, *etc.*: pp. 195-210, French translation. [B.M.

3355. Kwang Ki Chaou. Dictionary of English phrases. . . . To which are added . . . a selection of Chinese proverbs and maxims, *etc.*
Pp. 817-825, Chinese proverbs and wise sayings in English. *See* **607.**

3356. Lister (Alfred). Chinese proverbs and their lessons.

8°. Hongkong, 1874-75.

In The China Review, Vol. 3, pp. 129-138. An article containing numerous examples in English. These proverbs in the original Chinese are given in a list at the end. [B.M.

3357. Loomis (A. W.). Chinese proverbs.

8°. San Francisco, 1873.

In Overland Monthly, Vol. 10, pp. 82-85. [B.M.

3358. Mémoires. Mémoires concernant l'histoire . . . des Chinois, par les missionaires de Pe-kin. 4°. Paris, *Nyon*, 1779.

Vol. 4, pp. 268-286, maximes, proverbes, sentences, pensées et réflexions morales sur la piété filiale. In French. [B.M.

3359. National Proverbs. National proverbs: China. pp. 81.

1/-. 8°. London, *Palmer*, [1913].

Proverbs in English; no notes. [F.-L.S.

3360. Neumann ( ). Sinesische Sprüchwörter und Maximen.

8°. Göttingen, 1839.

In Zeitschrift für die Kunde des Morgenlandes, Bd. 2, pp. 74-77. [B.M.

3361. Perny (Paul Hubert). Proverbes chinois, *etc.* pp. 135.

8°. Paris, *Firmin Didot*, 1869.

Chinese proverbs in the original with transliterations and French translations. [B.M.

3362. Philosophy. Chinese proverbial philosophy.

8°. London, 1865.

In The Chinese and Japanese Repository, Vol. 3, pp. 395-398, 488-490, 539-540.

3363. Prémare (Joseph Henri de). Notitia linguae Sinicae. *First edition.* pp. 262, 28.

4°. Malaccae, *Accademia Anglo-Sinensis*, 1831.

English translation. pp. 328.

8°. Canton, *Office of the Chinese Repository*, 1847.

Another edition. pp. 255.

8°. Hongkong, *Société des Missions Étrangères*, 1893.

Contains a collection of proverbs in Chinese characters, in transliteration, and in Latin translation. [B.M.

3364. Rochet (Louis). Manuel pratique de la langue chinoise vulgaire, *etc.* pp. xiv, 216. 8°. Paris, *Legrand*, 1846.

Pp. 95-97, proverbes. 50 Chinese proverbs in the original. [B.M.

3365. ———: Sentences, maximes et proverbes mantchoux et mongols, accompagnés d'une traduction française, *etc.* pp. iv, 166. 8°. Paris, *Maisonneuve*, 1875.

[B.M.

3366. Scarborough (William). A collection of Chinese proverbs, *etc.* pp. viii, xxxvi, 478.

8°. Shanghai, *American Presbyterian Mission Press*, 1875.

Ditto, revised and enlarged by the addition of some six hundred proverbs by C. Wilfrid Allan. pp. vi, 381, xiv.

8°. Shanghai, *American Presbyterian Mission Press*, 1926.

2720 Chinese proverbs with transliterations and English translations. In the introductory essay under " Sources " the author refers to a number of Chinese books of proverbs, maxims, *etc.* [B.M.

3367. Smith (Arthur Henderson). Proverbs and common sayings from the Chinese. *First edition.* pp. 2, 384.

8°. Shanghai, *American Presbyterian Mission Press*, 1888.

New and revised edition. pp. vii, 374, xxx.

la. 8°. Shanghai, *American Presbyterian Mission Press*, 1902.

Most of the material was published in the Chinese Recorder from 1882-1885. Proverbs are given both in Chinese and English. Contains a large amount of commentatorial matter. [F.-L.S. (Stephens collection).

3368. Stevens (H. J.). Cantonese apophthegms, *etc.* pp. ii, 155.

8°. Canton, 1902.

In the original, with transliterations, English translations and notes. Pp. 127-129, proverbs. [B.M.

3369. W. Proverbs and metaphors drawn from nature in use among the Chinese.

In The Chinese Repository, Vol. 7, pp. 321-327. 104 entries, in English. [B.M.

3370. Williams (Samuel Wells). The middle kingdom, *etc.* 2 vols. 8°. New York, London, *Wiley & Putnam*, 1848.

Another edition. 2 vols. 8°. London, *Allen*, 1883.

Contains a small collection of Chinese proverbs in English. [B.M.

2. KOREAN.

3371. Griffis (William Elliot). Corea. The hermit nation, *etc.* pp. xxiii, 462 + map. 8°. London, *Allen*, 1882.

Seventh edition. pp. xxvii, 495.

8°. London, *Harper*, 1905.

Chap. 35, pp. 317-319, Proverbs and pithy sayings. The following chapter on " The Corean Tiger " also contains a number of proverbs concerning that animal. In English. [B.M.

3. JAPANESE.

3372. Aston (W. G.). Japanese proverbs. 4°. London, 1872.

In The Phoenix, Vol. 2, pp. 127-129. 40 proverbs, transliterated and with English translations. Pp. 151-152, Some remarks on the Japanese proverbs by W. T. Mercer. [B.M.

3373. Bibra (Reinhard von). Japanische Sprichwörter.

8°. Stuttgart, *etc.*, 1896.

In Deutsche Revue, 21. Jahrgang, pp. 112-117. Containing numerous examples, in German. [B.M.

3374. Chamberlain (Basil Hall). A romanized Japanese reader, *etc.* 3 pts. 8°. London, *Trübner*, [1886].

Pt. 1, No. 1, 20 Japanese proverbs. Pt. 2, No. 1, their English translation. Pt. 3, No. 1, notes. [B.M.

3375. Ehmann (Paul). Japanische Sprichwörter und sprichwörtliche Redensarten. 4°. Tokyo, 1893.

In Mittheilungen der deutschen Gesellschaft für Natur- und Völkerkunde Ostasiens, Bd. 6, pp. 71-102. 365 Japanese proverbs with transliterations and German translations. [B.M.

3376. ———: Die Sprichwörter und bildlichen Ausdrücke der japanischen Sprache, *etc.* pp. xxii, 428.

8°. Tokyo, *Tokyo Tsukiji Type Foundry*, 1897, *etc.*

In progress. Supplement der Mittheilungen der deutschen Gesellschaft für Natur- und Völkerkunde Ostasiens. 3729 proverbs, *etc.*, with transliterations, German translations, and occasional notes. [B.M.

3377. Fleury (Jules). Le musée secret de la caricature, par Champfleury [Jules Fleury]. pp. x, 249.

8°. Paris, *Dentu*, 1888.

Pp. 175-186, Proverbes japonais. Discusses and explains various proverbs. In French. [B.M.

3378. Gattinoni (Giulio). Grammatica giapponese della lingua parlata, *etc.* pp. viii, 168, 28.

L.8. 8°. Venezia, *Manuzio*, 1890.

Pp. 161-166, Alcuni proverbi popolari giapponesi illustrati. 25 entries transliterated from the Japanese with Italian translations. [B.M.

3379. Griffis (William Elliot). The Mikado's empire. 2 vols.

8°. New York, *Harper*, 1876.

Tenth edition. 2 vols.

8°. New York, London, *Harper*, 1903.

Vol. 2, Chap. 14, Japanese proverbs. In English. [B.M.

3380. Harris (M. C.). Japanese proverbs. 8°. Yokohama, 1881.

In The Chrysanthemum, pp. 41-45, 87-91, 222-225, 347-349. Over 100 Japanese proverbs transliterated and with English translations and notes. [B.M.

3381. Hearn (Lafcadio). In ghostly Japan. pp. 241 + plates.

8°. London, *Sampson Low*, 1899.

Pp. 167-194, Japanese Buddhist proverbs. 100 proverbs transliterated, with English translations and footnotes, which serve to illustrate certain effects of Buddhist teaching upon popular thought and speech. [B.M.

3382. Horie (Otoya) and **Konisi** (Tatehiko). Weather folk-lore.

1924.

Suiro Yôhô (Hydrographic Bulletin), 3 (1924), pp. 41-47, 63-78, 93-105. 399 popular sayings on weather-forecasting on the coast of Japan. Collected and arranged according to the ports by Horie and discussed by Konisi.

3383. Knobloch (A. von). Japanische Sprichwoerter und Redensarten.   fol. Yokohama, 1873.

In Mittheilungen der deutschen Gesellschaft für Natur- und Völkerkunde
Ostasiens, Bd. 1, Heft 4, pp. 23-26. Japanese proverbs in transliteration with
German translations. Additions were made to this list by Dr. Lange. See
next entry.   [B.M.

3384. Lange (   ). Noch einige Sprichwoerter und sprich-
woertliche Redensarten der Japaner.
                                              fol. Yokohama, 1875-1880.

In Mittheilungen der deutschen Gesellschaft für Natur- und Völkerkunde
Ostasiens, Bd. 1, Heft 8, pp. 50-52, Heft 9, pp. 59-60, Heft 10, pp. 34-37;
Bd. 2, pp. 415-421. Japanese proverbs transliterated and with German trans-
lations. See notes to last entry.   [B.M.

3385. National Proverbs. National proverbs: Japan. pp. 76.
                          1/-. 8°. London, *Palmer*, [1913].
Proverbs in English only; no notes.   [B.M.

3386. Okoshi (N.). Japanese proverbs and some figurative expressions of the Japanese language.   8°. London, 1895.

In Transactions . . . of the Japan Society, Vol. 2, pp. 3-21. A paper
containing, besides numerous examples cited in the text, a list of 50 proverbs
with literal translations and equivalent English and French examples. Pp.
22-27 contain the subsequent discussion on the paper.   [B.M.

3387. Pfoundes (C.). Folk-Lore of old Japan.
                                    8°. Birmingham, [1881].
In Proceedings of the Birmingham Philosophical Society, Vol. 2, pp. 255-71.
Pp. 270-271, Japanese proverbs transliterated and with English translations.
                                                                  [B.M.

3388. Reed (*Sir* Edward James). Japan: its history, traditions
and religions, *etc.* 2 vols.   8°. London, *Murray*, 1880.
Vol. 2, pp. 105-112, proverbs and phrases of the people. In English. [B.M.

3389. Sandaya (H.). Japanische Sprichwörter . . . übersetzt.
pp. 42.   8°. Leipzig, 1913.

3390. Sarazin (François). Nihon-no koto-waza. Dictons et proverbes japonais, *etc.* pp. 7.
                          8°. Paris, *Bouchard-Huzard*, 1873.
In Bulletin de l'Athénée oriental, 1873.

3391. Seidel (August). Praktische Grammatik der japanischen
Sprache, *etc.* pp. viii, 198 + 10 tables.
                          8°. Wien, *etc.*, *Hartleben*, [1890].
Die Kunst der Polyglottie, Th. 22. Pp. 150-151, Sprichwörter und Sentenzen.
In Japanese, transliterated.   [B.M.

3392. Starr (Frederick). Japanese proverbs and pictures. pp.
50.   Tokyo, Chicago, 1910.

3393. Steenackers (Francis) and **Tokonosuke** (Uéda). Cent proverbes japonais. pp. iv, 214. 4°. Paris, [1886].

Proverbs transliterated and with French translations, accompanied by Japanese drawings and a full explanation of the same. The illustrations and text
need to be carefully studied before their bearing on the proverbs is compre-
hensible; some of the applications seem far fetched. Not a very good selection.
[B.M.

3394. Valenziano (Carlo). Sul letterato giapponese Kai-Bara
Yosi-Huru, e sulla sua opera Kotowaza-Gusa.
8°. Roma, 1892.

In Rendiconti della Reale Accademia dei Lincei, Classe di scienze morali,
Serie 5, Vol. 1, pp. 167-189. An article on the Japanese author of a collection
of proverbs and his book. 39 proverbs are quoted with notes. These proverbs
are continued in Vol. 3, pp. 707-747; Vol. 4, pp. 317-333, 399-417; Vol. 5,
pp. 299-319. [B.M.

4. ANNAMESE.

3395. Bocsq ( ). Chants populaires et proverbes annamites.
8°. 1896.

3396. Cùa (P.). Maximes et proverbes. pp. 35.
12°. Saigon, *Imprimerie du Gouvernement*, 1882.

Bernstein, 762. In the original.

3397. Degeorge (J. B.). Proverbes, maximes et sentences Tays.
la. 8°. Wien, 1927- .

In progress. *In* Anthropos, Bd. 27, pp. 911-32. 112 proverbs, in the original,
transliterated, and with explanations. [F.-L.S.

3398. J. (M. J.). Notions pour servir à l'étude de la langue
annamite. pp. 381.
8°. Tân Dinh, *Imprimerie de la Mission*, 1878.
Second edition. pp. 308.
8°. Saigon, *Imprimerie de la Mission*, 1914.

Contains a good selection of proverbs, maxims, *etc.*, some with French translations and some without. [B.M.

5. SIAMESE.

3399. Pallegoix (Jean Baptiste). Description du royaume Thai
ou Siam, *etc.* 2 tom. 12°. Paris, 1854.

Tome 1, pp. 401-402, 8 Siamese proverbs in French. [B.M.

6. MALAY.

3400. Beauregard (G. M. Ollivier). Dictons et proverbes malays.
8°. Paris, 1888-1890.

In Revue des traditions populaires, Tome 3, pp. 490-492; Tome 4, pp. 28-30,
352-354; Tome 5, pp. 722-723. In French. [B.M.

3401. Hoëvell (G. W. W. C. van). Vocabularium van vreemde woorden, voorkomende in het Ambonsch-Maleisch, *etc.* pp. iv, 58.   8°. Dordrecht, *Blussé en Van Braum*, 1876.

Bernstein, 4734. Pp. 39-53, Ambonsche spreekwoorden, *etc.*

3402. Klinkert (H. C.). Eenige Maleische spreekwoorden en spreekwijzen, *etc.*   8°. 's Gravenhage, *Nijhoff*, 1866.

In Bijdragen tot de Taal-, Land-, en Volkenkunde van Nederlandsch Indië, 3 Volgreeks, Deel 1, pp. 37-87.   [B.M.

3403. ———: Vervolg op die maleische spreekwoorden benevens eenige maleische raadsels en kinderspielen.
8°. 's Gravenhage, *Nijhoff*, 1869.

In Bijdragen tot de Taal-, Land-, en Volkenkunde van Nederlandsch Indië, 3 Volgreeks, Deel 4, pp. 24-67.   [B.M.

3404. Maare de Marin (Aristide). Proverbes et similitudes des Malais, avec leurs correspondants en diverses langues d'Europe et d'Asie. pp. 26.   8°. Torino, *Clausen*, 1898.

In Atti della R. Accademia delle Scienze di Torino, Vol. 33. 367 Malay proverbs translated into French, with equivalents from many other languages.
[U.C.L.

3405. ———: Sourat per oupama an Malayou. Le livre des proverbes malais, *etc.* pp. 38.   8°. Paris, *Leroux*, 1889.

In Recueil de textes et de traductions, publié par . . . l'École des Langues orientales vivantes, Vol. 2. Proverbs transcribed with literal French translations.

3406. Maxwell (*Sir* William Edward). Malay proverbs.
8°. Singapore, 1878-9.

In Journal of the Straits branch of the Royal Asiatic Society, 1878, pp. 85-98, 136-162; 1879, pp. 19-51. 301 proverbs, with English translations and notes.   [B.M.

3407. Skeat (Walter William) and **Blagden** (Charles Otto). Pagan races of the Malay peninsula. 2 vols.
la. 8°. London, *Macmillan*, 1906.

Vol. 2, pp. 679-80, Besisi proverbs; p. 692, proverbial sayings of the Bëlandas of Selangor.

3408. Swettenham (*Sir* Frank Athelstane). British Malaya, *etc.* pp. xi, 354 + plates.
8°. London, New York, *Lane*, 1907 [1906].

Pp. 169-171, proverbs in English.   [R.A.I.

3409. Wilkinson (Richard James). Malay proverbs on Malay character. pp. 48.
8°. Kuala Lampur, *F.M.S. Government Press*, 1907.

Papers on Malay subjects. Malay literature, Pt. 3. Pp. 1-20, proverbs. A general survey quoting a number of examples in English, which are given in the original in a list at the end.   [B.M.

7. INDONESIAN.

3410. Bowring (*Sir* John). A visit to the Philippine Islands. pp.
vi, 434 + plates and music.
8°. London, *Smith, Elder*, 1859.
Spanish translation. pp. xiii, 460.   8°. Manila, 1876.
Chap. 19 (pp. 286-91), popular proverbs. In the original, with English translations.   [B.M.

3411. Eck (R. van). Balische spreekwoorden en spreekwoordelijke uitdrukkingen.
8°. Batavia, *Bruining & Wijt*, 's Hage, *Nijhoff*, 1872, 1875.
In Tijdschrift voor Indische Taal-, Land-, en Volkenkunde, Deel 18, pp. 170-
188; Deel 21, pp. 122-145, 377-402.   [B.M.

3412. Helfrich (O. L.).   Lampongsche raadsels, spreekwoorden
en spreekwijzen.   8°. 's Gravenhage, *Nijhoff*, 1891.
In Bijdragen tot de Taal-, Land-, en Volkenkunde van Nederlandsch Indië,
5 Volgreeks, Deel 6, pp. 612-619.   [B.M.

3413. Hoezoo (W.).   Eenige Javaansche spreekwoorden.
8°. Rotterdam, *Wijt*, 1865.
In Mededeeling van wege het Nederlandsche Zendelinggenootschap, Negende
Jaargang, pp. 283-288.   [B.M.

3414. Holle (K. F.).   Honderd en een Soendasche spreekwoorden.
8°. Batavia, *Lange*, 1860-69.
In Tijdschrift voor Indische Taal-, Land-, en Volkenkunde, Deel 10 (4 Serie,
Deel 1), pp. 62-79; Deel 19 (6 Serie, Deel 1), pp. 271-295.   [B.M.

3415. Hurgronje (Christiaan Snouck).   Mekkanische Sprichwörter und Redensarten, *etc.* pp. 144.
8°. Haag, *Nijhoff*, 1886.
Published by the Koninklijk Institut voor de Taal-, Land-, en Volkenkunde
van Nederlandsch Indië. 77 proverbs in the original, with German translations
and explanations. Reviewed and criticised at great length in Landberg's Critica
Arabica, Pt. 1.   [B.M.

3416. Martin (Gregorio) and **Martinez Cuadrado** (Mariano).
Collección de refranes, frases y modismos tagalos traducidos
y explicados en Castellano. pp. 231.
12°. Guadalupe, *Asilo de Huerfanos de Nuestra Señora*
Bernstein, 2091.   *de la Consolación*, 1890.

3417. Uilkens (J. A.).   Soendasche spreekwoorden.
8°. Batavia, *Bruining & Wijt*, 1872-5.
In Tijdschrift voor Indische Taal-, Land-, en Volkenkunde, Deel 18 (6 Serie,
Deel 1), pp. 395-417; Deel 20 (6 Serie, Deel 3), pp. 327-349; Deel 21, pp. 183-
208.   [B.M.

3418. Warneck (Lic. Johann).   Die Religion der Batak. Ein
Paradigma für die animistischen Religionen des indischen
Archipels. pp. vi, 136.
la. 8°. Göttingen, *Vandenhoek & Ruprecht*,
Leipzig, *Hinrichs*, 1909.
Many references to proverbs.

AFRICAN

1. GENERAL.

3419. Bouche (Pierre).   Les noirs peints par eux-mêmes.   pp.
144.   8°. Paris, *Poussielgue*, 1883.
Proverbs with French translations and explanations.   [B.M.

3420. Philosophy. African proverbial philosophy.
8°. New York, 1854.
In Putnam's Monthly Magazine, Vol. 4, pp. 362-371. An article containing
numerous examples.   [B.M.

3421. Rowling (F.), *Canon*, and **Wilson** (C. E.).   Bibliography
of African Christian literature.   Conference of Missionary
Societies of Great Britain and Ireland.   pp. 130.
London, 1923.
Section H, Miscellaneous—proverbs, *etc.*

3422. Schoelcher (Victor).   Des colonies françaises, *etc.* pp. lii,
443.   8°. Paris, *Pagnerre*, 1842.
Gratet-Duplessis, 391. Pp. 417-434, proverbes et locutions nègres. Given in
the patois or corrupted French of the colonies, followed by brief explanations.
Particularly interesting for the light they throw on condition of slavery at that
period.   [B.M.

3423. Seidel (August).   Geschichten und Lieder der Afrikaner,
etc. pp. xii, 340.   8°. Berlin, *Schall & Grund*, [1896].
Contains many small lists of proverbs of various tribes. These proverbs are
given in German only.   [B.M.

3424. Wullschlaegel (H. R.).   Deutsch-negerenglisches Wörterbuch, *etc.* pp. x, 340.   8°. Löbau, *Duroldt*, 1856.
Pp. 301-340, 700 proverbs with German translations and equivalents.   [B.M.

2. MOROCCO AND ALGERIA.

3425. Cadoz (François).   Le secrétaire de l'Algérie, *etc.* pp. 180.
8°. Alger, *Bernard*, 1850.
Pp. 162-175, proverbes usités dans le langage vulgaire. 28 proverbs with
transliterations, French translations, and notes.   [B.M.

3426. Fischer (A.). Marokkanische Sprichwörter.
8°. Berlin, Stuttgart, *Spemann*, 1898.

In Mittheilungen des Seminars für orientalische Sprachen zu Berlin, Abth. 2, pp. 188-230. Some 70 proverbs accompanied by translations and full notes. Pp. 200-201, list of authorities. [B.M.

3427. Fitzner (R.). Sinnsprüche und Sprichworte der magribinischen Moslemîn. 8°. Leipzig, 1892.

In Zeitschrift für Volkskunde, Bd. 4, pp. 128-131. In German. [B.M.

3428. Luederitz (H.). Sprüchwörter aus Marokko mit Erläuterungen im Dialekt des nördlichen Marokko.
8°. Berlin, Stuttgart, 1899.

In Mittheilungen des Seminars für orientalische Sprachen, Jahrgang 2, Westasiatische Studien, pp. 1-46. 92 proverbs with transliterations and German translations. [B.M.

3429. Masqueray (Émile). Observations grammaticales sur la grammaire touareg, *etc.* pp. ii, 272.
8°. Paris, *Leroux*, 1896.

École des Lettres d'Alger, Publication 18. Pp. 185-192, proverbs. 42 proverbs in the original, with transcriptions and French translations. [B.M.

3430. Meakin (James Edward Budgett). An introduction to the Arabic of Morocco, *etc.* pp. xii, 255.
8°. London, *Kegan Paul*, 1891.

Pp. 217-222, useful proverbs, *etc.* Transcribed, and with English translations. [B.M.

3431. Muhammed Ibn Abi Shanab. Proverbes arabes de l'Algérie et du Maghreb, *etc.* 3 tom. 8°. Paris, *Leroux*, 1905-07.

Publications de l'École des Lettres d'Alger, 30-32. A large collection of proverbs in the original, with French translations and notes. Tome 1, pp. v-xiv, bibliography. [B.M.

3432. Proverbes. Proverbes des Musulmans d'Afrique.
4°. Paris, 1882.

In Le Magasin Pittoresque, 1882, pp. 118-120. In French. [B.M.

3. EGYPT.

3433. Budge (*Sir* Ernest Alfred Thompson Wallis). Facsimiles of Egyptian hieratic papyri in the British Museum. . . . Second series. pp. 51 + 128 plates.
fol. London, *British Museum*, 1923.

Pp. 41-51, hieroglyphic transcript of the admonitions of Amen-em-apt, the son of Kanekht. Egyptian text probably dates *c.* 1000 B.C., and therefore probably translated at Solomon's court. Furnishes direct parallels to Bible, Proverbs, chap. 22, verse 17—chap. 23, verse 11. [B.M.

3434. ———: The literature of the ancient Egyptians. pp. xiii, 272 + plates. 8°. London, *Dent*, 1914.

Chap. 13 deals with moral and philosophical literature, including the precepts of Ptah-hotep. [B.M.

3435. Budge (*Sir* Ernest Alfred Thompson Wallis). The precepts of life by Amen-em-apt, the son of Ka-nekht, *etc.*

8°. Paris, *Champion*, 1922.

In Recueil d'études égyptologiques dédiées à la mémoire de Jean-François Champollion, pp. 431-436. [B.M.]

3436. ——: The teaching of Amen-em-apt, son of Kanekht. The Egyptian hieroglyphic text and an English translation, with translations of the moral and religious teachings of Egyptian kings and officials, *etc.* pp. xv, 260 + plates.

8°. London, *Hopkinson*, 1924.

Includes the teaching of Ptah-hotep, *etc.* [B.M.]

3437. Erman (Adolf). Eine ägyptische Quelle der Sprüche Salomos. 8°. Berlin, 1924.

In Sitzungsberichte der preussische Akademie der Wissenschaften, Philosophisch-historische Klasse, 1924, No. 15, pp. 86-93. On the proverbs of Amen-em-ope compared with those of Solomon. [B.M.]

3438. ——: Die Literatur der Aegypter. Leipzig, 1923. *English translation.* pp. xliv, 318.

8°. London, *Methuen*, [1927].

Pp. 86-121, proverbial literature of ancient Egypt, *i.e.* the Instructions of Ptah-hotep, *etc.* [B.M.]

3439. ——: Das Weisheitsbuch des Amen-em-ope.

4°. Berlin, 1924.

In Orientalistische Literaturzeitung, Jahrgang 27, Nr. 5, pp. 241-252. [B.M.]

3440. Gardiner (Alan Henderson). The admonitions of an Egyptian sage, from a hieratic papyrus in Leiden, *etc.* pp. vi, 116 + plates. 4°. Leipzig, *Hinrich*, 1909. [B.M.]

3441. Gressmann (H.). Die neugefundene Lehre des Amen-em-ope und die vorexilische Spruchdichtung Israels.

8°. Giessen, 1924.

In Zeitschrift für die alttestamentliche Wissenschaft, N.F. 1, pp. 272-96. Gressmann's results are stated in popular form in his booklet, "Israels Spruchweisheit im Zusammenhang der Weltliteratur," Berlin, 1925. [B.M.]

3442. Griffith (Frank Llewellyn). The proverbs of Ptah-hotep, *etc.* 8°. [London], 1891.

In Proceedings of the Society of Biblical Archaeology, Vol. 13, pp. 72-76, 145-147. Ideographs with English translations and comments. [B.M.]

3443. ——: The teaching of Amenophis, the son of Kanakht. Papyrus B.M. 10474. 4°. London, 1926.

In Journal of Egyptian Archaeology, Vol. 12, pp. 191-231. [B.M.]

3444. Grimme (Hubert). Weiteres zu Amen-em-ope und Proverbien. 4°. Berlin, 1925.

In Orientalistische Literaturzeitung, 1925, coll. 57-62. See also, coll. 371-375, a review of P. A. A. Boeser's "Transkription und Übersetzung des Papyrus Insinger." [B.M.]

3445. Haggenmacher (Carl). Grammatik des ägyptisch-arabischen Vulgärdialektes, *etc.* pp. viii, 113.

8°. Cairo, *Boehme and Anderer*, 1892.

Pp. 82-83, Sprichwörter. Arab proverbs used in Egypt transcribed, and with German translations.

3446. Haigh (Richmond). An Ethiopian saga. pp. 207.

8°. London, *Allen and Unwin*, [1919].

Composed of 45 sections, each headed by a proverb.   [B.M.

3447. Hanki (Joseph). A collection of modern Egyptian proverbs, *etc.* pp. 133.

8°. Cairo, Egypt, *Al-Baian Printing Office*, 1897.

Proverbs with English translations, explanations, and equivalents.

3448. Leeder (S. H.). Modern sons of the Pharaohs. A study of the manners and customs of the Copts of Egypt, *etc.* pp. xvi, 355 + plates.

8°. London, *etc., Hodder & Stoughton*, [1918].

Pp. 32-34, proverbs in English.   [R.A.I.

3449. Lexa (François). Papyrus Insinger. Les enseignements moraux. . . . Texte démotique avec transcription, traduction française, commentaire. . . . Tome 1er, *etc.* pp. xx, 113, viii, 32.   4°. Paris, *Geuthner*, 1926.
                                                          [B.M.

3450. Linder (Josef). Das Weisheitsbuch des Amen-em-ope und die Sprüche von Weisen [Proverbs, 22, 17-23, 11].

8°. Innsbruck, 1925.

In Zeitschrift für katholische Theologie, Bd. 49, pp. 138-46.   [B.M.

3451. Mercer (Samuel A. B.). A new-found Book of Proverbs.

8°. Lancaster, U.S.A., 1926.

In Anglican Theological Review, Vol. 8, pp. 237-44. On the proverbs of Amen-em-ope.   [B.M.

3452. Oesterley (William Oscar Emil). The wisdom of Egypt and the Old Testament in the light of the newly discovered " Teaching of Amen-em-ope." pp. viii, 109.

8°. London, *etc., S.P.C.K.*, 1927.
                                                          [B.M.

3453. Ptah-hotep. The instruction of Ptah-hotep, *etc.* pp. 75.

8°. London, *Murray*, 1906.

Wisdom of the East Series. A translation [by Battiscombe G. Gunn]. Pp. 73-75, bibliography. Includes various translations, *etc.*, not given in this bibliography.   [B.M.

3454. ———: Les maximes de Ptahhotep, . . . par Eugène Dévaud. Texte. pp. 11, 53.   fol. Fribourg, Suisse, 1916.
                                                          [U.C.L.

3455. Rawnsley (Hardwicke D.).   Notes for the Nile, together with a metrical rendering of . . . the precepts of Ptah-hotep, *etc.* pp. xv, 324.   8°.   London, *Heinemann*, 1892.

Pp. 281-324, the precepts of Ptah-hotep.   [B.M.

3456. Revillout (E.).   Le premier et le dernier des moralistes de l'ancienne Égypte.   pp. 184.   8°.   Rome, 1905.

In Bessarione—revue des études orientales, 1905.   The precepts of Ptah-hotep, *etc.*, in French.   [B.M.

3457. Sayce (Archibald Henry).   Cairene folklore.
8°.   London, *F.-L.S.*, 1900.

In Folk-Lore, Vol. 11.   Pp. 382-383 contain a few proverbs.   [F.-L.S.

3458. Seidel (August).   Arabische Sprichwörter aus Egypten.
8°.   Berlin, *Reimer*, 1897.

In Zeitschrift für afrikanische und oceanische Sprachen, Jahrgang 3, pp. 338-343.   49 proverbs with German translations.   [B.M.

3459. Simpson (D. C.).   The Hebrew book of proverbs and the teaching of Amenophis.   4°.   London, 1926.

In Journal of Egyptian Archaeology, Vol. 12, pp. 232-239.   [B.M.

3460. Spitta (Wilhelm).   Grammatik des arabischen Vulgär-dialectes von Aegypten.   pp. xxxi, 519.
8°.   Leipzig, *Hinrich*, 1880.

Pp. 494-516, Amsâl.   301 proverbs transliterated and with German translations.   [B.M.

See also **3122.**

4. ABYSSINIA.

3461. Faïtlovitch (Jacques).   Proverbes abyssins, *etc.*   pp. 86.
8°.   Paris, *Geuthner*, 1907.

120 proverbs in the original, with transcriptions, French translations, and explanatory notes.   [B.M.

3462. Guidi (Ignazio).   Proverbi, strofe e racconti abissini, *etc.* pp. v, 131.   8°.   Roma, *R. Accademia dei Lincei*, 1894.

Originally published in the Giornale della Società Asiatica Italiana, Vol. 5, 1891, pp. 27-82.   Pp. 1-65 and 99-122, 119 proverbs in the original with Italian translations.   [B.M.

3463. ———: Nuovi proverbi, strofe e racconti abissini.   pp. 36.
8°.   Roma, 1892.

3464. Littmann (Enno).   Publications of the Princeton expedition to Abyssinia.   4 vols.   4°.   Leyden, *Brill*, 1910-1915.

Vol. 1, Nos. 36, 39, 40, the origin of three proverbs, Tigrē text.   Vol. 2, Nos. 36, 39, 40, the same proverbs translated into English.   [R.A.I.

3465. Mondon-Vidailhet (C.). Proverbes abyssins.

8°. Paris, 1904.

In Journal asiatique, 10ème série, tome 4, pp. 487-495. 25 proverbs with French translations and brief notes. [U.C.L.

3466. Petreius (Theodorus). Prophetia Jonae, ex Æthiopico in Latinum ad verbum versa, et notis atque adagiis illustrata etc. pp. 36.

4°. Lugduni Batavorum, *sumptibus Auctoris*, 1660.

Gratet-Duplessis, 86. Pp. 16-24, Adagia et sententiae quaedam Æthiopum.
[B.M.

3467. Praetorius (Franz). Tigrina-Sprüchwörter.

8°. Leipzig, *Brockhaus*, 1883-88.

In Zeitschrift der deutschen morgenländischen Gesellschaft, Bd. 37, pp. 443-450 : Bd. 38, pp. 481-485 : Bd. 39, 322-326 : Bd. 42, pp. 62-67. In the original, with German translations and notes. [B.M.

3468. Reinisch (Simon Leo). Die Saho-Sprache. 2 Bde.

8°. Wien, *Hölder*, 1889-90.

Bd. 1, pp. 299-306, 76 proverbs with German translations. [B.M.

3469. Schreiber (J.). Manuel de la langue Tigraï, *etc.* 2 pts.

8°. Vienne, *Hœlder*, 1887-93.

Pt. 2, pp. 191-197, 53 proverbs in the original, with French translations.
[B.M.

5. CENTRAL EAST.

GENERAL.

3470. Beech (Mervyn Worcester Howard). Aids to the study of Ki-Swahili, *etc.* pp. xvi, 159.

8°. [London], *Kegan Paul*, New York, *Dutton*, [1918].

Pp. 117-132, Enigmas and aphorisms with explanations as given by Wa-Swahili. [B.M.

3471. Capus (A.). Contes, chants et proverbes des Basumbwa dans l'Afrique Orientale. pp. 24. 4°. Berlin, 1897.

In Zeitschrift für afrikanische und oceanische Sprachen, Jahrgang 3, Heft 4, 1897. 10 proverbs with French translations and explanatory notes. [B.M.

3472. Steere (Edward). Swahili tales, as told by natives of Zanzibar. With an English translation. pp. xvi, 503.

sm. 8°. London, *Bell*, 1870.

Second edition. pp. xvi, 501.

8°. London, *S.P.C.K.*, [1889].

Pp. 191-195, a few proverbs with English translations. [R.A.I.

3473. Taylor (William Ernest). African aphorisms; or, saws from Swahili-land, *etc.* pp. xi, 182.

8°. London, *S.P.C.K.*, 1891

667 proverbs and sayings, with English translations and notes. [B.M.

6. UGANDA.

3474. Baskerville (George Knyfton) and **Pilkington** (George Lawrence). The Gospel in Uganda. pp. 52.

3d. 8°. London, *Church Missionary Society*, 1896.

Pp. 35-37, twenty proverbs out of several thousand in common use in Uganda. Translations and explanations are also given.   [B.M.

3475. Baskerville (Rosetta), *Mrs.* The king of the snakes, *etc.* pp. viii, 88 + 4 plates.   8°. London, *etc.*, *Sheldon Press*.

Pp. 87-88, 30 Luganda proverbs in English.   [B.M.

3476. Driberg (Jack Herbert). The Lango, a Nilotic tribe of Uganda. pp. 468. la. 8°. London, *Fisher Unwin*, [1923].

Pp. 136-137, proverbs with English translations.   [U.C.L.

3477. Kitching (Arthur Leonard). On the backwaters of the Nile: studies of some child races of Central Africa, *etc.* pp. 24, 295 + plates and 1 map.

8°. London, Leipsic, *Fisher Unwin*, 1912.

Pp. 132-138, proverbs, mostly in English, with explanations.   [U.C.L.

3478. Pilkington (George Lawrence) and **Cook** (Albert Ruskin). Engero za Baganda. Luganda proverbs. pp. 31.

8°. London, *S.P.C.K.*, 1901.

100 proverbs with notes. No translations.   [B.M.

3479. Roscoe (John). The Baganda. An account of their native customs and beliefs. pp. xix, 547. [Illustrated].

la. 8°. London, *Macmillan*, 1911.

Pp. 485-491, proverbs and sayings with English translations and explanations.   [U.C.L.

7. KENYA.

3480. Fokken (H.). Spruchweisheit der Masai.   Leipzig, 1914.

3481. Fuchs (Hanns). Sagen, Mythen und Sitten der Masai. Nach der Masaisprache und dem Englischen. pp. 144.

8°. Jena, *Costenoble*, 1910.

Pp. 63-67, proverbs of the Masai in German.   [R.A.I.

3482. Hollis (Alfred Claud). The Masai, their language and folk-lore. pp. xxviii, 356 + plates.

8°. Oxford, *Clarendon Press*, 1905.

Pp. 238-252, 75 Masai proverbs with English translations and notes: two indexes.   [U.C.L.

3483. ———: The Nandi, their language and folk-lore. pp. xl, 328 + plates and one map.

8°. Oxford, *Clarendon Press*, 1909.

Pp. 124-132, 57 Nandi proverbs, with literal and free English translations and notes.   [U.C.L.

3484. Hollis (Alfred Claud). Nyika proverbs.
8°. London, New York, *Macmillan*, 1916.
In Journal of the African Society, Vol. 16, pp. 62-70. With translations and notes. [B.M.

3485. ———: Taveta sayings and proverbs.
8°. London, New York, *Macmillan*, 1910.
In Journal of the African Society, Vol. 9, pp. 255-66. [B.M.

3486. Merker (M.). Die Masai, *etc*. pp. xvi, 424 + 6 plates.
la. 8°. Berlin, *Reimer*, 1904.
Pp. 219-220, Sprichwörter : in original and German.

8. TANGANYIKA.

3487. Dundas (*Hon*. Charles Cecil Farquharson). Kilimanjaro and its people, *etc*. pp. 349 + plates.
8°. London, *Witherby*, 1924.
Chapter 11, pp. 341-346, Chagga proverbs, with English translations and notes. [U.C.L.

3488. Seidel (August). Sprichwörter der Wa-Bondeï in Deutsch-Ostafrika. 8°. Berlin, *Reimer*, 1899-1900.
In Zeitschrift für afrikanische und oceanische Sprachen, Jahrgang 4, p. 287 : Jahrgang 5, pp. 76-78. 23 proverbs with literal German translations. [B.M.

3489. Woodward (Herbert Willoughby). Stories in the Bondei language, *etc*. pp. 59. 8°. London, *S.P.C.K.*, [1894].
Pp. 57-59, 85 proverbs, without translations or notes. [B.M.

9. NYASALAND.

3490. Johnson (William Percival). Chinyanja proverbs, *etc*. pp. 26. 8°. Cardiff, *Smith*, 1922.
101 proverbs in the original, with English translations and explanations. [B.M.

3491. Rattray (Robert Sutherland). Some folk-lore stories and songs in Chinyanja, *etc*. pp. 224.
8°. London, *S.P.C.K.*, 1907.
Pt 1, section 25, concludes with seven proverbs in the original. The translations are given in Pt. 2. [B.M.

10. MAURITIUS.

3492. Baissac (Charles). Étude sur le patois créole mauricien. pp. lvii, 233. 8°. Nancy, *Berger-Levrault*, 1880.
Pp. 146-171, proverbes et dictons. With French translations. [B.M.

11. MADAGASCAR.

3493. Clemes (S.). Malagasy proverbs.
8°. Antananarivo, *London Missionary Society*, 1885.
In Antananarivo Annual, Vol. 1, pp. 427-431. Malagasy proverbs with English translations. [R.A.I.

2 c

3494. Dahle (L.). Specimens of Malagasy folk-lore. pp. xiii, 457.   8°. Antananarivo, *Kingdon*, [1877].

Pp. 40-55, Hain-teny fohifohy sahalahala amy ny ohabolana. 302 entries in the original.   [B.M.

3495. Griffiths (David). A grammar of the Malagasy language, in the Ankova dialect. pp. xii, 244.

8°. Woodbridge, *Pite*, 1854.

Pp. 236-237, the proverbs or adages, Ohabolana. Examples. Half a dozen proverbs with English translations.   [B.M.

3496. Houlder (John Alden). Madagascar and its proverbs. Proverbial illustrations of Malagasy life and character. [Two articles in the Antananarivo Annual.

8°. Antananarivo, *London Missionary Society*, 1896.
    [R.A.I.

3497. ———: Ohabolana or Malagasy proverbs, illustrating the wit and wisdom of the Hova of Madagascar. . . . With translations into French by Henri Noyer. . . . Edited by James Sibree. Part 1, including 1236 proverbs. pp. [vi], 146, iii. 2 pts.   8°. Faravohitra, *Friends Foreign Mission Association*, 1915-16.

Arranged under subjects, in Malagasy, French, and English. The publication of these proverbs was begun in the Christmas 1894 number of the Antananarivo Annual, but discontinued in 1900. Explanatory notes are given.
    [F.-L.S. (1 pt.), B.M.

3498. Linton (Margaret M'Intosh). Madagascar proverbs.

8°. Boston, Mass., 1927.

In Atlantic Monthly, Vol. 139, pp. 352-354. Contains numerous examples in English.   [B.M.

3499. Marre de Marin (Aristide). Grammaire malagache, *etc.* pp. 126.   8°. Paris, *Maisonneuve*, 1876.

Pp. 115-120, Cent-et-un proverbes malagaches. In the original.   [B.M.

3500. Matthews (Thomas T.). Thirty years in Madagascar, *etc.* pp. xi, 384 + plates.   8°. London, *R.T.S.*, 1904.

Pp. 29-30, Malagasy proverbs about God.   [R.A.I.

3501. Moudain (G.). Des idées religieuses des Hovas avant l'introduction du Christianisme. pp. 175.

la. Paris, *Fischbacher*, [19—].

Pp. 5-7, on proverbs; pp. 62-68, Dieu dans les proverbes.

3502. Sibree (James), *Junior.* Madagascar and its people, *etc.* pp. 576.   8°. London, *R.T.S.*, [1870?].

Pp. 397-399, proverbs and sayings, some in Malagasy, about a God. [U.C.L.

3503. Standing (H. F.). Les fady malgaches, recueillis par H. F. Standing, traduits par A. Jully. pp. 120.

8°. Tananarive, *Imprimerie Officielle*, [190—].

From Bulletin de l'Académie malgache. 1768 examples in original and French.

12. NORTHERN RHODESIA.

3504. Melland (Frank Hulme). In witch-bound Africa. An account of the primitive Kaonde tribes and their beliefs. pp. 316 + plates and 3 maps. 8°. London, *Seeley*, 1923.

Chapter 24, pp. 279-282, Kaonde and Lunda proverbs with English translations. [U.C.L.

3505. Smith (Edwin William) and **Dale** (Andrew Murray). The Ila-speaking peoples of Northern Rhodesia. 2 vols.

8°. London, *Macmillan*, 1920.

Vol. 2, Chapter 27, pp. 311-324, proverbs. A statement of their importance for gaining an insight into the character of the people, followed by many examples : with English translations and notes. See also index for other proverbs quoted. [U.C.L.

13. SOUTH AFRICA.

3506. Beiderbecke (H.). Omiano vi Ovaherero. Proverbs of the Ovaherero. 8°. Cape Town, *Darter*, London, *Nutt*, 1880.

In Folk-Lore Journal [of the S.A. Folk-Lore Society], Vol. 2, Part 5, pp. 84-87. 12 proverbs with English translations and explanations. Vols. 1 and 2 of this journal contain a few other brief lists of proverbs. [B.M.

3507. Boas (Franz) and **Simango** (C. Kamba). Tales and proverbs of the Vandau of Portuguese South Africa.

la. 8°. 1922.

In Journal of American Folk-Lore, Vol. 35, pp. 151-204.

3508. Brown (John Tom). Among the Bantu nomads, *etc.* pp. 272 + plates. 8°. London, *Seeley*, 1926.

Pp. 197-203, proverbs with English translations (Bechuanaland). [R.A.I.

3509. Casalis (Eugène). Les Bassoutos, *etc.* pp. xvi, 370 + plates and map. 8°. Paris, *Meyrueis*, 1859.
English translation. pp. xix, 355 + maps.

8°. London, *Nisbet*, 1861.

Chap. 15 contains 50 proverbs in translation. [R.A.I.

3510. Crisp (William). The Bechuana of South Africa. pp. 60 + frontispiece. sm. 8°. London, *S.P.C.K.*, 1896.

Pp. 27-37, proverbs and fables. Some fifty proverbs are quoted in English. [B.M.

3511. German Colony. From a vanished German colony. . . . With an introduction by Odette St. Lys. pp. 195.

8°. London, Dublin, *Gypsy Press*, [1916].

P. 87, Setshuana proverbs : pp. 101-102, Herero sayings or proverbs : pp. 171-172, proverbs of the Ovaherero. [B.M.

3512. Jacottet (Édouard). Contes populaires des Bassutos, *etc.* pp. xiii, 292. 8°. Paris, *Leroux*, 1895.

Pp. 271-81, 60 proverbs with French translations. Pp. 282-289, bibliography of folk-lore. *Reviewed* in Folk-Lore, Vol. 7, 1896. [B.M.

3513. Junod (Henri A.). The life of a South African tribe. Second edition. 2 vols. la. 8°. London, *Macmillan*, 1927.

Vol. 2, pp. 176-84, Thonga folk-lore—A. Proverbial sayings and riddles.

3514. Kidd (Dudley). The essential Kafir. pp. xv, 436 + plates and a map.   8°. London, *Black*, 1904.
Second edition. pp. xiv, 435 + plates.
                                       8°. London, *Black*, 1925.

Pp. 294-297, Kafir proverbs in English. See also index for other proverbs mentioned. These proverbs are chiefly taken from Casalis " Les Bassoutos " and from " Zulu Izaga,' *q.v.*, No. **3522.**   [R.A.I.

3515. Mayr (Fr.). Zulu proverbs.   la. 8°. Wien, 1912.

In Anthropos, Bd. 7, pp. 957-963.   [U.C.L.

3516. Plaatje (Solomon Tshekisho). Sechuana proverbs, with literal translations and their European equivalents. pp. xii, 98 + plates.   obl. 8°. London, *Kegan Paul*, 1916.

Pp. ix-xii, preface : pp. 1-17, introduction : pp. 19-98, proverbs.   [R.A.I.

3517. Sekese (Azariele). Buka ea pokello ea mekhoa ea Ba-Sotho, le maele, le litsomo.   Moria, 1893.

A collection, in Sesuto, of the customs, proverbs and tales of the Basutos.

3518. ———: Mekhoa le Maele a Basotho (The customs and pro-verbial sayings of the Basuto). pp. 408.   8°.   1907.

Explication of 825 Sesuto proverbs.

3519. Theal (George McCall). A few Kaffir proverbs and figura-tive expressions.   8°. Cape Town, *Juta*, 1881.

In Cape Quarterly Review, October, 1881, pp. 67-74.

3520. ———: Kaffir folk-lore ; or, a selection from the traditional tales current among the people living on the Eastern border of the Cape Colony. pp. xii, 212.
                       8°. London, *Sonnenschein*, [1882].
Second edition. pp. xii, 226.   8°. London, 1886.

First edition, pp. 180-194, proverbs and figurative expressions. The same chapter in the second edition, pp. 191-206.   [F.-L.S.

3521. Vedder (   ), *Missionary.* Spruchweisheit der Herero. 4°. Braunschweig, *Vieweg*, 1914.

In Archiv für Anthropologie, N.F., Bd. 12, pp. 220-224. With numerous examples in German.   [B.M.

3522. Zulu Missionary. Zulu Izaga; that is proverbs, or out-of-the-way sayings of the Zulus; collected, translated, and interpreted by a Zulu missionary. pp. iii, 28 + plate.
              sm. 8°. Natal, *Sanderson*, London, *Trübner*, 1880.

Reprinted from the Natal Colonist. 189 proverbs with English translations and notes.   [U.C.L.

14. ANGOLA.

3523. Cordeiro da Matta (J. D.). Philosophia popular. Proverbos angolenses, *etc.* pp. 187.

8°. Lisboa, *Typographia Moderna*, 1891.

15. BELGIAN CONGO.

3524. Bittremieux (Leo). Mayombsche volkskunst, *etc.* pp. 227. 8°. Levven, *etc.*, *De Vlaamsche Boekenhalle*, [1924].
Pp. 71-88, proverbs in the original and Dutch.   [R.A.I.

3525. Claridge (G. Cyril). Wild bush tribes of tropical Africa, *etc.* pp. 314 + plates.   8°. London, *Seeley*, 1922.
Pp. 247-259, wisdom and wit of native folklore. Chiefly on proverbs and their importance, with many examples in English.   [R.A.I.

3526. Hurel (R. P. Eugène). La poésie chez les primitifs, ou contes, fables, récits, et proverbes du Ruanda (Lac Kivu). pp. 260.   Bruxelles, *Goemaere*, 1923.
Bibliothèque Congo, tome 9.

3527. Ruskin (E. A.). Mongo proverbs and fables. pp. [viii], 100.   sm. 8°. Bongandanga, *Congo Balolo Mission Press*, 1921.
Pp. 1-58, proverbs with English translations.   [F.-L.S.

3528. Samain (A.). Proverbes Baluba.
In Congo, revue générale de la colonie belge, 3e II, pp. 354-365.

3529. Starr (Frederick). Proverbs of Upper Congo tribes.
8°. Davenport, 1909.
In Proceedings of the Davenport Academy of Sciences, Vol. 12, pp. 176-200. Part of a paper entitled Ethnographic notes from the Congo Free State, *etc.* Also issued separately.   [B.M.

3530. Weeks (John H.). Among the primitive Bakongo. pp. 318 + plates and 1 map.   8°. London, *Seeley*, 1914.
Pp. 79-85, proverbs.   [F.-L.S.

16. FRENCH EQUATORIAL AFRICA.

3531. Bufe (   ), *Missionary*. Die Poesie der Duala-Neger in Kamerun, *etc.*   4°. Braunschweig, *Vieweg*, 1914.
In Archiv für Anthropologie, Neue Folge, Bd. 13. Pp. 55-58, Sprichwörter. 105 proverbs with German translations.   [B.M.

3532. Delafosse (Maurice). L'âme nègre. pp. 180.
Paris, *Payot*, 1922.
Contains proverbs of the natives chiefly of the Sudan and French equatorial colonies.

3533. Goehring (M.).   Aus der Volkslitteratur der Duala in Kamerun.   8°. Berlin, *Reimer*, 1900.

In Zeitschrift für afrikanische und oceanische Sprachen, Bd. 5, pp. 342-53.
100 proverbs, with notes in German.   [B.M.

3534. Hecklinger (Philipp).   Duala Sprichwörter, *etc.*
                                           8°. Berlin, Hamburg, 1921.

In Zeitschrift für eingeborenen Sprachen, Bd. 11, pp. 35-70, 125-160, 220-239,
306-315.   [B.M.

3535. Ris (Hans Nicolaus).   Elemente des Akwapim-Dialects der Odschi-Sprache, *etc.* pp. xviii, 232.
                                   8°. Basel, *Bahnmaiers Buchhandlung*, 1853.

Grammatical outline . . . of the Oji-language, *etc.* pp. viii,
276.   8°. Basel, 1854.

The English version is not a literal translation from, though it contains the
same material as, the original German. There is a list of 268 proverbs with
translations and notes.   [B.M.

3536. Seguin (C.).   Salutations et proverbes des Galoas.
                                           8°. Paris, 1909.

In Revue du mois, tome 8, pp. 319-30.   In French; commentary and
examples.   [B.M.

3537. Storbeck (Friedrich).   Fulsprichwörter aus Adamaua, Nord-Kamerun.   8°. Berlin, Hamburg, 1920.
In Zeitschrift für eingeborenen Sprachen, Bd. 10, pp. 106-22.   [B.M.

3538. Talbot (Percy Amaury).   In the shadow of the bush. pp. xiv, 500.   la. 8°. London, *Heinemann*, 1912.
P. 323, Ekoi proverbs, in original with translations.

3539. Trilles (H.).   Proverbes, légendes et contes Fangs. pp. 247.   8°. Neuchâtel, *Attinger*, 1905.
In Bulletin de la Société neuchâteloise de géographie, 1905.

17. NIGERIA.

3540. Banfield (A. W.).   Gamaga nya Nupe (Nupe proverbs), by A. W. B. pp. 124. sm. 8°. Shonga, *Niger Press*, 1916.
Contains 623 proverbs.

3541. —— and **Macintyre** (John Lester).   A grammar of the Nupe language, *etc.* pp. 186.   8°. London, *S.P.C.K.*, 1915.
Pp. 134-150, Some proverbs and common sayings. 150 entries with English
translations.   [B.M.

3542. Basden (George Thomas).   Among the Ibos of Nigeria. pp. 306 + plates and a map.   8°. London, *Seeley*, 1921.
Pp. 283-284, 160 proverbs, with English translations.   [U.C.L.

3543. Bowen (Thomas J.). Grammar and dictionary of the Yoruba language, *etc.* pp. xxi, 71, 136 + map.

4°. Washington, *Smithsonian Institution*, 1858.

In Smithsonian Contributions to Knowledge, Vol. 10, No. 4. Pp. 56-69, 100 proverbs in the original with English translations and notes. [U.C.L.

3544. Burton (*Sir* Richard Francis). Wit and wisdom from West Africa; or, a book of proverbial philosophy, idioms, enigmas, and laconisms. pp. xxxi, 455. 8°. London, *Tinsley*, 1865.

Pp. xi-xxx, preface, giving principal sources. Pp. 3-37, proverbs in the Wolof tongue. Pp. 39-59, proverbs in the Kanuri tongue. Pp. 61-130, proverbs in the Oji tongue. Pp. 131-175, proverbs in the Ga or Accra language. Pp. 177-320, proverbs in the Yoruba language. Pp. 321-412, proverbs in the Efik, or Old Calabar, language. Pp. 413-436, varia variorum. Pp. 437-442, proverbial sayings and idioms in the Mpangwe (Fan) tongue. Pp. 443-455, miscellaneous phrases and expressions. All the proverbs have English translations, and the more obscure have notes and explanations. *Reviewed* in the Quarterly Review, Vol. 125, pp. 217-254, and in the Shilling Magazine, Vol. 1, May, 1865, pp. 44-48. The latter review is also to be found in Stirling-Maxwell's collected works, Vol. 6, pp. 41-50. [U.C.L.

3545. Charlton (L.). A Hausa reading book. pp. 83 + 45 of facsimiles. 4/6. 12°. London, *Oxford University Press*, 1908.

Pp. 8-9, 15 proverbs.

3546. Crowther (Samuel). A vocabulary of the Yoruba language, together with introductory remarks by O. E. Vidal. pp. v, 287. 4°. London, *Seeley*, 1852.

Pp. 17-37, remarks on Yoruba proverbs, with examples and English translations. These occur in Vidal's introductory remarks, and are therefore not to be found in various other editions. [U.C.L.

3547. Edgar (Francis). Gbari grammar and dictionary. pp. 373. 15/-. 8°. Belfast, *printed by W. & G. Baird*, 1909.

Pp. 99-100, proverbs.

3548. ———: Litafi na tatsuniyoyi na Hausa. Litafi na-biyu, pp. xvi, 463. 10/6. 8°. Belfast, *Mayne*, 1911.

Pp. 427-450, proverbs, in the original. [B.M.

3549. Ellis (Alfred Burdon). The Yoruba-speaking peoples of the slave coast of West Africa, *etc.* pp. vii, 402.

8°. London, *Chapman*, 1894.

Pp. 218-240, Yoruba proverbs in English. [R.A.I.

3550. Fletcher (Roland S.). Hausa sayings and folk-lore, with a vocabulary of new words. pp. 173.

sm. 8°. London, *Frowde*, 1912.

Pp. 9-40, sayings in Hausa, with English translations. [F.-L.S.

3551. Koelle (Sigismund Wilhelm). African native literature, or proverbs, . . . in the Kanuri or Bornu language, *etc.* pp. xiv, 434. 8°. London, *Church Missionary House*, 1854.

Pp. 1-6, proverbs and sayings, *etc.* With English translations and notes.

[B.M.

3552. Leonard (Arthur Glyn). The Lower Niger and its tribes. pp. xxii, 564 + map.

8°. London, New York, *Macmillan*, 1906.

Pt. 2, Chapter 4, pp. 69-75, proverbs and fables. Discusses the prevalence and appropriateness of native proverbs, and gives many examples in English.

[U.C.L.

3553. Lethem (Gordon James). Colloquial Arabic. Shuwa dialect of Bornu, Nigeria and of the region of Lake Chad, etc. pp. xv, 487. 8°. London, *Government of Nigeria*, 1920.

Pp. 183-234, sayings, proverbs, riddles and songs.   [B.M.

3554. Merrick (George Charleton). Hausa proverbs, pp. viii, 113.   8°. London, *Kegan Paul*, 1905.

Between four and five hundred proverbs, common sayings, *etc.*, with English translations and notes.   [B.M.

3555. Mischlich (Adam). Lehrbuch der hausanischen Sprache. pp. 184.   8°. Berlin, *Reimer*, 1902.

Pp. 116-127, proverbs.

Lehrbuch der Hause-Sprache. pp. 250.

8°. Berlin, *Reimer*, 1911.

Pp. 130-143, 70 proverbs with transliterations, German translations and notes.

[B.M.

3556. Paddon (E. M.). Hausa proverbs and Hausa character.

8°. London, 1915.

In The Moslem World, Vol. 5, pp. 409-412.   [B.M.

3557. Prietze (Rudolf). Haussa-Sprichwörter und Haussa-Lieder, etc. pp. 85.   8°. Kirchhain N.-L., *Schmersow*, 1904.

Pp. 1-22, 103 proverbs with German translations and notes.   [B.M.

3558. Rattray (Robert Sutherland). Hausa folk-lore, customs, proverbs, etc. 2 vols. 8°. Oxford, *Clarendon Press*, 1913.

Vol. 2, pp. 251-278, proverbs in the Hausa language, transliterated, and in English.   [R.A.I.

3559. Schoen (Jacob Friedrich). Magána Hausa. Proverbs and tales in the Hausa language. pp. xx, 288.

8°. London, *S.P.C.K.*, 1885.

Pp. 5-10, 117 proverbs in the Hausa language. A second part entitled "African proverbs, tales," *etc.*, gives the translation of the other Hausa texts, but the proverbs appear to have been omitted.   [B.M.

3560. ——: Appendix to Dictionary of the Hausa language (1876). pp. 206. 8°. London, *Church Mission House*, 1888.

Pp. 204-6, a continuation of the proverbs in **3559,** Nos. 118-188, in Hausa only.

3561. Stirling (William), *afterwards* **Stirling-Maxwell** (*Sir* William), *Bart*. Wit and wisdom of West Africa. Review of " Wit and Wisdom from W. Africa." . . . Compiled by Richard F. Burton. [*q.v.* **3544**.] 8°. London, 1865.

First published in the Shilling Magazine, Vol. 1, May, 1865, pp. 44-48. Later included in his collected works (1891), Vol. 6 (Miscellaneous essays and addresses), pp. 41-50. [U.C.L. (Works).

3562. Thomas (Northcote Whitridge). Anthropological report on the Ibo-speaking peoples of Nigeria. 6 parts.
8. London, *Harrison*, 1913-1914.

Part 3, pp. 3-47, proverbs arranged by subjects. Part 6, pp. 1-75, over 1000 Ibo proverbs, with English translations, arranged in subject.
[F.-L.S. (Part 3), U.C.L. (Part 6).

3563. Trautmann (René). La littérature populaire à la Cote des Esclaves. Contes. Proverbes. Devinettes. pp. vii, 105.
fr.30 France et colonies; fr.45 étranger.
Paris, *Institut d'Ethnologie*, 1927.

Travaux et Mémoires de l'Institut d'Ethnologie, tome 4.

3564. Tremearne (Arthur John Newman). Hausa superstitions and customs. pp. xv, 548 + plates and a map.
8°. London, *Bale*, 1913.

P. 13, Hausa fondness for proverbs : pp. 60-66, Hausa proverbs in English.
[U.C.L.

18. TOGOLAND.

3565. Prietze (Rudolf). Beiträge zur Erforschung von Sprache und Volksgeist in der Togo-Kolonie.
8°. Berlin, *Reimer*, 1897.

In Zeitschrift für afrikanische und oceanische Sprachen, Jhrg. 3, pp. 17-64. Contains a list of 117 proverbs with German translations and explanations.
[B.M.

3566. Schoenhaerl (Josef). Volkskundliches aus Togo, *etc.* pp. x, 204. 8°. Leipzig, *Koch*, 1909.

Reviewed in Folk-Lore, Vol. 21. Pp. 85-99, 137-142, 200 proverbs with German translations.
[B.M.

3567. Spieth (Jakob). Die Ewe-Stämme. Material zur Kunde des Ewe-Volkes in Deutsch-Togo. pp. 80, 962.
la. 8°. Berlin, *Reimer*, 1906.

Pp. 599-612, Das Geistesleben der Hoer—E. Sprichwörter, lododowo. Proverbs in original, translated into German, with explanation.

19. GOLD COAST.

3568. Buergi (E.). Sammlung von Ewe-Sprichwörtern.
4°. Braunschweig, *Vieweg*, 1915.

In Archiv für Anthropologie, N.F., Bd. 13, pp. 415-50. 925 proverbs with German translations and notes.
[B.M.

3569. Cardinall (Allan Wolsey). In Ashanti and beyond, *etc.* pp. 288 + 16 plates.

8°. London, *Seeley, Service & Co.*, 1927.

Chap. 18, pp. 268-70, Conundrums and proverbs.

3570. Christaller (J. G.). Twi mmebusem mpensãahansĩa mmoaano. A collection of three thousand and six hundred Tshi proverbs in use among negroes . . . speaking the Asante and Fante language, *etc.* pp. xii, 512.

8°. Basel, *Basel German Evangelical Missionary Society*, 1879.

Proverbs arranged alphabetically, without translations or explanations. [B.M.

3571. Ellis (Alfred Burdon). The Ewe-speaking peoples of the slave coast of West Africa, their religion, manners, customs, laws, languages, *etc.* pp. viii, 331 + map.

8°. London, *Chapman*, 1890.

Pp. 258-268, proverbs in English. [F.-L.S.

3572. O'Kraku (John Atua Simeon). Dagomba grammar. pp. 152. sm. 8°. Cambridge, *University Press*, 1917.

Pp. 83-90, proverbial expressions.

3573. Rattray (Robert Sutherland). Ashanti. pp. 348 + plates.

8°. Oxford, *Clarendon Press*, 1923.

See index for proverbs and sayings represented by weights. [R.A.I.

3574. ———: Ashanti proverbs. . . . Translated from the original with grammatical and anthropological notes, *etc.* pp. 190.

8°. Oxford, *Clarendon Press*, 1916.

Arranged under subject headings in Ashanti and English. *Reviewed in* Folk-Lore, Vol. 28, pp. 108-11. [R.A.I.

3575. Schlegel (J. B.). Schlüssel zur Ewe-Sprache, *etc.* pp. xxiv, 328. 8°. Stuttgart, *Steinkopf*, 1857.

Pp. 122-148, Abeo-Sprichwörter. 130 proverbs with German translations and notes. [B.M.

3576. Zimmermann (J.). A grammatical sketch of the Akra— —or Gâ—language, *etc.* 2 vols.

8°. Stuttgart, *Steinkopf*, 1858.

Vol. 1, pp. 158-177, 220 proverbs with English translations. [B.M.

20. SIERRA LEONE.

3577. Douglin (P. H.). A reading book in the Soso language. pp. viii, 120. 8°. London, *S.P.C.K.*, 1887.

Pp. 99-105, proverbs : no translations or notes. [B.M.

3578. Ellis (George Washington). Negro culture in West Africa ; a social study of the negro group of Vai-speaking people, with . . . one hundred and fourteen proverbs, *etc.* pp. 290.

New York, *Neale Publishing Co.*, 1914.

Chapter 8, Vai proverbs.

3579. Koelle (Sigismund Wilhelm). Outlines of a grammar of the Vei language, *etc.* pp. vi, 256.

8°. London, *Church Missionary House*, 1854.

Pp. 67-68, a few proverbs with English translations. [B.M.

3580. Migeod (Frederick William Hugh). A view of Sierra Leone. pp. xi, 351. la. 8°. London, *Kegan Paul*, 1926.

Chap. 23 (pp. 276-80), Mende, Vai, Temne, and Kuranko proverbs in the original, with English translations. [F.-L.S.

3581. Schlenker (Christian Friedrich). A collection of Temne traditions, fables and proverbs, *etc.* pp. xxii, 298.

8°. London, *Church Missionary Society*, 1861.

Pp. 98-101, 10 proverbs, with English translations, notes, and comparisons.
[B.M.

21. FRENCH WEST AFRICA.

3582. Moussa Travélé (   ). Proverbes et contes bambara, *etc.* pp. 240. 8°. Paris, *Geuthner*, 1923.

Pp. 35-50, 101 proverbs with French translations and notes. [B.M.

AMERICAN

3583. Anderson (Izett) and **Cundall** (Frank). Jamaica negro proverbs and sayings, collected and classified according to subjects. pp. 48.
1/. 8°. Kingston, Institute of Jamaica, 1910.
737 proverbs. [B.M.]

3584. Armbrister (Hilda). Proverbs from Abaco, Bahamas.
8°. Lancaster, Pa., New York, 1917.
In Journal of American Folk-Lore, Vol. 30, p. 274. 15 entries. [B.M.]

3585. Audain (J. J.). Recueil de proverbes créoles. . . . 2me édition, etc. pp. 40.
8°. Port-au-Prince, Imprimerie Audain, 1877.
1011 proverbs, without notes or translations. [B.M.]

3586. Banbury (T.). Jamaica superstitions; or, the obeah book, etc. pp. iv, 43.　　　　　8°. Jamaica, de Souza, 1894.
Pp. 39-43, maxims and proverbs of the people. [B.M.]

3587. Bartlett (John Russell). Dictionary of Americanisms, etc. pp. xxvii, 412. 8°. New York, Bartlett and Welford, 1848. Fourth edition. pp. xlvi, 813.
8°. Boston, Little, Brown, 1877.
In the first edition proverbs are included in the body of the work, in later editions they form a separate list at the end. Fourth edition, pp. 801-806, proverbs. [B.M.]

3588. Bates (William C.). Creole folk-lore from Jamaica. **1.** Proverbs.
8°. Boston, etc., American Folk-Lore Society, 1895.
In Journal of American Folk-Lore, Vol. 9, pp. 38-42. 76 entries. [B.M.]

3589. Beckwith (Martha Warren). Jamaica proverbs, collected by M. W. Beckwith. pp. 137.
8°. Poughkeepsie, N.Y., 1925.
Publications of the Folk-Lore Foundation, Vassar College, No. 6. A collection of 972 proverbs, arranged alphabetically under the first word, with British and African parallels. The material has been collected from young women students, negro servants, and published collections. Reviewed in Folk-Lore, Vol. 37, pp. 411-412. [F.-L.S.]

3590. Bigelow (John). The wit and wisdom of the Haytians. pp. 112. 8°. New York, *Scribner & Armstrong*, 1877.

Originally published in Harper's Magazine, Vol. 51, pp. 130-136, 288-291, 438-441, 583-587. 92 proverbs with comments explanatory and illustrative.

[B.M.

3591. Blanco y Sánchez (Rufino). Refranero pedagógico hispano-americano. Tercera edición. pp. 17.

40 centimos. 12°. Madrid, 1920.

An alphabetical list. [B.M.

3592. Bonaparte (Roland Napoléon), *Prince*. Les habitants de Suriname, *etc.* pp. viii, 226. fol. Paris, *Quantin*, 1884.

Pp. 182-186, proverbes nègres, avec leur traduction française et leur interprétation par les proverbes européens. [B.M.

3593. Brueyre (Loys). Proverbes créoles de la Guyane française. 8°. Paris, *Maisonneuve*, 1883.

In Almanach des traditions populaires, 1883, pp. 110-111.

3594. Cannobbio (Agustin). Refranes chileños. pp. 118.

Barcelona, 1901.

3595. Clews, *afterwards* **Parsons** (Elsie Worthington). Riddles and proverbs from the Bahama Islands.

8°. Lancaster, Pa., *American Folk-Lore Society*, 1919.

In Journal of American Folk-Lore, Vol. 32, pp. 439-41.

3596. Espinosa (Aurelio M.). New-Mexican Spanish folk-lore. 4. Proverbs.

8°. Lancaster, Pa., *etc.*, *American Folk-Lore Society*, 1913.

In Journal of American Folk-Lore, Vol. 26, pp. 97-122. [B.M.

3597. ———: Spanish folk-lore in New Mexico.

Santa Fé, *New Mexico*, 1926.

In New Mexico Historical Review, Vol. 1, No. 2, pp. 135-155. Pp. 146-148 deal with proverbs; some fifty examples are given, half with assonance or rhyme and half without.

3598. Fortier (Alcée). Bits of Louisiana folk-lore. pp. 69.

8°. Baltimore, 1888.

Separate publication of an article in Transactions and Proceedings of the Modern Language Association of America, Vol. 3. Pp. 60-62, a few Creole proverbs. [B.M.

3599. Franck (Harry A.). Jamaica proverbs.

8°. New Haven, Conn., 1921

In Dialect Notes, Vol. 5, Pt. 4, pp. 98-108. A list of 468 proverbs. These are later to be used as illustrative sentences in a forthcoming article on the dialect of Jamaica. [B.M.

3600. Franklin (Benjamin). Poor Richard, 1733. An almanack for the year of Christ 1733. . . . By Richard Saunders Philom. [*pseud.* of B. Franklin].
12°. Philadelphia, *Franklin*, 1733.
Poor Richard's almanack. . . . Selections . . . with a facsimile in reduction of the almanack for 1733, *etc.* pp. 221 + facsimile.
sm. 8°. New York, *Century Co.*, 1898.

The numerous almanacks of Poor Richard were very popular, and contained large numbers of proverbs. These are gathered together in the Selections. Another excellent edition of the 1733 almanack was published in 1894, with a foreword by J. Bigelow. "The Way to Wealth," which is full of proverbial wisdom, was prefaced to the almanack for 1758 and was frequently reprinted. It was translated into French as the "Science du Bonhomme Richard" and enjoyed a great vogue. It was also translated into other languages. [B.M.

3601. Grant (Cyril F.). Negro proverbs collected in Jamaica, 1887.
8°. London, 1917.
In Folk-Lore, Vol. 28, pp. 315-317. [F.-L.S.

3602. Haurigot (Georges). Littérature orale de la Guyane française. Proverbes.
8°. Paris, *Lechevalier*, 1893.
In Revue des traditions populaires, Vol. 8, pp. 164-173, and pp. 291-394. Proverbs in the dialect of French Guiana with French translations and occasional explanatory notes. [B.M.

3603. Hearn (Lafcadio). Gombo Zhèbes; little dictionary of Creole proverbs selected from six Creole dialects, *etc.* pp. 42.
4°. New York, *Coleman*, 1885.
A collection of 352 Creole sayings with French and English translations, with footnotes. Contains a small bibliography. [B.M.

3604. Hoffmann (W. J.). Folk-lore of the Pennsylvania Germans.
8°. Boston, 1889.
In Journal of American Folk-Lore, Vols. 1-2. Vol. 2, pp. 197-202, 79 proverbs. [B.M.

3605. Johnson (John H.). Folk-lore from Antigua, British West Indies.
8°. Lancaster, Pa., New York, 1921.
In Journal of American Folk-Lore, Vol. 34, pp. 82-83. 5 proverbs. [B.M.

3606. Jones (D. Hedog-). West Indian studies. 4 pts.
8°. Grenada, 1916.
Pp. 22-28, proverbs in English. [R.A.I.

3607. Knortz (Carl). Folkloristische Streifzüge. Bd. 1, pp. 431.
8°. Oppeln, Leipzig, *Maske*, 1899.
No more published. Pp. 210-223, Amerikanische Sprichwörter und Redensarten. [B.M.

3608. Loscombe (A. R.). Jamaica wit and wisdom.
8°. London, 1903.
In Gentleman's Magazine, Vol. 295, pp. 564-70. [B.M.

3609. Morison (O.), *Mrs.* Tsimshian proverbs.
> 8°. Boston, New York, *American Folk-Lore Society*, 1889.

In Journal of American Folk-Lore, Vol. 2, pp. 285-286.   [B.M., F.-L.S.

3610. Newell (W. W.). Proverbs and phrases.
> 8°. Boston, New York, *American Folk-Lore Society*, 1889.

In Journal of American Folk-Lore, Vol. 2, pp. 153-154.   [B.M.

3611. Proverbs. Jamaica proverbs and John Canoe alphabet.
Illustrated by Miss Heaven.   Kingston, [1896].

3612. ———: Proverbs.   8°. Lancaster, Pa., New York, 1919.

In Journal of American Folk-Lore, Vol. 32, pp. 441-442. 12 proverbs from
Eleuthera, followed by 25 Geechee and other proverbs. 3 proverbs from Virginia
are given on p. 375.   [B.M.

3613. Radcliffe (John). Lectures on negro proverbs, with a preliminary paper on negro literature. Kingston, Jamaica, 1869.

3614. Rampini (Charles). Letters from Jamaica, *etc.* pp. 182.
> 12°. Edinburgh, *Edmonston & Douglas*, 1873.

Pp. 175-182, Negro proverbs.   [B.M.

3615. Santa-Anna Nery (Frederico-José de), *Baron.* Folk-lore
brésilien, *etc.* pp. xii, 272.   8°. Paris, *Perrin*, 1889.

Pp. 85-94, Quatrains populaires. . . . Proverbes, *etc.* The proverbs are few,
and are given in French only.   [B.M.

3616. Speirs (James). The proverbs of British Guiana.
> Demerara, 1902.

3617. Starr (Frederick). Notes upon the ethnography of southern
Mexico.   la. 8°. Davenport, 1901.

In Proceedings of the Davenport Academy of Sciences, Vol. 8. Pp. 130-1,
some Tlaxcalan (Aztec) proverbs.   [U.C.L.

3618. Thomas (J. J.). The theory and practice of Creole
grammar. pp. viii, 134.
> 8°. Port-of-Spain, *Chronicle Publishing Office*, 1869.

Pp. 120-127, Creole proverbs.

3619. Waugh (F. W.). Canadian folk-lore from Ontario.
> 8°. Lancaster, Pa., New York, 1918.

In Journal of American Folk-Lore, Vol. 31. Pp. 34-37, proverbs, sayings,
etc.   [B.M.

3620. Wintemberg (W. J.). Folk-lore collected in the counties of
Oxford and Waterloo, Ontario.
> 8°. Lancaster, Pa., New York, 1918.

In Journal of American Folk-Lore, Vol. 31. Pp. 141-142, proverbs, sayings,
expressions, and witticisms. For a few examples from Grey county, Ontario,
see p. 103.   [B.M.

See also **612, 945.**

AUSTRALASIAN AND PACIFIC

3621. Best (Elsdon). Maori eschatology, *etc.*
8°. Wellington, 1906.

In Transactions and Proceedings of the New Zealand Institute, Vol. 38, 1905, pp. 148-239. Pp. 226-227, expressions, proverbs, aphorisms, *etc.*, pertaining to decay and death. [U.C.L.

3622. Colenso (W.). Contributions towards a better knowledge of the Maori race. Part 2. Proverbs and proverbial sayings.
8°. Wellington, 1880.

In Transactions and Proceedings of the New Zealand Institute, Vol. 12, 1879, pp. 108-147. 235 proverbs with English translations and notes. [U.C.L.

3623. Collocott (E. E. V.) and **Havea** (J.). Proverbial sayings of the Tongas. Honolulu, *Bishop Museum*, 1922.

3624. Firth (Raymond). Primitive economics of the New Zealand Maori. pp. xxiv, 505.
25/-. la. 8°. London, *Routledge*, 1929.

Contains a great deal of material on proverbs, for which see the index.

3624a. ———: Proverbs in native life, with special reference to those of the Maori. 8°. London, 1926.

In Folk-Lore, Vol. 37, pp. 134-153, 245-270. Many proverbs in Maori, with English translations included as illustrations of points in the text. [F.-L.S.

3625. Green (Laura S.). Hawaiian stories and wise sayings. pp. x, 65. 8°. Poughkeepsie, N.Y., 1923.

Vassar College : Publications of the Folk-Lore Foundation, No. 3. Pp. 55-65, Olelo Noeau : wise sayings. [F.-L.S.

3626. Grey (*Rt. Hon. Sir* George). Ko nga whakapepeha me nga whakaahuareka a nga tipuna o aotea-roa, *etc.* pp. v, 120. 8°. Cape Town, *Solomon*, 1857.

Stirling-Maxwell, p. 41. New Zealand proverbs with translations, arranged in alphabetical order. At the end of the book are given a few fables from which some proverbs have been taken. Most of these proverbs are founded on local legends. The appendix contains the proverbs of Te Paki, with a translation ; a treatise drawn up by a native from the dictation of a native chief. [B.M.

3627. Hadfield (Emma). Among the natives of the Loyalty group. pp. xix, 316. [Illustrated].
8°. London, *Macmillan*, 1920

Pp. 310-312, Lifuan proverbs with English translations. [U.C.L.

3628. Hochstetter (Ferdinand von). Neu-Seeland, *etc.* pp. xx,
   555 + plates and maps.   4°. Stuttgart, *Cotta,* 1863.
   English translation.   8°. Stuttgart, 1867.
   Pp. 518-519, Sprichwörter. Maori proverbs in the original, with German
   translations.   [B.M.

3629. Ivens (Walter George). Melanesians of the south-east
   Solomon Islands. la. 8°. London, *Kegan Paul, etc.,* 1927.
   Pp. 401-403, proverbial sayings.   [B.M.

3630. New Zealand. New Zealand legends and proverbs.
                                        8°. London, 1876.
   In All the year round, New Series, Vol. 16, pp. 175-180. [U.C.L.

3631. Shortland (Edward). Traditions and superstitions of the
   New Zealanders. *First edition.* pp. xii, 300.
                          8°. London, *Longmans,* 1854.
   Second edition. **pp. xi, 316.**
                          8°. London, *Longmans,* 1856.
   Chap. 10, Whakatauki, or proverbs with English translations.
                              [U.C.L. (1856 edition), B.M.

3632. Smith (T. H.). On Maori proverbs.
                          8°. Wellington, 1890.
   In Transactions of the New Zealand Institute, Vol. 22, 1889, pp. 111-118.
                                                         [U.C.L.

3633. Taylor (Richard). Te Ika a Maui; or New Zealand and
   its inhabitants. . . . Illustrating the origin, manners . . .
   proverbs . . . of the Maori and Polynesian races in general.
   First edition. pp. xiv, 490.
                  8°. London, *Wertheim & Macintosh,* 1855.
   Second edition. pp. xv, 730.
              8°. London, *Macintosh,* Wanganui, *Jones,* 1870.
   Chap. 9 (1st edition), Chap. 16 (2nd edition), 85 proverbs with translations.
                              [F.-L.S., U.C.L. (1870 ed.), B.M.

2 D

NON-REGIONAL

1. ANIMALS.

3634. B. (A.). Pies i wilk w zdaniach i przysłowiach w porządku abecadłowym ułożonych, *etc.*
4°. Warszawa, 1856.

Bernstein, 2576. *In* Józefa Ungra Kalendarz Warszawski popularno-naukowy na rok przestępny 1856, pp. 114-119. The author is probably Adam Bartoszewicz. Proverbs on the dog and wolf.

3635. Brinkmann (Friedrich). Die Metaphern. . . . 1. Band Die Thierbilder der Sprache. pp. [v], 600.
8°. Bonn, *Marcus*, 1878.

A large number of the metaphors quoted are true proverbs. They deal with domestic animals, and are in many different languages. [B.M.

3636. Brunet (Jean). L'âne dans les proverbes provençaux.
8°. Paris, 1890, 1893-95.

In La Tradition, tom. 4, 7, 8, 9. [B.M.

3637. Daumas (Melchior Joseph Eugène). Les chevaux du Sahara, *etc.* pp. 384. 8°. Paris, *Chamerot*, 1851.
Fifth edition. pp. 438. 12°. Paris, *Michel Lévy*, 1858.
English translation. pp. xi, 355.
8°. London, *Allen*, 1863.

The early chapters contain a few proverbs and sayings about horses. [B.M.

3638. Dutailly (M. A. J.). Proverbes, dictons, et locutions diverses à propos de chats et de chiens, par M. A. J. D[utailly]. pp. 101. 12°. Noyon, *Andrieux*, 1885.
3rd edition. Paris, 1887.

3639. ———: Proverbes, dictons et locutions diverses à propos de singes, par M. A. J. D[utailly]. pp. 25.
12°. Noyon, *Andrieux*, 1885.

3640. Fumagalli (Giuseppe). Popolarità dei gatti. Milano, 1890.

In L'Illustrazione italiana, anno 17, No. 2. An article on the proverbs and popular superstitions about cats.

3641. Gay (Jean). Les chats. . . . Chansons, proverbes, superstitions . . . concernant la gent féline, *etc.* pp. 300.
12°. Paris, *chez l'auteur*, Bruxelles, *Gay*, 1866.

Pp. 201-208, proverbs in various languages concerning cats. [B.M.

3642. Genthius (Hermannus). Epistula de proverbiis Romanorum ad animalium naturam pertinentibus, *etc.* pp. 12.

4°. Hamburgi, *Meissner*, 1881.

Bernstein, 1268.

3643. Gesner (Conrad). Historiae animalium, *etc.* 5 vols.

fol. Tiguri, *Froschoverus*, 1551-1587.

Another edition. Thierbuch, *etc.*

fol. Zurych, *Froschoverus*, 1563.

Another edition. fol. 1669.

Gratet-Duplessis, 569. Proverbs and sayings are given at the end of some of the descriptions of animals. These proverbs are more numerous in the Latin edition.

3644. Gregor (Walter). Hippic folk-lore from the north-east of Scotland. 8°. London, 1884.

In Folk-Lore Journal, Vol. 2, pp. 106-109. Contains some fifty proverbs on horses. [F.-L.S.

3645. Guerrazzi (Francesco Domenico). L'Asino, *etc.* pp. 625.

4°. Torino, *Franco*, 1857.

Another edition. pp. 413. 8°. Roma, *Perino*, [1885].

Contains a list of some sixty Italian proverbs concerning the ass. [B.M.

3646. Houghton (H. P.). The moral significance of animals as indicated in Greek proverbs. Baltimore, *Hopkins*, 1915.

3647. Koehler (Carl Sylvio). Das Tierleben im Sprichwort der Griechen und Römer. Nach Quellen und Stellen in Parallele mit dem deutschen Sprichwort. pp. viii, 221.

8°. Leipzig, *Fernau*, 1881.

Arranged alphabetically by the German names of the animals. [F.-L.S.

3648. Labat-Lapeyrière ( ). Dictons et proverbes relatifs au cheval. Paris, 1900.

3649. Mantica (Nicolò). Raccolta di proverbi e dittati ippici pp. 110. 8°. Udine, *Tipografia del Patronato*, 1883.

741 proverbs, of which 177 are in either the Venetian or Friuli dialects. Many of the proverbs are merely variants of each other. Pp. 11-15, bibliography.

3650. Medicus (Wilhelm). Die Naturgeschichte nach Wort und Spruch des Volkes. pp. 231.

8°. Nördlingen, *Beck*, 1867.

Contains amongst other sayings, *etc.*, a number of proverbs. [B.M.

3651. ——: Die niedere Thierwelt im Dichter- und Volksmunde. pp. 57. 8°. Leipzig, *Thiel*, 1882.

Bernstein, 2128.

3652. ——: Das Thierreich im Volksmunde. Eine humoristische Naturgeschichte. pp. 244. 8°. Leipzig, *Thiel*, 1880.

Bernstein, 2127.

3653. Mezger (Moritz). Beitrag zur Erklärung der Satiren des Horatius, *etc.* pp. 46. 4°. Augsburg, *Pfeiffer*, n.d.

Bernstein, 2183. Pp. 22-45, Anhang. Der Esel im griechischen und lateinischen Sprichworte. (83 entries.)

3654. Moliné y Roca (Miguel). Paremiografía taurina, *etc.* pp v, 26. 8°. Barcelona, 1888.

A collection of proverbs, maxims, anecdotes, *etc.* 100 copies published.

3655. Otto (A.). Zu den Tiersprichwörtern. 8°. Leipzig, 1886.

In Archiv für lateinische Lexikographie, Jahrgang 3, pp. 388-397. [U.C.L.

3656. P. Zu den lateinischen Sprichwörtern und sprichwörtlichen Redensarten. 8°. Leipzig, 1886.

In Archiv für lateinische Lexikographie, Jahrgang 3, pp. 59-69. Paper on animals in Latin proverbs. [B.M.

3657. P. (R.). Der Esel im deutschen Sprichwort.
8°. Leipzig, *Brockhaus*, 1864.

In Deutsches Museum, October, 1864, pp. 512-517. [B.M.

3658. Pitrè (Giuseppe). The swallow book. . . . Rendered into English . . . by Ada Walker Camehl. [Illustrated]. pp. 158. 8°. New York, *etc., American Book Company*, [1912].

Pp. 105-115, The swallow in proverbs and riddles. [B.M.

3659. ———: Tradizioni e proverbi siciliani intorno alle api.
la. 8°. Jesi, *Flori*, 1885.

In Le Api e i Fiori, periodico mensile, *etc.*, anno 3, No. 5, pp. 33-35.

3660. Rolland (Eugène). Faune populaire de la France, *etc.* 6 tom. 8°. Paris, *Maisonneuve*, 1877-1883. *Nouvelle série*, tom. 7-13. 8°. Paris, 1906-[1911].

No more published. Contains many proverbs concerning animals, chiefly in French. [B.M.

3661. Rozan (Charles). Les animaux dans les proverbes. 2 tom.
8°. Paris, *Ducrocq*, [1902].

The second part deals with birds. This is not merely a list of proverbs, but rather a commentary on the popular view of the characteristics of various animals, and its crystallization and development in proverbs. [B.M.

3662. Sébillot (Paul Yves). Les crustacés. la. 8°. Paris, 1892.

In Revue des traditions populaires, tome 7, pp. 608-9. Some twenty proverbs concerning crabs, oysters, *etc.* The collection from which the proverb is taken is indicated in each case. [B.M.

3662a. Steiner (C. J.). Die Tierwelt nach ihrer Stellung in Mythologie . . . im Sprichwort und Volksfest. pp. xi, 323.
8°. Gotha, 1891.

3663. Thuengen (C. E. von), *Freiherr.* Der Hase . . . dessen Naturgeschichte, Jagd und Hege, *etc.* [Illustrated]. pp. xiv, 431. 8°. Berlin, *Wiegandt, Hempel & Parey*, 1878.

Pp. 13-14, German proverbs about hares.

3664. Udziela (Seweryn). Pies w przysłowiach polskich i zwrotach mowy. Zestawił S[eweryn] U[dziela], *etc.* pp. 11. 8°. w Krakowie, *Nakładem autora: Drukarnia Koziańskiego*, 1887.

A separate issue of an article in Opiekun Zwierząt, *etc.* Rok 1, Nos. 5-7. 143 entries.

3665. Van Vechten (Carl). The tiger in the house. pp. 367 + plates. 8°. London, *Heinemann*, 1921.

Pp. 137-143, proverbs concerning cats. [B.M.

3666. Volpini (Carlo). 516 proverbi sul cavallo, *etc.* pp. xxiii, 172. 12°. Milano, *Hoepli*, 1896.

Italian proverbs, with notes. [B.M.

3667. Weryho (Maryja). Z życia zwierząt. Pies, *etc.* pp. 68. 16°. Warszawa, *Kassa Dr. Mianowskiego*, 1889.

Contains several proverbs concerning dogs.

3668. Willems (J. F.). Reinaert de vos, *etc.* pp. lxvii, 352 + plates. 8°. Gent, *Gyselynck*, 1836.

Pp. 295-301, Nederlandsche spreekwoorden van den vos, den wolf, *etc.* [B.M.

3669. Wójcicki (A.). Przysłowia o zwierzętach.—Dalszy ciąg przysłów myśliwskich o ptakach.

8°. w Warszawie, 1838, 1840.

Bernstein, 4090. Two articles in Sylwan, *etc.*, 1838, pp. 524-528, and 1840, pp. 557-563. Besides the Polish proverbs, there are some from other countries given in the original languages.

3670. Wossidlo (Richard). Mecklenburgische Volksüberlieferungen, *etc.* 3 Bde. 8°. Wismar, *Hinstorff*, 1897-1906.

Bd. 2, pp. 29-42, Sprichwörter, in welchen Thiere redend eingeführt werden. A few proverbs are also given in Bd. 3. [B.M.

See also index at end for references to animals in other sections.

2. THE BODY.

3671. Griessbach (Michael Gottlieb). Abhandlung von den Fingern, deren Verrichtungen und symbolische Bedeutungen, *etc.* pp. [xxiv], 312, [24].

8°. Leipsig, Eisenach, *Griessbach*, 1756.

Gratet-Duplessis, 640. Contains the explanation of a number of German proverbs. Nopitsch, p. 64, attributes it to M. G. Griessbach. [B.M.

3672. Mensinga (J. A. M.). De haan. Eene oudheidkundige voorlezing, gehouden in de Amsterdamsche afdeeling der Hollandsche Maatschappij van fraaije Kunsten en Wetenschappen. pp. 177-220. 8°. [Amsterdam, 1849].

Bernstein, 2156, says this is taken from an unknown book published at Amsterdam in 1849. Pp. 210-219, Spreekwijzen en spreekwoorden aan de haan ontleend.

3673. Otto (A.).   Der menschliche Körper und seine Teile im Sprichwort.   8°. Leipzig, 1889.

In Archiv für lateinische Lexikographie, Jahrgang 6, pp. 309-340.   [U.C.L.

3674. Scarlattini (Ottavio).   L'huomo e sue parte figurato e simbolico, *etc.* 2 tom.   fol. Bologna, *Monti,* 1684.
Latin translation. 2 tom.
                          fol. Augustae Vindelicorum & Dilingae, 1695.

The description of each part of the body is followed by a section dealing with the proverbs which concern it.   [B.M.

3. CALENDAR, WEATHER, AGRICULTURE.

3675. Allen (Wilfrid).   Weather wisdom from January to December. pp. 71.   8°. London, n.d.

3676. Annuaire. Annuaire historique pour l'année 1847. pp. xii, 276.   18°. Paris, *Renouard,* 1846.
—— pour l'année 1848, *etc.*
              12°. Paris, *Société de l'Histoire de France,* 1847.

Gratet-Duplessis, 374. Contains proverbs and sayings relative to each month.
                                                        [B.M.

3677. Baldit (   ).   Recueil de proverbes agricoles.   1854.

In Bulletin de la Société d'Agriculture, Industrie, Sciences et Arts du Département de la Lozère, 5, 20.

3678. Banfi (Giuseppe).   Il tesoro del contadino.   Raccolta di lettere . . . proverbi, poesie, *etc.* pp. 191.
                          16°. Milano, *Pagnoni,* 1872.

Agricultural proverbs on pp. 8, 48, 143, 164.

3679. Boebel (Theodor).   Die Haus und Feldweisheit des Landwirths, *etc.* pp. [v], 147.   12°. Berlin, *Jeanrenaud,* 1854.

Contains many proverbs concerning the weather, agriculture, *etc.*   [B.M.

3680. Boudevillain (   ).   L'oracle des champs, ou recueil de proverbes à l'usage des gens de la campagne.
                                      Châteaudun, 1869.
Friesland, 258.

3681. Braga (Theophilo).   Cancioneiro popular. pp. vii, 223.
              16°. Coimbra, *Imprensa da Universidade,* 1867.

Pp. 182-196, Aphorismos poeticos da lavoura. Portuguese calendar rhymes.
                                                        [B.M.

3682. Bujault (Jacques).   Oeuvres, *etc.* pp. xx, 520.
                          8°. Paris, *Malteste,* 1845.
Another edition. pp. iv, 527.   8°. Niort, *Favre,* [1871].

Gratet-Duplessis, 372. A collection of articles on agriculture, *etc.*, which were first published in a periodical and later collected and republished as above. These articles are written in the style of Franklin and Paul-Louis Courier, and contain numbers of proverbs, chiefly concerning agriculture and domestic economy, some of which the author invented himself. The proverbs are also gathered together in the last ten pages of the introduction. The 1871 edition has not got the proverbs in a special list.   [B.M. (1871 edition).

3683. Camerarius (Joachimus). De re rustica opuscula non-nulla, *etc.* ff. 55.   4°. Noribergae, 1577.
Another edition.   8°. Noribergae, 1596.
Gratet-Duplessis, 142. Contains a list of proverbs, as well as a number of maxims, *etc.*   [B.M.

3684. Carnegy (Patrick). Agricultural folk-lore notes. Gathered from Carnegy's " Kachahrî technicalities." . . . With fresh translations by R. C. Temple.   8°. London, *F.-L.S.*, 1882.
In Folk-Lore Record, Vol. 5, pp. 33-49. Folk-lore catches and proverbs.   [F.-L.S.

3685. Castagna (Niccola). Calendario del popolo.   Milano, 1866.
In Almanacco del popolo, 1866.

3686. Čelakovský (František Ladislav). Kalendářík z přislovi slovanských.   8°. v Praze, *České Museum*, 1850.
In Časopis Českého Museum, 1850, pp. 206-220. Slavonic proverbs arranged in calendar form.   [B.M.

3687. Celi (Ettore). Il maestro del villaggio, almanacco pel 1866.
Modena, 1866.
Contains some agricultural proverbs.

3688. Ciani (Osvaldo). Prime nozioni pratiche di agricoltura con proverbi agricoli e morali.   San Daniele, *Pallarini*, 1882.
Pitrè, 2581.

3689. Claridge (John), *Shepherd.* The shepherd of Banbury's rules to judge of the changes of the weather. *First edition.* pp. viii, 64.   1/-. 8°. London, *Bickerton*, 1744.
Another edition. pp. xi, 56.
2/-. 8°. London, *Hurst*, 1827.
Another edition.   obl. 16°. [Banbury, *Walford*, 1920].
Contains various proverbs and adages concerning the weather. The Shepheards legacy. 8°. London, 1670, should perhaps be counted the first edition, as it forms the nucleus of these weather rules, but the true proverbs in this are very few.   [F.-L.S. (1827), (Stephens collection).

3690. Corbis (G.). Recueil des dictons populaires sur le temps.
8°.

3691. Cuppari (Pietro). Proverbi agrari.
Firenze, *Vieusseux*, 1849.
In Bullettino Agrario (Nuova Serie), Tomo 23, N. 5, del Giornale Agrario Toscano. Cuppari gives many agricultural proverbs in different numbers of this periodical.

3692. Daire (L. Fr.). Almanach perpétuel, pronosticatif, proverbial et gaulois, *etc.* pp. 210.
18°. Wiflispurg, Paris, *Desnos*, 1774.
Gratet-Duplessis, 319. A collection of proverbs and sayings concerning the seasons, the weather, agriculture, *etc.*, interspersed with useful information and curious anecdotes. It is frequently attributed to a Père Daire who was librarian of the Célestines at Paris.

3693. Denham (Michael Aislabie). A collection of proverbs and popular sayings relating to the weather, and agricultural pursuits; gathered chiefly from oral tradition. pp. iv, 73.

8°. London, 1846.

Percy Society's Publications, Vol. 20. Contains some uncommon proverbs. In verse. [U.C.L.

3694. ———: Proverbial rhymes and sayings for Christmas and the New Year. [Subscribed M. A. D., *i.e.* M. A. Denham]. pp. 12. 8°. Civ. Dunelm., 1853.

Only 50 copies printed. [B.M.

3695. Dralet (M.). Traité de la pierre à plâtre. . . . Avec recueil méthodique . . . des préceptes, maximes, proverbes français et étrangers relatifs à l'agriculture, *etc.* pp. iv, 136.

8°. Paris, 1837.

Pp. 87-136, proverbs taken from Olivier de Serres, **3733.**

3696. Dunwoody (Henry Harrison Chase). Weather proverbs, *etc.* pp. 148 + map.

8°. Washington, *Government Printing Office*, 1883.

U.S.A. War Department; Signal Service Notes, No. 9. Reprints the paper on weather prognostics by Abercromby and Marriot in the Journal of the Meteorological Society. Part 2 deals with scientific data. On the whole gives a good collection of proverbs relating to weather, animals, birds, *etc.* [B.M.

3697. Empson (C. W.). Weather proverbs and sayings not contained in Inwards' or Swainson's books. 8°. London, 1881.

In Folk-Lore Record, Vol. 4, pp. 126-132. Old style dates are given. The arrangement follows that of Inwards' book. [F.-L.S.

3698. Fages de Roma (Narciso). Aforismos rurales, *etc.* pp. xvi, 158. 12°. Figueras, *Matas de Bodalles*, 1849.

A French translation appeared in the Bulletin de la Société agricole, scientifique et littéraire des Pyrénées Orientales, 1854.

3699. Fapanni (Agostino). I proverbi del buon contadino. Almanacco per l'anno 1822, *etc.* [By A. Fapanni].

18°. Milano, *Silvestri,* 1821.

Also for the years 1829, 1837, 1838, 1840.

3700. Ferrario (Ercole). I principali proverbi relativi all' agricoltura, *etc.* pp. 95.

8°. Milano, *Riformatorio Patronato*, 1888.

Proverbs divided into twelve chapters, with full notes.

3701. Gomis (Cels). Meteorología y agricultura populars, ab gran nombre de confrontacions. pp. ix, 176.

8 rals. 8°. Barcelona, *Verdaguer*, 1888.

Biblioteca popular de la Associació d'Excursions Catalana, Vol. 5. Contains a large number of Catalan weather and agricultural sayings, compared with those of other languages (principally French, Italian, and other Spanish).

[B.M.

3702. Haffer (W.). Ueber Wetterprophezeihung und die natürlichen Wetterpropheten. fol. Neubrandenburg, 1864.

In Allgemeiner Mecklenburgischer Anzeiger, 1864, Nos. 38-43. Contains weather and agricultural proverbs.

3702a. Haldy (B.). Die deutschen Bauernregeln. Gesammelt von B. Haldy. Mit Monatsbildern von J. L. Gampp.
Jena, *Diederichs.*

3703. Hall (H. C. van). Spreekwoorden en voorschriften in spreuken, betreffende Landbouw en weêrkennis, *etc.* pp. vi, 80. 8°. Haarlem, *Kruseman,* 1872.
Bernstein, 3824.

3704. Hombres-Firmas (d'). Recueil de proverbes météorologiques . . . des Cévennois. *See* **1266.**

3705. Hoermann (Ludwig von). Die Frühlingsvorboten im Sprüchwort. Wien, 1894.

In Wiener Tagblatt, Jahrgang 1894, Nr. 67, 68.

3706. Horn (G. von). Die Kunst des Wetterprophezeiens, *etc.* pp. v, 103. 8°. Altona, *Verlags-Bureau,* 1869.

Pp. 51-99, Die Bauernregeln. Agricultural and weather sayings. [B.M.

3707. Humphreys (William J.). Weather proverbs and paradoxes. pp. viii, 125 + 16 plates.
7/-. 8°. London, *Baillière,* 1923.

3708. Inwards (Richards). Weather lore: a collection of proverbs, sayings and rules concerning the weather. Compiled and arranged by R. Inwards. pp. 91.
sm. 8°. London, *Tweedie,* 1869.
Third edition. pp. xii, 233 + plates.
8°. London, *Elliot Stock,* 1898.

Divided into such sections as, times and seasons, wind, *etc.* The two later editions (1893 and 1898) contain a bibliography of weather lore at the end. This capital compilation makes good reading and is done in a careful and painstaking fashion. There are proverbs from many countries, but all are given in English. Wherever possible the origin is indicated. [F.-L.S. (Stephens collection).

3709. K. Maj w przysłowiach. [Signed K.].
fol. Warszawa, 1899.

In Wędrowiec. Pismo Tygodniowe Ilustrowane, Rok 37, No. 20. The month of May in proverbs.

3710. Kerdellec (Gabrielle Marie Couffon de). Trésor des laboureurs . . du canton de Lamballe. *See* **1180.**

3711. Leistner (Ernst). Des deutschen Landwirths Sprüchwörterbuch . . . 1800 auserlesene und bewährte Bauernregeln und Sprüchwörter, *etc.* pp. xvi, 144.
8°. Leipzig, *Douffet,* [1876?].
Bernstein, 1890.

3712. Le Maout (Charles). Le trésor des laboureurs. Adages, maximes et proverbes agricoles, *etc.*

8°. Saint-Brieuc, 1853.

[Bristol Public Library.

3713. Maginu (Antoine). Le kalendrier perpetuel aux bons laboureurs, *etc.* 12°. Rouen, 1678.

Another edition. Prognostications perpetuelles des laboureurs, jardiniers et vignerons, *etc.* pp. 72.

sm. 12°. Saint Mihiel, *Duval,* [*circa* 1700].

Gratet-Duplessis, 294. A book of little importance, containing a medley of proverbs concerning agriculture, domestic economy, the seasons, *etc.*

3714. Malfatti (Antonio). Nozioni pratiche di agraria, proverbi e pronostici agrari, *etc.*

50 centesimi. 16°. Milano, *Marchi,* 1872.

Pp. 94-105, agricultural proverbs.

3715. Manni (Domenico Maria). Del fare i lavori della campagna in tempo. 4°. Firenze, 1770.

Gratet-Duplessis, 447. Agricultural and weather proverbs in use amongst the peasants of Tuscany.

3716. Masclet ( ). Adages des champs. 8°. Douai, 1823.

Gratet-Duplessis, 347. *In* Journal d'Agriculture du Département du Nord, août, 1823. Agricultural proverbs.

3717. Menu (Henri). Les dictons de l'année. 8°. Paris, 1893.

In La tradition, tome 7, pp. 44-48, 215-216. [B.M.

3718. Merkens (Heinrich). Das Wetter im Sprichwort.

8°. Lunden, 1893.

In Am Ur-Quell, Bd. 4, pp. 184-185. [B.M.

3719. Mese. Il mese che viene e i suoi proverbi. Roma, 1889.

In L'Opinione, an. 42. From March to September : in each case, a few calendar and weather proverbs. [B.M.

3720. Mirandolo. Il gran mirandolo, pronostico per l'anno 1842. . . . Contiene . . . proverbi per gli agricoltori, *etc.* pp. 64.

16°. Verona, *Bisesti,* [1841?].

Ditto for 1843 and 1844.

3721. Muedener (Rudolf). Das Buch vom Wetter oder das Wetter im Sprüchwort. pp. 153.

8°. Bernburg, Leipzig, *Bacmeister,* n.d.

3722. Otto (A.). Landswirthschaft, Jagd und Seeleben im Sprichwort. 8°. Leipzig, 1889.

In Archiv für lateinische Lexikographie, Jahrgang 6. pp. 9-24. [U.C.L.

3723. Petri (Rudolph Wilhelm Theodor). Das Landwirth's-Orakel, *etc.* pp. xvi, 116. 8°. Breslau, *Kern,* 1866.

A collection of weather and calendar proverbs and sayings, from many parts of Europe. [B.M.

3724. Philopère. Almanach nouveau, fait aux dépens des temps
passés, *etc.* pp. 96.   32°. Paris, *Bouquet*, 1812.

Gratet-Duplessis, 340.   Hécart, Bibliographie parémiographique, p. 38.   Proverbs concerning the weather and agriculture arranged under each day of the
year.

3725. Pouplin (   ). L'agronome des quatre saisons.
                                                Paris, *Béraud*, 1820.

Gratet-Duplessis, 342.   Hécart, Bibliographie parémiographique, p. 38.   Proverbs about agriculture.

3726. Predizioni. Le predizioni del mese ed i proverbii di
Gennaio.
Le predizioni del mese ed i proverbii di Febbraio.
                                                Palermo, 1890.

In Giornale di Sicilia, Anno 30, Nos. 3, 11.   Republished from the Opinione
of January and February.

3727. Procacci (Pietro).   Proverbi agrari.
                L.1.   16°.   Rocca S. Casciano, *Cappelli*, 1888.

In Almanacco per i Campagnuoli . . . Anno 3, pp. 185-9.

3728. Proverbi. I proverbi meteorologici del mese di Novembre.
                                                Roma, 1889.

In L'Opinione, Anno 42, No. 327.   30 proverbs.   [B.M.

3729. Refranes. Refranes de sanidad.—Refranes agrícolas.
                        12°.   Barcelona, 1896.

In Almanaque [Universal], para 1896.   Util—Instructivo—Ameno.   Hygienic
and agricultural proverbs for each month.

3730. Reinsberg-Düringsfeld (Otto von), *Baron.*   Das Wetter im
Sprichwort. pp. vii, 216.
                        20 Sgr.   8°.   Leipzig, *Fries*, 1864.

A collection, with commentary, of weather sayings of all nations, given in
German.   A bibliography is given at the end.   [B.M.

3731. Schaffler (Karel).   Z mudrosloví rolníkův.   Stručná sbírka
pranostik a přísloví haspodářských.   pp. 68.
Bernstein, 3213.   sm. 8°.   v Praze, *Knapp*, 1881.

3732. Sébillot (Paul Yves).   Dictons rimés sur les mois.
                        la. 8°.   Paris, 1886, 1888.

In Revue des traditions populaires, Tome 1, pp. 1, 29-30, 61-62, 93-94, 125-
126; Tome 3, pp. 345, 392, 434, 521, 590, 639.   [B.M.

3733. Serres (Olivier de), *Seigneur de Pradel.*   Le théâtre d'agriculture. . . . Nouvelle édition, *etc.*   2 vols.
                4°.   Paris, *Société d'Agriculture du*
                        Département de la Seine, 1804.

Gratêt-Duplessis, 25 and 884.   Tome 1, pp. 81-92, agricultural proverbs from
the French, Flemish, Spanish, Italian, German, English, Russian, and Chinese.
This is an interesting though by no means exhaustive collection.   Duplessis

gives the work from which each of these selections is extracted. In this edition the proverbs, which are scattered through the text of the original work, have been collected together by François de Neufchâteau, one of the editors : consequently the earlier editions are not worth noting. Duplessis, p. 419, reprints the Russian proverbs (in French). [B.M.

3734. Spiegel (Henrik L.). Hart-spiegel, *etc.*
sm. 8°. Amsterdam, *Colom*, 1650.

Another edition. 8°. Amsterdam, *Wetstein*, 1694.

Another edition. 8°. Amsterdam, *Van Damme*, 1723.

The above, but not all, editions contain Spiegel's Byspraax Almanack, which includes many calendar and other proverbs. [B.M.

3735. Statistique. Statistique de la France. . . . Agriculture. Résultats généraux de l'enquête décennale de 1862. pp. 51, clxxi, 272. 8°. Strasbourg, *Berger-Levrault*, 1868.

Pp. cxxxv-clxxi, proverbes et dictons agricoles. [B.M.

3736. Steinmetz (Andrew). A manual of weathercasts, *etc.* pp. 208. 8°. London, New York, *Routledge*, 1866.

Chap. 3 contains a number of proverbial rhymes concerning the weather, and others are to be found scattered throughout the book. [B.M.

3737. Swainson (Charles). A handbook of weather folk-lore: being a collection of proverbial sayings in various languages relating to the weather, with explanatory and illustrative notes. pp. x, 275.
6/6. sm. 8°. Edinburgh, London, *Blackwood*, 1873.

Part 1, pp. 1-171, proverbs relating to the weather and the calendar. Part 2, pp. 172-275, proverbs relating to the planets, animals, *etc.* Pp. vii-viii, list of works consulted. [F.-L.S. (Stephens collection).

3738. Tusser (Thomas). A hundreth good pointes of husbandrie, *etc.* 4°. [London, *Tottel*, 1557].

Five hundreth points of good husbandry, *etc.* [Together with the points of huswifrie]. 4°. London, *Tottel*, 1573.

A hundreth good pointes of husbandrie. . . . Copied from the first edition, 1557. pp. 19. 4°. London, 1810.

Five hundred points of good husbandry, *etc.* pp. xxxi, 347.
8°. London, *English Dialect Society*, 1878.

The hundred good points were greatly enlarged and published as Five hundred points. The points consist of agricultural precepts or maxims in verse. Another excellent edition was published in 1812, edited by W. Mavor.
[B.M. (1557, 1573, 1580, and other editions),
U.C.L. (1812, 1848, 1878 editions).

3739. Ventué y Peralta (Benito). Baturrilo de paremiología, ó tratado de frases celebres, apotegmas proverbiales, y refranes con aplicación á las ciencias y en especial á la agricultura, *etc.* pp. 207. 8°. Granada, *Lozano*, 1889.

3740. Ventura Intorrella (Giambattista). Proverbii agrarii illustrati. pp. 124. 8°. Modica, *Delia*, 1878.

Bernstein, 3860.

3741. Vergara y Martín (Gabriel Maria). Refranes meteoro-
lógicos referentes a los diferentes meses del año.
4°. Madrid,

3741a. Wallace (R. Hedger) *and others*. Proverbs of the dairy.
sm. 4°. High Wycombe, 1924-29.
In Notes and Queries, Vol. 146, pp. 192, 237, 308-9, 326-27; Vol. 157, pp. 227-
29, 246-48, 265, 319-20, 341, 431. Many examples, not all in English.

3742. Weather. Weather wisdom, *etc.* pp. 32.
16°. London, *Groombridge*, [1861].
P. 15, Weather proverbs. 13 rhymed proverbs; one or two others are given
in the text. [B.M.

3743. Witkowski (Władysław). O porach roku w naszym klimacie
i o ważności narodowych przysłów meteorologicznych. pp. 28.
8°. Warszawa, *Berger*, 1871.
Bernstein, 2071. A reprint from Biblioteka Warszawska.

3744. Wójcicki (Kazimierz Władysław). Archiwum domowe, *etc.*
pp. [vi], 578, v.
8°. w Warszawie, *Drukarnia Sprawiedliwości*, 1856.
Pp. 561-576, calendar proverbs. [B.M.

3745. ———: Przysłowia rolnicze miejsce kalendarza u ludu
zastępujące, *etc.*
4°. Warszawa, *Księgarnia bióra informacyjnego*, 1838.
In Nowy Kalendarz Powszechny na rok zwyczajny 1838, pp. 1-8. Polish
compared with Ruthenian and Russian.

3746. Wright (M. E. S.). A medley of weather lore. Collected
by M. E. S. Wright. pp. 144.
sm. 4°. Bournemouth, *Commin*, 1913.
A few weather proverbs included, arranged under months.
[F.-L.S. (Stephens collection).

*See also index at end for references to Calendar, Weather,
Agriculture, in other sections.*

4. CLOTHES.

3747. Kaden (Woldemar). Anzahl italienischer Sprichwörter über
Kleidung und Schönheit. Berlin, 1876.
In Der Bazar, Nos. 2, 10.

3748. ———: Italienische Gyps-Figuren. pp. iv, 454.
8°. Oldenburg, *Schulze*, 1881.
Pp. 151-168, Italienische Sprüchwörter über Kleidung und Schönheit. [B.M.

3749. Otto (A.). Kleidung und Wohnung im Sprichwort.
8°. Leipzig, 1888.
In Archiv für lateinische Lexikographie, Jahrgang 5, pp. 1-15. [U.C.L.

5. FAMILY AND DOMESTIC.

(Women and Children.)

3750. B. (B.). Raccolta di provuerbi. pp. [12].
8°. Verona, *Merlo*, 1861.

Pitrè, 6072. A few proverbs on women, love, and marriage.

3751. Boniforti (Luigi). La donna e la famiglia. Scelti pensieri, moniti e proverbi a tutela della domestica felicità. pp. vii, 95.
16°. Milano, *Pizzi*, 1889.

3752. Buelow von Dennwitz (Gertrud), *Gräfin.* Die Frauen und der Ehestand im deutschen Sprichwort.
fol. Frankfurt a. M., 1894.

In General-Anzeiger der Stadt Frankfurt a. M., Nr. 111, 1894.

3753. Canziani (Estella). Piedmontese proverbs in dispraise of women. *See* **2362.**

3754. Castro (Giovanni de). Laura [*pseud.* of De Castro]. Caro nodo! Consigli ed auguri. 24°. Milano, *Brigola*, 1881.

Pp. 21-40, proverbi sulla casa.

3755. ————: I proverbi sulla donna. Napoli, *Carluccio*, 1881.

In Rivista nuova di Scienze, Lettere ed Arti, Fasc. 4. Considered to be by De Castro.

3756. Cecchi (Silvio). La sapienza del popolo intorno al matrimonio. Proverbi, *etc.* L.1.25. 8°. Siena, *Gati*, 1878.

Another edition. pp. 11.
4°. Firenze, *Tipografia del Fieramosca*, 1886.

A booklet of advice and remarks suggested by certain proverbs concerning marriage. 1878 edition contains 17 proverbs. [B.M.

3757. Cock (Alfons de). Spreekwoorden en Zegswijzen over de vrouwen en liefde en het huwelijk. Gent, *Hoste,*

3758. Doświadczyński (Agricola Prosper). Kobieta. Zbiór aforyzmów, zdań, myśli i przysłów. pp. 93.
16°. Warszawa, *Leppert* [1896?].

Bernstein, 4354. A collection of proverbs, *etc.*, on women, from different languages, with translations.

3759. Dyer (Thomas Firminger Thiselton-). Folk-lore of women, *etc.* pp. xvi, 253. 8°. London, *Elliot Stock*, 1905.

Proverbs, anecdotes, superstitions, *etc.*, about women. No special list of proverbs, but numbers of them are included in each chapter. Reviewed in Folk-Lore, Vol. 18. [B.M.

3760. Frau. Die Frau im Sprichwort.
fol. Frankfurt a. M., 1889.

Bernstein, 1169. *In* Kleine Presse, Nr. 73, Blatt 2. Contains proverbs from various countries concerning women.

3761. Jeaffreson (John Cordy). Brides and bridals. . . . *First edition.* 2 vols. 8°. London, *Hurst & Blackett,* 1872. *Second edition.* 2 vols.

8°. London, *Hurst & Blackett,* 1873.

Vol. 1, pp. 343-362, Old proverbs about marriage and women. [B.M.

3762. Kornmann (Heinrich). Tractatus de virginitate, *etc. See* **2266.**

3763. Leistner (Ernst). Mädchen und Frauen, Liebe, Heirath und Ehe im Sprüchwort-Wahrwort, *etc.* pp. xii, 222.

Bernstein, 1891. 8°. Berlin, *Gultentag,* 1877.

3764. Lespy (V.). Les femmes d'après les proverbes.

8°. Condom, 1866.

In Revue d'Aquitaine, 1866, pp. 457-463. A commentary with examples. [B.M.

3765. Milin (G.). Proverbes bretons sur les femmes. *See* **1184.**

3766. Otto (A.). Familie und Freundschaft im Sprichwort.

8°. Leipzig, 1888.

In Archiv für lateinische Lexikographie, Jahrgang 5, pp. 369-386. [U.C.L.

3767. Pitrè (Giuseppe). Proverbi siciliani sulla donna.

Firenze, 1865.

In La Civiltà Italiana, Anno 1, 2⁰ trimestre, No. 4, pp. 59-60. 42 proverbs.

3768. Quitard (Pierre Marie). Proverbes sur les femmes, l'amitié, l'amour et le mariage, *etc.* pp. vi, 416.

12°. Paris, *Garnier,* 1861.

Another edition. pp. viii, 416. 8°. Paris, 1889.

An interesting book; the illustrations of the proverbs are excellent. [B.M.

3769. Raphael (Alfred). Die Sprache der proverbia quae dicuntur super natura feminarum, *etc.* pp. 50.

8°. Berlin, *Schade,* 1887.

Bernstein, 2947. An inaugural lecture delivered at the University of Berlin.

3770. Reinsberg-Düringsfeld (Otto von), *Baron.* Die Frau im Sprichwort. pp. viii, 208. 8°. Leipzig, *Fries,* 1862.

First published in the Magazin für die Literatur des Auslandes, No. 49. A large collection of proverbs, given in German only. [B.M.

3771. ———: Das Kind im Sprichwort. pp. 105.

sm. 8°. Leipzig, *Fries,* 1864.

Proverbs from many countries concerning children. In German. [U.C.L.

3772. Strafforello (Gustavo). Il male che i proverbi han detto delle donne.

Il po' di bene che dissero i proverbi delle donne.

Firenze, 1865.

In La Civiltà italiana, anno 1, Nos. 3 and 4. Proverbs concerning women, in various languages. The unfavourable ones are in the majority.

3773. Tanini (Francesco). La donna secondo il giudizio dei dotti e dei proverbii di tutti i popoli. *First edition.* pp. viii, 288.
8°. Firenze, *a spese dell' editore*, 1872.
Third edition. pp. iv, 480. L.4. 16°. Prato, *Tanini*, 1884.
Fourth edition. 16°. Prato-Toscana, 1884.

The fourth edition is practically the same as the third, though with a slightly altered title. This is a popular book and has no scientific interests. Proverbs of all times and all languages, together with quotations from famous authors, are translated into Italian and collected together without any distinction. [B.M.

3773a. ———: Proverbi sulle donne, contenendo 2000 sentenze tutte riguardanti la donna. pp. 320. 8°. Roma, 1887.

3774. Tobler (Adolph). Proverbia que dicuntur super natura feminarum. 8°. Halle, 1886.

In Zeitschrift für romanische Philologie, Bd. 9, pp. 287-331. Also at pp. 139-144 of Ernesto Monaci's Crestomazia italiana, *etc.*, fasc. 1. 4°. Città di Castello, 1889. Quatrains in Italian which frequently contain proverbs, taken from a medieval manuscript. [U.C.L.

3775. Ungarelli (Gaspare). I proverbi bolognesi sulla donna, *etc.* pp. 43. 8°. Bologna, *Fava e Gargnani*, 1890.

Pp. 1-27, a discourse on women in proverbs : pp. 29-43, 87 proverbs of Bologna.

3776. Waesberge (P. van). Sermoen over het vrijen, zamengesteld uit vaterlandsche spreuken en spreekwoorden.
sm. 8°. Schiedam, *Goude*, 1839.

Harrebomée, 117. *In* Schiedamschen Almanak, pp. 51-67.

3777. Wójcicki (Kazimierz Władysław). Niewiasty polskie, *etc.* pp. xxxx, 311. 8°. Warszawa, *Strabski*, 1845.

Pp. 25-34, 113-119, some Polish proverbs on brides. [B.M.

6. FOOD.

(Eating and Drinking.)

3778. Bernoni (Domenico Giuseppe). L'igiene della tavola dalla bocca del popolo ossia proverbi che hanno riguardo all' alimentazione raccolti in varie parti d'Italia. pp. 96.
L.1. 16°. Venezia, *Cecchini*, 1872.

Parte 1, l'alimentazione : parte 2, gli alimenti. There are 270 proverbs in the first part and 633 in the second, nearly all in Italian but with some Latin and dialect ones. The author also published two chapters of Proverbi igienici and Proverbi fisionomici in the *Tradizione popolare veneziane: Medecina.* [London Library.

3779. Fos (Augustin Léon Fortuné de). Gastronomiana. Proverbes, aphorismes, préceptes et anecdotes en vers, *etc.* pp. xxv, 169.
12°. Paris, *Rouquette*, Clermont-Ferrand, *Boucard*, 1870.

Pp. 1-126, gastronomic proverbs and aphorisms in rhyme. [B.M.

3780. Heilly (   ). Gastronomia. Proverbes, aphorismes, préceptes et anecdotes en vers. Paris, 1872.

Friesland, 277.

3781. Macadam (J. H.). A collection of proverbs of all nations, on bread and baking. pp. 136.

8°. London, *Maclaren*, [1924].

Proverbs arranged alphabetically by languages, the foreign ones with translations. [B.M.

3782. Ofellus (Q.), *Junior*. Philosophie des Magens in Sprüchen aus alter und neuer Zeit. pp. viii, 142.

8°. Leipzig-Reudnitz, *Schmidt*, 1886.

Bernstein, 2389. Contains German and Latin proverbs concerning food, and analogous subjects.

3783. Otto (A.). Essen und Trinken im Sprichwort.

8°. Leipzig, 1887.

In Archiv für lateinische Lexikographie, Jahrgang 4, pp. 345-357. [U.C.L.

3784. Palmireno (Lorenço). El estudioso cortesano, *etc.* [viii], 151 leaves.

sm. 8°. Alcala de Henares, *Iñiguez le Lequerica*, 1587.

Gratet-Duplessis, 492. Contains a long list of proverbs concerning food and health entitled Refranes de mesa, salud y buen criança; cogialos de muchos autores y conversaciones Lorenço Palmireno en Valencia, año 1569. This date indicates that there must have been an earlier edition. Reprinted by Sbarbi in Vol. 1 of his " Refranero general español," **1420.** [B.M.

3785. Reinsberg-Düringsfeld (Ida von), *Baroness*. Das Sprichwort als Gastrosoph. fol. Berlin, *etc.*, 1863.

In Magazin für die Literatur des Auslandes, 32. Jahrgang, pp. 555-556, 569-571, 603-605. A collection of proverbs in different languages with German translations. [B.M.

3786. Sébillot (Paul Yves). Traditions et superstitions de la boulangerie. pp. [vi], 70 + frontispiece.

8°. Paris, *Lechevalier*, 1892.

Contains various proverbs concerning bread.

7. FOOLS AND JESTING.

3787. Floegel (Karl Friedrich). Geschichte der Hofnarren. pp. xx, 530. 8°. Leignitz, Leipsig, *Siegert*, 1789.

Gratet-Duplessis, 674. Pp. 74-75, about 40 proverbs concerning court and other fools. A good book on an unusual subject. [B.M.

3788. Leistner (Ernst). Witz und Spott, Scherz und Laune in Sprüchwörtern und Volksredensarten. pp. 122.

12°. Lahr, *Schauenberg*, 1879.

Bernstein, 1893.

2 E

3789. Moenkemoeller (Otto). Narren und Toren in Satire, Sprichwort und Humor. Zweite Auflage. pp. 262.

8°. Halle a. S., *Marhold*, 1912.

[B.M.

3790. Nick (A. Friedrich). Die Hof- und Volks-Narren, *etc.* 2 Bde. 12°. Stuttgart, *Scheible*, 1861.

Bd. 1, pp. 83-88, Hundert deutsche Sprüchwörter in Bezug auf Narren und Narrheit. [B.M.

8. HUNTING.

3791. Berg (Carl Heinrich Edmund von), *Baron.* Pürschgang in Dickicht der Jagd- und Forstgeschichte. pp. xx, 250.

8°. Dresden, *Schönfeld*, 1869.

Pp. 187-222, Jäger, Jagd und Jagdthiere : pp. 222-250, der Wald und seine Bäume. Proverbs with brief notes. [B.M.

3792. Denham (Michael Aislabie). Rhymes and proverbs relating to hawking and the chase. [By Autolycus, *i.e.* M. A. Denham]. pp. [2]. 8°. 1857.

Only fifty copies printed. [B.M.

3793. Fos (Augustin Léon Fortuné de). Proverbes cynégétiques, ou aphorismes à l'usage des chasseurs.

8°. Paris, *Proux*, 1845.

Gratet-Duplessis, 373. Bibliographie de la France, No. 1501. In verse.

3794. Jaegerbrevier. Jägerbrevier. Jagdaltherthümer : Waid-sprüche und Jägerschreie, Jagdcalendar, Jägerkünste und Jägeraberglauben, Jägersagen. pp. iv, 180.

8°. Dresden, *Schönfeld*, 1857.

Bernstein, 1588, declares the author to be J. G. T. Grässe. Pp. 57-59, Jagd-Sprüchwörter. Other proverbs are to be found scattered throughout the book. [B.M.

3795. Minà-Palumbo (Francesco). Proverbi cinegetici.

Palermo, 1859.

In L'Empedocle, Nuova serie, Anno 1, pp. 27-41. 32 proverbs, chiefly Sicilian and Italian, on hunting.

3796. Otto (A.). Landwirthschaft, Jagd und Seeleben in Sprich-wort. *See* **3722.**

3797. Wildungen (L. C. E. H. F. von). Wildungen's Neujahrs Geschenck für Forstmänner . . . Zweyte Auflage. pp. iv, 148.

8°. Marburg, *Akademische Buchhandlung*, 1795.

Gratet-Duplessis, 690. Contains Forst- und Jagdparömien und Sprichwörter

9. LAW AND CRIME.

3798. Bogišić (Valtazar). Gragja u odgovorima iz različnih krajeva Slovenskoga juga, *etc.* pp. lxxiv, 714.
8°. u Zagrebu, *Župan*, 1874.
Contains a number of legal proverbs of the Southern Slavs. No special lists.
[B.M.

3799. ————: O važnosti sakupljanja narodnijeh pravnijeh običaja kod Slovena. 8°. u Zagrebu, *Albrecht*, 1866.
In Književnik, God. 3, pp. 1-47, 161-241, 408-476. Serbian law proverbs, compared with Polish, Russian, and Czech.

3800. Borkowski (Arthurus). De veterum Germanorum jure consuetudinario paroemiarum habita ratione, *etc.* pp. 73.
8°. Halis, 1852.

3801. Bouthors (Jean Louis Alexandre). Les proverbes, dictons et maximes du droit rural traditionnel, *etc.* pp. 215.
8°. Paris, *Durand*, Amiens, *Caron*, 1858.
Contains the explanation and illustration of numerous legal sayings concerning country life. [B.M.

3802. Catherinot ( ). Les axiomes du droit françois. pp. 8.
4°. Bourges, 1683.
Gratet-Duplessis, 291. A very rare pamphlet containing a long but confused list of maxims, aphorisms, and sayings concerning law. Not of much use, since there is neither commentary nor explanation. A work of the same kind, but far better, is that of Loisel, *q.v.*, **3825.**

3803. Čelakovský (František Ladislav). Slovanská právnická přísloví. 8°. v Praze, *České Museum*, 1851.
In Časopis Českého Museum, 1851, pp. 16-40. [B.M.

3804. Chaisemartin (A.). Proverbes et maximes du droit germanique étudiés en eux-mêmes et dans leurs rapports avec le droit français. pp. xxx, 585.
8°. Paris, *Larose & Forcel*, 1891.
Bernstein, 580. The proverbs are given in the original German and in French translations.

3805. Cohn (Georg). Das neue deutsche bürgerliche Recht in Sprüchen. 1. Allgemeiner Teil. pp. viii, 95.
Bernstein, 636. 8°. Berlin, *Liebmann*, 1896.

3806. Conradi (Friedrich Christian). Grundsätze des teutschen Rechts in Sprichwörtern. pp. 27. 4°. Helmstädt, 1745.
Gratet-Duplessis, 627. This little work was an original of the larger one by J. F. Eisenhart, *q.v.*, **3809.**

3807. Drago (Luigi). I criminali-nati, *etc.* pp. xxxix, 135.
8°. Torino, *Bocca*, 1890.
Bernstein, 898. Pp. xxiv-xxv, Raccolse pure alcuni proverbi portoghesi che alludone al crimine, assai curiosi.

3808. Duval (M. Y.). Le droit dans ses maximes, *etc.* pp. viii, 208. 8°. Paris, *Legrand & Bergounioux*, 1837.

Bernstein, 936.

3809. Eisenhart (Johann Friedrich). Grundsätze der deutschen Rechte in Sprüchwörtern, mit Anmerkungen erläutert. pp. [xxiv], 614. 8°. Helmstädt, *Weygand*, 1759.

Another edition. 8°. Leipzig, 1822.

Gratet-Duplessis, 642. This is the fully developed work founded on the next entry. The best of its kind in German, and has been frequently reprinted.
[B.M.

3810. ———: Kurze Abhandlung von dem Beweise durch Sprichwörter. pp. 20. 4°. Erfurt, *Nonne*, 1750.

Gratet-Duplessis, 635. A prelude to the last entry.

3811. Estor (Johann Georg). Bürgerliche Rechtsgelehrsamkeit der Teutschen, *etc.* 3 pts. 8°. Marburg, Frankfurt am Main, *Weidigens*, 1757-1767.

Gratet-Duplessis, 641. Contains a large number of law proverbs explained and applied. [B.M.

3812. Fasterling (Martin Luther). De utilitate brocardicorum. Altdorfi, 1693.

Gratet-Duplessis, 180. A dissertation on law proverbs or brocards and their utility for students, professors, lawyers, and judges.

3813. Gentius (Gulielmus). Adagia aliquot e jure scripto, *etc.*

In various editions of the Adagia of Erasmus and Grynaeus. [B.M.

3814. Gilhausen (Ludwig). Fasciculus proverbiorum et sententiarum ex utroque iure, *etc.* Mülhausen, 1600.

3815. Graf (Eduard) and **Dietherr** (Mathias). Deutsche Rechtssprichwörter, unter Mitwirkung der Professoren J. C. Bluntschli und K. Maurer gesammelt und erklärt, *etc.* pp. xvi, 606. 8°. Nördlingen, *Beck*, 1864.

Second edition. pp. xvi, 606.
8°. Nördlingen, *Beck*, 1869.

Numerous law proverbs illustrated and explained. [B.M.

3816. Hasselt (Jan Jacobus van). Annotationes ad Antonii Matthaei paroemias Belgarum jurisconsultis usitatissimas. 8°. Neomagi, *Van Campen*, 1780.

3817. Hedegaard (Christian Ditlev). Trifolium juridicum, *etc.* 3 pts. 4°. Odensöe, *Brandt*, 1748.

Pt. 3, Jurisprudentia proverbialis, eller een samling af gamle danske ordsprog, *etc.* [B.M.

3818. Hertius (Joannes Nicolaus). Epidipnides paroemiarum juris privati et publici germanicarum. 4°. Giessae, 1689.

Ejusdem, satura paroemiarum juris germanici nova.
4°. Giessae, 1698.

Ejusdem, de paroemiis juris germanici, libri tres.
4°. Francofurti, 1700.

Gratet-Duplessis, 577. These law proverbs of Germany were included in various editions of the author's works, notably in that of Frankfort, 1700. It is probable that the particular edition of these proverbs given above is merely a separate publication of part of this collection of 1700. [B.M. (Works).

3819. Hillebrand (Julius Hubert). Deutsche Rechtssprichwörter, *etc.* pp. xxiii, 247. 8°. Zürich, *Meyer & Zeller*, 1858.

373 law proverbs, with explanatory notes. [B.M.

3820. Illyustrov (Iakinth I.). Юридическія пословицы и поговорки русскаго народа, *etc.* pp. 72, iv.
8°. Москва, *Чичеринъ*, 1885.

Russian legal proverbs, *etc.*, with brief notes. [B.M.

3821. Kindius (Johann Adolf Theoph.). Programma de jurisprudentia Germanorum paroemiaca eiusque cauto usu. pp. 24. 4°. Lipsiae, 1776.

Gratet-Duplessis, 650.

3822. Koehne (C.). Gewerberechtliches in deutschen Rechtssprichwörtern. pp. 82. 8°. Zürich, 1915.

3823. Kornemann (Heinrich). Enucleatae questiones complectentes perjucundum tractatum de virginum statu ac jure. *See* **2266.**

3824. Kreittmayr (Wiguläus Xaver Alois). Rechtsregeln und Sprüche, *etc.* pp. viii, 247. 8°. München, *Weiss*, 1848.

Contains many law proverbs, Latin and German.

3824a. Lobe (A.). Neue deutsche Rechtssprichwörter für jedermann aus dem Volke. Volksausgabe. pp. 141.

3825. Loisel (Antoine). Institutes coutumières, *etc.*
8°. Paris, *Legras*, 1637.

Another edition. pp. 164. 8°. Paris, *Legras*, 1646.

Another edition. 2 vols. 12°. Paris, *Sanson*, 1784.

Another edition. 2 vols.
12°. Paris, *Durand Videcoq*, Leipzig, *Franck*, 1846.

Gratet-Duplessis, 262. This book contains a number of legal axioms which have, in course of time, acquired a true proverbial character. The first edition appeared at the end of the " Institution au droit françois," by Guy Coquille, 4°, 1607. The editions of 1784 and 1846 are both good ones. Duplessis also quotes others. *See* **1038.** [B.M.

3826. Lombroso (Cesare). L'uomo delinquente, *etc.* pp. xxxv.
610 + plates. 8°. Roma, *etc.*, *Bocca*, 1884.
Fourth edition. 2 vols. 8°. Torino, *etc.*, *Bocca*, 1889.

Contains a page or two of proverbs concerning criminals, *etc.* These are
not included in the 1876 edition. [B.M.

3827. Matthaeus (Antonius). Paroemiae Belgarum jurisconsultis
usitatissimae, quibus, praeter Romanorum aliarumque
gentium mores et instituta, jus ultrajectinum exponitur. . . .
Opus posthumum. pp. 392.
sm. 8°. Ultrajecti, *Smytegelt*, 1667.

Gratet-Duplessis, 806. This contains a well-developed commentary on nine
law proverbs of Flanders. *See also* **3816.**

3828. Murray (David). Lawyers' merriments.
8°. Glasgow, *MacLehose*, 1912.

Pp. 47-59, proverbs. Comments on legal proverbs and maxims. [B.M.

3829. Osenbrueggen (Eduard). Die deutschen Rechtssprichwörter, *etc.* pp. 40.
8°. Basel, *Schweighauserische Verlagsbuch-
handlung*, 1876.

Oeffentliche Vorträge gehalten in der Schweiz, Bd. 3. A commentary with
many examples. [B.M.

3830. Pistorius (Georg Tobias). Thesaurus paroemiarum ger-
manico-judicarum, *etc.* 2 vols.
4°. Lipsiae, *Müller*, 1716-1725.

Gratet-Duplessis, 592. The first edition of a part of this curious work
appeared at Leipsig, 1714, 8°, and there were others, but these partial editions
have been more or less superseded by the above edition of 1716-25. It contains
the explanation in Latin of a number of German law proverbs. [B.M.

3831. Reyscher (A. L.). Die Ueberlieferung der Rechte durch
Sprichwörter. 8°. Leipzig, *Wigand*, 1841.

In Zeitschrift für deutsches Recht und deutsche Rechtswissenschaft, Bd. 5,
pp. 189-209. [B.M.

3832. Rybička (Antonín). Wýpisky z archiwu Chrudimskèho.
8°. v Praze, *Českè Museum*, 1845.

Bernstein, 3103. In Časopis Českého Museum, 1845, Swazek 3, pp. 358-364,
Řehole právní. Legal proverbs. [B.M.

3833. Scherzius (Jo. Ge.). Paroemiae juris Germanici. pp. 24.
4°. Argentorati, 1722.

Gratet-Duplessis, 607. Contains the explanation of seven law proverbs.

3834. Schjørring (P.). Juridske ordsprog. pp. 32.
[Copenhagen], 1866.
In Tidsskrift f. Retsvaesen, Vol. 4.

3835. Thuriet (Charles). Proverbes judiciaires. pp. xii, 181.
fr.10. 8°. Paris, *Lechevalier*, 1891.

Translations of some 500 law proverbs embodied in verse.

3836. Volkmar (Leopold). Paroemia et regulae juris Romanorum, Germanorum, Franco-Gallorum, Britannorum, *etc.* pp. 513.
12°. Berolini, *Allgemeine deutsche Verlags-Anstalt*, 1854.
Law proverbs and rules arranged alphabetically. [B.M.

3837. Woelcker (Simon Tobias). J. J. Epidipnides paroemiarum juris Germanicarum . . . praeside D. Joanne Nicolao Hertio . . . submittit S. T. Woelcker. pp. 71.
4°. Gissae-Hassorum, *Müller*, 1710.

3838. Woldenberg (Christian). Micarum iuris manipulis tres, *etc.* 4°. Rostock, 1665.
Contains Proverbia juris.

10. MEDICINE AND HYGIENE.

3839. Baier (Johann Jacob). Adagiorum medicinalium centuria, quam recensuit variisque animadversionibus illustravit Jo. Jac. Baierus. pp. [xii], 196.
4°. Francofurti et Lipsiae, *typis J. G. Kohlesii*, 1718.
Gratet-Duplessis, 190 and 599. Explains various German medical proverbs.
[U.C.L.

3840. Bailly (Pierre). Questions naturelles et curieuses . . . où se voient plusieurs proverbes populaires, *etc.* pp. [xxiv], 733.
sm. 8°. Paris, *Bilaine*, 1628.
Gratet-Duplessis, 272. An excellent collection of the medical proverbs then current in France. Each proverb is accompanied by a brief explanation designed to show its truth or falseness. [B.M.

3841. Bernoni (Domenico Giuseppe). L'igiene della tavola dalla bocca del popolo ossia proverbi che hanno riguardo all' alimentazione, *etc. See* **3778.**

3842. Bremser (Johann Gottfried). Medizinische Parömien. . . . Ein Nachtrag zum Gesundheittaschenbuch. pp. 309.
sm. 8°. Wien, *Schaumburg*, 1806.
Gratet-Duplessis, 730. The author explains and comments on 35 medical proverbs. [B.M.

3843. Buecking (Johann Jacob Heinrich). Medicinische und phisikalische Erklärung deutscher Sprichwörter und sprichwörtlicher Redensarten. pp. 290.
8°. Stendal, *Franz & Grosse*, 1797.
Gratet-Duplessis, 698. Medical and practical explanations of various German proverbs. [B.M.

3844. Corvinus (Georg Ludwig). Adagia quaedam medicinalia, . . . praeside Ioh. Iac. Baiero . . . proponet G. L. Corvinus. pp. 24. 4°. [Altdorf], *Kohlesius*, 1713.
[B.M.

3845. Couhé (G. M.). Essai sur quelques expressions proverbiales et sentences populaires relatives à la médecine, *etc.* pp. 35.
4°. Paris, *Didot*, 1808.

Gratet-Duplessis, 337. Hécart, Bibliographie parémiographique, p. 52. The author gives observations on the origin and history of each proverb. [B.M.

3846. Delanoue (Arthur). Choix de proverbes . . . français et étrangers . . . suivis de proverbes relatifs à la santé, l'hygiène, l'économie domestique, l'agriculture . . . rangés par ordre de matières par Arthur Delanoue [*pseud.*]. pp. 62.
sm. 8°. Paris, *Passard*,

Some 1200 proverbs from different languages translated into French.

3847. Ehinger (Johann). Adagiorum medicinalium sylloge, quam sub praesidio Io. Iac. Baieri . . . proponet I. Ehinger. pp. 20.
4°. Altorfii Noric[orum], *Kohlesius*, 1717.
[B.M.

3848. Francus (Johannes Georgius). Adagia quaedam medicinalia . . . praeside Joh. Jac. Baiero . . . ad disputandum proponet J. G. Francus. pp. 24.   4°. [Altdorf], *Kohlesius*, 1711.
[B.M.

3849. Hertel (E.). Gesundheitslehre in Sprichwörtern.
8°. Stuttgart, *Zimmer*, 1894.

In Hygieia, Jahrgang 8, pp. 21-26, 69-71.   [B.M.

3850. Johannes *de Mediolano.* Schola Salernitana, sive, de conservanda valetudine praecepta metrica.
sm. 8°. Parisiis, *Marnes*, 1580.

Nova editio. pp. [xlviii], 517, [10].
sm. 12°. Roterodami, *Leers*, 1667.

Another edition. Regimen sanitatis salernitanū, *etc.*
4°. Louvain, *J. de Westphalia*, 1480?

Gratet-Duplessis, 169. Versified aphorisms on hygiene and medicine, which were probably written for the use of students, but which rapidly became popular and familiar to everyone, and certainly deserve to be considered as true medical proverbs. There were many editions of this work, one of the best being that of Stendal, 8°, 1790. There is a good French translation :

L'art de conserver la santé, . . . avec une traduction, en vers français, des vers latins de l'École de Salerne; par M. J. F. Alexandre Pougens. pp. viii, 320, 90.   8°. Montpellier, Paris, *Béchet*, 1825.
[B.M.

3851. Krauss (Friedrich Saloman). Südslavische Pestsagen, *etc.* pp. 43.   8°. Wien, 1883.

Bernstein, 4513. Pp. 9-10, die Pest im Sprichwort. Separate publication of an article in Mittheilungen der anthropologischen Gesellschaft in Wien, Bd. 13 (N.F., Bd. 3).

3852. Medicus. Poetischer Medicus, oder Sammlung auserleszner medicin- und physicalischer Gedancken, Verse, Sprichwörter, Sentenzien, *etc.*   8°. Berlin, Leipzig, n.d.
[Bristol Public Library.

3853. Melle (Franciscus Jacobus a). Adagiorum medicinalium sylloge,—quam, sub praesidio Io. Iac. Baieri . . . proponet F. J. a Melle. pp. 24.
4°. Altorfii Noric., *Kohlesius*, [1717].
[B.M.

3854. Miller (August Wolfgang). Adagia quaedam medicinalia . . . praeside Ioh. Iac. Baiero . . . proponet A. W. Millerus. pp. 16.
4°. [Altdorf], *Kohlesius*, 1714.
[B.M.

3855. Millingen (John Gideon). Curiosities of medical experience.
2 vols.
8°. London, *Bentley*, 1837.
Second edition.
8°. London, *Bentley*, 1839.
Gratet-Duplessis, 863. Vol. 1, pp. 371-374, proverbs and sayings regarding health and disease. No explanations.
[B.M.

3856. Miró y Borrás (Olaguer). Aforística medica popular catalana, confrontada ab la de altres llengues, *etc.* pp. 473.
8°. Manresa, *Esparbé*, 1900.
Biblioteca popular del " Centre escursionista de Catalunya," Vol. 8. Over 1000 Catalan sayings compared with those of other languages.

3857. Pasqualigo (Cristoforo). 280 proverbi veneti (médicaux) . . . traduits . . . par Dutertre-Deléviéleuse. pp. 77.
8°. Paris, *Maloine*, 1918.
An interesting and informative introduction. The proverbs are medical ones selected from Pasqualigo's Proverbi Veneti, and given here with a French translation. There are frequent comparisons with proverbs of other languages, chiefly Scotch.
[B.M.

3858. Pauli (Tobias Ferdinandus). Adagia quaedam medicinalia . . . praeside Ioh. Iac. Baiero . . . proponet T. F. Pauli. pp. 24.
4°. [Altdorf?], *Kohlesius*, 1714.
[B.M.

3859. Refranes. Refranes de sanidad. *See* **3729.**

3860. Rorie (David). On Scottish folk-medicine. IX.—Scottish proverbs bearing on medicine.
8°. Glasgow, *Caledonian Medical Society*, 1929.
In Caledonian Medical Journal, Vol. 14, pp. 20-27. Classified according to subject. Many examples given.

3861. Seiz (Johann Friedrich). Adagia quaedam medicinalia . . . praeside Joh. Jac. Baiero . . . proponet J. F. Seiz. pp. 24.
4°. [Altdorf], *Kohlesius*, [1712].
[B.M.

3862. Sonntag (Heinrich). Adagia quaedam medicinalia . . . praeside Joh. Jac. Baiero . . . proponet H. Sonntagius. pp. 16.
4°. [Altdorf], *Kohlesius*, [1712].
[B.M.

3863. Sorapan de Rieros (Juan). Medicina española, contenida en proverbios vulgares de nuestra lengua, *etc.* 2 pts.

4°. Granada, *Muñoz*, 1616, 1615.

Another edition. pp. [xx], 517.

4°. Madrid, *Zambrano*, 1616.

Gratet-Duplessis, 498. This book is a veritable treatise on medicine founded on proverbs. The author takes a proverb (they are not all exclusively Spanish in origin) and makes it the text for information, anecdotes, and observations of all kinds. Duplessis prints the list of proverbs used in this book. *Reprinted* from the edition of Madrid, 1616, in Vol. 3 of Sbarbi's "Refranero general español, *q.v.*, **1420.** [B.M.

3864. Stagioni. Le quattro stagioni. . . . Consigli igienici per la gente che lavora, *etc.* pp. 64.   16°. Milano, 1875.

Contains 106 proverbs and maxims.

3865. Widmannus (Johann Wilhelm). Adagia quaedam medicinalia . . . praeside Joh. Jac. Baiero . . . proponet Joh. Guil. Widmannus. pp. 24.   4°. [Altdorf], *Kohlesius*, 1721.

3865a. Zimmermann (W.). Arzt- und Apothekerspiegel, Sprichwörtersammlung.   8°. Dresden und Stuttgart, 1924.

11. MOON AND STARS.

3866. Brunet (J.). Bachiquello e prouvèrbi sus la luno. pp. 14.

8°. Avignoun, *Aubanel*, [1876].

Provençal proverbs on the moon. On the back of the paper cover is the following announcement : En preparacioun, dòu meme felibre : La Sagesso prouvèncalo. Culido di prouvèrbi o refrin recata dins touti li caire e cantoun dòu Miejour, eme traducioun francèso. [B.M.

3867. Gomis (Cels). La lluna segons lo poble. pp. 16.

4°. Barcelona, *Ullastres*, 1884.

Third edition. pp. 59.

fol. Barcelona, *tip. L'Avenç*, 1912.

The first edition contains some 50 proverbs about the moon. The third edition is greatly enlarged, and contains comparisons with proverbs in other languages.

3868. Ostermann (Valentino). Superstizioni, pregiudizi e credenze popolari relativi alla cosmografia, *etc.*

Pp. 20-9, Proverbi friulani relativi alla luna. *See* **2432.**

3869. Soerio de Brito (J. Maria). Collecção Silva Vieira. Astronomia, meteorologia e chronologia populares. pp. 42.

16°. Espozende, 1890.

Bernstein, 3447.

3870. Swainson (Charles). A handbook of weather folk-lore, *etc.*

Pp. 172-275, proverbs relating to the planets, *etc. See* **3737.**

12. MUSIC.

3871. Kastner (Georges). Parémiologie musicale de la langue française, ou explication des proverbes . . . qui tirent leur origine de la musique, accompagnée de recherches sur un grand nombre d'expressions de même genre, empruntées aux langues étrangères, *etc.* pp. xx, 657.

4°. Paris, *etc.*, *Brandus & Dufour*, n.d.

Contains the explanation of various proverbs, sayings, expressions, *etc.*, concerning music or musical instruments. [B.M.

3872. Peeris (William). The musicall proverbis in the garet at . . . Lekingfelde. Edited by Philip Wilson.

8°. London, *Milford*, 1924.

Musical maxims in verse taken from an ms. in the British Museum. The author or compiler is apparently William Peeris. [B.M.

3873. Schranka (Eduard Maria). Der neue Demokrit, *etc.* 2 Bde.

8°. Berlin, *Lüstenöder*, 1890-1891.

Bd. 2, pp. 209-219, die Musikinstrumente in Sprichwort.

13. PICTORIAL.

3874. Adam (V.). Proverbes en actions. Album composé et lithographié par V. Adam. fol. *Aubert.*

22 lithograph plates.

3875. Aken (F. van). [Plates representing Dutch proverbs, for children]. 3 vols. 12°. Amsterdam, 1806.

Gratet-Duplessis, 800.

3876. Alken (Henry). British proverbs.

fol. London, *M'Lean*, 1824.

Bernstein, 61. Coloured plates.

3877. Bennett (Charles Henry). Proverbs, with pictures.

4°. London, *Chapman & Hall*, 1859, [1858].

A series of 48 plates illustrating various proverbs. [B.M.

3878. Browne (Gordon Frederick). Proverbial sayings, *etc.* pp. 59. obl. 4°. London, *Wells Gardner*, [1901].

Coloured plates. [B.M.

3879. Demarteau (Servais). Le roman des proverbes en action, *etc.* 2 tom. 8°. Paris, *Didier*, n.d.

Bernstein, 799.

3880. Fernandez Villabrille (Francisco). Los cien proverbios, ó la sabiduria de las naciones. Obra imitada del Frances.

8°. [Madrid, 1850?].

Imitated from the " Cent proverbes " of Grandville, **3882.** A collection of drawings illustrating proverbs, accompanied by brief anecdotes. [B.M.

3881. Garnerey. Le petit Sancho. Suite de 24 proverbes mis en action et lithographiés. 24 plates.   4°. Paris, *Noel*, n.d.
Bernstein, 1239.

3882. Gerard (Jean Ignace Isidore), *called Grandville.* Cent proverbes, par J. J. Grandville et par trois têtes dans un bonnet. [Illustrated].   8°. Paris, *Fournier*, 1844.
Gratet-Duplessis, 371. This book is principally a series of illustrated proverbs, for which the text seems only a framework. The artist is mentioned first, and the writers afterwards.   [B.M.

3883. Goya (Francisco). Proverbios. 21 plates.   fol. 1920.
Edition of 500 copies.

3884. Lagniet (Jacques). Recueil des plus illustres proverbes, . . . mis en lumière par J. Lagniet.   4°. Paris, [1657-63].
Gratet-Duplessis, 284. A collection of plates representing proverbs. In an example in the library of Méon the number of pictures is 314 (in the B.M. copy there are 123), but it is difficult to say if this is complete or if some extraneous illustrations have been included. Duplessis discusses this point and gives further details; he regards Lagniet as the editor or even the bookseller of these proverbs, and not the artist or engraver.   [B.M.

3885. Matéaux (C. L.). Old proverbs with new pictures by Lizzie Lawson. Rhymes by C. L. Matéaux. pp. 64.
        4°. London, *etc.*, *Cassell*, n.d.
A picture book for children.   [B.M.

3886. Mitelli (Giuseppe Maria). Proverbi figurati, *etc.* 48 plates. *See* **2283.**

3887. Nelli (Niccolo). Proverbii.   Venetia, *Bertelli*, 1564.
A series of engravings illustrating 33 rhymed Italian proverbs.

3888. Ogilvie (Alexina). Profitable proverbs. . . . Five and twenty woodcuts illustrating as many proverbs, *etc.*
        4°. London, *The Cayme Press*, 1923.
        [B.M.

3889. Piattoli (Giuseppe). Raccolta di quaranta proverbi toscani espressi in figure.   fol. Firenze, 1786.
Another edition.   8°. Firenze, 1811.
Gratet-Duplessis, 449. 40 coloured plates.

3890. Pigal (   ), **Pajon** (   ), and **Arago** (J.). Proverbes et bons-mots mis en action, *etc.*   fol. Paris, *Dauty*, 1823.
Gratet-Duplessis, 344. A series of 66 coloured lithographic plates accompanied by a brief explanatory text. The collection was discontinued after the sixty-sixth plate.

3891. Poisle Desgranges (Joseph). Proverbes mis en action, ou morale récréative.   obl. 16°. Paris, *Ponthieu*, 1824.
Gratet-Duplessis, 348. A series of plates.

3892. Proverbs. Pictorial proverbs for little people. [With coloured illustrations]. pp. 16.

4°. London, Brighton, *S.P.C.K.*, [1889].

Pictures and anecdotes illustrating 12 proverbs. [B.M.

3893. ———: Русскія пословицы. . . . Тетрадь 1.

fol. С.-Петербургъ, 1862.

Lithographs without text. [B.M.

3894. Raccolta. Nuova raccolta di xxiv proverbi toscani rappresentati in figure, *etc. See* **2491.**

3895. Richter (Ludwig). Der deutschen Sprichwörter und Sprüchreden. Mit Illustrationen von L. Richter. *See* **1732.**

3896. Spruechwoerter. Deutsche Sprüchwörter und Spruchreden in Bildern und Gedichten. Ausgeführt im lithographischen Institut von Arnz und Comp. 20 plates + pp. 40.

4°. Düsseldorf, *Arnz*, [1852?].

Plates illustrating German proverbs. [B.M.

3897. ———: Sprüchwörter in Wort und Bild.

4°. Düsseldorf, *Bagel*, n.d.

A book for children.

3898. ———: Sprüchwörter und Redensarten. Erbaulich zu lesen für Jung und Alt. ff. 12.

4°. München, *Braum & Schneider*, n.d.

Münchener Bilderbücher, 7. Coloured prints illustrating German proverbs.

3899. Trusler (J.). Proverbs exemplified, and illustrated by pictures from real life. . . . By the author of " Hogarth moralized " [J. Trusler]. pp. viii, 196.

3/-. 16°. London, *Trusler*, 1790.

Proverbs in verse, *etc.* pp. 122.

16°. London, *Souter*, [1800?].

The second book is a paraphrased version of the first. Very poor; the cuts by J. Bewick are the only redeeming feature. [B.M.

3900. Tueshaus (Fritz). Deutsche Sprichwörter, nach Federzeichnungen von Fritz Tüshaus, in Holzschnitten von R. Brend'amour, *etc.* 12 plates. 4°. Leipzig, *Barth*, 1872.

Bernstein, 3775. 12 plates illustrating German proverbs.

3901. Visscher (N.). 96 spreekwoorden in prent verb. 96 plates.

4°.

An album consisting of 96 coloured plates. Each picture presents a scene from Dutch life and illustrates a Dutch proverb. Several bear the inscription : Visscher excu. Bernstein, 3903, reproduces six of these pictures.

14. PLANTS.

3902. Costa (Joaquin). Influencia del arbolado en la sabiduria
popular. 8°. Palermo, *Lauriel*, 1882.

In Archivio per lo studio delle tradizioni popolari, Vol. 1, pp. 120-125. [B.M.

3903. Dyer (Thomas Firminger Thiselton-). The folk-lore of
plants. pp. 328.
6/-. 8°. London, *Chatto & Windus*, 1889.

Pp. 128-144, plant proverbs. Slightly reminiscent of Trench's style, but
matter quite different. [U.C.L.

3904. Friend (Hilderic). Flowers and flower lore, *etc.* 2 vols.
8°. London, *Sonnenschein*, 1884.
Another edition. 2 vols. 8°. London, *Sonnenschein*, 1892.

Vol. 1, pp. 203-230, contains an interesting chapter entitled Proverbs of
flowers and plants. [B.M.

3905. Gomis (Cels). Botánica popular, *etc.* pp. 157.
8 rals. 8°. Barcelona, *tip. L'Avenç*, 1891.

Biblioteca popular de la Associació d'excursions Catalana, Vol. 6. Contains
a large number of Catalan botanical proverbs, weather sayings, proverbs about
the moon, *etc.* [B.M.

3906. Mylius (Martinus). Hortus philosophicus.
8°. Gorlicii, *Rhamba*, 1597.

Anmütiger Weisheit Lust-Garten. . . . Erstlich von dem
Wohlgelehrten Herzen M. Martino Mylio . . . in lateinischer
Sprache beschrieben : und unter dem Titel : Hortus philosophicus : in Truck gegeben, *etc.* pp. 763.
8°. Strassburg, *Carolus*, 1621.

Most chapters contain a special section of proverbs on trees, *etc.* [B.M.

3907. Otto (A.). Das Pflanzenreich im Sprichwort.
8°. Leipzig, 1887.

In Archiv für lateinische Lexikographie, Jahrgang 4, pp. 189-196. [U.C.L.

3908. Rolland (Eugène). Flore populaire, *etc.* 11 tom.
8°. Paris, *Rolland*, 1896-1914.

Contains a number of proverbs and sayings concerning flowers. 13 volumes
should have appeared, but owing to the War the eleventh seems to have been
the last. [B.M.

3909. Rozan (Charles). Les végétaux dans les proverbes. La
terre, l'eau, *etc.* pp. 288. 12°. Paris, n.d.

3910. Sébillot (Paul Yves). Traditions et superstitions de la
Haute-Bretagne.

Tome 2 contains proverbs concerning plants, *etc. See* **1188.**

3911. Sobotka (Primus). Rostlinstvo a jeho význam v národních písních, pověstech, bájích, obřadech a pověrách slovanských, *etc.* pp. 344. 8°. v Praze, *Matice Česká*, 1879.

No special list, but contains a number of proverbs and sayings, amongst the songs, superstitions, *etc.*, of the Slavs in general. [B.M.

3912. Unseld (Wilhelm). Die Pflanzen in den schwäbischen Sprichwörtern und Redensarten.

8°. Bonn, *Hanstein*, 1898.

In Alemannia, Jahrgang 25, pp. 114-126. [B.M.

3913. Wagler (Paul). Die Eiche in alter und neuer Zeit, *etc.* 2 Thle. 4°. Wurzen, *Jacob*, 1891.

Theil 1, pp. 27-31, Die Eiche in sprichwörtlichen Redensarten. [B.M.

15. POLITICAL ECONOMY.

3914. Breugel (J. F. van). Alphabetisch vaderlandsch kijkje in de staatshuishoudkunde, met zinrijktoegepaste spreekwoorden uit oud spaansche, italiaansche en portugesche schrijvers. pp. xv, 96. 8°. Utrecht, *Terveen*, 1861.

[B.M.

3915. Britten (James). Proverbs and folk-lore from William Ellis's " Modern Husbandman " (1750). 8°. London, 1880.

In The Folk-Lore Record, Vol. 3, Part 1, pp. 80-86. Proverbs from the eight volumes of the " Modern Husbandman," excluding those to be found in Ray's collection (Bohn's edition). [F.-L.S.

3916. Cock (Alfons de). Proverbes et dictons flamands et hollandais sur différents métiers. 8°. Paris, 1895.

In Revue des traditions populaires, tome 10, pp. 397-405. In Flemish and Dutch, with French translations. [B.M.

3917. Code. Code de commerce, *etc.* 18°. Paris, *Roset*, 1829.

Gratet-Duplessis, 352. Hécart, Bibliographie parémiographique, p. 42. Pp. 244-255, catéchisme proverbial-industriel.

3918. Henisch (Georg). De asse et partibus eius. pp. [iv], 233, [24]. 8°. Augustae Vindelicorum, *Francus*, 1606.

Pp. 227-233, Proverbia sumta ex asse et partibus eius. 21 Latin and German proverbs concerning money. [B.M.

3919. Marperger (Paul Jacob). Fragen über die Kauffmann-schaft. 8°. Leipzig, 1715.

Gratet-Duplessis, 593. Pp. 429-446, Sprichwörter bei Kauffmannschaft.

3920. Modderman (A.). Bijdragen tot de huishoudkunde . . . uit spreuken, spreekwijzen en spreekwoorden. pp. 155.

8°. Groningen, *Schierbeek*, 1852.

A commentary rather than a list. [B.M.

3921. Otto (A.). Geldverkehr und Besitz im Sprichwort.
8°. Leipzig, 1889.

In Archiv für lateinische Lexikographie, Jahrgang 6, pp. 47-58. [U.C.L.

3922. ———: Staatliche und private Einrichtungen und Berufs-
arten im Sprichwort. 8°. Leipzig, 1892.

In Archiv für lateinische Lexikographie, Jahrgang 7, pp. 1-23. [U.C.L.

3923. Penny. The penny: a blessing or a curse. An essay treated
proverbially. pp. 36.
8°. London, *Cradock*, Stoke Newington, *Miller*, 1852.

An essay written almost entirely in proverbs, concerning money, thrift, *etc.*
The origin of each one is briefly indicated, as a general rule the collector's
name being given for English ones and the language for foreign ones, which
are all given in English. Contains some unusual proverbs. [B.M.

3924. Prato (Stanislao). Il concetto del lavoro nella mitologia
vedica e nella tradizione popolare. 8°. Palermo, 1886.

In Archivio per lo studio delle tradizioni popolari, Vol. 5, pp. 569-582. The
article contains various Indian, Turkish, and Arabian proverbs, with Italian
translations.

3925. Sébillot (Paul Yves). Légendes et curiosités des métiers,
etc. 20 pts. 8°. Paris, *Flammarion*, [1895].

Contains a large number of proverbs and sayings in all languages relative
to various trades. [B.M.

3926. Silva (Carlos Martínez). Los refranes y la economía
política. Leido ante la Academía Columbiana.
4°. San Salvador, 1895.

In La Universidad, Serie 5, No. 7, pp. 241-252.

3927. Waesberge (P. van). Sermoen over geld en geldzaken
zamengesteld uit vaderlandsche spreekwijzen en spreekwoorden. 12°. Schiedam, *Goude*, 1838.

Harrebomée, 113. *In* Schiedamschen Almanak, pp. 160-172.

16. RELIGION.

(God ; Saints ; Devil ; Superstition.)

3928. Freybe (Albert). Deutsche Sprüche.
8°. Leipzig, *Ungleich*, 1896.

In Allgemeine konservative Monatsschrift für das christliche Deutschland,
1896, pp. 745-746, 860-864, 968-972, 1083-1087. Proverbs about God.

3929. Gianandrea (Antonio). La festa di S. Giovanni nei proverbi e negli usi marchigiani. 8°. Palermo, 1889.

In Archivio delle tradizioni popolari, Vol. 8, pp. 334-336.

3930. Goetze (Johann August Ephraim). Natur, Menschenleben
und Vorsehung, *etc.* 1789.

Another edition. 7 Bde. 8°. Leipzig, *Weidmann*, 1796.
Gratet-Duplessis, 673. Contains a chapter on Abergläubische Sprichwörter.
[B.M.

3931. K., *Dr.* Der Teufel im deutschen Sprichworte.
8°. Gotha, *Perthes*, 1863.

In Protestantische Monatsblätter für innere Zeitgeschichte, Bd. 22, pp. 108-112. [B.M.

3932. Klosterspiegel. Klosterspiegel in Sprichwörtern, Spitzreden, Anekdoten und Kanzelstücken. pp. viii, 121.
8°. Bern, *Jenni*, 1841.

Pp. 1-81, Des Volkes und seiner Weisen Sprüchwörter und Spitzreden über die Klöster.

3933. Koerner (Friedrich). Deutsche Götter und Göttersagen *etc.* pp. iv, 412. 8°. Leipzig, *Douffet*, 1877.

Pp. 357-360, der Teufel in Sprüchwort. [B.M.

3934. Leistner (Ernst). Wie das Volk über die Pfaffen spricht. Neuer Kloster- und Pfaffenspiegel enthaltend Sprüchwörter, geschichtliche Aussprüche und Volksredensarten, *etc.* pp. viii, 248. 12°. Lahr, *Schavenberg*, 1877.

Bernstein, 1892.

3935. Lipiński (Tymoteusz). Przysłowia tyczące się Świętych.
4°. Warszawa, 1858-60.

In Jana Jaworskiego Kalendarz, 1858, pp. 83-87; 1859, pp. 166-167; 1860, pp. 160-162.

3936. Lysthenius (Johannes). Paroemihagiographia, das ist Beschreibung der geistlichen Sprüchwörter.
4°. Leipzig, 1638.

3937. Margalits (Ede). Isten a világ közmondásaiban, *etc.*
8°. Budapest, *Szerző Sajátja*, 1910, *etc.*

Proverbs concerning God, in Italian, Slovak, Roumanian, Polish, *etc.*, with Hungarian translations. [B.M.

3938. Otto (A.). Die Götter und Halbgötter im Sprichworte.
8°. Leipzig, 1886.

In Archiv für lateinische Lexikographie, Jahrgang 3, pp. 207-229. [U.C.L.

3939. Stirling (William), *afterwards* **Stirling-Maxwell** (*Sir* William), *Bart.*
A few Spanish proverbs about friars. *See* **1424.**

3940. Teirlinck (Is.). Le folklore flamand.
Pp. 33-35, proverbes . . . dans lesquels intervient le nom de Dieu : pp. 94-97, proverbes . . . se rapportant au diable. *See* **1952.**

3941. Unseld (Wilhelm). Der Herrgott in schwäbischen Sprichwörtern und Redensarten. 8°. Bonn, *Hanstein*, 1892.

In Alemannia, Jahrgang 20, pp. 290-293. 76 entries. [B.M.

3942. ——— : Schwäbische Sprichwörter und Redensarten.
8°. Bonn, *Hanstein*, 1898.

In Alemannia, Jahrgang 25, pp. 131-132. 40 proverbs about Heaven, *etc.* [B.M.

2 F

3943. Unseld (Wilhelm). Der Teufel in schwäbischen Sprichwörtern und Redensarten. 8°. Bonn, *Hanstein*, 1892.

In Alemannia, Jahrgang 20, pp. 203-206. 84 entries. [B.M.

3944. ———: Der Tod in schwäbischen Sprichwörtern und Redensarten. 8°. Bonn, *Hanstein*, 1894.

In Alemannia, Jahrgang 22, pp. 87-89. 74 entries. [B.M.

3945. Valera (Cipriano de). Dos tratados. El primer es del Papa y de su autoridad. . . . El segundo es de la Missa, *etc.* [By C. D. V., *i.e.* Cipriano de Valera]. pp. [xvi], 488, [8].

sm. 8°. [London?], *Hatfildo*, 1588.

Another edition. 8°. [Madrid?], 1851.

Bernstein, 4733. The first part contains a section, De la mala vita de los Eclesiásticos. These proverbs are taken from the collection of Nuñez. There is an English translation of the book, 4°, London, 1600. [B.M.

3946. Vergara y Martín (Gabriel María). Refranes y cantares referentes a curas, frailes, monjas y sacristanes, reunidos por Garevar [*pseud.* of G. M. Vergara y Martín].

16°. Madrid,

3947. Wall (James Charles). Devils, *etc.* pp. x, 152 + plates.

8°. London, *Methuen*, [1904].

Pp. 126-135, proverbs. [U.C.L.

3948. Wander (Karl Friedrich Wilhelm). Christliche Glaubens- und Sittenlehre in Sprichwörtern. Erster Theil, *etc.* pp. xii, 264. 8°. Hirschberg, *Zimmer*, 1836.

[B.M.

3949. ———: Das Sprichwort, angewandt zu Unterredungen über die Sonn- und Festtagsevangelien, *etc.* pp. x, 203.

8°. Berlin, *Heymann*, 1836.

Over 1100 proverbs concerning festivals, saints' days, *etc.*, with notes, and comparisons with the Scriptures. [B.M.

3950. Weisheit. Die Weisheit auf der Gasse. Deutsche Sprichwörter religiösen und sittlichen Inhaltes, *etc. See* **1828.**

3951. Woerle (J. G. C.). Materialen zu fünfzehnhundert Vorschriften aus dem Gebiete der Pflichten- und Religionslehre, *etc.* pp. 202. 8°. Ulm, *Ebner*, 1844.

Bernstein, 4121. Pp. 11-16, 30-33, 54-65, 82-85, 116-120, proverbs.

3952. Wossidlo (Richard). Gott und Teufel in Munde des mecklenburgischen Volkes. 8°. Hamburg, *Soltau*, 1891.

In Korrespondenzblatt des Vereins für niederdeutsche Sprachforschung, Jahrgang 1891, Heft 15, pp. 18-32, 44-48. [B.M.

17. THE SEA, SAILORS AND FISHERMEN.

3953. Bassett (Fletcher S.). Proverbes et dictons relatifs à la mer. fol. Paris, 1889.

In Mélusine, Tome 4, col. 490-494. [U.C.L.

3954. Bayon (Paul). Proverbes et dictons de marins. Haute Bretagne. 8°. Paris, *Leroux*, 1889.

In Revue des traditions populaires, 4e année, tome 4, pp. 391-392; *see also* tome 5, p. 35. Proverbs about sailors and the sea. [B.M.

3955. Celesia (Emanuele). Linguaggio e proverbi marmareschi. pp. 174.

L.2. 8°. Genova, *Tipografia de R. Istituto Sordo-muti*, 1884.

Pp. 102-174, proverbs, some in Venetian and other dialects. An extremely interesting little book. [B.M.

3956. Corbière (Édouard). Des proverbes nautiques. 8°. Rouen, 1845.

In Revue de Rouen et de la Normandie, Année 13, No. 3. [B.M.

3957. Cowan (Frank). Dictionary of the proverbs and proverbial phrases of the English language relating to the sea, *etc.* pp. 144.

8°. Greenesburgh, Penn., *Oliver Publishing House*, 1894.

Accompanied by explanatory notes, literary references, *etc.* The prolegomenon contains some interesting remarks on the arrangement of proverbs. A good and interesting collection. [B.M.

3958. Fischer (Christian August). Reiseabentheuer, *etc.* 2 Bde. 8°. Dresden, 1801.

Another edition. 8°. Dresden, *Gerlach*, 1803.

Gratet-Duplessis, 796. Bd. 1, Chap. 18, contains "Holländische Sprichwörter aus dem Seeleben." Proverbs in Dutch and German. Very few are given. [B.M.

3958a. Lypkes (W.). Seemannssprüche, Sprichwörter und sprichwörtliche Redensarten über Seewesen, Schiffer- und Fischerleben in den germanischen und romanischen Sprachen. M.3.75. 8°. Berlin, 1900.

3959. Otto (A.). Landwirthschaft, Jagd und Seeleben in Sprichwort. *See* **3722.**

3960. Prato (Stanislas). Proverbes relatifs à la mer. 8°. Paris, 1889.

In La Tradition, 3e année, nos. 3, 4, 6. Some 50 Italian proverbs. In the next volume are another half dozen Spanish ones. [B.M.

3961. Rolland (Eugène). Proverbes et dictons relatifs à la mer. fol. Paris, 1886.

In Mélusine, Tome 3, col. 14-19, 233-244. [B.M.

3962. Sébillot (Paul Yves). Le folk-lore des pêcheurs. pp. xii,
389.   sm. 8°. Paris, *Maisonneuve*, 1901.

Les Littératures Populaires, tome 43. Pp. 380-382, a few proverbial sayings
about fishermen. [R.A.I.

3963. ———: Légendes, croyances et superstitions de la mer.
2 séries.   8°. Paris, *Charpentier*, 1886.

Reference to the index will show that brief lists of proverbs in various
languages are included in most of the chapters. [B.M.

3964. ———: La mer et les eaux. Les navires. Proverbes et
comparaisons.   8°. Paris, 1903.

In Revue des traditions populaires, tome 18, pp. 340-346. Proverbs, sayings,
etc., from all countries. [B.M.

3965. Scolari (Filippo). Lettere filologiche di marina. pp. xi, 58.
                        8°. Venezia, *Gattei*, 1844.

Pp. 24-33, Lettera quarta : proverbi. [B.M.

3966. Winschooten (Wigardus a). Seeman: behelsende een
grondige Uitlegging . . . der Spreekwoorden . . . uit de see-
vart sijn ontleend, *etc.* pp. [xiv], 368 + plates.
                        8°. Leiden, *Vivic*, 1681.

Gratet-Duplessis, 795. An alphabetical list of nautical words, phrases, proverbs, sayings, *etc.*, with explanations. [B.M.

3967. Witsen (Nicolaus). Aeloude en hedendaegsche scheeps-
bouw en bestier, *etc.* pp. 516, 40.
                        fol. t'Amsterdam, *Commelijn*, 1671.

Pp. 481-516, Verklaringen van scheeps spreeck-woorden, en verscheiden eigen
benamingen. [B.M.

18. WINE, BEER AND TAVERNS.

3968. Graesse (J. G. Th.). Bierstudien. Ernst und Scherz. . . .
Mit Illustrationen und Musikbeilagen. pp. viii, 262 + 4.
                        8°. Dresden, *Zahn*, 1872.

Bernstein, 1340. Pp. 231-237, Sprichwörter vom Bier.

3969. Harrebomée (Pieter Jakob). Bacchus in Spreekwoorden
taal, . . . door A. E. B. Herroem [*anagram* of Harrebomée].
pp. viii, 152.   8°. Gorinchem, *Schook*, 1874.

3970. Ricek-Gerolding (L. G.). Gelehrter Zecher goldnes Alphabet, *etc.* pp. 110.   16°. Leipzig, *Reclam*, [1897?].

Bernstein, 3023. Pp. 50-55, Sprichwörter und Sprüche. Proverbs and
sayings about wine, drunkenness, *etc.*

3971. Scalici (Emanuele). Lu veru codici di lu toccu arriccutu
. . . di un discursu supra la putenza di lu vinu. pp. iv, 9.
                        8°. Palermo, *Giliberti*, 1883.

In the introduction, pp. i-iv, 17 proverbs on wine are explained.

3972. Schranka (Eduard Maria). Ein Buch vom Bier, *etc.*
2 Bde. [in 1]. 8°. Frankfurt a. d. Oder, *Waldmann*, 1886.

Pp. 347-359, das Bier in Sprichwort.

3973. Sprueche. Sprüche der Weisheit aus Weinstube und
Keller, *etc.* pp. 16. 8°. Stuttgart, *Lemppenau*, 1881.

Bernatein, 3555.

3974. Waesberge (P. van). Sermoen over den wijn, zamengesteld
uit vaderlandsche spreuken en spreekwoorden.
12°. Rotterdam, *Wynands*, 1840.

Harrebomée, 120. *In* Rotterdamsch Jaarboekje, pp. 10-19.

19. MISCELLANEOUS.

3975. Crollalanza (Goffredo di). Almanach héraldique et drôla-
tique pour l'année 1885, *etc.* pp. xii, 256.
4°. Paris, *Plon*, Pise, *Journal héraldique*, 1884.

Pp. 148-150, Armoiries et proverbes comparés. 34 French or Italian heraldic
sayings and proverbs, in French.

3976. Denham (Michael Aislabie). A chapter of cuckoo cries
endeavoured by M[ichael] A[islabie] D[enham]. pp. 11.
8°. Civ. Dunelm., 1854.

Proverbs, sayings, rhymes, and superstitions concerning the cuckoo. [B.M.

3977. ———: A few popular rhymes, proverbs, and sayings
relating to fairies, witches, and gipsies. [Subscribed M. A. D.,
i.e. M. A. Denham]. pp. 8. 8°. Civ. Dunelm., 1852.

Only 50 copies printed. [B.M.

3978. Dutailly (M. A. J.). Proverbes et dictons . . . à propos de
cloches par M. A. J. D[utailly]. pp. 44.
8°. Noyon, *Andrieux*, 1884.

Bernstein, 2732.

3979. Eckart (R.). Der Wehrstand im Volksmund: eine Sammlung von Sprichwörten, Volksliedern, Kinderreimen und
Inschriften an deutschen Waffen und Geschützen. pp. 121.
8°. München, *Militarische Verlagsanstalt*, 1917.

Pp. 51-77, proverbs. No order, no notes. [B.M.

3980. Fabricius (Johann Albert). Hydrotheologie, *etc.* pp. 436.
8°. Hamburg, *König & Richter*, 1734.

Pp. 97-106, Ein hundert Sprüch-Wörter der Gleichnisse, vom Wasser herge-
nommen. [B.M.

3981. Fernand-Michel (François Fortuné). Histoire philosophique et anecdotique du baton, . . . par Antony Réal [Fernand-Michel], *etc.* pp. vi, 323.
12°. Paris, Société des Gens de Lettres, [1873?].

English translation. The story of the stick, *etc.* pp. x, 254.
12°. New York, Bouton, 1875.

Another edition. pp. xviii, 254.
8°. New York, Bouton, 1892.

Concludes with a few French proverbs concerning sticks. [B.M.

3982. Gatty (Margaret), *Mrs. Alfred Gatty.* The book of sun dials, *etc.* pp. xxvi, 152 + plates.
4°. London, Bell & Daldy, 1872.

Enlarged edition. pp. xvii, 529 + plates.
4°. London, Bell, 1900.

1682 alphabetically arranged sundial mottoes, quotations, proverbs, *etc.*, are given. They come from all parts; translations follow the foreign ones. The number of true proverbs is not great, but many of the mottoes have a certain proverbial character, and the labour of a search through them is sure to be repaid. [B.M.

3983. Gener (Hiob). Die bösen Schwiegermütter, *etc.* pp. 125.
8°. Berlin, Nachfolger, [1887].

Pp. 76-82, proverbs, principally German, concerning mothers-in-law. [B.M.

3984. Junker. Junker und Pfaffen im Gewande des Sprichworts und unter der Geissel des Volkswitzes. Vom Verfasser der "Allotria. Ungeflügelte Worte." Zweite, unveränderte Auflage. pp. xii, 41.
8°. Berlin, Denicke, [1874].

Third edition. pp. 84.
8°. Leipzig, Laudien, 1886.

[B.M.

3985. Krauss (Friedrich Saloman). Südslavische Hexensagen.
4°. Wien, 1884.

Pp. 17-18, die Hexe im Sprichwort. Separate publication of an article in Mittheilungen der anthropologischen Gesellschaft in Wien, Bd. 14 (N.F., Bd. 4), pp. 13-48.

3986. Krebs (Gotthold). Militärische Redensarten und Kunstausdrücke, *etc.* pp. 183.
8°. Wien, Seidel, 1892.

Militärische Sprichwörter und Redensarten (Der Redensarten und Kunstausdrücke neue Folge), *etc.* pp. vi, 213.
8°. Wien, Seidel, 1895.

[B.M.

3987. La Croix (Paul), **Duchesne** (Alphonse), and **Seré** (Ferdinand). Le livre d'or des métiers. Histoire des cordonniers. pp. 326 + plates.
4°. Paris, Librairie historique . . . de Seré, 1852.

Pp. 219-223, French and Latin proverbs concerning shoes and shoemakers.

[B.M.

3988. Lipiński (Tymoteusz). Przysłowia tyczące się świat.
4°. Warszawa, 1857.

In Jana Jaworskiego Kalendarz, 1857, pp. 174-176.

3989. Lukas (Jos.). Der Schulmeister von Sadowa. pp. viii,
502. 8°. Mainz, *Kirchheim*, 1878.

Pp. 374-382, Die Schule im Sprüchwort.

3990. Otto (A.). Die historischen und geographischen Sprichwörter. 8°. Leipzig, 1886.

In Archiv für lateinische Lexikographie, Jahrgang 3, pp. 355-387. [U.C.L.

3991. ———: Die Natur im Sprichwort. 8°. Leipzig, 1887.

In Archiv für lateinische Lexikographie, Jahrgang 4, pp. 14-43. [U.C.L.

3992. Perchaux ( ). Proverbes et barbiers. Étude sociale
et politique. Le Mans, 1885.

Friesland, 246.

3993. Pieri (Giovanni). Trattatello sull'arte del barbiere.
L.1. 8°. Capodistria, *Appollonio e Caprin*, 1875.

Pp. 53-60, proverbs and sayings originating from the barber's art, or concerning the hair and beard.

3994. Pitrè (Giuseppe). Proverbi siciliani illustrati: la suocera
e la nuora. 4°. Palermo, *Cristina*, 1867.

In Ore del Popolo, Anno 1, pp. 83-85. 36 proverbs and proverbial sayings
about mothers- and daughters-in-law.

3995. Reinsberg-Düringsfeld (Otto von), *Baron.* Internationale
Titulaturen. pp. viii, 316. 2 Bde.
Thaler 1. sm. 8°. Leipzig, *Fries*, 1863.

3996. Ricci (Corrado). I colori nei proverbi. pp. 47.
L.1. 16°. Bologna, *Zanichelli*, 1881.

Was reprinted in Note storiche e letterarie di Corrado Ricci, sm. 16°,
Bologna, 1881.

3997. Sébillot (Paul Yves). Les pendus. 8°. Paris, 1890, 1891.

In Revue des traditions populaires, tome 5, pp. 582-586, and tome 6, pp.
564-565. Tome 5 contains proverbs concerning hanging from various countries;
tome 6 contains 17 French ones only. [B.M.

3998. ———: Les personnages dans les proverbes.
8°. Paris, 1903.

In Revue des traditions populaires, tome 18, pp. 172-176. Proverbs from
different countries concerning Biblical characters. [B.M.

3999. ———: Les travaux publics et les mines, dans les traditions et les superstitions de tous les pays, *etc.* [Illustrated].
pp. xvi, 623 + 8 plates. 8°. Paris, *Rothschild*, 1894.

Pp. 76-82, proverbs relating to roads: pp. 259-262, proverbs relating to
bridges: pp. 587-588, proverbs relating to mines. These proverbs are in various
languages, the foreign ones with French translations.
[F.-L.S. (No. 96 of 770 numbered copies).

3999a. Steiner (C. J.). Das Mineralreich nach seiner Stellung in
Mythologie, . . . im Sprichwort und Volksfest. pp. x, 142.
8°. Gotha, 1895.

4000. Unterricht. Unterricht in Sprichwörtern durch passende
Erzählungen, Fabeln und Erklärungen, *etc.* pp. xii, 230.
8°. Duisberg, *Schmachtenberg*, 1837.

4001. Voss (Rudolph). Der Tanz und seine Geschichte, *etc.* pp.
402. 8°. Erfurt, *Bartholomäus*, n.d.
Another edition. pp. 402. 8°. Berlin, *Seehagen*, 1869.
Pp. 260-265, Der Tanz in deutschen Sprüchwort und in volksthümlichen
Redensarten. [B.M.

4002. Weber (Theophil). Sammlung von Denk-, Sinn- und
Trinksprüchen, Sprichwörtern, *etc.*, für Radfahrer. pp. 64.
8°. Leipzig, *Weber*, n.d.
Bernstein, 3990. Contains proverbs concerned with cycling, *etc.*

4003. Wick (W.). Geographische Ortsnamen, Beinamen und
Sprichwörter, *etc.* pp. 174. 8°. Leipzig, *Fock*, 1896.
Pp. 160-174, Sprichwörter und Beinamen zur Charakteristik von Land und
Leuten. [B.M.

4004. Wittstock (Albert). Die Erziehung im Sprichwort oder die
deutsche Volks-Pädagogik. pp. 281.
8°. Leipzig, *Naumann*, 1889.
Dissertations on proverbs concerned with education. [B.M.

INDEX

References are to entry numbers, not to pages.

Suchorowski (M.), 2845.
Suffolk, 683, 686.
Sukhadevaprasāda, 3259.
Sulaimān ibn Ya'kūb, al-Shāmī al-
Sālihānī, 3158.
Sulzer (F.), 2133.
Sumaran (J. A. von), 187.
Sumaran (A. A.), 188.
Sumatran. *See* Indonesian.
Sumtsov (N. T.), 3066.
Sun-dials, 90, 3982.
Superstition, 3930.
Suprian (K.), 1604.
Surinam, 3592, 3593, 3602.
Suringar (W. H. D.), 212n., 296, 1535, 1789a, 1947-9.
Susan (S.), 1790, 1950.
Sussex, 715, 715a.
Sutermeister (O.), 2134.
Sutor (A.), 1791.
Sutphen (M. C.), 297.
Svillić (M.), 2633.
Swabia, 2065, 2068, 2069a, 2072, 2073, 2079, 2083, 2084, 2087, 3912, 3941-4.
Swahili, 3470-3.
Swainson (C.), 3737.
Swallow, 3658.
Swedish, 816, 820-841, 847, 888.
Swettenham (*Sir* F. A.), 3408.
Świętek (J.), 2846.
Swiss, 2116-2136.
Sychra (M. J.), 2746.
Sykes (E. C.), 3179.
Syrian, 3118, 3123, 3141, 3145.
Syv (P.), 849n., 862n., 877, 878.
Sz. (M.), 2847.
Szabó (R.), 2696.
Szelinski (V.), 298.
Szent-Páli (S.), 2697.
Szirmay (A.), 2698.
Szyrma (W. S.). *See* Lach-Szyrma.

Tabourot (É), 1123.
Tagliabue (C.), 3260.
Tailliar (É.), 1124.
Takács (E.), 2699.
Talbot (P. A.), 3538.
Tallander (A.), *pseud. See* Bulbena y Tusell (A.).
Tallquist (K. L.), 3159.
Talmud, 155n., 432n., 435, 441, 442, 445, 449, 453n., 458, 464, 469, 471, 490, 494, 501-4, 508n., 509.
Tamil, 3289-3305.
Tammerlinus (L. R.), 2912.
Tanganyika, 3487-9.
Tanini (F.), 3773, 3773a.
Tannen (K.), 1869a.
Tappe (A. W.), 3026.
Tappius (E.), 1593, 1792.

Tarbé (L. H. P.), 1198.
Tarentaise, 1222.
Tarn-et-Garonne, 1277.
Taro, 2449.
Tartar, 3211, *et seq.*
Taschenbuch [*anon.*], 1793, 2085.
Tauber (I.), 299.
Taupiac (L.), 1282.
Taverner (R.), 189.
Taveta, 3485.
Taylor (A.), 645a.
Taylor (F. E.), 680.
Taylor (J.), 646.
Taylor (R.), 3633.
Taylor (W. E.), 3473.
Teacher, 3303.
Tcheng-Ki-Tong, 3339.
Tegg (W.), 647.
Teglia (F. del), 2493.
Teirlinck (I.), 1952.
Telugu, 3320-1.
Temne, 3580, 3581.
Temple (*Sir* R. C.), 3241, 3261, 3684.
Tenca (C.), 2346.
Tendlau (A.), 505.
Tennent (*Sir* J. E.), 3326.
Teodorescu (G. D.), 2670.
Teramo, 2515.
Tetzner (F.), 2849, 2890.
Teza (E.), 15n., 390.
Theal (G. McC.), 3519, 3520.
Theysbaert (M.), 1125.
Thiele (L.), 1674a.
Thiessing (J. B.), 1270.
Thiollière (J. C.), 1126.
Thirring-Waisbecker (I.), 1794.
Thiselton (W.), 648.
Thiselton (W. M.), 649.
Thiselton-Dyer (T. F.). *See* Dyer.
Thomas ( ), 1127.
Thomas (E. B.), 724.
Thomas (J.), 716.
Thomas (J. J.), 3618.
Thomas (N. W.), 667, 731, 3562.
Thomasson (P.), 837.
Thomaszik (E.), 1795.
Thompson (P.), 688.
Thonga, 3513.
Thorburn (S. S.), 3236.
Thorn (A. C.), 217.
Thuengen (C. E. von), 3663.
Thuriet (C.), 3835.
Thuringia, 2058-63.
Thurneysen (R.), 808.
Ticino, 2123, 2381.
Tigrē, 3464, 3467, 3469.
Tigri (G.), 2494.
Tiller *von Tscherlow, pseud. See* Sager (O.).
Tilley (M. P.), 650.
Timofeev (K.), 3027.

PRINTED IN GREAT BRITAIN BY ROBERT MACLEHOSE AND CO. LTD.
THE UNIVERSITY PRESS, GLASGOW.